RESPONDING TO HUMAN RIGHTS VIOLATIONS
1946–1999

International Studies in Human Rights

VOLUME 63

The titles published in this series are listed at the end of this volume.

Responding to Human Rights Violations

1946–1999

by

KATARINA TOMAŠEVSKI

Chair in Human Rights at the Riga Graduate School of Law,
Professor of International Law and International Relations at the University of Lund, and
External Lecturer at the Centre for Africa Studies at Copenhagen University

MARTINUS NIJHOFF PUBLISHERS
THE HAGUE / BOSTON / LONDON

Library of Congress Cataloging-in-Publication Data

Tomasevski, K. (Katarina)
   Responding to human rights violations, 1946–1999/by Katarina Tomasevski.
     p. cm. – (International studies in human rights; v. 63)
   Includes index.
   ISBN 9041113681 (HB: alk.paper)
   1. Human rights. 2. Economic sanctions. I. Title. II. Series.
JC571.T67 2000
327.1'17'09045–dc21

1003861885

ISBN 90-411-1368-1

Published by Kluwer Law International,
P.O. Box 85889, 2508 CN The Hague, The Netherlands

Sold and distributed in North, Central and South America
by Kluwer Law International,
675 Massachusetts Avenue, Cambridge, MA 02139, USA

In all other countries, sold and distributed
by Kluwer Law International, Distribution Centre
P.O. Box 322, 3300 AH Dordrecht, The Netherlands

Printed on acid-free paper

Printed and bound in Great Britain by Cromwell Press Limited.

Table of Contents

Part V: A look back and a look forward

Preface

This book chronicles Western responses to human rights violations, summarizing what has been said and done in the name of human rights, what effects it has had, and why events have unfolded as they have. This history is unfinished and is likely to be re-written if an international equivalent of truth commissions is created. Such bodies could then scrape below the surface of the records written while foreign and international interventions in the name of human rights are occurring. All such records are likely to be amended anyway, but this will take thirty or fifty years. Much as it was necessary for full five decades to elapse before Europe could begin probing into foreign responses to Nazism and to unravel a great deal of 'aiding and abetting,' it will take a change of generation to look back at the 1946–1999 period without our blinkers.

One purpose of this book is to remedy the short attention span which has become a key feature of international human rights politics in the 1990s. Each crisis disappears into oblivion, not to be recalled if another crisis erupts in the same country a few years later. There is no institutional memory of previous crises and responses. Another is to dismantle prevalent myths about solving human rights problems of other countries, which revolve around the ease and speed with which this can be done, at low or no cost. It describes and explains the recent history of each country that has appeared on the international human rights agenda, brings to light the process of creating this agenda, and looks into the layers of appearance and reality cloaked by human rights rhetoric. My decision to write it was triggered by two students who drove me to despair with their enthusiastically naive perception of the ease with which one can solve human rights problems in other countries.

Having written a polite letter about their desire to 'do something about human rights,' as they put it, these two students specializing in international development (again, their words) came to ask me what they could do to about human rights in China. China was a highly visible political issue at the time (March 1997) because Denmark had just tabled a draft resolution before the Commission on Human Rights, seeking China's condemnation for human rights violations; newspapers were overflowing with ideas and proposals. The two girls were bitterly disappointed with our encounter. I argued, reasonably as I thought, that they had never been to China, did not know anything about the country, could not understand the language, and it was unlikely that they could do anything useful. If they wanted to 'do something about human rights,' I suggested a number of things they could do in Denmark. This was not at all what they had expected. Having planned to get involved in some radical, decisive action against China, they did not take kindly to my mentioning Denmark. Indeed 'human rights' tends to be used in the Western media only for events in developing and 'transitioning' countries. My insistence that they should study and learn so as to acquire some professional competence in order to be useful to the human rights movement produced even less enthusiasm. No student likes being told to go home and study rather than venturing to change the world. The memory of two young disappointed faces was with me for a very long time; it still is. If we have led the new generation to believe that 'human rights' is simple and easy, the least I could do was to try to saw some seeds of doubt.

The memory of the two girls is visible in my effort to provide some background about individual countries and specific events in order not to leave human rights in a vacuum. For many of their peers, the Cold War is history, past finished, with no relevance for today's developments, while the long pre-human-rights history of international relations and international law is wished away. The ability to quote one or another of the many United Nations documents has been greatly facilitated by websites and it is ever so easy to find out what they say. Yet, what these documents *mean* cannot be downloaded from websites. One needs to *know* that a mere adoption of international human rights guarantees does not necessarily result from a commitment to human rights nor does it automatically engender codes of conduct for those wielding the power necessary to put those guarantees into practice. It has become an article of faith to assume that a mere enshrining of rights in formal documents will protect them, while a mere fact of publishing reports on violations of these rights will galvanize 'the international community' (however defined) into action. Domestically, human rights protection relies on well established patterns of political and institutional behaviour, which takes generations to build. This behaviour has to be established against the heritage of racism, sexism and xenophobia, which is global, against believing the 'the state' to be inherently evil or naturally benevolent but amenable to moulding. Knowledge about the gulf between aspiration and reality can only be created once both aspiration and reality are examined, and then the gap between the two. Such knowledge shatters believing that we can solve other countries' human rights problems without knowing anything about them or about human rights.

Simple solutions are always preferred to good ones. A simple diagnosis of a problem as human rights violations triggers a simple solution, condemnations and sanctions, presupposing our ability to micro-manage political change through remote control. And, if powerful and militant Western constituencies support the case, the next step might be military intervention. It seems deceptively easy to impute a single cause-and-effect to a chain of identifiable phenomena. It is easy to condemn violations, difficult to understand what makes and breaks human rights protection. The rationale for condemnations (and sanctions, and interventions) is grounded upon moral values rather than analysis. Violations trigger an occasional brief sentimental spasm and responses are based on emotional impulse.

The normative wording of human rights guarantees has made things worse by creating wildly unrealistic expectations. A host of inter-governmental actors have elaborated an endless stream of apparent human rights guarantees, and quite a few governments have been nudged or bullied into demonstrating, at least on the rhetorical level, a commitment to exactly the same ideas. Many of these are not home-grown and not even meant to be translated into local languages and circumstances. Anglo-American terms such as gender, or mainstreaming, or civil society, or prisoner of conscience, or NGO, cannot be translated into other languages and remain a part of a virtual reality shared amongst the initiated. This erasure of complexity is the normal fate of any icon. Disdain for the history of documents that made all these human rights promises as well as for the history of countries for which these are championed encourages off-the-shelf, cost-free solutions. Moralizing prevails over assembling evidence on the process of making and breaking human rights and the painstaking efforts necessary to build institutions that translate parchment promises into rules for governmental conduct.

The problem is, of course, that simple solutions do not work. What is defined as a human rights violation is itself a construct, a perception that varies in time and place and is not shared by all relevant actors. Perception produces its own reality; varying perceptions generate different realities. Political preferences are elevated to the status of axioms by the expedient of labelling them as violations. There is a controlled human rights vocabulary in international law but its effects on international human rights politics have been minuscule. Law is slow and cumbersome, it gives both the prosecutor and the violator an equal hearing, it requires adjudicators to be independent of both parties. It is thus ignored, but the price is a risk that the process of divorcing *human rights* from *human rights law* will empty the term 'human rights' of contents and transform it into a weasel-word, like 'development' or 'democracy,' to be filled with new contents with every change of the political fashion of the season.

The book argues that a criminal-justice rationale has led to a self-created right to define human rights violations, condemn the offenders, impose sanctions, or authorize interventions. The victim is, as in criminal justice, an afterthought. International human rights activism started in earnest in the 1960s, positing that universality of human rights necessitated acting for the benefit of victims in other countries. Varying levels of human rights protection pitted organizations based in the West against dictatorships – first in the West and then elsewhere – and led in the 1970s to inserting human rights into Western foreign policies. The original purpose of benefiting victims yielded to the desire to punish violators. This advanced in the 1990s to a self-granted right to harm others in the name of furthering their human rights.

This line of argument is based on the history of international and foreign responses to human rights violations which is discussed in the thirteen chapters that follow. Most of this is past-unfinished, yielding to tentative rather than conclusive interpretations of what happened, when and how. Official histories of quite a few dictatorships have been re-written by truth commissions; these have spanned, with only one exception, only domestic dimensions. Parliamentary commissions of inquiry into Western support for human rights violators are rare. This reflects a mistaken assumption about states' practice: active and passive support to dictatorships is the practice of states established through centuries; refusal of such support, condemnations, sanctions and interventions are new.

This book is a result of two years of writing preceded by ten years of research, and the number of people who have helped me along this tortuous path is much too long to allow individual acknowledgments to all. Lest it be thought that new generations could be typified by the two girls who forced upon me a sense of guilt about the simplistic portrayal of human rights they have been exposed to, I want to thank my students for their cheerful and irreverent challenge of the existing human rights research in this area, including mine. In contrast to the received wisdom whereby students are ill-advised to select as the topic for their thesis a pet subject of their professor's, a number of them did so with excellent outcomes and I have particularly fond memories of Karin Buhmann, Thomas Elholm, Dennis Janssen, Anders Krab-Johansen, Kristine Kruma, and Robbyn Wilkins.

At the Danish Centre for Human Rights, where I did most work for this book, Karen Lise Thylstrup never failed to get the book or document I sought, combining old-fashioned and new technologies, and never giving up. Agnethe Olesen always managed to figure out what I wanted, even if I only remembered a part of the author's name and the colour of the book cover. Hashil Seif Hashil made mountains of photocopies, greeted each new lot with a smile and a pat on the shoulder, and never wavered in supporting my writing, although it absorbed the time which we could have used to get his torturer to court.

I have had much joy in presenting parts of my research at various seminars and have benefited a great deal from the feed-back by different audiences. I am grateful to COPRI (Copenhagen Peace Research Institute) for quite a few lively debates we have had, to the Research Center on Development and International Relations of Aalborg University for building bridges across disciplinary boundaries, to my colleagues at Dansk PEN for organizing a debate about Western punitive human rights policies and to Niels Helveg Petersen for being such a nice man.

I owe a debt of gratitude to Peter Baehr, who read a much longer version of the manuscript while it was in an embarrassingly unfinished shape to provide a wealth of good ideas. Reed Brody has filled in the details which I was missing from his vast experience in getting things done. Håkan Wiberg has, as always, prevented me from any temptation to slide into moralizing. Niels Barfoed has prodded me to think through the profound changes that have taken place in the past decade. Mark Gibney has relentlessly rallied me on and, to acknowledge his help, I have mentioned the word 'ethics' at the beginning of the Introduction. Robin Clapp uncomplainingly sacrificed her Christmas and New Year's holidays to help me prepare the text for publication.

K.T.
Copenhagen, December 1999

List of tables

Introduction

Reality, being unruly, does not fit into a conceptual framework based on law or ethics. Both tell us how governments *should* behave, shying away from inquiring into how they *do* behave. Describing and analysing how governments, in the name of their states, behave towards each other within a coherent framework requires, as John Dewey wrote more than eighty years ago, a 'persistent endeavour to revise current beliefs so as to weed out what is erroneous, to add to their accuracy, and, above all, to give them such shape that the dependencies of the various facts upon one another may be as obvious as possible.'[1] This book maps out the states' practice in responding to human rights violations thus far, weaving together the bilateral and multilateral levels, the political and economic dimensions, and highlighting congruence or discordance between them. Like an audience in a Javanese *wayang* puppet play, which sees the shadows but not the reality because the master directs the puppets behind a lighted screen, determining 'the facts' necessitates the persistent endeavour which John Dewey urged so long ago. The official versions of events which have been labelled as human rights violations have often been presented differently by individual governments and inter-governmental organizations and the labels have thus varied. Differences in determining what is and is not a human rights violation have been exacerbated by non-governmental or journalistic versions, which have often contradicted the officialdom. Political judgments about rights and wrongs concerning other countries have often failed to influence the parallel track of aid and investment flows.

Condemnations of human rights violations and sanctions against violators are a recent phenomenon and are chronicled in their entirety. The beginning has been traced back to 1946, to India's quest for a condemnation of South Africa by the United Nations for institutionalized discrimination and Indian economic sanctions against South Africa. That first initiative had taken place before the Universal Declaration of Human Rights was adopted and pointed to the future pattern of targeting along the North-South and West-East lines. The end of resort to condemnations and sanctions is nowhere in sight. On the contrary, the menu has expanded to military interventions and international tribunals, hence states' practice is likely to become even more unruly than during the past five decades. The purpose of this book was to capture all cases so as to draw a complete record for 1946–1999. The end of 1999 has been chosen as a tidy, if somewhat arbitrary, cutoff point for all case histories.

This book treats condemnations and sanctions, which have evolved as typical responses to human rights violations in other countries, as empirical questions. They can be studied because official documents are available from the United Nations or individual governments, a great deal of literature has been generated.

---

[1] Dewey, J. – *Democracy and Education*, Macmillan, New York, 1916, p. 256.

These responses emerge as a reaction to some reported abuse which has been labelled as a human rights violation. These cases, many as they are, represent an unknown – certainly very small – proportion of abuses which were and are going on in the world. The process of creating a case is therefore an important object of study because it is necessarily selective.

Responses to human rights violations escalate from expressions of concern to condemnations and to various types of sanctions and interventions. The starting point of this book is that such responses are not established and accepted states' practice, not yet at least. Traditional, if unwritten, norms of states' behaviour towards each other developed through centuries endorse silence and inaction; the prevalent reaction to human rights violations by another state within that state, (that is, without foreign or international spillover effects), remains the absence of any response. Furthermore, this book probes into evidence of active and passive complicity in human rights violations by reviewing aid to countries in which violations have been taking place, diplomatic initiatives undertaken to shield violators from public exposure, mutually contradictory paths of condemning violations while at the same time facilitating them by enhancing financial flows to the government in question. Responses to human rights violations thus do not happen unless a political process has nudged, or forced, a government in this particular direction, and they are not necessarily negative. Flows of development finance have often appeared to be rewarding rather than penalizing violators.

The process whereby a case is created nudges governments towards atypical behaviour. Forging a response against violations in the form of a condemnation amounts to a political sanction and entails the risk of retaliation. Small, poor, remote, and friendless governments are thus a typical target. The imposition of diplomatic or economic sanctions necessitates rupturing the existing links between the two countries; it is easy is such links are few and far between, difficult if the bonds are numerous, and extremely burdensome if these bonds are beneficial for the country whose government is nudged to impose sanctions. The pattern of condemnations and sanctions, as this book shows, is not and cannot be guided by human rights alone.

CONCEPTUAL FRAMEWORK

Condemnations and sanctions are generally analysed within inter-state relations, omitting intra-state processes. The state may be perceived as an (many would say 'the') actor responding to atrocities committed by its peers. Underneath a veneer of conduct attributed to the state, there are interwoven, often conflicting, threads created by acts and omissions of many actors within it. 'The state' consists of an executive and a legislature that differ in defining both atrocities and condemnatory or punitive responses. The executive itself consists of various actors which represent foreign policy, trade, aid, migration, suppression of drug trafficking, that vary in laying down guidance for bilateral responses. The mass media promptly impart newsworthy atrocities, demanding instant reaction, which is generated through political processes which cannot isolate human rights from the multitude of inter-woven foreign policy concerns. The judiciary has remained outside the realm of condemnations and sanctions; these phenomena have remained extra-legal. Added to these three branches of the government is a maze of actors, ranging from exporters to trade unions, from established churches to associations of exiles. The role of human rights organizations has become particularly prominent in the creation of cases for which a foreign-policy response then needs to be forged.

The starting point of this book is that responses to human rights violations in other countries pertain to foreign policy, which is defined here as the promotion of our interests and values beyond borders. Attempts to account for foreign policy with a single theory have thus far failed, and one important reason has been the inevitable clash between interests and values in its creation. In the field of human rights, commercial interests or fears of immigration proverbially undermine human-rights values. Moreover, both granting and withholding aid can be defined in terms of promoting human-rights values. The resulting foreign policy ought to accom-modate a variety of conflicting interests and values, and a state can appear to be pursuing simultaneously several foreign policies. The way forward pursued in this book is an anti-generalizations approach. It furnishes a chronicle of the past half century by describing what has taken place and how, to then move on to explaining why things worked out the way they did.

The essential difference between responding to human rights violation at home and abroad revolves around the role of law. Human rights law was designed to hold each government accountable by its population. Rights and freedoms are defined through political processes for which international law serves as corrective. Violations are determined and remedied through domestic procedures; international procedures can only be viable if domestic procedures are effective. Responses to violations in other countries transpose assumptions derived from familiarity with one's own country to another; these routinely prove unfounded. The postulate that human rights are universal comes to rescue, and it not interpreted as a normative statement should be (human rights should be universally recognized) but rather as if it were an empirical statement (human rights are already recognized worldwide). A series of assumptions is then built on this basis, that identical phenomena constitute violations, that violations can be halted through a single recipe. The abyss between *should* and *is*, assumptions and analysis, is cloaked underneath a vocabulary of virtual reality, in which ratification of a human rights treaty is assumed to entail a commitment to human rights, that constitutional guarantees drafted by expatriate experts are endowed with local ownership, that individual entitlements originating from the welfare-state model are tenable without the welfare-state taxation on which they depend. This virtual reality hides away its unruly counterpart rather than trying to tackle it.

Two words – states should – are amply used in the field of human rights. An endless stream of declarations and resolutions abounds with 'states should' and is constantly supplemented. NGO reports on human rights violations routinely wind up with a series of 'states should,' addressed always to the violator and often also to its major donors. The underlying normative theories are derived from an image of the world as it should be, saying too little about the world as it is. A civilian government may well be under the control of the army, in opposition to the pre-requisites for human rights protection; individual security may depend on self-protection because the government does not have the capacity to constrain private armies and/or militias on the territory over which it has (in theory) the monopoly of armed force; the judiciary may be so poorly paid that the requirement for it to be independent can only be made in theory. And yet, if such a state has ratified human rights treaties (as is often the case), it will be assumed to be committed to human rights and capable of guaranteeing them. External and international pressure will then be defined as advancing the cause of human rights because both commitment and capacity are assumed to exist; forcing violators to alter their conduct necess-itates this assumption. If the very assumption proves untenable, the vocabulary changes into 'rogue states,' or targeting moves from states to individual leaders, who are identified as the cause of all ills.

The selection of atrocities which are defined as human rights violations changes in time and place and is divorced from the meaning of rights, violations and viol-ators in international law. The handful of *rights* that have generated political and legal commitment of most states in the world is replaced by an endless listing of desires and aspirations. At a drop of hat, a right to violence-free life or sexual rights is added to the listing, triggering lively academic debates about what such a right should mean. *Violations* refer to a broad range of phenomena, from excessive use of the death penalty to electoral fraud, from military coups to child labour, from corruption to violence against women. A state in which everybody, including chil-dren, has to work because poverty does not allow for the luxury of not working can then become a *violator*, as can a state in which husbands are reported to be rou-tinely beating their wives. Moving violations and violators away from the legally established human rights obligations of states transposes them into weasel-words that can be filled with different contents. Anything desirable can be elevated into a right and anything frowned upon labelled as violation, anybody's views and beliefs are then just as good as anybody else's. Emotional reactions to abuse and suffering, generally formulated as 'something should be done,' do not necessitate different-iating between symptoms and causes nor ascertaining concordance between ends and means.

Gunnar Myrdal has argued in 1957 that research into policy should proceed 'in terms of means and ends rather than causes and effects.'[2] The subject-matter which this book addresses, responses to human rights violations, requires prioritising concordance and discordance between means and ends. The rationale for this orien-tation is grounded in the fundamental human rights precepts. Because law is sym-metrical, freedom is correlated with responsibility hence the exercise of freedom to respond (or not) to violations in other countries, and the choice of how to respond, entails responsibility. As Hubert Védrine put it, 'the dividing line is not between

---

[2] Myrdal, G. – *Economic Theory and Underdeveloped Regions*, Methouen & Co., London, 1957, p. vi.

compassion and indifference, but between responsibility and irresponsibility.'[3] Free choice of means makes the pursuit of means which defy the professed ends possible, even likely if this choice can be exercised irresponsibly.

This book presents the pattern that has emerged thus far through the exercise of this freedom of choice in responding to human rights violations in other countries through an array of case histories. Below a coating of well-sounding abstract principles in formally adopted foreign policies there is a labyrinth through which information about atrocities abroad and suggested courses of action is filtered, necessarily resulting in a labyrinthine pattern of responses. The book weaves together two parallel tracks:

- it examines political processes to discern how governments acting collectively responded to human rights violations by their peers, and how Western human rights policies have been applied to violations and violators through globalized unilateralism;
- it reviews economic exchanges, focussing on government-to-government aid since it generally forms part of foreign policy,[4] to detect whether the two simultaneous tracks have followed the identical or similar line.

The progression from non-response (that is, silence), over exposure and condemnation, to sanctions and ultimately interventions, maps out the range of possibilities out of which the collective governmental responses have rarely ventured beyond public exposure and condemnation. Western human rights policies have broadened the spectrum through extensive resort to economic sanctions and, more recently, military interventions. Each case history compares the outcomes of multilateral and unilateral political processes, which have varied more often than not, adding the simultaneous developments in the realm of economic exchanges. The resulting mosaic demonstrates how few threads typifying responses to human rights violations can be extracted from the intricate pattern that the states' practice has woven.

Multilateral condemnations have been none too numerous, sanctions rare. In contrast, unilateral sanctions have been numerous and based on unilateral determinations of violators. Different outcomes of these two political processes hint at different dynamics of each. The precursor to identifying individual governments as violators was the emergence of the collective political will within the United Nations and governments started sitting in judgment of their peers. Decision-making is democratic and depends on the acquiescence of regional groups and votes of individual governmental delegations. This multilateral scheme was imme-

---

[3] 'Dans cette affaire, la ligne de clivage n'est pas entre sensibilité et insensibilité, mais entre responsabilité et irresponsabilité.' Védrine, H. – *Les mondes de François Mitterand a l'Elysée, 1981–1995*, Fayard, Paris, 1996, p. 637.

[4] In some countries, a single ministry encompasses foreign affairs and aid, in others a separate ministry (usually called ministry for development cooperation) deals with aid, in yet others the provision of aid might be spread over a large number of different ministries and public institutions.

diately supplemented by individual judgments of Western governments, strengthened by unilateral sanctions. Studying the two tracks in conjunction leads to domestic political processes rather than human rights or their violations in the target state as the key to understanding how and why this erratic pattern has evolved.

Condemnation of individual governments by the collective voice of its peers was initially anticipated as the only sanction for human rights violations. When the United Nations ventured into defining what governments should not do to their population, the painstaking process of building collective political and then legal commitments was initiated against the heritage of the exclusive state's power to treat its population as it pleased. Five decades later, a commitment to a handful of basic rights has been generated and is backed by a wavering willingness of governments, acting collectively, to nudge each other into behaving accordingly. The definition of rights and determination of their violations takes place through two different mechanisms, legal and political. The former requires a legal commitment by each individual state, the latter a majority of votes by governmental delegations in the United Nations Commission on Human Rights or General Assembly. Public exposure of abuses and condemnation of a particular government is an extra-legal phenomenon, a political sanction.

The term sa*nction* (as a noun) denotes *enforcement*; its purpose is to exact forcibly an action from the targeted state. In contrast, to *sanction* (as a verb) signifies approval. The linguistic potential of this oddity is immense because it endows *sanction* as a noun with the authority of law from which it is assumed to derive. The original meaning of *sanction* emphasizes authority rather than punishment, it means 'to invest with legal or sovereign authority, to make valid or binding.'[5] Studying sanctions thus requires crossing disciplinary boundaries between international relations and international law. The former leans towards an institutional approach and the latter follows a normative approach. A trans-disciplinary bridge is necessary to discern what happens to rights and violations when they are extracted from law to be implanted in international relations, whether sanctions re-enter law when they are applied against violators and thus need to borrow the authority of law, and what happens when sanctions apparently breach the existing legal prohibitions.

STRUCTURE AND CONTENT

This book describes and discusses all cases where the human rights rhetoric was used to justify condemnations and sanctions and starts with a simple question: What does the pattern of condemnations and sanctions ostensibly in response to human rights violations look like? The answer was developed on the basis of a

---

[5] *The Compact Edition of the Oxford English Dictionary*, vol. II, Oxford University Press, 1971, p. 82–83.

chronology of all cases in the past five decades. A chronological sequence is followed as much as the outcomes of decision-making within the United Nations and the erratic pattern of Western condemnations and sanctions permitted. The findings are striking: more than two-thirds of the world's governments have been placed on the UN agenda as violators, less than one-third were condemned. This demonstrates that UN's human rights work has progressed far beyond token condemnations of small and friendless countries. Simultaneously, more than one-third of non-Western countries were targeted by some form of economic sanctions with human rights violations cited among the justifications. The answer to an apparently simple question becomes complicated without correspondence between governments condemned by their peers and those targeted by Western sanctions.

Human rights are defined in this book as safeguards against abuse of power by the government. Chapter 1 traces the milestones amongst collective governmental decisions to constrain their own power through collective and individual self-policing. The scheme is simple: each government should police itself because governments are the principal violators as well as protectors of human rights. Governments acting collectively define the minimal standards of acceptable behaviour and supplement self-policing. Collective self-policing would require a commitment to human rights that was – and is – more than rudimentary. The outputs of inter-governmental decisions concerning individual governments are described in Chapter 1 and details concerning specific country situations are discussed throughout this book. Since inter-governmental decisions against human rights violators have been too few from the viewpoint of the proponents of the condemn-and-sanction practice, a parallel track was established through the institutionalization of 'a right' of individual governments to police and penalize others. Most sanctions have been unilateral and bypassed procedural rules of inter-governmental decision-making.

The time-frame, 1946–1999, coincides with the commitment to human rights by the collective decision of governments within the United Nations. The legal basis for such a commitment was provided in the UN Charter and human rights were moved from the exclusively internal matter for each individual state into the international arena. Before any legal framework was elaborated to define what governments should and should not do, South Africa was already on the agenda of the UN General Assembly for human rights violations. It took three decades for the United Nations to set up a mechanism for political accountability of individual governments to their peers, and one more decade to establish initial mechanisms for their legal responsibility.

The initial commitment forged within the United Nations in 1946–48 led to condemning individual governments as violators as late as 1967 and was followed in 1970 by the empowerment of the UN to investigate violations. The first sanctions were multilateral and had been imposed before the UN human rights bodies acquired the powers of determining a government as a human rights violator. They are described in Chapter 2. Rhodesia was the precedent-setting case of punitive UN response to the denial of the right to self-determination. South Africa, much more than Rhodesia, triggered off UN condemnatory actions, which were reinforced with sanctions as <u>the</u> external and international response to apartheid. Both cases pertain to pre-human rights times at the United Nations. Multiplicity of sanctions and differences between unilateral and multilateral sanctions is exemplified by South Africa. Sanctions can be traced to 1947 (unilateral sanctions by India) or 1962 (UN General Assembly) or 1973 (Convention against Apartheid) or 1986 (US anti-apartheid statute), or one or the other among the Security Council decisions.

Israel joined South Africa as a target of UN condemnations as a human rights violator, but has remained immune to sanctions, with the exception of the boycott by the League of Arab States. It is discussed in Chapter 3. The interplay between domestic politics and (foreign) human-rights policy is illustrated in the fate of Israel and Cuba (discussed in Chapter 4), with the USA leading in opposite directions – safeguarding Israel from multilateral sanctions while globalizing the reach of US unilateral sanctions against Cuba. Responses to these two notorious cases of economic warfare have changed a great deal over the past decades. US sanctions against Cuba had not originally been associated with human rights. The human rights rhetoric was added later, then reinforced through the placement of Cuba on the UN violations-agenda. A great deal of protest was generated because US domestic politics was transposed into its foreign policy. The attempt to impose US foreign policy as a constraint upon private businesses dealing with Cuban companies repeated the model of the Arab oil embargo against Israel: in both cases, individual companies – wherever based – were subjected to penalties if not conforming to the foreign policy of states with which they had no legal link. Although economic sanctions against Israel coincided with its founding, they were 'discovered' by countries outside the region in 1973–74 due to the secondary boycott, namely sanctions against companies that were dealing with Israeli companies. Opposition to such secondary boycotts was fierce in both cases.

Economic sanctions preceded multilateral determinations of violators or violations, and Chapter 4 reviews economic sanctions as a unilateral foreign policy tool introduced by the USA. Economic sanctions were institutionalized as a response to violations in the 1970s, reinforcing and globalizing unilateralism. This created two parallel tracks, with the United Nations condemning violators by majority vote and rarely calling for economic sanctions, with the international donor community (led by the USA as it used to be the biggest donor) globalizing unilateral punishment of violators on the basis of the US model.

Economic sanctions were globalized in the 1970s. Chapter 5 discusses the series of cases that emerged in the 1970s, Equatorial Guinea, Uganda, South Korea and Chile, which had nothing in common except being aid recipients and found by their donor to have violated human rights whereupon sanctions followed in the form of suspension or decrease of aid. Quite a few Western countries formally adopted a foreign human-rights policy in the 1970s as the basis for responding to human rights violations abroad. Foreign policy is exempt from legal restraints. Different practices based on similar wording suggest an inquiry into the domestic politics of foreign human-rights policy. Since the human rights pronouncements in foreign policies look very much alike, their meaning can be retrospectively inferred from the observable behaviour of the respective governments. Differences between rhetoric and conduct are frequent. They reveal the contributions of the relevant actors within the government, the parliament and the executive, and within the executive the foreign-policy and the development-aid establishments. Foreign-policy decisions respond to rapidly evolving political events while remoulding bilateral economic exchanges requires a longer lead time. The result is frequently the lack of correspondence between the behaviour of two parts of the same government. The available quantitative data, especially on aid flows, highlight such lack of correspondence: sanctions were sometimes threatened but not imposed, sometimes announced but implemented with much delay or as token gestures.

Chapter 6 reflects the prominence of South America in international human rights politics in the late 1970s. The dirty war in Argentina broke the UN's condemnatory mould by triggering thematic procedures. Argentina could not be condemned politically and so disappearances were placed on the agenda to rupture silence and inaction that would have resulted from political paralysis. A combination of warfare and repression in El Salvador and Guatemala made Central America the target of non-governmental human rights organizations, but US involvement precluded inter-governmental condemnations or economic sanctions. Two small and poor countries – Haiti and Suriname – exemplified the rule of thumb in the pattern of sanctions – remote, small and poor countries are the easiest to target by economic sanctions and to forget thereafter.

Chapter 7 discusses the fate of Middle Eastern countries in international human rights politics. Unrelated to the Cold War which was – unknown at the time – coming to its end, an ideological battle about universality of human rights started after the 1979 revolution in Iran. It entered international human rights politics much later because Iran was initially targeted by US sanctions as retaliation for hostage-taking, while the field of human rights was still dominated by the cold-war agenda. Western human rights policies towards Iran, Afghanistan, Turkey and Algeria reveal a retrospective scenario of replacing the previous ideological fault-line with the religious one, and the consequent focus of international human rights politics on Islam. A great deal of effort has been expended to focus international attention on real as well as apparent challenges of the postulated universality of human rights. With just a bit of cynicism, one could conclude that the underlying strategy was not to universalize human rights but to use them, much as before, as a justification for the condemnatory and punitive practices against re-defined targets.

Asia has been the most difficult region for Western human rights policies, and has also exposed the weakness rather than strength of the United Nations. Chapter 8 follows chronological sequence in which individual countries were placed on the UN human rights agenda, starting from Cambodia during the reign of Pol Pot, then addressing Sri Lanka at the time of the outburst of warfare in the early 1980s, mentioning briefly Pakistan because nothing resembling an international response to human rights violations ever emerged, to proceed to Burma. Different from all other Asian countries, Burma's government (the one that changed the name of the country to Myanmar) has been repeatedly condemned as well as targeted by economic sanctions. This exception is followed by cases which follow the rule:

China, Indonesia and Papua New Guinea exhibited a great deal of wavering as to condemnations and disunity as to sanctions.

Chapter 9 summarizes haphazard international and foreign responses to man-made disasters in Africa. A book could be written about the fate of each African country from the colonial times to the turn of the millennium from the viewpoint of its negative impact on human rights. The fate of the continent has been to serve as object of experiments. An early UN military intervention in Congo led to the subsequent reluctance to resort to forceful action to halt abuses until the military intervention in Somalia reinforced the previous reluctance. The three decades in between were marked by proxy wars fought along the cold-war lines. The end of the Cold War triggered an outburst of enthusiasm for democracy, which soon gave way to anguish interspersed with oblivion. Africa's vulnerability to economic sanctions made it the most frequent target for human rights violations and every other reason. Africa's disposal of a large numbers of votes within the United Nations made condemnations rare.

As Chapter 9 describes, African countries have been targeted the most, on various grounds, Asian countries have been targeted the least because the rhetoric of human rights in Western foreign policies encountered domestic opposition. The importance of Western aid was incomparably smaller for Asia than for Africa, with a disproportionately larger commercial potential of Asia. The attraction of the largest market to be conquered permitted little interference; foreign policies duly adjusted, incorporating promotion of domestic commercial interests as their objective. Chapter 9 demonstrates that Western human rights policies were not implemented with regard to large Asian countries, such as India, China or Indonesia, but were also difficult to discern with regard to small ones, such as Fiji or Papua New Guinea. One part of the explanation is the West's limited leverage over Asia, as different from Africa. Another part, partially related to this leverage, is the resistance of Asian governments to accepting the Western human rights discourse, evidenced *inter alia* in the absence of a regional human rights organization.

Long, comprehensive and strictly enforced sanctions against Iraq, discussed in Chapter 10, highlighted a question seldom posed before: are economic sanctions promoting or undermining human rights? Are sanctions depriving the target government of capacity to guarantee human rights although the actors enforcing sanctions claim the opposite? If the effect of sanctions is impoverishment and disempowerment, how could they be beneficial for the population in the name of whose rights they are imposed and enforced? These types of questions were forced upon international human rights agenda due to the cross-fire in which the Iraqi population found itself, whose devastating outcome has been publicised by the government of Iraq for obvious reasons, but also by increasing numbers of institutions and individuals who found it difficult to reconcile the rhetoric of sanctions with their reality.

The final part of the chronology of condemnations and sanctions looks at what used to be Eastern Europe during the Cold War in Chapter 11. Their immunity to condemnations and sanctions during the Cold War was ruptured with Albania and Romania. The former was placed on the UN human rights agenda, the latter had already been an object of US sanctions. The Baltic countries exhibited the quick-sand in which Western human rights policies drowned trying to design simple recipes for unruly reality: assumptions that human rights would blossom with the demise of their main ideological target proved unfounded. Rather, targets have multiplied. Warfare in the Former Yugoslavia overwhelmed all other priorities and UN condemnatory resolutions lengthened. Condemnations were reinforced by economic sanctions, to then try to stop war by waging war.

Much as with the previous wars between the worlds' major Western powers, after the end of the Cold War the victors have elevated their political platform to the global model for all to follow. The collapse of cold-war structures, from national to global, unleashed conflicts and problems upon a world both unwilling and unable to cope with them. Condemnations and sanctions became an attractive coping strategy – Western governments could be seen as acting while not creating any costs for themselves.

As Chapter 11 describes, the post-cold-war Eastern Europe exhibited a striking change of Western, especially West European, foreign policies. The initial *democracy cum human rights* rhetoric was short-lived. A great deal of warfare ensued from the rapid dismantling of the previous states and was exacerbated by disem-powerment of new states. The affected countries elicited chaotic Western responses, similarly to warfare in Africa. If a strategy could be discerned, it was containment: preventing a possible flood of refugees and even excessive concern by cloaking unsolved or mishandled problems under a veneer of *democracy cum human rights* structures (such as Bosnia and Herzegovina) or away from Western mass media (such as Albania). Similarly to Asia, trade-and-investment jeopardized a possible priority for human rights in Western foreign policies, fear of migration to Western Europe overwhelmed all other considerations.

SCOPE AND METHODS

Analysing decision-making within the United Nations is easy because formally established procedures are well known and official documents are widely available. Supplementing missing pieces of an occasional puzzle necessitates an un-scientific but efficient expedient of knowing who to ask. Studying the process whereby individual Western states have responded to human rights violations abroad is, in contrast, difficult. Even within the executive alone, a response mechanism which would combine multilateral with bilateral, and political with economic response, does not exist. Different facets of the analytical path can be exemplified as follows:

– Quite a few Western governments committed themselves in their law or foreign policy to respond to violations in other countries. To discern how this com-mitment is translated into practice, one has to ask a series of questions: Which actor within the government has the authority to decide that a violation has taken place? Which actors outside the government are likely to prod the government towards such decision? On the basis of what definition of violations is such a decision made? How is the choice between multilateral fora (the United Nations or a regional analogue) and bilateral response made? Which actors are supposed to put into practice the government's response and how much leeway do they have in interpreting what should be done?

– Where silence (i.e. non-response to human rights violations) was the chosen option despite a legal or foreign policy commitment to react, one ought to identify substantive and procedural obstacles within decision-making: Which violations triggered off condemnations and/or sanctions and which did not? Which countries were targeted by condemnations and sanctions and which ones remained immune?

– While condemnations seldom amount to more than mobilization of shame, economic sanctions entail purposeful impoverishment of the people whose rights are being championed, while a military intervention risks killing its purported beneficiaries. The progression from a verbal condemnation to economic sanctions and military intervention broadens the entities within the government that have to be involved in decision-making. A long series of questions ought to be asked: How is a political decision to halt aid reconciled with aid policy which by definition cannot accommodate a stop-go recipe for development? What happens when two constituencies are at odds with each other, one advocating sanctions to punish violators, another championing un-interrupted aid to foster development?

– The escalation of responses to violations beyond sanctions to military interventions has opened new questions, thus far having provided no answers. It is difficult to predict whether the future of Bosnia and Herzegovina, Kosovo, and East Timor, which have furnished the first but probably not the last field-testing for a military intervention followed by an international protectorate, will prove such experiments to have led in the desired or opposite direction. Their very design raises profound questions about the difference between protecting people and their rights, or the abyss between international law and international politics.

This book discusses the fate of individual countries in alternating multilateral and unilateral responses to human rights violations. Shifts in Western strategies[6] between these two tracks have been numerous. Efforts to generate condemnations within the United Nations routinely originate from WEOS (the Western Group), which tables the largest number of condemnatory proposals. These are not always a reflection of a commitment to exposing and opposing violations. Intra-state processes combine human rights with a range of other foreign policy concerns, and then inter-governmental and inter-regional politics molds outputs. The case-by-case

---

[6] Although the Western Group (WEOS) is an established entity within the United Nations, and the West (or North) is seen as a homogeneous entity from the outside, the emergence of the European Union as an international actor has consolidated what could be called 'Western European human rights policy' which is often distinct from that pursued by the USA:

examination of different responses to human rights violations compares multi-lateralism with Western unilateralism – some governments were condemned for human rights violations by their peers within the United Nations and became targets of Western sanctions, others were condemned for violations but sanctions did not follow, yet others became targets of Western sanctions without a UN condemnation.

The raw material on which this book is based – states' practice – profiles the final product. This focus on the states' practice originates from its status as a source of international law. The bias in the human rights literature towards explicit provisions of international human rights treaties (supplemented by what is fondly called 'soft-law,' namely resolutions, declarations, platforms, programmes of action, guidelines, that should be called 'non-law') has generated high expectations by blurring the difference between the normative and the empirical. An assertion that everybody has the right to life is often interpreted as if it were an empirical statement, positing that everybody's right to life is already secured rather than everybody's right to life should be secured by individual states within the definition to which each is legally committed. This leads to a further step whereby every killing can be defined as human rights violation, and another which fails to distinguish between protecting human lives and the right to life. Condemnations and sanctions are generated through domestic and international political processes in which the legal grounding of human rights can easily be ignored. The price is arbitrariness. It is in the interest of those states that are likely to become targets of condemnations and sanctions to challenge such arbitrariness, although the reasons may have nothing to do with human rights.

The large number of condemned and sanctioned countries and the long time-span enables comprehensive stocktaking. Cross-country comparisons illustrate varying foreign policy responses to similarly repressive regimes. Some repressive regimes were rewarded by increased foreign and international financial inflows, others were penalized by withheld aid and denied access to other sources of funding. The reasons were obviously not their human rights records. Changes of regime in the countries subjected to condemnations and/or sanctions furnish the background for comparison in time: international financial support increased and also decreased with a transition from a violator to a protector of human rights.

Analyses of the individual cases include retrospective overviews of the determination of human rights violations on the basis of which sanctions were imposed and the role which sanctions played in shaping the target country's future. The early cases, Rhodesia and South Africa, highlight the orientation of sanctions towards political transitions and disregard for an economic underpinning of post-transition regimes. Chile requires seeking an answer to a question which human rights activists prefer to avoid: didn't the economic success of the Pinochet regime – with the price which Chileans paid through human rights violations – provide the economic basis for the subsequent political transition? And was not the discrepancy between Chilean and Western reactions to the attempt to bring General Pinochet to trial in Europe in 1998–99 indicative of different answers to that painful question? This book emphasizes, for Chile and all other countries, detrimental consequences of dissociating political reforms from their economic underpinning, and the harm done to human rights through damaging the capacity of states to comply with all their human rights obligations. The trend of *americanizing* Western human rights policies by restricting them to civil liberties and political rights has led to lop-sided and unsustainable transitions, exacted costlessly for the West but at a great past and future cost for the countries that have been the target of such Western policies.

Although many cases chronicled in this book can be classified as past-finished, developments unfolding well after condemnations stopped and economic sanctions were lifted demonstrate that all are likely to appear as past-unfinished sometime in the future.

TERMINOLOGY, ACRONYMS AND INDEXES

Reliance on official governmental and inter-governmental documents makes writing difficult because multiple vocabularies have impeded anything resembling terminological consistency in the text. There is no controlled vocabulary in the field of human rights. The vocabulary of the United Nations human rights bodies includes a bewildering array of organs, standards and procedures which are familiar only to a fairly small circle of the initiated. The European Union has followed suit and created its own terminology. Individual governments use human rights rhetoric differently, as do human rights organizations, journalists, and scholars, and so the term 'rights' or 'violations' appears in this text endowed with array of meanings. The terms as used by different actors have not been altered because, in human rights more than in other fields, language is a weapon rather than a label. The opprobrium inherent in the term 'violation' or 'violator' is the reason for using such terms and no attempt to remedy the prevailing terminological inconsistency has been made. Citations and references are amply used so as to clarify the origin and authorship in the terminological mosaic which this text contains.

In contrast to human rights, the area of aid, investment and trade enjoys a controlled vocabulary, even if disputes about the contents defined by each terms have never stopped nor are they likely ever to end. DAC/OECD (the Development Assistance Committee) was used as the source for all data on aid flows wherever possible so as to make the figures comparable. They are, as is customary, always expressed in million US dollars.

Resort to abbreviations and the creation of acronyms has entered the *modus operandi* of each international organization, whether inter-or non-governmental, and the resulting alphabetical soup is, without doubt, a constant source of irritation for everybody. This author could not resist this temptation herself, having created EUrope[7] to denote the European Union (and all its previous incarnations) in its role of an international actor, and the only apology she can offer is the frustration of having to constantly shift between different acronyms. Each abbreviation and

---

[7] Tomaševski, K. – *Between Sanctions and Elections*, Pinter/Cassell, London, 1997, p. 41.

acronym is spelled out in full when first used and all are included in a separate index at the end of the book. The text is followed by two more indexes, which should considerably facilitate the orientation of those who have not been forced by circumstances to navigate through this labyrinth. Because the book spans many countries and deals with developments over five decades, an index of geographical and personal names is attached separately from an analytical index which is customary in such books.

Part I

Evolution of multilateralism

Chapter 1

Multilateral Passage from Rights to Violators

Human rights are safeguards against the abuse of power by governments and hence rely on governmental self-restraint. These safeguards always emerge retroactively, through mobilisation of shame which compels governments into self-restraint. A merger of domestic and peer pressure nudges individual governments to behave accordingly. Because international law is horizontal, and there is no supra-state structure to impose human rights safeguards upon governments, such peer pressure is crucial for translating political commitments into legal rules and, ultimately, into state practice.

The protection of human rights is a *process* which depends on institutions and procedures for challenging their denials and violations. Unless there are institutions willing and able to effectively oppose abuses, substantive human rights guarantees remain parchment promises. The number of such promises is, of course, immense. The United Nations (UN) is notorious for generating them and academics thrive on describing and analysing the wording of each and every resolution or declaration.

The evolution of collective self-restraint and its translation into correctives for state practice is summarized in this Chapter. The UN uses uses *standard-setting* to denote the process of generating normative statements, both legal and extra-legal, and documents embodying these standards are referred to as *instruments*. This terminological choice is purposeful – human rights instruments are merely tools that have no effect unless they are used. This book does not focus on what these various instruments say. Rather, it maps out the procedures and institutions that have evolved to hold governments accountable for breaching their very spirit.

The first task before the United Nations was to lay down substantive human rights standards in order to develop a globally applicable yardstick, to define <u>what</u> before proceeding to <u>how</u>. Collective governmental acquiescence in the 'what' and the 'how' was necessary to make these safeguards viable. Human rights protection does not occur spontaneously because some governments are 'good' while others can be made 'good' if one or two 'bad' individuals can be replaced. Because exercise of power constitutes the key word in defining governance, abuse of power occurs unless and until it is prevented and such prevention necessitates structural and institutional safeguards. Human rights thus constitute obligations for governments. This was normatively accomplished with the very establishment of the United Nations, but it then took two decades to empower the UN to respond to gross abuses of power.

A list of those phenomena that reflect gross abuses of power and embody denials and violations of human rights has evolved slowly and gradually over the past decades, defining specific conduct as an apparent violation to then determine that the respective government is a violator. The functional equivalents of the prosecutor, judge and law enforcement agency have not evolved into a coherent system as in the domestic criminal justice system, however. The political process of defining violations and identifying violators takes place within an inter-governmental structure, through democratic decision-making, founded upon the one-state-one-vote principle. To determine that a state is a violator, its peers have to decide so by a majority vote The government's peers have the role of the judge, while the role of the prosecutor shifts between governmental and non-governmental actors, with non-governmental organisations routinely taking the lead in exposing governmental abuses. There is no international law enforcement agency. Multilateral sanctions are rare; they are imposed for human rights violations even more rarely, and even then their enforcement depends on each individual government.

Governmental conduct is routinely found to be inconsistent with human rights standards. Even those that take a great deal of pride in their human rights record lose cases. These will not be about torturing prisoners or disappearing political opponents, but about securing that women are not discriminated against in social security or that minority children are educated in their own language.

Human rights standards tell us how states *should* behave not how they *do* behave. The number of states listed in annual reports documenting torture is large and increasing. Nevertheless, this finding does not undermine the prohibition of torture, on the contrary. It proves that this normative statement is increasingly applied as the yardstick for measuring governmental performance, worldwide. The states' collective and individual acceptance of this yardstick provides legitimacy for challenging the gap between the *should* and the *is*. This process is never-ending.

UN's work on defining human rights and delineating violations evolved through three stages. The first, from 1946 to 1967, started with a post-war surge of goodwill but was immediately paralysed by the Cold War. In the 1960s, the process of decolonisation ruptured that cold-war paralysis and led to political procedures for condemnation of human rights violations, initially for collective rather than individual rights. The second stage, from 1967 to 1970, established the foundations for the public identification of human rights violators, to then open the way for denouncing violations of individual rights and for initiatives to come from governments and non-governmental organisations, witnesses and victims, anywhere around the world. This process vastly expanded UN's violations-agenda in the 1980s and early 1990s to face an uncertain future.

WESTERN DOMINANCE AND COLD-WAR PARALYSIS, 1946–60

The initial decades of UN's human rights work were marked by profound ideological and political disagreements about the meaning and implications of human rights. The idea was new and there were no precedents to follow. Governments had formerly been free to treat their populations as they pleased, shielded by the prohibition of interference in internal affairs and the sovereign equality of states. A break away from the past had taken place on the normative level with the adoption

of the UN Charter and the Universal Declaration of Human Rights, but their substantive provisions did not lead to procedures whereby their apparent breach could
be challenged until twenty years later.

The UN Charter affirmed the significance of human rights in its preamble, pro-
claiming the promotion of human rights as one of the main purposes of the United
Nations. According to the Charter, all members of the United Nations are legally
bound to strive towards the full realization of all human rights and fundamental
freedoms. Human rights were thereby elevated from a noble aim to an obligation of
all governments. It is important to add here that the United Nations never did – nor
could – oblige itself to ensure that governments comply with their human rights
obligations. Rather, words like 'encourage' and 'promote' described UN's methods
of work. The initial caution in the UN's response to human rights violations
reflected the absence of the collective political will of governments. An exception
was the mission statement of the first UN High Commissioner for Human Rights,
whereby he committed himself 'to ensure the universal enjoyment of all human
rights by giving practical effect to the will and resolve of the world community.'[1] A
promise to *ensure* human rights went too far and was, much as the first UN High
Commissioner for Human Rights, soon forgotten.

A general plan was forged in 1947 to adopt a human rights declaration, then a
convention (i.e. treaty), and thereafter to specify implementation measures. Only
the first step materialised, with the adoption of the Universal Declaration of Human
Rights in 1948. Because the Cold War had already broken out, the voting pattern
reflected it: the majority of 48 votes were cast in favour, with the abstention of
eight members. The latter were all the Eastern European members of the time,
namely Byelorussia (as of 1991 Belarus), Czechoslovakia (as of 1993 the Czech
Republic and Slovakia), Poland, Ukraine, the Soviet Union (Russian Federation as
of 1991), and Yugoslavia (as it then was), joined by Saudi Arabia and South Africa.
The Cold War prevented the adoption of a human rights treaty. The two Covenants
were adopted in 1966 and ten years later came into force. Thus, the division of
human rights into civil and political on one hand, and economic, social and cultural, on the other, was transposed from ideology into law and formalised in the
names of two Covenants.

The third planned step, implementation, was silently dropped. The ideological
and political polarisation along the West-East line was later complemented by
another, along the North-South line. No overall design for implementation ever
evolved. The practise of institutionalised *ad-hoc-ism* resulted in a patchwork of
procedures for a specific country or topic around which the collective will of
governments of the time could be mobilised.

---

[1] The mission of the then High Commissioner was reproduced at the front page of each issue of
HCHR News, the monthly bulletin issued by the Office of the High Commissioner from November 1995
until his departure in March 1997.

This collective will of governments has reflected the changing UN membership. Its initial membership was less than a third of today's, merely 51.[2] The Commission on Human Rights was the main forum for negotiating the human rights commitments of governments and the corresponding UN's role, with one-third of its membership belonging to WEOS (the 'Western and Other States' group).[3] Out of the initial 18 seats, WEOS had six and Eastern Europe three. The other half pertained to the rest of the world: Latin America had four seats as did Asia, and Africa had one. Within each region, governments to hold a seat in the Commission are selected through more or less democratic methods, one unwritten rule being that the five permanent members of the Security Council traditionally hold a seat in the Commission.

Evan Luard has described the first decade of the Commission on Human Rights, from 1945 to 1955, as the years of Western domination.[4] Western input went beyond its seats and/or votes to the substance of future human rights standards. All drafts of the future Universal Declaration of Human Rights had originated in the West and were in English, except two in French.[5] Howard Tolley has added that the non-Western members of the Commission tended to be American-educated diplomats, which then created verbal duels where, for example, the 'influential diplomat P.C. Chang of China [Taiwan] held a Columbia University Ph.D., but challenged the Western orientation of the Harvard-educated Malik [Lebanon]'. Tolley thus summed up the geopolitical profile of the first two decades of the Commission:

A United States delegate served as Chair for six consecutive sessions, and no Eastern block member ever held that office. The Soviets were excluded from the initial three-member drafting committee for the Universal Declaration, and two anti-American NGOs were stripped of their consultative status. The Peoples

---

[2] The largest regional group was Latin America with 20 states, and its composition has hardly changed since. The second largest group was WEOS (Western Europe and Others) with 13 members. The Asian group initially had 8 members (China, India, Iran, Iraq, Lebanon, Philippines, Saudi Arabia, and Syria), Eastern Europe had six, and Africa was the smallest region with merely four states (Egypt, Ethiopia, Liberia, and South Africa). It should be recalled that China's UN seat was held by Taiwan until 1971.

[3] The Western European and Other States (WEOS) group has nominally twenty-six members (Andorra, Australia, Austria, Belgium, Canada, Denmark, Finland, France, Germany, Greece, Iceland, Ireland, Italy, Liechtenstein, Luxembourg, Malta, Monaco, the Netherlands, New Zealand, Norway, Portugal, San Marino, Spain, Sweden, Turkey, and the United Kingdom). For the purpose of elections to the Commission on Human Rights WEOS has two additional members, the United States and Japan. Two states based in Europe, the Holy See and Switzerland, are not members of the United Nations but have observer status.

[4] Luard, E. – *A History of the United Nations. The Years of Western Domination*, 1945–55, vol. 1, MacMillan, London, 1982.

[5] Humphrey, J.P. – *Human Rights and the United Nations: A Great Adventure*, Dobbs Ferry, New York, 1984, p. 31–32; Robinson, J. – *Human Rights and Fundamental Freedoms in the Charter of the United Nations. A Commentary*, Institute of Jewish Affairs, New York, 1946, p. 98–99.

Republic of China was blocked from membership, the Asian region was generally underrepresented, and there was no black African representative before
1964.[6]

Expectations raised by the human rights language used in the UN Charter led to
complaints of violations as soon as the United Nations had been established. While
the Universal Declaration of Human Rights was still being drafted, the Commission
on Human Rights was already receiving complaints and decided that it had no
power to take any action,[7] declining to respond to violations. Not only the
Commission, but all other UN bodies were expected never to acquire such powers.
Complaints received by the United Nations were rendered anonymous; both the
identity of the complainant and the name of the target government were withheld
because complaints had to be forwarded to the target governments. The substance
of processed complaints was thereupon summarised and presented in the form of an
anonymised global pattern. Different from a widespread perception that the West
has been championing the cause of human rights within the United Nations since its
very establishment, 'in the 1950s it was left to countries like Egypt, India and the
Philippines to push for the establishment of a procedure to examine petitions from
individuals.'[8]

THE FIRST ENLARGEMENT AND THE RIGHT TO SELF-DETERMINATION, 1960–67

Two parallel processes took place within the United Nations in the 1950s: bodies
having 'human rights' in their title pursued human rights standard-setting, with an
exclusive focus on individual rights, while the General Assembly dealt with
decolonisation, but without reference to human rights. The two tracks merged in the
1960s, when self-determination was added to the human rights agenda and affirmed
as *the* collective human right. Much as with other issues, human rights standards
were developed retroactively after a vocal inter-governmental constituency had
been formed. In this case, its objective was decolonisation and its first target
southern Africa.

   The process of decolonisation, and UN's subsequent policy facilitating further
decolonisation, was the basis of the formation of this constituency, which was
strongly supported by the Soviet Union and its allies. Verbal condemnations were
soon broadened to sanctions against those colonial states that defied demands for
independence by their colonies ('non-self-governing territories' in UN parlance),

---

   [6] Tolley, H. – *The U.N. Commission on Human Rights*, Westview Special Studies in International
Relations, Westview Press, Boulder, 1987, p. 11 and 187.

   [7] Commission on Human Rights – Report of the First Session, U.N. Doc. E/259, para. 22.

   [8] Zuijdwijk, T.J.M. – *Petitioning the United Nations. A Study in Human Rights*, Gower, Aldershot and
St. Martin's Press, New York, 1982, p. 14.

and such policies were complemented by support for liberation movements, thus affirming the legitimacy of armed struggle for independence. Obligatory sanctions could only be imposed by the Security Council and only against states jeopardizing international peace and security. The arming of liberation movements was aimed, *inter alia*, to provoke South Africa or Portugal into overreacting.[9] Since many, if not all these wars were also part and parcel of the Cold War, human rights could not be safeguarded from ideological and political abuses. Ultimately, support for armed struggle backfired when liberation movements turned their weapons against each other. The decolonisation of former Portugese colonies, especially Angola and Mozambique, plagued the United Nations long after their political independence because warfare did not stop once decolonization was attained. (In Angola, warfare has not stopped throughout its history as an independent country and it is discussed in Chapter 9.)

The 1955 Bandung Conference (predecessor to the Non-Aligned Movement, NAM) elaborated a common anti-apartheid platform to be pursued within the United Nations and developed a broader human rights strategy focused on anti-colonialism and/or attainment of self-determination.[10] As UN human rights bodies were drafting standards only for individual rights, definitions of 'human rights' by NAM and the UN differed a great deal. With the admission of seventeen African countries to the United Nations in 1960, an Afro-Asian bloc emerged within the UN and made South Africa, Rhodesia and Portugal its priority, defining self-determination as a human right and its denial, consequently, as a violation.

The first wave of African UN members gave priority to anti-colonialism and political independence for other potential members. In 1961, the Commission on Human Rights was enlarged to 21 members, and in 1967 to 32, altering its geo-political profile. WEOS shrank from its initial one-third of seats to become a minority with eight equaling in size the African group, Asia and Latin America had six seats each and East Europe four. This altered balance between the North (divided between West and East) and the growing South led to profound changes in the UN's human rights agenda.

The most notable change was the placement of collective rights, the right to self-determination, on the human rights agenda. Whether human rights should apply to people in colonies ('non-self-governing territories') had been debated during the adoption of the Universal Declaration of Human Rights. An amendment favouring full application of human rights had been tabled by the Soviet Union and rejected by a counter-proposal of the United Kingdom. The vote was close: 29-17-10.[11] The eagerness of the newly independent countries to extend human rights to those who had yet to attain independence was supported by the then-East and opposed by the (then and now) West.

---

[9] Bissell, R.E. – *Apartheid and International Organizations*, Westview Press, Boulder, 1977, p. 95.

[10] McTurnan Kahin, G. – *The Asian-African Conference, Bandung, Indonesia, April 1955*, Cornell University Press, Ithaca, 1955.

[11] United Nations – *Yearbook of the United Nations. Special Edition: UN Fiftieth Anniversary 1945–1995*, Martinus Nijhoff Publishers, The Hague, 1995, p. 303.

Before the expansion of the membership of Commission on Human Rights in 1967, initiatives related to decolonization and self-determination had little resonance. The principal battleground was the UN General Assembly. Increasing majorities were mobilized around constantly increasing numbers of condemnatory resolutions relating in particular to southern Africa. UN's intergovernmental structure would have had the colonial countries represented by their sovereigns (Portugal or South Africa), and because these had been declared illegitimate a way was opened to bring into the United Nations actors other than governments. Furthermore, condemnations of violations necessitated a great deal of factual material to be compiled and verified and thus testimonies by the victims themselves as well as missions to the field gradually became accepted working methods. This process had led to the first complaints procedures, which were subsequently transposed from the General Assembly downwards to the Commission on Human Rights. The General Assembly adopted in 1960 the Declaration on the Granting of Independence to Colonial Countries and Peoples and established one year later the Special Committee on Decolonisation[12] to facilitate its putting into practice. The Committee was empowered to examine petitions against governments accused of impeding decolonisation and to organise hearings. A model for subsequent human rights complaints procedures had thus been developed. The General Assembly and its Decolonization Committee prodded the Commission on Human Rights into action by placing human rights violations in several Portuguese colonies as well as South West Africa and Southern Rhodesia on its 1965 agenda.

The powers of the United Nations to hold individual states accountable for denials and violations of human rights were extended in the 1970s to individual rights in individual countries, and in the 1980s to particularly egregious phenomena embodying abuses of power such as disappearances, torture and arbitrary executions wherever they occur. These changes were made through a series of political decisions influenced, besides UN's changed membership, by increasing political visibility of human rights. Neither the UN Charter nor the Universal Declaration of Human Rights have ever been amended. And yet, while they had initially been interpreted to deny the United Nations the powers to respond to human rights violations, subsequent re-interpretations have bestowed such powers upon the Organisation.

The United Nations was originally mandated to protect and enforce peace, but only to 'promote' human rights. When the General Assembly dealt with human rights issues, these were classified as political problems, while the Commission on Human Rights pertained to social and humanitarian issues on the agenda. Once the former victims of the denial of self-determination obtained a political voice, the

---

[12] The official name of this Decolonization Committee was the Special Committee on the Situation with regard to the Implementation of the Declaration on the Granting of Independence to Colonial Countries and Peoples, and it was established by General Assembly resolution 1654 (XVI) of 27 November 1961.

precedent was made in the 1960s through defining denials of self-determination as human rights violations, condemning (and sometimes sanctioning) violators, to be then applied also to individual rights.

EMERGING POWERS TO NAME VIOLATORS, 1967–70

Two years of political and organisational debates within the Commission on Human Rights led in 1967 to the first procedure for dealing with complaints of human rights violations. The convoluted UN language revealed that the principal target was southern Africa, but an opening was made to address gross and/or consistent violations worldwide.[13] This procedure, known by the number of the authorizing resolution as the '1235 procedure', leaves the initiative to individual governments and is public. (Its sister, the '1503 procedure,' which is confidential and enables any individual to denounce violations by any government, was set up in 1970 and is described below.)

As mentioned earlier, the changed membership of the United Nations explains the priority for southern Africa. While only four African countries had been founding members of the United Nations, by 1960 they were twenty-six.[14] The importance of the right to self-determination for decolonisation was obvious as was the focus on Africa. That first wave of independence brought with it the first challenges to the ideologically divided bipolar world and added the division into South and North. Although the South was divided geographically between different UN regions, it forged common positions outside the UN, within the Non-Aligned Movement (NAM). The NAM was instrumental in creating an initial political platform for what was later to become the South, Third World, Group of 77, or developing countries. This initial platform prioritised southern Africa and led to the Commission on Human Rights to publicly name the first violator – South Africa – in 1967.

After South Africa had become the first entry on the violators-agenda in 1967, as Table 1.1. shows, it stayed there for more than three decades. Southern Rhodesia

---

[13] ECOSOC (the Economic and Social Council) resolution 1235 (XLII) of 6 June 1967 empowered the Sub-Commission and the Commission on Human Rights to 'examine information relevant to gross violations of human rights and fundamental freedoms, as exemplified by the policy of apartheid as practised in the Republic of South Africa and in the Territory of South West Africa under the direct responsibility of the United Nations and now illegally occupied by the Government of the Republic of South Africa and to racial discrimination as practised notably in Southern Rhodesia.' The use of 'as exemplified by' opened the possibility for inquiring into gross violations beyond the three explicitly identified culprits. If the initial investigation revealed 'a consistent pattern of violations', the Commission was empowered to carry out a thorough study.

[14] The founding members of the United Nations were Egypt, Ethiopia, Liberia and South Africa, joined by Libya, Morocco, Sudan and Tunisia in 1955–56, Ghana and Guinea joined in 1957–58, and sixteen in 1960 (Benin, Burkina Faso, Cameroon, Central African Republic, Chad, Congo, Côte d'Ivoire, Gabon, Madagascar, Mali, Niger, Nigeria, Senegal, Somalia, Togo and Zaire).

Table 1.1: Chronological list of human rights violators, 1967–1999

1967–1973	1974–1979	1980–1989	1990–1998
South Africa (1967)	Chile (1975)	Afghanistan (1980)	Cuba (1990)
Israel (1968)	Cyprus/Turkey (1975)	Guatemala (1980)	Panama/USA (1990)
	Kampuchea/Cambodia (1979)	Malawi (1980)	Iraq (1991)
	Equatorial Guinea (1979)	Bolivia (1981)	Burma/Myanmar (1992)
	Nicaragua (1979)	El Salvador (1981)	Somalia (1992)
		Western Sahara (1981)	Sudan (1992)
		Iran (1982)	Zaire/Congo (1992)
		Mauritania (1982)	[Yugoslavia] (1992)
		Poland (1982)	Papua New Guinea/Bougainville (1993)
		Indonesia/East Timor (1983)	Togo (1993)
		Grenada/USA (1984)	Angola (1994)
		Haiti (1984)	Burundi (1994)
		Sri Lanka (1984)	Georgia (1994)
		Lebanon/Israel (1985)	Rwanda (1994)
		Paraguay (1985)	Nigeria (1996)
		Pakistan (1985)	
		Uruguay (1985)	
		Albania (1988)	
		Romania (1989)	

Note: Only states whose governments were explicitly named as human-rights violators by the Commission on Human Rights are listed, and the year when the first such resolution was adopted is noted. Square brackets are used for states which have changed their identity thereafter.

and the Portugese colonies had already been dealt with by special bodies established by the General Assembly, before the Commission on Human Rights
obtained powers to name violators and never obtained South Africa's prominence.

The 1235 resolution had indicated what type of violations should be sought and
where these should be looked for, but this narrow focus encountered immediate
opposition. As soon as the rule of anonymity had been lifted, the Sub-
Commission[15] (a smaller body composed of nominally independent experts) duly
named South Africa, South West Africa, Rhodesia and Portugal (because of
Angola, Mozambique and Guinea Bissau) as violators. It wanted, however, to add
Greece and Haiti to the list.[16] Greece was at the time ruled by the military which
had taken power through a coup in 1967, while Duvalier-ruled Haiti later attained
notoriety for abuses that had been taking place at the time. However, the Greek
delegation was formed by its military government and the delegation of Haiti by
the Duvalier regime and neither acquiesced in broadening the notion of violators
beyond the originally intended culprits in southern Africa. Haiti and Greece – and
their supporters within the United Nations – prevailed.[17] Similar political battles
have continued to this day, but the power of the United Nations to identify violators
had come to stay.

The first years of the UN's public exposure of violators did not divide governmental delegations into two neat camps, one supporting and the other fighting such
practise. The West did not champion public condemnation of violators. When the
Commission on Human Rights obtained powers to react to complaints of human
rights violations, none of the eight Western members voted in favour but the
motion carried nevertheless.[18] The Western reluctance to accept the right of self-
determination, which automatically placed all colonial powers among prospective
violators, made their human rights policy appear hypocritical. The Soviet Union
routinely challenged UN's powers to determine violations and identify violators
while supporting every action against colonialism and the colonial powers, to later
champion UN's action against Pinochet's Chile. Members of NAM launched all

---

[15] The Sub-Commission on Prevention of Discrimination and Protection of Minorities had originally
been set up as one of the two subsidiary bodies of the Commission on Human Rights (the other one was
supposed to be a sub-commission on freedom of information which was never established) to then function as the Commission's subsidiary body throughout the past five decades. In 1999, it officially changed
name into Sub-Commission on the Promotion and Protection of Human Rights.

[16] Sub-Commission on Prevention of Discrimination and Protection of Minorities – Report on the
Twentieth Session (1967), U.N. Doc. E/CN.4/947, para. 95.

[17] Reporting on human rights violations. Introduction by Nigel Rodley, *Netherlands Quarterly of
Human Rights*, 1994, No. 3, p. 310.

[18] The voting record on the first proposal to endow the Commission with powers to deal with
individual complaints, contained in its resolution 2(XXII) is found in U.N. Doc. E/4184 (1966),
paras. 165–221.

initiatives against South and southern Africa and supported those against foreign occupation (targeting Israel), while protecting its own members from becoming a target. Alliances have thus often changed according to the issue and the country.

Battles were – and are – fought about each particular country and specific issue as well as about abstract principles, especially about reconciling the prohibition of interference in internal affairs and UN's powers to interfere in internal affairs so as to expose and oppose gross abuses of power. The real question has become which violators can mobilise a sufficient majority within the Commission to remain immune to public exposure and to being publicly labeled as violators.

As shown in Table 1.1, condemnations of violators started in 1967 with South Africa, with Israel following one year later, and Chile joining in 1974. With Chile (discussed in Chapter 5), UN's definition of violators moved beyond colonial and foreign occupation to military coups in independent countries and institutionalised rule by force. This extended UN's remit worldwide. Many countries were brought up on the agenda, although few were condemned, as the rest of this book shows. At least one-third of governmental delegations taking part in discussing how to deal with human rights violations also have the unpleasant task of responding to allegations of violations of which their own governments are accused.

The first steps towards exposing and opposing institutionalised violations of individual rights legitimised UN's powers to carry out investigations, publicise their results, and publicly condemn individual governments. Public exposure and condemnation represent political sanctions and are reinforced by the peer pressure inherent in decision-making by fellow-governments.

After the breakthrough in 1967, it took the UN three years to overcome the obstacle of governmental reluctance to publicly name others amongst their peers as violators. A powerful governmental constituency to parallel those against South Africa and Israel would have been difficult to find. Broadened targeting was accomplished through the procedural expedient of giving standing to non-governmental entities for gross and systematic violations. That decision was approved narrowly. In fact, each part of what was to become the 1503 procedure was voted on separately, and each of the four votes was a narrow approval.[19]

This confidential procedure is also known by the number of the authorising ECOSOC resolution and was created to operate alongside the public 1235 procedure to enable the United Nations to process individual complaints ('communications' in UN jargon) which alleged gross and systematic violations.

---

[19] Commission on Human Rights – Report of the Twenty-Fifth Session, U.N. Doc. E/4621, 1969, paras. 407–435.

The 1503 procedure[20] reveals the multi-layered paradox inherent in UN's work to identify individual governments as violators. To begin with, the complainant is only an informant and not a party to the procedure. In a typical criminal justice model, the victim is left out in the cold. In contrast to the complainant, the target government is very much a party to the procedure. Before any decision can be made, the government is asked to respond to allegations and faces possible public censure if it refuses to enter into dialogue. Public exposure has been used as a sanction against governments that consistently remained silent (such as Equatorial Guinea during the Macias regime, as discussed in Chapter 5). Entering into a dialogue, no matter how remote from the substance of the allegations, has thus evolved into a useful shield. As long as a government is 'dialoguing' about its alleged gross and systematic violations under the 1503 procedure, public debate is pre-empted. This was the case, for example, with Idi Amin's Uganda (discussed in Chapter 5) and Argentina during the dirty war (dealt with in Chapter 6).

During the early years of the 1503 procedure, neither the names of countries nor the substance of alleged violations had been made public. Since 1978, and because of a controversy about Idi Amin's Uganda discussed in Chapter 5, the names of countries are revealed while the substance remains confidential. It is thus impossible to know whether a government kept 'under review,' in UN parlance, may be responsible for slaughtering its minorities or refusing to compensate owners of nationalized property or failing to accord human rights protection to patients in mental hospitals. Some initially confidential cases have subsequently become

---

[20] The 1503 procedure consists of seven steps. (1) Complaints from individuals and organizations are received and registered by what used to be the UN Centre for Human Rights and is now the Office of the UN High Commissioner for Human Rights. The secretariat acknowledges the receipt and sends a copy to the government of the country where the alleged violation took place for its reply. (2) The secretariat analyses and summarizes received complaints in a monthly confidential document. The monthly summary identifies the governments complained against and the substance of the complaints. (3) The Working Group on Communications meets annually before each session of the Sub-Commission on Prevention of Discrimination and Protection of Minorities and considers all communications as these are prepared by the secretariat, including replies from governments. It decides which communications appear to reveal a consistent pattern of gross and reliably attested violations and should be brought to the attention of the Sub-Commission. (4) The Sub-Commission, on the basis of the confidential report of the Working Group, decides at a closed meeting which country situations to refer to the Commission on Human Rights, and for which to defer action or decide to take no action. (5) The Working Group on Situations meets annually before each session of the Commission and examines cases referred to in the confidential report of the Sub-Commission. It elaborates recommendations to the Commission on what type of action to take regarding specific country situations. (6) The Commission on Human Rights examines at closed sessions country situations which appear to reveal a consistent pattern of gross and systematic violations. This includes a dialogue with the respective governments about possible measures to remedy the situation. The lack of any form of reply from the government concerned sometimes leads to the conversion of confidential to public procedure. (7) The Commission may use its powers to carry out a study by appointing a working group or a special rapporteur, and may ultimately condemn individual governments for violations of human rights.

prominent in international human rights politics. Burundi is one example, discussed in Chapter 9. It had first been placed on the agenda in 1974 only to come under the spotlight twenty years later.

Explicit and public condemnations of human rights violators have not been all that many, as Table 1.1 reveals. Not all stopped with a mere condemnation. The appointment of a Special Rapporteur (or a working group as was practised earlier) followed for prominent cases, culminating in the creation of a separate agenda item for the violators elevated to the highest rank of public opprobrium. Table 1.2 lists chronologically those countries that triggered such heightened attention on the UN's human rights agenda to illustrate its geopolitics.

The immense and long-lasting political attention for South Africa is obvious and is discussed in more detail in Chapter 2. South Africa was followed by Israel (addressed in Chapter 3) and Chile (discussed in Chapter 5). Chronologically, they were followed by Cyprus, which was placed on the UN agenda in 1974, although nothing has been accomplished thereafter and this case history is thus not included in this book. The background was Turkey's military invasion in 1974, allegedly prompted by a plot to unify Cyprus with Greece (which was under military rule at the time). Although Turkey was found to have violated much of the European Human Rights Convention,[21] the UN Commission on Human Rights has never named it as a violator. Following the Sub-Commission's failed attempt to list Greece as a violator in 1967–68, Cyprus has remained on the agenda ever since, and Turkey has remained an absentee. Some of the reasons are explained in Chapter 7.

After Cyprus (which still holds its specific agenda item), only one country was accorded special attention in the 1970s – Equatorial Guinea (dealt with in Chapter 5). The violators-agenda broadened in the 1980s, during the last decade of the Cold War. The disappearance of one block opened the way for cold-war victors to enlarge the list of violators. As Table 1.2 shows, eight more countries were added. Three were a part of the cold-war battleground (Poland, Afghanistan, and Cuba) and four were in Central and Latin America (Bolivia, El Salvador, Guatemala, and Haiti). No less than nineteen followed in the 1990s. Because all such procedures or institutions or 'field presences' (in UN parlance) or courts require resources which are, as a rule, beyond what the United Nations can do or have done, this expansion is unlikely to continue. The slant which it has taken, with mergers between condemnatory and assistentialist tasks, or dismissed boundaries between human rights and humanitarian law, has vastly extended UN's human rights remit. This expansion has not substantially altered the process of creating UN's human rights agenda, however.

---

[21] Cyprus *versus* Turkey, *1975 Yearbook of the European Convention on Human Rights*, pp. 82–124.

Table 1.2: Country-specific UN institutions and procedures

South Africa	1952	Ad Hoc Committee (General Assembly)
	1962–94	Special Committee against Apartheid (General Assembly)
	1963	Group of Experts (Security Council/Secretary-General)
	1965–93	Trust Fund for South Africa
	1967–90	United Nations Council for Namibia (General Assembly)
	1967–94	Special Rapporteur (Commission)
	1967–94	Working Group of Experts (Commission)
	1967–95	Ad Hoc Working Group on Southern Africa (Commission)
	1974–93	Special Rapporteur on adverse consequences of aid (Commission)
	1978–95	Group of Three (Commission)
	1992–94	Observer Mission (General Assembly)
	1993–95	Special Rapporteur to monitor transition (Sub-Commission)
Israel	1968	Special Working Group of Experts
	1968–97	Special Committee on Israeli Practices (General Assembly)
	1975	Committee on Palestinian Rights (General Assembly)
	1993–	Special Rapporteur (Commission)
Chile	1975–79	Ad Hoc Working Group (Commission)
	1978–81	UN Trust Fund for Chile (General Assembly)
	1977–90	Special Rapporteur (Commission)
	1980–90	Working Group on missing persons (Commission)
Cyprus	1975–97	Committee on Disappearances
	1974–	UNFICYP (Security Council)
Equatorial Guinea	1979–80	Special Rapporteur (Commission)
	1980–92	Independent Expert (Commission)
	1993–	Special Rapporteur/Expert (Commission)
Bolivia	1981–84	Special Rapporteur/Expert (Commission)
El Salvador	1981–92	Special Rapporteur (Commission)
	1991–96	ONUSAL (Security Council)
	1992–96	Independent Expert/Rapporteur (Commission)
	1992–94	Truth Commission (United Nations)
Poland	1982–84	Special Rapporteur (Commission)
Iran	1984–	Special Representative (Commission)
Guatemala	1983–86	Special Rapporteur (Commission)
	1987–90	Independent Expert (Commission)
	1990–96	Independent Expert/Rapporteur (Commission)
	1994–	MINUGUA (Security Council)
Haiti	1984–87	Special Rapporteur (Commission)
	1987–90	Independent Expert (Commission)
	1991	ONUVEH (General Assembly)
	1991–94	Sanctions (Security Council)
	1991–94	Special Rapporteur (Commission)
	1993–96	UNMIH/MICIVIH (UN/OAS)
Afghanistan	1984–	Special Rapporteur (Commission)
Cuba	1988	Field mission (Commission)
	1991–97	Special Rapporteur (Commission)
Romania	1990–92	Special Rapporteur (Commission)
Iraq	1990–	Sanctions (Security Council)
	1991–	Operation Provide Comfort (Security Council)
	1991–92	Special Rapporteur on Iraqi-occupied Kuwait (Commission)
	1991–	Special Rapporteur (Commission)
Cambodia	1991–93	UNTAC (Security Council)
	1992–	Special Rapporteur/Expert (Secretary-General)
	1993–	Field office (Commission)

Former Yugoslavia	1991–	Sanctions (Security Council)
	1992	Two special sessions of the Commission
	1992–93	Commission of Experts (Security Council/Secretary-General)
	1992–	Special Rapporteur (Commission)
	1993	International Conference (United Nations)
	1993–	Monitors/HRFOY (Commission)
	1994–97	Rapporteur on missing persons (Commission)
	1993–	International Tribunal (Security Council)
Burma/Myanmar	1992–	Special Rapporteur (Commission)
Somalia	1992	Sanctions (Security Council)
	1993–	UNOSOM (Security Council)
	1993–	Independent expert (Commission)
Angola	1993–	Sanctions/UNITA (Security Council)
	1995–97	UNAVEM III (Security Council)
	1997–	MONUA (Security Council)
Liberia	1992–98	Sanctions (Security Council)
	1993–98	ECOMOG/UNOMIL (OAU/UN)
Sudan	1993–	Special Rapporteur (Commission)
	1996–	Sanctions (Security Council)
Zaire/Congo	1994–	Special Rapporteur (Commission)
	1997	Investigative team (Secretary-General)
Rwanda	1994	Special Session of the Commission
	1994	Commission of Experts (Security Council)
	1994	Commission of Inquiry (Security Council)
	1994–	Special Representative (Commission)
	1994–	International Tribunal (Security Council)
	1994–98	Field presence/HRFOR (Commission)
Burundi	1994–	Field office (UNHCHR)
	1995–	Special Rapporteur (Commission)
	1995–	Human rights observers (Commission)
Armenia/Azerbaijan	1995–97	Independent Expert (Commission)
Chad	1995–99	Independent expert/1503 (Commission)
Georgia/Abkhazia	1996–97	Field office (UNHCHR)
Colombia	1996–	Field office (Commission)
Nigeria	1996	Mission (Secretary-General
	1997–	Special Rapporteur (Commission)
Indonesia/East Timor	1999	UNAMET (Security Council)
	1999	Special session (Commission)

Note: Bodies created by the Security Council or the Secretary-General are included only if they had an explicit human rights mandate. For many of these bodies, the time between decision and deployment can be considerable and the time of decision is recorded in the table.

The terminology used by the United Nations is confusing. The term 'Special Rapporteur' is normally used to denote appointments mandated to investigate human rights violations, but such individuals can also be called 'representatives' or 'envoys'. The term 'Individual expert' denotes a mandate to provide advice and/or assistance to the government, but was used in the case of Chad to denote investigation of alleged gross and systematic human rights violations. There is no clear-cut distinction between different terms nor between different functions and mandates. 'Human rights monitors' denotes what is often referred to as 'field presence' where the purpose is reporting on violations, while 'field office' is used to denote provision of assistance. The terms and functions are, however, blurred in practice.

CREATING CASES: A LOOK BACK AND A LOOK FORWARD

Human rights violations will be found wherever they are sought. Where one goes to look for them, and what phenomena one is looking for, are determined by an implicit definition of human rights and their violations. Although international human rights instruments are routinely cited, their huge number and abstract formulation give grounds for defining nearly anything as a human rights violation. Interest for particular countries and specific human rights violations is then created according to a specific political agenda. The initial provision of information creates demand for condemnation as well as additional information through further investigation.

The process of investigating and condemning violators is not only, nor mainly, inter-governmental politics. In this area, non-governmental actors routinely lead and governments follow, collectively pressurized to balance their role as violators and protectors of human rights. New actors have emerged in the form of non-governmental organisations (NGOs) and in the form of the victims themselves, notably the indigenous. Pressurized by growing numbers of human rights organizations, inter-governmental politics has had to accommodate some human rights concerns. Increased public interest for human rights, especially in the West, has turned the spotlight on Western foreign policies, especially their response to human rights violations elsewhere.

Because the United Nations can only act in response to the information it receives, an outside initiative is a necessary first step. Non-governmental organisations rather than governments, take the lead in exposing violations. From a handful that started in the West in the 1960s, their number has grown to thousands in the 1990s. Theo van Boven has pointed out that the number of NGOs grew from 15 at the time when the United Nations had been established to 150 in 1968, at the time of the first World Conference on Human Rights, to 1,500 at the time of the second World Conference, in Vienna in 1993.[22] Most information originates from intermediaries rather than victims; most of the intermediaries are either based in the West or their funding originates in the West.

The absence of a controlled vocabulary among non-governmental organisations and within the Commission on Human Rights has divorced human rights from their grounding in law and transplanted them into international politics. Definitions of violations change in time and place and vary from one non-governmental organisation to another. What does not change has been highlighted by David Weissbrodt and James McCarthy:

---

[22] van Boven, T. – Fifty years of the Universal Declaration of Human Rights – Balance and challanges of the international protection of human rights, in: Baehr, P. et al. (eds.) – *Innovation and Inspiration: Fifty Years of the Universal Declaration of Human Rights*, Royal Netherlands Academy of Arts and Sciences, Amsterdam, 1999, p. 7–8.

There is nothing which convinces the outside world so much as the statement 'We were there and we saw.'[23]

The geopolitics of the search for human rights violations is illustrated in Table 1.3, which summarises the most frequent destinations of NGO fact-finding missions in 1970–1986. The number of both non-governmental organisations and their

Table 1.3: Destinations of NGO fact-finding missions, 1970–86

Region and country	Number of missions
CENTRAL AMERICA	
29 to El Salvador	
25 to Nicaragua	
19 to Guatemala	111
ASIA	
11 to Philippines	
8 to Pakistan	
8 to Sri Lanka	65
SOUTH AMERICA	
19 to Chile	
9 to Argentina	
8 to Uruguay	58
NORTH AFRICA	
9 to Morocco	
7 to Egypt	
4 to Tunisia	51
MEMBERS OF COUNCIL OF EUROPE	
11 to Turkey	
5 to United Kingdom	
3 to Spain	29
MIDDLE EAST	
11 to Iran	
8 to Palestine	28
NORTH AMERICA	
4 to Canada	
1 to USA	5
OCEANIA	
1 to Australia	
1 to Papua New Guinea	4

Note: Regions are ranked by the total number of fact-finding missions. Only the most frequent target countries are singled out within each region and the figures therefore do not add up.
Source: Thoolen, H. and Verstappen, B. – *Human Rights Missions. A Study of the Fact-finding Practice of Non-governmental Organizations*, Martinus Nijhoff Publishers and Netherlands Institute of Human Rights (SIM), 1986.

---

[23] Weissbrodt, D. and McCarthy, J. – Fact-finding by nongovernmental organizations, in Ramcharan, B.G. (ed.) – *International Law and Fact-finding in the Field of Human Rights*, Martinus Nijhoff Publishers, The Hague, 1982, p. 190.

missions was small enough at the time to make such stocktaking possible. That period, 1970–86, also coincided with the first fifteen years of UN procedures for identifying human-rights violators. Similarities between the NGO-generated supply of information on abuses in specific countries and the UN human rights agenda are as obvious as are the differences. The process of creating a case involves choices – which country? what issue? – for which the abstract postulate of 'all human rights for all' does not help at all.

The focus on Central and South America – almost half of the NGO missions went there – reflects the international human rights politics of the time. The 1970s were the era of increasing domestic pressures to constrain US-supported abuses abroad, and NGO missions targeted those countries which were of particular interest to domestic US constituencies. The entry of human rights into the foreign policies of other Western countries contributed to slanting the search for violations towards those countries in which domestic constituencies had a particular interest because they were aid recipients.

Human rights organisations have opted for the term 'fact-finding' to depict their missions because it implied that the law was clear and only facts should be verified. Indeed, Hans Thoolen and Bert Verstappen, the authors of this stocktaking project, have found that half of such fact-finding missions did not make any reference to the law that was supposedly breached. Any abuses could be called 'violations'. The reliance on English as *the* working language (with French tailing behind with one-third of reports) rather than the languages of the visited countries, and the absence of non-Western non-governmental organisations as originators of such reports were the defining features of geopolitics of NGO missions.[24] A decade later, Ian Martin, a former Secretary-General of Amnesty International, has noted how tempting it must have been 'to use the economic power of the North to apply pressure on aid-dependent countries for civil and political rights protection.'[25] Amnesty International did not succumb to that temptation while Human Rights Watch took the opposite path, advocating the imposition of sanctions as well as human rights conditionality in aid, further to create 'the right to monitor.'[26]

This process of creating cases further politicised the inherently political determination of violators, splitting the international human rights agenda in two: one Western, with decision-making confined to individual governments or institutions in which developing countries had no say, while the other – the United Nations – underwent further changes in the 1990s. The second wave of independence increased UN membership through the fragmentation of Eastern Europe. The UN

---

[24] Thoolen, H. and Verstappen, B. – *Human Rights Missions. A Study of the Factfinding Practice of Non-governmental Organizations*, Martinus Nijhoff Publishers and Netherlands Institute of Human Rights (SIM), 1986, pp. 114–115 and 34.

[25] Martin, I. – The new world order: Opportunity or threat for human rights? A lecture by the Edward A. Smith Visiting Fellow presented by the Harvard Law School Human Rights Program, Cambridge, 1993, p. 17.

[26] *Human Rights Watch World Report 1993*, New York/Washington/Los Angeles, 1993, p. xvii.

Commission on Human Rights was enlarged in 1990 as was its agenda. From 'traditional' topics focusing on the most obvious abuses of power in areas where the state has a monopoly, namely the use of force, violence and coercion, the span has broadened to encompass topics ranging from foreign debt to income distribution, from mercenaries to terrorism, from violence against women to extreme poverty and the export of toxic waste. The underlying right often remained unclear while denounced violations proliferated.

The Commission on Human Rights started the 1990s enlarged from 43 to 53 members and consolidated into regional blocks. Regardless of what else it may have been doing, the coverage of its sessions in the mass media portrayed it as an arena of confrontation between those regional blocks. Seven consecutive sessions (1990 to 1997, and 1999) were marked by the Western (first the US, then EU, then Danish) attempts to condemn human rights violations in China; a parallel attempt against Indonesia (1992–1997) received much attention as well, as did confrontations with Islamic countries, especially Sudan. Adrien-Claude Zoller noted at the beginning of decade: 'the Soviet target has vanished, but the strategy of confrontation remains'[27] and has subsequently been proven right. Of the condemnatory draft resolutions before the Commission, more than half are initiated by the West although its membership is a mere one-fifth.

The rules of democracy require a majority of votes to condemn a country for human rights violations, and most votes are held by Africa (15), Asia and Latin America (12 and 11 respectively), the Western Europe and Others group (WEOS) has 10 votes and Eastern Europe five. Regional meetings of members and observers were institutionalised within the Commission a long time ago, and intra-regional solidarity became a noticeable feature of the Commission's output in the 1990s. Throughout the decade, Western initiatives have often failed to obtain the necessary majority and the West found itself targeted in retaliation. As Table 1.1 has shown, besides Cyprus, there have only been two condemnatory resolutions against Western countries, in both cases against the United States, and in both cases for its military interventions. A good illustration for changing agenda-setting (if unchanged outcomes of the Commission's deliberations) was 1995, when all five permanent members of the Security Council found themselves discussed under various items on the violations-agenda. Cuba had initiated a draft resolution on racial discrimination in the United States following the findings of the Special Rapporteur on racism. The United Kingdom had been placed on the violations-agenda earlier because of 'troubles' in Northern Ireland, and France arrived on the agenda following the findings of the Special Rapporteur on racism. A chairman's statement was adopted on Chechnya, acknowledging that violations were taking place (this is dicussed in Chapter 11).

---

[27] Zoller, A.-C. – 46th session of the United Nations Commission on Human Rights. Analytical report, *Netherlands Quarterly on Human Rights*, vol. 10, 1990, No. 2, p. 144.

To reduce, if not eliminate, possibilities for the identification and condemnation of violators, the Commission has shifted from voting to consensus-building. By 1997, more than two-thirds of all resolutions were adopted by consensus. Debates about 'rationalising' (UN language) the work of the Commission became embroiled in a mixture of budgetary and political battles. To a great degree, the need to streamline the work of the Commission has been dictated by excessive costs. As the Commission and its Sub-Commission, their meeting time, and agendas have been enlarged, the costs skyrocketed. Participation in the six-week-long annual session of the Commission on Human Rights exceeds 2,000 people (equally divided between governmental and non-governmental participants). Hundreds of documents, thousands of pages, have to be produced in all six official languages, and endless stream of speeches simultaneously translated. The system has reached the point where further expansion is neither politically nor financially possible.

Chapter 2

THE FIRST MULTILATERAL SANCTIONS

The two case studies in this Chapter, Rhodesia and South Africa, summarise the UN's rapid passage from condemnations to sanctions. Rhodesia was the target of the first and the longest UN sanctions applied to enforce the right to self-determination. The transformation of Rhodesia into Zimbabwe achieved the aim of the sanctions. In the case of South Africa, sanctions followed its numerous and repetitive condemnations and led to law-making in the form of the Convention against Apartheid. Sanctions also served as the rallying point of the incipient international human rights movement. The premise that everybody should react to human rights violations anywhere in the world characterised the anti-apartheid movement, as did the belief that sanctions constituted a necessary complement to condemnations.

With the benefit of hindsight, one can argue that sanctions against Rhodesia would never have happened had it not been for Britain's role. The United Kingdom, Rhodesia's sovereign, approached the United Nations calling for sanctions as an alternative to armed force. Because Britain was a member of the Security Council, it could 'multilateralise' and legalise sanctions. Not so for South Africa, which was dealt with by the General Assembly, and the UN human rights bodies joined in 1967.[1] South Africa dominated the *violations-condemnations-sanctions* agenda until the General Assembly lifted sanctions in 1993[2] and the country was ultimately taken off the violators-agenda in 1995. As late as 1988, the last year before the Cold War officially ended, South Africa (together with Israel) occupied half of each annual session of the UN Commission on Human Rights.[3]

The huge volume of condemnatory resolutions against South Africa included many calls for sanctions, leading eventually to the adoption of a convention aimed at mandating a halt in all exchanges with South Africa. International law is not self-enforcing, however, and translating sanctions from rhetoric to reality was left to each individual state. The Security Council could have imposed sanctions as it had done against Rhodesia but did not do so. Those permanent members of the Council who were also South Africa's main commercial partners kept economic

---

[1] The first inquiry into South Africa's treatment of its population had been initiated by pre-independence India in 1946. The inquiry concerned the plight of Indians in South Africa and pointed to the difficulties which that had created for relations between the two countries. The United Nations first addressed the treatment of the black population in South Africa in 1952, and phrased its concerns so as to stress the implications of that treatment for South Africa's relations with other countries.

[2] Resolution 48/1 on the lifting of sanctions against South Africa was adopted without a vote.

[3] Guest, I. – On the Brink of a Mid-Life Crisis: The United Nations at Forty, *HRI (Human Rights Internet) Reporter. Special Report*, vol. 12, No. 2, Winter 1988, p. 55.

sanctions voluntary and unilateral all the way to the1980s, almost to the eve of dismantling apartheid. While Rhodesia was the target of sanctions for fourteen years, economic sanctions against South Africa by its main commercial partners were short: EUrope's from 1985 to 1991, US sanctions from 1986 to 1991, and Japan's from 1988 to 1991.

Anti-apartheid sanctions served as a catalyst for human rights activism in the Western industrialised countries. The ultimate object of sanctions was far away but their immediate target was domestic. Individuals had to make daily decisions so as not to provide any support to or bestow legitimacy upon the apartheid regime or its beneficiaries. Moreover, they had to pressure their own governments into taking a stand against apartheid. The mobilising power of sanctions became an article of faith for the incipient human rights movement.

RHODESIA

The Security Council used its enforcement powers sparingly during the first four decades: between 1946 and 1990 it adopted only fourteen resolutions under Chapter VII of the UN Charter, which empowers the Council to impose sanctions which have to be implemented by all states, after it has determined a threat to peace, a breach of peace or an act of aggression.

Rhodesia first appeared on the Council's agenda in 1963. The Council urged the United Kingdom (Rhodesia's sovereign) not to transfer sovereign powers to an unrepresentative regime. The 1962 elections had effectively excluded the entire non-white population, which otherwise would have constituted 94% of the electorate. The United Kingdom vetoed a proposed resolution which would have impeded its transfer of sovereign powers to Rhodesia, thus paralysing the Security Council. The issue was transferred the UN General Assembly, which declared the situation in Southern Rhodesia to constitute a threat to international peace and security. Rhodesia nevertheless declared independence in 1965. The Security Council then, without a British veto, called on states not to recognise the Rhodesian 'illegal racist minority regime' nor to render it any assistance; it also imposed oil and petroleum embargoes.[4] Sanctions were justified by declaring Rhodesia to constitute a threat to international peace and security, although this was challenged by a claim that internal repression and denial of human rights did not endanger international peace and security. The challenge was not successful and thus began the first, fourteen-year long, United Nations sanctions. James Baldwin has commented:

Rhodesia will always be remembered as the first country against which the United Nations imposed mandatory sanctions. This historic event had a sym-

---

[4] Security Council resolutions 216(1965) and 217(1965).

bolic significance that went beyond inconvenience that might or might not have accompanied the act.[5]

The symbolic significance of sanctions aside, their effectiveness was questionable because no monitoring existed. Sanctions were thus imposed (or not) by individual states with little authoritative evidence for either. Moreover, most countries had no national legislation to implement international sanctions. Much as in subsequent cases, official data and information collected by non-governmental organisations and academics differed a great deal. The transition from Rhodesia to Zimbabwe was attributed to the war of liberation (with substantial involvement of the neighbouring countries) rather than to sanctions. Because an international military intervention was out of question due to Britain's commitment that armed force would not be used against Rhodesia, sanctions were the only complement to condemnations.

The creation of Rhodesia and its subsequent transformation into Zimbabwe was embedded in the regional process of decolonisation, in which the United Kingdom and South Africa were influential actors. In 1953, Southern Rhodesia (Zimbabwe), Northern Rhodesia (Zambia) and Nyasaland (Malawi) were joined to form the Federation of Rhodesia and Nyasaland, which was dissolved ten years later. Zambia and Malawi became independent in 1964. The fate of Southern Rhodesia was left to its domestic political processes, implicitly accepting the right to vote confined to taxpayers (one-quarter million whites) and excluding more than four million Africans. The United Kingdom accepted a promise that political rights would be gradually extended and majority rule attained by the year 2035. Moreover, Britain committed itself not to use military force to prevent Rhodesia's independence.[6] When challenged by the Security Council to secure a representative government in Rhodesia before relinquishing its international responsibility, the United Kingdom vetoed that draft resolution. The justification was that orderly dissolution of the Federation of Rhodesia and Nyasaland necessitated transferring sovereignty to Southern Rhodesia as it was at the time.[7]

Rhodesia's 1961 Constitution effectively denied human rights to the indigenous non-white population. Elections were held in 1962 on the basis of that Constitution and independence was declared in 1965 by the thus elected government. UN's appeals to the United Kingdom to secure basic rights for the non-European population fell on deaf ears. Although the United Kingdom had nominal sovereignty, Rhodesia had been self-governing as of 1923, including full control over the army and the police. Self-government was confined to the white population. Negotiations

---

[5] Baldwin, J. – *Economic Statecraft: Theory and Practice*, Princeton University Press, 1985, p. 192.

[6] Documents Relating to the Negotiations between the United Kingdom and Southern Rhodesian Governments, November 1963–November 1965, London, 1965, p. 124.

[7] U.N. Doc. 5/P.V. 1068, Official Records of the Security Council, vol. 18, 1963, 1068th meeting, p. 2.

between the United Kingdom and Rhodesia terminated inconclusively and Ian Smith, the chief negotiator, returned home to declare Rhodesia independent. The Unilateral Declaration of Independence of 11 November 1965 was followed the very next day by the Security Council's call on all states not to recognise the illegal racist minority regime of Rhodesia and to refrain from rendering it assistance. Thereupon the Council called upon all states to break off all relations with Rhodesia and in 1966 sanctions were made mandatory. They were broadened and strengthened in 1968, 1973 and 1976.[8]

Although the United Nations had not yet developed a response to denials and violations of human rights, human rights language had been amply used. Denials of equal rights were frequent in justifying sanctions. The involvement of the United Nations was based on Rhodesia's status as a non-self-governing territory and a determination that it threatened international peace and security. These grounds were irrelevant for practical purposes: the United Kingdom agreed to UN involvement, no other veto-wielding member of the Security Council disagreed. Hence, the United Nations acted on the basis of 'a factual and political judgment' rather than on interpretations of the UN Charter or general international law.[9]

These sanctions were a precedent for the United Nations. Co-ordinating and monitoring capacity was lacking, as was investigation or enforcement. A sanctions committee was duly established and processed governmental reports on compliance.[10] Reporting was voluntary. This set the model for the future: the reporting governments were self-selected and their reports were positive self-evaluations of compliance.

Sanctions by Rhodesia's neighbours had minuscule negative effects. For Zambia, they amounted to self-inflicted harm – Zambia had been dependent on Rhodesia for, *inter alia*, electricity and transport, not to mention the sole export route for its copper. The cost of Zambia's sanctions against Rhodesia was high for Zambia and negligible for Rhodesia.[11]

Few countries had economic exchanges with Rhodesia except its neighbours and Britain and sanctions were easy to impose where there was nothing to break off. South Africa, which opposed sanctions, was Rhodesia's major trading partner. Together with Portugal (and thus Mozambique and Angola until their independence), it openly flouted sanctions as well as assisting Rhodesia's government in

---

[8]   Security Council resolutions 216 and 217 (1965), 232 (1966), 253 (1968), 333 (1973) and 388 (1976).

[9]   Gowland-Debbas, V. – *Collective Responses to Illegal Acts in International Law: United Nations Action in the Question of Southern Rhodesia*, Martinus Nijhoff, Dordrecht, 1990, p. 451.

[10] The committee was established in 1968 and submitted its last report in 1980, when the sanctions were lifted. Twelfth Report of the Security Council Committee established in pursuance of resolution 253 (1968) concerning the question of Southern Rhodesia, Official Records of the Security Council, vol. 35, 1980, Special Supplement No. 2, U.N. Doc. S/13750.

[11] Anglin, D.G. – *Zambian Crisis Behaviour: Confronting Rhodesia's Unilateral Declaration of Independence, 1965–1966*, McGill-Queen's University Press, Montreal, 1994.

suppressing domestic opposition. Sanctions were less openly flouted by the United Kingdom and the United States.

The United States imposed sanctions against Rhodesia in 1971. They were difficult to impose because the Byrd Amendment impeded sanctions against a 'free world country' unless they were also imposed against Communist countries.[12] They were even more difficult to enforce and their breaches did not go unnoticed:

> In Washington the Rhodesian Information Office was allowed to remain open, disseminating information, lobbying on Capitol Hill, encouraging American tourism and recruiting Americans for the Rhodesian armed forces. In New York, the Air Rhodesia office worked closely with American airlines, travel agencies and credit card companies promoting tourism to Rhodesia. American tourists made up a fifth of the total Rhodesian tourist trade and brought in about £8,000,000 a year in much-needed foreign exchange.[13]

Studies of the impact of sanctions found them to have been effective at first. Statistical evidence on aid was clear. Britain's aid alone had been $11 million in 1963, but total aid to Rhodesia fell to an annual $0.3 million in 1966–67.[14] Besides Britain, other donors (Canada, Germany and Sweden) together contributed less than a million U.S. dollars annually before sanctions.

Rhodesia was a major exporter of tobacco, which had amounted to one-third of the total, while mineral exports constituted one-fourth of total. The value of Rhodesia's exports declined by one-third in 1966–69, but for 1970–74 statistics pointed in the opposite direction and Rhodesia's economy grew by an annual 9%.[15]

Table 2.1 highlights Rhodesia's increasing budgetary deficit in the last years before its transformation to Zimbabwe. The increasing deficit was due to the cumulative effects of enforcing minority rule, fighting a guerrilla war (estimated at 30–40% of the budget), and coping with sanctions.

Sanctions were not meant to merely inflict economic hardship upon Rhodesia, but to change minority to majority rule. They were a protest against its government and aimed at its demise by targeting its economic underpinning, therefore designed against the white population, who could – and ultimately did – alter governmental policy. Within the white population, however, the effect of sanctions was opposite to that intended. Rather than fostering opposition to the government, sanctions

---

[12] Carnegie Endowment for International Peace – Irony in chrome: The Byrd Amendment two years later, Interim report of the Special Rhodesia project, New York, 1973.

[13] Martin, D. and Johnson, P. – *The Struggle for Zimbabwe. The Chimurenga War*, Faber and Faber, London/Boston, 1981, p. 232.

[14] OECD – *Geographical Distribution of Financial Flows to Less Developed Countries (Disbursements) 1960–1964*, Paris, 1966, p. 84–85, and *1966–1967*, Paris, 1969, p. 40–41.

[15] Anglin, D.G. – United Nations economic sanctions against South Africa and Rhodesia, in Leyton-Brown, D. (ed.) – *The Utility of International Economic Sanctions*, Croom Helm, London, 1987, p. 33–34.

Table 2.1: Rhodesia's financial crisis, 1974–1980

	1975–75	1975–76	1976–77	1977–78	1978–79	1979–80
External finance	–	–	–	63.8	122.9	101.0
Domestic finance	45.2	24.5	109.0	88.0	165.8	280.9
Government revenue	400.5	462.3	530.9	610.2	580.2	675.9
Government expenditure	445.7	486.8	639.9	762.0	868.9	1057.9
Deficit	–45.2	–24.5	–109.0	–151.8	–288.7	–382.0

Note: Figures represent Rhodesian dollars in millions.
Source: Renwick, R. – *Economic Sanctions*, Center for International Affairs, Harvard University, Cambridge, 1981, p. 105.

stifled it. Increased repression of the black majority and all opponents was justified 'by the necessity to face the economic warfare being waged by Britain and the United Nations.'[16] Conversion from minority to majority rule was ultimately accomplished through all-encompassing suffrage. The economic underpinning for future majority rule was thus dissociated from political transition, and has been haunting post-transition Zimbabwe ever since.

Robin Renwick has found that sanctions did not affect 'the sophisticated sector of the economy' but instead ruined the subsistence sector. Tobacco constituted the primary target of sanctions, which were intended to harm the wealthy and politically powerful rural white community and, in particular, the owners of the large commercial farms involved in export-oriented agricultural production. Tobacco farmers were white, their labourers were black, but sanctions affected both. The tobacco farmers lost two-thirds of their income in the period between 1964 and 1968 and the number of white commercial farmers was halved. Losses inflicted upon black farm labourers were never quantified; they lost their jobs and there was no alternative employment to absorb the African labour force.[17]

There are two competing interpretations of the reasons for the guerrilla warfare against Rhodesia's minority regime. One concentrates on the political dimension; the other considers access to land as the principal driving force for indigenous opposition to white settlers. Jonathan Moyo, the chairman of *Inqama* (a ram in Ndebele) made his case thus:'our leaders made us fight a war for the land which is still not ours.'[18]

Land is, regretfully, a marginal issue in international human rights politics and access to land is not guaranteed as a human right. As a consequence, legally entrenched private ownership is protected while access to land for those who need

---

[16] Losman, D.L. – *International Economic Sanctions. The Cases of Cuba, Israel, and Rhodesia*, University of New Mexico Press, Albuquerque, 1979, p. 119.
[17] Renwick, R. – *Economic Sanctions*, Center for International Affairs, Harvard University, Harvard Studies in International Affairs, No. 45, Cambridge, 1981, pp. 32, and 56–57.
[18] Ngwenya, D. – Zimbabwe: Peasants revolt, *New African*, April 1997.

it to secure their survival cannot be invoked as a right. Yet land is the key to survival in Africa and also to the realisation of human rights.

In the Rhodesian case, political and economic governance were treated as distinct and unrelated issues. In the transition from Rhodesia to Zimbabwe, land ownership by the while minority was entrenched in the Lancaster House Agreement and made untouchable for a decade to become an explosive political problem as soon as that decade ended. Sanctions were then threatened to deter Zimbabwe from altering the pattern of land ownership. Majority rule was designed for the political domain and the will of the majority was precluded from tampering with minority land ownership. It was assumed that political governance founded upon majority rule and economic governance based on minority land ownership could go hand in hand.

Mandatory sanctions against Rhodesia were kept in place till 1979. The United Kingdom accepted responsibility for the transformation of Rhodesia into Zimbabwe and led the negotiations to the conclusion of the Lancaster House Agreement. This Agreement was followed by a cease-fire, a new constitution, elections based on universal suffrage, and Rhodesia became Zimbabwe. The Lancaster House Agreement, however, imposed constraints upon future majority rule: parliamentary representation for the white minority, protection of their large commercial farms from nationalisation, and impunity for abuses by the previous government as well as the opposition. In his broadcast on the eve of independence, prime minister Robert Mugabe said: 'The wrongs of the past must now stand forgiven and forgotten.'[19]

Post-sanctions Zimbabwe

Paula Park and Tony Jackson have thus described the pattern of land ownership in Rhodesia/Zimbabwe:

> Under the 1969 Land Tenure Act, 45 million hectares of land (formerly known as the Tribal Trust Lands) were set aside for black farmers and 45 million for white farmers. After independence, there were 680,000 black farmers, nearly three times the maximum number that the land could safely carry, while there were only 6,700 European farmers working 'their half'. Whites had access to a hundred times more land than blacks.[20]

At independence, 5,000 white-owned large commercial farms generated 90% of agricultural output. A small-scale resettlement programme gave 60,000 families five-year leases and compensated former landowners to be criticised both for not having gone far enough and for having gone too far. Demands that land be distributed according to need met a series of obstacles. Land cannot be multiplied and

---

[19] *Africa Today*, Africa Books, London, 1996, p. 1650.
[20] Park, P. and Jackson, T. – Lands of plenty, lands of scarcity. Agricultural policy and peasant farmers in Zimbabwe and Tanzania, Oxfam, Oxford, May 1985, mimeographed, p. 3.

its distribution is a zero-sum-game. Redistribution, without investment in agricultural inputs and vocational training, does not automatically meet the basic human needs of beneficiaries.

After the ten-year guarantee of white land ownership expired, land reform reverted to being an unsolved political and economic problem. Donors threatened aid cutoffs each time the government threatened to dispossess the white minority. The government's justification was an equitable racial balance of land ownership. The donors' justification was the government's self-granted power to deprive individuals of their legally recognised rights, the economic cost of diminished agricultural exports, and the government's record in allocating land on the ground of greed rather than need, in the form of self-allocation within the political elite.[21]

An economic system based on dispossession of the black majority thus continued alongside majority rule. Economic growth at first exceeded an annual 10% but thereafter Zimbabwe's economic performance worsened. Recurring drought was beyond governmental control. Worsening economic conditions led to indigenous opposition to the indigenous government and to its Rhodesia-styled suppression. Rhodesia's emergency rule (1965–79) was rescinded as late as 1990.[22]

By the 1992 Land Acquisition Act, the government gave itself powers to acquire land on its own terms, namely to select farms for compulsory purchase and to set the level of compensation, preventing any challenge by owners. Parliament, in which Robert Mugabe's party held 147 out of 150 seats, easily adopted the law. Legal challenges followed immediately as did donors' threats. Britain announced that it would discontinue its $36 million contribution to Zimbabwe's land resettlement programme to prevent these funds from supporting the government's abuse of power.[23] Attempts to declare the Land Acquisition Act unconstitutional failed after Zimbabwe's judiciary affirmed 'the state's right to compulsorily acquire property.'[24] Prime Minister Mugabe's justification was that the forefathers of the current owners had taken land by force, and their complaining grandchildren were a 'greedy bunch of racist usurpers.'[25] Subsequent scandals revealed that 're-appropriated' land was distributed among political leaders, generals and cabinet ministers, including among the beneficiaries Witness Mangwende, the minister who had introduced and defended the 1992 Act).[26]

---

[21] Economic scandals rock Zimbabwe, *New African*, July/August 1997; Duval Smith, A. – Gulf between needy and greedy, *Guardian Weekly*, 14 June 1998.

[22] Ncube, W. – State security, the rule of law and politics of repression in Zimbabwe, Third World Seminars, University of Oslo, mimeographed, 1990.

[23] Zimbabwe: Your land will be my land, *The Economist*, 15 February 1992; McIvor, C. – Zimbabwe: The fight for land, *New African*, July 1992.

[24] Zimbabwe: The price of food, land and rhetoric, *The Economist*, 2 October 1993; Zimbabwe farm seizure allowed, *Financial Times*, 11 November 1994.

[25] Moyo, B. – Zimbabwe: Landing the needy, *Africa Events*, October 1993; Kelso, B.J. – Farmers sue the Zimbabwe government, *New African*, November 1993.

[26] Beresford, D. – Mugabe backs down over 'land grab' plan, *Guardian Weekly*, 30 October 1994; Marion, G. – Cash crisis fuels Zimbabwe's racial tension, *Le monde*, 12/13 February 1995, reproduced in *Guardian Weekly*, 19 February 1995.

In November 1997, the government announced that half of the land owned by white commercial farmers, some 1500 farms out of a total of about 4500, would be nationalised following the 1998 harvest. The Commercial Farmers Union opposed the decision by claiming that 40% of foreign exchange was generated by agricultural exports from these white-owned farms.[27] They also employed 300,000 labourers, whose strikes for better pay and living conditions for themselves and their families (numbering more than 2 million) added fuel to fire.[28] The solution reverted back to the United Kingdom: 'Mr Mugabe insists that Britain is obliged to finance land nationalization, compensating the white farmers, under oral agreements made before independence.'[29]

Commentators pointed out that the government simply had no money to pay compensation, being in the dire economic straits of which the currency collapse and riots over increased food prices were visible symptoms. And yet, while the army was quelling riots, the government reportedly purchased 50 Mercedes cars for its ministers.[30] Aid was later suspected of funding Zimbabwe's military intervention in Zaire/Congo and suspended. At issue was the cost of warfare for Zimbabwe estimated at between $3 million per month and $1 million per day.[31] At a pledging conference held in September 1998, Zimbabwe sought half of the estimated cost of $2.2 billion for land reform, giving assurances that due process of law would be followed to rescind three months later and issue acquisition orders for 841 white-owned farms. A court ruling saying that the government failed to designate 520 out of 841 farms on time led to the government's verbal attacks on judges.[32]

Two views epitomise the planned redistribution of land. Joseph Msika, Zimbabwe's Minister of State at the time, emphasised that Zimbabwe had to succeed in altering the pattern of land ownership because 'it will be of tremendous importance for the entire southern African region.'[33] Morgan Tsvangirai, a trade union leader and spokesman for a newly formed opposition party, protested at the government's tendency to look back rather than forward:'every time we talk about the future, they bring up the past.'[34] Zimbabwe's experience has been instructive

---

[27] Hawkins, T. – Mugabe set for party triumph over land seizure plan, *Financial Times*, 3 December 1997.

[28] Gadaga, N. – Zimbabwe: The farm workers will suffer too!, *New African*, February 1998.

[29] Zimbabwe: Swapping land for votes, *The Economist*, 6 December 1997; Meldrum, A. – Zimbabwe to seize white farmland, *Guardian Weekly*, 19 October 1997 ; Holman, M. – Mr Mugabe lets slip an unsettling aside, *Financial Times*, 19–20 November 1994.

[30] Hawkins, T. – Cornered Mugabe still without challenger, *Financial Times*, 23 January 1998.

[31] Hawkins, T. – Mugabe's mind on foreign adventure as Zimbabwe slides further into mire, and IMF team suggests resuming lending to Zimbabwe, *Financial Times*, 5 November 1998 and 14 January 1999; Meldrum, A. – Zimbabwe hides the cost of Congo war, *Guardian Weekly*, 18 April 1999; Chinaka, C. – War haunts Mugabe, *New African*, November 1999.

[32] Cash, please, and Mugabe's battle, *The Economist*, 5 September 1998; Outburst by Mugabe may deter donors, and Zimbabwe to 'cut ties' with IMF, *Financial Times*, 11 February and 12 April 1999.

[33] Meldrum, A. – Mugabe responds to land squats with revived settlement plan, *The Guardian*, 6 July 1998.

[34] Jeter, J. – African liberator becomes a liability, *Guardian Weekly*, 25 November–1 December 1999.

for South Africa: political transition to majority rule was fostered through condemnations and sanctions, and greeted with loud international applause; Zimbabwe
was then left to its own devices to tackle the economic underpinnings of majority
rule.

SOUTH AFRICA

South Africa's treatment of its non-white population was raised before the General
Assembly during its very first session. India, in bringing up the topic, focused on the
plight of the Indian population in South Africa; the plight of the country's entire non-
white population had long historical roots.[35] India imposed sanctions and, in 1947,
South Africa accused India 'of seeking to force a solution by the imposition of unilateral sanctions'.[36] South West Africa was added to the United Nations agenda soon
thereafter, and apartheid finally 'discovered' to make South Africa *the* human rights
violator for four decades. Many states followed India and imposed sanctions.

Following the plight of Indians in South Africa, the United Nations prioritized
South Africa's status as a colonial power. When the General Assembly affirmed the
right to self-determination in 1950, South West Africa (today's Namibia) had
already been on its agenda for four years. In fact, the decision that a trusteeship
agreement should be negotiated between the United Nations and South Africa had
been taken by the General Assembly in 1946. Such an agreement was never concluded, and South West Africa continued on the United Nations agenda until
Namibian independence in 1990. The International Court of Justice (ICJ) found in
1971 South Africa's continued presence in Namibia illegal and declared all its acts
null and void. Moreover, the ICJ found that other states had an obligation to refrain
from any relations with South Africa that could bestow legality upon its reign over
South West Africa.[37] This justification for sanctions was complemented by the

---

[35] The Union of South Africa was established (as a British Dominion) in 1910, and in 1913 the
Native Land Act divided White and Non-White land ownership. Similarly to Rhodesia, the best land
was allocated to the whites. *Apartheid* was formally introduced in 1948 and legalized in 1950 through
the Group Areas and Population Registration Acts; the Bantu Education Act was added in 1953. The
classification by race and colour entailed a progressive denial of rights linked to progressively darker
pigmentation. Opposition to apartheid was initially outlawed through the Suppression of Communism
Act of 1950. The language combining the threat of terrorism and/or communism alluded to the Soviet
Union as the main source of danger. This came later and the Soviet Union started supporting the South
African Communist Party (SACP) in 1961 and in 1963 also the ANC (African National Congress) with
military training and arms supplies. Shubin, V. – The Soviet Union/Russian Federation's relations with
South Africa, with special reference to the period since 1980, *African Affairs*, vol. 95, 1996, pp. 5–6 and
15.
[36] United Nations – *United Nations Action in the Field of Human Rights*, Sales No. E.94.XIV.11,
New York and Geneva, 1994, paras. 1482–1485.
[37] International Court of Justice – Legal consequences for states of the continued presence of South
Africa in Namibia (South West Africa) notwithstanding Security Council resolution 276 (1970),
Advisory opinion, *ICJ Reports 1971*.

outrage against apartheid. Calls for sanctions proliferated, but the Security Council was indisposed to heed them.

In 1960, an annual conference of independent African states, predecessor to the future Organization of African Unity, asked all African states to break off diplomatic relations with South Africa and institute a comprehensive trade, transport and communications boycott.[38] That initiative evolved into two-tiered strategy – isolation and sanctions. South Africa's isolation was accomplished through its exclusion from the Commonwealth in 1961 and its enforced withdrawal from the International Labour Organization (ILO) in 1964, which resulted from a 1963 demand for expulsion. This was followed by South Africa's withdrawal from the Food and Agriculture Organization (FAO) in 1963 and, the following year, from the Universal Postal Union (UPU). In 1974, South Africa was deprived of voting rights in the United Nations. The battle to isolate South Africa spanned many international fora including international sports events.

In addition to this strategy to isolate South Africa, the General Assembly recommended sanctions in 1962 and the Security Council recommended a weapons embargo in 1963. Sanctions were gradually made both comprehensive and obligatory. The Security Council converted the arms embargo from voluntary to obligatory in 1977, but did not venture into economic sanctions. Other UN bodies counterbalanced the Council's reticence through an endless stream of condemnations and calls for sanctions.

A series of bodies was specially created to deal with apartheid and/or South Africa. (Those concentrating on the human rights dimensions have been listed in Table 1.2.) The General Assembly established its Special Committee against Apartheid in 1962. The UN Ad Hoc Working Group of Experts on Southern Africa was established by the Commission on Human Rights in 1967 and submitted its last report in 1995. In 1973, the International Convention on the Suppression and Punishment of the Crime of Apartheid was adopted by the UN General Assembly, and entered into force three years later. The Group of Three was established by the Commission on Human Rights to review reports on its implementation.[39] This Convention is nominally still in force, but the Group of Three has been suspended. Also in 1973, the Sub-Commission on Prevention of Discrimination and Protection of Minorities appointed the Special Rapporteur on Adverse Consequences for the Enjoyment of Human Rights of Political, Military, Economic and Other Forms of Assistance Given to the Racist and Colonialist Regime of South Africa. His last annual report was presented in 1992. In a typical UN fashion, yet another monitoring mechanism was established in 1989, on the eve of the dismantling of apartheid.

---

[38] *Second Conference of Independent African States*, Addis Ababa, 16–26 June 1960, pp. 102–105.

[39] Different from all other human rights treaties whose monitoring bodies are composed of independent experts, the members of the Group of Three were appointed by the chairman of the Commission on Human Rights out of the governmental delegations from those states that have ratified the Convention, and it reported to the Commission.

Mobilization against apartheid: Non-Western and Western strategies

The UN General Assembly first called for isolation of South Africa in 1962, asking states to break off economic and diplomatic relations. The first sanctions, after those imposed by India, followed the Sharpeville massacre in 1961 and the sentencing of Nelson Mandela to (initially) five years in prison. The Soweto uprising of 1976 and Steve Biko's death in 1977 prompted additional sanctions, and the 1984–85 townships revolt triggered further sanctions. These events are well-known and need not be described here. South Africa's debt crisis in 1986, however, blurred justifications for economic sanctions, adding its loss of creditworthiness to apartheid.

A great deal of effort was expended to strengthen and broaden sanctions. The Soviet Union and Guinea initiated the drafting of the Convention on the Suppression and Punishment of the Crime of Apartheid in 1971[40] with the aim of furnishing a legal basis for South Africa's isolation and sanctions. Although the General Assembly had proclaimed apartheid to constitute a crime against humanity, that was a political judgment and the Convention was intended to endow that it with legal force and to lay down the corresponding governmental obligations. It obliged governments to prevent private companies and individuals from complicity in apartheid and granted universal jurisdiction for identifying and prosecuting culprits.

The International Convention against Apartheid reflected the division of the world because no Western industrialised state ever ratified it.[41] As Table 2.2 shows, out of those that ratified it, a fairly small number referred to some imposed sanctions in their reports to the Committee of Three. The majority reported their support for the international anti-apartheid struggle and stopped there. Domestic measures were none too many as Table 2.2 illustrates. Some parties probably did not have much contact with South Africa to begin with and there was little they could do. African countries were politically and legally committed to isolation and sanctions, both within the OAU (Organization of African Unity) and as parties to the Convention. Their reports routinely indicated that all relations with South Africa had been severed, yet the *Financial Times* found in 1991 that South Africa was trading with every African country except Equatorial Guinea and Djibouti.[42]

Little is known about the domestic enforcement of the Convention. As Table 2.2 shows, the only enforcement measures were reported by Jamaica, Nigeria, Philippines and Sri Lanka. The Group of Three reported on 'the vigilant monitoring' of the Convention[43] but its reliance on governmental self-assessment as the only source of information made such vigilance impossible.

---

[40] U.N. Doc. A/C.3/L.1871 of 29 October 1971.

[41] United Nations – Status of the International Convention on the Suppression and Punishment of the Crime of Apartheid. Report of the Secretary-General, U.N. Doc. E/CN.4/1995/102 of 28 December 1994.

[42] Waldmeir, P. and Gawith, P. – Final barriers still to clear, *Financial Times*, 11 July 1991.

[43] United Nations – Implementation of the International Convention on the Suppression and Punishment of the Crime of Apartheid. Report of the Group of Three established under the Convention, U.N. Doc. E/CN.4/1995/76 of 25 January 1995, para. 13.

Table 2.2: Sanctions against South Africa by parties to the Convention against Apartheid

Argentina	– sports boycott – suspension of air links (1981) – trade embargo (strategic materials)
Bahamas	– denial of entry to South Africans (persons of non-Caucasian origin and members of anti-apartheid movements exempt)
Bulgaria	– arms embargo – denial of participation to South African teams (world gymnastic championship in 1974)
Burundi	– denial of diplomatic recognition (1963 and 1977)
Cameroon	– no relations with South Africa of any kind – denial of entry to South Africans – denial of landing rights and overflight (1963)
[Czechoslovakia]	– diplomatic and all other relations broken off (1963) – all economic links prohibited (1980)
Egypt	– arms embargo – prohibition of licensing (weapons, ammunition and military equipment)
Ethiopia	– all commercial and banking transaction prohibited – sports boycott – denial of landing rights and overflight
India	– sanctions originally imposed in 1946 – diplomatic representatives withdrawn (1954) – all commercial exchanges prohibited (1964)
Iraq	– trade with the South African regime prohibited
Jamaica	– denial of entry to South Africans – domestic cricket teams banned after playing in South Africa
Mexico	– trade embargo (1987) – oil embargo – denial of entry to South Africans
Nigeria	– foreign companies with links with South Africa excluded from public procurement – sports boycott – sanctions against companies dealing with South Africa (British Petroleum, Barclays Bank)
Philippines	– all commercial relations prohibited – travel (to and from South Africa) prohibited – entry to South Africans granted upon written renunciation of apartheid – participants in the Miss World competition (1977) withdrawn due to South Africa's participation – migrant work prohibited – seamen prohibited from working on South African ships
Qatar	– oil embargo (1973)
Rwanda	– all relations broken (1964) – denial of landing rights and overflight
Senegal	– legislation (1963) on sanctions against Portugal (until 1975) and South Africa – transport boycott – denial of entry to South Africans
Seychelles	– transport and tourism links broken off (1980)
Sri Lanka	– cricket teams banned for 25 years for playing in South Africa

Syria	– all relations broken off (1963) – Syrians prohibited from travelling to South Africa
Trinidad and Tobago	– trade embargo (1976) – sports boycott
Soviet Union	– oil embargo (re-export of Soviet oil to South Africa also prohibited)
Venezuela	– migration, tourism, investment, credit guarantees prohibited (1982) – oil embargo (re-export conditioned by end-user certificates)

Note: Only those parties to the Convention (23 out of the total number of 99) whose reports listed some specific implementations measures are included.

The target of the anti-apartheid movement were those states that did not ratify the Convention against Apartheid, namely the West. They were practising 'constructive engagement', a policy of continuing aid, trade and investment, which was supposed to gradually dismantle apartheid. Commercial engagement with South Africa correlated with opposition to sanctions. Japan, the United States, West Germany and the United Kingdom were South Africa's most important commercial partners and the most reluctant to take condemnatory and punitive initiatives.[44] Following the Nordic Joint Programme of Action, first adopted in1978, and strengthened in 1985 and 1988, Western sanctions were imposed in the mid-1980s. Sanctions imposed by individual Western countries are shown in Table 2.3.

In the United States, South Africa's access to international development finance was limited in 1983 by the Gramm Amendment, which mandated US delegates not to vote for loans. Suspension of new loans and new investment followed a year later. The Comprehensive Anti-Apartheid Act was adopted in 1986,[45] after Congress had overridden President Reagan's veto.[46] The Act merged previously fragmentary sanctions with institutionalised assistance to victims of apartheid and anti-apartheid organisations. On the punitive side, it spanned import and export restrictions, banned loans and new investment, prohibited South African planes from landing in the United States and US planes in South Africa, and mandated the executive to report on its implementation and on progress towards dismantling apartheid. Critics concentrated on what the Anti-Apartheid Act did not prohibit. It was the import of gold, which accounted for 48% of South Africa's foreign exchange earnings as the Act was being finalised;[47] the import of strategic minerals

---

[44] van Wyk, K. and Radloff, S. – Symmetry and reciprocity in South Africa's foreign policy, *Journal of Conflict Resolution*, vol. 37, 1993, No. 2, pp. 382–396.

[45] Pub. L. No. 99–440, 22 U.S.C. paras. 5001–5116, Supp. IV 1986.

[46] Fletcher, L. et al. – South Africa: United States sanctions and the impact on apartheid, *Human Rights Yearbook*, vol. 1,1988, pp. 236–247.

[47] United States Department of State – *A U.S. Policy Toward South Africa. The Report of the Secretary of State's Advisory Committee on South Africa*, Department of State Publication 9537, Washington, D.C., April 1987, p. 32.

Table 2.3: Sanctions against South Africa by Western countries

Australia	– import prohibition (krugerrands, coal, iron and steel, uranium and agricultural products); export prohibition (nuclear and computer technology) – prohibition of governmental loans – transport boycott (air links)
Austria	– import prohibition (krugerrands, iron and steel); export prohibition (computer technology) – prohibition of new loans and investment
Belgium	– import prohibition (krugerrands, iron and steel); export prohibition (nuclear technology)
Canada	– import prohibition (coal, iron and steel, uranium, agricultural products) – prohibition of government loans – transport boycott (air links)
Finland	– prohibition of new loans and investment – transport boycott (air links)
France	– import prohibition (krugerrands, coal, iron and steel); export prohibition (oil) – prohibition of new investment
Germany	– import prohibition (krugerrands, iron and steel); export prohibition (nuclear technology) – prohibition of new investment
Italy	– import prohibition (krugerrands, iron and steel)
Japan	– import prohibition (krugerrands, agricultural products); export prohibition (nuclear and computer technology) – prohibition of new loans and investment – transport boycott (air links)
Netherlands	– import prohibition (krugerrands, iron and steel, uranium); export prohibition (oil, nuclear technology) – prohibition of government loans
Nordic countries (Denmark, Norway, Sweden)	– import prohibition (krugerrands, coal, iron and steel, uranium, agricultural products); export prohibition (oil, nuclear and computer technology) – prohibition of government loans and new investment – transport boycott (air links)
Portugal	– import prohibition (krugerrands, iron and steel); export prohibition (nuclear technology) – prohibition of new investment
Spain	– import prohibition (krugerrands, iron and steel) – transport boycott (air links)
Switzerland	– export prohibition (nuclear technology) – prohibition of government loans
United Kingdom	– import prohibition (krugerrands, iron and steel); export prohibition (oil, nuclear technology) – prohibition of government loans
USA	– import prohibition (krugerrands, coal, iron and steel, uranium, agricultural products); export prohibition (oil, nuclear and computer technology) – prohibition of government loans and new investment – transport boycott (air links)

was also left out of the Act. Critics also noted that the prohibition of new investment came too late because investment had already been halted in 1984.[48] Trade sanctions could not be enforced because the State Department did not issue a list of goods subject to sanctions[49] and thus, despite sanctions, the annual value of trade for 1990–91 was estimated at $3 billion.[50]

At the time of the Security Council's arms-and-nuclear embargo in 1977, EUrope (the European Communities at the time) adopted a Code of Conduct for Companies in South Africa, a political gesture rather than a forceful anti-apartheid policy. It tried to adopt an oil embargo in 1985 but failed due to the lack of consensus. Similarly, EUrope's nuclear non-cooperation with South Africa was subjected to divergent interpretations. In 1986, EUrope prohibited trade in kruggerands, iron and steel as well as new investment. As mobilization against apartheid intensified, so did the naming-and-shaming of recalcitrant governments and companies. Japan introduced sanctions against South Africa in 1988, following wide publicity for its being South Africa's largest trading partner, with an annual $4 billion in bilateral trade. Sanctions were revoked in 1991.[51]

Effects of sanctions

While the Western strategy of 'constructive engagement' was seen as commercial opportunism, sanctions were deemed to be human-rights-friendly, but both extremes existed only in theory. South Africa's economic and financial problems translated into diminished commercial opportunism, which was seen as a success of the mobilization against apartheid. Sanctions were not necessarily human-rights-friendly, however. Indeed, the political transition to which they aimed to contribute may have been facilitated, but the economic basis necessary to *sustain* that political change was in fact, undermined through sanctions. Nor was this economic basis enhanced thereafter through 'counter-sanctions,' namely the minute economic support for the new South Africa.

International development finance can impede the protection of human rights or further their respect, and South Africa provided an ideal case study. The relationship between systematic human rights violations and continued international financial support has been depicted as a *circulus inextricabilis*: foreign economic assistance strengthens a repressive regime by making it economically viable and thus contributes to the perpetuation of violations. United Nations studies have con-

---

[48] Lawyers Committee on Human Rights – *United States Policy Toward South Africa*, Human Rights and U.S. Foreign Policy, 1988 Project Series, No. 1, New York, 1989, pp. 9–17.

[49] McAuliffe, D. – U.S. study discloses failure of sanctions, *International Herald Tribune*, 21 August 1989.

[50] Devroy, A. – Bush, citing gains, lifts sanctions on South Africa, *International Herald Tribune*, 11 July 1991.

[51] Sanger, D.E. – Japan revokes most sanctions on South Africa, *International Herald Tribune*, 23 October 1991.

cluded that 'all kinds of assistance eventually lead to, and should be considered a form of military support,' and dismissed Western 'constructive engagement'. 'Far from exerting leverage for changes in policy, increased foreign funds are bolstering the regime's resistance to change.'[52]

Studies of the effects of sanctions have been conducted on two levels, firstly to determine whether sanctions achieved their intended economic effects, and, if so, whether they resulted in the anticipated political changes. Those who exerted great effort to have sanctions imposed and sustained point to a decreased rate of economic growth or to disinvestment as evidence that sanctions resulted in economic hardship. While trade-related sanctions had negligible effects, disinvestment (especially in 1985–87) was visible, although its causes remained disputed: some pointed to fear of political turmoil, others to anti-apartheid advocacy, yet others to South Africa's diminished creditworthiness. Isolating effects of sanctions from the fluctuating price of gold (half of South African exports), the cost of enforcing apartheid, or of warfare against front-line states, estimated at $100 billion, was impossible[53] As foreign companies were pulling out, South African firms bought their assets and disinvestment thus produced the unintended consequence of concentration of ownership in a few large South African companies.[54] As sanctions were 'designed to pressurize and undermine the strength of those groups that either hold power in society or are responsible for creating, implementing or bolstering apartheid' and their success was to be measured 'by its impact on the business community'[55] they may have achieved exactly the opposite.

Research into sanctions has often concluded that analysing their effects or impact had to account for the fact that they were flouted. Even the area of internal security, where foreign help was most likely to facilitate abuses, retrospectively yielded evidence that sanctions had been flouted. Revelations before the Truth Commission about South Africa's biological and chemical arsenal have pointed to foreign complicity. Dr Wouter Basson, who testified about South Africa's biological warfare programme, claimed that some British scientists, as well as others from the United States, Germany, Japan and Canada, bartered with the South African team for information about chemical warfare programmes in Soviet-supported African countries.[56] As Dr Basson was referring to bartering in the early 1980s, it is possible that the ban came after such exchanges were no longer interesting for the Western countries because the South African side no longer had interesting data to barter.

---

[52] Adverse consequences for the enjoyment of human rights of political, military, economic and other forms of assistance given to the racist and colonialist regime of South Africa, by Ahmed M. Khalifa, Special Rapporteur, U.N. Doc. E/CN.4/Sub.2/1984/Rev.1, para. 17 and E/CN.4/Sub.2/1987/8/Rev.1, para. 26.

[53] Bell, T. – The impact of sanctions on South Africa, *Journal of Contemporary African Studies*, vol. 12, 1993, No. 1, p. 19–20.

[54] How do South African sanctions work? *The Economist*, 14 October 1989.

[55] United Nations – South Africa: The case for mandatory economic sanctions, Centre against Apartheid, Doc. 18/86, September 1986, paras. 4 and 36.

[56] Duval Smith, A. – 'Dr Death' tells of SA germ warfare, *Guardian Weekly*, 9 August 1998.

Regardless of their effects on or in South Africa, sanctions were immensely successful because they raised apartheid's visibility. Everybody had a decision to make as consumer, tourist, or sports fan. Richard Dowden asked in 1993:

> If you have not eaten a Cape grape or an Outspan orange for 30 years did you contribute to the collapse of apartheid?[57]

His answer was 'no'; the anti-apartheid movement's was a resounding 'yes'. History's judgment will probably be that economic sanctions were less successful than isolation. Indeed, it was the global mobilisation around sanctions, rather than their effects, that made them such a prominent issue.

After sanctions, what?

By the time apartheid was de-institutionalised in the early 1990s, 54,000 non-governmental organizations had been created, mostly with foreign and inter-national funding. A great deal of attention and funding focused on the ANC (African National Congress), which, after being un-banned in June 1989, conducted the protracted negotiations that ended apartheid. In 1994, the ANC formed a co-alition government, which was followed by an ANC government (May 1996), re-elected in 1999.

The process of lifting sanctions started in 1990, and international activism shifted to monitoring the transition. When international monitors started arriving in South Africa in 1992, the locals noted that 'the number of observers attending an event can almost outnumber the participants.'[58] Foreign observers of the 1994 elections in South Africa included 2,000 from the United Nations, 2,000 from non-governmental organizations, 600 from individual governments, 300 from the European Parliament, and 50 from the OAU (Organization of African Unity).[59] These numbers exceeded the previous record of 2,578 observers for the Nicaraguan elections in 1990.[60] Some soul-searching followed the observers' enthusiastic reports of the 1994 elections in South Africa. Under-reported 'irregularities' were described later.[61] How electoral registration had been carried out without knowl-edge of the size of the population to the nearest million remained a mystery. Elections were merely a means towards majority rule; hence, technicalities could be dispensed with as long as the desired end was in sight. For the United Nations,

---

[57] Dowden, R. – Fruits of boycott not so black and white, *The Independent*, 25 September 1993.

[58] What role is there for foreign monitors? *Democracy in Action*, vol. 6, No. 7, 17 December 1992, p. 5.

[59] Holman, M. – World offers democracy a helping hand, *Financial Times*, 25 April 1994.

[60] Beigbeder, Y. – *International Monitoring of Plebiscites, Referenda and National Elections. Self-determination and Transition to Democracy*, Martinus Nijhoff Publishers, Dordrecht, 1994, p. 168.

[61] Tjønneland, E.N. (ed.) – *South Africa's 1994 Elections*, Norwegian Institute of Human Rights, Human Rights Report No. 3, Oslo, October 1994, pp. 45–47; Reynolds, A. (ed.) – *Election '94 South Africa*, James Currey, 1994, p. 227.

however, elections were the end. The General Assembly congratulated itself and a host of other inter-governmental bodies for having supported 'the process of peaceful change *culminating in the elections* (emphasis mine).'[62] The elections and the Constitution were signposts of change, but they only spelled out in vague terms how the consequences of apartheid should be dealt with in the future.

Post-apartheid South Africa attracted much international praise but little aid. President Nelson Mandela's undiplomatic labeling of US aid as 'peanuts' created a diplomatic furore during his first official visit to the USA.[63] Mandela's criticism, however, also generated support: 'Washington is contributing $543 million over three years; Britain $94 million over the same period. 'Peanuts' Mr Mandela called it, and peanuts it is.'[64] Relations with the USA soured when the latter threatened to cut off aid because of South Africa's arms export to Syria.[65] Indeed, by 1994, weapons had became South Africa's second biggest export item.[66]

EUrope was not any more generous than the USA. Its initial promise of 400 million in trade concessions was decreased to 260 million during the first round of negotiations.[67] Negotiations on a free-trade agreement took twenty rounds and four years, and were described as 'hand to hand combat for each product.'[68] The initial enthusiasm for the new South Africa was replaced by resistance to agricultural imports. EUrope had reportedly promised favourable trade terms to South Africa at the time of the 1994 elections,[69] but its first offer excluded 40% of South Africa's potential exports, mainly fruit and wine, so as to protect EUrope's own producers. On the other hand, that same first offer demanded a free trade regime for EUrope's industrial exports to South Africa.[70] South Africa's exports to Europe were subjected to long negotiations. The last hurdles included 'EU insistence that South Africa phase out use of the names port and sherry for fortified wines' and a German initiative that a clause on suppression of illegal immigration be included in the trade agreement.[71] The latter seemed to have been overcome in time for the

---

[62] United Nations – Elimination of apartheid and establishment of a united, democratic and non-racial South Africa, resolution 48/258 of 6 July 1994, para. 5.

[63] Taylor, P. – Mandela criticises US aid, *The Washington Post,* reprinted in *Guardian Weekly,* 27 November 1994.

[64] Beresford, D. – South African fairy-tale can work its magic on the rest of Africa, *The Guardian,* 25 November 1994.

[65] Pretoria disappoints (editorial), *The New York Times,* reprinted in *International Herald Tribune,* 20 January 1997; Beresford, D. – Mandela angered by Washington's bullying, *Guardian Weekly,* 26 January 1997.

[66] Spence, J.E. – On becoming 'just another country', *The World Today,* March 1997, p. 69.

[67] Marshall, A. – Brussels trade deal with SA reduced, *The Independent,* 12 August 1994.

[68] Islam, S. – EU sees South Africa deal as model for future, *European Voice,* 22–28 July 1999.

[69] Ryle, S. – EU reneging on trade deal, says Pretoria, *Guardian Weekly,* 17 November 1996.

[70] Wise, E. – EU hopes for 'little present' from Pretoria, *European Voice,* 7–13 November 1996.

[71] Parker, A. – Blair aims to speed up talks on SA trade deal, *Financial Times,* 5 January 1999; Harding, G. – EU on verge of historic deal with South Africa, and Pretoria trade deal faces delay, *European Voice,* 28 January–3 February and 18–24 February 1999.

signing ceremony in October 1999, while the former was channelled into negotiating a separate agreement on wine and spirits.[72] Verbal duels about the use of the
term *grand cru* and the percentage of alcohol in whiskey continued.

Disappointingly, the initial enthusiasm for political change did not lead to
international financial support to sustaining that change. South Africa soon became
a byword for carjacking and armed robbery, and as the violence spread from the
cities to the countryside, it was amply described in Western media. Redistribution
was seen as a purely domestic problem: 'The real test of tolerance of the new order
will be when those whites, gracious in political defeat, start paying the price for the
years of privilege.'[73] Desmond Tutu, as the chairman of the Truth Commission
'urged South Africa's white business community to take some responsibility for the
apartheid system and consider offering financial help to those who had suffered
most.'[74] His criticism of the role of Shell, BP and Mobil broadened the circle of
those who should take some responsibility for what he called 'racial capitalism.'[75]

South Africa thus found itself in a catch-22 position: it needed to demonstrate
political stability in order to attract foreign investment, but it needed investment
(including foreign) in order to bolster political stability. The previous logic
whereby any foreign investment could lead to strengthening apartheid should have
been, but was not, reversed. Earlier critics of sanctions have advocated investment
in post-apartheid South Africa. One can recall that Haider Ali Khan doubted
whether sanctions would have positive effects on eradicating apartheid,[76] and
Daniel Bradlow opposed the single-minded focus of anti-apartheid organizations on
sanctions and proposed 'a development exception.'[77]

Domestically, one of the thorniest issues proved to be land redistribution. The
pattern of land ownership has been similar to that in Zimbabwe: the bulk of the best
land was – and is – owned by white farmers. It is therefore not surprising that one
of the most bitterly contested topics during the negotiations on the new South
African Constitution was the restitution of land expropriated by legislation initiated
in 1913. The ANC promised to redistribute 30% of white-owned land by the year
2000. Much as in Zimbabwe, funding for compensation could not be found.

A distinct pattern in the behaviour of what is fondly called 'the international
community' has emerged: previous punishment for apartheid has not been followed
by rewards for the valiant effort to dismantle it. Neither has there been a commitment to help the government of South Africa redress apartheid-generated

---

[72] Harding, G. – EU deal with Pretoria risks being delayed, *European Voice*, 7–13 October 1999.
[73] Survey: South Africa, *The Economist*, 20 May 1995.
[74] Matthews, R. – S African business faces apartheid past, *Financial Times*, 12 November 1997.
[75] Tutu, D.M. – *No Future Without Forgiveness*, Rider, Johannesburg, 1999, p. 181.
[76] Ali Khan, H. – *The Political Economy of Sanctions against Apartheid*, Lynne Rienner Publishers, Boulder and London, p. 76.
[77] Bradlow, D.D. – Debt, development, and human rights: Lessons from South Africa, *Michigan Journal of International Law*, vol. 12, 1991, No. 4, p. 688–689.

inequalities. Instead, foreign and international human rights assistance has concentrated on formalising human rights guarantees and a host of human rights institutions has been established. It is still too early to assess the long-term effects of such assistance. In the short-term, however, it has contributed to raising the expectations of those who suffered under apartheid, and, consequently, increasing the pressure upon the government to satisfy them.

Chapter 3

LIMITATIONS OF MULTILATERALISM:
ISRAEL BETWEEN THE WEST AND THE MIDDLE EAST

Economic sanctions against Israel began in 1948, just after India's against South Africa. Israel also tailed South Africa as the second government to be condemned for human rights violations and was, alongside South Africa, the only named violator in the 1960s. Both were condemned, *inter alia*, for the denial of the right to self-determination, which was the foremost human rights concern of the new UN majority. This is where similarities end, however.

After South Africa was taken off the UN agenda, Israel has become the longest-condemned violator. Nevertheless, thirty years of condemnations for human rights violations have not been accompanied by sanctions, despite recommendations by the UN Commission on Human Rights and the General Assembly. The United Nations first recommended sanctions in 1968, and calls for sanctions have intensified thereafter, yet political and financial support by the United States has given Israel immunity. The United States used its veto more than sixty times between 1970 and 1993; half of the vetoes blocked proposed sanctions against Israel.[1] Similarly, appeals for sanctions have been largely ignored by Western governments, with the exception of few suspensions of aid by EUrope. That pattern has continued in the 1990s.

Since its establishment as a state, Israel has been the principal target of sanctions by the League of Arab States. It is geographically but not geopolitically part of the Middle East; accordingly, it is a member of WEOS (the Western group) in the United Nations. Alongside being among the largest recipient of US aid throughout the ebb and flow of international opprobrium, Israel has also benefitted from Western guilt and shame for the Holocaust. West European (especially German) financial and political support has been considerable. This support from the West against economic and armed warfare by its neighbours was somewhat altered by the OAPEC's (Organization of Arab Oil Exporting Countries) oil embargo in 1973–74, tilting it away from Israel and towards Palestine.

---

[1] Bailey, S.D. – *The UN Security Council and Human Rights*, St. Martin's Press, New York, 1994, p. 127–128.

THE UNITED NATIONS

Responsibility for Palestine

UN's responsibility for Palestine is almost as old as the United Nations itself. The United Kingdom placed Palestine on the agenda in 1947, having administered it under a League of Nations mandate since 1922. It was seeking UN involvement after a plan to divide Palestine into an Arab and a Jewish state had failed. During the first round of warfare in 1948, Britain relinquished its mandate amidst protests against preventing the immigration of Holocaust survivors. Israel acquired statehood. Palestine did not. Palestine's territory and population size had diminished and thereafter its also lost its name to become 'occupied territories,' and was administered by Jordan in 1948–1967, with the Gaza Strip administered by Egypt.

A Palestinian state, as originally planned when the United Nations was born, came back on the agenda as the Organization turned fifty; problems which had not been solved at the outset continued to fester throughout those five decades. An endless stream of emergency sessions of the General Assembly, cease-fires, peace-keepers, aid providers, negotiators and mediators failed to solve these problems. Peace-making moved outside the United Nations, and during the 1970s the United States and the United Nations pursued different, sometimes conflicting policies. The US-sponsored 1978 Camp David Accords between Israel and Egypt were condemned by the UN as a flagrant violation of the rights of the Palestinian people.[2] The United States was deemed guilty of sidestepping the UN and cold-shouldering the Palestine Liberation Organization (PLO), but it did broker peace between Israel and Egypt, bearing its political and financial cost, reflected in the volume of US aid to both countries in the aftermath of Camp David.

The original charter of the Palestine Liberation Organization denied Israel's right to exist and committed the PLO to the liberation of Palestine through armed struggle. In 1987, however, the PLO accepted Security Council resolution 242 and formally renounced terrorism, thus paving the way towards negotiations with the United States, within the framework for peace-making laid out in the resolution itself. This required the withdrawal of the Israeli army from the occupied territories and affirmed the right of all states in the region to exist, including Israel's, previously denied. Yet Israel's withdrawal from the occupied territories was entangled in a grammatical cover-up for a political problem. The omission of 'the' before 'occupied territories' in the English text of the resolution was interpreted by the United States and Israel as deliberate vagueness, allowing Israel to withdraw from some occupied territories but not others.[3]

---

[2] United Nations – *The United Nations and the Question of Palestine*, DPI, New York, November 1985, p. 27.

[3] Chartrand, S. – Resolution 242: In a word, ambiguity, *International Herald Tribune*, 30 October 1991.

Negotiations continued outside the United Nations. Norway nurtured and brought to fruition the Oslo Agreements, and the United States then resumed its increasingly criticised role of the principal mediator. The Declaration of Principles on Interim Self-government Arrangements was signed in September 1993,[4] the Israel-PLO Agreement on the Gaza Strip and the Jericho area in Cairo in May 1994,[5] the Israeli-Palestinian Interim Agreement followed in September 1995, and the Hebron Protocol in January 1997.[6] That intricate web of mutual commitments combined abstract principles with precise timetables, adding explicit and implicit escape clauses. In brief, it has provided sufficient background for both parties, and anybody else for that matter, to claim both compliance and non-compliance.

Condemnations of Israel

Israel's condemnation for human rights violations followed the Six Day War. The very first resolution of the 1968 International Conference on Human Rights (one of the two held in the past fifty years) was entitled *Respect for and implementation of human rights in occupied territories*. The Conference condemned 'the violation of human rights in Arab territories occupied as a result of the June 1967 hostilities', and requested the General Assembly 'to appoint a special committee to investigate violations of human rights in the territories occupied by Israel.'[7] As the voting record demonstrates – sixty in favour and fifty-seven against or abstaining[8] – governments were divided in 1968. Nevertheless, the favourable vote by however small a margin, allowed the Assembly to immediately established the Special Committee, which has continued to function (under a slightly changed name) ever since.

The denial of inalienable rights of Palestinian refugees has been singled as the principal violation amongst the many for which the General Assembly has faulted Israel. Palestinian refugees (initially 700,000) have been assisted by the UN as of 1948, when within one day Britain pulled out, Israel declared independence, and the League of Arab States decided to invade Israel. The refugee problem was seen as a consequence of the denial of Palestinians' collective rights. Subsequent UN resolutions have affirmed collective and individual rights of the Palestinian people. In 1971, the General Assembly affirmed the legality of their armed struggle for

---

[4] Declaration of Principles on Interim Self-government Arrangements was signed by Israel and the Palestine Liberation Organization, and witnessed by the USA and Russia in Washington, on 13 September 1993, reproduced in *International Legal Materials*, vol. 32, 1993, pp. 1525–1544.

[5] Israel-PLO Agreement on the Gaza Strip and the Jericho Area (consisting of the Agreement itself, four protocols and an exchange of letters) was finalised in Cairo on 4 May 1994, reproduced in *International Legal Materials*, vol. 33, 1994, pp. 622–720.

[6] Cockburn, P. – A new Berlin on the West Bank, *The Independent*, 18 January 1997.

[7] United Nations – *Final Act of the International Conference on Human Rights, Teheran, 22 April to 13 May 1968*, U.N. Doc. A/CONF.32/41, p. 5.

[8] General Assembly – Resolution 2443 (XXIII) of 19 December 1968.

self-determination and in 1974 broadened collective Palestinians' rights to include national independence and sovereignty. Ten years later, the General Assembly found that Israel's occupation itself constituted a grave violation of human rights.

The number and length of General Assembly's annual resolutions dealing with the Middle East not only reflect the different facets of the problem, but also the mandates of various bodies which have been established to address it. (Those with a specific human rights mandate have been listed in Table 1.2) These bodies range from the oldest, the UNRWA (United Nations Relief and Works Agency for Palestine Refugees), to the already mentioned Special Committee to Investigate Israeli Practices Affecting the Human Rights of the Palestinian People and Other Arabs of the Occupied Territories, to the Committee on the Exercise of the Inalienable Rights of the Palestinian People, established in 1975. The UN Commission on Human Rights added one more in 1993, a Special Rapporteur, whose mandate is to investigate Israel's violations of human rights and humanitarian law until the end of the occupation.[9] Much as is the case with similar UN bodies, Israel refuses to co-operate with the Special Rapporteur, justifying its position by citing the unlimited nature of his mandate, to continue as long as the Israeli occupation lasts.

In his 1996 report, the Special Rapporteur acknowledged that his mandate was biased. Although both Israel and the Palestinian Authority were violating the human rights of Palestinians, his mandate was to investigate only Israeli violations.[10] The following year he called for a change so that he could 'study and recommend constructive human rights and humanitarian programmes to prevent violations or remedy their aftermath.'[11] Had such a change materialized, it would have constituted a break with the past. René Felber, a previous Special Rapporteur, noted in 1995 that 'neither the General Assembly nor the Commission [on Human Rights] has had any particular success in the area of enforcement of human rights in the occupied territories.'[12] A break with the past has remained impossible although the change of government in Israel in May 1999 offered a glimpse of hope for such a change in the year 2000.

Alongside its refusal to cooperate with human rights bodies established by the General Assembly and the Commission on Human Rights, Israel often ignored committees monitoring human rights treaties to which it had become a party. One such instance was an attempt by the CERD (Committee on the Elimination of

---

[9] Question of the violation of human rights in the occupied Arab territories, including Palestine, resolution 1993/2A of the Commission on Human Rights of 19 February 1993.

[10] Commission on Human Rights – Report on the situation of human rights in the Palestinian territories occupied since 1967, submitted by Mr. Hannu Halinen, Special Rapporteur, U.N. Doc. E/CN.4/1996/18 of 15 March 1996, paras. 28 and 43.

[11] Commission on Human Rights – Report on the situation of human rights in Palestinian territories occupied since 1967, submitted by Mr. Hannu Halinen, Special Rapporteur, U.N. Doc. E/CN.4/1997/16 of 19 February 1997, paras. 36–37.

[12] United Nations – Report on the human rights situation in the Palestinian territories occupied since 1967, U.N. Doc. E/CN:4/1995/19, p. 14.

Racial Discrimination) to enter into a dialogue with Israel following Baruch Goldstein's massacre of Palestinians during prayer at the Tomb of Patriarchs in Hebron. That request resulted in Israel's refusal to supply information. The Committee then reaffirmed Israel's human rights obligations under the Convention, concluded that a number of those apparently had been breached, and repeated its request for overdue reports.[13]

In another instance, the Committee against Torture (CAT) requested a special report from Israel following widespread publicity of the legalization of interrogation techniques apparently in breach of the prohibition of torture.[14] The Committee had already determined a breach of the Convention in 1994 because Israel's definition of torture had been too narrow and dependent upon an assessment by interrogators whether 'necessity' took precedence over the right to freedom from torture.[15]

The Committee's request for a special report came after the Israeli judiciary ruled in 1996 that physical pressure could be used in interrogation.[16] Since other governments hide similar practices from judicial scrutiny, the judicial endorsement of 'physical pressure' by Israeli courts seemed to be an open challenge to international human rights law. Israel submitted the requested special report, in which interrogation practices were only cursorily described. Such a description had been classified information and the justification was that interrogations would become ineffective if suspects knew interrogation techniques in advance. Attached to the report was the court judgment that had created the controversy. The court had affirmed that 'physical pressure is permitted in a situation where conditions for the defense of necessity exist.'[17] As the delegation of Israel stated before the UN Commission on Human Rights, 'the State of Israel was at war against terror and was exercising its right to self-defense.'[18]

The Human Rights Committee has acknowledged that Israel is at war, and has been throughout its existence, and thus emergency has spanned its entire existence as a state. It has, nevertheless, objected to the scope of emergency regulations and also posited that Israel should be applying not only humanitarian, but also human

---

[13] Report of the Committee on the Elimination of Racial Discrimination, U.N. Doc. A/49/18, paras. 73–91.

[14] A UN finding of torture. Israel is violating Convention, panel says, *International Herald Tribune*, 10–11 May 1997.

[15] Committee against Torture – Conclusions and recommendations relating to the initial report of Israel of 25 April 1994, U.N. Doc. CAT/C/SR.183 of 25 April 1994.

[16] *Legitimizing Torture: The Israeli High Court of Justice Rulings in the Bilbeisi, Hamdan and Mubarak Cases*, B'Tselem, Israeli Information Centre for Human Rights in the Occupied Territories, Jerusalem, January 1977.

[17] Committee against Torture – Special report by Israel submitted in accordance with a request made by the CAT on 22 November 1996, U.N. Doc. CAT/C/33/Add.2 of 6 January 1997, p. 7, para. 4.

[18] Commission on Human Rights – Statement of Mr. Landman (Observer for Israel), Summary record of the 3rd meeting, 19 March 1996, U.N. Doc. E/CN.4/1996/SR.3 of 30 April 1996, para. 24.

rights law in the occupied territories.[19] The representative of Israel has rejected that interpretation, invoking the existence and powers of the Palestinian Authority. Questions about their shared responsibility in the area of human rights, led the Israeli representative to doubt whether a joint Palestinian-Israeli delegation could appear before the Committee.[20]

Joint Palestinian-Israeli responsibility for the protection of human rights has been included in the wording of peace agreements. The path towards them was long and tortuous, international and external involvement considerable, albeit often pulling in opposite directions. Indeed, the contrast between the Arab oil embargo and Western aid to Israel as levers is illustrative of the crossfire in which human rights were placed by clashing foreign policies.

COUNTERVAILING PRESSURES

The Arab oil embargo

The first Arab-Israeli war in 1948–49 prompted an arms embargo, the second one in 1967 led to Israel's placement on the UN violations agenda, the third war in 1973 led to the Arab oil embargo. The embargo ruptured the pattern of sanctions as the West was the principal target rather than the initiator. It was reinforced by a huge increase in the price of oil, took place during heated diplomatic battles about a (or 'the') new international order within the United Nations, and was to some degree successful in changing Western foreign policies (with the exception of the United States) towards Palestine.

The embargo and the quadrupling of the price of oil triggered the 1974–75 economic crisis, which spread from the West worldwide, dividing the post-war economic history into two halves – a period of continuous growth beforehand and a period of lurching from one economic recession to another thereafter. Assertions that the 1974–75 crisis was caused by the Arab oil embargo remain unproven, but the coincidence in time is telling.

The embargo as a unique (thus far) resort to economic sanctions against the West was a precedent in many respects. Its explicit aim was to alter Western policies towards Palestine and Israel, its justification was Israel's denial of Palestinian rights. And yet, this embargo is routinely excluded from listings of sanctions for human rights violations in the Western human rights literature. The oil embargo, much as similar economic sanctions, generated more heat than light in academic literature. Scholars were divided with regard to its legality. The immediate US

---

[19] Human Rights Committee – Concluding observations: Israel, U.N. Doc. CCPR/C/79/Add. 93 of 18 August 1998, paras. 4 and 10.
[20] Human Rights Committee – Consideration of the initial report of Israel, U.N. Doc. CCPR/C/SR. 1676 of 28 September 1998, para. 14.

reaction was to claim that embargo was illegal because it coerced states to change their foreign policy. Many US sanctions had that same purpose, as was noted by many commentators.[21]

The first Arab oil embargo had been announced in 1967 against countries providing military aid to Israel.[22] Little is known about its effects. The second one was officially launched on 17 October 1973 and lifted on 18 March 1974. It was imposed by the OAPEC (Organization of Arab Petroleum Exporting Countries) but its purpose was subjected to endless speculation because the announcement had been issued in Arabic while translations into English varied. Its aim was Israel's withdrawal from the occupied territories and the realization of the legitimate rights of Palestinians. The main targets were the United States, the Netherlands, Portugal, Rhodesia and South Africa, and it was extended to countries that trans-shipped Arab oil to the embargoed countries. At the same time the price of oil was increased fourfold and exports to many countries were curtailed.

The background to the Arab oil embargo can be illustrated by a chronology of events. The Yom Kippur war started on 6 October 1973 and the next day the PLO called upon Arab states to halt the export of oil. The United States pledged military aid to Israel on 16 October and on 17 October the Arab oil ministers met in Kuwait and instituted the oil embargo. The principal target was the United States (as 'the principal and foremost source of the Israeli power'), and the embargo was intended to alert 'major consumer industrial nations' to their need to co-operate with the Arab nations in liberating the territories occupied by Israel.[23]

The principal object of the embargo – Israel – had been the target of Arab economic sanctions from its very establishment in 1948. These continued the previous economic boycott of the emerging Jewish communities. The Central Boycott Office of the Arab League had a co-ordinating role, but implementation remained within the discretion of each member state, while secrecy prevented insight by outsiders. The aim was known: to bring about the collapse of the state of Israel.[24] The Arab oil embargo of 1973–74 strengthened the pre-existing sanctions against Israel by targeting its existing and potential supporters, thus introducing secondary targets. Aid to developing countries from the OAPEC represented an attractive incentive for potential supporters of Israel to change sides. This focused international attention on the Middle East and succeeded in diminishing political support for Israel as political and economic warfare spread to the United Nations and its specialized agencies. In 1974, the ILO (International Labour Organization) adopted a resolu-

---

[21] Lowenfeld, A.F. – Sauce for gander ... the Arab Boycott and United States political trade controls, *Texas International Law Journal*, vol. 12, 1977, No. 1, pp. 1–61.

[22] Daoudi, M.S. and Dajani, M.S. – Economic leverage and Middle East Politics, *Third World Affairs 1987*, p. 128–129.

[23] Shihata, I.F.I. – Destination embargo of Arab oil: Its legality under international law, *American Journal of International Law*, vol. 68, 1974, No. 4, p. 592–593.

[24] Dewitt, D.B. – The Arab boycott of Israel, in Leyton-Brown, D. (ed.) – *The Utility of International Economic Sanctions*, Croom Helm, London, 1987, p. 149.

tion urging action against Israel's racism and violations of trade union freedoms, whereupon the United States left the ILO.[25] This created a shortfall in the ILO's budget, which was indemnified by the OAPEC. Taking economic warfare further, US Senate decided in 1975 to review aid to all states that voted for the expulsion of Israel from the United Nations or its specialized agencies.[26]

The Arab sanctions pulled in the opposite direction. Amongst the immediate outcomes of the oil embargo was the granting of the UN observer status to the PLO in 1974. Furthermore, in 1975 the UN General Assembly adopted a resolution equating zionism with racism, which intensified the on-going political and economic warfare. Many countries found themselves in the crossfire – facing the loss of Arab aid and oil for supporting Israel, or facing the loss of US aid for supporting the PLO. The impact of the Arab oil embargo was illustrated, for example, by the fact that only 70 states had embassies in Israel in 1988, while in 1993 their number grew to 120 and in 1996 to 161.[27]

As peace-making intensified in the early 1990s, Arab sanctions against Israel were suspended; when the process faltered, they were re-imposed. In April 1997, representatives of Arab states meeting in the Council of the Arab League called for reimposition of sanctions against Israel (the wording used was 'stopping all normalization steps').[28] The immediate cause was Israel's decision on the Har Homa and/or Jebal Abu Ghoneim housing project in East Jerusalem, while the underlying cause was disappointment with the stalled peace process. Much as before, that recommendation was subject to an individual decision by each member state. Sanctions were immediately put into practice by Oman through the exclusion of Israel from a computer fair in Muskat,[29] but could not be applied by Egypt, Jordan and the Palestinian Authority because each had a treaty with Israel. The most controversial facet of the previous sanctions, namely targeting third parties, was abandoned. Thus, sanctions were not expected to affect more than 1% of Israel's trade.[30]

Western aid to Israel

Israel's GDP per capita exceeds $16,000, placing it well above the upper limit of eligibility for aid. Nevertheless, Israel remains among the largest recipients of aid, immune to developmental or human rights criteria: 'Israel gets about $3 billion a

---

[25] Joyce, J.A. – *The New Politics of Human Rights*, The Macmillan Press, London, 1978, p. 111–112.

[26] Gross, E. – On the degradation of the constitutional environment of the United Nations, *American Journal of International Law*, vol. 77, 1983, No. 3, p. 571.

[27] Furfinkiel, M. – The peace dove's golden eggs, *The European*, 23–26 September 1993; Gardner, D. – Harvest of the first fruits. Survey of Israel, *Financial Times*, 15 July 1996, p. vi.

[28] Lancaster, J. – Arab states recommend sanctions on Israel, *International Herald Tribune*, 1 April 1997; Huband, M. and Machlis, A. – Arab states put closer links with Israel on hold, *Financial Times*, 1 April 1997.

[29] Will Arabs renew Israeli boycott, *South*, May 1997, p. 14.

[30] Israel and the Arab world: Little becomes even less, *The Economist*, 5 April 1997, p. 48.

year from the United States. About $1.8 billion is for loans to buy US weapons essential to Israeli defense. The rest is used to pay interest on past military loans to Israel.'[31] Aid earmarked for the repayment of military loans was until recently labeled as 'economic' rather than military aid.[32] These facts being well known, the UN Commission on Human Rights has occasionally expressed concern 'at the military, economic and political support given by some States to Israel' and called upon those states 'to bring adequate pressure to bear on the Government of Israel to put an end to its aggressive and expansionist policy.'[33] The states have not been named, the calls not heeded.

A mixture of motives has guided Western aid to Israel. Germany's guilt was reflected in ample aid to Israel during the first decades of Israel's existence, the Western guilt for having allowed the Holocaust to happen influenced Western foreign policies. French and British support ensued from Israel's participation in the 1956 Suez Canal military intervention, which established Israel as the indispensable Western cold-war ally in the Middle East.

Table 3.1: Aid to Israel from Germany and the USA in 1960–95
(in million US$)

	1960	1965	1970	1975	1980	1985	1990	1995
USA	41.0	36.9	29.0	414.0	780.0	1948.0	1296.0	328.0
Germany	62.6	74.9	34.1	51.0	110.0	25.8	39.3	−20.4
Total bilateral	105.0	122.0	62.4	466.0	892.1	1978.3	1370.6	330.9

Source: *Geographical Distribution of Financial Flows to Developing Countries*, DAC/OECD, Paris, various issues.

Table 3.1 shows aid to Israel from the two principal bilateral donors in the past decades, Germany and the USA, at five-year intervals. During the first decades, Germany's aid was a form of compensation for the Holocaust. US aid began increasing in the 1970s and thereafter the United States became the principal donor. In contrast to Germany, much US aid was – and is – military.

US aid to Israel started in 1949 and the first punitive suspension occurred in 1953 because of Israel's military raids into and dispute over access to water with Jordan. The second followed in 1956 for Israel's joining Britain and France in the military

---

[31] Rosenthal, A.M. – How Israel could do with less, *International Herald Tribune*, 20/21 March 1993.

[32] '$1.2 billion is considered economic aid, but it goes back to Washington to repay old Israeli debts for military purchases. Of the $1,8 billion in military aid, more than 70% must be spent on U.S.-made equipment and weapons.' Haberman, C. – How will Israel spend the money? U.S. watches closely, *International Herald Tribune*, 9 March 1993.

[33] Commission on Human Rights – Situation in occupied Palestine, resolution 1989/19 of 6 March 1989, preamble, and Situation of human rights in southern Lebanon, resolution 1989/65 of 8 March 1989, para. 3.

occupation of the Suez Canal.[34] Another occurred in 1991 with regard to US funding for the Israeli settlements in the occupied territories as is discussed below. The United States also suspended aid to Israel in 1997 because a 17-year old American fled there, having committed a particularly brutal murder, and escaped repatriation by claiming Israeli citizenship.[35] Suspensions of US aid have been, therefore, few and short-lived.

Pro-Israel lobby in the United States has been held up as a model of effectiveness for its success rate above 80% in transforming its lobbying platform into US foreign policy.[36] A key lobbying organization has been the American Israel Public Affairs Committee (AIPAC), which was founded in 1951 as a domestic US organization that 'plays American politics without apology.'[37] Occasional threats by the executive that the United States would 're-examine' its approach to the peace process have been undermined by 'Congress in which Mr Netanyahu [the Israeli prime minister at the time] enjoys greater support than in the Israeli Knesset.'[38]

Calls for sanctions against Israel were particularly frequent during *intifada*, the Palestinian unarmed uprising against Israeli occupation in the West Bank and Gaza Strip, which started in December 1987. The 1989 US State Department Report on Human Rights Practices acknowledged Israel's abuses, especially suppression of *intifada*. Images of heavily armed Israeli soldiers pitted against stone-throwing Palestinian teenagers were beamed across the world. Israel's own estimate was that 120,000 out of the total population of 2 million Palestinians were imprisoned in 1987–93.[39]

Table 3.2: Aid to Israel, 1982–94
(in million US$)

	1982	1985	1987	1989	1990	1992	1994
France	50.6	3.7	19.0	−60.5	−15.2	−11.1	36.1
Germany	61.4	72.2	145.6	−29.9	36.1	222.3	116.3
United Kingdom	3.0	13.2	13.8	76.7	47.5	23.9	−15.4
USA	1360.0	2470.0	1862.0	2107.0	1479.0	3090.0	3992.0
EUrope	167.4	88.5	233.5	−49.5	13.4	25.8	110.0
Total bilateral aid	1580.6	2561.9	2113.4	2029.6	1443.4	3096.1	4074.2
Multilateral aid	1551.0	2547.9	2092.2	2005.8	1470.8	3103.2	4103.5

Source: *Geographical Distribution of Financial Flows to Developing Countries*, DAC/OECD, Paris, various issues.

---

[34] Melman, Y. and Raviv, D. – *Friends in Deed. Inside the U.S.-Israel Alliance*, Hyperion, New York, 1994, pp. 74 and 83.

[35] Borger, J. – US murder suspect holds up Israeli aid, *Guardian Weekly*, 19 October 1997.

[36] Bard, M.G. – *The Water's Edge and Beyond*, Transaction Publishers, 1990.

[37] Erlanger, S. – Pro-Israel lobby in U.S. wields discreet power, *International Herald Tribune*, 27 April 1998.

[38] Gardner, D. and Gowers, A. Albright's trade offs, *Financial Times*, 7 May 1998.

[39] Gellman, B. – Israel frees Arab women, but the spirit is missing, *International Herald Tribune*, 13 February 1997.

Table 3.2 traces aid to Israel at the time of *intifada*, showing that it diminished between 1987 and 1992. Germany and EUrope suspended aid on several occasions and other Western countries imposed arms embargoes. After Israel had concluded a trade agreement with EUrope in 1975, attempts to broaden cooperation have routinely been linked to progress in peace-making.[40] In 1987–88, the European Parliament refused to give assent to an agreement with Israel because of human rights violations.[41] That agreement was subsequently approved but made conditional on progress towards an Arab-Israeli peace agreement and cooperation with Israel was suspended again in 1990.[42] In July 1995, EUrope (then the European Community) signed two agreements with Israel, one on trade and another on research and development, thus 'rewarding Israel for its efforts in the Middle East Peace process.'[43] Negotiations had lasted 18 months and the bottleneck was not human rights but non-tariff barriers which created Israel's large trade deficit with the EU.[44] The EUrope-Israel association agreement (including a human rights clause) was signed in November 1995 after the last hurdles had been overcome, the 'Spanish worries over imports of oranges, Austrian fears over apple juice imports, French difficulties over foie gras and maize.'[45]

Aid to Israel has been discouraged but never banned. The only actor that could have banned it, the Security Council, was unable to do so because of US vetoes. In 1980, the Security Council called upon states not to provide Israel with aid that would facilitate settlement in the occupied territories,[46] but that call was not heeded. Ten years later, foreign funding facilitating settlements created another rare suspension of US aid, leading to a 1992–96 freeze on new Israeli settlements. That suspension was intended to initiate a 'trialogue' between Israeli, Palestinian and US diplomats, the key obstacle to which was continued US financial support for Israeli settlements. Israel had requested the United States to underwrite commercial loans for the settlement of some 400,000 Jewish immigrants, mainly from the Soviet Union. Amongst other things, this controversy revealed that US aid to Israel was $77 billion in 1967–91, which translated into an annual $16,500 per capita.[47] President Bush postponed decision on Israel's demand for a $10 billion housing loan guarantee so as to enable the United States to mediate.[48]

---

[40] Carnegy, H. – EC links trade deal to Israeli peace progress, *Financial Times*, 11 July 1991.

[41] Zwamborn, M. – Human rights promotion and protection through the external relations of the European Community and the Twelve, *Netherlands Quarterly of Human Rights*, vol. 1, No. 1, 1989, p. 18.

[42] EC links trade deal to Israeli peace progress, *Financial Times*, 11 July 1991.

[43] Barber, L. – Hagglings ends with EU-Israel trade accord, *Financial Times*, 19 July 1995.

[44] Ozanne, J. – Israel sets terms for new trade pact with EU, *Financial Times*, 8 June 1995.

[45] EU and Israel initial co-operation accord, *EuroStep News*, No. 22, 31 October 1995, p. 19.

[46] United Nations – *The United Nations and the Question of Palestine*, DPI, New York, November 1985, p. 26.

[47] Bradsher, K. – Israel aid tally: $77 billion, *International Herald Tribune*, 25 September 1991.

[48] The sequence of events was vividly portrayed in the titles of newspaper reports: Israel plans to ask U.S. for $10 billion in loan guarantees for housing; Shock for Israel: U.S. firmness on loan; Shamir explodes at U.S. over loan delay; Israel, resigned, accepts loan delay, *International Herald Tribune*, 5 and 21–22 September, and 8 October, 1991.

The 1990s did not bring much change. In 1998–99, when the peace process seemed doomed by Israel's intransigence, its minister of foreign affairs, Ariel Sharon, was able to say: 'I can't remember Israel getting as much American aid in the past as it does now. Our relations with the US have never been better.'[49]

AIDING A PEACE WITHOUT HUMAN RIGHTS?

The tug of war between the United Nations and the United States has continued and little has changed with regard to Israel's susceptibility to UN condemnations and immunity to sanctions. A typical instance was the Security Council's resolution on the Hebron massacre in February 1994 (when Baruch Goldstein had killed 29 Palestinians and wounded many more while they were praying), which condemned the massacre and called upon Israel to 'continue taking measures' aimed at preventing 'illegal acts of violence by Israeli settlers.'[50] That language could not have been deemed too harsh even by the Israeli government. The Council's response to Israel's opening of a tunnel below Al Aqsa mosque was to regret the 'tragic events' and to call for reversing acts that led to them.[51] The United States abstained and that resolution was adopted, but it vetoed a proposed resolution which would have called upon Israel not to build a Jewish settlement in what used to be Arab East Jerusalem.[52]

In the meantime, peace-making triggered pledges for aid to Palestine which amounted to $2.4 billion for the planned five year transition period (1993–98).[53] The gap between pledged and disbursed aid was, much as elsewhere, considerable, with about half of committed aid actually disbursed. Terje Larsen, the UN Under-Secretary-General for Palestinian Territories at the beginning of the transition period, used exceptionally harsh words about this aid: 'the strategy is wrong, the priorities wrong, and the timetable wrong.'[54]

---

[49] Marion, G. – 'We won't give in to outside pressure,' *Le monde diplomatique*, reprinted in *Guardian Weekly*, 24 January 1999.

[50] This mildly worded text was a compromise acceptable to the USA. It abstained from endorsing two paragraphs in the preamble, one expressing the Council's concern at the number of Palestinian casualties and the other reminding Israel that international humanitarian law applied to all occupied territories. The text of Security Council's resolution 904 of 18 March 1994 is reproduced in *International Legal Materials*, vol. 33, 1994, pp. 548–549.

[51] Security Council resolution 1073 of 28 September 1996.

[52] Gardner, D. – Arab leaders question US role after veto, *Financial Times*, 10 March 1997.

[53] Garg, P. and El-Khouri, S. – Aiding the development effort for the West Bank and Gaza, *Finance & Development*, September 1994, p. 8.

[54] Ibrahim, Y.M. – PLO wants aid funds, fast, but its says donors' supervision is humiliating, *International Herald Tribune*, 10 June 1994; Gumbel, A. – $42m to halt Arafat cash crisis, *Guardian Weekly*, 19 June 1994; Palestinian aid programme 'has been failure', and EU signs $124m aid and loan package with Palestinians, *Financial Times*, 10 and 22 November 1994.

Aid to the Palestinian Authority (PA) involved donors in areas they tend to avoid, such as financing the police and/or security personnel. Because of the lack of revenue, the new Palestinian civil service had to be funded by donors, including more than 40,000 people in various police and security services.[55] The donors' direct payment of police salaries would have raised eyebrows, even without widespread publicity for their abuses, and so 'the United Nations Development Program [was put] in charge of disbursing $7 million every month for the salaries and other expenses of the Palestinian police.'[56] The UN Special Rapporteur has confirmed that 'human rights violations were not denied by the representatives of the Palestinian Authority.'[57]

The conduct of Palestinian police forces was closely related to Israel's security. Terrorist attacks within Israel multiplied in 1994 and proved impossible to prevent because most were suicide missions. They led to collective punishments of Palestinians through closures of the 'green line' which divides Israeli and Palestinian territories. These prevented migrant work, the main source of income for a large number of Palestinians, and led to calls for aid as a humanitarian gesture and also to prevent terrorism. It was cooperation between Israel and the Palestinian Authority that stopped terrorist incursions into Israel, at the cost of widespread allegations that PA's crackdown was carried out in disregard of human rights.

Condemnations of Israel's human rights record were therefore joined by 'concerns' about the Palestinian Authority. Nobody was quite sure whether Palestine should be treated as if it were a state: it exercised some powers associated with statehood but it could not become bound by any human rights treaties because it was not a state. 'Concerns' over abuses attributed to the Palestinian Authority proliferated, regardless of the absence of a proper legal formula. The UN Special Rapporteur noted in February 1998 that 'torture and ill treatment in the detention centres under the control of the Palestinian Authority have reportedly continued due to the pressure said to be placed on the Authority to deal with its own and Israeli security concerns.[58]

The pressure upon the Palestinian Authority increased with the Wye Agreement, which conditioned implementation of previous agreements by prevention and suppression of anti-Israeli violence, with the United States monitoring and refereeing. Predictably, a crackdown by Palestinian security forces against Palestinians who

---

[55] Shahin, M. – Palestine: Who will police the police?, *The Middle East*, January 1997, p. 12–13; Cockburn, P. – Did Arafat give a green light to terror?, *The Independent*, 25 March 1997.

[56] Immanuel, J. and Makovsky, D. – UN may disburse funds for Palestinian police, *The Jerusalem Post*, 20 August 1994.

[57] Commission on Human Rights – Report on the situation of human rights in the Palestinian territories occupied since 1967, submitted by Mr. Hannu Halinen, Special Rapporteur, U.N. Doc. E/CN.4/1996/18 of 15 March 1996, para. 28.

[58] Commission on Human Rights – Report on the situation of human rights in the Palestinian territories occupied since 1967, submitted by Mr. Hanu Halinen, Special Rapporteur, U.N. Doc. E/CN.4/1998/17 of 19 February 1998, para. 29.

were determined to constitute a threat followed. Human rights 'concerns' were raised by NGOs and the media but not by the negotiating parties.[59]

Pressures and counter-pressures have accompanied the ebb and flow of the peace process, but the level of frustration amongst the major funders increased in 1998. EUrope reportedly contributed $1.9 billion to the peace process in 1994–97 to then complain about not seeing any 'tangible peace dividends.'[60] Israel reportedly 'asked the US for an additional $1.3 billion for redeployment' of its military as anticipated by the Wye Agreement.[61] Tangible peace benefits of the Wye Agreement were not visible either until the government of Israel changed in May 1999, the newly elected government promising to make peace. Financial inducements did not prove decisive in moving forward the peace process, foreign and international condemnations did not seem to have played a major role either. Retrogression in human rights seemed to have been the price peace-making.

---

[59] Friedman, G. – For Israel, a victory and a time bomb, *International Herald Tribune*, 27 October 1998; Hockstader, L. – Palestinian security crackdown raises questions about human rights, *International Herald Tribune*, 30 October 1998; Palestinians: Early warning, *The Economist*, 31 October 1998.

[60] Dempsey, J. – Santer backs Palestinians, *Financial Times*, 9 February 1998.

[61] Said, E. – Arafat sells his people down the Wye river, *Guardian Weekly*, 15 November 1998.

Part II

The United States as trendsetter in unilateralism

Chapter 4

Containment of Communism

In 1949–89, humanity was held hostage to mutually-assured destruction, of which ideological and political confrontations between the United States and the Soviet Union were a constant reminder. Ideological and economic warfare was complemented by proxy wars fought to demarcate spheres of influence. The dismantling of the Soviet empire and the consequent demise of a hated and powerful enemy to rally against depleted US foreign policy of its principal objective and domestic politics has filled this void.

Domestic politics has been particularly lively in finding fault with other countries and imposing sanctions. The United States has been the trend-setter in economic sanctions, believing in its superpower status and the corollary ability to mould other governments' behaviour. Economic sanctions were initiated in 1947 as a cold-war weapon, to submerge aid, trade and investment under the foremost foreign policy objective of the time, the containment of communism. With the United States as the sole country whose economy had not been ruined by the Second World War, while other Western countries were its aid recipients, sanctions were easy to impose and enforce.

1947: INSTITUTIONALISATION OF AID CONDITIONALITY

The season of fiftieth anniversaries in mid-1990s revived interest for developments five decades ago. The fiftieth anniversary of the Universal Declaration of Human Rights, on 10 December 1998, was preceded by the fiftieth anniversary of the Marshall Plan in 1997. Human rights were intended to curtail the power of the state by affirming individual rights and freedoms, while the Marshall Plan intended to rebuild Western (but not Eastern) Europe.[1] The Cold War furnished the link between the two. The Council of Europe was established in the Western part of Europe in 1949 with an explicit commitment to human rights. The European Convention on Human Rights which followed one year later affirmed only civil and political rights, which became the West's key objection against Eastern Europe.

While the Universal Declaration of Human Rights was being negotiated, the Cold War had already become a fact. Indeed, The Soviet Union and Eastern Europe abstained in the final vote. The 'human rights' in the Universal Declaration were

---

[1] Milwards, A.S. – *The Reconstruction of Western Europe 1945–51*, Methuen & Co., London, 1984.

not associated with on-going economic warfare, which were deemed to be a lesser evil compared to much feared military confrontation. The Iron Curtain kept peace in Europe while wars were fought elsewhere. One of the first erupted in Korea. The countries which the United States defined as culprits – in this case North Korea and China – were subjected to economic sanctions. At the other side of the globe, the Cold War started in 1954 in Central America, with the US-supported military coup in Guatemala (discussed in Chapter 6) and economic warfare began in earnest with the US economic sanctions against Cuba in 1960. Moving back to Asia, Indonesia's suppression of communism in 1965–66 brought it Western support and aid as well as endorsement for its occupation of East Timor because of fears that it could become another Cuba. Africa was partitioned and re-partitioned along changing cold-war borders. This sequence of events could not be anticipated at the time, but circles of concern were clearly defined with Europe at their core.

George Kennan, the intellectual father of the containment of communism doctrine, predicted that the European Recovery Program (nicknamed the 'Marshall Plan' after the US Secretary of State, General George Marshall) would be 'the last major effort of this nature which our people could, or should, make.'[2] Marshall's definition of aid was instructive:

> Europe's requirements for the next three or four years of foreign food and other essential products – principally from America – are so much greater than her present ability to pay that she must have substantial additional help to face economic, social and political deterioration of a very grave character.
> It is logical that the United States should do whatever it is able to do to assist in the return of normal economic health in the world, without which there can be no political stability and no assured peace. Our policy is directed not against any country or doctrine but against hunger, poverty, desperation and chaos. Its purpose should be the revival of a working economy in the world so as to permit the emergence of political and social conditions in which free institutions can exist.[3]

The idea that US policy was not directed against any country or doctrine, as emphasised in Marshall's speech, was probably believed by nobody, given that both the country and the doctrine were known to all. The Marshall Plan did become the unique aid effort, called for many times but never repeated. The rationale whereby hunger, poverty, desperation and chaos ought to be eliminated before free political institutions can be established gradually disappeared from US foreign policy.

Kennan's memoirs tried retroactively to correct misinterpretations related to the containment of communism, which he had unwittingly made into a code-word for

---

[2] Quoted from Gaddis, J.L. – Containment: A reassessment, *Foreign Affairs*, vol. 55, No. 4, July 1977, p. 876.
[3] Address by General George C. Marshall, Secretary of State of the United States, at Harvard University, 5 June 1947, text available on http://www.oecd.org/about/ms-eng2.htm.

US foreign policy.[4] His early critics objected to waging the Cold War through sanctions against the Soviet Union and its allies, while providing aid to US allies and to regimes perceived as possible victims of Soviet expansionism. Walter Lippmann predicted that US sanctions against communist and inducements to anticommunist countries would lead to 'recruiting, subsidising, and supporting a heterogenous array of satellites, clients, dependents and puppets.'[5] Charles William Maynes took this line of argument one step further to point out that the Soviet Union was perceived as lawless and immoral hence 'Americans could match [it] only by lowering their own standards,'[6] and a downward spiral of ever-lowered constraints upon foreign policy because a defining feature of the past five decades. In his study into the Western economic warfare against communist countries, Gunnar Adler-Karlsson has found that sanctions were not imposed following a study into what they should achieve but were 'an expression of popular sentiments.'[7] Demonisation of the enemy, which replaced rational calculation with articles of faith, both created and reflected such popular sentiments.

In 1947–1951, the United States equipped itself with an arsenal of economic weaponry to fight the Cold War. The revival of war-related export controls was globalised through their linkage with US aid, which was easily secured because the United States was the single donor at the time and today's industrialised countries were recipients of US aid. Trade was subsumed under foreign-policy objectives, most importantly the containment of communism. The Export Control Act of 1949 defined US policy as 'the necessary vigilance over exports from the standpoint of their significance to the national security of the United States'.[8] In 1951, denial of trade preferences to communist countries became part of US law, while the Mutual Defense Assistance Control Act (known as the Battle Act) denied aid to any country which failed to comply with US export controls. The aim was to reduce Soviet military strength, as well as that of its allies, and to 'assist the people of the nations under the domination of foreign aggressors to re-establish their freedom.'[9]

Between 1949 and 1994, Cocom co-ordinated (as its name, Co-ordinating Committee, suggests) trade restrictions against communist countries. Its member-

---

[4] Kennan, G.F. – *Memoirs: 1925–1950*, Little Brown, Boston, 1967.

[5] Lippmann, W. – *The Cold War: A Study in U.S. Foreign Policy*, Harper, New York, 1947, p. 575.

[6] Maynes, C.W. – The role of power, law and morality in American foreign policy, *Proceedings of the 85th Annual Meeting, April 17–20, 1991*, American Society of International Law, Washington, D.C., p. 454.

[7] Adler-Karlsson, G. – *Western Economic Warfare 1947–1967. A Case Study in Foreign Economic Policy*, Stockholm Economic Studies, New Series No. 9, Almqvist & Wiksel, Uppsala/Stockholm, 1968, p. 31.

[8] The Export Control Act of 1949, as amended by Public Law 89–63, 89th Congress, Section 2, para. 1.

[9] Mutual Defense Assistance Control Act of 1951, Public Law 213, H.R. 4550, 82nd Congress, 65 Stat. 644 of 26 October 1951, preamble and Section 101.

ship was modelled after NATO's, as was its secretiveness.[10] During its first decade, the list of prohibited goods encompassed almost half of all traded goods and applied to all recipients of US aid. That list was shortened as Western Europe's dependence on US aid diminished. During the Marshall Plan period, the United States could impose restrictions on West-East trade upon recipients. In 1948–52, Iceland received an annual $72 per capita, Norway $50, the Netherlands $45, Greece $44, Belgium and Luxembourg $36, France $35, Denmark $29, United Kingdom $19, West Germany $15, and Italy $13.[11] These figures appear small and insignificant from the viewpoint of today's value of the US dollar and the high average incomes in these countries today, and so one should add a few zeroes to get a sense of the volume of US aid fifty years ago. Aid conditionality was precisely defined and strictly applied. US legislation envisaged the withholding of aid if the recipient was suspected of planning exports to Eastern Europe:

> The bilateral agreements were a systematic attempt by the United States to determine how far it should and could exact political and economic concessions in return for foreign aid and as such were an early determinant of a vital aspect of American foreign economic policy for the next [forty] years.[12]

Aid conditionality, as defined five decades ago, has not subsequently changed. In contrast, the geopolitical map of the world has changed, with the emancipation of Western Europe from the status of aid recipients to donors. Their policies had been tested with regard to Cuba, which became a veritable cold-war battlefield in the early 1960s to continue creating unanimity and dissent in Western foreign policies thereafter.

1960: US SANCTIONS AGAINST CUBA

Cuba exemplifies how little the addition of human rights rhetoric changed the pre-existing pattern of sanctions. Human rights had not been invoked in 1960, when the United States imposed sanctions against Cuba but were used in 1962 to justify Cuba's expulsion from the OAS. Then human rights were not were not mentioned when the OAS lifted sanctions against Cuba, but came to dominate US policy against Cuba in the 1990s.

---

[10] Greene, O. – Developing an effective successor to Cocom, Saferworld Briefing, London, September 1995, mimeographed.

[11] USAID (United States Agency for International Development) – *U.S. Overseas Loans and Grants and Assistance from International Organizations*, Washington, D.C., 1982.

[12] Milward, A.S. – *The Reconstruction of Western Europe 1945–51*, Methuen & Co., Cambridge, 1984, p. 114.

The entry of human rights into US foreign policy in the 1970s did not make Cuba a prominent item. Cuba was not a recipient of US but Soviet aid hence there was no aid to be cut off. The subsequent demise of the Soviet Union provided the United States with the possibility of ending the Cold War within its own sphere of influence. It placed Cuba on the UN violations-agenda and intensified economic sanctions to throttle the country. Impoverishment was expected to lead to public protest, which would be brutally repressed, leading to popular revolt against the government and, ultimately, its replacement. This scenario might have seemed feasible in theory but the first post-cold-war decade did not see it working in practice.

The low visibility of Cuba in global human rights politics lasted until the end of the Cold War. In contrast, Cuba had been a bone of contention in its region. Its expulsion form the OAS and sanctions had not been justified by human rights alone but rather by the incompatibility of Marxism-Leninism with the Inter-American definition of representative democracy. There was not much 'representative democracy' at the time, but the term denoted unacceptability of a doctrine which did not endorse it as a goal. Furthermore, Cuba was seen as the principal exporter of revolution in the Americas, the launch-pad of a communist offensive.[13] The real source of danger, 'an extracontinental power,' remained unnamed.[14]

Unilateral US sanctions against Cuba were first imposed in 1960 as a response to the nationalisation of US property in the aftermath of the 1958 revolution. Fidel Castro became the head of government on 1 January 1959. At first, his government had been recognised by the United States. In May 1959, Cuba adopted a new law on agrarian reform nationalising large landholdings, and offering compensation in the form of government bonds, which were deemed worthless. Many of these landholdings were owned by United States citizens and companies, notably 40% of the sugar plantations that generated the bulk of Cuba's foreign currency. Other large landholdings had been owned by some 200,000 Cubans who had fled to the United States following the revolution, settled mainly in Florida, and became naturalised US citizens ('Cuban-Americans'). The 1959 land reform affected more than a quarter-million-dollar American investment in agriculture (at 1959 prices) and protests of landowners were vehement.

Other foreign investment, notably in oil refineries, became embroiled in a Cuba-USSR-USA conflict. After Cuba concluded a sugar-for-oil barter agreement with the Soviet Union, some American-owned refineries refused to process Soviet oil

---

[13] Resolution I adopted by the Eighth Consultative Meeting of Ministers of Foreign Affairs was entitled 'Communist offensive in Americas' and resolution VI excluded the then-government of Cuba from participation in the Inter-American system. *Octava Reunion de Consulta De Ministros de Relaciones Exteriores, Punta del Este, Uruguay, 22–31 enero 1962, Actas y Documentos*, OAS Doc. OEA/Ser. F/III.8. Resolution I of the Ninth Meeting of Consultation of Ministers of Foreign Affairs on 21–26 July 1964 withheld recognition to the government led by Fidel Castro and imposed trade sanctions in response to Cuba's 'export of revolution.' (OAS Official Records, Doc. OEA/Ser. D/III.15, 1964, p. 3)

[14] Resolution I of the Seventh Meeting of Consultation of Ministers of Foreign Affairs, OAS Doc. OEA/Ser. C/II.7, p. 4–5.

and were seized by the Cuban government in retaliation.[15] In counter-retaliation, US aid to Cuba was cut off in May 1960 and two months later Cuba's sugar quota abolished. Export of Cuban sugar to the United States had constituted two-thirds of the total value of exports. The chain of retaliation and counter-retaliation went further and Cuba's government nationalised all American property in August 1960, and the United States retaliated by imposing an embargo on all exports to Cuba. US sanctions had been justified as economic counter-measures at the time and diplomatic sanctions followed. The United States broke off diplomatic relations with Cuba in January 1961 in retaliation for Cuba's cooperation agreement with the Soviet Union. The tit-for-tat intensified with the ill-fated Bay of Pigs invasion of 1961 and the Cuban missile crisis of 1962.[16] In 1962, the US Export Control Act was amended to describe 'the policy of the United States to use its economic resources and advantages in trade with Communist-dominated nations to further the national security and foreign policy objectives of the United States.'[17]

Human rights rhetoric was not used at the time, and battles were fought to outlaw Marxism-Leninism in the Americas, rupture Cuba's links with the Soviet Union, halt the export of revolution within Central and Latin America, and later to roll back Cuba's military deployment in Africa. The aims of US sanctions have not changed much in the past four decades, however. They were summed up forty years ago by the then US Secretary of State, Dean Rusk, as follows:

1) To reduce Castro's will and ability to export subversion and violence to other American States;
2) To make plain to the people of Cuba that Castro's regime cannot serve their interests;
3) To demonstrate to the peoples of the American republics that communism has no future in the Western Hemisphere; and
4) To increase the cost to the Soviet Union of maintaining a communist outpost in the Western Hemisphere.[18]

---

[15] Adler-Karlsson, G. – *Western Economic Warfare 1947–1967. A Case Study in Foreign Economic Policy*, Stockholm Economic Studies, New Series IX, Almqvist & Wiksell, Uppsala/Stockholm, 1968, p. 209–210.

[16] Thirty-six years after the Bay of Pigs invasion, the Inspector General's Survey of the Cuban Operation was brought to light through freedom of information legislation. The Survey revealed that agents had been infiltrated to topple Fidel Castro and that a CIA-formed government was to take over. President Kennedy's last minute rollback of a planned air strike led to the death of all infiltrated agents. (Weiner, T. – Bay of Pigs was fiasco, CIA admits, *Guardian Weekly*, 1 March 1998.) This was followed by the Cuban Missile crisis, a thirteen-day 'nuclear chess' between presidents Kennedy and Khruschev, triggered by the stationing of nuclear missiles on Cuba and solved by their withdrawal in exchange for the withdrawal of US missiles from Turkey. (May, E.R. and Zelikow, P.D. – *The Kennedy Tapes: Inside the White House during the Cuban Missile Crisis*, Belknap Press, 1997.)

[17] Berman, H.J. and Garson, J.A. – United States export controls – past, present and future, *Columbia Law Review*, vol. 67, No. 5, May 1967, p. 802.

[18] McKitterick, N. – *East-West Trade. The Background of U.S. Policy*, Twentieth Century Foundation, New York, 1966, p. 23.

US sanctions against Cuba were extended to all recipients of US aid in 1963. To remain eligible for US aid, recipients had to cut off, or at least curtail, links with Cuba. As Table 4.1 shows, that strategy was effective, and no aid to Cuba was provided, except by the Soviet Union. Data on Soviet aid were neither publicly available nor reliable. Thus, estimates vary a great deal. Determining prices and translating them into US dollars is an impossible task and much exchange between Cuba and the Soviet Union was barter and Cuban sugar was traded for Soviet oil, for example. One Cuban 'guesstimate' is that total Soviet aid in 1960–1989 amounted to $16.7 billion.[19] After the end of the Cold War and disintegration of the Soviet Union, Russia became liable to US sanctions due to the sugar-for-oil barter with Cuba, which enabled Cuba to have access to oil at below-market prices.[20]

Table 4.1: Aid to Cuba in 1960–95
(in million US$)

	1960	1965	1970	1975	1980	1985	1990	1995
Canada	–	–	–	0.4	–5.4	0.1	0.2	0.9
France	–	–	–	–	26.5	0.5	0.8	3.2
Germany	–	–	–	–	0.4	0.0	1.1	1.5
Italy	0.1	–	–	–	–0.3	0.1	10.5	5.7
Netherlands	–	–	–	0.2	3.8	0.0	0.0	0.8
Norway	–	–	–	1.2	0.1	–	0.1	0.6
Spain	n/a	n/a	n/a	n/a	n/a	n/a	17.5	15.4
Sweden	–	–	0.1	10.0	12.9	1.8	2.6	3.6
Switzerland	–	–	–	–	28.8	–	0.0	0.3
Total bilateral	0.1	0.0	0.1	14.2	19.7	2.5	33.6	33.6
CMEA (brutto)	n/r	n/r	n/r	n/r	400.0	689.0	n/r	n/a
EUrope	–	–	–	–	–3.1	0.7	30.1	46.8
Total multilateral	10.8	0.0	1.7	6.7	40.6	15.7	17.4	30.9

Source: *Geographical Distribution of Financial Flows to Developing Countries*, OECD, Paris, various issues.

Even if aid statistics for Soviet aid are non-existent of unreliable, a glimpse of its volume can be gauged from the few data that have been included in the DAC/OECD annual reports. The figures for officially reported aid through the

---

[19] Mesa-Lago, C. – The economy: Caution, frugality and resilient ideology, in: Dominguez, J. (ed.) – *Cuba: Internal and International Affairs*, Sage Publications, Beverly Hills, 1982, p. 150.

[20] Now, the Cuban endgame, editorial, *The Washington Post*, reprinted in *International Herald Tribune*, 14–15 September 1991; Cuba embargoes spark protest, Cuba sanctions threaten to sour US-EU relations, Russia vows to defy US on links with Havana, *Financial Times*, 2/3 March and 24 May 1966.

CMEA (Council for Mutual Economic Assistance)[21] are available only for the 1980s and illustrate how much Soviet/CMEA aid overshadowed all other sources.

The pattern of aid flows to Cuba illustrated in Table 4.1 highlights what an East-West battle field Cuba had been. The early aid embargo is clearly seen and is Cuba's predicament in the 1990s. The early aid embargo was related to diplomatic and political sanctions against Cuba. The Organization of American States (OAS) had been first mobilised by the United States to invoke collective security against the threat of international communism in 1954, at the time when the USA was retrospectively found to have fostered an 'anticommunist' military coup in Guatemala. Cuba was expelled in 1962 and OAS sanctions followed in 1964 to be formally lifted in 1975.[22] By that time, sanctions against Cuba had been imposed by other Western countries in response to military interventions in Africa, especially the deployment of Cuban troops in Angola in 1975 and in Ethiopia in 1978. As shown in Table 4.2, aid to Cuba noticeably diminished from the 1976 total of $357 million to $79 in 1977, and in1979–80 it fell below $40 million.[23] These sanctions were lifted once Cuban troops were withdrawn, although aid did not significantly increase, as Table 4.2 illustrates.

Table 4.2: Aid to Cuba, 1982–94
(in million US$)

	1982	1985	1987	1989	1990	1992	1994
Canada	–4.8	–1.9	2.0	–0.6	–1.3	–0.4	0.2
France	–41.0	34.0	–108.2	–48.3	37.7	–47.6	16.3
Italy	11.0	29.2	–50.2	46.0	17.5	18.7	–24.7
Spain	–	–	–	–	19.1	4.8	2.8
EUrope	–29.1	59.3	–148.5	46.6	97.4	–3.0	15.1
Total bilateral aid	–125.7	24.7	–169.7	42.5	140.9	–48.0	–41.0
Multilateral aid	–110.7	40.3	–146.7	55.6	158.3	–35.3	–12.2

Source: *Geographical Distribution of Financial Flows to Developing Countries*, DAC/OECD, Paris, various issues.

Reverse flows in Table 4.2 reflect Cuba's inability to service its previously incurred debts. Subsequent to the demise of the CMEA and the Soviet Union,

---

[21] The Council for Mutual Economic Assistance (known under two different acronyms, CMEA or COMECON) was established in 1949 and obtained its constituent charter in 1959. It was mandated for comprehensive economic cooperation 'based on consistent implementation of the international socialist division of labour in the interest of the building of socialism and communism' (Preamble to the CMEA Charter, *United Nations Treaty Series*, vol. 368, p. 253).

[22] Organization of American States – Final Act of the Sixteenth Meeting of Consultation of Ministers of Foreign Affairs, San José, 29 July 1975, resolution I, Doc. OEA/Ser.C/II.16, p. 4.

[23] DAC/OECD – *Geographical Distribution of Financial Flows to Developing Countries in 1975–81*, OECD, Paris, 1982.

foreign and international aid to Cuba virtually disappeared. Moreover, Cuba's previous Eastern European allies conditioned resumption of trade on Cuba's acknowledgement of its debts.[24]

Although Cuba has been complaining about the economic cost of US sanctions for a very long time, aid from the former Soviet Union neutralised much of that cost. With the disappearance of Soviet aid, Cuba's economy recorded negative growth: in 1990–94, its GNP decreased by 35%, to recover to an estimated growth of 2.5% in 1995 and a reported 7.8% in 1996.[25] Cuba's inability to service its external debt, estimated at between $7 and 9 billion, makes it ineligible for international development finance, even without the likely US veto of Cuba's membership in the International Monetary Fund (IMF) or the World Bank. Cuba's inability to export to Western markets and earn foreign currency has made debt servicing impossible.

The government declared in 1990 something resembling an economic emergency, the 'Special Period in Peacetime'. Free education and health care, which had previously kept Cuba at the top of the list of success stories in literacy and life expectancy levels – outperforming much richer countries – has become difficult to sustain. Rather than nudging the population to rebel against its own government in response to impoverishment and economic hardship, sanctions have been defined as 'the enemy,' provided justification for the economic decline, as well as for suppressing opposition, perceived as unpatriotic. The UN Special Rapporteur, Carl-Johan Groth, has noted that US hostility reinforced the regime in power, as did the 'fear of alternative policies represented by hard-line, politically influential Cuban-American groups'.[26] One year later, he has added:

The embargo serves as a ready pretext for keeping the population under strict control and for punishing or suppressing in various ways those who work for political change.[27]

The United Nations: USA versus Cuba, Cuba versus the USA

The United Nations became a double political battlefield at the end of the Cold War. *USA versus Cuba* has been fought as of 1988 within the Commission on Human Rights with regard to Cuba's condemnation for human rights violations;

---

[24] Mesa-Lago, C. – Assessing economic and social performance in the Cuban transition of the 1990s, *World Development*, vol. 26, 1998, No. 5, p. 866.

[25] Heroic illusions. A survey of Cuba, *The Economist*, 6 April 1996, p. 6; Cole, K. – *Cuba: From Revolution to Development*, Pinter, London, 1998, p. 56.

[26] United Nations – Report on the situation of human rights in Cuba, prepared by the Special Rapporteur, Mr. Carl-Johan Groth, U.N. Doc. E/CN.4/1995/52 of 11 January 1995, para. 59.

[27] United Nations – Report on the situation of human rights in Cuba submitted by the Special Rapporteur, Mr. Carl-Johan Groth, U.N. Doc. E/CN.4/1998/69 of 30 January 1998, para. 69.

Cuba versus USA has been fought as of 1991 within the UN General Assembly to condemn the United States for persisting with sanctions against Cuba.

The voting record of the General Assembly's resolutions on US sanctions against Cuba have demonstrated increasing self-isolation of the United States. They have attracted an increasing majority of votes, including Western. The annual resolution was entitled *Necessity of ending the economic, commercial and financial embargo imposed by the United States of America against Cuba*, and its voting pattern was as follows: 59-3-71 in 1992, 88-57-3 in 1993, 101-48-2 in 1994, 117-3-38 in 1995, and 137-3-25 in 1996.[28] In 1995, a good number of Western delegations voted against the US embargo, namely, Australia, Austria, Belgium, Denmark, Finland, France, Norway, Spain, and Sweden. In 1996 all members of the European Union voted against the US embargo. Only Israel and Uzbekistan voted with the USA.

The United States first tried – unsuccessfully – to have Cuba condemned for human rights violations in 1986 by the General Assembly and the following year by the Commission on Human Rights, also unsuccessfully. In 1988 the US delegation to the Commission was headed by Armando Valladares, himself a former Cuban prisoner, who presented to the Commission a number of people who claimed to have been disabled as result of ill-treatment in Cuban prisons. Nevertheless, support for a condemnatory resolution was not forthcoming, and a compromise was made whereby the Commission would field a visit to Cuba. The group consisted of governmental delegates selected by regions. It visited Cuba and reported evidence of abuses as well as evidence that abuses were decreasing. A condemnatory resolution was adopted by the Commission and political warfare continued. In 1991, a Special Representative of the Secretary General on human rights in Cuba was appointed to follow up on the 1988 visit. The government of Cuba refused to co-operate and continued not cooperating with the subsequently appointed Special Rapporteur. In 1997, the United States could not secure the necessary votes in the Commission on Human Rights and ten years of political battles seemed to be over. Yet in 1999 the Czech Republic, a previous cold-war ally, tabled a resolution against Cuba, which was adopted by a dramatic vote of 21-20-12.[29]

Neither these nor the previous votes were necessarily guided by human rights considerations. *Americas Watch* found in 1989 that US campaign against Cuba, marked by greatly exaggerated charges and a high level of politicisation, damaged the human rights cause.[30] US lobbying tactics included threats of cutting off aid to

---

[28] General Assembly resolutions 47/19 of 24 November 1992, 48/16 of 3 November 1993, 49/9 of 26 October 1994, 50/10 of 2 November 1995, and 51/17 of 12 November 1996.

[29] Commission on Human Rights – Human rights in Cuba, resolution 1999/8 of 23 April 1999.

[30] *Human Rights in Cuba. The Need to Sustain the Pressure*, Washington, D.C., January 1989, p. 95.

those recipients whose delegations did not join the condemnation of Cuba's human rights record,[31] and, for example, US aid to India was reduced by $15 million.[32]

Challenges to the privatisation and globalization of US sanctions

The strengthening and broadening of US sanctions against Cuba followed the demise of the Soviet Union, with the obvious intention of enforcing change through economic strangulation. It was done in two stages. In 1992 sanctions against Cuba were privatised domestically and in 1996 extended globally.

The *Cuban Democracy Act* of 1992 (known as the *Torricelli Act*) mandated sanctions against US companies whose foreign subsidiaries operated in Cuba or traded with it. A controversy concerning the extraterritorial reach of US law ensued, with Canada and Britain instructing their companies not to comply with US law.[33] Compliance with their own law would have made them breach US law, while compliance with US law would have forced them to violate domestic law.

Despite the absence of an international endorsement, US sanctions against Cuba were strengthened and broadened further. The United States tabled a resolution before the Security Council, proposing sanctions against Cuba, after two US planes had been shot down by Cuba's military.[34] There was no support for this, however, and the 1996 Cuban Liberty and Democratic Solidarity Act (known as Helms-Burton Act after its congressional sponsors) was adopted instead. It allows Cuban-Americans to file suits before US courts against anybody (any individual or company from any country) for 'trafficking' in property confiscated by Cuba in 1959–60. The underlying reasoning was that virtually all commercially useful property in Cuba had been confiscated when Fidel Castro came into power and thus all today's commercially useful property is likely to have been confiscated at the time and encompassed by the prohibition of 'trafficking.' By inhibiting commerce involving illegally obtained property (confiscation constituted theft), the United States was upholding property rights.[35]

The Helms-Burton Act found that '36 years of communist tyranny and economic mismanagement by the Castro government' ruined the economy, while

---

[31] Bone, P. and Onello, M. – United Nations Human Rights Commission: United States pressure for investigation of human rights abuses in Cuba, *Harvard Human Rights Yearbook*, vol. 2, 1989, note 46, p. 215.

[32] The US draft resolution on human rights violations in Cuba had been proposed in 1987, and followed by a draft resolution on human rights violations in the USA submitted by Cuba. The discussion reached a stalemate and India proposed that both items be suspended. Commission on Human Rights – Report on the Forty-third session, U.N. Doc. E/1987/18, p. 137–138.

[33] Petras, J. and Morley, M. – Clinton's Cuba policy: Two steps backward, one step forward, *Third World Quarterly*, vol. 17, 1996, No. 2, p. 270.

[34] Freedland, J. – US punishes Cuba for downing planes, *Guardian Weekly*, 3 March 1996.

[35] Clagget, B.M. – Cuba and U.S. sanctions and extraterritoriality; Title III of the Helms-Burton Act does not violate international law, American Society of International Law – *Proceedings of the 90th Annual Meeting*, March 27–30, 1996, Washington, D.C., pp. 368–373.

health and welfare deteriorated because of 'the refusal of the Castro regime to permit free and fair democratic elections in Cuba'. Things would not improve until free elections were held, and the USA should continue its 'effective sanctioning of the totalitarian Castro regime.' The international community was accused of 'ethically improper conduct' for its failure to follow the US lead.[36]

The *Financial Times* called the Helms-Burton Act 'silly and indefensible,'[37] adding to the veritable flood of protests in the West. Two points were made in these protests, firstly, that US legislation could not apply extraterritorially, and, secondly, that US foreign policy should not be imposed on other countries. Canada and France went further and enhanced economic and commercial relations with Cuba.[38] US legislation was challenged as a breach of the free trade principles embodied in NAFTA (the North American Free Trade Agreement).[39] The Inter-American Juridical Committee was asked by the OAS General Assembly whether the Helms-Burton Act was valid under international law and replied in the negative.[40] The European Union reached the same conclusion.[41]

The apparent conflict between the Helms-Burton Act and free trade principles induced EUrope to take the United States to the World Trade Organisation (WTO) so as to obtain an authoritative determination of a breach of international trade law. Because sanctions were part and parcel of US domestic politics, adjudication was postponed in the hope that US elections in November 1996 would diminish the importance of Cuban-American votes in Florida. In the meantime, the part of the Helms-Burton Act threatening companies to be taken to court as 'traffickers in confiscated property' was suspended for six months, then again.[42] Subsequently, these waivers were quietly continued. In November 1996, the European Council adopted a regulation which asked European companies not to apply the Helms-Burton law and enabled them, if sued before American courts as 'traffickers in

---

[36] The text of the Cuban Liberty and Democratic Solidarity (Libertad) Act of 1996 is reproduced in *International Legal Materials*, vol. 35, 1996, pp. 359–396.

[37] Brinkmanship over Cuba (leader), *Financial Times*, 4 february 1997.

[38] Crary, D. – Canada hits back at US law on Cuba, *Guardian Weekly*, 22 September 1996; Farah, D. – Cuba signs broad pact with Canada, *The Washington Post*, reprinted in *Guardian Weekly*, 2 February 1997; France increases Cuba credit, *Financial Times*, 18–19 January 1997; Fletcher, P. – France to sign deal with Cuba, *Financial Times*, 22 April 1997.

[39] U.S. boycott policy angers its allies, *The Washington Post*, 11 May 1996; U.S. isolated in the Americas for tighter embargo against Cuba, *International Herald Tribune*, 7 June 1996. Canada to retaliate against US over Cuba trade act, *Financial Times*, 13 June 1996; EU summit warns US on sanctions, *Financial Times*, 24 June 1996.

[40] Organization of American States – Opinion of the Inter-American Juridical Committee in response to resolution AG/DOC.3375/96 of the General Assembly of the Organization, entitled 'Freedom of trade and investment in the hemisphere', Doc. CJI/SO/II/doc.67/96 rev. 5 of 23 August 1996.

[41] Demarche by the Delegation of the European Commission of 5 March 1996, reproduced in *International Legal Materials*, vol. 35, 1996, p. 398–399.

[42] Clinton extends waiver on anti-Cuba law, *Financial Times*, 17 July 1998.

confiscated property', to recoup their penalty through a counter-suit before a European court.[43]

This EUrope *versus* USA case was diverted to political negotiations. The acquiescence of the United States was sought for 'secure and lasting waivers' as well as a commitment not to continue trying to globalise US legislation. (Besides US sanctions against Cuba, those targeting Iran and Libya were on the agenda as well.) Waivers were granted against EUrope's acknowledgment 'that many of the Castro nationalizations were illegal under international law' and foreign investors might be investing in illegally acquired property.[44] That political compromise enabled negotiators for both sides to claim victory, leaving interpretation of their agreements and disagreements to further political bargaining.

Although worded in the language of democracy and human rights, the Helms-Burton Act carefully singled out national security as the pre-eminent justification for sanctions against Cuba. The US position was that any adjudication within the World Trade Organization would 'infringe on the sovereign prerogative of governments to determine their national security arrangements.'[45] Article XXI enables governments to take measures necessary to protect their national security interests. There is no definition of 'national security' or of the measures necessary to protect it and exemption of such cases from adjudication provides limitless opportunities for abusing this clause with impunity. The then European Community used an identical justification when it had imposed economic sanctions against Argentina during the Falklands/Malvinas war.[46] There was also a possible application to Israel: a US demand for EUrope's commitment to deter investment in any property that was confiscated, anywhere in the world, was reportedly dropped when 'somebody asked about Palestinian claims against Israel' with regard to Palestinian properties that have never been compensated.[47]

The value of compensation owed by Cuba for the property confiscated after the 1959 revolution was estimated as high as $6 billion. Ernesto Betancourt, then the director of *Radio Martí*, a US-based broadcasting service transmitting to Cuba, announced that the CANF (Cuban American National Foundation) 'has buyers willing to pay $15 billion for 60% of Cuba's land and assets.'[48] These figures bring the issue to US domestic politics. The importance of the Cuban-American vote has been identified as the predominant factor explaining US sanctions against Cuba,

---

[43] European Communities – Proposal for a Council regulation protecting against the effects of the application of certain legislation of certain third countries, and actions based thereon or resulting therefrom, COM(96) 420 final of 31 July 1996.

[44] Buckley, N. – Tough talking looms on US laws, *Financial Times*, 15 May 1998; Cornwell, R. – Deal lets Europe trade with 'pariahs', *The Independent*, 19 May 1998; Walker, M. – Transatlantic trade deal placates EU, *Guardian Weekly*, 24 May 1998.

[45] de Jonquières, G. – Showdown on Cuba trade, *Financial Times*, 3 February 1997.

[46] de Jonquières, G. – US dodges Brussels onslaught, *Financial Times*, 21 February 1997.

[47] EU strikes deal on Cuba, *International Herald Tribune*, 12–13 April 1997.

[48] Betancourt, E.F. – As Castro's time expires, this pushing won't help, *International Herald Tribune*, 7–8 September 1991.

and their ebb and flow is deemed to reflects Florida politics, in which CANF is a crucial actor. *The Economist* has commented that, as well as providing money in congressional and presidential elections, CANF 'can usually deliver the Cuban vote at election time.'[49] When sanctions are shaped by domestic politics, their effects on a foreign target become irrelevant. Jorge Domínguez has concluded: '[the] United States has been a staunch enemy of Fidel Castro, but with the enemy like this one, he may not need friends.'[50]

Perhaps an even more influential factor than CANF is time. CANF's insistence on isolation and sanctions was initiated forty years ago, its main protagonists have become forty years older, and the original leader of CANF has long since died. The new generation of Cuban-Americans may not continue seeking Cuba's isolation and a fifth decade of sanctions. US sanctions against Cuba were softened in 1999 to allow US exports of food and agricultural inputs 'for the use of independent non-government entities' but that easing of sanctions did not show any practical results because it was difficult to identify 'independent non-government entities' as well as to obtain US export credits.[51] The hope has been that the attraction of a $1 billion market for US food exports could tip the scales for further relaxation of sanctions. It remains to be seen whether the tenth US Administration since Fidel Castro came to power will continue transposing Florida politics into US policy.

1970: FROM DÉTENTE TO THE SECOND COLD WAR

Different from uninterrupted sanctions against Cuba, US sanctions against the Soviet Union were relieved during a short-lived détente in 1970–75. Private and public dialogue was expected to reach beyond arms control and international trouble spots to ultimately develop into cooperation. A trade agreement was signed in 1972, only to be renounced by the Soviet Union in 1975. The reason was US public punitiveness at the expense of private Soviet concessions. Henry Kissinger's memoirs have described how Jewish emigration from the USSR had increased – from 400 in 1968 to almost 35,000 in 1973 – in response to US inducements, which included a commitment not to publicly exploit that change.[52] That changed practice was abandoned after a US shift from behind-the-scene inducements to its public conditioning of trade by demanding publicised Soviet compliance. The 1974 Jackson-Vanik amendment conditioned trade with communist countries on increased emigration, after which the 1974 Stevenson amendment diminished

---

[49] Cuban-Americans: The other Maximum Leader, *The Economist*, 29 November 1997.

[50] Domínguez, J.I. – The secret of Castro's staying power, *Foreign Affairs*, vol. 72, 1993, No. 2, p. 107.

[51] Fletcher, P. – US farm groups on sales mission in Havana, *Financial Times*, 13 January 2000.

[52] Kissinger, H.A. – *Years of Upheaval*, Little, Brown and Company, Boston, 1982, pp. 249–50.

Soviet access to trade-related credit. The latter meant that 'the Soviets would be eligible for less in credits over the subsequent four years that they had already over the previous two, before they had made any concession!' As a consequence, in 1976 Jewish emigration from the USSR plummeted to 13,000 from an anticipated 60,000.[53]

That shift from behind-the-scene inducements to public humiliation of the Soviet Union had an immediate negative effect on détente. Exactly at that time, the 1975 Helsinki Final Act had added human rights to the West-East dialogue. With the approach of the follow-up meeting to review its implementation after two years, the Carter Administration took office promising to make human rights a keystone of US foreign policy. Indeed, the 1980s were dubbed the 'Second Cold War' because cold-war battles dominated international human rights politics. The Helsinki process had legitimised human rights in West-East relations and a large number of human rights organisations devoted themselves to documenting breaches of the Helsinki commitments by Eastern European states. The Soviet military intervention in Afghanistan triggered sanctions and subsumed aid to the Afghani resistance under 'human rights.' The military take-over in Poland was less violent but nevertheless became a major issue on the UN violations-agenda and also triggered economic sanctions. Towards the end of the Cold War, countries such as Romania or Cuba were placed on the UN violators-agenda; previously this had been impossible.

Responses to the Soviet military intervention in Afghanistan and to the imposition of martial law in Poland exposed the split within the West. The best known controversy was related to the building of a gas pipeline as a conduit for Soviet natural gas to Western Europe. To punish the Soviet Union for its military intervention in Afghanistan, the United States prohibited US companies from participating in the project and this prohibition also encompassed their subsidiaries in Western Europe as well as European companies which used US-licensed technology or equipment. Protests in Western Europe were rapid and firm. Extending enforcement of US foreign policy into Europe was deemed illegal. An eleven-month-long US attempt to block the Soviet gas pipeline ended with the formal lifting of sanctions in November 1982. US policy was changed 'to minimize the impact of export controls on pre-existing contracts and business activities in allied countries when these controls are imposed for foreign policy reasons.'[54]

In the United Nations, the 1980s started with Eastern Europe on the UN violators-agenda. East Germany found itself publicly named in 1980 under the 1503 procedure (described in Chapter 1); Poland followed under public procedure in 1982. The strange case of East Germany had happened in August 1980, just before

---

[53] Yergon, D. – Politics and Soviet-American trade: The three questions, *Foreign Affairs*, vol. 55, No. 3, April 1977, p. 526 and 532.

[54] Desouza, P.J. – The Soviet gas pipeline incident: Extension of collective security responsibilities to peacetime commercial trade, in Reisman, W.M. and Willard, A.R. (eds.) – *International Incidents. The Law that Counts in World Politics*, Princeton University Press, Princeton, N.J., 1988, p. 110.

Ronald Reagan was elected to the presidency of the United States. According to widespread gossip, the Soviet member of the Sub-Commission, Vsefolod Sofinsky, could not come to Geneva in time for the meeting of the 1503 Working Group of the Sub-Commission and East Germany lost its principal protector. Complaints against East Germany dealt with denial of the right to leave the country, precisely the issue that subsequently led to the dismantling of the Berlin Wall.

In contrast to East Germany, about which nothing was officially known due to the confidentiality of the 1503 procedure, the United Nations made a public response to the military coup and imposition of martial law in Poland in December 1981. Three months after the imposition of martial law, the 1982 session of the Commission on Human Rights took place. By a vote of 19-13-10, the Commission requested a thorough investigation into the human rights situation in Poland. Rather than an independent expert, a UN Under-Secretary-General carried out the investigation with the cooperation of the Polish authorities.[55] The attitude of the Commission changed two years later: a draft resolution tabled to condemn Poland for human rights violations was defeated by a vote of 17-14-12.[56] One reason for the defeat was a widely held view that martial law had pre-empted a Soviet military intervention. Another was that the human toll had been minuscule in comparison with other countries on the violations-agenda: the Polish Helsinki Watch Committee identified no more than 54 people whose deaths could be blamed on the government.[57]

The Commission's decision to place Poland on the violations-agenda in 1982 had been preceded by NATO's warning to the Soviet Union against military intervention in Poland[58] and followed by US economic sanctions. These included cutting down Poland's minuscule trade with the USA, denial of export credits, and suspension of negotiations to reschedule Poland's debt. Poland's inability to service its foreign debt, both public and commercial,[59] made rescheduling urgent in order to prevent default. Therefore, the postponement of rescheduling was directed against Poland as well as its creditors. US trade sanctions against Poland attracted attention because they represented a violation of GATT (General Agreement on Tariffs and Trade) rules. These did not authorise withdrawals of MFN (Most

[55] Commission on Human Rights – Resolution 1982/26 of 10 March 1982, and report of the Secretary-General E/CN.4/1983/18.

[56] Commission on Human Rights – Decision 1984/110 of 14 March 1984, and U.N. Doc. E/CN.4/1984/L.66/Rev. 1.

[57] The Helsinki Committee in Poland – Memorandum to the Human Rights Commission of the United Nations, *Poland Watch*, No. 6, 1984; *1984 Violations of Human Rights in Poland. Report by the Polish Helsinki Committee*, U.S. Committee in Support of Solidarity, 1985.

[58] Marantz, P. – Economic sanctions in the Polish crisis, in Leyton-Brown, D. (ed.) – *The Utility of International Economic Sanctions*, Croom Helm, London, 1987, p. 133.

[59] Szlek Miller, S. – The Polish case, in Matthews, R.O. and Pratt, C. (eds.) – *Human Rights in Canadian Foreign Policy*, McGill-Queen's University Press, Kingson and Montreal, 1988, p. 254 and 260.

Favoured Nation) status on non-commercial grounds such as human rights violations, but there was no attempt to legally challenge the United States on this
score.[60]

A ping pong game of accusations and counter-accusations between the West and
the East featured in annual sessions of the UN Commission on Human Rights in the
early 1980s. The West would submit a draft resolution to condemn violations in the
Soviet Union, and the USSR would retaliate by a draft resolution on violations in
the West. In 1980 a draft resolution on the detention of Andrei Sakharov was tabled
by the United Kingdom, and the Soviet Union tabled a resolution on the ill-
treatment of prisoners in Northern Ireland. In 1981 a US draft resolution on
Sakharov was countered by a Soviet draft resolution on the victimisation of blacks
in the USA. The solution was routinely the withdrawal of both draft resolutions.[61]

Governmental delegations from countries that were not involved in cold-war
battles must have experienced a great deal of frustration throughout the years while
the Cold War constituted the foremost issue on the UN human rights agenda, whatever the item to be discussed was nominally supposed to be. The abuse of human
rights for ideological and political purposes had become established practice, and
the damage could not subsequently be remedied.

---

[60] Advisory Committee on Human Rights and Foreign Policy – *Human Rights and International
Economic Relations*, Report No. 12, The Hague, 29 May 1991, mimeographed, p. 66.

[61] Commission on Human Rights – Report on the Thirty-Sixth Session, U.N. Doc. E/1980/13, para.
274 and Report on the Thirty-Seventh Session, U.N. Doc. E/1981/25, para. 253.

Chapter 5

Wielding the Aid Lever

The United States initiated the linkage between human rights and foreign aid in the early 1970s, modelling it on the pre-existing institutionalisation of economic sanctions.[1] US aid cutoffs were not the first, as this Chapter shows, but the United States led in forging the link between human rights and aid in its foreign policy as well as legislation. Such a link was none too clear because it constituted an addition to the mosaic of different sanctions on different grounds. The most widespread type of economic sanctions designed to penalize countries for their human rights performance – aid cut-offs – could not be employed against ideological enemies because they were not aid recipients. Hence, aid cut-offs were employed against ideological allies (South Korea was a prominent example, discussed below) with patchy results.

Aid cutoffs were apparently aimed against particular recipients of US aid but these were their object rather than the principal target. The rationale for aid cut-offs was domestic: the principal message was directed against abuses of US aid to support human rights violations in the recipient countries. These countries were seen as objects of US meddling. The objective of linking human rights and foreign aid was to constrain the United States from committing or facilitating abuses beyond the reach of domestic legal and democratic safeguards. Domestic opposition to such meddling aimed to protect its objects (aid recipients) by developing safeguards to constrain the principal actor (US executive).

GLOBALISING UNILATERALISM: THE US MODEL[2]

Human rights have been introduced into foreign policy under the pressure of articulate domestic constituencies. Similarly to sanctions aimed at containment of communism, sanctions for human rights violations reflected popular sentiment

---

[1] Michael Malloy has chronicled US economic sanctions based on the presidential emergency powers first applied in 1950 against China. Malloy, M.P. – *Economic Sanctions and US Trade*, Little, Brown & Co., Boston, 1990, pp. 595–606.

[2] This section does not provide a detailed description of the design and application of the US model for linking aid and human rights. This is done in Tomaševski, K. – *Development Aid and Human Rights, Pinter Publishers*, London, 1989, pp. 50–53, and Tomaševski, K. – *Development Aid and Human Rights Revisited*, Pinter Publishers, London, 1993, pp. 84–86, as well as Tomaševski, K. – *Between Sanctions and Elections*, Pinter/Cassell, London, 1997, pp. 17–21.

rather than a thought-out foreign policy. Domestic pressures towards US dis-engagement from repression and warfare abroad built on the anti-Vietnam-war movement, adding an incipient human rights rationale.

The first target was US military and/or security assistance, including police training abroad. In 1973, the Subcommittee on International Organisations of the Foreign Affairs Committee started hearings on human rights in the major recipients of US military aid: Argentina, Brazil, Chile, El Salvador, Guatemala, Nicaragua, Paraguay, and Uruguay. By no coincidence, abuses that could be traced to US involvement were found in them all. Too little information was publicly available and David Forsythe has found that not even the exact number of recipients was known, then or later, let alone the precise type and scope of aid.[3] The first link was forged by positing that US military assistance should not be provided to countries where political imprisonment was practised. This automatically disallowed aid to all cold-war enemies, but also added South Korea and Chile (in 1975), Uruguay and the Philippines (in 1977), Argentina, Brazil, El Salvador, Ethiopia, Guatemala, Nicaragua, and Paraguay (in 1978), and in 1980–81 Zaire. Different from what US legislation indicated and congressional scrutiny aimed at, the linkage between aid and human rights violations was in practice haphazard. Aid is a notoriously un-transparent area and any outside scrutiny is hampered by labyrinthine channels through which aid is provided and endless possibilities of presenting aid figures as these should look like. Voluminous literature thus appeared exposing dis-crepancies between rhetoric and reality, congressional intentions and executive's performance. For example, one prominent gesture of the Carter Administration was to decrease (not suspend) military aid to Argentina in February 1977 as a response to 'dirty war' (discussed in Chapter 6). This pitted the USA. against a 'friendly' military regime rather than a communist adversary.[4] Indeed, the Argentine military claimed that the dirty war was fought against a 'communist insurgency'. Clearly, statutory requirements were not applied to all recipients. US policy toward the Philippines in the same period demonstrated the priority given to the maintenance of US military bases over the international outcry against the Marcos regime.[5]

The 1973 congressional initiative led to a report on human rights in the eighty-two recipients of US military assistance. The report became the first issue of the

---

[3] Forsythe, D.P. – Congress and human rights in US foreign policy: The fate of general legislation, *Human Rights Quarterly*, vol. 9, 1987, p. 383.

[4] US conduct with regard to Argentina during the 'dirty war' (1976–84) is chronicled in Lillich, R.B. – *International Human Rights. Problems of Law, Policy and Practice*, Little, Brown and Company, Boston, 1991, Second Edition, pp. 977–1013.

[5] The United States started providing military, security and police assistance to the Philippines in 1947 and continued to do so throughout the reign of Ferdinand Marcos. Although Marcos ruled by emergency decrees in 1972–86, US aid continued until 1985. Claude, R.P. – Human rights in the Philippines and US responsibility, in Brown, P.G. and MacLean, D. (eds.) – *Human Rights and US Foreign Policy*, Lexington Books, 1979, pp. 229–253.

annual review of human rights practices[6] that has continued thereafter, although with a changed aim and purpose. The initial focus on US military involvement was lost when annual reports were broadened to all recipients of US civilian aid. Finally, the link with US aid was severed altogether when the reports began to encompass all countries in the world.

The 1970s were a period of converging challenges for US foreign policy. The 'Vietnam syndrome' intensified as the war ended; the Watergate scandal lowered the prestige of the executive, making foreign policy – a prerogative of the executive – a political battlefield. Against this background, congressional initiatives to constrain US aid by attaching human rights conditions blossomed. At the beginning, in 1973, US military assistance had been tied to the absence of political prisoners in the recipient countries; conditions were subsequently broadened to include the absence of serious and systemic human rights violations. Because the United States was not providing aid to the Soviet Union or Romania, legislative changes in 1974 linked human rights to trade and the MFN (the most-favoured nation status) was conditioned by the right to leave a country. The targeting of the Soviet Union and its allies was a necessary complement to the targeting of cold-war allies. In 1976, human rights became a criterion for US votes in international development finance agencies, and sixteen countries were immediately affected by US vetoes. Additional legislation balanced the punitive behaviour of the US towards its allies by preventing multilateral banks from using US funds for its ideological enemies: Angola, Cambodia, Cuba, and Mozambique, as well as Idi Amin's Uganda.[7] In 1977, human rights were also added as criteria for agricultural export credits.

This legislative mosaic did not quite reflect the intended linkage between aid, trade and human rights but was a product of domestic politics. Originally, this linkage had aimed to constrain US conduct abroad, implicitly acknowledging past wrongdoing and trying to build safeguards for the future. The addition of a host of concerns advocated by various domestic constituencies resulted in a merger between aid and trade, or in exemptions of specific countries or particular exports based on self-interest of particular domestic constituencies and thus severing links with human rights. Even more importantly, as sanctions multiplied in law and in practice, the previous idea that the US conduct abroad was their principal target was gradually lost. Rather, sanctions targeted individual recipients, severing the conceptual bond between US conduct and US aid.

---

[6] *Human Rights Practices in Countries Receiving US Security Assistance*, report submitted by State Department to Committee on International Relations, House of Representatives, Washington, D.C., 25 April 1977.

[7] The sixteen countries were: Afghanistan, Argentina, Benin, Central African Republic, Chile, El Salvador, Ethiopia, Guatemala, Guinea, Laos, Paraguay, Philippines, South Korea, South Yemen, Uruguay, and Viet Nam. Center for International Policy – *International Policy Report: Multilateral Aid Law*, Washington, D.C., 1991, pp. 6–7.

A human rights policy which penalizes individual aid recipients became associated with the Carter administration. Not only was the United States the first to explicitly link aid to the absence of human rights violations, it was also the largest donor at the time. The US model became a battleground within domestic politics in other donor countries, where human rights were defined differently, sometimes in (implicit) opposition to the US model. The 'like-minded[8] donors', Canada, Denmark, the Netherlands, Norway and Sweden, had a domestic commitment to the welfare-state model, and a broader definition of human rights in foreign policy. Nevertheless, however broadly 'human rights' was defined in this period, it remained on the margins of aid. The elimination of poverty, for instance, was routinely defined as the primary objective of aid, but was not included in the definition of 'human rights'. There has never been a single case in which a donor has cut off aid because a recipient pursued a policy of impoverishment or increased income inequalities.[9]

The chronological overview of aid cutoffs justified by human rights concerns in this Chapter shows that Canada led, having responded to abuses in Equatorial Guinea as early as 1971, with the United Kingdom following in 1972 by cutting down aid and mobilising the United Nations against the mass expulsion of Ugandan Asians. Both Canada and the United Kingdom retroactively developed a human rights policy, much as other donors have done. Their early responses to what were intuitively perceived as gross human rights violations took place in a vacuum.

The United States was faced with need to respond to abuses in South Korea just as its future policy linking aid and human rights was being elaborated. Chile provided a rallying point for the entire human rights and donor communities. It was around Chile that UN human rights bodies for the first time forged a strategy for exposing and opposing institutionalised denials of human rights. It was also Chile that provoked inquiries into the divergence between political and economic dimensions in foreign policy: political dimensions were pushing towards sanctions, while economic considerations were pulling in the opposite direction, toward continuing financial support to violators. Western foreign policies thus split in the 1970s to accommodate conflicting demands upon them.

---

[8] The adjective 'like-minded' was originally used to denote those Western donors whose aid policy aimed to enhance human rights in developing countries. It has since developed into a self-descriptive label of a group of developing countries (such as India, Pakistan, China, and Cuba) within the UN Commission on Human Rights, which routinely rejects all Western human rights initiatives.

[9] Donors' policies of the 1970s are discussed in Tomaševski, K. – *Development Aid and Human Rights, Pinter Publishers*, London, 1989, pp. 53–59. Their changes in the 1980s are addressed in Tomaševski, K. – *Development Aid and Human Rights Revisited*, Pinter Publishers, London, 1993, pp. 86–92, while policies of all donors (with or without human rights) are examined in Tomaševski, K. – *Between Sanctions and Elections*, Pinter/Cassell, London, 1997, pp. 21–39.

THE EARLIEST CASES

1971: Equatorial Guinea

A tiny, Spanish-speaking West African country, Equatorial Guinea is absent from newspaper headlines and from the literature on the linkage between human rights and aid. Although it has been on the donors' agenda since 1971, when the first aid cutoffs took place, and has been on the UN violations-agenda since 1976, the country remains unknown. Suzanne Cronjé has blamed 'the protective wall of silence' around a dictatorship that lasted from independence in 1968 to a military coup in 1979, when a change of personalities, rather than governance, took place. This lack of publicity and negligible donors' sanctions have been possible because a significant donor such as Spain has failed to discuss human rights in its relations with Equatorial Guinea throughout the past decades.

Donors ranging from Spain, to the United States or the United Nations Development Programme (UNDP), were 'developing' Equatorial Guinea even as one quarter of its population was being driven into exile by repression and two-thirds of the first national parliament – including a minister of finance, a director of the central bank, and several ambassadors – were disappeared by the government. At the time, an abyss separated development and human rights. Spain, Guinea's former colonial power, coupled its financial support with silence about abuses. Information about Equatorial Guinea was classified in Spain until 1976,[10] when Equatorial Guinea was placed on the UN human rights agenda under the confidential 1503 procedure. The immediate reason was information about killings and detentions of foreign priests. In 1979, Guinea was moved to a public procedure because the Macias government failed to respond to UN's attempts to clarify the facts. Neither the change of regime in 1979 nor the expert assistance subsequently provided by the United Nations to the new government made an impact within the country.

The Macias dictatorship ended with a military coup, the former dictator was brought to trial before a military court, sentenced to death, and his property was confiscated. The prosecution relied a great deal on the Universal Declaration of Human Rights because 'for many years the regime had enacted hardly any legis-lation and there was no system of criminal law in operation.'[11] The post-1979 government was led by Teodoro Obiang, the nephew of the former dictator, who had led the military coup against his uncle. Obiang ruled for a decade without elections to then become the elected leader of the country.

---

[10] Cronjé, S. – *Equatorial Guinea: The Forgotten Dictatorship. Forced Labour and Political Murder in Central Africa*, Research Report No. 2, Anti-Slavery Society, London, 1976, p. 41.

[11] International Commission of Jurists – *The Trial of Macias in Equatorial Guinea. The Story of a Dictatorship by Dr. Alejandro Artucio, ICJ Observer*, Geneva, 1979, p. 58.

UN's response to human rights violations in Equatorial Guinea came too late. The exposure of abuses resulting from the shift from confidential to public procedure in 1979 coincided with the removal of the Macias regime. The new government, although it came to power through a military coup, was assumed to be committed to human rights and was provided with human rights assistance. The first UN expert mandated to assist the government, Fernando Volio, after a decade of futile efforts to design human rights assistance thus diagnosed Equatorial Guinea: 'a police state backed by the army and personally controlled by the omnipresent, omnipotent figure of the President.'[12]

After Canada had stopped aid to Equatorial Guinea in 1971, prompted by reports of abuses, other bilateral and multilateral donors continued their aid. Table 5.1 shows that colonial history placed Equatorial Guinea among EUrope's recipients and major bilateral donors were also European. This had not led to human rights conditionality but meant an adjustment to the donors' demand for elections in the 1990s. Indeed, various elections have taken place. In 1995, when Equatorial Guinea's government transformed itself from military to 'democratic', a new UN Special Rapporteur was appointed. It was Alejandro Artucio, who had been the ICJ observer of the Macias trial in 1979 and was thus acquainted with the country. While he indeed noted progress in some areas, he reported none in curbing the unrestricted powers of the military or in the widespread use of prisoners as unpaid labour.[13]

Table 5.1: Aid to Equatorial Guinea, 1987–94
(in million US$)

	1987	1989	1991	1992	1993	1994
France	14.4	14.0	10.4	11.4	12.9	8.0
Italy	3.6	1.9	–2.0	–9.8	–2.2	0.2
Spain	–	–	20.3	19.9	15.6	8.4
EUrope	28.4	47.3	33.5	27.0	28.8	20.3
Total bilateral aid	25.7	41.3	33.5	23.9	28.5	18.3
Multilateral aid	46.0	63.8	60.2	48.4	63.8	32.0

Source: DAC/OECD – *Geographical Distribution of Financial Flows to developing Countries, 1987–90 and 1990–94.*

Elections took place because Equatorial Guinea had to comply with the donors' requirement to democratise in order to continue being eligible for aid. The first

---

[12] United Nations – Report on the human rights situation in Equatorial Guinea submitted by the Expert of the Commission on Human Rights, Mr. Fernando Volio, U.N. Doc. E/CN.4/1993/48 of 31 December 1992, and E/CN.4/1992/51 of 17 January 1992, para. 93.

[13] Commission on Human Rights – Report on the human rights situation in the Republic of Equatorial Guinea submitted by Mr. Alejandro Artucio, Special Rapporteur, U.N. Doc. E/CN.4/1995/68 of 10 January 1995, para. 49 (c).

announcement of a forthcoming democratisation in 1991 had been accompanied by arrests of potential candidates. A constitutional referendum, held in November 1991, resulted in a 98% vote in favour of the new Constitution, despite the fact that its text had been released only 48 hours beforehand. The explanation was that a 'no' vote was black, while a 'yes' was red, and vote casting was monitored in the booths.[14]

Europe's efforts to democratise Equatorial Guinea were not successful. In September 1992, a statement on behalf of the European Political Co-operation (EPC) threatened an aid suspension unless detained opposition politicians were released,[15] but this threat did not enhance their electoral prospects. In February 1994, the European Parliament demanded suspension of aid to Equatorial Guinea 'in light of the fact that the 21 November 1993 elections were boycotted by 70% of the population, making their validity doubtful.'[16] Aid was suspended without dissent. The previous year, EUrope had failed to persuade Spain to cut off aid to its former colony.

EUrope then openly conditioned aid on observance of human rights 'as verified by the Commission on Human Rights through its Special Rapporteur.'[17] The Special Rapporteur, however, could not verify compliance because the necessary funding was not available.[18] Prospects for the future, according to knowledgeable commentators, depend on results of oil exploration rather than human rights monitoring.

Spain's previous neglect of human rights in Guinea was brought back home by the 1998 trial of 117 people for 'separatist violence' under criminal law that was exported from Spain to Equatorial Guinea in 1948, during the reign of General Franco. Defendants stood before judges with visible signs of recent mutilation, while the court rejected their assertion that they had been tortured. This might have gone unnoticed had four of the defendants not been Spanish citizens.[19]

1972: Uganda

In January 1971, Idi Amin became President of Uganda through a military coup. He stayed in power until 1979, when he was ousted by Tanzania's military intervention. Amin's rule made Uganda notorious for killings, disappearances and

---

[14] Lashmar, P. – Equatorial Guinea: Lurching forward, *Africa Report*, vol. 37, No. 2, March/April 1992, p. 69.

[15] *The Courier*, No. 136, November-December 1992, News round-up, p. iii.

[16] EP calls for suspension of aid to Equatorial Guinea, *Europa/Development Monthly*, February 1994.

[17] Letter dated 3 January 1995 from the Special Rapporteur addressed to the Chairman of the Commission on Human Rights, Annex to Report on the human rights situation in the Republic of Equatorial Guinea submitted by Mr. Alejandro Artucio, Special Rapporteur of the Commission, U.N. Doc. E/CN.4/1995/68 of 10 January 1995, p. 16–17.

[18] United Nations – Report on the human rights situation in the Republic of Equatorial Guinea submitted by Mr. Alejandro Artucio, Special Rapporteur of the Commission, U.N. Doc. E/CN.4/1996/67/Add.1 of 15 March 1996, para. 19.

[19] Hooper, J. – Trial allows glimpse of harsh regime, *Guardian Weekly*, 7 June 1998.

torture. However, what brought Uganda into the international limelight and prompted economic sanctions were not the atrocities against Ugandans[20] but the mass expulsion of Asians.

Unilateral sanctions against Idi Amin's Uganda were led by Britain, its biggest donor and former colonial power. Human rights violations were publicised after the 1972 mass expulsion of Asians, but UN investigative and condemnatory action started much later, towards the very end of Idi Amin's rule. Solidarity among African statesmen precluded condemnation. Furthermore, one may ask whether an international outcry would have taken place at all had it not been for the expulsion of Asians and Britain's involvement in their resettlement.

In August 1972, Idi Amin announced that all Asians, first those with British citizenship and then all Ugandan Asians (as they are still called) were going to be expelled, more than 75,000 people.[21] His justification was that Uganda's economy had been dominated by Asians, who were accused of sabotage and corruption. Uganda's Truth Commission noted two decades later that 'the expulsion was on the whole popular amongst Ugandans.'[22] The well-known pattern of choosing a foreign-looking scapegoat had had an added inducement of redistribution of Asian wealth in favour of the indigenous population. The Asians were given three months to leave and their property was confiscated. This provoked vehement protests, especially from the United Kingdom and India, and a great deal of debate about the legality of mass expulsion under international law. At the time, the international response was articulated in humanitarian rather than human rights language.

Idi Amin was honoured by election to the Chairmanship of the Organisation of African Unity (OAU) for 1976–77; the African group within the United Nations elected Uganda to membership of the Commission on Human Rights in 1976. Amin's election to the OAU chairmanship and Uganda's election to UN Commission followed the 1975 initiative of the late Julius Nyerere, then president of Tanzania, to develop a common stand within the OAU against human rights violations in Uganda.[23] Within the OAU and within the United Nations, a critical mass of governments willing to take a stand against violators did not exist at the time.

---

[20] The Uganda Commission of Inquiry into the Violation of Human Rights 1962–1986 reported, for example, that in 1973 more than 15,000 corpses had been collected in and around Kampala. The Uganda Commission of Inquiry into the Violation of Human Rights – *Pearl of Blood. Summary of the Report*, Kampala, October 1994, p. 6.

[21] Yash Tandon and Arnold Raphael found the number of Indians in Uganda to have been 76, 000 in 1970 to have diminished to 430 in 1980. Tandon, Y. and Raphael, A. – *The New Position of East Africa's Asians: Problems of a Displaced Minority*, Minority Rights Group Report No. 16, London, Second revised edition, November 1984, p. 2.

[22] The Uganda Commission of Inquiry into the Violation of Human Rights – *Pearl of Blood. Summary of the Report of the Commission*, Kampala, October 1994, p. 10.

[23] Ngom, B. – Human rights in Africa: The decisive steps, *The Courier*, No. 128, July/August 1991, p. 68.

UN human rights bodies were slow and hesitant. Uganda was discussed by the Sub-Commission in 1972. No resolution was adopted but a decision was made to study the human rights of non-citizens.[24] Information on killings and torture targeting African Ugandans was supplied by NGOs. The *International Commission of Jurists* reported that 80,000 people had been killed in 1971–73.[25] Uganda was debated under the confidential 1503 procedure in 1974 and 1976. The Commission on Human Rights discussed information submitted by NGOs and kept Uganda 'under review', meaning that clarification was sought from the government under the confidential 1503 procedure.[26] A draft resolution was tabled by the United Kingdom and Canada in 1977, supported by the Nordic countries, but could not be adopted because Uganda was 'under review' and thus a public procedure was pre-empted.[27] The chairman of the Commission was an African and reportedly unwilling to mention an African country 'under review' and the compromise was to read aloud the names of all countries. As mentioned in Chapter 1, this procedural gimmick led to a new rule, whereby the Chairman of the Commission of every session reads out the names of countries under review in order to identify those that should not be publicly discussed.

Finally, in 1978, the Commission authorized a study into the situation in Uganda.[28] A special representative to carry out this study was agreed upon by the Commission in 1979, but this initiative came too late – Idi Amin's government has been ousted. Uganda's armed attack on Tanzania led to Tanzania's counterattack in March 1979, which ended Idi Amin's regime. The new president of Uganda addressed the UN General Assembly and noted that 'the United Nations looked on with embarrassed silence [while] at least half a million people were murdered in cold blood.'[29]

While UN human rights bodies were keeping Uganda 'under review' and failing to mobilize a sufficient political will to act, donors needed no inter-governmental

---

[24] Sub-Commission on Prevention of Discrimination and Protection of Minorities – Report on the Twenty-fifth session (1972), U.N. Doc. E/CN.4/1101, pp. 23–24 and 60.

[25] International Commission of Jurists – Uganda: A lawless state, *The Review*, No. 7, December 1972. Subsequent to the UN's failure to act, the ICJ published all its complaints of violations as *Uganda and Human Rights: Reports to the UN Commission*, International Commission of Jurists, Geneva, 1977.

[26] Liskofsky, S. – Coping with the question of the violation of human rights and fundamental freedoms, *Human Rights Journal*, vol. 8, 1975, p. 906.

[27] Commission on Human Rights – Report on the Thirty-Third Session, U.N. Doc. E/5927, 1977, paras. 72–78; Rosas, A. – Nordic human rights policies, *Current Research on Peace and Violence*, vol. 9, 1986, No. 4, p. 177.

[28] During those early years in the procedure for gross and systematic human rights violations information was confidential and it was impossible to document what action was, or was not, taken. According to Howard Tolley, Uganda was referred to the UN Commission on Human Rights in 1974, 1976 and 1977, which must have culminated in the decision to carry out a study in 1978. Tolley, H. – The concealed crack in the citadel: The United Nations Commission on Human Rights' response to confidential communications, *Human Rights Quarterly*, vol. 6, No. 4, November 1984, p. 442.

[29] Statement of Godfrey Binaisa, President of Uganda, at the 14th plenary meeting of the General Assembly, Official Records of the General Assembly, vol. 34, p. 269–270.

consensus and could act individually. As Table 5.2 shows, the United Kingdom led in imposing sanctions against Idi Amin's Uganda and was followed by Canada, Sweden, Norway, the Netherlands, and later by EUrope (the European Economic Community at the time); the United States followed last. Alex Cunliffe has argued that Britain suspended aid to Uganda because it had to admit a large number of expelled Asians, not because of human rights violations against indigenous Ugandans.[30]

Table 5.2: Bilateral aid to Uganda 1971–1977
(in million US$)

Donor	1971	1972	1973	1974	1975	1976	1977
Australia	0.1	0.1	–	0.1	0.2	0.1	0.2
Canada	1.6	1.8	1.4	0.3	0.8	0.5	0.5
Denmark	1.7	3.1	0.8	0.5	0.1	0.1	–0.3
Germany	1.9	1.7	2.1	3.8	2.1	6.9	0.8
Italy	0.1	0.1	–	0.1	0.3	0.4	0.2
Japan	0.3	1.3	0.6	0.5	0.4	0.6	0.7
Netherlands	0.5	0.4	0.3	1.8	0.7	0.6	0.8
Norway	1.2	1.8	0.4	–	–	–	–
United Kingdom	7.9	7.9	1.4	–1.4	–0.1	–	0.7
United States	5.0	3.0	2.0	1.0	–	–	–
Total bilateral aid	20.3	21.3	9.1	6.7	4.5	9.2	3.6

Source: *Geographical Distribution of Financial Flows to Less Developed/Developing Countries*, OECD, Paris, various issues.

The problems of Asians in Uganda, and in other former British colonies in Africa, did not begin, nor did they end, with Idi Amin's rule. Having been moved from Asia to Africa when both were part of the British Empire, 'the British tried to shake off the Asian minorities in Africa by persuading the East and Central African countries during the negotiations for independence to take them on as their responsibility.'[31] An increasingly restrictive migration policy reduced possibilities for Ugandan Asians to settle in the United Kingdom. Negotiations about their fate had preceded Idi Amin's rule, and the British government tried to dissuade Amin from expelling them, obviously without success. Another event prompted the United Kingdom to break off diplomatic relations with Uganda: the killing of Dora Bloch, a British citizen, during the much-publicised Israeli raid at Entebbe airport in July 1976.

---

[30] Cunliffe, S.A. – British economic aid policy and international human rights: A comparative analysis of conservative and labour policies in the 1970s, *Political Studies*, vol. 33, 1985, p. 112.

[31] Tandon, Y. and Raphael, A. – *The New Position of East Africa's Asians: Problems of a Displaced Minority*, Minority Rights Group, Report No. 16, London, Third edition, November 1984, p. 11.

Table 5.2 shows that bilateral aid decreased from $21.3 million in 1972 to $9.1 million in 1973 and further to $4.5 million in 1975. Donors' sanctions are clearly reflected in the aid statistics for Canada, Denmark, Norway, the United Kingdom and the United States, but less so for the Netherlands. Germany's aid to Uganda increased at the time, while aid from Japan fluctuated.

The decrease of British aid translated into diminished aid flows in 1973. Canada followed the United Kingdom, and in January 1973 suspended its development projects in Uganda; the official explanation was 'a lack of commitment to development shown by the Amin regime'.[32] Because translating such decision into practice often takes time, the slump in Canada's aid appeared in aid statistics for 1974.

Uganda also triggered a re-examination of the Lomé Convention. After it had been signed in 1975, controversies emerged in 1977 relating to the human rights record of three countries – the Central African Empire (as it was at the time), Equatorial Guinea and Uganda. The Central African Empire was ruled by Emperor Bokassa at the time and did not develop into a human rights case because its main donor, France, prevented this. Equatorial Guinea was, as discussed above, was shielded by its main donor, Spain. Uganda, however, prompted a change in the delivery of aid under the Lomé Convention: projects that would strengthen the regime were excluded. In June 1977, the European Council took note of human rights violations in Uganda and declared that co-operation under the Lomé Convention should not contribute to violations. There was nothing about human rights or violations in the Lomé Convention at the time and a compromise was forged to redirect rather than suspending aid.[33]

The United States imposed an embargo on Uganda in October 1978.[34] Uganda had not been a recipient of US aid since 1973, when the US Embassy in Kampala had been closed and all development projects discontinued. The reason was, however, a diplomatic scandal rather than human rights violations. An embargo was subsequently seen as the only possibility for some form of economic sanctions as response to human rights violations. The Carter Administration doubted both the legality and effectiveness of the embargo, while some commentators saw the embargo as retaliation for Idi Amin's 'forging a close diplomatic relationship with Moscow.'[35]

---

[32] Keenleyside, T.A. – Development assistance, in: Matthews, R.O. and Pratt, C. (eds.) – *Human Rights in Canadian Foreign Policy*, McGill-Queen's University Press, Kingston and Montreal, 1988, p. 199.

[33] Kamminga, M. – Human rights and the Lomé Conventions, *Netherlands Quarterly of Human Rights*, vol. 7, 1989, No. 1, pp. 28–29.

[34] Ullman, R.H. – Human rights and economic power: the US vs. Idi Amin, *Foreign Affairs*, vol. 56, 1979, No. 3, pp. 529–543.

[35] Mayal, J. – The United States, in: Vincent, R.J. (ed.) – *Foreign Policy and Human Rights. Issues and Responses*, The Royal Institute of International Affairs and Cambridge University Press, 1986, p. 181.

Donors' reactions to Idi Amin's misrule can be seen in the diminished aid flows shown in Table 5.2. Critics claimed, however, that sanctions did not really affect Uganda because 'the Soviet Union, Saudi Arabia and Libya replaced the canceled aid.'[36] Their aid was not officially recorded at the time and this assertion cannot be verified. Richard Carver has claimed that officially recorded aid did not reveal all Western aid either, and that Britain continued to support Idi Amin's regime despite announcements to the contrary. He described the twice weekly 'whiskey run' destined for Amin's army flying from Stansted airport near London to Entebbe until a month before Amin was overthrown.'[37]

A retrospective overview of abuses during Idi Amin's reign was provided by the Commission of Inquiry into Violation of Human Rights, established in 1986 to investigate violations in 1962–86 to produce its report in 1994. As is customary, the report did not address foreign and international policies towards Amin's Uganda.

Uganda was subsequently not immune to donors' punitiveness, however. The shift from human rights to democracy made it a target for donors' insistence on multi-party elections. Uganda had initially rejected a multi-party system, held *sui generis* presidential and parliamentary elections, and a referendum on this peculiar movement[38] *versus* multi-party system is planned for the year 2000. Elections for the constitutional assembly were held in March 1994, with candidates campaigning in their own name rather than as representatives of political parties, on the fear that political parties would replicate and reinforce regional, ethnic and religious dividing lines.[39] This concern was based on the experiences of the previous decades, in which the prevailing chaos precluded the emergence of a shared vision of the future and of the institutions needed to unite a fragmented and divided society. The emergence of such a shared vision necessitates the free articulation of varying collective and individual interests, for which political rights and political parties are the normal channel.

The 1996 parliamentary and presidential elections followed Uganda's *sui generis* movement-based model of political representation, prompting a great deal of both praise and criticism. The developmental implications of alternative models of political organisation are hardly discussed, exacerbating the abyss between econ-

---

[36] International Commission of Jurists – *Human Rights in United States & United Kingdom Foreign Policy. A Colloquium*, Palace of Westminster, November 27–28, 1978, p. 41.

[37] Carver, R. – How African governments investigate human rights violations, *Third World Legal Studies 1988*, p. 169.

[38] Movement-based political representation is defined as broad-based, non-partisan and all-inclusive, envisaging that individuals contest elected posts on the basis of merit. The explicit assumption of this model is its ability to accommodate all different, often contradictory, interests in the society, thus excluding opposition. In practice, opposition to this model cannot be accommodated within the model itself and is therefore denied legitimacy.

[39] President Museveni's position has been that 'multi-partyism' was not suitable for African pre-industrial conditions where 'each tribe has its political party.' President Museveni: An interview, *The New Vision*, 28 February 1992.

omic and political governance. Donors' insistence on replicating multiple political parties diminished as Uganda became in the 1990s the pearl of Africa (as it had been named in colonial times), praised for its strict implementation of structural adjustment and diligent debt servicing.

1973: South Korea

Early US sanctions against Korea were revived in public memory at the time of rapid political and economic changes in 1997–98. The election of Kim Dae Jung as Korea's president recalled US efforts to save his life more than two decades earlier, while he had been *the* internationally known dissident. Korea's profound economic crisis brought about his electoral victory. It also brought into question 'the international financial infrastructure'[40] that had previously kindled Korea's economic growth.

Links between South Korea and the United States spring up with every political change in and around South Korea. US involvement goes back to the Potsdam Conference in 1945 when Korea was partitioned, and to the Korean War in 1950–53. The 1954 Mutual Defense Treaty committed the two countries to jointly meeting 'common danger', the un-named but recognisable North Korea, and this mutual commitment does not seem to have decreased with time.

South Korea was an early target of US economic sanctions. As a major recipient of US aid at the time when aid was first linked to the human rights records of recipients, it was the target of small reductions in aid accompanied by a great deal of publicity. Subsequent decreases in aid were associated with South Korea's increasing wealth rather than with human rights concerns, as Table 5.3 below shows. South Korea became a donor, with its own version of conditionality,[41] after its miraculous conversion from a developing into an industrialised country in the space of one generation. In 1996, it became a member of the Organisation for Economic Co-operation and Development (OECD), previously a club of Western countries with the exception of Japan. The crisis that erupted in 1997 proved that some of Korea's economic miracle might have been a mirage.[42] Much as with political changes, foreign and international influence on developments in Korea was debated a great deal.

---

[40] This nebulous term was coined in the aftermath of the Asian crisis in 1998 to denote the absence of any overview, let alone public control, over global financial transactions.

[41] South Korea reportedly conditioned its loans to Russia on the delivery of the flight recorder data ('the black box') of KAL flight 007 which had been shot down by the Soviet military in 1983. Seoul apologizes to nation over 'black box' error, *International Herald Tribune*, 3 and 4 December 1992.

[42] The president of the World Bank, James Wolfensohn, held up high savings, commitment to education, sound fiscal policies and outward orientation as the pillars of the South East Asian economic miracle that produced unprecedented rapid economic growth and reduction of poverty. Wolfensohn, J. – Asia: The long view, *Financial Times*, 29 January 1998.

Political changes had started much before the former dissident became president. The 1993 election of Kim Young Sam brought South Korea its first president without a military background. Prosecution of former military leaders followed in 1996, with accompanying calls to broaden co-responsibility for the military repression of the 1970s to the United States, the principal supporter of Korea's military governments of the previous decades.

The process of change was triggered by mass popular protests and street riots against military-authoritarian rule. The previously praised 'Korean model' brought the country from poverty to affluence within one generation, and the government's prestige, as well as its legitimacy, was based on its having created the economic miracle during military rule in the period 1961–79. During this time, South Korea was governed first by Park Chung Hee (a General before becoming President), who was assassinated by General Chun Doo Hwan, who became President in 1979. The 1996 trials probed into abuses of power by the consecutive military governments of the time, while the subsequent financial crisis brought to light the other side of the coin, fault-lines in economic governance on the domestic level, as well as the dark side of volatile global movements of short-term investments.

As Table 5.4 illustrates, Korea's economic growth was fuelled by private investment rather than public aid (shown in Table 5.3). This abundance of 'cheap foreign capital'[43] gravitated towards high-yield, quick-turnaround sectors, but could also be improperly allocated or misspent because the supply seemed boundless. A change in the flows of short-term capital created the financial crisis, first in Thailand, then in Malaysia, Indonesia and South Korea. 'The region managed to attract $97 billion in private capital inflows in 1996; [in 1997] there was an outflow of $12 billion, or a net reversal of $109 billion.'[44]

South Korea was held up as the prototype of the Asian miracle; the World Bank's 1993 book *The East Asian Miracle* was the final seal of endorsement. A mission fielded by the International Commission of Jurists found 'a country that has undergone staggeringly successful economic advancement but whose political development has been slow and fitful by comparison.'[45] The use of sanctions against South Korea by the USA was fitful as well, and not necessarily related to domestic changes in South Korea. William Gleysteen, the US Ambassador in South Korea at the time of US sanctions, did not think much of human rights or sanctions – he found the former hortatory and the latter symbolic.[46]

---

[43] Desai, V.V. – A new miracle needed, *Far Eastern Economic Review*, 25 December 1997–1 January 1998.

[44] Sender, H. – Asian capital markets: Competitive drive, *Far Eastern Economic Review*, 23 July 1998.

[45] Oxman, S.A. et al. – *South Korea: Human Rights in Emerging Politics. Report of an ICJ Mission from 25 March to 12 April 1987*, International Commission of Jurists, Geneva, 1987, p. 14.

[46] Gleysteen, W.H. – Korea: A special target of American concern, in Newsom, D.D. (ed.) – *The Diplomacy of Human Rights*, Institute for the Study of Diplomacy and University Press of America, Washington, D.C., 1986, pp. 85–99.

Table 5.3: Aid to South Korea, 1970–80
(in million US$)

	1960	1965	1970	1971	1972	1973	1974	1975	1976	1977	1978	1979
USA	249.0	164.8	175.0	175.0	230.0	91.0	33.0	88.0	273.0	99.0	324.0	196.0
Japan	–	45.9	86.8	124.2	112.7	156.6	167.8	87.4	114.4	144.3	634.2	505.9
Germany	–	4.5	1.7	4.1	5.1	11.7	17.0	34.7	133.1	86.4	43.5	193.5
Canada	–	–	–	–	–	–	–	14.5	23.3	40.8	44.9	186.5
France	–	–	–	–	–	–	–	–	106.7	61.8	7.7	31.4
Total bilateral aid	250.5	218.1	268.0	305.2	351.2	262.9	220.5	213.1	1012.6	1037.6	1096.6	1246.0
Multilateral aid	0.3	2.4	6.8	19.3	14.0	19.4	31.7	36.4	1455.3	1380.5	1539.6	1714.4

Source: OECD – Geographical Distribution of Financial Flows to Developing Countries, various issues.

Table 5.4: South Korea: Investment, export credits, exports and GNP per capita, 1970–80
(in million US$)

	1970	1975	1976	1977	1978	1979	1980
Private sector investment from OECD/DAC	n/r	n/r	688.0	726.2	580.0	912.0	236.3
Export credits	n/r	n/r	1091.8	1272.7	1222.7	1254.2	709.4
Exports to OECD/DAC	835	5081	6106.5	7304.5	9386.1	10791.8	11267.8
GNP per capita (in 1975 US$)	270	550	948.8	1113.5	1309.7	1500.8	1523.4

Note: The figures denoting investment and exports refer to members of the OECD/DAC, namely Western donor countries
Source: Geographical Distribution of Financial Flows to Developing Countries, 1976–1979 and 1977–1980.

Sanctions were used against South Korea at the very outset of the US linkage between aid and human rights because of worldwide publicity for the kidnapping of Kim Dae Jung, whose abduction from Japan by South Korean agents in 1973 made him a particularly prominent victim of governmental abuse. It is possible that he would have been killed on the high seas, had the United States not intervened. Two decades later, as Head of State, President Kim had to take responsibility in the name of the state for his own extra-territorial persecution while he had been a dissident:

> Kim ended wide speculation about whether he'd press Japan on the controversial subject [his own abduction in 1973] by assuring Japanese journalists in Seoul that he wouldn't bring it up. Japan and South Korea have agreed the incident, in which the agents nearly dropped Kim into the Sea of Japan to die, is officially off-limits. Why? Because if Kim protested, Tokyo would be entitled to ask for an official 'apology' from the Korean government for illegally sending agents to kidnap a private citizen from Japanese soil – a flagrant challenge to Japan's sovereignty. Now, of course, Kim heads that government – which would put him in the ridiculous position of having to apologize, on behalf of the government, for his own kidnapping.[47]

Back in 1973, Kim was brought back to Korea – alive – for detention, released, re-arrested and imprisoned for attempting to overthrow the government, released, then exiled to the USA. He returned to Korea in 1985, for the parliamentary elections, accompanied by 38 American observers to ensure his safety. Upon their arrival, Kim was forcibly separated from the American observers and placed under house arrest. The publicity in the United States was immense, and the Korean authorities ultimately apologised for having used force against the observers. The background had been Kim's trial by court-martial in 1980 and condemnation to death. Protests by the USA, Japan and Germany, each of which conditioned aid to Korea on commutation of Kim's sentence, brought about a change from death to life imprisonment.[48] Table 5.3 shows that aid flows decreased in 1974–75, especially from the USA and Japan.

The sequence of events in 1973, which was internationally monitored through the fate of Kim Dae Jung, followed a 1972 state of emergency. Respect for human rights had been formally suspended and restrictions upon individual rights and freedoms had been increased in 1973. The US Congress responded by diminishing military assistance to South Korea and mandating the executive to certify 'substantial progress in the observance of internationally recognized human rights' for military aid to be fully resumed. This congressional linkage found little support from three

---

[47] Awkward apology, *Far Eastern Economic Review*, 15 October 1998.

[48] Kamminga, M.T. – *Inter-state Accountability for Violations of Human Rights*, University of Pennsylvania Press, Philadelphia, 1992, pp. 20–21.

consecutive executives (the Ford, Carter and Reagan administrations) and sanctions amounted to a loud bark and a gentle bite, as Table 5.3 shows.

Hufbauer, Schott and Elliot have estimated that US sanctions against South Korea in 1973–77 diminished military aid by $333 million, and contributed to releasing political prisoners, but were not otherwise successful.[49] US-based human rights organisations claimed that sanctions were negligible: the United States supported Korea's consecutive governments and exercised quiet diplomatic pressure to ameliorate publicised abuses. Token gestures were reported. In 1977, the United States abstained rather than vetoing two loans from the Asian Development Bank. In 1980, following another emergency and the crushing of a demonstration in Kwangju, the United States asked for the postponement of a vote on loans to Korea.[50]

Domestic South Korea's problems of whatever type were never the only US concern. The government of South Korea justified consecutive emergencies by the threat of invasion by North Korea, and placed national security consistently above individual rights. Similarly, relations between the United States and South Korea were from the outset governed by the North Korean (and indirectly Chinese) communist security threat.

Despite unchanged perceptions of North Korea's threat, the change in South Korea has been profound. The first direct presidential elections in 1987, prompted by waves of popular protest against military rule, brought a disputed victory to Roh Tae Woo, a retired general, amidst challenges of electoral fraud by the opposition. International electoral observers were cautious and declared that the elections could 'lead to the first peaceful transfer of power in the Republic's history.'[51] The presidential elections were preceded by a constitutional referendum earlier that year, and followed by parliamentary elections in 1988. Foreign human rights observers routinely objected to the widespread harassment of the political opposition and the lack of safeguards against abuse of power by the military.

South Korea's political development has continued following its own pace and direction. As mentioned above, the first non-military president was elected in 1993, followed by the dissident-turned-president in 1997. His election was immediately followed, even before he was inaugurated, by negotiations with the International Monetary Fund (IMF) about early disbursements of a pledged $57 billion in loans. The United States conditioned its approval on human rights grounds, shifting from governmental abuses to workers' rights.[52]

---

[49] Hufbauer, G.C. et al. – *Economic Sanctions Reconsidered. History and Current Policy*, Institute for International Economics, Washington, D.C., 1990, Second edition, Case 73–2.

[50] International League for Human Rights and International Human Rights Law Group – *Democracy in South Korea: A Promise Unfulfilled. A Report on Human Rights 1980–1985*, Washington, D.C., April 1985, p. 105 and 136.

[51] *The 1987 Korean Presidential Election. Report of the International Delegation sponsored by the International Human Rights Law Group*, Washington, D.C., February 1988, p. viii.

[52] Dunne, N. – Congress may add strings to IMF funding, *Financial Times*, 27–28 December 1997.

1974: Chile

Political responses to the 1973 military coup in Chile were swift and decisive, and were followed by bilateral aid cutoffs. Sanctions against Pinochet's Chile were led by the like-minded donors. More importantly, Chile altered inter-governmental human rights politics – Western donors joined a Soviet-initiated UN condemnation of human rights violations and added a price tag by cutting down their aid. Yet foreign and international capital flows to Chile increased, revealing an abyss between public and private flows, multilateral and bilateral donors.

Condemnatory and investigative action within the United Nations had begun as one of many similar in the cold-war duels. The contribution of NGOs in mobilising the United Nations against human rights violations in Chile was enormous. Yet, Chile would not have been placed on the agenda had it not been for the Soviet Union – the ousting of Chile's socialist president by the US-supported military was too attractive a political issue to be missed. However, there would have been no UN action had it not been for Western Europe joining Eastern Europe in condemning the 1973 military coup and subsequent repression. Thus, a forceful and sustained United Nations response to human rights violations developed around Chile. One reason was effective opposition by Chileans themselves, both in exile and at home; another was the international outcry against the military coup that ousted the first Latin American democratically elected socialist president.

On 11 September 1973, General Augusto Pinochet carried out a military coup, President Salvador Allende was forced into suicide, parliament was dissolved, and the Constitution suspended. Pinochet's regime (1972–89) became notorious for systematic human rights violations. Nevertheless, it did not become past-finished after the change in 1990 but re-emerged in 1998–99. On 10 March 1998 General Augusto Pinochet retired as commander-in-chief of the armed forces and one day later became senator-for-life. Rather than falling into oblivion, he became the focus of a combined Spanish/British attempt to bring him to court for human rights violations, thus reviving unsolved questions about foreign and international involvement in Chile in 1972–89. The case was debated for its lifting of impunity for gross human rights violations from a former head of state, but it also raised interest for foreign support for Pinochet's dictatorship.

Much has been written about human rights violations in Pinochet's Chile and about the international response and only some highlights will suffice here. It was the first time that the United Nations abandoned its exclusive focus on the denial of self-determination by colonial regimes or occupying powers to look into violations of individual rights and freedoms through rule by force. Although the issue had been placed on the agenda as part of the cold-war battle, it became a genuine precedent.

Chile was also the principal precedent for suspending bilateral aid in response to systemic human rights violations. Aid was cut off from Pinochet's government in 1974 by a large number of donors: the Netherlands, Great Britain, Sweden, Canada, Finland, Denmark, Germany, Italy, Norway, and Belgium. Table 5.5 illustrates flows of bilateral aid to Chile in the 1970s. Because a decision to cut off aid cannot

Table 5.5: Bilateral aid to Chile 1971–77
(in million US$)

Donor	1971	1972	1973	1974	1975	1976	1977
Canada	1.1	2.2	1.2	1.4	0.1	–0.2	–0.2
Denmark	0.2	0.2	0.3	0.4	0.2	0.2	0.1
France	4.6	14.1	0.2	7.5	–2.8	–1.2	–5.6
Germany	7.0	8.1	12.5	16.6	19.8	–2.0	–5.4
Italy	–1.0	0.2	3.2	0.1	0.1	–	–4.8
Japan	0.1	0.1	1.3	8.1	1.2	1.3	2.2
Netherlands	1.4	0.6	3.8	3.8	1.1	1.8	3.0
Sweden	–	0.7	4.7	0.6	–0.4	–0.1	–
United Kingdom	–1.0	0.1	0.8	1.2	0.6	1.2	3.0
United States	7.0	5.0	5.0	–33.0	82.0	2.0	8.0
Total bilateral aid	20.6	32.9	35.0	8.7	104.3	4.6	2.1

Note: The table does not include aid from all donors hence figures do not add up to total aid.
Source: *Geographical Distribution of Financial Flows to Developing Countries. Data on Disbursements 1971 to 1977*, OECD, Paris, 1978.

be instantly reflected in aid flows, total bilateral aid to Chile was unaffected in 1973 (it had actually increased in comparison with 1972) but decreased from $32.9 to $8.7 million in 1974 when sanctions took effect. Japan decreased its aid in 1975 and Germany in 1976.

The position of the United States was peculiar; sanctions had been imposed in November 1970 due to expropriation claims, with the unspoken intention of bringing Allende's socialist – or rather, 'communist', by US classification – government to ruin. The United States resumed, and later increased, aid to Chile starting in September 1973, one week after the military coup, despite a 1974 congressional requirement to reduce it.

Allende's *Unidad Popular,* one of the largest socialist (or communist, as the US had it) parties in the world at the time, won the 1970 elections. A communist party thus came into power through multi-party elections, which would have been declared free and fair had electoral observation existed at the time, and Allende's overthrow through a military coup three years later triggered an international solidarity movement. It was seen as a communist plot by some, however. Moses Moskowitz has called the UN's response to Chile a 'Soviet vendetta against an ideological foe.'[53] Indeed, the Soviet delegation subsequently argued that UN's response had been justified because the military coup had been engineered by a

---

[53] Moskowitz, M. – *The Roots and Reaches of United Nations Actions and Decisions*, Sijthoff & Noordhoff, Alphen aan den Rhijn, 1980, p. 175.

foreign power.[54] At the time of legal proceedings against General Pinochet in 1998–99, the probing into US archives proved the Soviet Union to have been right.[55] Nevertheless, stripped of ideological overtones, a military coup followed by legalised repression merited an international response. Indeed, although the United Nations addressed human rights violations in Chile thanks to an agenda initially set by ideological opponents, Chile was soon liberated from this ideological baggage; it thus appeared on the international human rights agenda, becoming the prototype for responding to future violators of human rights.

The chronology of UN's response is well known: The first session of the Commission on Human Rights after the military coup and the death of President Allende was addressed by his widow. The 1974 session of the Sub-Commission had adopted a resolution on detainees and prisoners in Chile, which was endorsed by the General Assembly.[56] The subsequent session of the Commission on Human Rights established the Ad Hoc Working Group on Chile. The (military) government of Chile agreed, indeed welcomed, a UN fact-finding mission, provided that no East European country or other Soviet ally was included.[57] The Ad Hoc Working Group submitted eight reports and set a precedent for factual reporting as the background for clarifying the dynamics of human rights violations. Subsequent UN investigations looked further into their causation.

The mobilisation of the entire international human rights system was as unprecedented as was the expansion of human rights organisations in Chile. The international assistance Chilean human rights organizations received was comparable only to that enjoyed by anti-apartheid organisations. Such human rights work took more than fifteen long years, during which big donors financed Pinochet's government, while small donors funded human rights NGOs.

The background for this divergence was that Pinochet's Chile was praised as an economic miracle. This necessarily led to asking whether institutionalised human rights violations were the necessary price of an economic miracle. Chile's GNP was growing, inflation was falling, foreign trade and investment were blossoming, and Chilean debt-equity swaps were successful. International development banks continued aiding Chile after a suspension: the Carter Administration voted against

---

[54] Commission on Human Rights – Summary records of 10 March 1982, U.N. Doc. E/CN.4/1982/SR.57, p. 13.

[55] Franklin, J. – CIA files show Chilean blood on US hands, *Guardian Weekly*, 14–20 October 1999.

[56] Resolution 8 (XXVII) of the Sub-Commission (Report of the Sub-Commission on its Twenty-seventh Session, U.N. Doc. E/CN.4/1160, p. 53) and General Assembly resolution 3219 (XXIX) of 6 November 1974.

[57] Commission on Human Rights – Report on the Thirty-first Session (1975), U.N. Doc. E/5635, Supplement No. 4, paras. 93 and 102.

loans to Chile, the Reagan administration supported them. Nordic objections on human rights grounds did not carry enough weight to make a difference.[58]

The IMF/World Bank policy-prescriptions were duly implemented. Privatisation encompassed housing, health, education and public works. Its effects were both economic and political. In health, privatisation eliminated preventive programmes while making political control of the medical profession easier. Privatisation of education institutionalised access to school corresponding to the ability to pay. In a World Bank survey of measures to improve employment opportunities for the poor under structural adjustment, Chile's emergency employment programme was cited as a success.[59] The same programme was described by the late Jacobo Timerman (whose freedom from detention had been secured through US human rights conditionality) as follows:

> The Pinochet regime has seven percent of Chile's labour force in what was announced as a program to fight unemployment. But the regime has not gone in for Mussolini-like public works. Wages range from twenty to forty dollars a month, a sum that barely covers the cost of transport if you cannot walk to work. The real objective of the plan to fight unemployment is to keep Santiago clean, swept, and washed, and its parks and plazas watered, and its walls looked after.[60]

A thorough study into the effects of international financial flows on human rights was carried out by Antonio Cassese for the UN Sub-Commission on Prevention of Discrimination and Protection of Minorities. That study included detailed statistics on financial flows of all types, and analysed the effects on human rights of the application of IMF and World Bank policy prescriptions, which facilitated debt rescheduling. Cassese recommended that aid be conditioned by 'a basic reorientation of the general policy of the government, and full restoration of all the basic human rights and fundamental freedoms.'[61]

Total financial flows to Pinochet's Chile increased because Allende's Chile had been a target of US sanctions in 1970–73. The US lead was followed by major multilateral donors, and total aid from the United States, the World Bank, the International Monetary Fund, and the Inter-American Development Bank to Chile of $30 million during Allende's government increased to over $300 million in 1974, after Pinochet had taken over.[62] The donors that cut off aid to Pinochet's

---

[58] A detailed description of donors' responses to political and economic developments in Chile in 1972–89 is included in Tomaševski, K. – *Development Aid and Human Rights*, Pinter Publishers, London, 1989, pp. 69–71, and Tomaševski, K. – *Development Aid and Human Rights Revisited*, Pinter Publishers, London, 1993, pp. 100–102.

[59] Demery, L. & Addison, T. – The Alleviation of Poverty under Structural Adjustment, The World Bank, 1987, at 21–23.

[60] Timerman, J. – Chile. Death in the South, Picador, New York, 1987, at 79.

[61] Study of the impact of foreign economic aid and assistance on respect for human rights in Chile, Report prepared by Mr. Antonio Cassese, Rapporteur, U.N. Doc. E/CN.4/Sub.2/412 (vol.IV), para. 541.

[62] Dias-David, M., et al. – *Asistencia financiera externa a la junta militar de Chile*, Institute of Latin American Studies, Stockholm, 1978, mimeographed.

Chile were not those contributing the bulk of aid. Foreign investment also increased and surpassed aid. During the second half of the 1970s, bilateral aid fell below $100 million while private lending surged above $900 million. Similar data had been provided to the hearings on human rights and aid to Chile before the US Congress[63] by the former Chilean Ambassador to the United States, Orlando Letalier. His killing triggered off a prolonged legal dispute between the United States and Chile.

Cassese's study was never published nor was he reelected to the Sub-Commission after completing it. That unrecorded case of censorship was noted by Howard Tolley, who argued that Cassese's call for economic policies to be examined for their effect on human rights was unpalatable for the powers that be, and 'even the most independent experts on the Sub-Commission found that prospect too alarming.'[64] His conclusion has been that the suppression of civil and political rights was 'necessary to impose and enforce the economic and social policy of the military government.'[65] The result was prosperity for the few at the expense of poverty and powerlessness for the many, as captured by a 1987 UN report.[66] The proportion of people below the poverty line had increased from 20% in 1970 to 44% in 1986/87, but fell back to 33% in 1992.[67] Public spending had been halved during Pinochet's regime, and doubled after the restoration of civilian government.

The presidential plebiscite in October 1988 brought Chile a great deal of international attention. The sole candidate was, to nobody's surprise, General Pinochet. He lost. Thirteen Chilean political parties campaigned for a 'no' in an atmosphere of fear. Fear cannot be quantified by statistics nor conveyed by reports on human rights violations, nor did it enable Chile to comply with the US condition of 'an atmosphere free of fear and intimidation.'[68] Elections followed and a civilian government was inaugurated in 1990. Yet the powers of post-Pinochet civilian governments have been constrained by denying the (civilian) President's power to appoint and dismiss the highest ranking military officers and preserving the block of minority of senators appointed by the military regime into the 21st century.

After General Pinochet's constitutionally guaranteed position as commander-in-chief of the armed forces came to its constitutionally envisaged end in March

---

[63] US Congress – *Chile: The Status of Human Rights and Its Relationship to US Economic Assistance Programs*, Hearings before the Subcommittee on International Organizations of the Committee on International Relations, House of Representatives, 94th Congress, US Government Printing Office, Washington D.C., 1976.

[64] Tolley, H. – *The U.N. Commission on Human Rights*, Westview Special Studies in International Relations, Westview Press, Boulder, 1987, p. 175.

[65] U.N. Doc. E/CN.4/Sub.2/412, vol. III, para. 440.

[66] Question of human rights in Chile. Report submitted by the UN Special Rapporteur, U.N. Doc. E/CN.4/1988/7 of 5 February 1988, para. 124.

[67] Herzlich, G. – Bridging the gap between two Chiles, *Le Monde*, reprinted in *Guardian Weekly*, 22 May 1994.

[68] Testimony by Richard Schifter, Assistant Secretary of State, before the US House of representatives, Subcommittee on Human Rights and International Organizations, 17 May, 1988, p. 5.

1998 and he moved to his new position – also constitutionally prescribed – of senator-for-life, public protests affected even the parliament.[69] The background was a deep division between people who were unable to forget and unwilling to forgive, as governmental policy wished them to,[70] and those who glorified General Pinochet as Chile's saviour. The government's policy has been to reveal abuses and compensate victims, but to postpone prosecution of the responsible individuals into the future.

Prosecutions have indeed been few, although attempts to broaden them have been many. A 1978 amnesty law protects abuses that occurred in 1973–78, but Chilean courts have nevertheless made small inroads into the blanket impunity based on that law.[71] In 1993 General Manuel Contreras was convicted to imprisonment for the killing of Orlando Letalier in 1976; he started serving his sentence in 1995. A common interpretation was that he was tried 'because the United States pressed the issue.'[72] From prison, he pointed his finger at General Pinochet saying that he was always strictly obeying orders.[73]

Responding to similar accusations, General Pinochet has insisted that he defended Chile against aggression 'carried out by the terrorists' and that his sixteen-and-a-half-year government left Chile 'bigger and greater, and free.'[74] He has taken a great deal of pride in his 'accomplishments', described in five-volumes of memoirs, to which Jaime Velasco of the Chilean Human Rights Commission has published a thoughtful and well-founded response.[75]

The Truth Commission appears in retrospect to have been the beginning rather than the end of a dialogue intended to unearth multi-layered truth. Ultimately, any effort to postpone dialogue concerning responsibilities until the next century was ruptured with the case against General Pinochet in 1998. Whether the Western European initiative to hasten retroactive responsibility of General Pinochet for his acts and omissions while he had been the head of state in Chile will turn out to have

---

[69] Capozza, K. – Chile confronts its painful past, *Human Rights Tribune/Tribune des droits humains*, vol. 5, Nos. 1–2, April 1998, pp. 30–31.

[70] The Truth Commission hoped that 'a recognition of the veracity of the events [will contribute] to ending the long and painful division which has affected Chilean society during the period when these events were denied.' *To Believe in Chile. Summary of the Truth and Reconciliation Report*, Chilean Human Rights Commission, Centro IDEAS and Ministry of Foreign Affairs of Chile, Santiago de Chile, July 1991, presentation, p. 1.

[71] Salinas Rivera, A. – Two examples of battling impunity in Chile, *The ICJ Review*, No. 53, 1994, pp. 13–19.

[72] Symbolic justice in Chile (leader), *The New York Times*, reprinted in *International Herald Tribune*, 26 October 1995.

[73] Olivares, E. – Ally accuses Pinochet in murder case, *Le Monde*, 1–2 March 1998, reproduced in *Guardian Weekly*, 15 March 1998.

[74] Scott, N. – General Pinochet defies his critics, *Guardian Weekly*, 17 September 1995.

[75] Castillo Velasco, J. – *?Hubo en Chile violaciones a los derechos humanos? Comentario a las Memorias del General Pinochet*, Comisíon Chilena de derechos humanos, Santiago, 1995.

been beneficial could not be anticipated. The accounting at the end of 1999 high-lighted, on the benefits side, the precedent of bringing a former head of state and government to court for abuses and, on the harmful side, the likelihood that this Western European activism could have facilitated a change of the Chilean political landscape. The first round of elections in Chile, in December 1999, ended without an electoral preference for either main candidate; both obtained less than 50% of the votes cast with the difference between the two consisting of a mere 30,000 votes. The runoff has been scheduled for 16 January 2000. The expected victory of Ricardo Lagos, the candidate of *Concertación*, the anti- and post-Pinochet coalition which governed Chile from 1990 till 1999, seemed to have been impeded by econ-omic recession but also by Pinochet's prosecution in Europe. Jonathan Franklin has noted that a key element in the unexpectedly large percentage of votes cast for Joaquin Lavin 'was the arrest of General Pinochet in London in October [1998], which mobilized the right in common defence of the Chilean leader and of Chilean sovereignty.'[76]

---

[76] Franklin, J. – Pinochet disciple closes in on Chilean presidency, *Guardian Weekly*, 16–22 December 1999.

Part III

Unilateralism and Multilateralism in Practice

Chapter 6

South America

North-South relations in the Americas have throughout past decades elicited much attention, particularly because of the changing fate of human rights in US foreign policy. The United States has alternated between facilitating and opposing repression, aiding and penalising dictatorships. Yet the importance of South America in the area of human rights goes far beyond US unilateralism: it was the non-governmental human rights work in South America in the 1970s and early 1980s that influenced NGOs worldwide as well as altering UN's responses to violations.

The subsequent change from military to civilian government was often accompanied by the re-writing of contemporary history. Extensive NGO networks and vast documentation were instrumental in drawing up authoritative records of previous abuses. Truth commissions (with the exception of Guatemala, discussed below) stopped short of inquiring into foreign and international support to dictatorships. Nevertheless, such re-written domestic history has made supporters of dictatorships look like accessories, it has transformed silence into complicity, discredited official inter-governmental human rights records based on blanket denials of denounced abuses by dictatorships, and cast some light upon the political ploys of their peers within the United Nations and the Organization of American States.

Two factors were decisive in making South America prominent in international human rights politics in the late 1970s:

- denials and violations of individual rights were institutionalised through military rule in the most developed countries of the region,[1] eliciting a great deal of passive and active resistance in the urbanised and industrialised communities in Argentina, Chile and Uruguay, including exile[2] or refuge in the West through which Western attention was forced on abuses at home;
- institutionalised abuses of power and their human toll were rapidly and extensively documented. The human toll, 30,000 in Argentina,[3] for example, consisted

---

[1] Frühling, H. et al. – *Organizaciones de derechos humanos de América del Sur*, Instituto Interamericano de Derechos Humanos, San José, 1989, p. 14.

[2] Chile, Argentina and Uruguay generated a large number of political refugees becae exile was a form of punishment, individuals were given a choice of leaving the country rather than remaining in detention.

[3] Mignone, E.F. – Argentina: los desafios del fin de siglo, in Basombrío, C.I. (ed.) – ¿ ... *Y ahora qué? Desafíos para el trabajo por los derechos humanos en América Latina*, Diakonia, La Paz (Bolivia), 1996, p. 208.

of those selectively targeted by the military government to stifle and then prevent opposition to repression and was bound to generate publicity. Pressure upon governments – especially Western – followed, and they had to react both individually and collectively.

The landscape of international human rights politics changed with the mushrooming of NGOs throughout South America. Their work in collecting and publicising information on abuses was the background to international condemnations and sanctions. Nobel Prizes for human rights work to Amnesty International, then to Adolfo Perez Esquivel of Argentinian SERPAJ (*Servicio Justicia y Paz*), and later to Rigoberta Menchu (thus giving credit to Guatemala's growing indigenous movement), transformed human rights activists from subversives to celebrities.

International human rights organisations, such as Amnesty International, were based in the North, publicising information about – and collected in – the South. A circular mode of exerting pressure upon governments emerged.[4] Reports on human rights violations in South America were then launched in the United States or Western Europe in order to mobilise the respective governments, so that they would, in turn, mobilise inter-governmental human rights bodies or impose sanctions in order to constrain abuses by South America's recalcitrant regimes. As table 1.3 (in Chapter 1) has shown, the Thoolen-Verstappen study has revealed that in 1970–86 the largest numbers of NGO missions went to Central America, with El Salvador, Nicaragua and Guatemala accounting for thirty missions each, followed by Chile (with 19 missions), Argentina (9 missions) and Uruguay (8 missions). That pattern both reflected and influenced human rights geopolitics at the time.

Intra-regional differences also influenced international responses to abuses in particular countries. Central America was a cold-war battlefield in the litteral sense of this word, victimised by proxy wars which were blended with warfare of domestic origin, originating in grossly unequal pattern of land ownership or institutionalized racism. Nothing resembling the precision with which the number of victims of the dictatorship was calculated in urbanised Argentina could be replicated in rural El Salvador or indigenous Guatemala. In Guatemala, the indigenous majority had neither been officially registered as citizens nor officially recorded as individual victims. In the retrospective re-writing of the history of their victimisation, Central America's truth commissions were international rather than domestic and their influence on the domestic recognition of human rights is as yet uncertain.

---

[4] Margaret Keck and Kathryn Sikkink have studied this circular mode of creating human rights cases from the opposite entry point, namely discussing 'the boomerang pattern' as a strategy whereby 'NGOs bypass their state and directly search out international allies to try to bring pressure on their states from outside.' Keck, M.E. and Sikkink, K. – *Activists Beyond Borders: Advocacy Networks in International Politics*, Cornell University Press, Ithaca, 1998, p. 12.

A COMPARISON BETWEEN CONDEMNATIONS AND AID FLOWS

The effect of intra-regional differences and inter-governmental politics in funnelling information about abuses towards public condemnation of violators is shown in Table 6.1. Out of nineteen cases that were placed on UN's human rights agenda, eight were filtered out and condemnatory resolutions adopted for eleven governments. The list in Table 6.1 thus does not include Suriname (discussed below), although violations have been authoritatively determined by the Human Rights Committee and the Inter-American Court of Human Rights, and the Netherlands had cut off aid in response to one of the most serious incidents.

Cuba's initiatives against the United States (discussed in Chapter 4) have not led to a condemnation for reasons that do not require any comment. Countries like Guyana or Venezuela have not elicited much attention in international human rights politics and documentation on abuses has not been as extensive as for Argentina, which is discussed below. It constituted a precedent for the United Nations by forcing a shift from targeting an individual government to the phenomenon that exemplified its ill-deeds. In other words, Argentina could not be condemned as a human rights violator because too many governmental delegations argued and voted in accordance with their governments' friendly relations with Argentina's military government. Hence the first thematic procedure was set up to address disappearances, the phenomenon that symbolized ill-deeds of Argentina's military government, but Argentina was not named. This shift has broadened UN's remit with regard to violations, albeit at the price of diverting the focus away from individual violators and thus implicitly reinforcing their immunity to naming-and-shaming. The precedent was established for Argentina to be later applied to Brazil, Colombia or Peru and reinforcing the shift from violators- to violations-oriented procedures.

Within the less politicised realm of international human rights law, Honduras entered the history of human rights having generated one of the most important judgements in the history of international human rights litigation. The Inter-American Court of Human Rights rejected the widely used strategy whereby a government could evade responsibility for disappearances by claiming ignorance about them.[5] At the time when disappearances had been taking place, the background was thus described: 'the Hondurans got millions of dollars of aid (much of which went straight to the army), and America's blessing on the human-rights record of the police and the army.'[6]

Such constraints profiled the resort to international human rights system, both regional and global. As Table 6.1 shows, the easiest entry point within the United Nations was the 1503 procedure, widely used by NGOs. The number of governments denounced as violators diminished as documentation on abuses was

---

[5] Inter-American Court of Human Rights – *Velasquez Rodriguez* case, Judgment of 29 July 1988.
[6] Honduras: Breeze of change, *The Economist,* 3 April 1993, p. 49–50.

processed by inter-governmental mechanisms on the way upwards through the Sub-Commission to the Commission on Human Rights. Chile was the first prominent item on the violations-agenda and has been addressed in Chapter 5. It was atypical because the Soviet Union had mobilized the inter-governmental machinery. Nicaragua was condemned as a violator in 1979, just as the condemned Somosa regime was being ousted through armed rebellion, and is discussed below. Initially, it had also been a case where governments denounced a fellow-government for human rights violations. In contrast, Guatemala, El Salvador and Bolivia followed in 1980–81 not having generated consensus amongst governments, Grenada and Haiti were added in 1984, Paraguay and Uruguay in 1985, and Panama and Cuba completed the list in 1990. US aid to Guatemala and El Salvador muted international condemnations, while US military interventions in Grenada and Panama triggered verbal condemnations of the United States. Colombia followed in 1996 with an innovative UN's response similar to that of Argentina: it was not condemned for human rights violations because inter-governmental consensus has been lacking. Too much information on abuses has been available to enable collective silence of governments to persist. Hence, a murky compromise emerged in 1996 in the form of a field office with terms of reference that included some monitoring of abuses and some cooperation with the government.

Table 6.1: The Americas on the UN violations- agenda

Country	Commission	Sub-Commission	1503 procedure
Argentina	–	(1976), (1978)	1980–84
Bolivia	1981–83	1980	1977–81
Brazil	–	–	1974–76
Chile	1975–90	1974–88	1975–76, 1978–79, 1981
Colombia	(1995–96)	1995	1990
Cuba	(1988), 1990–96	–	–
El Salvador	1981–91	1981–92	1981
Grenada	1984	–	1988
Guatemala	1980–86, 1992, 1994	1982–86, 1989–95	1981
Guyana			1975–75
Haiti	1984,1987–90, 1992–94	1988, 1992–94	1981–87, 1989–90
Honduras	–	–	1988–89
Nicaragua	1979	1979	–
Panama	1990	1990	–
Paraguay	1985	1983–85, 1989	1978–90
Peru	–	1992–93	(1990)
Uruguay	1985	1983–84	1978–85
USA	(1995–96)	–	1997
Venezuela	–	–	1982

Within the OAS, where only North and South America are represented, attempts at investigative or condemnatory action required carefully elaborated strategy and a great deal of persistence. It is easy to envisage the obstacles encountered by the Inter-American Commission on Human Rights, with the OAS political organs composed of the very governments which the Commission was publicly denouncing as violators. The early OAS expulsion of Cuba (summarized in Chapter 4) was followed by its exceptional public condemnation of Somosa's regime in Nicaragua (discussed below). The two easily attained consensus of governmental delegations. Difficult targets followed – Chile and Argentina. The Inter-American Commission demonstrated a great deal of ingenuity in exposing abuses by the powers that be but, in contrast to the UN Commission, it has no power to condemn. Cecilia Medina noted that Pinochet's government was never condemned by the political organs of the OAS owing to, *inter alia*, the support of the military government of Argentina.[7]

Such support extended further, to the northern part of the region and outside it, and went beyond human wrongs and rights, and beyond cold-war alliances. When the UN's violations-agenda (Table 6.1) is compared with aid flows to the countries in question (Table 6.2), support for governments by their peers can be seen in its political and financial dimensions. The former reflects the paucity of explicit condemnations of violators, the latter illustrates the flows of aid to the governments that were likely to be using it, *inter alia*, to carry out the violations that were being discussed. This comparison is not guided by the often-posed question: did multilateral condemnations result in diminished aid flows? Research generated by that question has yielded inconclusive results, which are supported by the data in Table 6.2. These show that question to be pertinent only for three small countries, Grenada, Suriname and Panama.

For Grenada, the previously minuscule amounts of aid increased following the US military intervention of 1984–85. For Suriname, which is discussed below, aid suspension by the Netherlands was clearly reflected in the plummeting of total aid. Suriname is a fine illustration of the proverbial vulnerability of a small and poor recipient to the changing conduct of a single big donor. It is worth remembering here that, with the exception of Suriname, the United States was the main donor to South America. Indeed, Panama's vulnerability to changes in US preferences was no less significant than that of Suriname to the Netherlands.

Panama was targeted by economic sanctions followed by military intervention. The United States cut off aid to Panama in 1987 in response to anti-US demonstrations.[8] Congress made resumption of aid conditional on progress in

---

[7] Medina Quiroga, C. – *The Battle for Human Rights. Gross, Systematic Violations and the Inter-American System*, Martin Nijhoff Publishers, Dordrecht, 1988, pp. 312–313.

[8] 'For years the Reagan administration chose not to criticise the regimes controlled by Noriega, even as the general consolidated his power and corruption increased. The administration ignored the well-publicised fraud in the 1984 elections, in which the Defense Forces' favored candidate was bestowed victory ...When the Defense Forces ousted [the president elected in 1984] in September 1985, the administration withdrew $5 million in promised aid (a small portion of total U.S. aid to Panama) but recognized the successor government ... A decision to freeze further aid came after pro-government demonstrators attacked the U.S. embassy with rocks and red paint in July 1987.' Americas Watch – *Human Rights in Panama*, New York, April 1988, p. 45–46.

Table 6.2: Aid to South America, 1978–1988
(in million $)

Recipient	1978	1979	1980	1981	1982	1983	1984	1985	1986	1987	1988
Argentina	46	62	24	60	42	66	71	56	101	99	142
Bolivia	233	226	224	232	208	244	246	286	395	319	384
Brazil	177	131	106	320	292	144	235	177	207	292	197
Chile	13	-39	-13	-10	-11	0	3	57	-6	21	41
Colombia	113	78	119	140	136	121	127	88	72	78	58
Costa Rica	81	76	86	75	114	355	314	399	225	228	175
Cuba	78	56	42	19	24	18	17	26	21	30	19
El Salvador	88	87	128	229	308	409	376	492	392	426	392
Grenada	3	3	4	5	6	10	40	50	29	20	20
Guatemala	115	95	96	103	90	107	94	118	155	241	219
Haiti	148	134	139	145	177	196	193	217	212	219	137
Honduras	148	138	136	145	219	262	404	382	326	258	301
Jamaica	186	138	153	210	254	255	245	244	205	169	180
Mexico	29	108	74	137	197	186	120	207	290	156	161
Nicaragua	67	164	279	185	170	169	164	145	173	141	199
Panama	46	50	61	54	58	66	104	98	60	41	21
Paraguay	69	43	41	71	111	68	72	71	77	82	71
Peru	228	288	268	320	264	419	447	450	313	292	254
Suriname	105	137	108	133	143	6	7	9	7	14	20
Uruguay	18	20	13	10	6	4	6	7	31	18	38

Note: Figures represent net disbursements of aid (ODA) from all sources according to definitions ed at the time.
Source: DAC/OECD.

civilian control over the armed forces, but soon thereafter Panama's 'illegitimate Noriega regime'[9] was declared ineligible for aid. Panama's assets in the United States were frozen in retaliation for General Noriega's dismissal of a civilian president who had been favoured by the United States. Human rights rhetoric was not used because, according to cynics, Panama could by no definition be characterised as communist. The justifications for US sanctions were military abuses and the interruption of democracy.[10] General Noriega was in 1988 indicted by US courts on a dozen charges relating to drug trafficking and money laundering, and the United States requested his extradition. US sanctions were expected to ruin Panama because it used dollars as the national currency and operated extensive banking services, but when this did not happen, US military intervention followed in 1989. Its declared purpose was to, *inter alia*, help restore democracy and bring General Noriega to justice. The US military intervention was duly condemned by the United Nations.[11]

Uruguay is something of a counter-example because, as Table 6.2 shows, aid diminished in 1982–85, as if the country had been punished for the transition from military to civilian rule that was going on at the time. The United States had cut off first military then economic aid to Uruguay, and opposed loans from international development banks.[12] The change from Carter to Reagan administration in 1981 brought with it a change in foreign policy, diminishing the importance of human rights. Uruguay received scant international attention and never became a topical political issue. The creeping military coup[13] that instituted military rule in Uruguay had happened just a few months before the military coup in Chile, and international attention focussed on Chile. Uruguay was not a cold-war battleground nor did it have the international stature of Argentina, being its much smaller and poorer neighbour. The military rule was documented in a functional equivalent of the Argentine *Nunca más* (*Never Again*) report, but Uruguay's report also received scant attention.[14]

[9] Panama: Still there, alas, *The Economist*, 16 January 1988, p. 56; U.S. adds to Panama sanctions, *International Herald Tribune*, 12/13 March 1988.

[10] Nash Leich, M. – Economic measures against the illegal Noriega regime in Panama, *American Journal of International Law*, vol. 82, 1988, p. 566–567.

[11] Effects of the military intervention by the United States of America in Panama on the situation in Central America, General Assembly resolution 44/240 of 29 December 1989,

[12] Schoultz, L. – *Human Rights and United States Policy toward Latin America*, Princeton University Press, Princeton, 1981, p. 295.

[13] Uruguay's government empowered its military in 1971 to defeat Tupamaros, an urban guerrilla movement, having implicitly declared itself unable to halt bombings and assassinations. This was followed by a proclamation of the state of internal war in 1972 and suspension of constitutional guarantees. Although the military declared in 1973 that Tupamaros had been military defeated, constitutional guarantees were not re-instituted. Rather, the government of the time dissolved parliament and, together with the military, vested governance in bodies composed of individual appointees.

[14] SERPAJ (Servicio paz y justicia) – *Uruguay Nunca Más: Informe sobre la violación a los derechos humanos (1972–1985)*, Altamira, Montevideo, 1989.

In contrast to Grenada, Suriname and Panama, large and fairly developed countries, such as Argentina or Brazil, were not dependent on a single donor. Germany, Japan and Italy, alongside the United States, provided considerable aid. Nor were such countries dependent on aid, with per capita aid amounting to an annual $2 or less. Conversely, with aid per capita of an annual $100, El Salvador and Guatemala (discussed below), were dependent on aid, although such aid was mostly military. Rather than seeking any correspondence between condemnations of violators and diminished aid, one can then treat aid to the condemned, or 'almost-condemned', governments as states' practice which has been established in the pre-human-rights era to be only slightly and occasionally influenced by human rights considerations.

Table 6.2 reproduces data on aid flows to individual South American countries in 1978–88, the decade of institutionalised human rights violations in quite a few countries, some of which were associated with the Cold War. The most controversial case, Nicaragua, is discussed first, followed – in chronological sequence – by Argentina, Haiti, El Salvador, Guatemala and Suriname.

NICARAGUA[15]

The first target of OAS political action in response to human rights violations was Cuba in 1962–64, followed by Nicaragua in 1978–79. Human rights language was used against Cuba, the main assertion being that communist ideology denied human rights, but the focus was rather protection of the region against communism. A convoluted argument emerged whereby human rights violations were permissible so as to combat communism, because, if allowed, communism would deny human rights. Acceptance of ideological pluralism by the OAS had to wait till 1975.

In 1978, the OAS called for a change of government in Nicaragua, then ruled by the Somosa regime (1936–78). This was not at all a part of the cold-war battles. Post-Somosa Nicaragua, however, immediately followed Cuba in becoming a cold-war battlefield. The interplay of the US-supported contras, US sanctions against Nicaragua, and Soviet-Cuban (as well as some Western) assistance to 'Sandinista Nicaragua' to compensate for US sanctions, were typical of the geopolitics of human rights in the 1980s. Against such a multitude of intervening actors, inter-governmental human rights bodies were helpless.

---

[15] Having been one of the prominent cold-war battlefields, Nicaragua has been dealt with in detail elsewhere: Tomaševski, K. – *Development Aid and Human Rights*, Pinter Publishers, London, 1989, pp. 64–68; Tomaševski, K. – *Development Aid and Human Rights Revisited*, Pinter Publishers, London, 1993, pp. 96–99; Tomaševski, K. – Nicaragua, in *Human Rights in Developing Countries. 1995 Yearbook*, Martinus Nijhoff Publishers, Dordrecht, 1995, pp. 203–236.

Relations between Nicaragua and the United States went through four distinct phases:

- In 1977–79, aid had been suspended because of human rights violations by the Somosa regime. Its overthrow by the Sandinistas in 1978–79 was accompanied by an initial US commitment to assist Nicaragua.
- In 1979, US aid was conditioned on Nicaragua's abstention from subversion abroad ('aiding or abetting acts of violence in another country'); the prohibition of stationing Cuban or Soviet military in Nicaragua; the prohibition of using aid in projects involving Cuban advisors or teachers; and the absence of violations of freedom of expression and trade union freedoms. Furthermore, aid was tied to the purchase of US goods, and conditioned on informing the Nicaraguans that aid was provided by the United States.[16]
- US aid was suspended in 1981 because of Nicaragua's assistance to insurgents in El Salvador, described by the United States as 'support of terrorism'.[17] The following year, US covert, and later open, support to the *contras* (armed resistance to the Sandinista government) started, as did US opposition to loans to Nicaragua from multilateral and regional banks.
- US trade sanctions followed in 1985. Nicaragua's aid dependence had been aggravated by the 1978–79 war, by capital flight ensuing from the exodus of the defeated Somosa regime, and by the foreign debt which that regime had left to Nicaragua. The Sandinista government was repaying foreign debt until 1985 when further repayment became impossible because of inadequate loans from international development finance agencies, lack of foreign investment, and the increasing cost of warfare.

US sanctions against Nicaragua were at first compensated by the Soviet Union, which provided mainly military aid; by Cuba, which supplied all forms of aid, including military; and by Libya, which provided loans. The Netherlands provided grants and loans as of 1982 to offset vetoes in international development finance agencies. As Table 6.3 shows, aid to Nicaragua was halved between 1980 and 1982 and only increased in the 1990s. When the trade embargo was imposed in 1985, Canada, France, Germany, Italy, Portugal, Spain, and Sweden opposed it, declined to stop their trade with Nicaragua, and extended aid. Table 6.3 shows that Western aid indeed constituted virtually all aid to Nicaragua. sanctions against Nicaragua became a prominent global controversy. Intense publicity accompanied every facet of what was seen as David's battle against Goliath.

In 1987–89 a peace plan developed by Central American presidents (Esquipulas I and II) was translated into reality and internationally supported. US aid to

---

[16] US Congress – Congressional Record of 22 February 1980, pp. H2009-H2020.

[17] US Congress – Review of the Presidential certification of Nicaragua's connection to terrorism, Hearings before the Subcommittee on Inter-American Affairs, Committee on Foreign Affairs, Hoe of Representatives, 96th Congress, 2nd session, Washington, D.C., 30 September 1980.

Table 6.3: Aid to Nicaragua in 1977–80, 1982–85 and 1992–95 (in million $)

	1977–1980				1982–1985				1992–1995			
	1977	1978	1979	1980	1982	1983	1984	1985	1992	1993	1994	1995
USA	14.0	24.0	29.0	79.0	6.0	3.0	–	–	154.0	38.0	60.0	29.0
Canada	0.6	0.1	–	0.3	2.3	6.2	8.8	5.8	6.0	8.7	9.1	8.1
France	–	–	–	0.5	8.6	8.7	8.5	7.0	19.8	11.9	7.8	15.9
Germany	3.1	1.0	17.8	8.3	8.5	6.9	4.5	4.7	47.6	28.8	43.9	174.6
Japan	0.2	0.3	5.5	2.3	0.3	0.1	0.1	0.1	54.1	41.3	54.7	51.9
Netherlands	0.0	0.4	6.4	14.6	23.9	17.6	21.2	15.7	26.3	26.7	26.6	48.9
Norway	–	–	0.9	0.5	2.1	2.3	5.7	5.0	26.1	17.5	20.3	27.8
Sweden	–	–	8.1	7.7	9.3	10.6	13.7	12.6	68.5	36.3	30.7	31.8
EUrope	36.5	41.6	115.1	220.6	51.6	45.5	52.5	45.9	268.6	183.4	287.1	386.7
Total bilateral	18.7	26.5	73.8	116.6	76.9	72.9	71.7	67.2	472.9	275.0	417.6	490.6
Total multilateral	17.8	15.2	40.3	104.0	43.9	47.5	42.0	35.2	185.4	50.6	184.4	170.7

Source: OECD – *Geographical Distribution of Financial Flows to Developing Countries*, various issues.

Nicaragua was resumed in 1989, at first as assistance to UNO (the National Opposition Union), a coalition of opposition parties which defeated the Sandinista government in 1990. According to Gary Prevost, 'the 14-party UNO coalition was brought together under the auspices of the US embassy'.[18]

In June 1986, the International Court of Justice (ICJ) found that the United States had committed a multitude of breaches of international law.[19] The eight-year armed conflict had been fuelled by US support for the *contras*. The ICJ 1986 judgement obliged the United States to make reparations to Nicaragua, whose estimate of the amount due had been placed at $15 billion. The judgement could not be enforced, however, because the United States vetoed a proposed Security Council resolution. General Assembly resolutions recommended but could not enforce US compliance.[20] In September 1991 the changed government of Nicaragua stopped seeking enforcement, following a bilateral agreement with the United States aimed at enhancing Nicaragua's economic, commercial and technical development.[21]

US aid to Nicaragua following the 1990 elections remained enmeshed in internal politics. There was continued pressure to cleanse the new government of Sandinistas, and settle claims against Nicaragua by US citizens whose property had been expropriated during the Sandinista regime. In August 1993 the US again suspended aid to Nicaragua because Nicaragua was harbouring international terrorism.[22] Such incidents were a sideshow, as Nicaragua slid off the international political agenda with the electoral defeat of the Sandinistas in 1990 and the victory of Arnoldo Alemán in the subsequent elections.

Then came Hurricane Mitch and history repeated itself. In a previous era, the aid that followed the earthquake that had destroyed most of Managua in 1972 had been misappropriated by Anastasio Somosa. His demise had been hastened by the ensuing protest. Somewhat similarly, President Alemán was accused of excluding regions supportive of the Sandinistas in the distribution of aid that followed Hurricane Mitch.[23] Hurricane Mitch represented an unrepeatable opportunity, 'a dramatic, photogenic natural disaster,'[24] to place Nicaragua back on the agenda, at

---

[18] Prevost, G. – The Nicaraguan revolution – six years after the Sandinista electoral defeat, *Third World Quarterly*, vol. 17, 1996, p. 310.

[19] The Court found the United States responsible for a series of breaches of international law, including its own military actions against Nicaragua, such as the mining of its ports and territorial waters, but not for actions by the *contras*, arguing that these could not be imputed to the United States. This is discussed in Gibney, M., Tomaševski, K. and Vedsted-Hansen, J. – Transnational state responsibility for violations of human rights, *Harvard Human Rights Journal*, vol. 12, Spring 1999, pp. 267–295.

[20] General Assembly resolution 42/231 of 12 May 1988.

[21] Security Council does not adopt text calling for compliance with International Court ruling regarding Nicaraguan case, *UN Chronicle*, vol. 24, No. 1, February 1987, pp. 62–63; the letters of the two governments and the ICJ order on the discontinuance of proceedings in *Nicaragua v. United States* have been reproduced in *International Legal Materials*, vol. 31, 1992, pp. 103–106.

[22] Rillaerts, S. – Menaces d'extreme droite sur le Nicaragua, *Le monde diplomatique*, September 1994, p. 3.

[23] Gunson, P. et al. – Apocalypse now in fragile democracies, *Guardian Weekly*, 15 November 1998.

[24] Debt relief for central America (editorial), *The Economist*, 14 November 1998.

least for its disproportionately heavy debt burden. Although aid has constituted close to half of Nicaragua's GDP, most of it has been used for debt servicing and it therefore did not have much of an impact in the country. The disadvantage of photogenic natural disasters is that they are soon forgotten, and Nicaragua slid back into oblivion.

ARGENTINA

Argentina's 'dirty war' in 1976–83 became an object of immense international mobilisation amongst NGOs, but the response of inter-governmental organisations was muted. The Inter-American Commission on Human Rights encountered opposition within the OAS and similar obstacles hampered the United Nations.

The military takeover in 1976 introduced repression that was dubbed *guerra sucia* (dirty war), the very term which had been utilized by the army to justify repression against an assumed threat of communist and/or terrorist insurgency. Argentina's military government exploited its diplomatic and commercial support as well as the defence-against-communism slogan to full advantage in resisting placement on the violations-agenda by the United Nations. Consequently, a thematic procedure had to be created so as to enable the United Nations to tackle a government with too many friends amongst its peers.

The dirty war (1976–83) was initiated through a military coup and ended after the defeat of the Argentinian military in the Falklands/Malvinas war. The ensuing repression was typified in the practice of disappearances. The Never Again *(Nunca más)* book[25] retroactively described how the dirty war was fought, and in so doing became a precedent later followed by truth commissions in many other countries.

Most disappearances took place during the first the two years after the 1976 military coup, when the Carter administration had just came into office and declared its policy of cutting off military and development aid to regimes whose human rights performance matched a definition of institutionalised violations. However well Argentina fitted the definition, sanctions were negligible, as has been mentioned in Chapter 4. The promise of human rights in foreign policy thus encountered its first test – repression was open, widespread, brutal and well documented while Argentina was a recipient of US aid. In February 1977, US military aid to Argentina was reduced by more than half, from $48 to $15 million[26] and five months later Congress banned military aid to Argentina. This gesture actually followed Argentina's announcement that it would not accept any military aid from the United States, in protest against aid decreases and their linkage with human rights.[27]

---

[25] *Nunca Mas (Never Again). A Report by Argentina's National Commission on Disappeared People*, Faber and Faber & Index on Censorship, Boston and London, 1986.

[26] Lillich, R.B. – *International Human Rights. Problems of Law, Policy and Practice*, Little, Brown and Company, Boston, 1991, Second Edition, pp. 977–1013.

[27] Congressional Research Service – Human rights and foreign assistance: Experiences and issues in policy implementation (1977–78), Report prepared for the U.S. Senate Committee on Foreign Relations, November 1979, p. 106.

US economic aid was even more difficult to tackle. Since Argentina was hardly dependent on economic aid, which amounted to less than 1% of its GNP, a threat to cut off that aid would not have been much of a deterrent. US representatives in multilateral banks did not vote in favour of Argentina's applications for loans, but this did not stop their approval, as neither did they vote against. US export credits for Argentina created a short-lived controversy. US companies keen on contracts facilitated by export credits successfully lobbied for a legislative change. Thus, as of 1978, non-commercial reasons could only be used to deny export credits if the President determined that such denials would be in the national interest.[28]

The European Parliament condemned human rights violations in Argentina in July 1976 and advocated diplomatic rather than economic sanctions. A suspension of aid was suggested as late as 1980. The reason was, simply, that there was too little EUrope's aid to cut off, while the Commission's view was (rightly, as it happened) that trade agreements could not be suspended on human rights grounds.[29]

Similarly to the United States and Europe, difficulties in forging a response to abuses by Argentina's military government paralysed the United Nations and the Organization of American States. Iain Guest's book *Behind the Disappearances* was facilitated after transitions to civilian rule in Argentina and Uruguay furnished access to many background documents. Both new governments decided that UN archives could be opened. Much had been known about abuses, but next to nothing was publicly known about the politics within the United Nations which impeded an effective international response. What was known from the official records was that Argentina had been discussed by the Sub-Commission in 1976, just after the military coup and at the very beginning of the dirty war. Thereafter Argentina disappeared into the confidential 1503 procedure[30] to reappear in 1980 as the

---

[28] Guest, I. – *Behind the Disappearances. Argentina's Dirty War Against Human Rights and the United Nations*, University of Pennsylvania Press, Philadelphia, 1990, p. 172.

[29] Thun, T. – Europe, human rights and Latin America, in Latin America Bureau – *The European Challenge. Europe's New Role in Latin America*, London, 1982, pp. 166–169.

[30] The Sub-Commission had reacted in 1976, three months after the military coup, to reported killings of refugees in Buenos Aires but also pointed out that the human rights of Argentinians appeared to be in jeopardy. Statements about human rights violations in Argentina were also made in 1977, 1978 and 1979 before the Commission on Human Rights by Austria, France, Canada and Sweden. The necessary votes for Argentina's condemnation were, however, not forthcoming. Much documentation has been processed under the 1503 procedure which, after it was retroactively made public, convincingly showed violations to have been gross and systematic. The Sub-Commission, however, voted in 1977 and 1978 in favour of Argentina, changing its mind in 1979 and forwarding the case to the Commission. The Working Group on Disappearances was established in 1980 because a condemnation of Argentina was politically impossible. The Commission's obstacles were, *inter alia*, support for Argentina beyond its own region, in Asia and Africa, but also an unusual like-mindedness of the Soviet Union and the United States. The former would have deemed Argentina's military government to be an ideological foe had it not been for commerce, especially grain imports; the latter's human rights policy (especially during the Carter Administration in 1976–80) would have nudged it towards seeking Argentina's condemnation had the government translated its policy into practice.

main – but unnamed – target of the newly established Working group on Disappearances.[31]

The combination of international and domestic pressures upon Argentina's military government led to a decrease in visible manifestations of its abuse of power. Argentinian diplomats of the time aimed 'to delay criticism of supposed violations of human rights in order to gain time and permit the necessary freedom of manoeuvre so as to bring the struggle against subversion to a happy conclusion.'[32] That diplomatic strategy was effective. When the Working Group on Disappearances was set up in 1980, disappearances had almost stopped. The Group was able to report that no disappearances had been reported from Argentina after December 1983.[33] Human rights problems do not disappear with the suppression of their visible and quantifiable manifestations, however. Attempts to bring victimisers to court have continued ever since, as have parallel efforts to codify the rights of victims.

The United Nations found a way of addressing violations in Argentina (if anonymously) in 1980, which coincided with the report on Argentina by the Inter-American Commission on Human Rights. Having received hundreds of complaints from Argentina, the Commission requested a visit so as to be able to study the situation *in situ*.[34] This visit took place in 1979 and became the basis of the Commission's 374-page report,[35] which proved that violations were systematic and serious. During its visit, the Commission received more than 5,000 additional complaints, having become ever more aware of the scope of victimisation when its announcement that it would interview victims' families filled the street with thousands of people.

The key word utilized by Argentine diplomats in defending their government was terrorism, and all allegations were rebutted by the necessity to combat terrorism. All the disappeared were retroactively labelled as terrorists. If this was impossible, the claim was that they had been killed by terrorists. Argentine military leaders believed in rule by force and in immunity bestowed by military power: 'If the Reich's troops had won the last world war the tribunal would have been held not in Nuremberg but in Virginia.'[36]

---

[31] The Commission was able to draw upon the General Assembly's resolution on disappearances of 1978, which addressed the issue without mentioning the country, and adopted on 29 February 1989, by consensus, resolution 20 (XXXVI) on the 'Question of missing or disappeared persons.' This resolution led to the appointment of a five-member Working Group, at first for one year, which was alerted to the need 'to carry out its work with discretion.'

[32] Guest, I. – *Behind the Disappearances. Argentina's Dirty War Against Human Rights and the United Nations*, University of Pennsylvania Press, Philadelphia, 1990, p. 106.

[33] Commission on Human Rights – Report of the Working Group on Enforced or Involuntary Disappearances, U.N. Doc. E/CN.4/1988/19 of 31 December 1987, para. 38.

[34] According to the peculiar rules of inter-governmental human rights work, the Commission has had to requested an invitation to visit from the respective government. The invitation from Argentina came through in 1977, whereby the government tried to constrain the Commission's work in the country to a review of laws, only to agree to a visit on the Commission's terms almost two years later.

[35] Inter-American Commission on Human Rights – Report on the Situation of Human Rights in Argentina, Doc. OEA/Ser.L/V/II. Doc. 49, corr. 19, 11 April 1980.

[36] *Clarin* (Buenos Aires), 22 March 1981.

Subsequent governments in Argentina have gone through the stages of re-writing the history of the dirty war, making small dents into the victimisers' impunity, and thus demonstrating that the world has improved since the times when might was right. The Inter-American Commission on Human Rights has come to the aid of victims' families and human rights activists trying to combat amnesty (derived from Greek *amnestia*, best translated as oblivion). Self-amnesties by military regimes have been declared by the Commission to 'have no juridical validity.'[37] After it had faulted self-amnesty laws in Uruguay, Argentina and El Salvador,[38] two governments (Argentina and Uruguay) asked the Inter-American Court of Human Rights for an advisory opinion on the Commission's competence to assess the compatibility of national with international law. The Court reaffirmed the Commission's competence.[39]

HAITI

Haiti, a small, poor island country, is a textbook case in which sanctions should be effective and indeed have been imposed many times. It is dependent on the outside world for aid as well as for imports of food and fuel.

The 1991–94 sanctions, aimed at ousting a military government, were neither the first nor the last. Aid was cut off many times by individual governments because of human rights violations in 1986–90, and was not fully resumed after the legitimate government was re-instituted in 1994 because of, *inter alia*, Haiti's failure to carry out privatisation.

Haiti was on the UN violations-agenda in 1981–87. After the departure of 'Baby Doc' (Jean-Claude Duvalier) in 1986, a UN human rights expert was nominated to assist the first post-Duvalier government in the 'full restoration of human rights', but was prevented from carrying out this task.[40] The United Nations switched back to documenting violations in 1992, and Haiti was again moved to the assistance-agenda in 1996. An expert was nominated to provide assistance to the government but his mandate also included assessments of Haiti's compliance with its human rights obligations.[41] This wavering has demonstrated the mismatch between

---

[37] Annual Report of the Inter-American Commission on Human Rights 1985–1986, OEA/Ser.L/V/II 68, Doc. 8, Rev.1 of 26 September 1986, p. 192.

[38] The complaints from El Salvador were examined in Report No. 26/92 of 24 September 1992, Uruguayan cases were examined in Report No. 26/92 of 2 October 1992, and Argentine cases were in Reports No. 28/92 and 29/92 of the same date.

[39] Inter-American Court of Human Rights – Certain attributes of the Inter-American Commission on Human Rights, Advisory Opinion OC-13/93 of 16 July 1993.

[40] Commission on Human Rights resolution 1987/13 of 2 March 1987, and Advisory Services in Human Rights: Report on Haiti, U.N. Doc. E/CN.4/1988/38 of 3 February 1988.

[41] Commission on Human Rights – Situation of human rights in Haiti, Report by Mr. Adama Dieng, independent expert, U.N. Doc. E/CN.4/1996/94 of 24 January 1996, para. 3.

expectations that countries can change overnight and the obstacles to change ingrained in Haiti's heritage.

Haiti was ruled by the Duvalier family from 1957 to 1986, first by François Duvalier ('Papa Doc') and after his death in 1971, by his son Jean-Claude ('Baby Doc'). US involvement in Haiti preceded the Duvalier regime. The United States had invaded Haiti in 1914, ruled it until 1934, and supported the Duvaliers until the very end of their rule. In January 1986, the United States announced that aid to Haiti would not continue because of human rights violations, and in February 1986 Jean-Claude Duvalier ('Baby Doc') left Haiti. The United States thereafter resumed aid and Haiti's improved human rights record was certified by the Reagan administration. The National Governing Council, which governed Haiti after Duvalier's departure, did not, however, fulfil the standards represented by that certificate. It was supposed to facilitate the transition to an elected government, but bloodshed instead ensued. Killings encompassed presidential candidates and voters, culminating in November 1987 when elections were scheduled to take place. The United States again suspended aid. Canada did not, it protested against the complicity of Haitian authorities in the killings, but decided against suspending aid in order not to 'punish the people of Haiti for the actions of its government.'[42] The aftermath of Duvaliers' family rule was not marked by progress towards respect of human rights; rather, deterioration in the human rights situation ensued, aid cutoffs proliferated, the human rights situation deteriorated further to be followed by further aid cutoffs.

The *Washington Post* criticised the practice of suspending and resuming aid in a typical *Gringo's light switch* pattern, and argued that 'a better strategy is to increase aid and to do as much as outsiders can do to improve the conditions of life, while continuing to keep the money entirely away from the Haitian government and the Army.'[43] *The Economist* joined the choir, pointing out that 'the poor in the sodden slums will start to die'[44] as the consequence of donors' punitiveness. Besides stopping aid whenever consecutive governments misbehaved, donors were also criticised for inappropriate aid. More than 75% was spent in the capital, Porte-au-Prince, and much was wasted through rampant misappropriation, dubbed *kleptocracy.*[45]

Aid to Haiti was again stopped in response to the military coup in September 1991, which ended the first part of Jean Bertrand Aristide's presidency. The OAS/UN-supervised elections were duly proclaimed free and fair, 'with exemplary participation by political parties and the electorate in a historical break with a past

---

[42] Haiti: the election drowned in blood, *The Economist*, 5 December 1987, p. 65.
[43] How to help Haiti, editorial, *The Washington Post*, 21 June 1988.
[44] At the bottom of the barrel, *The Economist*, 9 January 1988, p. 56.
[45] Riddell, R. – *Foreign Aid Reconsidered*, Johns Hopkins University Press & James Currey, London, 1987, p. 255.

of electoral fraud.'[46] Although Aristide had been elected by a vast majority, a former military ruler, Henri Namphy, said that there was only one vote which counted in Haiti and that was the army's.[47] President Aristide was re-instituted by the US/UN military intervention in October 1994, proving Namphy's prophecy even though the army was foreign rather than Haitian. The path towards this military intervention led through sanctions.

Table 6.4 shows aid to Haiti in 1984–1995, listing major bilateral and multi-lateral donors. Its ebb and flow corresponds to political developments. There was a slight increase in 1987, when hopes for a smooth and swift transition from Duvalier-dictatorship to post-Duvalier democracy were alive. This was followed by a downswing in 1992, when aid was suspended in response to the military coup, and finally, by a huge increase in 1994, coinciding with the US/UN military intervention.

The 1991 military coup was condemned by the Organization of American States (OAS) a day after it had taken place, and six days later the OAS urged all its members to freeze Haitian assets and impose a trade embargo.[48] The Aristide government had been able to secure aid commitments of $511 million,[49] but all aid was suspended after the military coup. The OAS and the UN called for non-recognition of the military regime, dubbed *defactos*.[50] That call was heeded with the exception of the Vatican (Holy See).[51] Vatican's exceptionalism was retaliation for Aristide's endorsement of liberation theology and his confrontation with the Haitian army and the Catholic Church.[52] The OAS was meeting in emergency sessions, sending missions to Haiti, calling for strict enforcement of sanctions. The hope was that cutting off oil would nudge the military to step down because it would run out of fuel. On the contrary, the military was later described as 'awash in gasoline and profits.'[53]

The Security Council's sanctions followed the light-switch model: it imposed sanctions in June 1993, suspended them in August 1993, and re-imposed them in October 1993.[54] The imposition of sanctions had to be preceded by a finding that

---

[46] United Nations press release SG/SM/4531, 17 December 1990.

[47] Gold, H. – Haitian cleptocrats and their jackals, as usual, *International Herald Tribune*, 22 September 1988.

[48] Organization of American States – *Report on the Situation of Human Rights in Haiti*, Washington D.C., March 1993, pp. 3–4.

[49] Aristide, J.-B. – To refloat Haiti, throw the coup regime overboard, *The Washington Post*, 12 January 1993.

[50] The term *defactos* was developed in the United States as a neutral reference to Haiti's military government, referring to them being a *de facto* rather than legally recognised government.

[51] Alaux, J.-P. – Haïti à bout d'espérance. Quinze mois de dictature militaire, *Le monde diplomatique*, January 1993, pp. 26–27.

[52] Commission on Human Rights – Report on the human rights situation in Haiti by Mr. Marco Tulio Bruni Celli, U.N. Doc. E/CN.4/1992/50 of 31 January 1992, para. 174 (c).

[53] Booth, C. – Haiti: The bad embargo joke, *Time,* 21 March 1994, pp. 34–36.

[54] Security Council resolutions 841 of 16 June 1993, and 875 of 16 October 1993.

Table 6.4: Aid to Haiti, 1984–95
(in million $)

Donor	1984	1985	1987	1989	1990	1991	1992	1993	1994	1995
USA	41.0	54.0	92.0	68.0	50.0	66.0	38.0	57.0	541.0	376.0
France	4.8	20.2	19.3	27.3	32.1	36.6	16.0	17.9	10.1	25.1
Canada	8.0	6.0	8.9	9.1	10.4	12.8	9.4	14.6	14.9	18.4
Germany	8.0	7.7	10.7	14.4	12.8	8.0	21.5	3.8	1.6	6.4
European Union	5.1	4.1	4.5	20.8	20.8	12.9	12.6	10.0	13.6	85.8
IDA/IBRD	28.9	21.8	45.6	10.0	12.0	8.0	0.2	0.0	0.0	39.4
IDB	16.2	10.7	2.4	9.9	11.7	6.7	0.5	0.0	−15.5	67.4
UNDP	4.8	4.1	5.8	8.6	11.9	7.2	3.6	4.9	2.3	12.4
Total bilateral aid	71.2	94.5	143.8	138.0	114.7	125.8	91.0	92.5	592.3	498.0
EU&member states	24.9	30.1	34.0	66.4	68.3	48.6	53.9	29.7	34.7	173.8
Total multilateral aid	63.9	50.3	68.0	61.2	66.4	42.0	24.7	27.1	4.2	221.0

Note: Only the biggest bilateral and multilateral donors are included hence figures do not add up to total aid.
Source: OECD – *Geographical Distribution of Financial Flows to Developing Countries*, various issues.

international peace and security had been jeopardised. As a military coup with no visible international involvement or ripple effects, except for Haitians seeking refuge in the United States, the Council was careful to emphasise, twice, that the situation was unique and exceptional.[55]

Similarly to the Security Council, the United States was oscillating between imposing and enforcing, strengthening and weakening economic sanctions against Haiti. The United States had condemned the 1991 military coup and acquiesced to the OAS sanctions. This was closely observed[56] because there had been speculation about its involvement in that coup. Christophe Wargny argued that the coup had been organised with the acquiescence of the CIA and the US embassy in Port-au-Prince.[57] Four months after OAS sanctions had been imposed, the United States eased sanctions and then strengthened them again in May 1994. The sanctions included travel restrictions against 600 military officers who had allegedly participated in the 1991 coup. In June 1994, the United States banned commercial air traffic as well as financial transactions affecting 83 individuals and 35 Haitian institutions presumed to be *de facto* power-holders. The military was not weakened by the sanctions, however, one reason being the 'one ton of cocaine [passing through Haiti] each month from Colombia to the U.S.'[58] Additional sanctions followed in 1994 and were enforced by a naval blockade. Their effects could not materialise, however, because too little time elapsed between these sanctions and the subsequent US/UN military intervention.

Designing sanctions to protect the civilian population while inflicting harm upon its wrongdoing government is difficult even in theory. The UN Secretary-General at the time, Boutros Boutros-Ghali, concluded that the sanctions had not affected at all Haiti's 'mafia of racketeers.'[59] Sanctions are based on a trickle-up assumption: economic hardship hurts the most vulnerable but is expected to trickle upwards to power-holders. The first part worked out as intended and the poor were further impoverished. Much as in all other cases, the second part did not, and sanctions

---

[55] United Nations – Security Council resolution 841 (1993) of 16 June 1993.

[56] The United States was also closely observed with regard to the exodus of Haitians. This was an object of dispute during the Bush-Clinton electoral contest and policy changed after the Clinton administration took office in 1993. President-to-be Clinton's opposition to denying asylum to fleeing Haitians had received publicity and so did his reversal. Asylum was allowed in June 1995, produced a mass exodus, and was again reversed.

[57] Wargny, C. – Haïti so la férule de Washington et du FMI, *Le monde diplomatique*, July 1996, p. 28.

[58] U.S. Plans to ease embargo against Haiti, despite OAS displeasure, *International Herald Tribune*, 6 February 1992; Key accord on Haiti embargo: Island neighbour vows to plug border leaks, *International Herald Tribune*, 27 May 1994; US changes gear on Haiti sanctions, *Guardian Weekly*, 8 May 1994; Walker, M. – Clinton still talking tough on Haiti, *Guardian Weekly*, 19 June 1994; Smolowe, J. – Haiti: With friends like these, *Time*, 8 November 1993, p. 58.

[59] *The United Nations and Haiti, 1990–1996*, The Blue Series, United Nations, New York, 1997, para. 9.

never trickled up to hurt *defactos*. In order to make the powerful an explicit target of sanctions, their individualization is the obvious remedy. The switch to the individualisation of sanctions led to freezing the financial assets of Haiti's military elite, as authorised by Security Council's resolution 841 of 16 June 1993. That planned switch did not materialise, however, because *defactos* were subsequently promised all their assets in exchange for relinquishing formal power and leaving Haiti to open the way for US/UN military intervention.[60]

As is customary, sanctions against Haiti exempted humanitarian relief. Food and medicine should have been available, but public services that could have delivered relief had all collapsed. Moreover, people did not have money to buy food or medication. A UN report thus concluded that the humanitarian exemption did not achieve its purpose.[61] A study of sanctions against Haiti found fault with their very design:

(1) sanctions were tightened and loosened in a haphazard and inefficient manner;
(2) they did not appear to have an impact on the ruling elite;
(3) there was no monitoring of the effects of sanctions on the population;
(4) neither the OAS nor the UN elaborated a policy for prohibited targets and/or effects of sanctions.[62]

An additional reason why food or medicine could not reach the needy was that humanitarian goods could not be transported. Because of the oil embargo, fuel was available only on the army-controlled black market. The extent to which the sanctions worsened the survival prospects of the poorest was amply documented and critics concluded that sanctions 'killed more people than the military.'[63]

The US/UN military intervention to re-institute the Aristide government killed few people. It conformed to the practice of the Security Council acquiescing to a military intervention by a veto-wielding member within the latter's sphere of interest and at its own expense. The Security Council similarly endorsed the French military intervention in Rwanda or the Russian intervention in Georgia (Abkhazia). *The Washington Post* commented:

[60] Bardacke, T. – Haitian military's assets protected, *Financial Times*, 14 October 1994.
[61] United Nations – Report of the Secretary-General on efforts to resolve the Haitian crisis, U.N. Doc. A/47/599 of 3 November 1992, paras. 44–97.
[62] Simunovic, M. – Sanctions studies pose dilemmas, *PHR Record*, vol. 7, No. 1, Winter/Spring 1994, pp. 14–15.
[63] Barnes, E. – Sanctions and spoons. Aimed at defiant military leaders, the U.N. embargo is causing the starvation of many young children, *Time,* 22 November 1993, p. 42.

Amazingly, Clinton went to the United Nations for approval of military action inside our Western Hemisphere 'sphere of influence,' but evaded Congress-because he knew support was lacking.[64]

This support was lacking because the US/UN military intervention was controversial. Besides Congress, the then-president Aristide – the apparent beneficiary – did not endorse it, nor did the Organization of American States. The cost for the United States was estimated at $765 million.[65] The force was three times the size of Haiti's entire army, a murky Carter-Cedras agreement preceded its deployment, and the intervention was proudly described as a success because no American lives were lost.

The contents of the agreement negotiated between former US President Jimmy Carter and *defactos*, which preceded the US/UN military intervention, is unknown, although parts were revealed in the media and retrospectively clarified through subsequent events. Dante Caputo, the Special UN Envoy to Haiti, resigned in protest.[66] The agreement reportedly unfroze the assets of *defactos*, an additional financial incentive consisted of advance payments of rental for the villas that they could not take along. US-supplied charter flights took them into exile in Panama and the United States.[67] Haiti's Parliament was convened in October 1994 under US/UN military protection to adopt an amnesty law and secure impunity for *defactos*. Marco Tulio Bruni Celli, then UN Special Rapporteur on Haiti, noted that 'the scope and consequences of this legal instrument are not clearly established.'[68] *The Economist* clarified: 'The Carter-Cedras agreement offered an 'honourable retirement' to Haiti's military dictators, effective once Haiti's parliament had passed an amnesty law.'[69] Five months after that agreement, Jimmy Carter's visit to Haiti had been anticipated as an occasion for him to receive 'a hero's welcome' for 'one of his greatest diplomatic triumphs'. Rather, he found 'the capital covered with graffiti insulting him and no official representative of the government to greet him.'[70]

Foreign and international involvement in the various stages of Haiti's recent history is unlikely to become an object of in-depth accounting. Moreover, the very foreign involvement has impeded an accounting of the most recent period of repression in Haiti. The Commission on Truth and Justice was established to tackle 'the

---

[64] Broder, D.S. – Clinton hostage to Haiti's fortunes, *The Washington Post*, reprinted in *Guardian Weekly*, 2 October 1994.

[65] Schmitt, E. – U.S. plans to declare Haiti 'stable' and shift military authority to UN, *International Herald Tribune*, 16 January 1995.

[66] Tran, M. – Angry UN envoy quits in protest over Carter pact, *The Guardian*, 21 September 1994.

[67] Bardecke, T. – Haitian military's assets protected, *Financial Times*, 14 October 1994.

[68] Commission on Human Rights – Situation of human rights in Haiti. Report submitted by Mr. Marco Tulio Bruni Celli, Special Rapporteur, U.N. Doc. E/CN.4/1995/59 of 6 February 1995, para. 8.

[69] The nightmare next door, *The Economist*, 24 September 1994.

[70] Rohter, L. – Haitians give Carter a chilly reception, *International Herald Tribune*, 25–26 February 1995.

existence, both past and present, of paramilitary groups and unlawful private armed groups operating with complete impunity, under the protection of the State, and systematically committing politically-motivated crimes.'[71] The Commission's report *Si M Pa Reve* (*If I don't cry out*) reflected its limited access to information. Indeed, one of the notorious para-military organisations, FRAPH (*Front révolutionnaire armé du peuple haïtien*) remained beyond its reach. There were two reasons. Firstly, the United States was reported to have reached a secret settlement with FRAPH's leader, granting him a right to stay in the United States and immunity from prosecution. Secondly, US army took all archives from the FRAPH headquarters (allegedly 160,000 pages) to the United States.[73] An attempt to prevent the disclosure of assumed US complicity seemed the obvious reason. Perhaps it was not by coincidence that the Security Council subsequently advocated national reconciliation for Haiti. The Council welcomed President Aristide's return and urged the people of Haiti to 'consolidate democracy in a spirit of national reconciliation,' to assert later that the people of Haiti bore the sole responsibility for achieving reconciliation.[74]

A conflict between different foreign policy concerns came under the spotlight in the United States because of those airlifted documents. The United States was the principal donor to reform of Haiti's administration of justice, thus nominally committed to making Haiti's judiciary independent and empowering it to tackle abuses of power, especially by the government. A promised return of documents, related to the most recent period of gross abuse of power, was conditioned on their remaining secret or on US removal of all identifying information that might be damaging to American individuals or interests.[75]

Aid suspensions did not stop with President Aristide's return to Haiti nor after the series of elections that followed. Parliamentary elections were held in June and presidential elections in December 1995; another round of parliamentary elections followed in April 1997 and local elections in June 1997. Differences in their assessment became painfully visible. One end of the spectrum was represented by self-

---

[71] The National Commission on Truth and Justice was established by a presidential decision in March 1995 and submitted its report in February 1996, just as president Aristide was leaving office. Its report does not seem to have been disseminated, while its terms of reference were listed in Haiti's summary report to the Human Rights Committee, U.N. Doc. CCPR/C/105 of 28 February 1995, paras. 25–26.

[73] Human Rights Watch/Americas – Haiti: Thirst for Justice, Human Rights Watch/Americas Reports, vol. 8, No. 7 (B), Washington, D.C., September 1996, pp. 17 and 25–26.

[74] United Nations – Security Council resolutions 948 (1994) of 15 October 1994 and 975 (1995) of 30 January 1995, preamble. Brazil abstained from resolution 948 in disagreement with the US-led military intervention. China abstained from resolution 975, recording its disagreement with the planned deployment of foreign military and police officers. Both Brazil and China abstained from resolution 940 (1994) which endorsed the US-led military intervention in Haiti.

[75] United Nations – Situation of human rights in Haiti. Report by Mr. Adama Dieng, Independent Expert, U.N. Doc. E/CN.4/1997/89 of 7 February 1997, paras. 35–38.

congratulation. The Security Council spoke about 'the complete consolidation of democracy in Haiti,'[76] *The New York Times* said that 'thanks to the United States and other countries [Haiti] is now a democracy.'[77] Another end of the spectrum was reflected in electoral participation, which diminished with each subsequent election to sink as low as 5% in 1997.[78]

Even if all these elections led towards a democracy, they would not have enabled Haitians to survive nor would they have enabled Haiti to service its foreign debt. Marco Tulio Bruni Celli, UN Special Rapporteur on Haiti at the time, expressed in 1995 his concern about 'the slowness of international co-operation programmes'. Donors had been fast in cutting off aid and slow in resuming it. When resumed, aid tended to concentrate on elections or policing, and at a high price, since most work was done by expatriates financed out of aid from their own countries. Bruni Celli noted that pledged aid added up to $1.2 billion,[79] but pledges have not been converted to disbursements. The mandate of his successor, Adama Dieng, included verification of Haiti's compliance with its human rights obligations.[80] The question of Haiti's ability to meet their costs, with aid expected to finance 70% of the budget but not furnished, was not discussed. Aid was held up because privatisation was opposed by parliament while donors had made it a condition for resuming aid, or later because the whole government came to a standstill.[81] The year 1999 was marked by consecutive postponements of a fresh round of elections that were due to take place with most aid still suspended, and the government without resources to suppress and prevent crime and violence.[82] Summing up, one can diagnose conflicting foreign policies as described by Richard Falk:

---

[76] United Nations – Security Council resolution 1007(1995) of 31 July 1995, preamble.

[77] Keep helping Haiti (leader), *The New York Times*, reprinted in *International Herald Tribune*, 9 April 1997.

[78] Preval wins in Haiti amid voter apathy, *International Herald Tribune*, 20 December 1995; Crosskill, H. – Presidents in poverty, *The World Today*, vol. 52, No. 2, February 1996, p. 37; Haitians scorn polls, *The Washington Post*, reprinted in *Guardian Weekly*, 13 April 1997; Democracy, Haiti-style, *The Economist*, 7 June 1997; Cassen, B. – Haïti dans la spirale du désespoir, *Le monde diplomatique*, October 1997.

[79] United Nations – Situation of human rights in Haiti. Report submitted by Mr. Marco Tulio Bruni Celli, Special Rapporteur, U.N. Doc. E/CN.4/1995/59 of 6 February 1995, paras. 21–23.

[80] United Nations – Situation of human rights in Haiti, resolution 1996/58 of the Commission on Human Rights of 19 April 1996.

[81] Lippman, T.W. – U.S. delays economic aid to Haiti, *International Herald Tribune*, 11–12 November 1995; Farah, D. – Uncertainties cloud Haiti's democracy, *The Washington Post*, reprinted in *Guardian Weekly*, 3 December 1995; Haiti: Help wanted: One government, *The Economist*, 25 July 1998.

[82] Kovaleski. S. – Getting the message from Haiti's urban scrawl, *Guardian Weekly*, 11–17 November 1999; Haitians turn their back on President Preval – and politics, *The Economist*, 4 December 1999.

The potentially adverse impact of intervention on the goals of the intervening side highlights the contradictory nature of simultaneously promoting democracy (which is likely to generate economic nationalism in poor countries victimized by exploitative foreign investors) and the protection of property and economic rights of these investors.[83]

EL SALVADOR

El Salvador was governed in 1956–79 by a succession of military regimes. Civil war followed in 1980–92, and extensive UN involvement in peacemaking in 1992–96, after which El Salvador was taken off international human rights agenda. Micheal Czerny's 1992 prediction came through. He voiced fear 'that the war is El Salvador's last link to the world and, once it is over, the country will sink into oblivion of an indistinguishable poverty in which all human rights are abused indiscriminately.'[84]

Following a military coup in 1979 and the ensuing repression, the FMLN (*Frente Farabundo Martí para la Liberación Nacional*) was formed in1980 and warfare started. The United States supported the government, deeming the FMLN a replica of the *Sandinistas* in the neighbouring Nicaragua, who had come to power just one year earlier and were accused of supporting the FMLN. US aid to El Salvador was estimated at $4 billion in 1980–91,[85] which translates into an annual $100 per capita for this tiny country. Contrary to what this average suggests, the population did not benefit because aid was directed towards the army.

The war was terminated through a protracted process of peace-making from 1990 until 1995, which also led to a truth commission,[86] elections, and to international support to bridge the abyss from institutionalised denial of human rights

---

[83] Falk, R. – The Haiti intervention: A dangerous world order precedent for the United Nations, *Harvard International Law Journal,* vol. 36, No. 2, Spring 1995, p. 348.

[84] Czerny, M.F. – Liberation theology and human rights, in Mahoney, K.L. and Mahoney, P. (eds.) – *Human Rights in the Twenty-first Century: A Global Challenge*, Martinus Nijhoff Publishers, Dordrecht, 1993, p. 34.

[85] Americas Watch – *El Salvador's Decade of Terror*, New York, 1991, Appendix A, p. 141.

[86] The Truth Commission was established on the basis of peace agreements but was international in stature, being under the auspices of the United Nations. It was also foreign in composition, composed of 'three scholars from other countries,' according to their self-description. The Commission had a double task – to clarify serious acts of violence in 1980–91 and to tackle impunity. The Commission's investigative work was based on confidentiality for all witnesses and documents. Its moved from institutional to individual responsibility and identified military and civilian officials who were, as sanction, recommended for dismissal and a 10-year ban on holding public office. The Commission tried to identify the perpetrators of specific abuses and also to discern the command control as high upwards in the Salvadoran power structure as it could reach, but it did not extend its remit beyond El Salvador to foreign involvement.

towards the rule of law and civilian control over the military. Much as with other countries, El Salvador was taken off the international human rights agenda in 1996 and left to build this bridge on its own.

The uninterrupted political, financial and military support provided by the United States to consecutive Salvadoran governments throughout previous decades suggests US complicity in human rights violations. Only on few occasions was US aid suspended. In December 1983, an announcement was made that aid would stop unless killings by death squads diminished, and indeed they did,[87] to increase after aid was resumed. Such practice earned human rights conditionality the label of *Gringo's light switch*.

If US military aid has been widely denounced because it is more than likely that it facilitated human rights violations, it has been assessed by its proponents as 'one of the outstanding successes of the U.S. intervention in El Salvador.'[88] A dark side of that success was revealed in efforts to clarify the well-publicised killing of four American churchwomen in 1980. The US-based Lawyers Committee for Human Rights protested against the denial of access to information in the United States, which it suspected has been shielding a military cover-up. US residence granted to one of El Salvador's military officers implicated in killing of the four American churchwomen[89] increased those suspicions.

Alongside its military component, US aid supported elections. Many took place in South America after democracy had been substituted for the previous human rights conditions. This 1982 shift in US aid policy was dubbed the *Reagan doctrine*.[90] El Salvador furnished field-testing for this doctrine and the observers' reports on the 1982 and 1984 elections differed. The elections were praised by the US government and criticised by NGOs, while the United Nations Commission on Human Rights jointed the critics.[91] An NGO description of the elections has illustrated the type of objections that were voiced:

> On election day, multifaceted fraud took over. While voting appeared more or less normal in central San Salvador – where the majority of OAS and other international observers set up shop – it was a different story in poor neighbourhoods and rural areas. The intimidating presence of the military was everywhere.

---

[87] Lawyers Committee for Human Rights – *From the Ashes. A Report on Justice in El Salvador*, New York, 1987, p. 3–4.

[88] Evans, E. – El Salvador's lessons for future U.S. interventions, *World Affairs*, vol. 160, No. 1, Summer 1997, p. 47.

[89] Lawyers Committee for Human Rights – El Salvador: The case of four American churchwomen, media alerts of 24 June and 1 July 1998.

[90] Louis Henkin described the Reagan Doctrine as 'a claim of the right to intervene by force in another state to preserve or impose democracy.' Henkin, L. – The use of force: Law and U.S. Policy, in: Henkin, L. et al. – *Right v. Might. International Law and the Use of Force*, Council on Foreign Relations Press, New York and London, 1989, p. 44.

[91] Kamminga, M.T. – *Inter-State Accountability for Violations of Human Rights*, University of Pennsylvania Press, Philadelphia, 1992, pp. 98–99.

The process of issuing voter registration cards had bogged down to the point where, a few days before the election, the government succumbed to popular pressure and said that people would be able to vote by presenting the receipt showing they had applied for a voting card. An estimated 10 percent of the people who went to vote, however, *with and without* voter registration cards, were unable to find their names on the voting lists, and therefore couldn't vote. In some cases, the posted lists differed from the lists at the voting booth itself; supposedly they were carbon copies.[92]

The *Reagan doctrine* was found by Larry Diamond to have favoured formally elected civilian governments, disregarding the 'actual behaviour of the regime after the transition.'[93] This disregard also spanned the judiciary and USAID's programme aimed at reforming El Salvador's judiciary came under the scathing critique of US-based human rights organizations.[94] The Truth Commission also found that the judiciary allowed abuses to continue with impunity and suggested that it be completely overhauled. ONUSAL's findings were even more critical.[95] These retrospective assessments were made possible through a negotiated settlement, whose human rights components were facilitated and monitored by the United Nations until 1996.[96]

Despite dwindling international attention to El Salvador after the elections, efforts to clarify US complicity in abuses by previous regimes have intensified. Robert White, US ambassador to El Salvador in 1980–81, referred to his government's conduct at the time as 'one of the most disgraceful chapters in U.S. foreign policy.'[97] The extent of US involvement is gradually being revealed, step by step. In December 1981, the Salvadoran army killed between 500 and 750 peasants in El Mozote because their village was situated in a rebel-held area, hence they were assumed to have been supporters of the FMLN. Information on the massacre was publicised in US newspapers on 27 January 1992, but the very next day President Reagan certified to Congress that El Salvador was making a significant effort to comply with international human rights guarantees.[98]

---

[92] Jailer, T. – El Salvador: Another 'free and fair election', *Z Magazine*, Institute for Social and Cultural Communications, Boston, MA, May 1991, p. 27–28.

[93] Diamond, L. – *Promoting Democracy in the 1990s. Actors and Instruments, Issues and Imperatives*, A Report to the Carnegie Commission on Preventing Deadly Conflict, Carnegie Corporation of New York, December 1995, p. 53.

[94] Lawyers Committee on Human Rights – *Underwriting Injustice: USAID and El Salvador's Judicial Reform Program*, New York, April 1989.

[95] United Nations – From madness to hope: The 12-year war in El Salvador, Commission on the Truth for El Salvador, U.N. Doc. S/25500, 15 March 1993; Brody, R. – The United Nations and human rights in El Salvador's 'negotiated revolution', *Harvard Human Rights Journal*, vol. 8, 1995, p. 169–171.

[96] This is discussed in Tomaševski, K. – *Between Sanctions and Elections*, Pinter/Cassell, London, 1997, pp. 161–163.

[97] White, R.E. – The guilty men of Reagan years, *The Washington Post*, reprinted in *Guardian Weekly*, 26 January 1992.

[98] Danner, M. – *The Massacre at El Mozote*, Vintage Books, New York, 1994.

Early in peace-making, in September 1991, nine members of the armed forces were tried for the murder of six Jesuit priests: the Rector, Vice-Rector, Director of the Human Rights Institute, and three teachers at the Central American University. In addition, the priests' housekeeper and her daughter were killed in order to avoid leaving witnesses to the crime. The killings took place in November 1990, a time when the armed forces were faced with one of the strongest FMLN offensives. The killings created an international uproar, and a trial took place against the low-level officers who had carried out the killings, thus sheltering the upper strata of the military hierarchy and obscuring possible links to the civilian government of the time. Disappointments were therefore many, but it was the first time that military officers had been convicted for summary executions. Previous efforts had been forcefully resisted. People recalled that a judge who had presided over a trial of military officers suspected of kidnapping in 1988 was killed.[99] The 1991 trial pointed to a link with US military aid, although the trial itself could not address it:

> It is a stinging indictment of American policy that all of the soldiers who stood trial were products of U.S. military training. [That] explains why, a decade after the United States became heavily involved in El Salvador, the Salvadorean Army still does not understand why all those North Americans got so upset about the killing of a few priests.[100]

The Truth Commission's mention of US involvement was scant. It acknowledged that El Salvador was a victim of the Cold War and noted that peace negotiations became possible due to 'the recognition that the communism which had encouraged one side had collapsed, and perhaps also the disillusionment of the Power which had encouraged the other.'[101] That nameless Power was recognisable to all readers, as was the effort not to mention it.[102] This orientation conformed to the practice of previous truth commissions to 'domesticate' political accountability for abuses by previous regimes, excluding foreign involvement. The Commission attributed

---

[99] Prosecutors and judge will flee El Salvador, *International Herald Tribune*, 2 October 1991; Judge to quit El Salvador, *Guardian Weekly*, 6 October 1991.

[100] Arnson, C.J. – Bizarre justice in El Salvador, *The New York Times,* reprinted in *International Herald Tribune*, 4 October 1991.

[101] United Nations – Report of the Commission on the Truth for El Salvador: From Madness to Hope. The 12-year War in El Salvador, Annex to U.N. Doc. S/25500 of 1 April 1993, p. 10 and 172.

[102] The Commission's references to US involvement were confined to mentioning that US aid was suspended after the killing of four American churchwomen in 1980, and that aid was restored and increased in 1981. The Commission highlighted Vice-President Bush's 1983 visit as an illustration 'that United States diplomatic pressure could bring about a reduction in the number of violations'. US strategy at the time of the Truth Commission was to insist that the specific individuals named by the Commission be dismissed from their military or civilian duties, and the Commission duly emphasised the previous US pressure related to the trial of military officers who had raped and killed the four US churchwomen in 1984. Report of the Commission on the Truth for El Salvador, op. cit., p. 29, 31, 33 and 34.

specific abuses to the individual *Salvadoreños* who had carried them out or given orders. This found an echo in parallel domestic efforts to further limit accountability.

In January 1992, El Salvador's parliament adopted an amnesty law to encompass political crimes and crimes committed in connection with the armed conflict of 1980–91.[103] A response to the findings of the Truth Commission was postponed until its report could be finalized. Five days after the Commission had presented its report, parliament adopted another amnesty law. The United States suspended military aid until military officers responsible for gross abuses were dismissed from active service.[104]

Reed Brody, who had led ONUSAL's human rights programme, later pointed out that 'sustainable results of ONUSAL's presence would be seen in the institutions it would leave the country.'[105] Yet by 1996, only four UN human rights monitors remained in El Salvador. While the media reported the re-emergence of death squads,[106] El Salvador was taken off the international human rights agenda.

GUATEMALA

The Cold War was ushered into South America through the 1954 military coup, which also established three decades of military rule in Guatemala. Systematic human rights violations prevailed and thirty-six years of warfare ensued, with a human toll that will remain unknown, probably forever. Guatemala's Truth Commission (*Comisión de Esclarecimiento Histórico*, CEH) found that 'the aim of the perpetrators was to kill the largest number of group members possible' and the CEH could do no more than establish the number of major massacres and estimate that the number of people who had been killed was around 200,000.[107] As with other genocides, the individualisation of victims was impossible because the strategy had been elimination of the whole communities. All this happened with considerable US involvement,[108] which the CEH tackled by requesting access to US archives to obtain close to 1,000 documents in March 1998. Different from all other truth commissions, the CEH broadened its remit beyond Guatemala's borders.

---

[103] Kircher, I. – The human rights work of the United Nations Observer Mission in El Salvador, *Netherlands Quarterly of Human Rights*, 3/1992, p. 313–314.

[104] Truth will out, *The Economist*, 20 March 1993, p. 43–44.

[105] Brody, R. – The United Nations and human rights in El Salvador's 'negotiated revolution', *Harvard Human Rights Journal*, vol. 8, 1995, p. 169.

[106] Farah, D. – Violence plagues El Salvador, and El Salvador death squads reappear, *Guardian Weekly*, 24 March and 20 October 1996.

[107] *Guatemala: Memory of Silence. Report of the Commission for Historical Clarification*, Guatemala City, February 1999, para. 113. The text is available at http://hrdata.aaas.org/ceh/report.

[108] McClintock, M. – *The American Connection: State Terror and Popular Resistance in Guatemala*, Zed Press, London, 1985.

The investigative and condemnatory actions by UN human rights bodies look timid in retrospect. Guatemala was placed on the human rights agenda in 1979, a Special Rapporteur followed in 1983–85, and in 1986 Guatemala was taken off the violators-agenda to become a recipient of human rights assistance. This change followed the 1985 elections which re-introduced civilian government. A Law Group/WOLA (Washington Office for Latin America) electoral observer mission has thus explained the rationale for the 1985 elections:

The military's corporate interests required it to relinquish formal executive power in order to facilitate external aid [but there was doubt] as to whether the elections would lead to civilian control over the military or even over the non-military aspects of government.'[109]

The new Guatemalan government benefited from extensive international assistance in human rights education and training and in the setting up of various bodies with 'human rights' in their title. There was disagreement between the United Nations and NGOs, however; the latter were especially critical of Guatemala's transfer from the 'violators' to the 'assistance' agenda. The United Nations based its decision on 'the Government's firm political will to ensure respect for human rights.'[110] In contrast, NGOs doubted both the willingness and the capacity of that government to ensure respect for human rights:

The real power remains in the hands of the army and large landowners, and the Government has no interest, will or political power to clarify and investigate the situation of human rights violations in Guatemala.[111]

While the United Nations assisted the government, NGOs protested against abuses that continued with impunity, and objected to individual donors' aid to the military and the police as inappropriate and counterproductive.[112] After reviewing developments during the first years of that civilian government, Roger Plant has found 'an alarming escalation in political violence and a continuation of long-standing patterns of severe human rights violations.'[113]

---

[109] *The 1985 Guatemalan Elections: Will the Military Relinquish Power? Report of the Delegation sponsored by the International Human Rights Law Group and the Washington Office on Latin America*, Washington, D.C., December 1985, p. iv.

[110] United Nations – Advisory services in the field of human rights. Report by the expert on Guatemala, U.N. Doc. E/CN.4/1988/42 of 10 December 1987, para. 57.

[111] Report on human rights in Guatemala by Ernest Glinne, Jannis Sakellariou and Victoria Abellán, *Guatemala Human Rights Bulletin*, vol. 6, No. 32, March 1988, p. 5.

[112] *Political Transition and the Rule of Law in Guatemala. Report of the Follow-up Delegation of the International Human Rights Law Group and the Washington Office on Latin America*, Washington D.C., January 1988, p. v.

[113] Lawyers Committee for Human Rights – *Abandoning the Victims: The UN Advisory Services Program in Guatemala*, New York, February 1990, p. 1.

The second civilian government (1991–93) became a target of US sanctions because of a coup. A short-lived *autogolpe* (self-coup organized by the president himself) by president Serrano in 1993 was opposed not only by the United States but also by Guatemala's military because 'an overt grab for power would meet American objections and bring economic sanctions.'[114] The Clinton administration took considerable credit for upholding the statutory ban on aid to a regime that came to power through a coup. US aid was suspended and were GSP (Generalized System of Preferences) benefits.[115] Complemented with US negative votes for loans to Guatemala, these sanctions nudged Guatemala to quickly revert to its pre-coup regime. This reversal did not improve prospects for human rights; indeed, the civilian government of 1991–96 followed in the footsteps of the previous one (1986–91).

The United Nations also alternated between assistance and condemnation, appointing an Independent Expert in 1990, whose mandate combined the provision of assistance with reporting on violations. This was a hybrid solution, neither treating the government as violator nor merely providing assistance. In 1996, the government announced that it would continue receiving assistance but demanded that reporting on violations be stopped. The culmination of this sequence was the 1998 decision of the UN Commission on Human Rights, by consensus, to formally 'concluded its consideration of the human rights situation in Guatemala.'[116] The decision of the UN Commission on Human Rights to take Guatemala off the agenda was based on the findings of a mission whose mandate had been to assess whether further investigative and/or condemnatory action was necessary. It found that violations were still occurring on a large scale and were systematic, but they were no longer Guatemala's policy.[117] Just when the Commission on Human Rights had taken Guatemala off its agenda, Monsignor Juan Gerardi, the author of *Guatemala: Nunca Más* – a 1,400 page report documenting 55,021 apparent violations, mostly killings, during the previous three decades – was murdered. UN human rights officials condemned his killing,[118] but Guatemala remained off the agenda.

---

[114] Guatemala: On the brink, *The Economist*, 9 April 1994.

[115] Human Rights Watch/Americas – *Human Rights in Guatemala during President León Carpio's First Year*, June 1994, p. 114.

[116] Commission on Human Rights – Assistance to Guatemala in the field of human rights, resolution 1998/22 of 14 April 1998, para. 15.

[117] Commission on Human Rights – Assistance to Guatemala in the field of human rights. Report of the members of the Secretary-General's mission to Guatemala, Mr. Alberto Díaz Uribe, Mr. Diego García-Sayán and Mr. Yvon Le Bot, on the evaluation of the situation of human rights in Guatemala in the light of the implementation of the peace agreements, submitted in accordance with Commission on Human Rights resolution 1997/51, U.N. Doc. E/CN.4/1998/93 of 13 February 1998, para. 10.

[118] High Commissioner for Human Rights strongly condemns assassination of Monsignor Juan Gerardi Condera in Guatemala, and Chairman of Human Rights Commission condemns killing of Guatemala bishop, Press releases HR/98/30 and HR/98/31 of 28 and 29 April 1998.

US complicity in human rights violations in Guatemala can be traced to the US intervention in 1954, which set up 'an institutional structure built to violate human rights'[119] and strengthened it through US military aid. Congress prohibited further military aid to Guatemala in 1978 due to widely reported atrocities by the military. That ban was not implemented, however, and military aid was merely re-labelled.[120] In 1982, when the CEH ascertained that genocide had been taking place, the UN General Assembly called upon governments to refrain from providing military aid 'as long as violations continue to be reported'[121] but that call went similarly unheeded. US military aid was again suspended in 1990, yet it nevertheless continued, under a different guise, until 1994.[122]

Multiple links between the United States and Guatemala's military, which are being revealed slowly and gradually, provided some opportunities for initiating trials against individual military officers while they were in the United States. General Hector Gramajo, a former defence minister of Guatemala, was found responsible by US courts in nine cases of torture and summary executions and victims' families were granted $47.5 million punitive damages by US courts.[123] During his studies at the Kennedy School of Government at Harvard University, General Gramajo explained how he had improved Guatemala's development strategy: from the previous strategy of killing 100% of the rural population, his approach was to provide development for 70% and kill 30%.[124] General Gramajo was brought before a US court by US citizens. Other US-based efforts also focussed on victimised US citizens or their spouses.[125] The fate of Guatemalan victims without a US link remained beyond the pale. A comprehensive investigation into US complicity could implicate six former US presidents who may – or should have – known about abuses in Guatemala, including covert US operations, going back to the 1950s.[126]

The process of exposing abuses that were carried out during the past decades has generated a great deal of revulsion against previous silence. One reason for this silence was racism. Guatemala's indigenous majority was not recognised as such

---

[119] Herman, E.S. – The United States versus human rights in the Third World, *Harvard Human Rights Journal*, vol. 4, 1991, p. 91.

[120] Sikkink, K. – The effectiveness of US foreign policy, 1973–1980, in Whitehead, L. (ed.) – *The International Dimensions of Democratization. Europe and the Americas*, Oxford University Press, Oxford, 1996, p. 98.

[121] General Assembly resolution 38/100 of 16 December 1983.

[122] O'Shaughnessy, H. – UK to arm Guatemala regime of terror, *The Independent*, 13 October 1995.

[123] Daly, C.B. and Thomas, P. – $47.5m blow for Guatemalan general, *Guardian Weekly*, 23 April 1995.

[124] Guatemala: Let the trials begin, *The Economist*, 20 July 1991.

[125] Gomze, D. – The CIA in Guatemala, *Human Rights Tribune/Tribune des droits humains*, October/November 1995, pp. 19–21.

[126] Smith, J. – Priest, D. – U.S. embarrassed by Guatemala links, *The Washington Post*, reprinted in *Guardian Weekly*, 23 May 1995.

until the time of the peace treaties, nor were indigenous people the subjects of individual – let alone collective – rights. The Agreement on a Firm and Lasting Peace was signed on 29 December 1996 between the government and the URNG (*Unidad Revolucionaria Nacional Guatemalteca*)[127] and dotted with human rights guarantees. The funding needed to carry out the commitments made in peace agreements was estimated at $2.3–2.7 billion, out of which $1.5–1.7 was expected from donors.[128] The uncertain prospects for securing such large sums of money inspired the UN Commission on Human Rights to break its usual silence about the financial underpinning of human rights and a adopt an unusual statement, expressing its wish 'that the structure and goals of tax and fiscal reform, on which the country's development largely depends, be in accordance with the terms established in the peace agreements.'[129]

The Commission's 'wish' has reflected the uniqueness of the issue at hand. It is not customary for the Commission, or any other human rights body for that matter, to discuss the funding needed to translate governmental human rights commitments into reality. *The Economist* has noted that Guatemala's tax revenue was an exceptionally low 7% of GDP.[130] The World Bank has warned that peace agreements 'cannot be implemented because they are based on unrealistic assumptions of the availability of resources to finance them.'[131]

SURINAME

When the Netherlands cut off aid to Suriname in 1982–83, both the Netherlands and Suriname attained prominence in international human rights politics. Aid cut-offs were associated with the United States rather than the Netherlands, whose linkage between human rights and aid was designed not to be punitive. Little was – and is – known about Suriname. That small country (with a population of 400,000)

---

[127] The negotiations originally started in Mexico in 1991, after the first direct contacts in Spain in 1987. After the interruption of the first round of negotiations in 1992–93, a series of agreements were concluded in 1994–96. The first substantive agreement of 1994 related to human rights; nine more agreements followed: on the resettlement of the uprooted population and the truth commission in 1994 and on the identity and rights of indigenous peoples in 1995. Five substantive agreements were concluded in 1996: on socio-economic issues and the agrarian situation, on the strengthening of the civilian authorities and role of the armed forces, on constitutional reform and the electoral regime, and on the legal integration of the URNG. These were followed by the final agreement on implementation, compliance and verification, signed in Guatemala City on 29 December 1996.

[128] Central America (editorial), *Financial Times*, 30 December 1996; Ward Anderson, J. – Power in Guatemala 'shifts to civilians,' *The Washington Post*, reprinted in *Guardian Weekly*, 15 December 1996.

[129] Commission on Human Rights – Assistance to Guatemala in the field of human rights, resolution 1998/22 of 14 April 1998, para. 9.

[130] Guatemala: The peace police, *The Economist*, 28 June 1997.

[131] The World Bank – *Development and Human Rights. The Role of the World Bank*, Washington, D.C., September 1998, p. 24.

has never been in the international limelight, positive or negative. While legal human rights bodies dealt with the events which led to the Dutch aid cut off, the UN Commission on Human Rights has never had Suriname on its agenda.

Suriname, a former Dutch colony, attained political independence in 1975 and had a civilian government for five years thereafter, whereupon a military coup took place. Suriname's own description of developments thereafter goes as follows:

> The government before and after independence consisted of coalitions of different political parties, organized in large part on an ethnic basis. On 25 February 1980 a military coup d'etat took place, which removed the legitimately elected civilian Government. Suriname was governed by a military dictatorship until 25 November 1987 and then again from 24 December 1990 through 25 May 1991. In the 1980s the lack of respect for the constitutional State, serious violations of human rights, a devastating war in the hinterland of Suriname and a dramatic economic deterioration were manifest.[132]

Suriname's self-description also points out that a plantation economy was introduced during colonial times, which required large numbers of labourers to be imported from Africa, India and Java. Their descendants constituted the majority of the population in the post-colonial period, although they remained split ethnically among the three largest categories: Indians, Creoles, and Indonesians, with the next largest referred to as 'Bushnegroes' to label them as descendants of runaway slaves. The three largest categories were reflected in the three major racially and/or ethnically based political parties that took turns governing until the 1980 military coup.[133]

Similarly to Suriname's self-description, the Inter-American Commission on Human Rights has pointed out that 'the military authorities had proceeded to name successive governments which continued to perform their functions as long as the military could count on their complete allegiance.'[134] One of the most publicised atrocities seems to have taken place to deter anything other than such 'complete allegiance.' Fifteen opposition leaders were abducted and killed in December 1982, prompting the Dutch aid cut-off. The military rulers did not investigate those killings. Investigations have been carried out by international organizations, ranging from the non-governmental International Commission of Jurists to the Inter-American Commission on Human Rights or the International Labour Organization. They have all found the reluctance of military rulers to investigate

---

[132] United Nations – Core document forming part of the reports of States parties: Suriname, U.N. Doc. HRI/CORE/1/Add.39/Rev. 1 of 30 June 1998, para. 11.

[133] United Nations – Suriname. Core document forming part of the report of States Parties, U.N. Doc. HRI/CORE/1/Add. 39 of 7 February 1994, paras. 3, 6 and 43.

[134] Inter-American Commission on Human Rights – Second Report on the Human Rights Situation in Suriname, OAS Doc. OAS/Ser.L/V/II.66 doc. 21 rev. 1, 2 October 1985, p. 9.

the killings supportive of the assumption that they had been carried out following military orders. The Human Rights Committee confirmed the responsibility of the military government upon a complaint by the families of the murdered leaders of the opposition.[135]

In response to the killings, the Netherlands suspended its 15-year development co-operation treaty with Suriname and disbursement of $110 million in aid for 1983. Human rights were not mentioned in that decision. The Netherlands claimed that changed circumstances made aid to Suriname unfeasible, but the government's Human Rights Advisory Committee concluded that aid had been suspended because of human rights violations.[136]

As Table 6.5 reveals, total aid to Suriname plummeted. The loss of Dutch aid translated into a 25% decrease of Suriname's budget, and GNP declined in 1983–86. Aid from Libya and trade with Brazil redressed a part of the shortfall. Dutch aid was suspended until Suriname met specified conditions, one of which was protection of human rights. In January 1987, the Dutch Ambassador to Suriname was expelled for interfering in Suriname's internal affairs, while the UN investigated another series of killings.[137] The Netherlands resumed humanitarian aid in 1987, and towards the end of that year a new constitution was adopted by referendum, elections held, and a new civilian government was inaugurated in 1988.

The former leader of the military government, Desi Bouterse, had carried out the 1980 military coup and ruled seven years, to yield power to an elected government in 1987, thereupon to organize another military coup in 1990, and another round of elections took place in 1991. Desi Bouterse faced the electorate for the third time in 1996 but his civilian opponent, Jules Wijdenbosch, won to applause from the Netherlands to face calls for his resignation by more than half of parliament three years later,[138] while Desi Bouterse underwent a trial in absentia in the Netherlands for smuggling 1.5 tons of cocaine.[139]

Bouterse's coup of 1980 occurred before Suriname's donors had forged a response to such events. In contrast, EUrope (the European Community at the time) condemned the 1990 coup and aid was suspended. The elections of May 1991 ended another period of military rule, and the European Community congratulated the people of Suriname on free and fair elections, hoping that 'the people of Suriname will be spared all military interference in the democratic process' in the

---

[135] Human Rights Committee – Views concerning communications Nos. 146/1983 and 148–154/1983, *John Baboeram et al. v. Suriname*, U.N. Doc. A/40/40 (1985).

[136] Human Rights Advisory Committee – Supporting Human Rights. Human Rights in Suriname, The Hague, 18 June 1984, mimeographed, p. 14–15.

[137] Suriname: Running out of friends, *HRI Reporter*, vol. 12, No. 2, Winter 1988, p. 97.

[138] Surinam strongman seeks electoral comeback today, and Surinam president rejects offer, *Financial Times*, 23 and 29 May 1996; Suriname's wondrous botch, *The Economist*, 5 June 1999.

[139] Suriname: On trial, The Economist, 3 April 1999.

Table 6.5: Aid to Suriname in 1982–95
(in million US$)

	1982	1983	1984	1985	1987	1989	1990	1995
Belgium	0.7	0.8	0.8	0.9	1.2	1.3	4.8	2.9
Canada	0.2	0.0	0.0	0.0	–	0.1	0.1	0.0
France	0.3	0.1	0.1	0.1	0.2	0.1	0.1	0.0
Japan	–0.1	–1.7	–0.1	–0.1	–0.1	0.2	0.6	–
Netherlands	97.3	3.1	0.7	2.0	7.0	43.3	45.5	61.6
EUrope	100.0	4.7	4.6	4.0	9.8	49.5	55.2	69.8
Total bilateral	98.4	2.3	1.5	3.0	8.6	45.0	51.2	70.3
Total multilateral	3.1	1.6	3.6	3.1	5.7	5.9	6.4	6.8

Source: OECD – *Geographical Distribution of Financial Flows to Developing Countries*, various issues.

future.[140] Aid was resumed after the elections. In April 1993 a threat to suspend aid followed a high-level military appointment. A statement on behalf of the EPC (European Political Co-operation) pointed out that 'negative consequences for the co-operation between the European Community and Suriname' related to the appointment of the new commander of Suriname's armed forces.'[141]

As mentioned above, Dutch aid was resumed but it has never reached its pre-military-coup level, remaining at 40%.[142] Small, poor, far-off countries pro-verbially experience aid cut-offs on many different grounds, of which human rights is only one. The interplay of these different grounds routinely precludes full resumption of aid – if there is compliance with some grounds, the recipient is faulted on others. In the emblematic case of Suriname, if compliance with human rights criteria remained doubtful, additional criteria were introduced and the Netherlands suspended aid to Suriname because of its failure to implement a structural adjustment programme.[143]

---

[140] European Community – Declaration on elections in Suriname, *The Courier*, No. 129, September-October 1991, p. vi.

[141] *The Courier*, No. 139, May-June 1993, News round-up, p. iii.

[142] United Nations – Suriname. Core document forming part of the report of States Parties, U.N. Doc. HRI/CORE/1/Add. 39 of 7 February 1994, para. 9.

[143] *Human Rights in Suriname 1992–1994. Annual report by Moiwana '86, Human Rights Organization in Suriname*, Netherlands Human Rights Institute, SIM Special No. 14, Utrecht, 1994, p. 53.

Chapter 7

The Middle East and North Africa

Iran ruptured the centrality of the Cold War in the UN's human rights agenda in 1980. Following its 1979 revolution, Iran had launched a formidable challenge to the legitimacy of secular human rights law. This challenge, which has subsequently been amplified, went beyond the usual defence based on claims of interference in internal affairs to question the very normative basis of international human rights law. A decade later, after the Cold War had ended, this has led to much interest and even more negative publicity for Islam. The ideological struggles about Western *versus* socialist concepts of human rights were replicated, as Islam became a convenient ideological foe to replace communism. The strategy of containment was replicated as well. Unwanted 'exports' included people seeking refuge in the West. With people came their problems; hence, both people and problems were to be contained where they originated. Western political rhetoric posited that Islam was hostile to human rights, identified Islam with fundamentalism, fundamentalism with terrorism, thus reinforcing Western dis-involvement.

On the heels of the 1979 Iranian revolution came the Soviet military intervention in Afghanistan in December of the same year. The international response was Cold War driven: Afghanistan was not seen to have anything to do with Islam. Rather, a proxy war between the Soviet Union and the USA was transposed to the United Nations. That Afghanistan was an Islamic country was 'discovered' after the Soviet army had pulled out, the last remnants of the (previously) Soviet-supported government had been summarily executed, and the country had switched to rule-or-ruin warfare and a particularly radical version of Islamic law. Since women's human rights were in the meantime elevated from the margins of international human rights politics into its core, Afghanistan was brought back into the international limelight.

A military coup in Turkey in 1980 followed the Soviet military intervention in Afghanistan and prodded EUrope to forge a response consistent with its emerging human rights policy. Since it also had to accommodate Turkey's strategic importance, such a response has not yet been found. A facilitating factor in EUrope's dealings with Turkey has been its commitment to secularism, particularly by Turkey's military establishment, against Islam/fundamentalism/terrorism. The Bolshevik logic whereby the end justifies the means[1] had first crept into cold-war Western foreign policies. It had urged the combating of communism by all means, with human rights suspended, because communism embodied denial of human rights.

---

[1] Rogov, S. – A Kosovo plan to reconcile Russia and the West, *International Herald Tribune*, 4 May 1999.

This same logic was then replicated to the combating of Islam/fundamentalism/terrorism after the Cold War had ended.

The contrast between two prominent human rights controversies of the early 1980s – Iran and Turkey – reveals the low rank of human rights in international politics. Iran attracted UN condemnations; Turkey did not. In contrast to Iran, Turkey is governed by secular law, and one of its foreign policy goals was, probably still is, membership in the European Union. Problems with Turkey's human rights performance have tended to focus on its rejection of human rights safeguards in the work of the military and security apparatus, justified by the necessity of combating terrorism. The issue of terrorism brings Turkey and Iran together despite their dissimilarities – Turkey has been one of the prominent lobbyists for including terrorism on the UN human rights agenda, while Iran has been a prominent victim of the US strategy targeting supporters of international terrorism.

Table 7.1 presents a chronicle of attempts to tackle violations, showing that Cyprus arrived on the agenda in 1974, followed in that same year by complaints against pre-revolution Iran under the 1503 procedure. In the early 1980s, Afghanistan, Iran and Western Sahara appeared on the agenda. The first two have been kept there ever since; Western Sahara's fate has been similar to that of Cyprus and it is not discussed in this book.[2] The early 1990s were overwhelmed by Iraq's invasion of Kuwait, addressed in Chapter 10.

Table 7.1: The Middle East and North Africa on the UN violations-agenda, 1967–1999

Country	Commission	Sub-Commission	1503 procedure
Afghanistan	1980–91, 1993–99	1981–88, 1999	1981–84
Algeria	–	(1997–98)	–
Bahrain	–	1997	1991–93
Cyprus/Turkey	1975–88, 1990, 1996	1974–88, (1996)	–
Iran	1982–99	1980–96	1974–75, 1983
Iraq	(1989), 1991–99	(1989), 1990–91, 1993–96	1988–89
Kuwait/Iraq	1991	1990	1994
Saudi Arabia	–	–	1995–99
Syria	–	–	1989,1992, 1997
Turkey	–	(1995–97)	1983–86, (1990)
Western Sahara	1981–87, 1989–90, 1993, 1995–96, 1998–99	1987	–
Yemen	–	–	1998–99

---

[2] Western Sahara has been discussed in Tomaševski, K. – *Between Sanctions and Elections*, Pinter/Cassell, London, 1997, pp. 54–55 and 198.

Syria, Bahrain, Saudi Arabia, Algeria and Yemen figure in Table 7.1, none having elicited a condemnation, and Algeria is discussed below as an illustration of the influence of EUrope's policy (and the French influence therein) on the outcomes of the UN's human rights work. Algeria's post-1991 government – first military, then elected – professed anti-terrorism as its goal, combating violence with violence. The underlying rationale was to prevent the emergence of an Islamic government. Europe's *human rights cum democracy* policy was tested and failed: the 1991 elections were interrupted by a military take-over, which should have – but did not – trigger off condemnations and sanctions. A cycle of violence and counter-violence followed. EUrope's response has been a very loud silence.

IRAN

Human rights were not a prominent Western concern for pre-1979 Iran. US support has been vastly documented and need not be described here, and Iran hosted the 1968 International Conference on Human Rights organised by the United Nations. The 1979 revolution was initially seen as a window of opportunity for human rights, but international attention was quickly diverted from human rights. The occupation of the US embassy in Teheran[3] inflamed American public opinion and US sanctions followed.

The impossibility of disentangling human rights from a myriad of other grounds for sanctions is evidenced in the sequence of events. The 1979 revolution ousted Shah Reza Pahlavi – not known for his commitment to human rights – and brought to life the Islamic Republic of Iran. The US embassy in Teheran was the most publicised target, typifying the switch from Western-supported to anti-Western regime. Western involvement in the 1953 military coup in Iran, which brought Reza Pahlavi to power, was often forgotten in the West but not in Iran.

The siege of the US embassy prompted the United States to demand Security Council sanctions against Iran. No such resolution was adopted because the Soviet Union, predictably, vetoed the US draft resolution, whereupon the United States resorted to unilateral sanctions. These encompassed boycotting Iranian oil and freezing its assets. Jimmy Carter commented: 'I thought depriving them of about twelve billion dollars in ready assets was a good way to get their attention.'[4]

---

[3] Gunnar Lagergren, former President of the Iran-United States Claims Tribunal, has thus described the background: 'At the end of October 1979 the deposed Shah arrived in the United States for medical treatment in a New York hospital. Seeing the Shah's reception by the United States as an act of provocation, militant students seized the U.S. Embassy in Tehran on 4 November 1979, taking a large number of diplomats and other U.S. citizens as hostages. In exchange for the release of the hostages, the students demanded that the Shah be returned to Iran. On 14 November 1979, President Carter in retaliation froze Iranian assets in the United States banks, at home and overseas, valued at some 12 billion dollars. It took the death of the Shah, the outbreak of the Iran-Iraq war and the mediation of a friendly power to end the captivity of the 52 hostages, 444 days after it began.' Lagergren, G. – The formative years of the Iran-United States Claims Tribunal, *Nordic Journal of International Law*, vol. 66, 1997, p. 23.

[4] Carter, J. – *Keeping Faith: Memoirs of a President*, Bantam Books, New York, 1982, p. 464–465.

Sanctions were retrospectively legitimised by the authoritative finding of the International Court of Justice (ICJ) that Iran had breached international law.[5] EUrope, with the exception of Britain, imposed economic sanctions in solidarity with the United States. Iran's breach of diplomatic immunity was seen as serious enough to justify a punitive response by the entire international community.[6]

In that tense atmosphere, the new Islamic Republic of Iran challenged in 1981 the Universal Declaration of Human Rights for being secular. Iran argued that religious (divine) law was pre-eminent to secular (man-made) law, and that secular bodies were not qualified to interpret religious law.[7] The Committee on Human Rights objected to 'the lack of transparency and predictability in the application of Iranian domestic law'[8] resulting from the powers of religious bodies to determine the contents and interpretation of the law. Such a challenge had not been anticipated. International human rights law was built on the separation between the state and the church, and religion was confined to the private sphere. Controversy intensified when Iran questioned the powers of UN human rights bodies to assess its human rights law and practice.

In 1981, Iran's ambassador to the UN stated that the United Nations was a secular body and as such should not address religious matters since such an effort was out of place.[9] One year later, Iran dissociated itself from the Universal Declaration of Human Rights and international human rights treaties, although not formally renouncing them. It highlighted as reasons that those secular instruments would not be applied where they differentiated from Islamic law, and added that human rights treaties had been ratified by the previous, illegitimate regime.[10] Separation between the church and the state was abolished with the following rationale:

> God has assigned his prophets to guide people to salvation. The Shiite Imam, as the true successor to the Prophet Muhammed, has the responsibility to create a favourable atmosphere for the furtherance of moral values based on faith and

---

[5] The ICJ found that the initial occupation of the US embassy may have been a spontaneous act. However, subsequent approval of the occupation of the embassy by the new government of Iran, as well as the government's decision that the embassy staff should continue to be held as hostages, transformed that originally spontaneous action into an act of state for which Iran was responsible. International Court of Justice – United States Diplomatic Staff in Tehran, *ICJ Reports 1980*, p. 29 and 35.

[6] Kamminga, M.T. – *Inter-state Accountability for Violations of Human Rights, Pennsylvania Studies in Human Rights*, University of Pennsylvania Press, Philadelphia, 1992, p. 161–162.

[7] Statement of Ambassador of Iran to the United Nations before the Third Committee of the General Assembly, U.N. Doc. A/C.3/36/SR.29 of 26 October 1981, p. 4–5.

[8] Comments of the Human Rights Committee following its consideration of the second periodic report of the Islamic republic of Iran, U.N. Doc. CCPR/C/79/Add. 25 of 3 August 1993, para. 6.

[9] Statement of Ambassador Khorasani before the Third Committee of the General Assembly of 26 October 1981, U.N. Doc. A/C.3/36/SR. 29, p. 4–5.

[10] Meron, T. – Iran's challenge to the international law of human rights, *HRI Reporter*, vol. 13, No. 1, Spring 1989, pp. 8–10.

righteousness and to struggle against all manifestations of corruption. It is for this reason that in this last monotheist divine religion there is no separation between the State and religion.[11]

Controversies intensified as the UN response to the abuses that were taking place became increasingly condemnatory. Resolutions were passed placing Iran on the violations-agenda and, as in similar cases, this was followed by the appointment of a UN Special Rapporteur in 1984.[12] His efforts to document abuses were more strenuous than in comparable situations. Indeed, the Rapporteur noted in exasperation that 'there are no accounts of situations or specific cases whose accuracy and veracity are not disputed.'[13] UN's response to proven abuses was also exasperating. The subsequent Special Representative on Iran, Maurice Copithorne, found 'the politicised tone [of] the dialogue so pervasive that human rights are in danger of becoming a vehicle rather than an end in themselves.'[14]

Various facets of the West-Iran conflict about the meaning of human rights came to light in the case of Salman Rushdie, the *cause célèbre* of EUrope-Iran relations. On 14 February 1989, Ayatollah Khomeini announced that the author of *The Satanic Verses* and all those involved in the publication of that book and familiar with its contents were sentenced to death. Those who died trying to carry out that *fatwa* would be martyrs, rewarded by eternal heaven.[15] A series of protests against *The Satanic Verses* and Salman Rushdie followed in Algeria, Bangladesh, India,

---

[11] United Nations – Core document forming part of the reports of States parties: Islamic Republic of Iran, U.N. Doc. HRI/CORE/1/Add. 93 of 30 June 1998, para. 8.

[12] The Sub-Commission for Prevention of Discrimination and Protection of Minorities initiated the process by adopting a resolution on the persecution of the Baha'i community in 1981 and, the following year, a resolution on religious persecution, including through such phenomena as summary executions [Resolutions 8 (XXXIV) of 9 September 1981 and 1982/25 of 8 September 1982]. The Commission on Human Rights voiced its concern about grave human rights violations in Iran in 1982–83 and in 1984 appointed a Special Representative to establish contacts with the government of Iran and 'make a thorough study of the human rights situation' (resolution 1984/54). The first Special Representative, Reynaldo Galindo Pohl, reported on widespread, numerous, and serious abuses that had been taking place, but adopted a conciliatory approach concerning Iran's challenge to international human rights law. Rather than dismissing it, he tried to understand its causes and consequences so as to establish a dialogue with Iran. Pohl resigned in 1985, pointing out that a critical report would be the only sanction available to a UN Special Rapporteur but would also constitute the final stage, since dialogue with Iran would become impossible. He also suggested that all avenues for securing Iran's co-operation should be explored before that final step was taken (U.N. Doc. E/CN.4/1986/25, Annex II).

[13] General Assembly – Situation of human rights in the Islamic Republic of Iran. Note by the Secretary-General, U.N. Doc. A/45/697 of 6 November 1990, para. 265.

[14] Commission on Human Rights – Report on the situation of human rights in the Islamic Republic of Iran, prepared by the Special representative of the Commission on Human Rights, Mr. Maurice Copithorne, U.N. Doc. E/CN.4/1996/59 of 21 March 1996, para. 2.

[15] Bedford, C. – *Fiction, Fact and Fatwa. 2,000 Days of Censorship*, Article 19, London, August 1994, p. 1.

Indonesia, Malaysia, Mali, Senegal, Somalia, Sri Lanka, Sudan, and the United Arab Emirates;[16] a series of protests against the *fatwa* ensued in Western Europe. Some Western European governments withdrew their ambassadors from Iran, others condemned the call for Rushdie's execution, and quite a few publicly condemned the government of Iran for not distancing itself from that call.

Much time and effort was expended to negotiate freedom from summary execution for Salman Rushdie. EUrope proclaimed itself alarmed by 'Iran's continued failure to repudiate the incitement to [his] murder'.[17] EUropean officials tried to negotiate a 'fatwa-free zone' for Salman Rushdie, following the precedent set by Denmark in 1994, when the ambassador of Iran signed a pledge that the *fatwa* would not be carried out in Denmark so as to facilitate an official visit.[18] The response of Iran was that the *fatwa* was a religious issue and defined as a duty of individual Muslims.[19] The weight of Khomeini's edict was – and remains – immense because 'the Leader is the highest religious and political authority of the country.'[20] Indeed, following a bomb attack against a publishing house and bookshop in Tehran in 1995 for 'Rushdie-like' reasons, Iran's religious leaders were quoted as approving of that attack in the name of Ayatollah Khomeini's political testament, noting that his will was above the law.'[21]

EUrope's response to domestic lobbying aimed at putting pressure on Iran to rescind the *fatwa* against Salman Rushdie was torn between commercial and non-commercial objectives. The European Parliament asked the Commission to negotiate with Iran 'a very strong clause requiring respect for human rights with an option to suspend any such agreement in the event of violation.'[22] Counter-pressures not to interfere with commercial relations prevailed.

The interplay between diverse pressures and counter-pressures was also evidenced in UN's policy towards Iran. In March 1991, the UN Commission on Human Rights adopted a consensus resolution on human rights in Iran instead of previous –

---

[16] Information provided by Iran's Permanent Representative to the United Nations at Geneva to the UN Special Representative on the human rights situation in the Islamic Republic of Iran, U.N. Doc. E/CN.4/1992/34 of 2 January 1992, para. 19.

[17] Statement of Mr. Larsen on behalf of the European Community and its Member States before the United Nations Commission on Human Rights, 49th session, 1 March 1993, U.N. Doc. E/CN.4/1993/SR.45 of 8 March 1993, para. 44.

[18] Rushdie may get fatwa-free zone in EU, *The Independent*, 11 April 1995, and Europe defends Rushdie, *Financial Times*, 8 June 1995.

[19] Ali Akbar Velayati, minister of foreign affairs, explained that *fatwa* had been decreed by Imam Khomeini on the basis of Islamic law, and was confirmed by the Organization of Islamic Council, by 52 Muslim countries. Velayati offers no word of hope for Rushdie, *The Independent*, 31 May 1995.

[20] United Nations – Core document forming part of the reports of States parties, U.N. Doc. HRI/CORE/1/Add. 93 of 30 June 1998, para. 11.

[21] Commission on Human Rights – Report of the Special Rapporteur on the promotion and protection of the right to freedom of opinion and expression, Mr. Abid Hussain. Report on the mission of the Special Rapporteur to the Islamic Republic of Iran, U.N. Doc. E/CN.4/1996/39/Add.2 of 11 March 1996, paras. 45 and 48.

[22] Europan Parliament – Violations of human rights in Iran, resolution of 12 March 1992, para. 7.

and subsequent – condemnations.[23] Iran subsequently described to the Special Rapporteur the negotiations that had led to that change, and he included it in his report, revealing the layers of behind-the-scenes agreements and disagreements hidden behind official UN documents and publicly adopted resolutions:

> The Iranian representatives alluded to the negotiations that led to the consensus resolution, during which, they said, it had been understood that the only question at issue was the diplomatic termination of United Nations supervision of the human rights situation in the Islamic republic of Iran; and that the fact that the General Assembly had not included that item on the agenda of its forty-seventh session (1991) also tended in that direction. With that understanding, official circles in Tehran had announced the cessation of the mandate [of the UN Special Representative on human rights] immediately after the Commission on Human Rights had adopted [by consensus, which included Iran as it was a member at the time] resolution 1991/82 on 7 March 1991. The Special Representative refused to interpret resolution 1991/82 in terms of the negotiations that had led up to it and therefore refrained from considering any promises and understandings or misunderstandings that might have arisen during such negotiations. … [A]ny promises or interpretations that might have come into play during the efforts to obtain a consensus, unless they were unequivocally reflected in the text, were only binding on the delegations that had made or endorsed them.[24]

Similar to the – albeit temporary – change in UN's approach in 1991, in the same year a co-operative mood replaced EUrope's previously condemnatory policy towards Iran. EUrope re-established dialogue with Iran and lifted the sanctions which had been imposed in response to the Iran-Iraq war (1980–88) in which EUrope had supported Iraq. An official statement during a visit to Tehran emphasised Iran's role in regional security[26] as Western sanctions in the meantime

---

[23] Details of the negotiations that took place behind closed doors are, of course, not known with the exception of the Iranian version as quoted here by the Special Representative. A similar situation was repeated in 1995, when Iran agreed to an initial visit by this new Special Representative, in the belief that it signified a forthcoming deletion of Iran from the UN violators-agenda. When that belief proved unfounded, Iran refused to accept any further visits. Commission on Human Rights – Report on the situation of human rights in the Islamic Republic of Iran, prepared by the Special representative of the Commission on Human Rights, Mr. Maurice Copithorne, U.N. Doc. E/CN.4/1997/63 of 11 February 1997, para. 9.

[24] Commission on Human Rights – Report on the human rights situation in the Islamic Republic of Iran by the Special representative of the Commission on Human Rights, Mr. Reynaldo Galindo Pohl, U.N. Doc. E/CN.4/1992/34 of 2 January 1992, paras. 376–377.

[26] Iran and Europe: Seeking the inside track, *The Middle East*, July 1991, p. 11.

turned from Iran to Iraq. EUrope's unchanged relations with Iran were defined as *critical dialogue*, in contrast to the *dual containment* of Iraq and Iran by the United States. Germany, Italy and France led in strengthening commercial relations, with Germany becoming Iran's largest trading partner.

The focus on the fate of Salman Rushdie and underlying human rights issues slackened somewhat as a result of the US classification of Iran, followed by Libya, as a 'terrorist state'.[27] US sanctions against Cuba were replicated, prohibiting individual companies world-wide from investing in Libya and Iran. Alfonse D'Amato, the main congressional supporter of these sanctions, explained that any commercial agreement providing outside funds to the blacklisted regimes was a direct threat to US security.[28]

US sanctions against Iran threatened the four billion US dollars generated annually by selling Iranian oil to (or through) American oil companies.[29] Sanctions targeted any company that invested more than $40 million in Iran's oil industry or was involved in the oil trade with Iran, as well as any bank that lent Iran more than $10 million.[30] Iran's support of international terrorism allegedly encompassed Hezbollah in Lebanon, Hamas in Palestine, and the Muslim Brotherhood in Egypt and Jordan. In a revival of cold-war rhetoric, Tehran was seen as 'the center of the world's new Comintern.'[31]

Neither Western Europe nor Japan supported the United States.[32] EUrope did not approve of US unilateral sanctions, particularly objecting to their extraterritorial extension. It oscillated between threatening to resort to the World Trade Organization to secure an authoritative finding that the United States was violating

---

[27] The grounds cited for classifying Iran as a 'terrorist state' were the acquisition of weapons of mass destruction and the means to deliver them and support of international terrorism; the latter included an accusation that Iran used its diplomatic facilities abroad to promote acts of international terrorism. For Libya, the listed grounds were Libya's lack of compliance with Security Council resolutions relating to Lockerbie, support of international terrorism, and efforts to acquire weapons of mass destruction. The text of the Iran and Libya Sanctions Act of 1996 has been reprinted in *International Legal Materials*, vol. 35, 1996, pp. 1273–1279.

[28] Berley, M. – French warned of sanctions. U.S. Senator cites Total's business with Iran, *International Herald Tribune*, 3 June 1996.

[29] Iran bid to beat US sanctions, *Financial Times*, 26 July 1994.

[30] Thoenes, S. et al. – US driving Iranian regime into Russian arms, *Financial Times*, 21 March 1996.

[31] Krauthammer, C. – One source of the new world disorder is Tehran, *International Herald Tribune*, 4 January 1993.

[32] Japan: Iran loan delayed, *Far Eastern Economic Review*, 11 May 1995; Iran shrugs off sanctions, *International Herald Tribune*, 22 June 1995.

international trade law[33] and bilateral negotiations. The latter prevailed because sanctions on national security grounds would not have been justiciable.

The Iran-Libya Sanctions Act, known by its acronym, *Ilsa*, became an object of EUrope-USA dispute, just as had US sanctions against Cuba. Ilsa's declared objectives ranged from halting Iran's support for international terrorism and its acquisition of nuclear technology, to preventing human rights violations, to the defence of Israel against possible Iranian military threats. In 1995, President Clinton chose the World Jewish Congress as the forum in which to announce forthcoming US economic sanctions against Iran.[34]

The aims of sanctions against Iran and Libya were sidelined by debates about their costs. Imposing sanctions meant losses for US oil companies; not imposing them meant admitting that Ilsa did not mean what it said.[35] A waiver was ultimately granted for investments whose total worth was not to exceed $2 billion – by Total, based in France, Gazprom in Russia, and Petronas in Malaysia[36] – thus opening the door to future investment.

Although EUrope did not endorse the US response to Iran's involvement in killings abroad, it had to tackle those that were carried out within the Western Europe. In 1990, Kazem Rajavi, a prominent exile and a frequent NGO spokesperson before UN human rights bodies, was killed in Switzerland. Another politically active exile, Shahpour Bakhtiar, was killed in France, bringing the issue geographically into EUrope. Furthermore, a group of Kurdish exiles was killed in Germany[37] and that case was, different from others, adjudicated. EUrope suspended its critical dialogue with Iran following a 1997 German judicial finding that Iran had been responsible for the 1992 killing of Kurdish exiles.[38] EUropean ambassadors were withdrawn as a form of diplomatic sanction; they returned after seven months.[39]

---

[33] EUrope lodged a complaint against the United States before the WTO (World Trade Organization) to suspend it after 'an understanding' that a compromise would be negotiated bilaterally. A great number of media reports followed those negotiations, unkindly but accurately described by *The Economist* as a search for a 'face-saving fudge' (Down with free trade, *The Economist*, 4 October 1997). A compromise was reached in May 1998, whereby the USA waived sanctions against oil firms, including the French firm, Total, for their $2 billion investment in Iran, and apparently promised that further waivers would be forthcoming (What to do about Iran, *The Economist*, 23 May 1998). Guarantees that foreign investment from EUrope would not be diverted to financing terrorism were apparently given. (Collet, N. – Iran looks west for oil sector investment, *The Middle East*, August 1998, p. 21).

[34] Walker, M. – Clinton stumbles over foreign affairs, *Guardian Weekly*, 22 June 1997.

[35] Lippman, T.W. – U.S. torn over punishing France, Russia and Malaysia for ventures in Iran, *International Herald Tribune*, 7–8 March 1998.

[36] Jonquieres, G. – Europe may escape Iran and Libya sanctions, *Financial Times*, 11 May 1998.

[37] Commission on Human Rights – Final report on the situation of human rights in the Islamic Republic of Iran by the Special representative of the Commission on Human Rights, Mr. Reynaldo Galindo Pohl, U.N. Doc. E/CN.4/1993/41 of 28 January 1993, paras. 60–67.

[38] Barber, L. – EU to allow Iran contacts, *Financial Times*, 24 February 1998.

[39] EU compromise on Mykonos affair, *ARTICLE 19 Bulletin*, Issue 25, December 1997, p. 3.

A further step away from confrontation was made through a reported rescinding of the *fatwa* against Salman Rushdie. A great deal of uncertainty nonetheless remained, as the then government of Iran claimed that it had no authority to rescind the *fatwa* and doubted its powers to prevent it from being carried out. It seems that a pledge not to carry out the *fatwa* was exchanged for the upgrading of British-Iranian relations to ambassadorial level.[40]

The twentieth anniversary of the 1979 revolution was celebrated on 1st February 1999, to mark the return of Ayatollah Khomeini from exile. Much changed during these twenty years, however. The students who had seized the US embassy in November 1979 were protesting against restrictions upon freedom of expression twenty years later. The elections in 1997 and 1999 instituted the accountability of the government to its population. Much as with similar transitions, Western condemnations and US sanctions were not rescinded and George Joffé noted that no Western support was forthcoming to facilitate the momentous changes in Iran.[41]

AFGHANISTAN

Western observers have often found warfare in Afghanistan in the 1990s incomprehensible – war should have ended with the pullout of the Soviet army in 1989 or at least with the fall of the (previously) Soviet-supported government in 1992. It did not. The foundations for continued warfare were laid in the 1980s and Barnett Rubin used an old Persian rhyme, 'if you do not like the image in the mirror, do not break the mirror, break your face', as the *leitmotif* of his book on Afghanistan.[42]

The United States, West Germany and France suspended civilian aid to Afghanistan in 1980 in response to the Soviet military invasion. Table 7.2 shows how aid diminished in the 1980s to increase subsequent to the pullout of the Soviet army. This was all humanitarian aid, however, exempt from post-invasion sanctions but routed to Afghan refugees in Pakistan. Afghanistan's major donor in 1980–89 was the Soviet Union, which provided two-thirds of aid, estimated at an annual $537 million.[43]

US military aid followed the Soviet military invasion. It was provided to a large number of different armed groups with the imputed rationale of preventing the emergence of a united Afghani armed resistance. By one count, no less than nineteen armed Afghani movements – ten based in Pakistan and nine in Iran[44] – were

---

[40] Cornwell, R. – Rushdie thaw is boost to oil firms, *The Independent*, 26 September 1998; Black, I. – Britain and Iran revive diplomatic relations, *Guardian Weekly*, 18 April 1999.

[41] Joffé, G. – Iran: At the turning point, *The World Today*, April 1999, p. 13.

[42] Rubin, B. – *The Fragmentation of Afghanistan: State Formation and Collapse in the International System*, Yale University Press, 1995.

[43] Hyman, A. – Afghanistan: Putting back the pieces, *The Middle East*, December 1988.

[44] Ali, S. – Afghanistan: Guerrillas, Iran, Pakistan reach consensus, *Far Eastern Economic Review*, 15 August 1991.

Table 7.2: Aid to Afghanistan in 1979–95
(in million US$)

	1979	1980	1982	1985	1990	1991	1992	1993	1994	1995
Canada	6.0	2.2	–	–	2.7	5.3	4.7	7.6	7.2	7.1
Denmark	0.0	1.8	1.0	0.0	1.6	2.7	3.2	4.3	2.0	5.6
France	–	0.7	1.1	3.2	1.9	1.5	1.4	2.1	4.4	3.5
Germany	12.9	1.4	-0.7	1.3	8.1	5.5	15.0	16.1	21.6	15.6
Netherlands	0.2	0.2	–	–	3.1	0.7	5.2	10.0	12.4	26.6
Norway	–	–	–	0.7	3.4	8.0	8.5	8.9	8.9	9.2
Sweden	–	1.1	0.1	1.0	16.1	4.8	13.0	9.1	12.4	15.3
USA	12.0	2.0	-2.0	–	56.0	59.0	65.0	42.0	53.0	2.0
EUrope	16.1	5.2	1.3	5.0	19.7	27.6	57.6	70.3	84.9	105.4
Arab donors	8.5	1.5	0.4	-1.5	36.8	375.3	3.5	3.4	6.6	0.0
Total bilateral	47.0	11.4	0.4	6.9	100.4	101.8	126.7	107.3	134.6	105.5
Total multilateral	52.5	19.4	8.4	11.4	38.2	34.8	74.2	116.6	88.8	109.1

Source: *Geographical Distribution of Financial Flows to Developing Countries*, OECD, Paris, various issues.

formed with foreign military support in 1979–89. Besides Pakistan and Iran as the closest foreign military supporters, Soviet support to Afghanistan's government and US support to armed opposition groups completed the landscape.

Estimates of US military aid to the anti-Soviet resistance in 1979–89 range between an annual $600 million and a total of $6–8 billion.[45] Less is known about Soviet military aid, but it is estimated to have been about the same. Military aid was at least ten times larger than civilian aid but cannot be tabulated because precise figures are never available. Table 7.2 reproduces officially recorded aid (mainly civilian) to illustrate this gap. Peace-making mirrored the symmetry between the two main providers of military aid: both the United States and the Soviet Union pledged to halt aid as long as the other side did the same.[46]

The chronicle which led to the Soviet military intervention can be reduced to three consecutive military coups: a coup d'etat had transformed Afghanistan from monarchy to republic in 1973; another followed, and a third coup brought a communist regime to power in 1978. Domestic opposition to communist rule, especially within the military, led to Soviet military intervention in 1979. Ten years of warfare followed, amidst considerable international attention and interference, ending with the Geneva Accords of 1988 and the pullout of Soviet troops the following year. Official forecasts optimistically anticipated a major international aid programme to follow peace-making, while unofficial suspicions that Afghanistan would 'return to chaos that prevailed when the Soviet troops intervened in 1979.'[47] persisted.

Afghanistan was placed on the UN human rights agenda in 1980, and has remained on it ever since despite profound changes in the definition of human rights problems. Subsequent to the withdrawal of Soviet troops, international attention diminished because what was considered to be the principal human rights problem – the denial of self-determination and/or the Soviet military presence – was solved. *Amnesty International* has claimed that previous international warmongering entailed responsibility for its aftermath,[48] but nobody has heeded *Amnesty's* call.

Afghanistan disappeared from the agenda of the Security Council when Soviet troops pulled out; its reappearance in 1996, seven years later, illustrated the changed definition of human rights: the human rights of women were mentioned

---

[45] Harrison, S.S. – A tightrope to peace in Afghanistan, *International Herald Tribune*, 10 April 1992; Brown, D. – Descent into anarchy, *Guardian Weekly*, 17 May 1992; Rashid, A. – Underground in Afghanistan, *Far Eastern Economic Review*, 28 January 1999.

[46] Friedman, T.L. – U.S. and Soviets agree to end arms sales to Afghans, *International Herald Tribune*, 14–15 September 1991.

[47] Kamm, H. – Chaos is Afghan destiny: Geneva Accord papers over war's reality, *International Herald Tribune*, 16–17 April 1988.

[48] Amnesty International – Afghanistan: International Responsibility for Human Rights Disaster, London 1995.

for the first time in the history of the Security Council. This would have been unthinkable in 1980–89. The Council denounced discrimination against girls and women, noting 'with deep concern possible repercussions on international relief and reconstruction programmes in Afghanistan [but called upon] all States and international organizations to extend all possible humanitarian assistance to the civilian population of Afghanistan.'[49] Thus the Security Council provided support both to those who curtailed aid because women were denied their human rights and to those who continued providing aid.

For example, UNICEF suspended work in those areas where discriminatory practices prevented girls and women from benefitting from aid. The Taliban's rules had in 1994 banned women's work outside the home, denied girls access to education, and confronted foreign humanitarian agencies with a requirement not to employ female staff. Even the UN Special Rapporteur, whose report detailed these developments, was prevented from bringing along a female human rights officer.[50] In contrast to UNICEF, but in similarity to the UN Special Rapporteur, who went to Afghanistan alone, some NGOs neither pulled out nor threatened to do so, professing 'respect for the local cultures of Afghanistan' and clarifying that they were not human rights organizations but assistance programmes.[51]

The approaches of these organizations mirrored the practice that had been institutionalised within the United Nations during previous decades, and was expressed in the existence of two parallel tracks, one for aid and another for human rights.[52] In its 1995 resolution on emergency relief, the General Assembly pleaded for aid; in another, it urged respect of human rights. The former apparently prevailed, as the Assembly mandated forthcoming UN assistance for constitution-making and elections – which did not materialize – to pay due regard to Afghan tradition.[53]

---

[49] Security Council resolution 1076 (1996) of 22 October 1996, paras. 11 and 12.

[50] Commission on Human Rights – Final report on the situation of human rights in Afghanistan submitted by Mr. Choong-Hyun Paik, Special Rapporteur, U.N. Doc. E/CN.4/1996/64 of 27 February 1996, paras. 69, 70, 72–73, 76, and 86–87.

[51] Steele, J. – Aid agencies bite bullet in Kabul, *Guardian Weekly*, 13 October 1996.

[52] In 1992, for example, the General Assembly hailed 'the establishment of the Islamic State in Afghanistan [as] a new opportunity for reconstruction of the country' and appealed for all possible assistance (Emergency assistance for the reconstruction of war stricken Afghanistan, General Assembly resolution 47/119 of 18 December 1992, preamble and para. 3), while its sister resolution on human rights listed armed confrontations, violations of civil and political rights, and denial of access to prisons to the ICRC (International Committee of the Red Cross) and the Special Rapporteur (Situation of human rights in Afghanistan, resolution 47/141 of 18 December 1992, preamble). The lack of cross-referencing illustrated the separation between these two tracks within the UN.

[53] United Nations – Emergency international assistance for peace, normalcy and reconstruction of war-stricken Afghanistan; Situation of human rights in Afghanistan, resolutions 50/88 of 19 December 1995 and 50/189 of 22 December 1995.

The dilemma for foreign and international agencies working in Afghanistan was simple. Providing aid on the Taliban's terms meant acquiescing in the denial of women's rights; not providing aid meant pulling out, or not going in, and thus not aiding anybody. Aid to Afghanistan had been decreasing even before the Taliban. In 1995, the United Nations sought $124 million and obtained $53, the year before it had sought $122 million and obtained $94 million.[54] The Taliban's policy led to further decreases in humanitarian aid.

The UN Special Rapporteur found in January 1995 that 'the human rights situation in Afghanistan continues to be conditioned by the absence of an effective central government' and so the fate of people in different parts of the country 'depends on the intensity of the power struggle between the rival groups.'[55] The discrepancy between the absence of a government – legally obliged to guarantee human rights – and the insistence on human rights guarantees addressed to warring parties typifies another facet of the changed definition of human rights. A look back at the 1980s illustrates the background against which this change took place.

In its first resolution on Afghanistan, the Commission on Human Rights called upon states to refrain from providing assistance to 'the imposed regime' (that is, the Soviet-supported government), pleading instead for 'assistance to the people to recover their right to determine their destiny,'[56] and reflecting the Commission's implicit endorsement of military aid to anti-Soviet resistance. The key aim was combating Soviet occupation and aid was primarily intended to support armed struggle. As long as the key problem was defined as self-determination, in its narrow meaning of liberation from foreign occupation, individual human rights had been marginalized and women's rights never mentioned.

A 1988 UN report anticipated the Soviet pullout and predicted that 'Afghanistan could become a test case for the effectiveness of the [human rights] advisory services system.'[57] This became an embarrassingly wrong prediction. The first Special Rapporteur, Felix Ermacora, had posited – against historical evidence to the contrary – that 'a nation cannot achieve self-determination through armed struggle'. He subsequently acknowledged that 'the political status of the country is dependent on

---

[54] Rashid, A. – Afghanistan: Austere beginning, *Far Eastern Economic Review*, 17 October 1996; Commission on Human Rights – Final report on the situation of human rights in Afghanistan submitted by Mr. Choong-Hyun Paik, Special Rapporteur, U.N. Doc. E/CN.4/1996/64 of 27 February 1996, para. 35.

[55] Commission on Human Rights – Final report on the situation in Afghanistan submitted by the Special Rapporteur, Mr. Felix Ermacora, U.N. Doc. E/CN.4/1995/64 of 20 January 1995, paras. 46–47.

[56] Commission on Human Rights, resolution 3 (XXXVI) of 14 February 1980.

[57] Commission on Human Rights – Report on the situation of human rights in Afghanistan, U.N. Doc. E/CN.4/1988/25 of 26 February 1988, para. 82.

the outcome of armed struggle for political power' and to add 'that important parties to the conflict are seeing a military solution.'[58]

The reference to 'Afghani resistance' survived the withdrawal of Soviet troops in 1989 and the fall of the communist regime in 1992. Thereafter, no ready-made vocabulary could accommodate Afghan realities. In 1992, the General Assembly acknowledged 'a situation of armed confrontation' but could not define its protagonists except as 'Afghan parties'.[59] Previous military aid left these 'Afghan parties' awash with weapons, channeled through Pakistan:

> In close coordination with [the] CIA, the ISI [Pakistan's military intelligence agency Inter Services Intelligence] organized the *mujahideen*, directed their military operations inside Afghanistan and managed their political image abroad.[60]

Liberation from foreign occupation was achieved in 1989 with the withdrawal of the Soviet Union, but the proxy war was then transformed into domestic war. Assumptions that the foreign military was the only problem, and external parties the key to peace making, proved unfounded. The common outside enemy had provided a focus for resistance movements; its absence revealed a patchwork of fiefdoms built by leaders of armed movements and inter-regional proxy-wars between Pakistan, Iran and Saudi Arabia, with different degrees of involvement of the Central Asian republics of the former Soviet Union: Turkmenistan, Uzbekistan and Tajikistan.[61] To make things even more complicated, the subsequent military victory of the Taliban was also attributed to foreign interference.

When the Taliban emerged as a new military actor in Afghanistan in 1994, it was initially referred to, in the West at least, as a 'students army',[62] leading readers to believe that this meant university students. In reality, the term meant pupils from religious schools, who may have only been instructed in a 'village version of village Islam.'[63] A great deal of international opprobrium then focused on the denial of women's rights, competing with other issues ranging from opium exports

---

[58] Commission on Human Rights – Final report on the situation of human rights in Afghanistan submitted by the Special Rapporteur, Mr. Felix Ermacora, U.N. Doc. E/CN.4/1995/64 of 20 January 1995, para. 45, E/CN.4/1993/42 of 18 February 1993, para. 59, and A/45/664 of 31 October 1990, para. 107.

[59] General Assembly – Situation of human rights in Afghanistan, resolution 47/141 of 18 December 1992.

[60] Rashid, A. – Afghanistan: A peep into the mysterious spy network, *Far Eastern Economic Review*, 17 October 1991, p. 21.

[61] Ali, S. and Rashid, A. – Afghanistan: Separate ways, *Far Eastern Economic Review*, 24 September 1992, pp. 18–20; Roy, O. – La crise afghane au miroir des ambitions étrangères, *Le monde diplomatique*, July 1993, pp. 22–23.

[62] Rollnick, R. – Religious zeal is the new ruler in Kabul, *The European*, 10–16 October 1996.

[63] Christensen, A. – *Aiding Afghanistan. The Background and Prospects for Reconstruction in a Fragmented Society*, Nordic Institute of Asian Studies, Copenhagen, NIAS Reports, No. 26, p. 68.

to a planned oil-and-gas pipeline, to the harbouring of Osama bin Laden. The output of the vast poppy fields of Afghanistan, transformed into opium in Pakistan, has been valued at an annual $2.5 billion[64] and explains the financing of continued warfare. Additional income was expected from an anticipated pipeline through Afghanistan. Efforts by Unocal, based in the USA, and Bridas, based in Argentina, to outbid each other so as to secure approval and funding for a pipeline between Turkmenistan and Pakistan were reportedly an incentive to peace-making and to the recognition of the Taliban as the legitimate government of Afghanistan.[65] This might have ruptured the lack of international recognition of the Taliban as government of Afghanistan, except by Pakistan, Saudi Arabia, and the United Arab Emirates, was it not for the United States. Suspecting Osama bin Laden's involvement in the bombing of US embassies in East Africa, the United States tried to bomb him out of existence and then imposed sanctions against the Taliban, which were followed by Security Council's sanctions.[66] These were founded upon the Council's assertion that the Taliban was providing safe heaven to Osama bin Laden and aimed at his surrender for trial in the United States. With global attention thus switched to terrorism, human rights have again sank on the international agenda as they did in the 1980s.

TURKEY

A wide range of human rights issues has been raised in EUrope's relations with Turkey in the past two decades: the lack of safeguards against torture, an open-ended definition of 'terrorism' which includes publication of texts critical of the government's human rights policy, the protracted armed conflict in south-eastern Turkey and the denial of minority rights to Kurds, and finally, the military occupation of Northern Cyprus (the Turkish Republic of Northern Cyprus is recognized by Turkey alone). Human rights in Turkey's relations with EUrope have been weighed against two countervailing interests: the strategic importance of Turkey and consequent US support on one side, on the other, Greek intransigence over any concessions to Turkey. In addition, Germany's anxiety about its own Turkish and Kurdish resident population has worked at cross-purposes with its extensive trade with Turkey.

Turkey, as a member of the Council of Europe as of 1949 and of NATO since 1952, is formally a member of Western inter-governmental organizations. An association agreement with EUrope (the European Communities at the time) followed in 1963, as did Turkey's first application for membership, rejected in 1989. This

---

[64] Rashid, A. – Drug overdose. Bumper opium harvest threatens social order, *Far Eastern Economic Review*, 15 December 1994, pp. 23–24.

[65] Rashid, A. – Energy: Second front, *Far Eastern Economic Review*, 19 June 1997.

[66] Security Council resolution 1267 (1999) of 15 October 1999.

rejection implicitly classified Turkey as non-western and was remedied in December 1999, when the Helsinki Summit elevated Turkey to a formally recognized applicant for membership in the European Union. Since Turkey's human rights record was held up many times as the biggest obstacle to its membership, as described below, one might be tempted to attribute EUrope's change of heart to Turkey's improved respect of human rights. The main arguments seemed to have been Turkey's membership in NATO (and thus its say in a planned European Defence Identity), pipeline politics (enhancing Turkey's position of a bridgehead to Caspian and Caucasian countries), coupled with an apparent 'thaw in Greek-Turkish relations after earthquakes in both countries.'[67]

Turkey's possible membership in the European Union has had numerous ups and downs, dotted with even more numerous – and undiplomatic – exchanges. Former Germany's chancellor, Helmut Kohl, was intransigent: 'From my geography lessons at school, I cannot recall being told that Anatolia was part of Europe.'[68] The Dutch minister of foreign affairs at the time, Hans van Mierlo, speaking on behalf of the EU Presidency, said that Turkey was 'a large Muslim state. Do we want that in Europe?'[69] After a murky compromise was forged in 1997–98 about Turkey being (but not quite) included in EUrope's planned enlargement,[70] the European Commission singled out human rights violations, 'important deficiencies in the treatment of minorities,' and the absence of civilian control over the military as important obstacles.

Such verbal exchanges have had only some impact on aid to Turkey. Table 7.3 gives aid flows to Turkey in 1960–1995 at five-year intervals. The dominance of bilateral over multilateral aid is clearly visible, as is the ebb and flow of bilateral aid that could possibly have been associated with donors' human rights policies. Efforts to condition aid to Turkey on human rights criteria first came to public attention in 1981–82, when Germany suspended a loan to Turkey in response to a 1980 military coup. The Commission of the European Community followed by suspending the financial protocol and the European Parliament called for suspension of the Joint EEC-Turkey Committee.[71] Aid to Turkey was resumed in 1983, following

---

[67] The European Union decides it might one day talk Turkey, *The Economist*, 18 December 1999.

[68] Paterson, T. – Germany shuts door to Europe on the Turks, *The European*, 3–9 April 1997.

[69] Mather, I. – Turkey talks tough as Union shies from Islam, *The European*, 6–12 February 1997.

[70] At the Luxembourg Summit in 1997, three categories of countries eligible for membership were defined. The first one was comprised of frontrunners such as the Czech Republic, Hungary and Poland. The second included countries that would not become members in the first expansion but would take part in negotiations, such as Bulgaria and Romania, and the third category was Turkey, which would be invited to participate in an annual conference of the existing and future members. This formula proved 'acceptable to its old enemy, Greece' and Turkey's relations with EUrope were made conditional on a 'satisfactory and stable relationship with Greece.' Turkey was asked to support a negotiated settlement in Cyprus, which was made urgent due to the latter's inclusion among frontrunners for membership. Tucker, E. – Turkey dispute hangs over expansion talks, *Financial Times*, 13–14 December 1997.

[71] This is described in more detail in Tomaševski, K. – *Between Sanctions and Elections. Aid Donors and their Human Rights Performance*, Pinter/Cassell, London, 1997, pp. 119–123.

Table 7.3: Aid to Turkey in 1960–1995
(in million US$)

	1960	1965	1970	1975	1980	1985	1990	1995
France	–	–	2.7	0.6	33.2	0.8	65.0	18.3
Germany	31.3	21.7	34.7	12.0	326.7	38.1	241.5	13.4
Italy	0.8	–6.5	1.4	–7.3	0.6	22.2	21.9	–6.0
Japan	0.0	–	0.2	4.8	5.4	26.0	324.2	33.7
Sweden	–	0.6	1.0	–0.3	11.8	–0.4	0.7	3.7
Switzerland	–	1.0	0.4	–0.3	–0.5	–0.2	1.1	5.9
United Kingdom	–1.8	18.6	10.2	–2.1	18.7	7.4	–8.2	–0.1
USA	108.0	111.4	95.0	8.0	265.0	38.0	–76.0	101.0
Arab donors	–	–	–	–	275.4	27.2	630.6	140.1
EUrope	–	–	–	–	388.9	73.9	299.8	19.5
Total bilateral (DAC/OECD)	137.5	154.6	152.6	23.5	713.8	136.7	598.7	173.7
Total multilateral	–3.0	9.0	22.7	47.8	20.7	12.4	–9.8	–10.1

Source: OECD – *Geographical Distribution of Financial Flows to Developing Countries*, various issues.

the adoption of a new constitution and parliamentary elections. Neither the brevity of suspension nor the small amount of aid could have had a significant economic impact on Turkey. That suspension cannot be seen in Table 7.3, which reproduced figures at five-year intervals but the ebb and flow of aid is shown in Table 7.4.

Many findings of Turkey's non-compliance with minimum human rights guarantees and calls for sanctions resulted in diminished aid. Table 7.4 lists Turkey's major donors in the 1980s in order to illustrate the obvious decrease of aid flows in the early 1980s, following the 1980 military coup. A decrease of aid was not uniform for all donors. The United States supported the Turkish military government by providing military and economic aid as well as enthusiastic human rights reporting. The *1993 State Department Country Report on Human Rights Practices* noted the 'declining numbers of complaints of torture by prisoners, and increasing numbers of convictions of police personnel for torture.'[72]

Table 7.4: Aid to Turkey, 1982–93
(in million US$)

	1982	1983	1985	1987	1989	1991	1993
France	89.6	47.7	105.6	19.3	169.8	214.9	477.2
Germany	45.7	−20.0	108.7	716.9	474.6	815.7	2019.0
Italy	238.8	70.5	213.4	−123.0	31.3	29.3	49.4
Japan	−13.6	−15.2	82.2	545.8	259.1	711.3	2084.7
USA	519.0	245.0	−234.0	−156.0	333.0	342.0	579.0
EUrope	417.4	95.0	581.7	1159.2	802.4	1307.2	2722.2
Total bilateral	893.0	248.7	418.6	1687.3	1419.1	2139.2	5627.0
Total multilateral	1540.1	703.3	1134.5	2415.3	1447.2	2846.3	5476.4

Source: *Geographical Distribution of Financial Flows to Developing Countries*, OECD, Paris, various issues.

The European Parliament's involvement in human rights began with public hearings on Turkey in 1983. Indeed, Turkey has remained an almost-permanent item on its agenda. The extent to which this attention for Turkey has been related to Greece is difficult to assess because the Parliament's punitive initiatives towards Turkey have regularly been couched in general human rights language. For example, EUrope's aid worth 375 million ecu ($470) under the 1995 customs union was blocked by the Parliament in September, citing human rights violations as the reason, although Greece was identified behind that initiative.[73] Greece and Turkey

---

[72] Department of State – *Country Reports on Human Rights Practices for 1983*, Washington, D.C., February 1984, p. 1108.

[73] Buonadonna, P. – Union struggles with human rights, *The European*, 26 September–2 October 1996; Turkey: Two-faced, *The Economist*, 26 October 1996..

have had a number of unsolved conflicts, ranging from Cyprus to the division of the continental shelf. The Parliament's initiatives, such as its refusal to give its assent to EUrope's agreements with Turkey (and Israel) in 1987, citing human rights violations, have routinely revealed that human rights have not been the sole motivation.[74]

In 1995–96, the European Parliament made human rights in Turkey its most widely publicised agenda item, first refusing and then granting assent to EUrope's customs treaty with Turkey. The background to this was the Parliament's decision in December 1994, having just overcome Greek resistance,[75] to suspend negotiations of a customs union treaty with Turkey. The minimum requirements for resuming negotiations were the release of political prisoners and the abrogation of the anti-terrorism legislation under which many of them were held. In fact, security courts had tried some 5,500 people for statements or publications that were subsumed under the prohibition of 'terrorism.'[76] Subsequent cases before the European Commission on Human Rights have demonstrated just how broad the definition of terrorism had been.[77]

Turkey's eventual response was to amend both the Constitution and anti-terrorism legislation and to release some political prisoners. Approval of the customs union treaty duly rewarded this.[78] Commentators attributed Parliament's change of heart to the inducement of an estimated $1.5 billion in import duties on European goods, combined with 'one of the fiercest lobbying campaigns ever mounted,' including trips to Turkey (paid by Turkey) by 'more than 120 MEPs [Members of European Parliament] out of a total of 626.'[79] Two EUrope's institutions articulated two distinct sets of criteria: the Parliament focused on human rights, the Council emphasised Turkey's geopolitical importance as well as the fact that half of Turkey's trade was with EUrope.[80] Human rights conditionality was defined in terms of constitutional and legislative changes,[81] thus facilitating

---

[74] Zwamborn, M. – Human rights promotion and protection through the external relations of the European Community and the Twelve, *Netherlands Quarterly of Human Rights*, 1989, No. 1, p. 18.

[75] Greece may lift veto on EU deal with Turkey, *The European*, 3–9 March 1995; EU link to Turkey is final. Greece ends veto for Cyprus talks, *International Herald Tribune*, 7 March 1995.

[76] Pope, N. – Open to change. Cosmetic surgery on its repressive laws has done little to change the face of Turkey's onslaught on its writers, *Index on Censorship*, vol. 25, No. 2, March/April 1996, p. 155.

[77] Ward, S. – British lawyers accuse Turkey, *The Independent*, 2 September 1995.

[78] Pope, H. – Kurdish MPs freed for 'Europe's sake', *The Independent*, 27 October 1995.

[79] Vernet, D. – Turkey woos the European Parliament, *Le Monde*, reprinted in *Guardian Weekly*, 26 November 1995; Southey, C. – MEPs vote under shadow of Islam, *Financial Times*, 13 December 1995.

[80] van der Klaauw, J. – European Community: EC – Turkey relations, *Netherlands Quarterly of Human Rights* 1992, No. 3, p. 334–335.

[81] European Commission – *General Report on the Activities of the European Union 1994*, Brussels/Luxembourg, 1995, para. 760.

Turkey's compliance. The treaty did not have a positive economic impact on Turkey because aid was subsequently blocked by Greece[82] while benefits accrued to EUrope – within the first six months, trade with Turkey increased by 41.5%.[83]

Just after the customs treaty was approved, ten contributors to a book published by the Human Rights Foundation of Turkey under the title *We Protect Human Rights with Imperfect Constitution and Laws* were indicted for a criminal offence of insulting the 'laws of the Republic of Turkey'.[84] Perhaps an improvement was that previously they would have been charged with terrorism. The European Parliament approved the customs union treaty anticipating that it could be suspended in such cases, but the Council of Ministers held that consulting Parliament 'about every human rights abuse in Turkey would be too time-consuming.'[85]

Responding to individual abuses might have seemed too time-consuming, but Turkey also raised a far more profound problem of respect for international human rights law, which triggered little international opprobrium. In 1992, Turkey refused to co-operate with the European Committee for the Prevention of Torture (CPT) and then defied a judgement of the European Court of Human Rights in 1998.[86] Political and legal human rights tracks are separate, however. The former, pursued by EUrope, has ignored law developed within the Council of Europe and laid down its own human rights criteria. The Council of Europe has failed to follow up on Turkey's disregard of human rights law, revealing an abyss between its legal and political organs. The former had the authority to fault Turkey's respect of human rights law but no enforcement powers, the latter could – but did not – apply sanctions such as suspension or expulsion.[87]

Such problems did not emerge in the 1990s, however. In 1982, Turkey was brought to court by Denmark, France, the Netherlands, Norway and Sweden under the European Convention on Human Rights. One of the main issues was torture. The case ended in 1985 with a friendly settlement, about which little was known at the time.[88] Torture did not disappear from Turkey but the friendly settlement

---

[82] Greece blocks billion-dollar aid to Turkey, *The European*, 7–13 March 1996; Ankara turns to Santer for reassurance during impasse, *European Voice*, 30 May–5 June 1996; Mortimer, E. & Hope, K. – Thaw pierces the Aegean chill, *Financial Times*, 24 July 1997; For the record: General Affairs Council 27 April, *European Voice*, 30 April–6 May 1998.

[83] Wise, E. – Turkey cries foul over treatment by Union, *European Voice*, 19 December 1996–8 January 1997.

[84] International Helsinki Federation for Human Rights – Once again, Turkey prosecutes human rights defenders. Their 'crime': Criticising Turkey's laws, Press release of 15 December 1995.

[85] Ciller provides testing ground for foreign policy debate, *European Voice*, 7–13 March 1996.

[86] Walker, M. – Money cannot buy happiness for Brussels, *Guardian Weekly*, 6 September 1998.

[87] Zwaak, L. – The Council of Europe and Turkey, *Netherlands Quarterly of Human Rights*, vol. 14, 1996, No. 4, pp. 387–388; Reidy, A. Et al. – Gross violations of human rights: Invoking the European Convention on Human Rights in the case of Turkey, *Netherlands Quarterly of Human Rights*, vol. 15, 1997, No. 2, pp. 161–173.

[88] Kamminga, M.T. – Is the European Convention on Human Rights sufficiently equipped to cope with gross and systematic violations?, *Netherlands Quarterly of Human Rights*, vol. 12, 1994, No. 2, pp. 153–164.

reportedly nudged Turkey to bestow the right of individual petition to the European Commission on Human Rights, which it did in 1987, and in 1991 it also accepted compulsory jurisdiction of the European Court of Human Rights. These two gestures resulted in a veritable flood of complaints – over 1,000 were registered by 1997,[89] many originating from victims of torture.

Additionally, the European Committee for the Prevention of Torture (CPT) issued in 1992 a public statement against Turkey, the only sanction at its disposal, after Turkey had breached its obligations under the European Convention for the Prevention of Torture.[90] The CPT's public statement recorded Turkey's failure to implement the Committee's key recommendations to strengthen safeguards against torture and constrain the power of anti-terrorism units.[91] A similar path was followed by the Committee against Torture (CAT) within the United Nations. The CAT found that torture in Turkey was systematic ('habitual, widespread and deliberate') and made its conclusions public.[92] It was, in the words of Gündüz Aktan, Turkey's ambassador to the United Nations, the most serious sanction against a government.[93] Indeed, it was the most serious sanction at the disposal of the CAT, while the UN's political bodies duplicated the conduct of their regional counterparts by failing to resort to any of the political and/or diplomatic sanctions at their disposal. As has been shown in Chapter 1 and is revisited in Chapter 12, Turkey has never been condemned for human rights violations by UN's human rights bodies.

Representatives of the Turkish government routinely attributed human rights problems to terrorism, blamed on PKK (Kurdistan Workers' Party), and thus legitimizing the government's response as suppression of terrorism. The spectacular capture and subsequent trial of Abdullah Ocalan raised hopes that repression blamed on terrorism could stop, but also fears that the battleground could shift to

---

[89] De Bellaigue, C. – Islamists set to muscle in as Turkey nurses a cold shoulder, *The European*, 9–15 January 1997.

[90] That Convention obligates parties to allow CPT access to all places where people are held in detention, to co-operate with CPT, and to follow up on its recommendations. The Committee is a unique international body, with a preventive rather than condemnatory role. It issues confidential reports based on visits to prisons, addressed to the respective government, suggesting measures to improve protection against ill-treatment of detainees. The government itself decides whether to make Committee's reports public, and in practice they all do. Despite harsh criticism to which the Committee subjects all governments, all co-operate with the Committee.

[91] European Committee for the Prevention of Torture and Inhuman or Degrading Treatment or Punishment – Public statement on Turkey of 15 December 1992, Doc. CPT/Inf (93)1, para. 2.

[92] Committee against Torture – Summary account of the results of the proceedings under article 20 of the Treaty against Torture concerning Turkey, U.N. Doc. A/48/44/Add. 1 of 9 November 1993, para. 39.

[93] Committee against Torture – Summary account of the results of the proceedings concerning the inquiry on Turkey, U.N. Doc. A/48/44/Add.1 of 9 November 1993; Statement of 24 November 1993 on behalf of the Republic of Turkey, *Human Rights Law Journal*, vol. 14, 1993, No. 11–12, p. 430.

EUrope, with 'a disciplined and coordinated campaign of awareness-raising [by the Kurdish expatriate community] within the European Union could prove infinitely more damaging to Turkey's long-term political and economic prospects than Ocalan's guerrilla campaign could ever have done.'[94] That guerrilla campaign had triggered military raids to root out PKK, often waged with Western-supplied weaponry[95] and thus implicit Western support. The translator and local publisher of one report about Western military aid were prosecuted in 1997 because the report was found to 'defame and belittle' Turkey's army',[96] the second largest in the NATO.

The father of modern Turkey, Kemal Ataturk, like six of his eight successors, had been a soldier. Three military coups took place in 1960–80, another in 1980 triggered Europe's aid suspension. Yet another occurred in 1996–97, called a 'soft' coup, and it ousted a government that had been deemed excessively Islamic. That government had also been unable to exert any control over the army:

> Mr. Erbakan's [Turkey's prime minister and the leader of the Welfare Party, thereafter outlawed] south-east policy bordered on the farcical when he announced in June that the Turkish army campaign against the Marxist PKK rebels sheltering in northern Iraq was over. Half an hour later, the Chief of the General Staff, General Ismail Hakki Karadayi, issued a press statement that his army's campaign was far from over and that cleansing operations against the PKK would continue.[97]

An assumption whereby the civilian government controls the army is one of the pillars of human rights protection. Indeed, human rights safeguards do not anticipate a situation in which the army controls the government. International human rights politics seldom heeds prerequisites for human rights protection, however, and EUrope has continued tackling individual abuses in Turkey within its Euro-Meda initiative.[98] The European Parliament demanded 'to inspect each programme

---

[94] McDowall, D. Own goal for Turkey?, *The World Today*, April 1999, p. 10.

[95] Turkey: Hold the funds, *Newsweek*, 4 July 1994; Arms aid to Turkey?, editorial, *New York Times*, reprinted in *International Herald Tribune*, 18 October 1995; Turkey bans arms from Denmark, *International Herald Tribune*, 1 June 1995; Human Rights Watch/Arms Project – *Weapons Transfers and Violations of the Laws of War in Turkey*, New York, November 1995, p. 36.

[96] Human Rights Watch – The United States and Europe plan further weapons sales to Turkey despite continuing violations of human rights, Press release of 17 January 1997.

[97] Parker, M. – Turkey's very democratic coup, *South*, July 1997, p. 38.

[98] EUropean-Mediterranean partnership was launched in October 1994 with Morocco, Algeria, Tunisia, Egypt, Jordan, Syria, Lebanon, Israel, Palestine, Turkey, Cyprus and Malta; Libya was excluded. It was designed to encompass economic development and trade, social stability, immigration, environment and security, specifically to double EUrope's aid ($6 billion was pledged for 1995–99) and lead to a free-trade zone by the year 2001. European Commission – *General Report on the Activities of the European Union 1994*, Brussels/Luxembourg, 1995, para. 845; Gardner, D. – EU turns strategic eyes to south, *Financial Times*, 17 May 1995.

to see if it would benefit Turkey and, if so, to block it,'[99] pursuing its punitive approach. Although the funding at issue was minuscule, the symbolic importance has been huge because Euro-Meda encompassed also Algeria, with structural obstacles to human rights protection similar to Turkey's.

ALGERIA

In contrast to Turkey, human rights have not been an obstacle for EUrope's aid to Algeria, and the Commission reported in 1996 that 'financial cooperation under the fourth protocol with Algeria continued to run smoothly.'[100] Nevertheless, Algeria did create an immense problem for EUrope's human rights policy. Similarly to Turkey, support for Algeria's military (justified by the need to combat terrorism and fears of a mass exodus towards Europe) has prevailed over human rights or democracy. Differently from Turkey, Algeria is rich in oil; this further tips the scales against EUrope's human rights policy.

A comparison between statements by the European Union and the USA before the 1998 UN Commission on Human Rights exemplifies how the violators-agenda is generated. Such *tour d'horizon* by the two actors which initiate the bulk of condemnatory resolutions aim to delineate the Commission's agenda. In April 1998, the spokeswoman for the European Union listed no less than thirty-seven states whose human rights performance EUrope faulted. Algeria was a terminological exception as 'allegations' was used rather than 'violations.' This was preceded by EUrope's unreserved condemnation of 'terrorist attacks against the Algerian population,' and followed by calling 'on the authorities to make every effort to protect them.'[101] No condemnatory resolution was even tabled, let alone adopted, and the Commission was criticised, not only by NGOs and the media, but by its own Chairman.[102]

The background to this state of affairs is well known and can be briefly summarized. The 1995 presidential elections in Algeria followed four years of bloodshed triggered by the interruption of the 1991 elections. Donors welcomed the 1995 elections because they lifted the burden of explaining why their postulated linkage

---

[99] Wise, E. – Turkey cries foul over treatment by Union, *European Voice*, 19 December 1996–8 January 1997.

[100] European Commission – *General Report on the Activities of the European Union 1994*, Brussels/Luxembourg, 1995, para. 855.

[101] United Nations – Statement by United Kingdom on behalf of the European Union before the Commission on Human Rights of 14 April 1998, U.N. Doc. E/CN.4/1998/SR.42 of 18 April 1998, paras. 69–70.

[102] Frustration, *The Economist*, 18 April 1998; Williams, F. – UN's human rights body under fire, *Financial Times*, 24 April 1998.

between aid and democracy had been suspended in 1991–95.[103] Indeed, when the government annulled the first round of elections at the end of 1991, which had been won by the Islamic Salvation Front (FIS, *Front islamique du salut*), donors' support for democracy had been put to a test.[104] The 1991 elections had been intended to constitute the final stage of the process of political liberalisation begun in 1989. In the aftermath of the 'bread riots' of 1988, the formation of political parties was allowed. These riots had been triggered by rapidly deteriorating living conditions, caused by a gradual fall in oil prices coupled with mounting government debt, which had led to a typical structural adjustment programme that further fuelled popular resentment. Political liberalisation was the government's – or the military's, as some would have it – response, and it opened political space for the FIS, whose electoral victories in the 1990 local elections and in the 1991 parliamentary elections led to its banning in 1992.

Contrary to donors' pledge to suspend aid when a democratic process is interrupted, their conduct exhibited a preference for 'a police state [rather than] an Islamic democracy.'[105] It was not *any* interruption of democratic process that would be penalized. As in Turkey, the military was associated with democracy and the opposition labeled as anti-democratic. A typical comment illustrates the tone adopted by the Western press: 'If the army fails, there is nothing else,' to which 'the danger of a massive wave of exiles leaving Algeria in the event of a FIS victory'[106] was routinely added.

Commenting on Europe's relations with Algeria, Lionel Jospin noted in 1997 that 'nobody moves in Europe because France does not move.'[107] France was – and remains – the originator of EUrope's policy towards Algeria and its principal donor, with an annual $1.2 billion in military and civilian aid.[108] Official aid statistics, reproduced in Table 7.5, show much lower figures because military aid is excluded. Zafar Masud has claimed that official figures do not reflect all civilian aid: 'Paris has been buying Algerian gas for the past 10 years at rates much higher than the market price in order to disguise its generous financial aid' to Algeria.[109]

---

[103] 'The Commission has asked member states to allow it to negotiate an association accord with Algeria which would cover political, economic and social cooperation as well as trade.' Wise, E. – Move to boost Euro-Med ties picks up pace, *European Voice*, 9–14 May 1996.

[104] The Human Rights Committee diagnosed that the Algerian authorities prevented forces that they considered hostile to democracy from taking advantage of democratic procedure in order to harm democracy. Algeria. Comments of the Human Rights Committee, U.N. Doc. CCPR/C/79/Add.1 of 25 September 1993, para. 4.

[105] Wright, R. – Islam, democracy and the West, *Foreign Affairs*, vol. 71, No. 3, Summer 1992, p. 137.

[106] Fisk, R. – Algeria's last-chance president is sworn in, *The Independent*, 1 February 1994; Muslim fundamentalists thwarted by coup, *Guardian Weekly*, 19 January 1992.

[107] Paris rejects call for move on Algeria, *International Herald Tribune*, 28 January 1997.

[108] Kepel, G. & Pierre, A,J, – For persuasion and pressure to rescue Algeria, *International Herald Tribune*, 9 July 1996.

[109] Masud, Z. – Parisian whispers, Under fire: Ethics in diplomacy and trade, *South*, December 1997, p. 21.

French and EUropean aid constituted four-fifths of total aid to Algeria, as Table 7.5 shows, and this support was further reflected in the decisions of major financial actors:

> A group of eight international banks, led by Crédit Lyonnais, approved on February 26, 1992, a $1.5 billion foreign loan to ease Algeria's debt repayments. The refinancing of Algeria's debt paved way for disbursement of a $510 loan from the European Community. Offers of credit from the World Bank ($1 billion), France ($877 million) and Italy ($300 million) were all aimed at soothing the country's economic distress.[110]

Table 7.5: Aid to Algeria, 1993–1997
(in million US$)

	1993	1994	1995	1996	1997
Belgium	4.6	1.4	6.6	11.7	4.5
France	199.5	209.3	183.9	241.1	136.7
Germany	5.2	11.0	27.1	−23.8	13.5
Italy	26.3	22.6	17.8	23.2	15.0
Spain	29.5	55.1	28.8	6.2	15.8
EBRD	46.0	37.1	18.3	22.0	34.0
Total aid from EUrope	306.3	408.8	304.1	282.1	222.6
Total aid	348.6	419.6	312.2	309.0	248.1

Source: *Geographical Distribution of Financial Flows to Aid Recipients, 1993–1997*, OECD, Paris, 1999.

Figures in Table 7.5 reproduce development aid as defined by DAC/OECD, showing France and EUrope as the largest donors. Alongside them, the IMF approved $1 billion in April 1994, which was followed by rescheduling Algeria's $26 billion debt in June 1994. This was followed by the World Bank's emergency rehabilitation loan of $200 million in October 1994 while France reportedly committed $3.1 billion to Algeria in 1994 alone. In May 1995, $1.8 billion was approved by the IMF so as 'to restore political stability in order to create an environment to encourage private sector investment,' and additional debt rescheduling followed.[111] EUrope followed the French lead, arguing that 'Algeria must be given

---

[110] Monshipouri, M. – *Democratization, Liberalization & Human Rights in the Third World*, Lynne Rienner Publishers, Boulder, 1995, p. 81.

[111] IMF pledges $1 billion after Algeria devaluation, *International Herald Tribune*, 11 April 1994; Randal, J. – Algerian peace hopes sabotaged, *Guardian Weekly*, 12 June 1994; Loan planned for Algeria, *Financial Times*, 3 October 1994; Kutschera, C. – Algeria: Does France have a policy? *The Middle East*, November 1994, p. 12; France and the IMF press aid for Algeria, *International Herald Tribune*, 10 January 1995; Khalaf, R. – Algeria wins rescheduling of $3.2 debt, *Financial Times*, 13–14 May 1995; Khalaf, R. – IMF board agrees $1.8bn Algerian loan facility, *Financial Times*, 23 May 1995; Algerian rescheduling agreed, *Financial Times*, 22–23 July 1995.

the maximum financial support to revive its economy and undercut popular support for radical Islam.'[112] The European Parliament called for suspension of military aid, implicitly endorsing all other forms of aid.[113] EUrope position was explained by Manuel Marin, at the time the Commissioner in charge of Euro-Meda:

> The EU cannot isolate Algeria. That would be counterproductive. Algeria has after all signed the Barcelona Declaration for a Euro-Mediterranean zone of shared prosperity. I assure you, however, that we are not helping the government of Algeria; we are neutral.[114]

It is unlikely that anybody believed EUrope's assertion that it has not been helping Algeria's government, but aid was indeed not its biggest source of revenue. Rather, it is oil and gas, whose export accounts for 95% of foreign exchange earnings. The oil industry is nationalized and the territory where oil wells are situated a veritable exclusion zone.[115] No less than thirty-two foreign oil companies from seventeen countries work in Algeria, through contracts with Sonatrach, Algeria's state oil and gas company.[116] The income from oil, supplemented by aid, is an even more heavily guarded exclusion zone, 'totally controlled by those who hold the reins of political power in Algeria.'[117]

Le Monde pointed to indissoluble links between France and Algeria, noting that even all others could be made to disappear, the bond created by bloodshed would tie the two countries.[118] The 1954–62 war was bloody, as was the massacre of protesting Algerians in Paris in October 1961, whose details only came to light in 1998.[119] Some four million North Africans live in France and fear of further 'export' of refugees *domesticated* French foreign policy: its effects in France were far more important than its effects for France. For example, the hijacking of Air

---

[112] Algeria: A downpayment from the West, *Africa Confidential*, vol. 35, No. 12, 17 June 1994, pp. 5–6; European Commission to prepare global plan for aid to Algeria, *Europe/Development Monthly*, No. 54, May 1994.

[113] Algeria, *Eurostep*, No. 20, April-June 1995, p. 15.

[114] Rollnick, R. – Algeria 'must not taint friendships across the Med,' *The European*, 13–19 March 1997.

[115] The territory around oil and gas installations is 'a restricted zone requiring special permission for entry by visitors,' it is guarded by Algeria's armed forces, and further protected by 'three sets of of electrified fences patrolled by Doberman dogs and screened by cameras.' Khalaf, R. – BP prepares to join Algeria's desert fortress, *Financial Times*, 19 December 1995.

[116] Corzine, R. – Algeria exploits its sea of sand, and Algerian killings fuel oil group's concern, *Financial Times*, 27 December 1995 and 6 January 1998; Martin, J. – Algeria pursues foreign investment, *The Middle East*, February 1997, p. 17–18.

[117] Dhombres, D. – 'Some Algerians are profiting from war': Interview with Gilles Kepel, *Le Monde*, reproduced in *Guardian Weekly*, 2 March 1997.

[118] France cannot disown links with Algeria (editorial), *Le Monde*, 26 December 1996, reproduced in *Guardian Weekly*, 5 January 1997.

[119] French admit hiding Algerians' toll in 1961 protest in Paris, *International Herald Tribune*, 5 May 1998.

France airliner in December 1994 was reported to be retaliation for France's support for the Algerian government, but focused instead on dangers of terrorism in France. Francis Ghilès commented:

> The sparse coverage of the brutality on both sides is in the Algerian government's interest. It is well aware that television reporting in particular could lead some in Europe to question the largely uncritical support afforded it until now by western powers since 1992. Most western leaders, notably President François Mitterand of France, tacitly endorsed the coup of January 1992. For the past three years the same leaders have been keen to denounce fundamentalist violence but are notably coy about the brutal methods of the army.[120]

The methods of the army may not have improved a great deal, but the government changed from military to civilian. Presidential elections were held in November 1995, and Liamine Zéroual (unelected head of state since January 1994, when his predecessor had been killed) continued in office, announcing that 'the state will pursue its struggle against what is left of the terrorist violence.'[121] The main opposition party, FIS, remained illegal, two others boycotted the elections, polling took place under heightened security. The presidential elections of 1995 were followed by a referendum on constitutional change in 1996, legislative and local elections in 1997, and new presidential elections in 1999. Abdelaziz Bouteflika, 'a smooth diplomat who might improve the country's tarnished image abroad,'[122] won the 1999 presidential elections after other six candidates had withdrawn.

Algeria's post-election diagnosis[123] prioritized the eradication of *terrorisme résiduel*. The human rights situation did not improve as *éradicateurs* pursued a policy which outsiders could not easily understand. The army was often faulted not to have prevented massacres, indicating negligence (to use the most generous term). Speculation ensued about 'residual terrorism' having been instigated by the army while it was talking about 'eradicating' it.[124] The intransigence of Algeria's government in precluding independent investigation supported such speculation.

---

[120] Ghilès, F. – Attention is focused on Algeria's hidden war, *Financial Times*, 28 December 1994.

[121] Simon, C. – Algeria's president blows hot and cold, *Le monde*, reprinted in *Guardian Weekly*, 10 December 1995.

[122] Khalaf, R. – Algerian regime's man runs on the reconciliation ticket, *Financial Times*, 11 March 1999.

[123] Algeria established its national institution for human rights, *Observatoire national des droits de l'homme*, which set forth – in French, English and Arabic – justifications for government's policy:'Facing the increase of breaches to public order and to the security of people and property as a result of extremist terrorist groups' actions of the Islamic fundamentalist movement which called for Djihad (holy war) in other to establish a totalitarian State, measures to fight subversion and terrorism were taken.' People's Democratic Republic of Algeria, National Observatory of Human Rights – *Legal Instruments and Agents in Charge of the Implementation of the Law and Exceptional Internal Circumstances in Algeria*, January 1997, p. 29.

[124] Addi, L. – L'armée algérienne confisque le pouvoir, *Le monde diplomatique*, February 1998.

EUrope's need to define its policy towards Algeria was heightened with the start of negotiations for an EU-Algeria association agreement.[125] Accepting Algeria's rejection of fact-finding by outsiders, EUrope fielded a diplomatic mission so as to establish dialogue with the government. That mission took place in January 1998 on 'a delicate 24-hour visit to Algiers' to return 'with no tangible results.'[126] It was followed by a four-day mission fielded by the European Parliament, which was also not allowed to visit sites of massacres or talk to anybody who had not been approved by Algeria's government. That second mission returned with tangible results, having agreed to a series of visits by Algerian parliamentarians to Europe.[127]

Diplomatic activity was thereafter transferred to the United Nations, which sent to Algeria a Panel of Eminent Persons, led by Mario Soares, former President of Portugal. The Panel noted that it was not allowed access to all people they wished so meet (such as detained FIS leaders and representatives of the Berber community) nor was it mandated to conduct investigations. While recommending international support for Algeria in its fight against terrorism (limited by human rights safeguards), the Panel pointed out that the country should 'reach a stage in which the government elected by the people would be the unquestionable political authority in the country.'[128] EUrope's reaction to that report failed to mention human rights, or the need for the civilian government to control the army rather than the other way around, emphasizing instead its support for 'the Algerian Government's efforts to consolidate democracy and to protect citizens from terrorism.'[129]

---

[125] EU optimistic new accord will favour ties with Algeria, *European Voice*, 19 December 1996–8 January 1997.

[126] EU sees progress in Algeria talks, and Faint hopes as Algeria mission ends, *Financial Times*, 21 and 22 January 1998.

[127] Khalaf, R. – Euro MPs to pursue peace in Algeria, *Financial Times*, 9 February 1998.

[128] United Nations – *Report of Eminent Panel, July – August 1988*, DPI, New York, 1999, p. 9.

[129] Declaration by the Presidency on behalf of the European Union on the Report of the United Nations Panel of Eminent Persons on the situation in Algeria, press release of 23 September 1998, PESC/98/108.

Chapter 8

Asia

The enormously varied landmass, home to two-thirds of humanity, which we call simply 'Asia' has evoked diverse responses to human rights violations. All inter-governmental responses have come from outside because there is no Asian inter-governmental organisation to have articulated an indigenous human rights policy and generated peer pressure towards its observance. Peer pressure coming from Western governments has routinely prompted Asian governments to circle their wagons, and verbal duels between the West and Asia have proliferated. The topics have ranged between prerequisites for human rights protection, such as civilian control over the military, to excessive resort to capital punishment or child labour, and verbal clashes have been guided by international human rights politics rather than by law. The legal commitments of Asian governments, expressed through their ratification of international human rights treaties and reservations to them, have seldom been used as yardstick. Indeed, the absence of an Asian human rights treaty has exacerbated incertitude about the meaning of 'human rights.' In the early 1990s, such controversies were subsumed under the umbrella-notion of *Asian values*. Similarly to cold-war duels about Western and Eastern definitions of human rights, *Asian values* was a code-word for underlying ideological and political disputes, reaching far beyond human rights. In the field of human rights, the bone of contention (both before and after *Asian values*) has been the Western linkage between aid and human rights and parallel Western condemnatory initiatives within the United Nations.

CONTRAST BETWEEN CONDEMNATIONS AND COMMERCIAL ENGAGEMENT

The diversity of responses to human rights violations in Asia has spanned both tracks, multilateral and bilateral, and has been complemented by the voluminous documentation on human rights violations produced outside inter-governmental circles. The paucity of international condemnatory or punitive response to the mass killings in Cambodia in 1975–79, or to abuses during the reign of Ferdinand Marcos by emergency decrees in the Philippines (1972–86), has not been followed by a substantively altered pattern. The chronological examination of all country situations as they were placed on the UN's or donors' agenda is complemented in Chapter 12 by looking into those countries that remained beyond the reach of these two established tracks.

The sequence of responses to human rights violations can be divided into four phases:

- International responses to violations were in their incipient phase in the 1970s. South Korea was discussed in Chapter 5 as an early target of US sanctions although, as Table 8.1 shows, it did not elicit a UN condemnation for violations. Cambodia (discussed below) triggered a UN condemnation in 1979, at the time when Pol Pot's regime had just been ousted by Vietnam. The target of condemnation was Vietnam and the United Nations reverted to addressing abuses by the Khmer Rouge twenty years later.

- In the 1980s, the focus was on government-to-government aid, and incipient NGO lobbying targeted Western donor governments. The Philippines, Sri Lanka and Bangladesh were typical examples of Western mobilization around abuses in aid recipients. Sri Lanka is discussed below; the Philippines and Bangladesh are addressed in Chapter 14 as cases that could have – but did not – prompt condemnatory and punitive responses.

- The suppression of Burmese demonstrations in 1988, the Chinese students' demonstration in 1989, and the killing of demonstrators in Dili in 1991 reversed the previously scant attention for Asia, converting Burma, China and Indonesia into focal points of international human rights politics. Burma triggered many UN condemnations and attempts to replicate the anti-apartheid sanctions strategy. China was a counter-example, with Western governments undermining their own human rights policies so as to help their companies gain a foothold in China. Indonesia elicited muted condemnations and split the donor community with regard to sanctions; its political transition in 1998–99 was triggered by the preceding economic crisis.

- The fourth phase started with international rescue packages of 1997–98. These were intended to help the limping Asian tigers, whose resort to *Asian values* in countering Western accusations of human rights violations plummeted. Paradoxically, the conditions embodied in these rescue packages did not include protection of human rights. On the contrary, high social costs were anticipated but silence prevailed as to how governments would cope with the resultant turmoil.

This Chapter discusses countries in the chronological order of their placement on the UN violations-agenda. As Table 8.1 shows, the UN's record in responding to human rights violations in Asia is uneven. Many attempts were made to have various Asian governments condemned for human rights violations but few condemnatory resolutions followed.

Out of sixteen countries which have been placed on the agenda through the confidential 1503 procedure, only six elicited condemnatory resolutions by the Commission on Human Rights. Nine countries: Bangladesh, Brunei, South Korea, Laos, Malaysia, Nepal, the Philippines, Thailand and Vietnam, were never moved outside the 1503 procedure and thus the substance of reported violations has remained confidential. Bangladesh and the Philippines are discussed in Chapter 12 because a great deal of information was generated without triggering donors' punitiveness or UN condemnations, and one can thus venture into speculating as to why neither case generated the response that might have been expected. A similar donor-recipient bond has recently coloured responses to human rights violations in Nepal.

The donor-recipient relations typical of previous decades have not necessarily followed the cartoon-type image of a powerful Western donor and a vulnerable Asian recipient. Regional superpowers, China and India, forged their own strategies of resisting Western dominance, domestically and internationally, each exhibiting immunity from Western punitiveness in the area of human rights. Asian tigers had altered their relations with the West from aid to trade and investment, and thus

Table 8.1: Asian countries on UN's violations-agenda

Country	Commission	Sub-Commission	1503 procedure	
Bangladesh	–	–	(1988)	
Brunei Darussalam	–	–	1988–90	
Burma/Myanmar	(1989–90), 1992–99	1991, 1993	1979–80, 1990–92	
Cambodia	1979–80, 1984–89, 1994–99	1978–88, 1991	1979	
China/Tibet	(1993–97; 1999)	1989–91, (1993)	–	
Indonesia/East Timor	1983, (1993–96), 1997, 1999	1982–84, 1987, 1989–90, 1992–93	(1973–75), 1978–81, 1983–85	
Korea, South	–	–	1977–82	
Laos	–	–	1995	
Malaysia	–	–	1984	
Nepal	–	–	1996	
Pakistan		1985	1985 1984, 1985, 1988	
Papua N.G./Bougainville	1993–95	1992, 1994	–	
Philippines	–	–	1984–86	
Sri Lanka	1984, 1987, (1994)	1983–84	–	
Thailand	–	–	1995, 1996	
Viet Nam	–	–	(1974–75), 1994	

from cooperation to competition, shifting also conditionality towards labour standards or environmental protection.

Promoting trade and investment, on one hand, and verbal condemnation of human rights violations on the other, formed two parallel, unlinked tracks. Table 8.2 depicts the volume of financial inflows into the main Asian destinations of investment before the 1997–98 crisis, when investors collectively pulled out of emerging markets. Table 8.3 features countries of origin of foreign investment.

The growth of investment in China or Indonesia was unhindered by parallel diplomatic efforts to respond to human rights violations. As Table 8.2 shows, between 1990 and 1997, while China was on the UN human rights agenda, foreign investment constantly and rapidly grew. The list of countries from which the bulk of investment originated included only the United States among non-Asian

Table 8.2: The most favoured countries: Foreign direct investment in Asia, 1990–97 (in US$ billion)

	1990	1991	1992	1993	1994	1995	1996	1997
China	3.5	4.4	11.2	27.5	33.8	35.8	40.2	43.0
Singapore	5.6	4.9	2.2	4.7	8.4	8.2	9.4	9.0
Malaysia	2.3	4.0	5.2	5.0	4.3	4.1	7.7	7.6
Indonesia	1.1	1.5	1.8	2.0	2.1	4.3	8.0	5.7
Thailand	2.4	2.0	2.1	1.8	1.4	2.1	2.3	3.0
Vietnam	0.2	0.3	0.5	1.0	1.5	2.0	2.5	3.0
India	0.1	0.1	0.3	0.6	1.0	2.1	2.2	2.7
South Korea	0.8	1.2	0.7	0.6	0.8	1.8	2.3	2.3
Philippines	0.5	0.5	0.2	1.2	1.6	1.5	1.5	1.3

Source: *Asia Pacific Profiles 1998*, Singapore, May 1998.

Table 8.3: Foreign direct investment in Asia by the country of origin

Burma/Myanmar	Cambodia	China	Indonesia	Philippines	Sri Lanka	Thailand	Vietnam
United Kingdom	[Expatriates]	Hong Kong	Hong Kong	USA	Hong Kong	USA	Singapore
Singapore	Singapore	USA	Australia	Hong Kong	South Korea	Hong Kong	Hong Kong
France	United Kingdom	Taiwan	United Kingdom	Taiwan	Singapore	Japan	Switzerland
Thailand	Thailand	Japan	South Korea	Bermuda	Australia	Taiwan	Taiwan
USA	Malaysia	Singapore	Japan	Malaysia	Japan	United Kingdom	Japan

Source: Who's whose biggest investors. Foreign direct investment in Asia, *Far Eastern Economic Review*, 12 October 1995.

countries, while the rest were Asian, if one counts Japan among them. Thus, a Western policy of discouraging investment would not have made a noticeable dent in the inflow of foreign investment into China. Table 8.3 points out that investment was intra-Asian rather than exclusively, or even mostly, Western. Thus Western leverage was obviously none too great and led to prioritising investment-and-trade at the expense of all other considerations so as not to lose out to Asian competitors in conquering large emerging markets.

CAMBODIA

Cambodia has been victimised by a long series of events: French colonial rule; US bombing in 1969–73 as a side-show to the Viet Nam war; the 1970 military coup and ensuing civil war against the US-supported government; wide-scale killings during the Khmer Rouge regime in 1975–78; and Viet Nam's occupation (or some would say liberation from the Khmer Rouge) in 1979–91. International peace-making intervention in 1991–93 did not significantly change the heritage of rule by force, which returned in 1997. Elections followed in 1998, amidst suspensions of aid, and an elected government was restored. International and domestic silence about previous abuses, especially during Pol Pot's reign, was ruptured in 1998–99 to attain symbolic importance as a signpost of transition from rule by force to rule of law.

The aid suspensions of 1997–98 fell into a previously established pattern. With the exception of 1991–93, the international response to developments in Cambodia was inevitably aid cut-offs. Cambodia was placed under what was then called an 'aid embargo' in 1980–91, aid was suspended for a short time in 1996 due to the illegitimate export of timber by Cambodia's military, and again following a self-coup by the second prime minister in 1997. Partial resumptions of aid were undertaken so as to make the 1998 elections possible, while full resumption might have been conditioned on bringing former Khmer Rouge leaders to trial.[1]

Human rights in Cambodia were placed on the United Nations agenda in 1979 as a self-determination issue. Pol Pot's regime was retroactively made notorious for abuses through the powerful symbol of the killing fields, although international

---

[1] The United Nations initiated the process towards establishing an international tribunal following the request by the government of Cambodia in June 1997, which was endorsed by the General Assembly. An expert committee was fielded to assess the existing evidence of responsibility of Khmer Rouge leaders. (Commission on Human Rights – Report of the Special Representative of the Secretary-General for Human Rights in Cambodia, Mr. Thomas Hammarberg, U.N. Doc. E/CN.4/1998/95 of 20 February 1998, paras. 73 and 75) The surrender of the last Khmer Rouge leaders in December 1998 opened the way for such a trial and proposals were discussed within the United Nations in January 1999. Anna Husarska anticipated that the donors' meeting of February 1999 would condition resumption of aid on Cambodia's performance concerning the trial of the Khmer Rouge. (Husarska, A. – Dictators are watching the Khmer Rouge case, *International Herald Tribune*, 14 January 1999)

responses had been muted in 1975–79. Self-determination defined the problem as foreign (that is, Vietnamese), armed intervention and illegal occupation. Aid to Cambodia was cut off in 1980 so as to deny financial support to the Vietnamese as well as to the country thus ruled. Aid was made conditional on the withdrawal of Vietnamese forces and a negotiated political settlement, which had to wait until 1991.

Although Cambodia was placed on the UN's human rights agenda in 1979, an attempt had been made in 1978 by the Commission on Human Rights to respond to abuses in Cambodia under the confidential 1503 procedure. Although nothing was known about the substance, it is safe to assume that gross abuses during the Pol Pot regime were at issue. Cambodia's government was asked to respond,[2] but denied the veracity of the information, and the Commission abandoned a planned investigation. The 1979 change of regime shifted the Commission's attention to the Vietnamese occupation, and it denounced 'foreign armed intervention and illegal occupation [as] the primary violation of human rights.'[3] The Commission's resolution departed from the UN practice of appealing for aid to the Cambodian people, although circumstances would have warranted it.

While the resolutions of the Commission on Human Rights were silent on aid, those of the General Assembly supported on-going humanitarian relief.[4] NGOs provided much relief and launched a campaign against the denial of aid. Thirty-four NGOs summarised their platform in a book entitled *Kampuchea:*[5] *Punishing the Poor.*[6] They argued that denying aid to Cambodia worked against prerequisites for human rights protection. Their recommendations were to grant aid free of political conditions, while withdrawing all forms of support from Khmer Rouge leaders.

Development aid was denied to Cambodia due to the Vietnamese occupation; aid to Vietnam, however, continued. As Table 8.4 illustrates, bilateral aid to Cambodia plummeted in the early 1980s. The exception was Australia – it provided aid to Cambodia but not to Vietnam. Humanitarian relief, which was exempt from punitive denial of aid as is customary, was channelled to the refugees on the Thai–Cambodia border rather than the population within the country. Some of that relief benefited the Khmer Rouge, creating safe heavens for them amongst refugees in Thailand.

As Table 8.4 reveals, Cambodia was a target of US sanctions,[7] and US aid was only resumed in 1990, but Cambodia also had two other superpowers to reckon

---

[2] Commission on Human Rights – Report on the Thirty-fourth Session, U.N. Doc E/1978/34. Supplement No. 4, p. 137.

[3] Commission on Human Rights – Situation on Kampuchea, resolution 1988/6 of 22 February 1988.

[4] General Assembly resolution 42/3 of 14 October 1987, preamble.

[5] The official name of the country was changed from Cambodia to Kampuchea but this change is not referred to here except when 'Kampuchea' appears in quotas and citations from that time.

[6] Mysliwiec, E. – *Punishing the Poor: The International Isolation of Kampuchea*, OXFAM, Oxford, 1988.

[7] Charny, J. et al. – *Obstacles to Recovery in Vietnam and Kampuchea. U.S. Embargo of Humanitarian Aid*, OXFAM America, 1980.

Table 8.4: Aid to Cambodia in 1973–95
(in million US$)

	1973	1974	1975	1976	1979	1980	1982	1985	1990	1991	1992	1993	1994	1995
Australia	1.8	0.6	0.3	0.2	4.8	4.5	3.4	2.3	4.3	4.8	7.7	10.4	14.3	25.8
Canada	–	0.6	–	–	–	–	–	–	0.2	2.8	3.3	3.5	3.2	4.2
France	-0.4	5.4	-0.6	–	–	3.5	–	0.3	3.0	5.3	8.7	16.8	28.4	53.4
Japan	10.8	8.4	0.2	0.1	0.1	0.1	0.4	–	0.2	0.5	4.7	61.3	64.5	152.0
Netherlands	–	0.1	0.2	–	1.5	6.8	2.2	0.4	4.1	7.8	13.6	12.6	11.0	11.8
Sweden	–	–	–	–	4.7	6.8	3.6	1.4	2.9	3.8	18.5	11.8	10.1	10.9
USA	125.0	288.0	78.0	–	–	–	–	–	5.0	6.0	13.0	29.0	16.0	33.0
EUrope	–	–	–	0.7	48.8	51.2	5.7	1.6	12.9	33.8	75.6	103.2	87.0	151.5
Total bilateral	138.7	305.1	78.6	0.5	25.0	48.6	14.5	5.6	28.5	49.9	95.4	196.6	181.0	341.0
Total multilateral	2.6	2.2	2.3	0.2	83.3	231.6	29.4	7.3	13.1	41.1	111.4	120.0	155.6	225.8

Source: OECD – *Geographical Distribution of Financial Flows to Developing Countries*, various issues.

with – China and the USSR. The Soviet Union supported Vietnam's occupation of Cambodia, while China supported the Khmer Rouge and was hostile to Vietnam. Both main adversaries in Cambodia (the Vietnamese-supported government and the Khmer Rouge) professed adherence to communism; China and the Soviet Union each supported their preferred model. The Khmer Rouge were the most powerful part of the anti-Vietnamese armed resistance and later of the Coalition Government. They were supported by China, but also by the West. In fact, the US defeat in Vietnam reinforced incentives for the denial of aid to the Vietnamese-supported government of Cambodia.

Cambodia was represented in the United Nations by the Khmer Rouge until 1982 and thereafter by the Coalition Government, a government-in-exile. The government in the country was ignored as a stooge of Vietnam. Aid could not be provided through the Coalition Government because it was outside the country, nor could it be provided through the government effectively running the country because the latter was not deemed legitimate. The many reports of human rights violations in 1980–90 added another justification for the denial of aid. Consequently, a split emerged between Western NGOs, with development NGOs criticising human rights NGOs for emphasising abuses and thus legitimising the denial of aid to Cambodia.[8]

As with other cold-war orphans, peace making followed the end of the Cold War. Once warfare was de-internationalised, it was assumed that it would simply and easily stop. The peace treaty was followed by the deployment of UNTAC (United Nations Transitional Authority in Cambodia), whose main task was to organise elections. The 1991 Paris Agreements provided for a powerful role of the United Nations, but the concentration on elections overshadowed all competing tasks. Thus, neither disarmament nor demilitarisation preceded the elections, and the government which followed them was internally divided.[9]

The media declared UNTAC to have been an expensive flop almost as soon as it was terminated. The expense was estimated at between $1.6 and $3 billion.[10] Serge Thion thus summed up the aftermath of UNTAC:

---

[8] Jackson, T. – Amnesty International and Human Rights in Kampuchea, OXFAM, November 1987, mimeographed.

[9] The UN endorsed power-sharing between, on the one hand, the previous tripartite anti-Vietnamese movements consisting of Funcinpec (Front uni national pour un Cambodge indépendent, neuter, pacifique et coopératif), the Khmer Rouge and Khmer People's National Liberation Front, and, on the other hand, the Cambodian People's Party which originated from the Vietnamese-supported government of 1980–91. The Khmer Rouge opted out; the Khmer People's National Liberation Front (restyled as the Buddhist Liberal Democratic Party) had a tiny fraction of divided positions. Governing was left to Funcinpec and the Cambodian People's Party, represented by two co-prime ministers, Prince Ranariddh, a son of King Sihanouk, and Hun Sen, the previous head of the Vietnamese-supported government.

[10] New world disorder, *Far Eastern Economic Review*, 3 December 1992; Cambodia's road to purgatory, *The Economist*, 15 August 1992; The UN's success in Cambodia? Look again, *International Herald Tribune*, 11 December 1995.

A bankrupt economy. All-out liberalization, along with the inflation generated by 20,000 highly paid UN personnel, the return of 300,000 refugees without income, the looting of natural resources by commercial networks.[11]

Two years after the UN-organised elections promoted Cambodia into democracy, threats of aid cut-offs proliferated. Aid was expected to cover one half of the government's budget and $1.5 billion were pledged for 1992–94.[12] As is customary, less than one-third was disbursed. An unnamed Western ambassador said that donors were 'looking for any excuse to cut back assistance.'[13] Such excuses were many. The killing of three Western hostages in October 1994 prompted calls for cutting off aid. In 1995, such calls encompassed, *inter alia*, press censorship, corruption, drug trafficking, and harassment of opposition leaders.[14] Calls upon donors to conditions aid on respect for human rights multiplied but were not heeded. One important reason was that this would have entailed an implicit acknowledgement that the 1991–93 intervention had failed.

Military expenditure amounted to almost half of the budget (46%) in 1995,[15] this proportion being attributed to the need to combat the Khmer Rouge. In July 1994, Cambodia's Parliament outlawed the Khmer Rouge, following protracted and unsuccessful negotiations. In fact, the Khmer Rouge had signed the 1991 Peace Agreement but had reneged less than one year later, refusing demilitarisation and elections. Warfare started in earnest in 1994, with the Khmer Rouge apparently winning at the beginning. The Security Council then imposed sanctions against the Khmer Rouge, but these were about as easy to impose as they were impossible to enforce: the jungle was outside governmental control.[16] Incentives to defect were more effective. The Khmer Rouge could change sides with guaranteed amnesty, regardless of efforts outside Cambodia to bring them to justice.

Although the Khmer Rouge were outside the government, they were ultimately decisive for its fall. Negotiations between Funcinpec and the Khmer Rouge were on the verge of success when the second prime minister, Hun Sen, carried out a coup against the first prime minister, Prince Ranariddh, in July 1997.[17] The background

---

[11] Thion, S. – Failure in Cambodia, *Far Eastern Economic Review*, 21 January 1993.

[12] Friedland J. – Aid: Someone in trust, *Far Eastern Economic Review*, 24 March 1994.

[13] Thayer, N. – Cambodia: Shut out, *Far Eastern Economic Review*, 6 July 1995, p. 20.

[14] Anger over hostage deaths may cut into military aid, *Far Eastern Economic Review*, 10 November 1994, p. 16; Cambodia's press comes under the gun, *Guardian Weekly*, 15 January 1995; Cambodia: Compassion fatigue, *Far Eastern Economic Review*, 16 February 1995, p. 19; Cambodia: Medellin on the Mekong, *Far Eastern Economic Review*, 23 November 1995, pp. 24–31; Cambodia's crumbling democracy, *The Economist*, 2 December 1995, p. 17.

[15] Square one: Cambodia strives for central control of economy, and Cambodia past and future, *Far Eastern Economic Review*, 20 January 1994 and 27 April 1995.

[16] Tasker, R. – Fortunes at risk: Sanctions threaten Thai-Khmer Rouge trade, Morello, T. and Thayer, N. – Cambodia: The Pol Pot trial, *Far Eastern Economic Review*, 12 and 26 November 1992.

[17] Thayer, N. – Cambodia: Ambiguous alliances, Cambodia: Law of the gun, *Far Eastern Economic Review*, 3 and 17 July 1997.

consisted of allegations that Funcinpec was forming a coalition of political parties, which, if joined by the Khmer Rouge, without Pol Pot, could enable it to govern the country. Military build-up and troop movements by both prime ministers preceded the coup. Three days of armed struggle followed, as did summary executions and detentions.

International censure included a postponement of Cambodia's admission to the ASEAN (Association of Southeast Asian Nations) and the refusal of the United Nations to accept the credentials of both prime ministers, Hun Sen and Prince Ranariddh.[18] Cambodia's seat was thus vacant once again for one year. Most donors suspended aid: the USA, Germany, EUrope, Australia, the IMF (International Monetary Fund) and the World Bank, while Japan, China and France did not, and Australia resumed aid after two months.[19] The 1998 elections were declared free and fair by international observers the very day after polling had ended.[20]

Tony Kevin, Australia's former ambassador to Cambodia, asserted that 'the U.S. aid boycott since mid-1997 has further damaged business confidence, economic growth and the growth of civil society – without any political benefits.'[21] Such political benefits may – or may not – have ensued from the 1998 elections, but critiques of donors' resort to sanctions have started in earnest. One point has been the focus on reporting abuses without building domestic capacity to respond to them.[22] Any strategy to rupture impunity necessitates moving away from condemnations or sanctions. John Pilger added a question:

> Will those foreign governments that backed Pol Pot while wringing their hands now help to rebuild the country they helped to devastate?[23]

---

[18] Richardson, M. – ASEAN delays admission of Cambodia, *International Herald Tribune*, 11 July 1997; Cambodia's many-headed monster, *The Economist*, 1st November 1997.

[19] Holloway, N. – Foreign relations: Confused signals, and Hiebert, M. and Vatikiotis, M. – Foreign relations: Conflict of interests, *Far Eastern Economic Review*, 24 July 1997; Lloyd Perry, R. – West washes its hands of Cambodia, *The Independent*, 28 July 1997; Hiebert, M. – Economies: Submerging market, *Far Eastern Economic Review*, 31 July 1997; Smith, R.J. – Hun Sen forces accused of executions, *Guardian Weekly*, 14 September 1997; Barnes, W. – Cambodia finance support suspended, *Financial Times*, 24 September 1997; Gilley, B. – Cambodia: Dancing with the dragon, *Far Eastern Economic Review*, 11 December 1997.

[20] Richardson, M. – Cambodia's neighbours expect vote Sunday to open way to join ASEAN, *International Herald Tribune*, 25–26 July 1998; Thayer, N. and Tasker, R. – Cambodia: Unfree, unfair, *Far Eastern Economic Review*, 13 August 1998.

[21] Kevin, T. – U.S. errs in Cambodia policy, *Far Eastern Economic Review*, 21 May 1998.

[22] Fernando, B. and Wickremashinghe, T. – An absence of genuine courts: A fundamental obstacle to democracy in Cambodia, *Human Rights Solidarity*, vol. 7, No. 7, December 1997, p. 13.

[23] Pilger, J. – Pol Pot: The monster we created, *Guardian Weekly*, 26 April 1998.

SRI LANKA

The outburst of attention for warfare between the LTTE (Liberation Tigers of Tamil Eelam) and the government in the early 1980s juxtaposed the outflow of refugees and the inflow of non-governmental fact-finding missions. The two were closely related, with the exiles, mostly Tamils, creating attention for governmental abuses in the countries of refuge, and foreign NGOs visiting their country of origin to document these abuses. The war continued thereafter, but Sri Lanka slowly disappeared from international human rights politics. This sequence highlighted the process of creating an international human rights case. Collective governmental condemnation of Sri Lanka as a violator followed in 1984, as shown in Table 8.1, and donors followed by suspending or decreasing aid, as is described below. Sri Lanka has vividly illustrated the inter-play between non-governmental and inter-governmental actors, condemnations and sanctions.

A short-lived attempt at peace making in 1994–95 failed. President Chandrika Kumaratunga had committed herself to peace making in her electoral platform before she was elected for the first time, and put such plans into practice after the elections. A four-month cease-fire followed at the beginning of 1995. Warfare resumed. President Kumaratunga made another attempt at peacemaking with a planned transformation of Sri Lanka into 'a federation of regions'. Neither attempt was successful. The government and the LTTE blamed each other.[24] Some outsiders took sides; others acknowledged that it was impossible to do so, while donors unanimously supported the government. Warfare erupted in earnest in 1996, and Sri Lanka's army ejected the LTTE from their stronghold in northern Jaffna. The ebb and flow of warfare continued to the turn of the millennium, with President Kumaratunga re-elected in December 1999 with a smaller majority than in 1994, probably because she failed to make peace as she had originally promised, but re-elected nevertheless. This electoral verdict was influenced by her wounding by one of LTTE's notorious 'black tigers' on the eve of elections, and the general change of attitudes towards the LTTE 'given that it has made a habit of killing any moderate Tamil figure who tries to find an area of agreement with the government.'[25] At the international level, a profound change in the status of the LTTE had happened in 1997:

Years of patient diplomacy by Colombo bore fruit in October 1997 as the United States classified the Liberation Tigers of Tamil Eelam (LTTE) as a foreign terrorist organization.[26]

---

[24] According to Sri Lanka's delegation before the Human Rights Committee during the consideration of its report under the ICCPR, LTTE had refused to enter into political dialogue or accept foreign mediation, and unilaterally resumed hostilities. Summary record of the meeting of the Human Rights Committee on 28 July 1995, U. N. Doc. CCPR/C/SR. 1436 of 28 July 1995, paras. 5–6.

[25] Chipaux, F. – Sympathy votes seals President's victory, *Le Monde*, 23 December, reproduced in *Guardian Weekly*, 6–12 January 2000.

[26] Far Eastern Economic Review – *Asia 1998 Yearbook*, Hong Kong, December 1997, p. 198.

Before the 1990s, the LTTE had been seen as a liberation movement, in accordance with a fairly typical orientation of NGO reporting in which the exposure of abuses by the government had been coupled with an implicit support for the armed movement against that government. UN human rights bodies authoritatively found Sri Lanka's protection of human rights lacking, thus supporting the thrust of NGO reporting. The seesaw of international opprobrium shifted from the government in the 1980s to the LTTE in the 1990s. This oscillation converted a search for right and wrong into the truism that two wrongs do not make a right.

Table 8.5: Aid to Sri Lanka in 1985–1993
(in million US dollars)

	1985	1987	1989	1991	1993
Canada	20.4	20.8	14.4	8.8	5.9
Germany	60.6	38.3	38.0	10.1	26.1
Japan	123.4	153.3	185.3	258.0	219.2
Norway	11.3	15.6	13.3	13.2	12.3
United Kingdom	42.3	50.1	249.0	20.1	67.8
USA	86.0	33.0	40.0	78.0	77.0
Total bilateral	434.8	369.4	591.5	443.9	482.7
Total multilateral	587.6	544.0	744.9	868.4	816.4

Source: OECD – *Geographical Distribution of Financial Flows to Developing Countries*, various issues.

The linkage between human rights and aid flows was visible, if controversial. Publicity for Sri Lanka's non-compliance with its obligations under international human rights law led to aid cut-offs by Norway and Canada. Norway justified its decision with the government's failure 'to do its utmost to assure the security and human rights for the citizens of the country.'[27] Canada justified cutting off aid by invoking human rights violations, but Keith Hay argued that aid 'tailed off due to perceived business risks from the continuing insurgency and guerrilla attack situation in the country.'[28] The donor community did not speak with one voice, however. While Norway and Canada cut aid, other donors increased it as an inducement to the government to end the armed conflict. At a donors' meeting in June 1987, pledges amounted to $625 million and fully met Sri Lanka's demands. Indeed, 'donors urged the Government to negotiate a settlement and the World

---

[27] Prospects for Peace in Sri Lanka. Report of a Seminar held in Oslo, 24 October 1986, [mimeographed] p. 1.

[28] Hay, K.A.J. – Aid to South Asia in the 1990s: Canada's role and some implications for trade. *Journal of Developing Societies*, vol. 7, 1991, No. 1. p. 95.

Bank announced that it would make a special effort to commit additional resources for reconstruction of affected areas should the Government and the Tamils agree on a peaceful settlement.'[29] As shown in Table 8.5, Canada's aid noticeably decreased; Norway's aid less so while total aid to Sri Lanka was not affected at all.

These donors' decisions were preceded by a large number of NGO fact-finding missions to Sri Lanka, at least twenty in 1981–84.[30] All the missions reported violations, in particular noting the absence of safeguards for personal integrity and security. Similarly, all demanded changes which were required by international human rights law. Last but not least, every mission – and most studies based on secondary sources – objected to Sri Lanka's ethnic policy, in particular pointing to language, religion, and education, as well as access to civil service.[31] Much as with other countries, inquiries into the causation of warfare went beyond ethnic to economic policy. The introduction of the free market in 1977 was identified as an aggravating factor, as it had undermined Sri Lanka's previous excellent performance in the social sector. Economic hardship, worsened through institutionalised discrimination, erupted in what was alternatively called communal violence or ethnic rioting.[32]

UN political bodies, the Commission on Human Rights and its Sub-Commission, examined human rights violations in Sri Lanka in 1984 and 1987;[33] while the Human Rights Committee discussed Sri Lanka in 1984 and again a decade later. In its 1994 report to the Human Rights Committee, Sri Lanka reaffirmed that self-determination did not apply to sovereign independent states because it would lead to their dismemberment.[34] The Committee objected to Sri Lanka's restrictive interpretation of the right to self-determination, which prohibited peaceful advocacy of 'separatism'. Additionally, Sri Lanka's policy against

---

[29] *Development Co-Operation. 1987 Report*, DAC/OECD, Paris, 1988, p. 90.

[30] The International Commission of Jurists organised a first mission to Sri Lanka in 1981, a second one in 1983, and a third in 1984. The International Human Rights Law Group had two missions, in 1982 and 1983. Amnesty International had a mission in 1982, the World Council of Churches in 1983, and the Lawasia Human Rights Standing Committee in 1984. Added to these, and larger in number, were missions by parliamentarians, ministries for development co-operation, independent institutions, and those by inter-governmental organisations.

[31] Experimentation with ethnic quotas, whereby recruitment to public service was apportioned as follows, 75% for the Sinhalese, 12.7% for Tamils, 8% for Muslims, and 5.5% for Indians, was declared unconstitutional by Sri Lanka's Supreme Court. U.N. Doc. CCPR/C/SR. 1436 of 28 July 1995, para. 20.

[32] Rupesinghe, K. – The effects of export-oriented industrialisation in Sri Lanka, *The Ecologist*, vol. 15, 1985, No. 5/6, pp. 246–256; Gunasinghe, N. – The open economy and its impact on ethnic relations in Sri Lanka, *Lanka Guardian*, vol. 6, No. 17, January 1984, p. 6.

[33] The Sub-Commission resolution 1984/32, of 30 August 1984, and the Commission decision 1984/111, of 14 March 1984, appealed to the parties in conflict 'to restore harmony.' The Commission resolution 1987/61, of 12 March 1987, called for the application of humanitarian law and a negotiated political solution, and invited the Government to allow the ICRC 'to fulfil its functions of protection of humanitarian standards, including the provision of assistance and protection to victims of all affected parties.'

[34] Human Rights Committee – Third periodic report of Sri Lanka, U.N. Doc. CCPR/C/70/Add. 6 of 27 September 1994, p. 1–2.

'separatist terrorists' was found incompatible with international human rights law, especially because there was no investigation of those abuses that had apparently been committed by persons acting in an official capacity.[35] A decade later, in 1994, the Human Rights Committee identified a long list of symptoms evidencing a lack of protection of human rights on the part of the Sri Lankan authorities. A host of administrative bodies, nine altogether, which the government had established with 'human rights' in their titles was not deemed to compensate for the lack of protection. The Committee's general finding was that 'the domestic legal system of Sri Lanka contains neither all the rights set forth in the Covenant nor all the necessary safeguards to prevent their restrictions beyond the limits established by the Covenant.'[36]

The UN Working Group on Disappearances visited Sri Lanka in 1991, having recorded more than 12,000 disappearances in 1980–90, the highest number for any single country. It confirmed that official tolerance of violence, diagnosed by the Human Rights Committee back in 1984, had continued. The Working Group found that all counter-insurgency methods were apparently deemed to be legitimate, adding that 'it was publicly indicated that troops were not afterwards going to be questioned how they have achieved their tactical and strategic objectives.'[37]

Sri Lanka invited the Working Group for a second visit in the aftermath of repeated calls for its condemnation by the UN Commission on Human Rights. These calls had not led to a condemnation but to a chairman's statement.[38] This procedural remedy is used when the adoption of a condemnatory resolution is uncertain and thus a text negotiated with the government in question represents a milder option. While preparations for that session of the Commission were in the final stage, Sri Lanka's donors were meeting in Paris. They acknowledged Sri Lanka's financial 'burden imposed by the domestic political and security situation,' recalled that human rights concerns had been raised at previous annual meetings, and pledged $825 in aid.[39]

Five years later, in 1997, the UN Special Rapporteur on arbitrary executions visited Sri Lanka and found the human rights situation to be deteriorating. Although he acknowledged the challenge facing the government, embodied in 'the pervasive violence generated by armed LTTE members,' he nevertheless faulted the government's human rights performance:

[35] Report of the Human Rights Committee, U.N. Doc. A/39/40, para. 100.

[36] Concluding comments of the Human Rights Committee, U.N. Doc. CCPR/C/79/Add. 56 of 27 July 1995, para. 10.

[37] United Nations – Report of the Working Group on Enforced or Involuntary Disappearances on the visit to Sri Lanka by three members of the Group (7–18 October 1991), U.N. Doc. E/CN. 4/1992/18/Add. 1 of January 1992, paras. 194–199.

[38] United Nations – Human Rights Commission expresses concern over human rights in Sri Lanka, Press release HR/3048 of 27 February 1992.

[39] The World Bank – Sri Lanka Aid Group Meeting, Press release of 7 February 1992.

the violations have been so numerous, frequent and serious over the years that they could not be dealt with as if they were just isolated or individual cases of misbehaviour by middle- and lower-rank officers, without attaching any political responsibility to the civilian and military hierarchy. On the contrary, even if no decision had been taken to persecute the unarmed civilian population, the Government and the high military command were still responsible for the actions and omissions of their subordinates.[40]

Donors did not probe into the political accountability of the government as the Special Rapporteur had suggested but instead displayed sympathetic indulgence. For instance, the 1995 donors' meeting blamed the LTTE for resumed hostilities, commending the government on its efforts at peace making and improving respect of human rights.[41] It is worth recalling that Sri Lanka's main donor has traditionally been Japan, with South Korea being its main investor, while its main arms suppliers have been Russia, Ukraine, Indonesia and Israel.[42] Western donors, such as Norway or Canada, have therefore had little influence, particularly because Sri Lanka's policy has been to rely on trade and investment rather than on aid.

The importance of aid was highlighted by Francis Deng, the UN Rapporteur on internally displaced persons. He has articulated the difficulties faced by donors in making their aid human-rights-friendly. He suggested that donors should ensure that 'assistance advances the cause of peace, security and stability in the country' but acknowledge that 'the international community does not have a mandate to intercede with the Government.'[43] In Sri Lanka, aid remained necessary to cover the government's budget deficit, much of which resulted from the civil war, the suppression of terrorism and resulting militarisation.[44] The cost of waging the war has been estimated at an annual 1 or 6% of the GDP,[45] partially offset by the economic benefits of the war: more than 500,000 Tamil refugees settled in the West and send remittances home.[46]

---

[40] Commission on Human Rights – Extrajudicial, summary or arbitrary executions. Report of the Special Rapporteur, Mr. Bacre Waly Ndiaye on his visit to Sri Lanka, U. N. Doc. E/CN. 4/1998/68/Add. 2 of 12 March 1998, para. 151.

[41] Donors urge greater role for private sector, *Tamil Information*, Tamil Information Centre, London, No. 44/45, March/April 1995, p. 11.

[42] Sri Lanka: Diplomatic advantage, *Far Eastern Economic Review*, 8 June 1995, p. 27.

[43] United Nations – Report of the Representative of the Secretary-General on internally displaced persons. Mr. Francis Deng, on the profiles of displacement in Sir Lanka, U.N. Doc. E/CN. 4/1994/44/Add. 1 of 25 January 1994, para. 146.

[44] Cooke, K. – The economy: Separatist war is still critical factor, Survey: Sri Lanka, *Financial Times*, 27 October 1993.

[45] Sri Lanka: Wages of war, *Far Eastern Economic Review*, 27 March 1997.

[46] Sri Lanka: Blood and money, *The Economist*, 8 August 1998.

PAKISTAN

Pakistan has a demonstrated immunity from donors' human rights conditionality and from UN condemnation of human rights violations – with one exception, as discussed below. The nuclear tests in May 1998 made a difference with regard to donors' policy, but no change has taken place concerning the UN's country-oriented procedures, As exposure of denials and violations by NGOs took root in the late 1970s, there was no shortage of problems brought to the UN's attention. These ranged from rule by the military,[47] to trials of political opponents by military courts, flogging and executions, to extraction of confessions by torture, and the denials of women's and minority rights. Pakistan's immunity from UN investigation and condemnation originated in its being 'the most allied of America's allies', in the oft-quoted words of Ayub Khan, one of Pakistan's earliest military rulers, which strengthened as the Cold War evolved. The Soviet military invasion of Afghanistan in 1979 confirmed Pakistan as the most allied of US allies,[48] while post-1979 Iran heralded an Islamic resurgence within the UN's human rights bodies, fending off challenges of Islamisation in Pakistan.

Pakistan's high military expenditure attracted greater attention on the part of donors than did human rights, culminating in financial sanctions in response to nuclear tests. Despite recent changes that have empowered development finance agencies to demand reduction of military budgets and restraint from nuclear weapons programmes, pressures have been verbal rather than financial. Pakistan's military expenditure translated in 1997 into 40% of its budget, 'with the luxury of financing deficits with foreign grants and loans.'[49] International financial institutions, usually criticised for decreasing social expenditure within structural adjustment programmes, advocated Pakistan's increased spending on health and education.[50] This unusual reversal of roles did not receive much attention because such conditionality did not advance very far, either before or after nuclear tests. In

---

[47] Pakistan embarked on independence with a civilian government (1947–1958), but reverted to military rule in 1958–1971; this was followed by another civilian regime, led by Zulfikar Ali Bhutto (1971–1977), and another military coup in 1977. Its leader, Zia ul Haq, dismissed national and provincial assemblies, banned political parties, tried and executed Zulfikar Al Bhutto, and also replaced previously secular law by Islamic edicts and courts. His rule (1977–1988) ended with his death in an accident, whereupon elected government was re-introduced. In 1988–1990 the government was led by Benazir Bhutto, followed by another (1990–1993) led by Nawaz Sharif. Benazir Bhutto led the government once again in 1993–1997, and was again followed in 1997 by a government led by Nawaz Sharif, and yet another military coup took place in October 1999.

[48] '[Prime Minister Nawaz] Sharif's mentor, Zia, used the Soviet invasion of Afghanistan to get out of a deep financial hole and growing international isolation after his coup and execution of Zulfikar Ali Bhutto.' Akbar, M.J. – Peace on the Subcontinent? *Far Eastern Economic Review*, 12 August 1999.

[49] Lodhi, M. – Belief in potential remains, Survey of Pakistan, *Financial Times*, 12 August 1997.

[50] Islam, R & Rashid, A. – Talking tough: Donors tell Pakistan to clean up its fiscal act, *Far Eastern Economic Review*, 9 May 1996; Islam, S. – Show time: Pakistan tries hard to impress its donors, Far Eastern Economic Review, 8 May 1997.

November 1998, the IMF decided on its seventeenth bail out for Pakistan,[51] despite the fact that its budgetary allocations remained unchanged, with 70% allocated to debt servicing and military expenditure.

In response to the nuclear tests, the United States immediately imposed the sanctions mandated by its 1994 Nuclear Proliferation Prevention Act. Aid was suspended,[52] as well as export/import credits; bank loans were banned, and negative US votes for loans by international development finance agencies threatened. Japan followed suit by suspending aid, as did Sweden, Norway and Denmark. Others did not. The G-7 only agreed that it would support negative US votes in development finance agencies.[53] Most sanctions were lifted after six months.[54] One reason for the lifting of economic sanctions was that they could have driven Pakistan to default on its foreign debt of $42 billion. Indeed, preventing default was given priority over punishment for nuclear tests, and negotiations started two months after the nuclear tests with a view to raising the funding necessary to offset sanctions.[55] Negotiating Western-funded loans to offset Western-imposed financial sanctions might have appeared self-defeating had it not been for the need to balance conflicting requirements: some sanctions were necessary in the name of non-proliferation, and some loans to prevent Pakistan's default on debt servicing.

If nuclear tests prompted only short-term financial sanctions, it should not be surprising that human rights violations triggered none. US support had generally permitted 'the military to stifle internal dissent with externally supplied strength.'[56] The single condemnation of Pakistan by the UN Commission on Human Rights in 1985[57] was preceded and followed by silence, and the situation had not improved a decade later. In 1994, for instance, the Committee against Torture prevented Canada

---

[51] India and Pakistan Survey, *The Economist* 22 May 1999.

[52] Suspensions of aid to Pakistan dated back to 1990, when military aid was cut off to penalise Pakistan for developing nuclear weapons. The Pressler Amendment to the Foreign Assistance Act then conditioned US aid to Pakistan on the President's certification that Pakistan did not possess a nuclear explosive device. That policy was not particularly effective because Pakistan had obviously enhanced its nuclear capabilities during the Soviet military intervention in Afghanistan, while it was receiving much US military and civilian aid to support the anti-Soviet war effort.

[53] The price for India, and U. S. penalties on India get scant support, *International Herald Tribune*, 14 May 1998; G8 to step up pressure on India and Pakistan, *Financial Times*, 13–14 June 1998.

[54] Lippman, T. W. – South Asia sanctions lifted, *The Washington Post*, reprinted in *Guardian Weekly*, 15 November 1998.

[55] Rashid, A. – Economies: It's no party, *Far Eastern Economic Review*, 16 July 1998; Bokhari, F. – Pakistan caught between low taxes, retailers, and the IMF, *Financial Times*, 24 September 1998.

[56] Richter, W.L. – Prospects for political freedom in Pakistan, in Gastil, R.D. (ed.) – *Freedom in the World. Political Rights and Civil Liberties 1981*, Freedom House & Clio Press, New York and Oxford, 1981, p. 124.

[57] The Commission on Human Rights emphasised 'the relationship between violations and human rights and mass exoduses' (resolution 1985/40 of 1 March 1985), which the Sub-Commission on Prevention of Discrimination and Protection of Minorities reinforced by pointing out denials of the rights of religious minorities and the potential for mass exodus, especially by the Ahmadi community (resolution 1985/21 of 29 August 1985).

from expelling a Pakistani back to his country because 'torture is widely practised in Pakistan.'[58] The UN Special Rapporteur on torture had this to say in 1996:

> For much of its 49 years of independence, Pakistan has had a tormented existence. For most of that period the country was ruled by a series of more or less brutal military regimes. The country is racked by intercommunal and intersect strife. The language and style of competitive politics goes beyond adversarial debate in a framework of respect, taking the form of a hostile, confrontational and self-interested maneuvering. There is a very small, very rich class (frequently described as feudal) from which most of the political elite come, and a large majority of very poor people. Law enforcement agencies have traditionally been used more to serve the narrow interests of those in office than to defend the rule of law.[59]

Pakistan's placement on the UN violators agenda in 1985 was preceded by extensive NGO documentation of abuses[60] but was not followed by any UN investigation or condemnation. Abuses publicised by NGOs revealed a deeper problem: Pakistan's consecutive governments displayed no commitment to human rights. The Human Rights Commission of Pakistan faulted the government for not accepting the very premise for human rights protection – that human rights are worth guaranteeing.[61]

UN human rights bodies have traditionally focused on the plight of victims who were prominent opposition leaders, journalists, judges or university students. In the 1990s, proposals to prohibit the importation of products of child labour moved attention to the plight of the majority, adding to international human rights politics new forms of punitiveness, such as consumer boycotts. EUrope pursued a non-punitive approach at the inter-governmental level,[62] while punitiveness prevailed at the non-governmental level.[63] Concerns about child labour have linked Pakistan

---

[58] Committee against Torture – *Khan v. Canada*, Communication No. 15/1994.

[59] Commission on Human Rights – Report of the Special Rapporteur, Mr. Nigel Rodley. Visit by the Special Rapporteur to Pakistan, U.N. Doc. E/CN. 4/1997/7/Add. 2 of 15 October 1996, para. 88.

[60] Amnesty International reported in 1983 trials of political prisoners by military courts, with sentences ranging from flogging to execution, and widespread use of administrative detention affecting prominent opposition leaders (Amnesty International – *1984 Report*, pp. 245–250). No improvement was reported for 1984; additional arrests and detentions targeted opposition to the referendum endorsing islamisation and to the denial of religious freedom to the Ahmadi community. (Amnesty International – *1985 Report*, pp. 233–237). For 1985, Amnesty noted no betterment and submitted documentation on on-going denials and violations of human rights to the UN under the 1503 procedure (Amnesty International – *1986 Report*, pp. 246–249).

[61] Human Rights Commission of Pakistan – *State of Human Rights in 1994*, Lahore, 1995, p. 153.

[62] Bokhari, F. – EU and Pakistan to seek closer ties, *Financial Times*, 22 July 1996.

[63] Child labour campaigner murdered in Pakistan, *Anti-Slavery Reporter*, vol. 1, No. 2, June 1995, p. 1; Clarke, H. – Pakistan faces sanctions over child labour, *The European*, 2–8 November 1995; Hilowitz, J. – Social labelling to combat child labour, *International Labour Review*, vol. 136, 1997, No. 2, pp. 215–232.

and India, as have mutual accusations of human rights violations relating to Kashmir.

The problem of Kashmir is rooted in the creation of the two states in 1947, when Kashmir was undecided whether to join predominantly Muslim Pakistan or pre-dominantly Hindu India. The first war between the rival states also took place in 1947, and Kashmir joined India when its Maharaja needed India's armed forces against Pakistani insurgents. The Security Council was faced in 1948 with India's accusation that Pakistan had militarily invaded Kashmir, and Pakistan's accusation that Kashmir's accession to India had been illegal and its fate should be decided by an internationally supervised plebiscite. While attempts at mediation failed, the UN deployed observers who have stayed on five decades.[64] Two more bouts of warfare between Pakistan and India followed in 1965 and 1999. The UN's inability to halt abuses had led to calls for sanctions against India and Pakistan, but 'Washington has offered nothing but rhetoric.'[65]

The International Commission of Jurists (ICJ) fielded a mission to Kashmir in 1993 to investigate the low-level civil war that started in 1989. Its report was pub-lished with a two-year delay because the draft had been sent to Pakistan and India, as was customary at the time, to allow governments to comment before publication. The outcome of that long process was that one government accused the ICJ of bias, the other of lack of objectivity. The government of Pakistan 'had sincerely hoped that the final version of the report would project the true picture of continuing gross violations of human rights in the Indian held Kashmir.' The government of India dismissed the report for its focus 'on the issue of so-called »self-determination« in Jammu and Kashmir.'[66] As the responses to the ICJ report indicate, the lack of a common language to define the problem of Kashmir is a major obstacle to halting the killings.

India has tended to dismiss international criticism of its human rights record as 'part of [the] disinformation campaign by Pakistan.'[67] And indeed, Pakistan's tabling a resolution against India before the Commission on Human Rights[68] reinforced the view that the two sides use the label of human rights violations

---

[64] Birgisson, K.T. – United Nations Military Observer group in India and Pakistan, in: Durch, W.J. (ed.) – *The Evolution of UN Peacekeeping. Case Studies and Comparative Analysis*, Macmillan, London, 1993, pp. 273–283.

[65] Davidson, A. and Brown, B. – India keeps failing the democracy test in Kashmir, *International Herald Tribune*, 30 January 1995.

[66] International Commission of Jurists – *Human Rights in Kashmir. Report of a Mission*, ICJ, Geneva, 1995, Response of the Government of Pakistan, p. 148, and Response of the Government of India, p. 99.

[67] Sidhva, S. – Vicious circle of violence, *Financial Times*, 8 November 1994.

[68] Pakistan tabled a draft resolution on violations of human rights of the people of Jammu and Kashmir, which would have authorised a fact-finding mission, on 28 February 1994. It obtained the support of the delegations of Bosnia and Herzegoniva and Saudi Arabia, and withdrew the draft on 9 March 1994 upon a request by the delegation of Iran. Commission on Human Rights – Report on the fiftieth session (31 January–11 March 1994), U.N. Doc. E/CN. 4/1994/132, paras. 483–492.

to score points against each other. International involvement has proved futile thus far.

BURMA/MYANMAR[69]

The Western policy of condemning, isolating and sanctioning Burma has been based on the hope that Burma would democratise rapidly, rather than on Burma's heritage of military rule. Rule by force seemed to have ended in 1988–90, but instead continued for another decade, and perhaps will continue much longer. Previous military rule (1962–1988) had brought the country to the verge of bankruptcy, and in 1988 widespread demonstrations were suppressed. The human toll was estimated at between 1,000 and 10,000, although the exact number may never be known. In contrast to China's suppression of the students' demonstration on Tiannanman Square one year later, there were no foreign film crews in Rangoon and information leaked out slowly; thus, there was no immediate international outrage.

International attention focused on Burma during the 1989–90 elections, won by the National League for Democracy despite the house arrest of its leader. That landslide – the League obtained 392 parliamentary seats out of 485 – resulted in arrests and prison sentences for the victors. An attempt to form a government could only be made outside Burma. In 1995, Bertil Lintner noted that 'Burma's democracy movement now exists almost entirely in exile.'[70]

The 1988 demonstrations, which led to the elections, were portrayed in the West as a democracy movement although they were as much, if not more, a protest against impoverishment. The arbitrariness of pre-1988 military rule had been illustrated, *inter alia*, in changing denominations of the national currency and the loss of savings for all who did not exchange old for new banknotes. An estimated one-third of the currency had been rendered worthless, and public demonstrations followed.

Although post-1988 military rule continued denying political freedoms, economic reforms were initially rapid and radical. Political freedoms were suppressed in the name of the stability necessary for economic reforms. In contrast to 1962, when all-encompassing nationalisation introduced socialism (outlined in Ne Win's familiar *Burmese Way to Socialism*), in 1988 the military committed itself to the free market. Ted Bradacke summed up that new Burmese way as 'free-market incentives combined with a generous amount of coercion.'[71] A foreign-investment

[69] Although the name of the country was officially changed from Burma to Myanmar by the post-1988 military government, Burma is used in this text or Burma/Myanmar where cited or quoted sources used Myanmar.
[70] Lintner, B. – Burma: Arrested development, *Far Eastern Economic Review*, 2 March 1995.
[71] Bradacks, T. – Burma's economic mini-boom helps junta stay in power, *Financial Times*, 6 December 1995.

law was rapidly adopted and investment concentrated on the exploitation of Burma's natural resources.[72] The main holding company, Union of Myanmar Economic Holdings (UMEC) held a monopoly over the inflow of foreign investment. Its biggest shareholder (40%) was, and probably still is, the ministry of defence.[73]

Nevertheless, the public investment necessary to redress the chronic shortage of electricity or build roads and railways was not forthcoming. An estimated 30 or even 60% of governmental budget was spent on defence,[74] thus crowding out all non-military items. Burma's military government[75] gave itself full legislative, administrative and judicial power; a new constitution was expected to institution-alise the political role of the army, replicating the model of *dwifungsi*, the army's dual function in Indonesia during Sukharto's rule. The justification was that the army was 'the single disciplined organization in the country.'[76] By 1997, the dimin-ishing value of the national currency and high inflation shed doubt on the success of Burma's economic reform, while the economic crisis affecting the ASEAN contributed to diminishing foreign investment. The cost of living increased eleven times,[77] triggering fears of a repetition of the 1988 protests and their suppression.

The massacre of unarmed demonstrators in 1988 and the retroactive annulment of the 1990 elections led to a condemnation of Burma/Myanmar by the United Nations. The fate of Burma, at least in the West, became identified with Daw Aung San Suu Kyi. Suu Kyi – the elected leader of the country – had been placed under house arrest in 1989, elected in 1990, awarded the Nobel Peace Prize in 1991, and freed from house arrest in 1995, although neither fully nor permanently. Her release was hailed as a sign that external pressure on Burma's government was effective.[78]

---

[72] The UN Centre on Transnational Corporations found that the bulk of foreign investment went into oil exploration and oil companies formed 'the major legal source of financial support' for the govern-ment. Teak wood was second, Burma being the world's principal supplier. Commission on Human Rights – Transnational investments and operations in the lands of indigenous people. Report of the Centre on Transnational Corporations, U. N. Doc. E/CN. 4/Sub. 2/1994/40 of 15 June 1994, paras. 33–41.

[73] Lintner, B. – Military: Absolute power, *Far Eastern Economic Review*, 18 January 1996.

[74] Fairclough, G. – Investment: Enter at own risk, *Far Eastern Economic Review*, 15 August 1996; Goldenberg, S. – Military junta turns on itself as the Burmese economy sinks, *Guardian Weekly*, 28 December 1997.

[75] The government originally called itself the State Law and Order Restoration Council (SLORC), but changed its name in 1997 into the State peace and Development Council (SPDC). The rationale was that peace and national 'reconsolidation' had been accomplished and 'disciplined democracy' could be gra-dually instituted. Commission on Human Rights – Note verbale dated 25 March 1998 from the Permanent Mission of Myanmar to the United Nations Office at Geneva addressed to the secretariat of the Commission on Human Rights, U. N. Doc. E/CN. 4/1998/150 of 27 March 1998, pp. 2 and 6.

[76] Note verbale dated 19 March 1997 from the Permanent Mission of the Union of Burma to the United Nations Office at Geneva addressed to the secretariat of the Commission on Human Rights, U.N. Doc. E/CN. 4/1997/123 of 21 March 1997, p. 8–9.

[77] Economic monitor: Burma, *Far Eastern Economic Review*, 13 November 1997.

[78] Suu Kyi speculated that the government deemed the National League for Democracy 'a spent force' and her release would not 'make any difference'. Pilger, J. – Brutal facts lay bare the land of fear, *Guardian Weekly*, 12 May 1996.

The government's subsequent vacillating between increasing and decreasing harassment of Suu Kyi typified the inherently arbitrary nature of rule by force.

External reactions ranged between supportive and condemnatory, seemingly in accordance with a criterion of geographical proximity: the support of neighbouring countries in contrast to the condemnations of the West. In response to the annulment of elections, the detention of the elected leader, and the continuance of military rule, the West cut off aid while The ASEAN opted for constructive engagement. The neighbouring countries, China, Thailand, Singapore, South Korea, and Hong Kong, were Burma's main trading partners and sources of investment. China concluded a border-trade agreement with Burma in August 1988, while demonstrations were still being suppressed, and became the major source of arms.[79] The ASEAN's constructive engagement was then construed as an attempt to counterbalance Burma's dependence on China.

Thailand, whose official delegation was the first to visit Burma after the suppression of the 1988 demonstrations, had initially been at the forefront in the ASEAN's constructive engagement policy.[80] Subsequently, however, the flow of refugees into Thailand, resulting from armed conflicts between Burma's government and ethnic minorities,[81] led to changed Thailand's position. That change was evidenced in Thailand's assertion that ASEAN was not ready to accept Burma.[82]

Burma's membership in the ASEAN was nevertheless approved in November 1996, with the ASEAN deciding, by consensus as is customary, that Burma, Laos and Cambodia would become members at the same time.[83] That decision was preceded and followed by an inter-regional dispute – Burma become a political battlefield between the ASEAN and EUrope. Its participation in meetings of the two regional blocks was a constant bone of contention. EUrope cancelled the first post-admission meeting with the ASEAN.[84] Every subsequent meeting was preceded by a minor diplomatic crisis, with EUrope preventing Burma's attendance at meetings, or refusing Burma's 'anonymous' and silent presence behind a nameplate reading *Asean – New member*.[85]

---

[79] Richardson, M. – China–Burma ties upset neighbours, *International Herald Tribune*, 7 April 1995.

[80] Position of ASEAN's 'constructive engagement' policy towards the SLORC, *DAWN News Bulletin* (Bangkok), vol. 3, No. 12, August–September 1992, p. 15; Cooke, K. – Singapore welcomes Rangoon pariahs, *Financial Times*, 9 June 1995.

[81] Problems with neighbouring countries emerged when armed conflicts within Burma spilled across its borders. The Communist Party had initiated an armed insurgency in 1948, which more than a dozen minorities – also armed – joined. By 1992, the military government had, in the name of stability, negotiated cease-fire agreements with several of these groups, while others continued their armed struggle, amidst allegations that some of these armed movements derived revenue from heroin production and trafficking.

[82] Vatikiotis, M. – Foreign relations: Seeds of division, *Far Eastern Economic Review*, 17 October 1996.

[83] McBeth, J. – Burma road, *Far Eastern Economic Review*, 12 December 1996.

[84] Lintner, B. – Burma: Just as ugly, *Far Eastern Economic Review*, 27 November 1997.

[85] Doors slam on Burma, *Far Eastern Economic Review*, 8 October 1998; General Affairs Council, 25 January, *European Voice*, 28 January–3 February 1999.

Burma's admission to the ASEAN in July 1997 took place just after the United States had banned new investment in Burma, strengthening sanctions stemming from the 'de-certification' of Burma for its failure to suppress drug production and trafficking.[86] US sanctions could not diminish Burma's access to multilateral funds, since it had had none beforehand and US aid had already been suspended. A great deal of attention thus focused on private finance, and calls for sanctions targeted commercial companies and investors. Much capital came from Asia rather than the West. Foreign investment in Burma was estimated at $1.3 billion in 1989–94; by 1996 commitments reached $3.8 billion.[87] Investment originated mostly in the neighbouring countries, and return from tourism, oil, gas and timber, was expected in foreign currency. Long-term investment in infrastructure was not forthcoming, while investment in social development was not even discussed.

Table 8.6 illustrates aid to Burma in 1990–94. The many negative figures reveal the government's inability to service previous loans, which, alongside human rights considerations, have contributed to diminished aid. The table also reveals that Japan's aid constituted half or two-thirds of total bilateral aid to Burma.

Table 8.6: Aid to Burma/Myanmar in 1990–1994
(in million US$)

	1990	1991	1992	1993	1994
Australia	2.2	0.6	0.5	0.2	0.4
Austria	–4.5	–4.4	–	–	–
Belgium	–0.8	–0.2	2.1	0.1	0.1
Canada	1.7	0.1	0.1	0.3	2.6
France	9.2	5.1	1.4	5.1	4.8
Germany	31.0	28.2	21.8	24.7	13.0
Japan	15.3	60.0	75.9	64.9	135.7
Netherlands	0.9	1.1	–3.5	–4.2	–3.1
Norway	–10.2	0.2	–1.6	–6.4	–1.6
Total bilateral aid	27.9	93.8	96.3	87.5	153.0
Multilateral aid	108.5	166.9	128.2	111.2	171.0

Note: Negative figures indicate that outflows (owed debt) exceeded inflows.
Source: *Geographical Distribution of Financial Flows to Aid Recipients 1990–1994*, OECD, Paris, 1995.

---

[86] Boucard, A. & L. – En Birmanie, répression sur fond de narcotrafic, *Le monde diplomatique*, November 1998.

[87] Mallet, V. – Exchange rate imprisons Burmese economy, *Financial Times*, 11 November 1994; Burma attracts investors, *International Herald Tribune*, 27 May 1994; Economic monitor: Burma, *Far Eastern Economic Review*, 7 November 1996.

In 1988–89, EUrope, the United States and Japan, as well as the World Bank and the IMF suspended aid to Burma. Diminished aid flows, except for Japan, are noticeable. The upward trend in aid flows as of 1991 was due to Japan's increasing aid, which compensated for diminished Western aid. It is worth bearing in mind that Japan is sometimes classified as Western, sometimes as an Asian country; its policy towards Burma accommodated both categorisations.

Japan's suspension of aid in 1988 followed the suppression of the '8-8-88' demonstrations, as they became known having taken place on 8 August 1988; however, this was not the only reason. Economic reform had been a bone of contention before the suppression of the demonstrations, whereupon a 'political component' was added[88] and Japan resumed aid at a lower level. In 1986–88 Japanese aid to Burma had been an annual $200 million; in 1990–91 it was $70 million.[89] (Table 8.4 reflects lower figures since these refer to aid flows which are officially recorded by DAC/OECD.) Following the release of Suu Kyi from house arrest, Japan announced that its aid would be fully resumed[90] and was reportedly supportive of the IMF's loans to Burma.[91]

Burma had been placed on the UN violations-agenda in 1979 under the 1503 procedure. Nothing was publicly known about the substance of the complaints or the dialogue between UN human rights bodies and the government. Complaints resumed in 1988–89 and the Commission on Human Rights fielded a fact-finding mission under the 1503 procedure, condemning Burma in 1992. By that time, worldwide publicity generated by the large numbers of exiles and Burmese organizations in the West had raised Burma to prominence in international human rights politics.

Only after a certain delay did the United Nations condemn Burma for human rights violations. In March 1989, the Commission on Human Rights adopted a decision, not yet a resolution, focusing on obstacles to the 'democratic aspirations of the Burmese people.'[92] In 1990, Sweden's initiative before the UN General Assembly to condemn Burma did not succeed: 'at Japan's request, the resolution was withdrawn for a year following fierce opposition from Singapore, China, Cuba

---

[88] Burma: Muted harping *Far Eastern Economic Review*, 16 March 1989; Lintner, B. – Wartime allies forge enduring relationship, and Burma: A yen for self-interest, *Far Eastern Economic Review*, 11 July 1991 and 14 May 1992.

[89] Jeff Kingston's figures for Japan's aid to Burma were $61 million in 1990 and $85 million in 1991. Kingston, J. – A Burmese test for Japanese aid, *International Herald Tribune*, 22 April 1993.

[90] Aid for Burma, *Far Eastern Economic Review*, 10 August 1995.

[91] Kevin Murphy attributed the IMF's resumption of contacts with Burma after seven years of suspension to 'behind-the-scenes lobbying led by Japan'. Murphy, K. – Burma's economy starts to mend, *International Herald Tribune*, 23 November 1995.

[92] Commission on Human Rights – Situation in Burma, decision 1989/112 of 8 March 1989.

and Mexico.'[93] Such a resolution was adopted one year later and continued on the agenda of the General Assembly thereafter.[94]

Calls upon the United Nations to react to human rights violations extended beyond its human rights bodies. The All Burma Students' Democratic Front sent in 1990, from exile, an open letter to the UNDP (United Nations Development Programme) protesting the approval of $20 million in development aid to 'an illegitimate military regime which has been condemned for the killing of its own people.'[95] Similarly, an ICJ (International Commission of Jurists) mission to Burma recommended that human rights be linked to aid in a non-punitive sense and that 'financial assistance for the education and training of the political dissidents' be provided.'[96] On the punitive side, the International Human Rights Law Group called upon the General Assembly to recommend an arms embargo against Burma because 'public exposure had done nothing to deter violations' but the Assembly did not heed such calls.[97]

As in similar cases, condemnations were accompanied by investigation, and a Special Rapporteur was appointed. The first, now former Rapporteur, Yozo Yokota, was allowed into the country but prevented from visiting prisons through a catch-22 scheme. He had first been told that the higher authorities do not interfere with the running of the prison and that the request should be made to the prison authorities. When he made such a request to the prison authorities, he was told stated that they required authorization from the higher authorities.[98]

He visited Burma annually in 1992–96, routinely complaining that he was not given access to the persons to whom he wished to speak confidentially, or that security agents had warned such people against talking to him. He managed to overcome these catch-22 obstacles and visited imprisoned political leaders to establish, as in the case of U Tin U, that three and then ten more years of imprisonment constituted punishment for:

(a) inciting the entire population for democracy and human rights;
(b) corresponding with parliamentarians of the European Community, Japan, and the United States of America; and
(c) meeting with military personnel and others in groups.[99]

---

[93] Lintner, B. – Reward for resistance, *Far Eastern Economic Review*, 24 October 1991.

[94] General Assembly resolutions 46/132 of 17 December 1991, 47/144 of 18 December 1992, 48/150 of 20 December 1993.

[95] An open letter to the UNDP Conference, *Voices* (Hong Kong), vol. 15, No. 1, February 1991, p. 5–6.

[96] International Commission of Jurists – *The Burmese Way: To Where? Report of a Mission to Myanmar (Burma)*, Geneva, 1991, p. 94.

[97] Pushing the UN to push Burma, *The Docket*, vol. 8, 1993, No. 2, p. 20; United Nations – Situation of human rights in Myanmar, General Assembly resolution 48/150 of 20 December 1993.

[98] United Nations – Report on the situation of human rights in Myanmar, prepared by Mr. Yozo Yokota, Special Rapporteur of the Commission on Human Rights, in accordance with Commission resolution 1992/58, U.N. Doc. E/CN. 4/1993/37 of 17 February 1993, para. 64.

[99] Commission on Human Rights – Report on the situation of human rights in Myanmar, prepared by Mr. Yozo Yakota, Special Rapporteur, U.N. Doc. E/CN. 4/1995/65 of 12 January 1995, para. 73.

The subsequent Special Rapporteur (as of 1996) never obtained permission to visit Burma, but has continued to record human rights violations, and the Commission on Human Rights has continued adopting condemnatory resolutions. This has triggered no change within Burma and the lack of UN-generated progress has led to numerous calls for economic sanctions.

The United States, generally militant in similar cases, was initially inactive, although no strategic interests were cited as obstacles. Rather, the obstacles were embodied in the very US foreign policy. One had pitted human rights against anti-narcotics policy. Burma was estimated to generate 60% of heroin and human rights lost out to attempts to diminish the supply of heroin.[100] Another has pitted human rights against investment. In 1995, the United States was Burma's fourth largest investor after Singapore, Thailand, and France, and Congress rejected a proposal to ban new investment in Burma.[101] Proposals continued in 1996, and the Cohen-Feinstein amendment empowered the President to impose sanctions 'if Slorc physically harms, rearrests, or exiles Daw Aung San Suu Kyi, or continues its repression of the democracy movement.'[102] This was a compromise between proponents and opponents of sanctions. The former, a combination of human rights groups and trade unions, secured a foothold to continue pressure. The latter, investors, postponed the ban. Nevertheless, it took effect in May 1997, when the President found that repression was increasing, as was Burma's involvement in drugs production and trafficking.[103]

Across the Atlantic, EUrope's aid to Burma has had its ups and downs. It had been suspended in 1990, but a review ensued because the Danish 'furniture industry is heavily reliant on Burmese teak.'[104] In 1994, EUrope's punitiveness was declared ineffective, and was to be replaced by dialogue,[105] patterned after the critical dialogue applied to Iran. At the time, Burma's military government held two widely publicised talks with Suu Kyi. EUrope's attitude was reversed again in 1996, with Denmark calling for sanctions against Burma because its honorary consul had been detained and died in prison, but no agreement on sanctions was reached. Leo Nichols had been honorary consul for five Western European countries besides Denmark. His offence had been two unregistered faxes and nine

[100] Lintner, B. – Burma: Hooked on the junta. US drug agency assailed for links to Burmese generals, *Far Eastern Economic Review*, 18 November 1993; Shenon, P. – Burma offers U.S. a deal on drug warlord, *International Herald Tribune*, 16–17 July 1994; Weymouth, L. – Time for America to do something about the drug lords in Burma, *International Herald Tribune*, 27 March 1995.

[101] Vatikiotis, M. – Sanctions: Talking tough, *Far Eastern Economic Review*, 13 July 1995.

[102] U. S. and Japan raise pressure on Burmese junta, *International Herald Tribune*, 25–26 May 1996; Doublethink in Myanmar, *The Economist*, 5 October 1996.

[103] Burma: U.S. imposes sanctions, *Far Eastern Economic Review*, 1 May 1997; Mydans, S. – Burma is said to arrest dissidents as U.S. sanctions take hold, *International Herald Tribune*, 22 May 1997.

[104] *Asia 1991 Yearbook*, Far Eastern Economic Review, Hong Kong, 1991, p. 87.

[105] ASEAN: Constructive cave-in, *The Economist*, 30 July 1994, p. 53; Ching, F. – Movement on Burma policy, *Far Eastern Economic Review*, 25 August 1994, p. 29.

telephone lines, but the reason seemed to have been his support for Suu Kyi. The official explanation for his death in prison, by Burma's minister of foreign affairs, was 'the excessive fats and richness of food' in prison.[106] That same year, mass arrests of some 200 members of the National League for Democracy in May and more than 500 in October led to denials of visas for members of the Burmese government and key military officials.[107]

Trade unions were more successful in lobbying for EUrope's sanctions, and they were imposed in March 1997 because of forced labour. GSP[108] benefits were cut off. This meant 2–5% higher import tariffs for Burmese industrial products, not affecting Burma's agricultural exports (more than half of the total); the value of Burma's exports to Europe was estimated at $50 million.[109] Although Burma's financial loss was thus not great, rescinding GSP benefits had had an important symbolic value, as it was the first application of EUrope's new GSP regulations.[110] A similar case had been initiated by a complaint filed by the ICFTU (International Confederation of Free Trade Unions), whereupon the International Labour Organization sent a mission to Burma in September 1997 and confirmed EUrope's finding that forced labour was widely used.[111] Burma objected to the use of the term 'forced labour' but acknowledged that 'citizens are upon occasion requested to donate their labour.'[112]

Alongside such cases, the involvement of Western oil companies in Burma was tackled through the mobilisation of shareholders, negative publicity, and legal challenges. The mobilisation of shareholders, for instance, worked well against Unocal, a Californian company involved in the construction of a pipeline for natural gas. 14.1% of Unocal's shareholders voted in favour of a report on the

---

[106] Palmer, J. and Cumming-Bruce, N. – Asean backs Burma as EU mulls sanctions, *Guardian Weekly*, 21 July 1996; Kyonge, J. – EU criticism of Burma irritates Asean nations, *Financial Times*, 20/21 July 1996; Leahy, J. – ASEAN: Round one to Rangoon, *Far Eastern Economic Review*, 1 August 1996.

[107] Pilger, J. – The betrayal of Burma, *The World Today*, November 1996, p. 279.

[108] The Generalized System of Preferences (GSP) was set up for the benefit of developing countries to allow duty-free entry for their products or lower import tariffs. Because such preferential treatment was unilateral, decisions were left at the discretion of countries granting them. The GSP enabled Western countries to grant preferential treatment to developing countries applying a range of conditions to grant or withhold such preferences, such as trade union freedoms (right to organise and bargain collectively, freedom of association) or prohibition for forced and child labour.

[109] Wise, E. – Human rights abuses in Burma threaten trading, and Burma trade sanctions set for approval, *European Voice*, 5–11 December 1966 and 23–29 January 1997; European Union: Burma loses benefits, *Far Eastern Economic Review*, 3 April 1997, p. 57.

[110] Regulation 3281/94 of 19 December 1994, *Official Journal of the European Communities*, L 348, p. 1.

[111] Council regulation 552/97 of 24 March 1997 temporarily withdrawing access to generalized tariff preferences from the Union of Myanmar, *Official Journal of the European Communities*, L 85, p. 8.

[112] Note verbale dated 19 March 1997 from the Permanent Mission of the Union of Myanmar to the United Nations Office at Geneva addressed to the secretariat of the Commission on Human Rights, U.N. Doc. E/CN. 4/1997/123 of 21 March 1997, p. 21.

human rights implications of Unocal's activities in Burma.[113] Unocal's involvement had begun with a 1995 agreement between Burma's state-owned Myanmar Oil & Gas Enterprise, Unocal and Total, partially owned by the French government.[114] The planned project had been valued at $1 billion[115] or one-third of annual foreign investment in Burma, and its ambition was to build a pipeline for offshore natural gas through Burma to Thailand. Opposition brought Unocal to court in a case initiated by Burmese exiles in the United States, some of whom were members of a government-in-exile. They claimed that Unocal was liable for the forced removal of some 30,000 people who had been in the way of the planned pipeline, for forced labour used to build the pipeline, and for environmental destruction.[116] Forced removal led to armed attacks against Total/Unocal's personnel by armed Karen groups. Because the pipeline was passing through minority-populated areas and some of the minorities were not yet 'pacified', in the words of an unnamed Total executive,[117] Burma's army provided security for the pipeline and the associated personnel. Judge Richard Perez found for the applicants. He found that Unocal's contract included paying the government for furnishing labour and providing security, thus making Unocal liable if labour was forced and security entailed abuses.[118] An opening was thus made towards holding individual companies legally responsible for benefiting from the lack of human rights protection in countries where they operate.

Mobilisation against individual companies operating in Burma has targeted their public image rather than only their possible legal responsibilities. Threats of boycotts by Western consumers led to corporate withdrawal by Levi Strauss, Eddie Bauer, Liz Claiborne, Pepsi Cola, Reebok, Carlsberg, Heineken, Kodak, Walt Disney, and Apple Computers.[119] Such boycotts could be threatened against individual companies whose products had an easily identifiable market, such an clothing. The rationale behind them has revealed chains of relationships which need to

---

[113] Clifford, M. – Pressure tactics: U. S. activists target companies doing business in Burma, *Far Eastern Economic Review*, 12 May 1994.

[114] France provided investment guarantees for Total's operations in Burma emcompassing possible sanctions against Burma. Burma: French guarantee, *Far Eastern Economic Review*, 20 March 1997.

[115] Vatikiotis, M. – Burma: Catching the wave, *Far Eastern Economic Review*, 15 February 1995.

[116] Holloway, N. – Energy: Long arm of the law, *Far Eastern Economic Review*, 19 September 1996; Bobin, F. – French oil firm accused on Burma rights, *Le monde*, 24 October 1996, reproduced in *Guardian Weekly*, 3 November 1996.

[117] Bardacke, T. – Burma gas pipeline rouses opposition, *Financial Times*, 24 January 1996.

[118] Iritani, E. – U.S. court links Unocal to Burma rights abuses, *International Herald Tribune*, 19 April 1997.

[119] Liz Claiborne to suspend business links with Burma, *International Herald Tribune*, 16 November 1994; Macy's no longer shops in Myanmar, *The Economist*, 22 April 1995; Burma: Pepsi pulls out, *Far Eastern Economic Review*, 2 May 1996; Usborne, D. – Heineken bows out of $30 million Burma deal, *The Independent*, 11 July 1996; Burma: Beer deal goes flat, *Far Eastern Economic Review*, 18 July 1996; Burma hits back at European beer companies, *Financial Times*, 6 August 1996; Bardacke, T. – American Burma boycotts start to bite, *Financial Times*, 6 February 1997; Texaco considers sale of stake in Burmese gas field, *Financial Times*, 11 June 1997: Burma: Texaco pulls out, *Far Eastern Economic Review*, 2 October 1997.

be tackled. A typical scenario would look something like this: a clothing factory in Burma would be owned by a Hong-Kong-based company and selling clothes to US-based companies, while the identities of owners of various links in such a chain regularly remained unknown. A boycott of Burma-produced clothing would lead the Hong-Kong-based intermediary to halve the number of workers in Burma. Newly unemployed textile workers thus lost their jobs – and the ability to feed their families – because this was supposed to benefit their rights. The complexity of punitive usages of human rights thus came to light. Proponents of punitiveness have argued, however, that ordinary Burmese had nothing to lose because only the privileged profited. The rationale was thus summed up:

> Ms Suu Kyi and the NLD argue that because the private sector elite and their military allies are those most affected by the slump in foreign investment, economic hardship could result in internal disintegration, eventual dialogue and political opening.[120]

Thus supported by the National League for Democracy, US sanctions moved from the federal level downwards. The city authorities in Berkeley, California, set the tone by subjecting to boycott companies that did not pull out of Burma. Such selective purchasing laws became popular and spread to Santa Monica (also in California), Madison (Wisconsin) and Ann Arbor (Michigan),[121] with other cities following. The momentum moved upwards and Massachusetts adopted a selective purchasing law; the blacklist included 150 foreign companies.[122] EUrope submitted a complaint to the World Trade Organization in June 1997, claiming a breach of free-trade rules, because the Massachusetts law excluded companies, wherever they might have been based, from public procurement in Massachusetts if they operated in Burma.[123] The human rights rationale has thus entered international trade law, promising to create much disagreement not only between Asian and Western countries but also between the Western countries themselves. Such disagreement has been a hallmark of Western policies with regard to China.

CHINA

There has been enormous publicity for human rights in China in the West as of 1989, as if to compensate for previous decades of silence. International attention

---

[120] Bardacke, T. – Burmese junta digs in its heels as sanctions bite harder, *Financial Times*, 5 May 1998.

[121] Vatikiotis, M. – The business of America, *Far Eastern Economic Review*, 6 June 1996.

[122] Bardacke, T. – American Burma boycotts start to bite, *Financial Times*, 6 February 1997; Dunne, N. – Massachusetts' Burma law row flares, *Financial Times*, 14–15 June 1997.

[123] Burma, EU v. Massachusetts, *Far Eastern Economic Review*, 3 July 1997; Dunne, N. – EU in Burma law protest, *Financial Times*, 13 July 1998.

reached its first peak in the aftermath of the Tiananmen massacre in June 1989 and for the first time in history as superpower was almost condemned for human rights violations by the United Nations. The second peak was related to de-linking human rights from US–China trade in 1994, and the third to the 1995 UN Commission on Human Rights, when US efforts to condemn China almost succeeded. Thereafter international attention diminished.

Publicity for human rights in China in the early and mid-1990s concentrated on two annual events: the UN Commission on Human Rights in March/April, and US debate about China's MFN (most favoured nation) status in June/July. Intense publicity preceded these two annual events but vote-counts usually represented an anti-climax. Human rights violations in China were described in a flood of publications, from trials and imprisonment of scholars and activists to the export of goods produced by prison labour, from limitations upon freedom of expression or association to a coercive population policy, with Tibet and later Hong Kong adding fuel.

The explosion of international attention in 1989 resounded against the silence that preceded it. Little was known about China and even less about Chinese human rights policy or practice, but the immense publicity for the Tiananmen massacre necessitated a response. The typical response would have been a UN condemnation coupled with Western economic sanctions, but neither quite materialised. The former was impossible because an insufficient number of governments supported the West against China in the United Nations; the latter was undermined by the attraction of one-and-a-half billion consumers for Western exports.

Although there was almost no publicity for human rights in China before 1989, China has been a target of economic sanctions for various non-economic reasons throughout its post-1949 history. The United States initiated sanctions against the 'communist-held mainland' before the People's Republic of China was established, and the 1950 Treaty of Friendship, Alliance and Mutual Aid between China and the Soviet Union formally extended anti-Communist sanctions to China.[124] One year later, the UN General Assembly recommended an embargo against China and North Korea 'to support and supplement military action' in the Korean War.[125] Thus, two different reasons for sanctions became blurred, communism and warfare. The Korean War ended in 1953, just a year after the establishment of Chincom, the functional equivalent of Cocom. As discussed in Chapter 4, containment of communism had its commercial underpinning in restrictions upon international trade. The Western isolation of China continued, even after it became the target of Soviet sanctions following their split in 1960.

[124] Evans, P.M. – Caging the dragon: Post-war economic sanctions against the People's Republic of China, in Leyton-Brown, D. (ed.) – *The Utility of International Economic Sanctions*, Croom Helm, London, 1987, pp. 61–62.

[125] Progress of embargo measures against China and North Korea, *United Nations Bulletin*, vol. 9, No. 1, July 1951, pp. 4–6.

One obvious consequence of this isolation was ignorance about China in the West, coupled with considerable sympathy for a country attempting to design and implement a non-western, egalitarian model of development. China replaced Taiwan as UN member as late as 1971 and was recognised by the United States in 1972; it was neither a recipient of Western aid nor a tourist or businessmen's destination. Another consequence of China's isolation was that the country became an object of scrutiny *after* the human rights situation had considerably improved. The first mention of human rights in China by the US government can be traced to 1978, when the Carter administration hailed China's official acknowledgement of abuses which had taken place during the Cultural Revolution.[126] A change in economic policy, also in 1978, created the background for subsequent rapid economic development, and Western interest for China augmented.

In her study into delayed international interest for human rights in China, Roberta Cohen identified the absence of a human rights lobby in the West as an influential factor.[127] Post-Tiananmen, on the other hand, produced an abundance of such lobbies; a vast number of NGOs, including those formed by exiles, dedicated themselves to meeting and creating interest for China. The annual ritual of the UN Commission on Human Rights and the MFN debate in the USA provided obvious foci for an endless stream of reports and studies on human rights in China.

Although Tibet has been on and off the UN agenda since 1959,[128] China was tackled for the first time by the UN human rights bodies only in 1989. The European Parliament had been a pioneer, having adopted its first resolution on human rights in China in October 1985. It criticised the extensive use of the death penalty, the ill treatment of prisoners and censorship.[129] A follow-on resolution in October 1987 criticised China's policy concerning Tibet, but led 'to a "fence-mending" public statement by Parliament's enlarged Bureau.'[130] In response to Tiananmen, EUrope's Commission imposed sanctions against China without consulting Parliament, and lifted them in the same manner. The European Parliament nevertheless continued calling for sanctions. In 1996 alone 'the Greens initiated a record 22 parliamentary resolutions condemning China for violating human rights.'[131] This parliamentary enthusiasm was matched by US Congress as discussed below.

---

[126] China commended for acknowledging past rights abuses, *The Washington Post*, 29 November 1978.

[127] Cohen, R. – *People's Republic of China: The Human Rights Exception*, A Report to the Parliamentary Human Rights Group, London, 1987, pp. 21–23.

[128] General Assembly resolution on Tibet were adopted in response to China's military occupation. China was not mentioned because Taiwan held China's UN seat at the time. The Assembly called for respect of the fundamental human rights of the Tibetan people, and their right to self-determination. General Assembly resolutions 1353 (XIV) of 21 October 1959 and 1723 (XVI) of 20 December 1961.

[129] European Parliament – Second report on human rights in the world for the year 1984, Doc. A2-121/85/1 of 11 October 1985, p. 20.

[130] Boumans, E. and Norbat, M. – The European Parliament and Human Rights, *Netherlands Quarterly of Human Rights*, vol. 1, No. 1, 1989, p. 38.

[131] Eye on the dragon, *Far Eastern Economic Review*, 6 February 1997.

In August 1989, less than three months after the Tiananmen massacre, with memories of world-wide broadcasts of tanks advancing on students still fresh, the UN Sub-Commission adopted a resolution entitled 'Situation in China'. NGOs were leading, as usual, and prodded governments into action – indeed, although the Sub-Commission is nominally composed of independent experts, its output belies this characterisation. Fierce opposition by the Chinese delegation led to voting by secret ballot, and the resolution was adopted. Its language was fairly neutral: the Sub-Commission expressed concern 'about the events which took place recently in China and about their consequences in the field of human rights'. China unyieldingly objected, declaring the resolution to be 'null and void,' and adding that 'the United States and the European Community had viciously slandered and attacked the Chinese Government and had offered support for a handful of criminals.'[132] In February 1990, the Commission on Human Rights took no decision on a proposed resolution on China by a vote of 17 against, 15 in favour and 11 abstentions.[133] The Sub-Commission's almost-condemnation was adopted by secret ballot so as to ensure anonymity for its members. Governmental delegations in the Commission on Human Rights could not vote anonymously.

The annual meeting of the Commission thereafter fell into a pattern: the United States – later the European Union, then Denmark, and then again the United States – would introduce a draft resolution on human rights in China. China (or Pakistan) would propose a no-action motion, and the members of the Commission would have to take sides. A procedural motion is put to vote before a substantive resolution, and the no-motion proposals carried from 1990 until 1994. In 1995, the vote was 22–22–9 and, because it was a tie, expectations were raised that the forthcoming session would lead to a condemnation. It did not. The majority switched to China's side, and in 1996 the vote was 27–20–6.[134] China's delegation commented:

> Under the pretext of caring about the human rights situation in China, a great Power, supported by some developed countries, had since 1990 been tabling draft resolutions against China that it had never managed to have adopted. Curiously, it was precisely during those past years that the situation in China had improved enormously.[135]

With the seventh repetition of a pre-vote count in the UN Commission on Human Rights in 1997, neither the United States nor the European Union tabled a

---

[132] Situation in China. Note by the Secretary-General submitted pursuant to Sub-Commission resolution 1989/5. U.N. Doc. E/CN. 4/1990/52 of 30 January 1990, para. 3; Press release HRR/3038, 20 February 1992, p. 12.

[133] Commission on Human Rights – Decision 1990/106 of 4 March 1990, U.N. Doc. E/CN. 4/1990/94

[134] Commission on Human Rights – U.N. Doc. EN/CN. 4/1995/176, pp. 389–391, and E/CN. 4/1996/SR. 59, p. 11.

[135] Statement of Mr. Wu Jianmin (China) before the Commission on Human Rights on 23 April 1996, U.N. Doc. E/CN. 4/1996/SR. 59 of 29 May 1996, p. 7.

resolution on China. It was tabled by Denmark, subsequent to extensive publicity for disagreement within EUrope. France, Germany, Italy and Spain were against repeating for the seventh time a gesture that had not succeeded the previous six times. Jacques Chirac explained that it was 'a perfectly sterile procedure' which 'produced absolutely no results.'[136] President Chirac was proven right because the vote was even more favourable for China: 27–17–9.[137] *Human Rights Watch* depicted the outcome as 'Chinese diplomacy coupled with Western hypocrisy.'[138]

China countered accusations of human rights violations with various versions of *Human Rights in China* 'in a choice of six languages, suitable for presentation to visiting delegations when they make their by-now customary representations about human rights before getting down to business-as-usual.[139] Commentators interpreted such moves differently. Ann Kent saw them as an acceptance of the human rights language as well as an opportunity to discern China's approach to human rights.[140] Others were cynical: 'China's leaders have simply decided that to retain most-favoured-nation privileges and be visited by Western politicians, they must pretend to listen to the West's concerns.'[141]

In contrast to developments within the United Nations, donors' response to the Tiananmen massacre on 4 June 1989 was rapid, though short-lived. Announcements that aid to China was suspended were made by the United States on 6 June, by the World Bank on 26 June, by EUrope (European Community at the time) on 27 June, and by the G-7 on 15 July 1989.[142] Japan, China's main donor, announced resumption of economic relations with China within six months; EUrope lifted the ban on export credits in December 1989, as did the USA, and in January 1990 the World Bank resumed loans to China, which was retroactively approved by G-7 in July 1990. The *International Herald Tribune* summed this up in an indicative title: 'All is forgiven as foreign funds return to China'.[143]

---

[136] Barber, L. – EU fails to build common foreign policy, *Financial Times*, 7 April 1997; Read, J. – Danes take on China over rights, *The European*, 10–16 April 1997; Interview/Jacques Chirac: Leading Europe east, *Far Eastern Economic Review*, 22 May 1997, p. 24.

[137] Yanni, C. – Anti-China move defeated, *China Daily*, 17 April 1997.

[138] Human Rights Watch/Asia-Chinese diplomacy, Western hypocrisy and the U.N. Commission on Human Rights, vol. 9, No. 3 (C), March 1997.

[139] The rights stuff, *Far Eastern Economic Review*, 14 November 1991.

[140] Kent, A. – *Between Freedom and Subsistence. China and Human Rights*, Oxford University Press, Hong Kong, 1993, pp. 222–230.

[141] China: First steps in human rights, *The Economist*, 3 August 1991.

[142] Foreign devils pack their bags, *The Economist*, 10 June 1989; Proper pressure on China, *International Herald Tribune*, 23 June 1989; No further action on Peking, *Financial Times*, 17 July 1989; World bankers weigh China debt repayments, *International Herald Tribune*, 15 August 1989; China can survive sanctions and continue change, Li says, *International Herald Tribune*, 17 August 1989.

[143] U.S. move opens door to major China loans, *International Herald Tribune*, 13–14 January 1990; World Bank sets China loan, *International Herald Tribune*, 9 February 1990; Far Eastern Economic Review – *Asia 1991 Yearbook*, Hong Kong, December 1990: Japan lends $1 billion to China, *International Herald Tribune*, 28–29 September 1991; *International Herald Tribune*, 16 June 1992.

Table 8.7 shows aid flows to China in 1989–94 and reveals how short-lived aid suspensions were. Suspensions by Denmark, Japan and the USA are reflected in aid statistics for 1990; others were so short that they could not be captured in annual statistics, while the over-all increase in aid belied donors' punitive rhetoric.

Table 8.7: Aid to China in 1989–94
(in million US dollars)

	1989	1990	1991	1992	1993	1994
Australia	35	67	69	84	120	130
Austria	50	183	205	121	573	527
Belgium	3	4	94	39	573	124
Canada	70	267	211	241	29	124
Denmark	2	−9	−16	14	−12	−9
France	713	673	728	813	754	607
Germany	350	376	227	109	294	953
Japan	2402	1368	2016	2027	3084	4973
Norway	10	17	10	20	12	128
United Kingdom	345	642	248	196	408	202
USA	120	−82	−487	−236	995	1906
Total multilateral aid	4436	4833	4685	4602	6832	10164
Multilateral aid	5620	4842	5133	6093	9001	12575

Source: OECD/DAC – *Geographical Distribution of Financial Flows to Aid Recipients, 1986–1993 and 1990–1994.*

Following the Tiananmen massacre, Canada suspended aid to China, but aid was soon resumed and reached its pre-Tiananmen level. One part of the rationale was that Canada possessed no leverage with the Chinese government, another the prominence of commerce in Canada's foreign policy.[144] Norway's aid to China increased fivefold in 1990–95, not without domestic protest. A visit by China's president, Jiang Zemin, resulted in a minor scandal with Norwegian police suppressing pro-human-rights demonstrations in Oslo.[145] Previously like-minded donors exhibited a new type of like-mindedness.

The credibility of donors' *condemnations-cum-sanctions* rhetoric was undermined by their widely publicised rush to secure a foothold in the largest emerging global market. Reports on governmental and/or commercial delegations to China emphasised the value of signed contracts and the underlying intra-Western com-

[144] *Canadian Development Co-operation in Asia: China*, Ottawa, 1991; *The Reality of Aid 95. An Independent Review of International Aid*, Earthscan Publications, London, 1995, p. 42.
[145] Norweigian aid to China increases five-fold in the 90s, *Development Today*, vol. 5, No. 12/13, 27 July 1995; Smith, F. – Norway penalty for China trade, *The European*, 18–24 July 1996.

petition.[146] Inter-regional differences in the portrayal of such visits were depicted for Britain's Prime Minister at the time, John Major, in 1991. While a Western newspaper reported that 'Britain would maintain "unremitting and relentless pressure" on human rights', an Asian newspaper pointed out that Major's human rights rhetoric created 'almost as much discomfort to his own officials as to the Chinese.'[147]

In the United States, publicity peaked each year at the time of the annual renewal of MFN status for China. The Jackson-Vanik amendment, originally intended for the Soviet Union, applied to China as of 1980 and the US president had to request MFN renewal each June. In the immediate aftermath of Tiananmen, political duels were fought between the Democratic majority in Congress and the Republican White House.[148] The signature of the US–China trade agreement in October 1992 triggered protests. President Bush's veto of the congressional decision to make MFN status for China dependent on the observance of human rights was overturned by a two-third majority in the House.[149] With President Clinton's election, such 'cuddling dictators in Beijing' (as he had put it during his campaign) was expected to stop. These expectations were frustrated by his de-linking human rights and MFN in 1994.[150] Immense publicity and fierce criticism accompanied that change, as did praise for successful commercial engagement with China.[151]

Diametrically opposed views fuelled such debates. Some argued that sanctions should be used to punish bad human rights performance. Sydney Jones, the director of Human Rights Watch for Asia, stated that 'by criticising United States policy on China, the human rights organizations have been able to exert some pressure on China itself.'[152] Others insisted that the use of human rights to impede trade 'is the economic equivalent of dropping in nuclear bomb on a civilian population, hoping that some of the perpetrators of outrages will be killed at the same time.'[153] Views

---

[146] *Financial Times*, 9 November 1994; *The European*, 14–20 April 1995; *Financial Times*, 6 July 1995; *The Economist*, 22 April 1995; *European Voice*, 31 October – 6 November 1996.

[147] *Guardian Weekly*, 15 September 1991; *Far Eastern Economic Review*, 12 September 1991, p. 12.

[148] Boudreau, D.G. – Beyond Tiananmen Square: China and the MFN debate, *World Affairs*, vol. 153, No. 4, Spring 1991, pp. 141 and 143–144.

[149] China praises Bush for vetoing sanctions; House overrides Bush's China veto, *International Herald Tribune*, 30 September and 1 October 1992.

[150] President Clinton's de-linking human rights and China's MFN status was accompanied by what he called 'a continuing aggressive effort in human rights,' which consisted of increased broadcasting by Radio Free Asia, increased support for human rights NGOs, and 'the development with American business leaders of a voluntary set of principles for business activity in China.' Most-favored-nation trade status: China, *American Journal of International Law*, vol. 88, 1994, p. 745–746.

[151] Walker, T. and Dunne, N. – US super-salesmanship discount human rights, *Financial Times*, 7 September 1994; Kaye, L. – Commerce kowtow: Human-rights concerns lost in rush of U.S. deals *Far Eastern Economic Review*, 8 September 1994.

[152] Crossette, B. – U.S. human rights office grows in influence, *New York Times*, 19 January 1992.

[153] Ching, F. – Hit where it hurts, *Far Eastern Economic Review*, 11 July 1991.

about the effectiveness of linking trade and human rights also fell into two extremes. Some claimed that 'no policy has been as effective in achieving modifications of Chinese human rights policy as the threat of MNF withdrawal.'[154] Others questioned whether any modifications were achieved, or even sought, and quoted illustrative incidents such as this one:

> At a meeting earlier this month [November 1992], U.S. diplomats are believed to have tried to give the Chinese Foreign Ministry an unofficial written inquiry about political prisoners. The Chinese refused to take it, so the Americans left it on a chair as they left. The Chinese then picked it up and said that there would be no response. But the Americans apparently were heartened that the Chinese at least picked it up.[155]

Threats of sanctions against China have encompassed a long list of issues: human rights in general and Tibet in particular, insufficient protection of intellectual property rights, prison labour, nuclear tests, the export of nuclear technology and ballistic missiles, the export of chemicals that might be used to manufacture poison gas, the absence of environmental safeguards, the denial of the right to emigrate, the enforcement of population policy, the treatment of orphans, freedom to carry out human rights fact-finding in China, the death penalty, the denial of trade union freedoms, the suppression of religious freedoms, the preservation of Hong Kong's autonomy after its hand-over to China, the future of Taiwan, and finally, the US trade deficit with China. Critics depicted the threat of sanctions as 'knee-jerk' reaction,[156] but legislative proposals for US economic sanctions against China continued unabated.[157]

By the mid-1990s, China had became the World Bank's largest borrower with an annual $3 billion,[158] the second largest destination for foreign investment in the world after the United States, and the recipient of more than one-third of total investment in developing countries. China received commitments for more than $20 billion in foreign direct investment in 1993, after which the surge diminished.[159] Nicholas Lardy calculated that foreign investment accounted for 70% of

---

[154] Statement of Andrew Nathan, of Columbia University, quoted in Foreign policy; Chinese boxes, *The Economist*, 30 April 1994.

[155] Silently, China signals an end to rights talk, *International Herald Tribune*, 25 November 1992.

[156] This formulation was concocted by US Senator John Danforth (China: Most-favored-nation treatment and U. S. policy on the Chinas, American Society of International Law – *Proceedings of the 87th Annual Meeting, March 31–April 3, 1993*, Washington, D. C., p. 442) and the latter by William Taylor of the Centre for Strategic and International Studies (Taylor, W. J. – Unilateral Sanctions on China aren't the solution, *International Herald Tribune*, 27 October 1993).

[157] Manning, R. – Foreign relations: Split personality, and Lutterbeck, D. – Foreign relations: China bashing, *Far Eastern Economic Review*, 27 November 1997 and 25 June 1998.

[158] World Bank in pledge to China, *Financial Times*, 6 July 1995.

[159] Norman, P. – The Chinese superlative, *Financial Times*, 3 October 199; Investment: The fever cools, China: Trade & investment, *Far Eastern Economic Review*, 31 August 1995; Walker, T. – Slowdown in rush to invest in China, *Financial Times*, 21 July 1997.

China's exports, most of which was labour-intensive industrial production.[160] Table 8.8 illustrates that most investment was intra-Chinese: more than half originated from Hong Kong and Macau.

Table 8.8: Foreign direct investment in China by country of origin, 1989–1995 (in billion $US)

	1989	1990	1991	1992	1993	1994	1995
Macau	2.077	1.913	2.487	7.710	17.861	20.175	20.499
Hong Kong	2.036	1.880	2.405	7.507	17.275	19.665	20.060
Taiwan	0.155	0.222	0.466	1.050	3.139	3.391	3.004
USA	0.284	0.460	0.323	0.511	0.206	0.249	0.308
Japan	0.356	0.503	0.532	0.710	1.324	2.075	3.108
Korea	0.004	0.017	0.396	0.119	0.374	0.723	1.043
United Kingdom	0.028	0.133	0.353	0.383	0.220	0.689	0.914
France	0.005	0.211	0.010	0.045	0.141	0.192	0.287
TOTAL	3.310	3.487	4.366	11.007	27.515	33.766	37.736

Source: Ridding, J. – China: FDI flood meets barriers, *Financial Times*, 27 June 1996

EUrope launched its new 'proactive policy' towards Asia in July 1994, emphasising co-operation instead of verbal confrontation. Human rights were to be raised in bilateral dialogue without affecting 'the steady growth in trade relations.'[161] Individual Western European countries preceded this change in policy, others followed.

One of the leaders was Germany, prompting domestic criticism of the commercialisation of its relations with China at the beginning of 1992. The parliamentary (Bundestag's) decision to suspend co-operation with China was ignored by the executive.[162] Commercial relations continued unhindered and China was by 1996 in a position to condition the continued flourishing of commerce on Germany's suppression of domestic protest. China protested against a conference on Tibet, which was held in Germany and funded by the Friedrich Naumann Foundation and the German government. The latter heeded China's protest and withheld funding, but the conference was held nevertheless and the Bundestag adopted a resolution opposing repression in Tibet. In retaliation, China closed down the Beijing office of the Friedrich Naumann Foundation and announced that a

---

[160] Lardy, N.R. – *China in the World Economy*, Institute for International Economics, Washington, D.C., April 1994.

[161] European Commission – *General Report on the Activities of the European Union 1994*, Brussels/Luxembourg, 1995, paras. 875–877 and 888.

[162] Nuscheler, F. – Development policy and its double standards on human rights, in Tetzlaff, R. (ed.) – *Human Rights and Development. German and International Comments and Documents* Development and Peace Foundation, Bonn, 1993, p. 82–83.

planned visit by Germany's minister of foreign affairs was 'not appropriate'.[163] An implicit threat was that relations between China and Germany, characterised by more than $15 billion in annual trade, would deteriorate. That threat proved effect- ive. Conditionality was effectively transformed into China's right to demand that freedom of expression be constrained in Germany so as to prevent criticism of China. The underlying reason was the need to balance two domestic constituencies in the creation of foreign policy:

> The politicians want to reap benefits of China trade for the sake of German industry, the economy and millions of blue-collar jobs. To satisfy their white- collar constituents, they also need to stage a morality play depicting themselves as morally superior to Asian or Islamic counterparts.[164]

Such balancing has typified all Western countries, not Germany alone. The Western donor community was hindered in forging a common response by the operative – as distinguished from rhetorical – criteria for aid allocation. While rhetorical cri- teria assigned priority to human rights, operative criteria favoured export promo- tion. Domestic constituencies pursuing exports won over those lobbying for punitiveness. Ultimately, only symbolic sanctions were imposed against China, thus avoiding self-inflicted punishment for Western exporters or investors.

INDONESIA

Indonesia has had a much longer tug of war with the West about its human rights record than China. It has been on and off UN's violations-agenda since 1983 because of East Timor, whose assimilation into Indonesia followed military occu- pation in 1976 and whose independence at the turn of the millennium was ushered by the United Nations. East Timor triggered a special session of the Commission on Human Rights in 1999, which had been prompted by Indonesia's implosion at the end of the Soeharto regime and the ensuing bloodshed that had affected first and foremost East Timor. In a chain of events that is recent enough to be remembered and thus need not be described in detail, the referendum in East Timor ('popular consultation' for the government of Indonesia) resulted in an overwhelming pre- ference for independence which triggered waves of violence inflicted upon the East Timorese. The Commission decided to establish an international commission of

---

[163] Lindemann, M. – Beijing calls off German visit as rift over Tibet grows, *Financial Times*, 24 June 1996; Williamson, H. – Kohl comfort: German chancellor disappoints Tibet support groups, *Far Eastern Economic Review*, 27 June 1996; Fornay, M. and Islam, S. – Back off, jack. China tries to mute European critics, *Far Eastern Economic Review*, 11 July 1996.

[164] Germany in Asia: Advertising supplement, *Far Eastern Economic Review*, 7 November 1996.

inquiry by a 27–12–11 vote,[165] which reinforced the usual West-Asia split, while the Security Council authorized a peace-keeping force.[166] These developments marked the final stages (for East Timor at least) of a long process dotted with shifts between silence and over-reaction, economic sanctions and inducements.

As Table 8.7 reveals, foreign investment in Indonesia grew, if unevenly, until 1996. Reasons for its ebb and flow might have included investors' concerns about human rights violations in East Timor but were more likely to have reflected their concerns about Indonesia's increasing inability to service its growing foreign debt. Indonesia's foreign, mainly private, debt was in 1994 reported by the government to be $88 billion, while 'the markets' reported a higher figure of $100 billion.[167] With the benefit of hindsight, one could argue that the outflow of funds from Indonesia precipitated the economic crisis that led to its political transition in 1998–99. Much as in similar cases, the crisis had not been predicted.

Before this quick sequence of events in 1997–99, Indonesia had belied the typical image of powerful Western donor *versus* vulnerable aid recipient. Rather, it was the opposite. Portugal, the main defender of East Timor, advocated sanctions against Indonesia within EUrope without much success.[168] Bernie Malone, an Irish MEP, lamented: 'There isn't a session of the European Parliament that doesn't open with a resolution on East Timor proposed by Portuguese MEPs.'[169] In response to a massacre of East Timorese civilians by Indonesia's army in Dili in 1991, the Netherlands, followed by Canada, suspended aid to Indonesia but met with a lack of success in swaying the donor community equal to Portugal's. The donor community pledged an annual $5 billion in aid to Indonesia and the annual value of foreign investment exceeded aid by a factor of four. The voting blocks within the United Nations at the time enabled Indonesia's Minister of Foreign Affairs, Ali Alatas, to claim that Indonesia would win a vote on East Timor in the General Assembly.[170]

Although international attention for East Timor peaked after the Santa Cruz massacre in Dili in 1991, problems with East Timor originated in its annexation in 1976–77. It was never recognised by United Nations. Portugal continued representing East Timor internationally until 1999, and took Australia, which recognised

---

[165] United Nations – Special session of Commission on Human Rights adopts resolution on East Timor, Press release HR/CN/99/70 of 27 September 1999.

[166] Security Council resolution 1264 (1999) of 15 September 1999.

[167] Far Eastern Economic Review – *Asia 1995 Yearbook*, Hong Kong, December 1994, p. 138.

[168] Maddening silence. Lisbon blamed for muted EC response on East Timor, *Far Eastern Economic Review*, 30 January 1992, p. 11; Stumbling block: Indonesia-EC agreement ditched by Timor issue, *Far Eastern Economic Review*, 30 July 1992.

[169] Vatikiotis, M. and McBeth, J. – No deal: Jakarta rebuffs Lisbon's initiative on Timor, *Far Eastern Economic Review*, 21 March 1996.

[170] Montagnon, P. and Saragosa, M. – Indonesia threatens showdown on E Timor, *Financial Times*, 3 June 1996.

Indonesia's annexation, to the International Court of Justice, trying to legally challenge Indonesia's sovereignty over East Timor. The case ended inconclusively.[171] A solution was sought in the UN-sponsored negotiations between Indonesia and Portugal that started in 1983 and intensified in 1992, aiming to 'ameliorate the human rights situation in East Timor' and then seeking a negotiated solution through 'an all-inclusive intra-Timorese dialogue.'[172] Indonesia's position was to dissociate human rights from the 'resolution of a political question'.[173] It took the fall of the Soeharto regime for Indonesia to announce that East Timor could have its freedom. Somewhat ironically, the announcement was made by the very same Minister of Foreign Affairs, Ali Alatas.[174]

As mentioned earlier, the donor community was mobilised in response to the Dili massacre in November 1991. A Japanese delegation to Indonesia – reportedly for the first time – had 'raised' (as diplomatic jargon has it) human rights in its dialogue with Indonesia already in March 1991; Japan had 'hoped that Indonesia would pay due regard to its human-rights problems.'[175] That hope was frustrated. World-wide reports of the Indonesian army opening fire on unarmed civilians who were mourning the death of a young man, also attributed to the army, at Santa Cruz cemetery in Dili generated a great deal of publicity. The mourners were carrying banners protesting Indonesia's annexation. 271 demonstrators were reportedly killed, 382 wounded, and a couple of hundred disappeared.[176] Probably thanks to the loud and immediate international outcry, the government appointed a commission of inquiry. Competing diagnoses of what had actually happened were reached by Indonesia and the United Nations:

> Indonesia informed that Commission on Human Rights in February 1992 that 'contrary to some misleading foreign reports, the demonstration of 12 November 1991 in Dili, East Timor, had not been an entire peaceful affair. The procession had from the outset been taken over by a small group of agitators whose belligerent acts culminated in the stabbing of a Deputy Battalion Commander and the wounding of a private from the security forces. It was in these conditions

---

[171] International Court of Justice – Case concerning East Timor: Portugal *versus* Australia, *ICJ Reports*, 1995, p. 90.

[172] United Nations – Update on the good offices activities of the Secretary-General concerning the question of East Timor, Situation in East Timor. Note by the secretariat, U.N. Doc. E/CN. 4/Sub. 2/1994/14 of 11 July 1994, paras. 5 and 9.

[173] Letter dated 12 April 1996 from the Permanent Mission of Indonesia to the United Nations Office at Geneva addressed to the Chairman of the Commission on Human Rights, U.N. Doc. E/CN. 4/1996/165 of 22 April 1996, p. 4.

[174] Aglionby, J. – East Timor 'can have its freedom,' *Guardian Weekly*, 7 February 1999.

[175] do Rosario, L. – Reluctant convert: Tokyo begins to speak up on human rights, *Far Eastern Economic Review*, 22 August 1991.

[176] Catry, J.-P. – Timor-Oriental est-il exempté de droit international? *Le monde diplomatique*, January 1992.

and in an atmosphere of rising tension and confusion that, most unfortunately, the shootings had taken place. The Government had acted firmly and swiftly in facing this tragic affair.'[177]

In contrast, Bacre Waly Ndiaye, the UN Special Rapporteur on Summary Executions, concluded:

The procession that took place in Dili on 12 November 1991 was a peaceful demonstration of political dissent by unarmed civilians; the claims of some officials that the security forces had fired in self-defence ... are unsubstantiated. There are, therefore, reasons to believe that the actions of the security forces were not a spontaneous reaction to a riotous mob, but rather a planned military operation designed to deal with a public expression of political dissent in a way not in accordance with international human rights standards.'[178]

Before the facts were authoritatively – if differently – clarified, the Dili massacre had been placed before the UN Commission on Human Rights. Having failed to agree on a condemnatory resolution, it merely deplored the massacre. The draft of a condemnatory resolution had been proposed by the WEOS (Western Group) to create a split: 'A team of heavyweight powers, the U.S., Australia, Japan – plus Britain as a member of the EC troika – all leant upon Portugal' and the proposed condemnatory resolution was not put to vote.[179] Indonesia argued that only consensus could form a basis for investigations or condemnations by the United Nations thus advocating a rule whereby a government could only be condemned for human rights violations if it acquiesced. This rule was immediately translated into practice and a consensus statement adopted for Indonesia.[180]

In contrast to the United Nations, where Indonesia could mobilise a sufficient number of votes to prevent condemnation, the donor community does not give recipients a voice in decision-making. In response to the Dili massacre, the Netherlands suspended aid.[181] As a small donor – its $91 million constituted a mere 1.9% of annual aid to Indonesia – it was not able to influence the donor community. The subsequent donors' meeting was held in July 1992 in Paris, having been

---

[177] Press release HR/3042, 24 February 1992, p. 5.

[178] United Nations – Report by the Special Rapporteur on extrajudicial, summary or arbitrary executions, Mr. Bacre Waly Ndiaye, on his mission to Indonesia and East Timor from 3 to 13 July 1994, U.N. Doc. E/CN. 4/1995/61/Add. 1 of 1 November 1994, para. 48.

[179] Human rights omissions and too quiet diplomacy, *Guardian Weekly*, 15 March 1992.

[180] Comments by the Government of Indonesia on the adoption of a Chairman's consensus statement on the human rights situation in East Timor by the fiftieth session of the Commission on Human Rights, U.N. Doc. E/CN. 4/Sub. 2/1994/14/Add. 1 of 5 August 1994, paras. 2 and 5.

[181] Dutch halt Jakarta aid over Timor massacre, *International Herald Tribune*, 22 November 1991; Schwartz, A. – Tilting at windmills. Cancellation of Dutch aid unlikely to affect economy, *Far Eastern Economic Review*, 9 April 1992.

moved there from the Hague, and chaired by the World Bank, which replaced the Netherlands. The World Bank pledged $4.94 billion, thus preventing any decrease in aid and indicating that aid was not tied to human rights.[182] Although the Netherlands did not make a dent in the total aid to Indonesia, it nevertheless prompted a vehement reaction. Indonesia asserted that it did not want any aid from the Netherlands, and prohibited Indonesian NGOs from receiving any 'even if assistance was channelled through Dutch NGOs.'[183] Canada followed the Netherlands and suspended its aid amounting to $30 million, less than 1% of total aid.[184] The United States remolded only its military aid through a half-way measure, whereby funding for the Indonesian military in US training programmes was withdrawn, although Indonesia could continue participating at its own cost. A ban on military sales, including crowd-control equipment, was imposed pending significant progress in human rights.[185]

Table 8.9: Aid to Indonesia in 1990–1994
(in million US$)

	1990	1991	1992	1993	1994
Australia	252.8	223.3	172.7	151.3	155.8
Austria	17.4	62.5	136.5	106.9	141.2
Belgium	43.6	145.6	169.4	−38.9	109.1
Canada	69.8	68.2	30.7	21.2	24.4
Denmark	−11.2	−9.1	226.1	12.2	−7.8
France	62.5	41.7	77.2	44.5	337.1
Germany	33.5	140.0	424.0	590.6	848.9
Japan	1521.8	2948.9	2819.0	282.4	1434.3
Netherlands	269.3	81.3	−162.1	58.1	241.2
United Kingdom	−203.9	157.7	−90.2	10.1	143.1
USA	145.0	358.0	927.0	1361.0	2083.0
Total bilateral aid	2166.7	4351.7	4870.1	2757.0	5338.6
Multilateral aid	3377.9	5766.4	5832.1	3877.7	5415.3

Source: OECD/DAC – *Geographical Distribution of Financial Flows to Aid Recipients 1990–1994.*

Table 8.9 demonstrates that total aid to Indonesia increased in 1990–94 with the exception of 1993, while Australia, Canada and the Netherlands decreased aid. The figures highlight the disunity among donors. Different from Canadian and

---

[182] Loans of US$4.8 billion sought for Indonesia, *Far Eastern Economic Review*, 11 June 1992; The poll Indonesia dares not hold, *The Economist*, 19 September 1992.

[183] Indonesia arranges aid despite Dutch withdrawal, *International Herald Tribune*, 18–19 July 1992; NGOs knocked: Jakarta extends ban on Netherlands aid, *Far Eastern Economic Review*, 14 May 1992.

[184] Aid to Indonesia, *Au courant*, January 1992, p. 10.

[185] U.S. Senate limits sale of arms to Indonesia, *International Herald Tribune*, 16–17 July 1994.

Dutch, Japanese or German aid to Indonesia was not interrupted by the Dili massacre. France and the United Kingdom counterbalanced the loss of Dutch and Canadian aid, and France became the third largest donor after Japan and Germany. Britain also increased aid to Indonesia 'by a record 250 per cent on the previous year', while Australia offset the cuts in US military aid.[186]

These varying donors' policies both instigated and reflected domestic disagreements. In Australia, public demonstrations against Indonesia's government (and Australia's policy towards Indonesia) were numerous and much publicised. When Australia's Prime Minister visited Indonesia in April 1992, the press commented:

> During the visit, the two countries consciously tried to separate political issues from mutually beneficial trade relations. Canberra is also trying to distance itself from Australian public sentiment, which generally takes a harder stand towards events in Indonesia.[187]

A campaign of burning Indonesian flags during the summer of 1995 prompted Indonesia's protests. A request to the government to prevent such incidents followed so as to prevent a boycott of Australia's exports to Indonesia.[188] In Japan, a Free East Timor Japan Coalition reported in June 1993 that petitions, including one signed by 262 members of Japan's parliament, the Diet, urged Japan to condition aid on the withdrawal of Indonesia's army from East Timor.[189] In the United Kingdom, protests against arms exports to Indonesia intensified after British police equipment was used in the suppression of anti-government demonstrators in July 1996. In a much-publicised court case four women, members of a Christian-feminist movement, were acquitted after damaging a military aircraft destined for Indonesia. Their defence was that the aircraft had been intended for use by Indonesia's army against East Timor, and they had used the minimum necessary force – disabling the aircraft with hammers – to prevent a much more serious crime.[190] It is likely that results of the 1999–2000 investigations into abuses in East

---

[186] Timor incident will not affect Tokyo aid, *Far Eastern Economic Review*, 27 February 1992; Guest, I. – Japan aid plan assailed. NGOs urge curbs on funds for Indonesia and Burma, *Terra Viva*, 12 June 1993; Pilger, J. – Deathly silence of the diplomats, *Guardian Weekly*, 30 October 1994; Indonesia: Filling the void, *Far Eastern Economic Review*, 11 August 1994; Australia and Indonesia sign security cooperation accord, *International Herald Tribune*, 19 December 1995; *The Reality of Aid 95. An Independent Review of International Aid*, Earthscan Publications, London, 1995, p. 52.

[187] The shadow of Dili, *Far Eastern Economic Review*, 7 May 1992.

[188] Senior Jakarta minister enters fray over flag; Indonesia decries Australian move; Indonesian importers threaten Australia – Warn of boycott over flag burning, *International Herald Tribune*, 21, 22/23, and 24 August 1995.

[189] Double standard! Japan's stand on East Timor, A submission by the Free East Timor Japan Coalition to the UN World Conference on Human Rights, June 1993, mimeographed.

[190] Harrison, D. – Indonesian deals row, and Beavis, S. – Angry investors protest against Bas [British Aerospace] arms sales, *Guardian Weekly*, 8 October 1995; Bellamy, C. et al. – British riot controls used in Indonesia, *The Independent*, 2 August 1996; Brown, A. and Cohen D. – The respectable revolutionaries, *The Independent*, 1 August 1996; Wainright, M. et al. – Peace women cleared over jet attack, *Guardian Weekly*, 11 August 1996.

Timor by Indonesia's army and militias, if they span more than just the final stage of violence in 1999, will retroactively prove them to have been one of the few foreign obstacles to the foreign facilitation of abuses.

Although Indonesia became prominent on the donors' human rights agenda in the 1990s, withdrawals of aid went back to 1965, when Canada terminated food aid following an Indonesian attack against Malaysia, arguing that aid was being diverted from development to finance external aggression.[191] The borderline between the two usually distinct type of budgetary allocations – developmental and military – was difficult to draw because Indonesia's army had a broadly defined developmental role (*dwifungsi*) and the very constitutional structure titled the balance of power in the army's favour.[192] The importance of the army became apparent in 1998, when Indonesia was left rudderless after the downfall of President Soeharto. His rule from 1965 to 1998 left a centralised and militarised regime, difficult to alter during an economic crisis which was caused by systemic fault-lines in the regime itself.

The end of the Soeharto regime was not predicted. Rather, the expectations had been that the regime itself would gradually change under foreign and international pressure. Freedom of expression provided in 1993–94 an illustrative example of the difference between symptoms and causes. The government's apparent tolerance of criticism was interpreted as improved respect for human rights. *The Economist* pointed out the previously taboo topics were discussed in newspapers, with journalists and editors not penalised, to then ask: 'Does the absence of a bark from the government mean that dissent is becoming more tolerated?'[193] That question was answered in June 1994, when the government closed down three newspapers and the riot police suppressed demonstrations in protest against the closures.[194] Although the government's tolerance of dissent proved to have been apparent rather than real, and even that for a short while, a donors meeting that took place within a month of the closures increased aid to Indonesia.[195]

If the donors' generosity seemed to conflict with their human rights criteria, they could cite valid reasons for aiding Indonesia. The routinely cited successes of the Soeharto regime included: increasing GNP per capita tenfold (from $90 in 1965 to $900 in 1993), a 6% rate of economic growth, and the reduction of absolute poverty from 80 to 15% in a population of some 200 million, scattered over 13,700 islands.

---

[191] Matthews, R.O. and Pratt, C. (eds.) – *Human Rights in Canadian Foreign Policy*, McGill-Queen's University Press, Kingston and Montreal, 1988, pp. 196–197.

[192] Vatikiotis, M.R.J. – *Indonesian Politics under Soeharto: Order, Development and Pressure for Change*, Routledge, London, 1993; Nasution, A.B. – *The Aspiration for Constitutional Government in Indonesia: A Socio-legal Study of the Indonesian Konstituante 1956–1959*, Doctoral thesis, University of Utrecht, November 1992; Lubis, T.M. – *In Search of Human Rights: Legal-Political Dilemmas of Indonesia's New Order, 1956–1990*, Gramedia Pustaka Utama, Jakarta, 1994.

[193] The regime that did not bark, *The Economist*, 4 September 1993, p. 63.

[194] Rude awakening. Press bans shock the emerging middle class, *Far Eastern Economic Review*, 7 July 1994, p. 18.

[195] Article 19 – *The Press under Siege. Censorship in Indonesia*, London, November 1994, p. 25.

As in similar cases, speculation about an association between such successes and political stability, and between repression and political stability, was endless. It typified the ASEAN, most of whose original members followed the route of economic growth through political stability. The positive aspects of that route, such as poverty-eradication or investment in education, proved unsustainable once the 1997–98 economic crisis shattered ASEAN.

Indonesia has set two world records. The first was a GDP growth rate of an annual 4% sustained in 1965–88 and increasing thereafter to 7%. The second was reversing the GDP growth rate of +7% in 1997 to –14% in 1998.[196] The turmoil that prompted and hastened the end of the Soeharto regime focused international attention on restoring economic and political stability. Similarly, stability was the main objective of international involvement in Papua New Guinea.

PAPUA NEW GUINEA

International attention for Papua New Guinea focused on the armed and political conflict in Bougainville (1988–98), with corollary abuses, as well as the role of its principal donor, Australia. The conflict revealed a multi-layered chain of causation and could not be solved by tackling one cause alone. Foreign and international involvement wavered between addressing different symptoms. Tackling causes was left for the future.

The armed conflict between the government forces and the Bougainville Revolutionary Army (BRA) started in 1989. It was the escalation of a deeply rooted conflict about the distribution of benefits and burdens in the exploitation of natural resources. The two sides were the local population and Panguna mining corporation, which had originally been Australian-owned; failure to negotiate an agreement led to violence.[197] After the armed conflict had erupted, Bougainville was isolated. Papua New Guinea withdrew all essential services, including communications and travel. In May 1990, an interim government was formed in Bougainville and declared independence. Papua New Guinea tried to re-take the island militarily,

---

[196] Vaitikiotis, M. & Schwarz, A. – Indonesia: A nation awakes, and Economic monitor: Indonesia, *Far Eastern Economic Review*, 4 June 1998 and 21 January 1999.

[197] The CERD (Committee on the Elimination of Racial Discrimination) singled out large-scale mining operations in Bougainville, without due regard to the rights of the population or to environmental degradation, as a major human rights problem. (U.N. Doc. CERD/C/SR. 1007 of 19 August 1993). The UN Special Rapporteur on Summary Executions went back into history to identify the roots of the problem. He traced it back to the times when Papua New Guinea had been an Australian colony. The mining licence was awarded by the Crown; prospecting had begun in Panguna in 1963 and mining in 1972. Under Australian law, the Crown owned the mineral wealth while the local population did not have entitlement to profit sharing. The Rapporteur calculated that local landowners had obtained less than 5% of profits between 1972 and the beginning of the conflict in 1989. (U.N. Doc. E/CN. 4/1996/4/Add. 2 of 27 February 1996, paras. 18–21).

and warfare erupted again. Attempts at peace-making were intermingled with other methods of ending the conflict, including the hiring of mercenaries.

The chain of causation reached further than warfare or mining. Underlying reasons included the lack of cultural or geographical proximity between Bougainville and Papua New Guinea. Bougainville is 500 miles away and had expressed a wish not to be part of Papua New Guinea at the time of independence from Australia in 1975. Demands for self-determination intensified after 1989, as did opposition: the Panguna mine had contributed 40% of Papua New Guinea's foreign exchange earnings.[198]

International involvement was triggered by the exposure of abuses reported to the UN human rights bodies with parallel attempts at peace-making. A truce was concluded in 1998, and international observers, led by Australia, were deployed to await further developments. These were anticipated to lead towards the independence of Bougainville from Papua New Guinea, against the wishes of Papua New Guinea, or to some compromise solution for Bougainville to remain within Papua New Guinea, against Bougainville's wishes.

Many abuses had been reported in 1988–98. The government's initial response was to deny that abuses were taking place and reject external interference so as not to prolong 'the unfortunate crisis'. It has thus explained the background:

> A perfectly legitimate resource benefit dispute between a mining company and the traditional landowners was taken advantage of by criminal elements whose activities derailed the negotiations for a just solution on compensation for the use of land for the development of the giant Panguna copper mine, at the time the biggest foreign exchange earner for the country.[199]

In August 1994, the Sub-Commission called upon the government to allow humanitarian aid and lift the military blockade[200] in breach of customary humanitarian principles. By the 1995 session of the Commission on Human Rights, the government had replaced its previous 4-page denunciation of 'external interference' with a 45-page document describing agreements reached in the early stages of the peace negotiations.[201] Six rounds of negotiations and 15,000 deaths later, a peace agreement was reached through the good offices of New Zealand, between a

---

[198] Pacific waves, *The Economist*, 27 March 1993, p. 72.

[199] Commission on Human Rights – Letter dated 25 February 1994 from the Secretary of Foreign Affairs and Trade of Papua New Guinea addressed to the Chairman of the fiftieth session of the Commission on Human Rights, U.N. Doc. E/CN. 4/1994/120 of 2 March 1994, p. 2.

[200] United Nations – Situation in Bougainville, resolution 1994/21 of the Sub-Commission on the Prevention of Discrimination and Protection of Minorities of 25 August 1994, para. 2.

[201] Commission on Human Rights – Human rights violations in Bougainville. Report of the Secretary-General, U.N. Doc. E/CN. 4/1995/60 of 16 February 1995, pp. 5–51.

changed government of Papua New Guinea and a changed rebel leadership, in an atmosphere of war-weariness.[202]

The population of Bougainville is 110,000, and the armed conflict involved less than 1,000 combatants on both sides. The fate of that tiny pacific island would hardly have prompted so much international attention had it not been placed on the UN agenda. The UN involvement did not alter the donors' support for the government, however, showing the abyss between multilateral and unilateral policies. At their annual meeting in May 1990, donors 'strongly commended the government of PNG [Papua New Guinea] for the prompt and decisive steps it had taken in responding to economic challenges,'[203] keeping conspicuously silent about human rights or their violations.

Australia was implicated in the conflict from the very outset, having been – and remaining – the largest donor to Papua New Guinea, as Table 8.10 illustrates. In 1984, Australia provided 30% of the government's revenue and 85% of total aid to Papua New Guinea.[204] Australia's treaty on development co-operation with Papua New Guinea was renewed in 1992 and did not include human rights. Instead, the emphasis was on 'maintaining political stability in the region'.[205] The explanation for not linking aid to human rights was that 'Australia's aid does not have sufficient clout to persuade truant nations to toe a line'.[206] In its review of Australia's aid, the DAC (Development Assistance Committee of the OECD) noted that one-third of Australia's aid was allocated to Papua New Guinea, while four-fifths of Papua New Guinea's aid came from Australia.[207] As Table 8.10 illustrates, Australia's aid continued throughout the Bougainville conflict.

The one step that donors deemed objectionable was the hiring of mercenaries. These were provided by the Sandline company, well-known for its involvement in similar mining-focused operations in Africa, especially in Sierra Leone. Australia declared the use of mercenaries unacceptable, and the World Bank announced a review of its loans to Papua New Guinea.[208] Domestic political opposition to mercenaries prevented their hiring. The story was amply described in the media: a contract was signed between the prime minister of Papua New Guinea and Sandline International, for the provision of 40 or 50 (depending on the source) 'military advisors' for a fee of $28 million. The armed forces denounced that contract, leading to a

---

[202] Bougainville – a new spirit and new deal? *The Courier*, No. 171, September–October 1998, pp. 24–27.

[203] Papua New Guinea, *Asia 1991 Yearbook*, Far Eastern Economic Review, Hong Kong, December 1990, p. 194.

[204] *Report of the Committee to Review the Australian Overseas Aid Programme*, Australian Government Publishing Service, Canberra, March 1984, p. 158.

[205] AIDAB – Australia and PNG (Papua New Guinea). A Developing Partnership, 1993, p. 2.

[206] Dias Karunaratne, N. et al. – A critical review of contemporary Australian foreign policy, *Scandinavian Journal of Development Alternatives*, vol. 11, No. 1, March 1992, p. 97.

[207] Development Co-operation Review Series – *Australia*, Development Assistance Committee (DAC), Paris, No. 18, 1996, p. 35 and 37.

[208] Suter, K. – Mercenaries, mines and mistakes, *The World Today*, vol. 53, No. 11, November 1997, p. 278.

Table 8.10: Aid to Papua New Guinea, 1990–94.
(in million US$)

	1990	1991	1992	1993	1994
Australia	319.9	519.9	430.0	339.9	234.5
Belgium	13.1	1.6	19.4	–4.7	25.6
France	23.0	–10.1	–23.8	–8.8	–1.2
Germany	1.1	–11.0	–18.3	–12.2	–9.9
Japan	43.2	21.3	87.6	8.2	–57.2
New Zealand	2.6	3.4	2.9	3.7	3.7
United Kingdom	22.8	20.7	18.2	0.5	–0.4
USA	1.0	1.0	10.0	2.0	3.0
Total bilateral aid	432.9	545.6	528.9	330.4	200.8
Multilateral aid	604.2	682.5	631.9	367.2	241.7

Source: OECD/DAC – *Geographical Distribution of Financial Flows to Aid Recipients 1990–94.*

bitter political dispute and a change of government in subsequent elections,[209] where-upon this new government negotiated a peace agreement with the rebels.

Table 8.10 reveals that aid to Papua New Guinea decreased in the mid-1990s. This coincided with the UN's concerns over human rights violations but was not associated with them. Rather, donors' concerns focused on macro-economic funda-mentals, and the ebb and flow of aid followed their improvement or deterioration. Improvements were expected from an anticipated income to be generated by a gold mine, operated by (British-based) Rio Tinto,[210] and thus continuing Papua New Guinea's reliance on mining. Yash Ghai has pointed out Papua New Guinea's key problem: the exploitation of natural resources is exempt from domestic human-rights safeguards. Thus, while formal human rights guarantees were introduced into the constitutional and legal system of Papua New Guinea, the economy – charac-terised by mega-projects in mining and oil – was 'surrendered to foreign corpora-tions.'[211] The abyss between subsistence agriculture, which determines the fate of the majority of the population and highly technologised enclaves in mining and oil has not been captured by domestic human rights laws and policies. Such enclaves, being highly technologized, are not employment-generating, and the export of natural resources generates financial benefits for the few while excluding the many. Bougainville-type conflicts are thus likely to continue.

---

[209] Tait, N. – PNG military chief resigns, *Financial Times*, 19 March 1997; Zinn, C. – South Pacific fears mercenary influx, and Papua army in revolt over mercenaries, *Guardian Weekly* 9, and 23 March 1997; Papua New Guinea: Line in the sand, *The Economist*, 29 March 1997.

[210] Callick, R. – Papua New Guinea: Treading water, *Far Eastern Economic Review*, 17 July 1997.

[211] Ghai, Y. – Establishing a liberal political order through a constitution: The Papua New Guinea experience, *Development and Change*, vol. 28, 1997, p. 325.

Chapter 9

Africa

Africa elicited scarce interest in international human rights politics until the Cold War had ended, and then a short-lived bout of enthusiasm for democracy again diverted attention from human rights.[1] One reason for that meager attention for Africa in the previous decades were proxy wars fought to demarcate cold-war spheres of influence, which facilitated rather than constraining abuses of power by African governments. Another and closely related reason was the delayed development of prerequisites for human rights protection. Many African countries obtained their political independence in the 1960s, some even later. The OAU (Organization of African Unity) and African governments focused first and foremost on de-colonization, as has been described in Chapter 1, prioritizing collective over individual rights. The focus on decolonization channeled all attention to southern Africa, highlighting Portugal, Rhodesia and South Africa as principal violators, as has been described in Chapter 2. South Africa remained the one and only violator until the 1990s. The two countries that have been discussed in Chapter 5, Equatorial Guinea and Uganda, did not trigger an intra-continental condemnation because regional solidarity against extra-continental onslaught was strong. The African Charter on Human and People's Rights was adopted by the OAU in 1981; the majority of leaders who signed it were military officers who had come to power through military coups and ruled by force.

Numerous cold-war battles that were fought in Africa strengthened the power and influence of the military and further aggravated prospects for human rights. The UN intervention in Congo in 1960–64 had discouraged its subsequent involvement until the 1990s, and then the US/UN military intervention in Somalia produced the same effect. The keyword was, in both cases, supporting African solutions for African problems. The future will show whether the turn of the century will bring Africa freedom from external intervention and, if so, what its effects will be.

Throughout the Cold War, proxy wars were fought in Africa between the United States and the Soviet Union with impunity, subsequently leaving a range of cold-war orphans. External interventions, even if they were benevolent such as aid, retroactively proved none too beneficial. The cold-war dividers reinforced colonial partitions, creating endless barriers for economic, political or human-rights development.

---

[1] This has been analysed in Tomaševski, K. – *Between Sanctions and Elections*, Pinter/Cassell, London, 1997, pp. 155–212.

Responses to the many man-made disasters have followed a distinct lack of pattern, by the West or by the United Nations alike. Human rights violations were identified in some armed conflicts while not in others, some military coups were condemned but not others, some countries pressurized into elections, others not. Table 9.1 lists African countries that were placed on the UN violations-agenda. With the exception of Portugal and South Africa, which were both targets of OAU-led UN sanctions under the colonialist and/or racist label, regional solidarity is evidenced in rare condemnations of human rights violations. As Table 9.1 illus-

Table 9.1: African countries on the UN violations-agenda

Country	Commission	Sub-Commission	1503 procedure
Angola	1994	–	–
Benin	–	–	1984–85, 1988
Botswana	–	–	1997
Burundi	1994–99	1988, 1994–96	1974–75
Central African Republic	–	–	1980–81
Chad	–	1993–94	1991–99
Congo/Brazzaville	–	1997, 1999	–
Equatorial Guinea	1979–85, 1989–90, 1992–99	1979–80	1976–79
Ethiopia	(1986)	–	1978–81
Gabon	–	–	1986
Gambia	–	–	1997–99
Kenya	–	–	1993
Liberia	(1996–97)	–	–
Malawi	1980	–	1977–80
Mali	–	–	1996
Mauritania	1982, 1985	1982, 1984–85	(1990)
Mozambique	–	–	1981
Nigeria	(1995), 1996–98	–	–
Rwanda	1994–99	1994–96	1993–95
Sierra Leone	1998	–	1996–97
Somalia	1992, 1994	1991–92	1989–94
South Africa	1967–94	1967–93	–
Sudan	1992–99	–	1991–93
Tanzania/Zanzibar	–	–	1974–75, 1997
Togo	1993–95	1994	(1993)
Uganda	–	(1972), (1979)	1975–81, 1995
Western Sahara	1981–87, 1989–90, 1993, 1995–96, 1998	1987	–
Zaire/Congo	1992–93, 1995–99	–	1985–89, 1991–93

trates, the confidential 1503 procedure has been used much more than public pro-cedures. The output of UN bodies deciding by majority vote, including the Commission on Human Rights, has reflected the growing numerical strength of African votes – naming-and-shaming African violators has been rare.

Ethiopia was placed on the violations-agenda, if not condemned, in 1978–81 and again in 1986. Angola elicited UN's attention late in the process of (failed) peace-making, in 1993–94. Burundi was placed on the violations-agenda in 1973, after the first aid cutoffs had already started but elicited little international attention until twenty years later. Since the fate of Burundi was interwoven with that of Rwanda and Zaire/Congo, the three are dealt with together. The section on the Great Lakes vividly illustrates the haphazard manner in which international responses to human rights violations took place: Zaire was shielded for a long time from any condemnation by its Western allies; Rwanda became the target of inter-national interventions in the aftermath of genocide, which had been foretold a year earlier by UN human rights bodies; genocide-prone policies in Rwanda and Burundi had been foretold by scholars researching genocide three decades earlier. If one compares the cursory treatment of Africa by UN human rights bodies with vehement Western condemnations of human rights violations in the 1990s, as is done below in case histories, the difference between multilateralism and uni-lateralism is apparent. The large number of African states in the United Nations has made the African group the largest in the Commission on Human Rights, and resulted in the correspondingly small number of condemnations. In contrast, aid dependance has made African countries vulnerable to shifts in donors' priorities, while steadily diminishing aid budgets provided a considerable incentive for punitive withdrawals of aid. Human rights have been only one of many grounds for such withdrawals.

This Chapter follows chronological sequence in which individual African coun-tries were placed on UN's violators-agenda and complements this multilateral track by looking into the conduct of major donors. Exceptions have been made where these are dictated by the shared fate of neighbouring countries; the Great Lakes sub-region and the Horn of Africa are discussed together. Alongside South Africa (dealt with in Chapter 2), Equatorial Guinea and Uganda (addressed in Chapter 5), Burundi was the earliest country for which complaints of systemic human rights violations were forwarded to the United Nations. Burundi was discussed under confidential 1503 procedure in 1974 to be condemned for similar violations in 1994. Since the underlying causes of violations link the fate of Burundi with that of Rwanda and Zaire/Congo, the three are discussed below first in the sequence in which they exploded and/or imploded.

Ethiopia followed Burundi in 1978 and came close to being condemned as a violator in 1986. Between these two signposts, the United Nations was internally divided – the human rights bodies dealt with violations, unsuccessfully as it turned out, while humanitarian bodies concentrated on providing relief, especially food aid. The two paths were merged in Somalia in the early 1990s, again unsuccess-fully. The underlying rationale was based on an article of faith. The hope was that the end of the Cold War would make it possible to swiftly end domestic warfare because outside warmongering had stopped. Domestic fault-lines were previously cloaked underneath the fiction of statehood, whose apparatus was funded and supported from the outside rather than home-grown. Domestic and regional fault-lines have also emerged in Sudan: racial and religious dividing lines split the country into the north and the south, while all Sudan's neighbours interfered, for worse more often than for better. A host of reasons was used at different times to justify condemnations and sanctions – military coups, human rights violations, Islam, inability to service foreign debt, warfare, terrorism.

Alongside these two sub-regional powder kegs – the Great Lakes and the Horn of Africa – the rest of the continent never obtained prominence in international human rights politics. The immunity of the French *chasse-gardée* to human-rights challenges was ruptured only in the 1990s. Togo was condemned for human rights violations by the Commission on Human Rights in 1993. Angola followed later that same year, adding a lusophone dimension, but in a reverse sense. In explicitly mentioning Angola, the Vienna Conference on Human Rights had breached its own procedural rule whereby individual countries should not be discussed. The exception was made for Bosnia and Herzegovina, and Angola was promptly added by the African Group so as to channel attention also to Africa's needs in peace-making. Perhaps there will be some retrospective regret expressed by the African leaders for having emphasized Angola's victimhood in 1993, in view of its subsequent return to rule-or-ruin warfare. As similar wars proliferated, the search for their causes gradually moved from recitals of ethnic differences within artificially created states towards inquiries into the economics of warfare. Accordingly, halting wars then had to move towards designing international responses which addressed their causes:

> In Liberia, the control and exploitation of diamonds, timber and other raw materials was one of the principal objectives of the warring factions. Control over those resources financed the various factions and gave them the means to sustain the conflicts. Clearly, many of the protagonists had a strong financial interest in seeing the conflict prolonged.[2]

Export of oil and diamonds have been fueling warfare in Angola and in Zaire/Congo, while diamonds re-appeared as the major fuel for warfare in Sierra Leone and Liberia. Different from a widespread perception of poverty being Africa's key problem, in warfare this proved to be wealth rather than poverty. Wealth has also been elevated, implicitly, through a major international orientation towards exposing and opposing corruption, to a key problem in peace-time. Nigeria created a veritable precedent for intra-African mobilization against human rights violators in 1995, as is described below. Oil was in the background, as was misappropriation of

---

[2] United Nations – The causes of conflict and the promotion of durable peace and sustainable development in Africa. Report of the Secretary-General, U.N. Doc. S/1998/318 of 13 April 1998, para. 14.

income from its export. This came to light when Nigeria's foreign debt mounted while the price of oil diminished and political transition started in 1998–99.

THE GREAT LAKES

The Great Lakes region imposed itself upon the world at large as the foremost man-made disaster of the mid-1990s and thus also upon the reluctant United Nations. The UN did not come out of that disaster covered with glory. Its policy towards Rwanda was much criticised, and little praise accompanied its responses to developments in the Great Lakes in general. A common pattern of problems was identified for all three countries – Burundi, Rwanda and Zaire/Congo – fairly late as mass population movements, coupled with illegal arms sales and exacerbated by incitement to racial and/or ethnic hatred.[3] The most visible consequence of these problems was warfare, and responding to it required the international community to speak with one voice, which it never could. The arms embargoes, imposed to prevent escalation of warfare, were poorly enforced, if at all; assistance to refugees and displaced populations involved a myriad of foreign and international actors and managed to accomplish little, at astronomic expense. Such assistance also contributed to subsequent warfare by failing to differentiate between armed groups and refugees, sheltering and feeding both. Many different facilitators of political negotiations all too often concentrated on the justifications proffered for warfare rather than its causes. The negotiations then resulted in parchment promises while warfare continued. To make things even more difficult, previously separate international policies were merged: peace-making was extended to encompass human rights protection, peace-keeping was mixed with humanitarian relief, and all such policies implemented on shoe-string budgets.

The model of development that had been applied within the affected countries contributed to the creation of problems but was absent from problem-solving. Development aid was routinely suspended when security and peace collapsed and its resumption tied to a host of conditions; none of the needy countries could meet them all. The multiplication of international and foreign actors that were involved, each with its separate agenda and source of funding, made things even more cumbersome.

All these international and foreign policies and actors have some impact on human rights, positive or negative. This impact is – at best – an object of retroactive assessments, and such assessments are likely to be negative rather than positive. The absence of a foreign and/or international human rights policy during the previous decades regarding Burundi, Rwanda or Zaire/Congo shifted in the 1990s to hectic efforts to include human rights into international interventions of

---

[3] Commission on Human Rights – Coordination meeting on the human rights situation in the Great Lakes region. Note by the High Commissioner on Human Rights, U.N. Doc. E/CN.4/1996/69 of 15 February 1996, paras. 13–14.

various types, within and without the United Nations. The UN had been designed to be the key global actor mandated to create a human rights policy, but a host of human rights policies emerged. The OAU created an indigenous African vision of human rights, if not an operative policy. Individual Western governments each had its own (explicit or implicit) version of a human rights policy, EUrope developed an explicit human rights policy for its relations with Africa and individual African countries. Different from the United Nations or the Organization of African Unity, Western policies have been backed up by funding to translate them into practice, which the OAU has always lacked and the UN has been increasingly lacking. UN's evolving responses to developments in Burundi, Rwanda and Zaire/Congo have demonstrated obstacles which such a multitude of human rights policies created in practice. A single human rights policy would have necessitated consensus amongst African countries, acquiescence of the former colonial powers, political and financial support by the superpowers, and an established human rights infra-structure through which such a policy could be translated into practice. None of these is likely to materialize and international responses seem doomed to alternate between silence and short-term-shoe-string-budget interventions as in the previous decades.

The first African country that emerged on the UN violations agenda was Burundi in 1973. It was dealt with under the confidential 1503 procedure, although it probably was not dealt with at all despite being on the agenda. The lack of col-lective political will to respond to massacres continued until the mid-1990s and was ultimately triggered by the 1994 genocide in Rwanda. The fate of two small, poor, overpopulated, agricultural, and landlocked countries tended to be attributed to ethnicity and/or the heritage of dominance by the Tutsi minority over the Hutu majority.

Burundi

Many proposals have been made to institute an early warning mechanism so as to enable the United Nations to preempt crises from exploding. An early warning had been given for Burundi but did not prove beneficial. Knowledge about past and emerging massacres has been available for a very long time but there was no commitment to act upon it. Information alone does not generate a commitment to act.

As mentioned above, Burundi was brought up under the confidential 1503 pro-cedure for gross and systematic human rights violations in 1973. One can go a bit further into history to recall the internationally organized and supervised elections which had brought independence to quite a few African countries, Rwanda and Burundi amongst them. The United Nations supervised a referendum on the separa-tion of Ruanda-Urundi as well as the subsequent pre-independence elections. These had been triggered by widespread violence in 1959. With the benefit of hindsight, one may wonder whether the fate of these two countries would have been different without elections and without their separation into two states. Such questions may appear to be futile because history cannot be retroactively reversed so that one

Table 9.2: Aid to Burundi in 1960–95 at five-year intervals

	1960	1965	1970	1975	1980	1985	1990	1995
Belgium	7.5	3.6	9.8	16.3	27.7	19.1	39.5	7.0
Canada	–	–	0.1	0.1	0.0	1.2	0.4	2.1
France	–	–	1.1	6.6	12.9	22.6	37.7	16.6
Germany	–	0.0	0.5	1.5	10.0	12.6	30.4	30.9
USA	–	0.1	–	1.0	4.0	9.0	18.0	23.0
EUrope	–	–	–	–	63.9	69.9	152.1	91.0
Total bilateral	7.5	3.7	11.6	26.3	59.8	77.1	156.8	101.7
Total multilateral	0.8	1.2	6.3	23.0	54.2	59.3	109.4	181.4

Table 9.3: Aid to Rwanda, in 1960–95 at five-year intervals

	1960	1965	1970	1975	1980	1985	1990	1995
Belgium	7.5	4.7	11.2	25.6	36.2	20.1	43.4	18.0
Canada	–	0.7	1.2	4.1	5.7	10.7	13.8	16.8
France	–	–	1.2	12.0	15.8	15.4	33.9	5.1
Germany	–	0.4	1.0	5.3	16.8	23.6	31.8	51.7
EUrope	–	–	–	–	94.8	78.5	156.4	148.6
Total bilateral	7.5	6.9	16.7	53.6	96.6	103.1	182.2	285.3
Total multilateral	0.8	1.5	5.1	29.1	57.5	73.0	98.9	373.4

Table 9.4: Aid to Zaire/Congo in 1960–95 at five-year intervals

	1960	1965	1970	1975	1980	1985	1990	1995
Belgium	71.0	87.9	50.4	113.0	169.7	78.7	95.4	45.5
Canada	0.0	0.6	0.7	4.1	13.5	17.7	14.3	0.5
France	–	–	3.8	20.3	39.4	28.5	174.2	16.9
Germany	0.0	0.3	1.4	8.5	36.8	20.0	112.4	7.0
USA	–	44.8	11.0	4.0	11.0	38.0	32.0	1.0
EUrope	–	–	–	–	555.3	161.8	588.0	177.5
Total bilateral	71.2	136.2	70.3	154.2	623.2	208.5	628.5	166.4
Total multilateral	18.6	13.2	19.0	50.4	129.1	324.2	194.4	76.8

Note: All figures are in US$ million.
Source: OECD – *Geographical Distribution of Financial Flows to Developing Countries/Aid Recipients*, various issues.

could find out answers to what-if kind of questions. However, the 1993 elections in Burundi made such probing questions pertinent. These elections were internationally supported and hailed for the electoral victory of the majority. Because the army remained the power-base of the political party which had lost because it disposed of a minority of votes, the military was able to dismantle the electoral outcome in two days only four months after the elections had taken place. Two presidents were killed in as many years and the military took over again in 1996.

A multi-party straightjacket produced in 1993 electoral victory for the numerically superior ethnic group at the expense of the numerically inferior, but powerful minority. The *ethnic-party-equals-ethnic-vote* model[4] equated democracy with demography and produced the inevitable outcome, imposing a question – as yet unanswered – as to what alternative types of political mobilization could replace the imported Western political-party model. The certain electoral victory by the Hutu majority led one of its radical groupings to indicatively call itself *Conseil national pour la défense de la démocratie* (CNDD) and its armed wing the *Front pour la défense de la démocratie* (FDD). Nevertheless, the conflict was perhaps not about democracy or ethnicity. As the Tutsi minority has been described as the 'elite caste consisting of members of the military and of townfolk, traders, civil servants and businessmen,'[5] the conflict can also be seen as struggle for retaining – or obtaining – privileges typifying the lifestyle of the urban elite.

The cycles of violence and elections and return to violence have dotted the history of Burundi. The pre-independence elections of 1961 were followed by political violence; elections of 1993 were followed by both political violence and a coup d'etat; elections of 1966 were followed by a coup d'etat. At the time of writing (December 1999), Burundi is ruled by the military, led by Pierre Buyoya, after yet another coup. Sanctions were imposed by the Western countries in response to that latest coup, but have been invisible because aid had been suspended already. Economic sanctions were also imposed by the neighbouring countries as a response to the 1996 military coup to be lifted in January1999.[6]

Shifts from elections to violence and to coups in Burundi and shifts from silence to condemnations to sanctions at the international level have only subdued the fear of a genocide, which persists. Leo Kuper has described the donors' knowledge and silence in 1972, when 'the Belgian Prime Minister had informed his cabinet that according to the information at his disposal Burundi was confronted with a veritable genocide.'[7] As Kuper has found, France, China, North Korea and the OAU supported the government of Burundi at the time, while Belgium (or the United Nations) did not respond to the massacres of 1972 nor prevented their

---

[4] Although neither main politic party defines itself as ethnic, the victor of 1993 elections, FRODEBU (*Front pour la démocratie au Burundi*) is seen as the Hutu party, and UPRONA (*Union pour le progrès national*) as Tutsi party.

[5] Commission on Human Rights – Initial report on the human rights situation in Burundi submitted by the Special Rapporteur, Mr. Paulo Sérgio Pinheiro, U.N. Doc. E/CN.4/1996/16 of 14 November 1995, para. 19.

[6] Otieno, B. – Burundi's blockade lifted, *New African*, March 1999.

[7] Kuper, L. – *Genocide: Its Political Uses in the Twentieth Century*, Yale University Press, New Haven, 1981, p. 162.

repetition one year later. An attempt was made to mobilize the UN human rights bodies, but it failed to secure the necessary governmental support. The biggest obstacle was OAU's support for the government of Burundi.

International attention focused on Burundi, as it did on Rwanda, in the mid-1990s and the word *genocide* was mentioned again. The Security Council decided in August 1995 to set up an international commission of inquiry to look into the most recent massacres, to identify perpetrators and, in an bout of optimism, to eradicate impunity.[8] The UN High Commissioner for Human Rights announced in June 1994 'a large programme of technical co-operation in the field of human rights which includes expert advice, institution-building, training, education and information activities'.[9] Preventive action was initiated alongside probing into past atrocities, signifying a welcome departure from the proverbial retroactivity in-built in human rights responses. That planned UN preventive programme did not materialize, however. *Africa Confidential* lamented 'the lack of any effective preventive diplomacy or international mediation in Bujumbura,' while *Amnesty International* called for civilian and military monitors to be urgently deployed.[10]

Although the interest for Burundi followed the 1994 genocide in Rwanda, donors had been faced with reports of killings in Burundi many times before. Indeed, massacres were documented in 1965, 1972, 1988 and 1991, before the cycle of violence started again in 1993. In 1987, the then-government of Burundi reported to the United Nations that 'it is no longer possible to identify different ethnic groups or tribes, given the homogeneity of the population.'[11] Much as that statement might have resembled the usual governmental self-praise, which has brought the reporting system under human rights treaties into disrepute, there was truth in it: distinguishing who should be killed as Tutsi or Hutu was easy in Rwands because this detail was included in everyone's identity papers. Not so in Burundi. Differences are not visible, nor is the language or religion different. Defining and identifying an enemy is, however, an attribute of power.

That power has been abused in Burundi for a very long time and donors started responding to repetitive massacres in the 1970s by cutting off aid. Disunity prevailed and some donors would cut off aid so as to punish the government for abuses while others would increase aid in order to assist the government in coping with the human toll of those abuses. Belgium was the first donor to cut off aid in 1972 and

---

[8] Security Council resolution 1012 of 28 August 1995.

[9] Address of the High Commissioner for Human Rights before the meeting of special rapporteurs/representatives/experts and chairpersons of working groups of the special procedures of the Commission on Human Rights in Geneva on 30 May–1 June 1994, U.N. Doc. E/CN.4/1994/5/Add.1 of 15 June 1994, p. 6.

[10] Burundi: On a knife's edge, *Africa Confidential*, vol. 35, No. 16, 12 August 1994, p. 1–2; Amnesty International – Burundi: Briefing paper for press conference on Amnesty International visit to Burundi 25 July–4 August 1994, Doc. AFR 16/17/94 of 10 August 1994.

[11] Committee on the Elimination of Racial Discrimination – Fifth periodic report of Burundi, U.N. Doc. CERD/C/145/Add. 1 of 3 November 1987, para. 4.

again in 1983–87, but Belgian aid increased in 1988 to support national reconciliation.[12] No reconciliation took place and mass killings again attracted donor
attention in 1988. The media reported that 5,000 Hutus had been massacred and
30,000 fled to Rwanda. Belgium did not decrease aid, explaining that it was was
necessary in anticipation of the return of Hutu refugees who fled to Rwanda during
massacres.[13]

Less international attention was generated in 1991 when, according to *Amnesty
International,* at least 1000 Hutus were killed by the military, following a Hutu
attack against Tutsis.[14] According to the government, which responded to the
Amnesty report, the number of victims had been 500 while 560 suspects were
arrested.[15] Human rights NGOs brought up Burundi before the Commission on
Human Rights in 1992, calling upon donors to condition their aid by demanding
from the government to halt institutionalized ethnic discrimination and noting that
they were 'astonished to see that assistance to the Government of Burundi continued without restrictions or conditions, even though fresh massacres had been
reported in November 1991.'[16] The representative of Burundi replied that 'disturbances' mentioned by NGOs 'had not involved a confrontation of a generalized
discriminatory nature,' but were caused by refugees who had entered Burundi clan-
destinely, formed an alliance with some local population, and attacked military
camps and police forces. The representative of Burundi 'was able to assure the
Commission that the situation was under control, that the population as a whole had
rejected the terrorist acts and that steps had been taken to ensure public and fair
trial for the guilty parties.'[17] Burundi's subsequent report under the ICCPR
(International Covenant on Civil and Political Rights) pointed out that the government had 'succeeded in preventing an escalation of the violence.[18]

The government was not successful, however, because massacres continued.
The government, civilian or military, was mostly Tutsi, with the majority of the
population being Hutu. Following the 'disturbances' of 1988 the Government had
indeed appointed a commission to study causes of ethnic strife, composed of equal
numbers of Tutsi and Hutu, which produced a long report. Following this report,

---

[12] Renard, R. and Reyntjens, F. – Aid and conditionality: The case of Belgium, with particular
reference to Burundi, Rwanda and Zaire, in Stokke, O. (ed.) – *Aid and Political Conditionality,* EADI
Book Series 16, Frank Cass, London, 1995, p. 96.

[13] Developments in Burundi during the previous decades and the donors' responses are described in
Tomaševski, K. – *Development Aid and Human Rights Revisited,* Pinter Publishers, London, 1993,
pp. 110–112.

[14] Amnesty International Doc. AFR 16/WU 01/91 of 18 December 1991.

[15] Rights advocates target Burundi, *International Herald Tribune,* 28 May 1992; Burundi: Tribal
tensions, *New African,* February 1992.

[16] U.N. Doc. E/CN.4/1992/SR.13, para. 63.

[17] U.N. Doc. E/CN.4/1992/SR.13, paras. 10–11.

[18] Human Rights Committee – Initial report of Burundi, U.N. Doc. CCPR/C/68/Add.2 of
19 November 1991, para. 9.

Burundi adopted the Charter of National Unity in 1990, which emphasized the respect of human rights and non-discrimination. Translating proclaimed principles into practice was not as easy. That period constituted the first presidency of Pierre Buyoya, who came to power through an internal military coup in 1987 and handed over to an elected government in 1993. He was credited not only for that Charter and a new Constitution, but for having appointed the majority of Hutu ministers in his government.[19] He had also been credited for his 1987 coup, which 'the Western powers and domestic churches applauded.'[20] Buyoya's re-emergence in 1996, again through a military coup, did not trigger applause but it did not prompt condemnations either.

One reason for this lack of opprobrium against military coups and their leaders have been disappointments with experiments in democracy. With the benefit of hindsight, the multi-party elections of a winner-takes-all type, as applied in 1993, deepened the divisions along the ethnic line. Ali Mazrui has found that multiparty pluralism can be disastrous in Africa.[21] Divisions along ethnic lines were exacerbated by the speed with which elections had been organized. The model established in Eastern Europe, with the creation of ethnically homogeneous states within the previously multi-ethnic countries, contributed to equating democracy and demography while the recognition of ethnically-based states by the international community legitimized that process. A replication of ethnically-based states from Eastern Europe was feared from the very establishment of the OAU, which committed in 1964 all its members to observe the prohibition of changing borders inherited from the colonial times.

Legitimacy was bestowed upon ethnically-based governance in Burundi through the UN human rights assistance programme, however limited or invisible it may have been. Since the government in power is routinely the UN's sole partner, its choice of what and who should be assisted is often unchallenged. Louis Joinet, a member of the Sub-Commission for Prevention of Discrimination and Protection of Minorities objected to the fact that UN's human rights assistance in Burundi was provided to '98% of the judges [who] were Tutsi, although the Tutsi ethnic group was a minority in the country.'[22] The UN Special Rapporteur on Summary Executions, Bacre Waly Ndiaye, added to the critique noting that 'the application of an overwhelmingly Tutsi judicial system to mainly Hutu defendants creates tension and distrust,' to then assert that ethnicity was not the cause of Burundi's problems:

---

[19] Misser, F. & Ankomah, B. – Burundi: Buyoya's sea change, *New African*, July 1989; Boyer, A. – Burundi: Unity at last, *Africa Report*, vol. 37, No. 2, March/April, 1992, pp. 37–40.

[20] Misser, F. & Rake, A. – Buyoya: Bogeyman of Burundi?, *New African*, October 1996.

[21] Mazrui, A.A. – Towards containing conflict in Africa: Methods, mechanisms and values, *East African Journal of Peace & Human Rights*, vol. 2, 1995, No. 1, p. 82.

[22] Summary record of the 4th meeting of the forty-sixth session of the Sub-Commission, 2 August 1994, U.N. Doc. E/CN.4/Sub.2/1994/SR.4 of 8 August 1994, para. 25.

Ethnicity as such is not the main factor in the conflict. Rather, the violence is rooted in the artificial ethnic boundaries and the discriminatory structuring of power introduced by the former colonial rulers and later used to gain access to or maintain political power.[23]

Indeed, Burundi's large and largely monoethnic (Tutsi) army has reversed electoral outcomes many times and proved resistant to changes envisaged by elections or new constitutions.[24] The UN General Assembly condemned the military coup of 1993 and demanded that 'perpetrators of the putsch lay down their arms and return to their barracks.'[25] They did not. Donors suspended (civilian and/or development) aid,[26] while flow of weapons continued unimpeded. François Misser has claimed that the reason for the 1993 coup 'was fear by the army that President Ndadaye was trying to build up an alternative Hutu-dominated presidential gendarmerie to counterbalance the primarily Tutsi army.'[27] Abuses continued with impunity and president Ndadaye was killed. An anonymous Western diplomat was quoted asserting that his assassins were known but no arrests were made for fear of sparking violence. 'He scoffed at the idea of bringing them to justice. 'What justice', he said, 'the whole legal system is manned by Tutsis.'[28] That Western diplomat was proved partially wrong when 35 government officials and military officers were brought to trial for killing president Ndadaye, but partially right when the UN Special Rapporteur concluded that only lower ranks had been brought to court.[29] Furthermore, the asymmetry has remained unchanged with 90% judges being Tutsi and 90% of prisoners Hutu.[30]

In designing solutions for such problems, international human rights bodies have an easy task in pinpointing what is wrong and what should be done to put it right. The Human Rights Committee has suggested that 'the army should be brought under the effective control of the civilian authorities,' and Burundi 'should receive resolute support of the international community.'[31] How should these aims be

---

[23] United Nations – Report of the Special Rapporteur on extrajudicial, summary or arbitrary executions on his mission to Burundi from 19 to 29 April 1995, U.N. Doc. E/CN.4/1996/4/Add. 1 of 24 July 1995, paras. 13–14.

[24] Reyntjens, F. – The proof of puddings is in the eating: The June 1993 elections in Burundi, *The Journal of Modern African Studies*, vol. 31, 1993, No. 4, pp. 563–583.

[25] United Nations – The situation in Burundi, General Assembly resolution 48/17 of 3 November 1993.

[26] Burundi: Turning the clock back, *Africa Events*, November 1993, p. 6.

[27] Misser, F. – Burundi: Democracy at stake, *New African*, December 1993, p. 30.

[28] Dowden, R. – Burundi looks for UN 'miracle' to avert famine, *The Independent*, 16 February 1994.

[29] Commission on Human Rights – Third report on the human rights situation in Burundi, submitted by the Special rapporteur, Mr. Paulo Sérgio Pinheiro, U.N. Doc. E/CN.4/1998/72 of 13 February 1998, para. 78.

[30] Committee on the Elimination of Racial Discrimination – Consideration of seventh to tenth periodic reports of Burundi, 19 August 1997, U.N. Doc. CERD/C/SR.1238 of 8 December 1997, para. 13.

[31] Human Rights Committee – Burundi: Comments of the Human Rights Committee, U.N. Doc. CCPR/C/79/Add. 41 of 3 August 1994, paras. 14–15.

achieved is a question which the Human Rights Committee, and other human rights bodies, deem to lie outside their mandate. Their mandate has become blurred with broadened definitions of human rights violations, however. The UN General Assembly found in 1995 that some unnamed entities 'from within and outside the country [are] heedlessly violating human rights [by] attacking innocent populations [or] arming extremists.'[32] How such unnamed entities fitted into the international legal framework has remained an open question.

Burundi has been affected by the warfare in and around Zaire/Congo. The justification for its active involvement was that the armed opposition was based there[33] and had initiated armed attacks against Burundi in 1994.[34] The main target of those attacks was Rwanda as well as Burundi. The fate of all neighbouring countries has become inextricably linked with the warfare spilling over borders and arms trade flourishing. The boundaries between domestic and cross-border warfare and between governmental and non-governmental armies have become blurred; international responses have necessarily become confused and confusing.

The lack of response to genocide-prone policies in Burundi and Rwanda in the previous decades have turned to hasty and excessive responses in the 1990s. The UN's attention for Burundi, never matched by that for Rwanda, has subsided after the military coup in July 1996, to which the OAU responded by imposing sanctions. Different views were expressed, some favouring sanctions in the hope that the country would become so much impoverished that further warfare would become impossible, others arguing against punitiveness and in favour of building a better future:

> The fact that the current Government of Burundi had no constitutional status should not prevent the international community doing all it could to help the country lay the foundations for the rule of law by encouraging wherever possible positive initiatives by the authorities.[35]

The 1996 coup returned to power Pierre Buyoya, the military ruler who had handed power over to a civilian government in 1993. Western economic sanctions followed

---

[32] United Nations – The situation in Burundi, resolution 50/159 of 22 December 1995, para. 134.

[33] Dowden, R. – The state has melted, the killing continues, *The World Today*, December 1996, p. 306.

[34] Braeckman, C. – Hantise du génocide au Burundi, *Le monde diplomatique*, March 1996.

[35] Statement by Mr. Pinheiro, Special Rapporteur on the situation of human rights in Burundi, before the Commission on Human Rights on 16 April 1998, U.N. Doc. E/CN.4/1998/SR.42 of 18 April 1998, para. 17. The Special Rapporteur's sympathy for the government was probably based on his findings about abuses by the rebels: 'The population increasingly fears direct contacts with the rebels and prefers in some cases to cooperate with the army or the civilian administration in order to be better protected. The rebels for their part take revenge by harassing or taking reprisals against civilians who refuse to follow them.' Commission on Human Rights – Third report on the human rights situation in Burundi, U.N. Doc. E/CN.4/1998/72 of 13 February 1998, para. 69.

without much impact because little aid had been going to Burundi anyway,[36] while the Security Council only threatened sanctions.[37] The lead towards an African solution for an African problem had been provided by the late Julius Nyerere, who had been the mediator for the Burundi conflict(s) and had initially advocated deployment of an international military force.[38] Resistance to such a foreign military presence had reportedly been one of the reasons for the 1996 military coup[39] and such plans were apparently abandoned in favour of sanctions. These required the government to lift restrictions upon political parties, un-suspend parliament, restore constitutional order (which probably meant that the military government should step down) and start peace negotiations. The sanctions were affective in preventing legal trade while encouraging smuggling. Prices of food increased because transportation costs skyrocketed. The export of coffee, Burundi's main foreign exchange earner, virtually ceased. The UN Special Rapporteur first 'applauded the determination of those African countries which decided to impose economic sanctions' to subsequently find sanctions to have 'a disastrous effect on the population of Burundi' as well as being ineffective as means of coercion.[40]

Moreover, the sanctions have radicalized politics. The politics of scarcity brings development into the picture to recall that development aid had been halted. Beforehand, the words Hutu or Tutsi did not figure in the World Bank's documents about Burundi. Their reader would not be aware of the fact that Burundi was ruled by the military or that military coups or massacres took place. Reading between the lines, terms such as 'the sensitive sociopolitical environment' or 'the delicate political climate'[41] alluded to obstacles for de-politicising development. The absence of massacres or military rule from the development policies had been prevalent

---

[36] 'The US and the European Union cut off crucial support to Burundi's war-battered economy after aid officials said the government lacked the will to end political and ethnic violence.' (*Guardian Weekly*, 14 April 1996). However, out of the European Union's 112 million ecu committed to Burundi only 23 million had been disbursed in 1990–95 (Wise, E. – Union lends backing to regional peace effort for Burundi, *European Voice*, 10–16 October 1996).

[37] The Security Council condemned 'the overthrow of the constitutional order in Burundi' (Statement by the President of the Council of 29 July 1996, Doc. S/PRST/1996/32) and vaguely threatened sanctions unless 'unconditional negotiations among all Burundi's political parties and factions, inside and outside the country' proceeded immediately; the anticipated sanctions were an arms embargo and/or 'measures targeted against the leaders of the regime and all factions who continued to encourage violence.' (Security Council resolution 1072 (1996) of 30 August 1996, paras. 6 and 11).

[38] Burundi: Tutsi-led army seizes power, *Africa Research Bulletin*, vol. 33, No. 7, 1–31 July 1996, 12326–12327.

[39] Woollacott, M. – A land split down the middle, *Guardian Weekly*, 4 August 1996.

[40] Commission on Human Rights – Second and third reports on the human rights situation in Burundi submitted by the Special Rapporteur, Mr. Paulo Sérgio Pinheiro, U.N. Doc. E/CN.4/1997/12 of 10 February 1997, para. 74 and E/CN.4/1998/72 of 13 February 1998, paras. 80–83.

[41] Englebert, P & Hoffman, R. – Burundi: Learning the lesson, in Husain, I. & Faruqee, R. (Eds.) – *Adjustment in Africa. Lessons from Country Case Studies*, World Bank Regional and Sectoral Studies, Washington, D.C., 1994, pp. 11 and 14.

until the 1990s. In some cases, as is described below for Rwanda, in the 1990s the donors have switched from silence about human rights violations to an overemphasis.

Rwanda

Rwanda was given prominence in the *DAC/OECD 1994 Development Co-operation Report* as the major humanitarian disasters of that time. The role of aid had been prominent because Rwanda had received an annual $1 billion[42] and no punitive suspensions or withdrawals had taken place until after the genocide. (Because a flood of literature followed the 1994 genocide in Rwanda, no description is included here.) The European Union suspended aid in 1995 because, as is discussed below, the new government (less than one year old at the time) was held responsible for the forceful dismantling of the Kibeho refugee camp, which involved a death toll of 300 or 5,000.[43]

The shift from the pre-1994 disregard for human rights protection to the post-1994 stringent human rights conditionality in aid coincided with the change of government in Rwanda. The new government formed after the military victory of the Rwandan Patriotic Front became immediately a target of donors' punitiveness. Belgium, the Netherlands and the European Union were in the lead and the EU Council reminded the government of Rwanda that development aid 'is conditional on the respect of human rights and progress towards national reconciliation.'[44] The search for reasons for the donors' punitiveness has gone behind the official justification (human rights violations) to find Rwanda's *anglicisation*[45] as an influential factor in Western foreign policies – the previous government had been Francophone. France was criticised for its military support to that government, even after the Security Council's embargo; for the *Opération Turquoise* (which provided a safe conduit to Zaire for *génocidaires*); for shielding and arming paramilitary troops which continued genocide they had started in 1994. France

---

[42] Overview of the DAC Chair, James Michel – Sustainable development for human security, *Development Co-operation. 1994 Report*, OECD, Paris, 1995, p. 3.

[43] The international commission of inquiry found that the chaotic closure of the Kibeho camp had involved the killing of unarmed refugees by the Rwandan armed forces, that the killing had not been planned but was an accident which could have been avoided. (Rwanda killings 'not planned', *Financial Times*, 20–21 May 1995). Previous media reports had placed the human toll at 5,000 (Bedford, J. and McGreal, C. – 5,000 killed in Rwanda massacre, *Guardian Weekly*, 30 April 1995), the UN's estimate was 2,000 killed, while Rwanda's government reported the number of 300. (Lorch, D. – Rwanda massacre: The grim reality, *International Herald Tribune*, 25 April 1995).

[44] Rwanda, *EuroStep News*, No. 20, April – June 1995, p. 24.

[45] Rwanda: Blocked aid, *EuroStep News*, no. 18, November – December 1994, p. 25; Rwanda: Kigali under Europressure, *Africa Confidential*, vol. 35, No. 22, 4 November 1994, p. 4.

exonerated its conduct through a commission of inquiry in 1997–98, not without domestic and international protest.[46]

The new government of Rwanda was not similarly exonerated. In May 1995, the International Commission of Inquiry finished its investigation of the Kibeho massacre, found the government not guilty and recommended that aid be resumed.[47] This did not happen, however. An important reason for the Commission's exoneration of the Rwandese government was that soldiers had overreacted. However strongly that was condemned, it was 'no great surprise that the RPA [Rwanda's Patriotic Army] has finally cracked, the pressure cooker blown.'[48] The RPA military commander was court martialed in December 1996 and found guilty of having failed to prevent the soldiers under his command from carrying out the killings.[49]

EUrope's aid to new Rwanda's government was neither generous (5 million ecu was approved in 1994) nor unconditional, but linked to 'the legal guarantees offered to the population.'[50] Insistence on legal guarantees for a country depleted of laws and lawyers was a condition difficult to meet. Most aid was, however, furnished to the Rwandan population but outside Rwanda. A vast international aid programme was carried out for Rwandan refugees in 1994–96, especially in Zaire, despite knowledge that refugees included armed (and re-armed) militias that had been involved in the 1994 genocide and despite protests by some aid-providers.[51] Probably because of such critiques, the European Union partially resumed aid to Rwanda and the World Bank initiated a $4 million programme to restore Rwandan agriculture.[52]

---

[46] Leymarie, P. – Litigieuse intervention française au Rwanda, and La politique française au Rwanda en questions, *Le monde diplomatique*, July 1994 and September 1998; Malley, S. – Rwanda: Le bilan tragique de l'Opération Turquoise, *Le Nouvel Afrique Asie*, No. 60, September 1994; Mitterrand defends Africa record, *Financial Times*, 9 November 1994; Paris must come clean on Rwanda arms (editorial) *Le monde*, reproduced in *Guardian Weekly*, 1 December 1995; Trueheart, C. – French panel faults U.S. for failure to act in Rwanda, *International Herald Tribune*, 16 December 1998; Ourdan, R. – France exonerates itself over Rwanda, *Le Monde*, 17 December, reproduced in *Guardian Weekly*, 27 December 1998.

[47] Rwanda: Kibeho inquiry results, *Africa Research Bulletin*, vol. 32, No. 5, 27 June 1995, p. A11861.

[48] Rwanda: Army triggers massacre, *Africa Research Bulletin*, vol. 32, No. 4, 25 May 1995, p. C11808-A11809.

[49] Commission on Human Rights – Human rights field operation in Rwanda. Report of the United nations High Commissioner for Human Rights, U.N. Doc. E/CN.4/1998/61 of 19 february 1998, para. 40.

[50] Rwanda; The new European commitment. International Conference in the Hague, *The Courier*, No. 148, November-December 1994, p. 15.

[51] Bonner, R. – Aid is taken 'hostage' in Rwandan camps. People behind earlier massacres terrorize refugees and divert aid, *International Herald Tribune*, 1 November 1994; Luce, E. – Aid workers want UN protection from militias, *Guardian Weekly*, 13 November 1994; Hélèle, J. – Goma prepares for the worst, *Le monde*, reproduced in *Guardian Weekly*, 6 August 1995.

[52] Brussels frees Rwanda aid funds, *International Herald Tribune*, 14 July 1995; World Bank bid to aid Rwanda farming, *Financial Times*, 12 December 1994

Alongside human rights conditionality, Rwanda's inability to service debt inherited from the previous government made it ineligible for aid. In 1995, a UNDP's (United Nations Development Programme) effort to mobilize donors resulted in pledges for $634 million, out of which only $69 million was disbursed, and out of this $29 million had constituted the payment of debt arrears[53] and had thus been paid from one donors' bank account into another.

The pre- and post-genocide role of aid was reviewed in the *Joint Evaluation of Emergency Assistance to Rwanda*. This study has revealed that the structural adjustment programme of 1990 disregarded potentially explosive consequences of Rwanda's economic retrogression. Internally, increased impoverishment of the rural (mainly Hutu) population was likely to have created a fertile ground for the anti-Tutsi propaganda. Internationally, the donor community found itself torn between conflicting aims:

[Strict enforcement of structural adjustment and fiscal reform] reduced the incentives for donors to insist on human rights, [while] democratization came to be seen as a solution to the growing problem of civil violence. Support for democratization and the related peace process implied continuous economic and political engagement in Rwanda. From this perspective, the threat of ultimately imposing sanctions by withdrawing aid – as Western human rights organizations called for in 1992–93 – was counter-productive. Donors thus became hostage to their own policies.[54]

The increased military expenditure (which grew from 2 to 8% of GDP in 1989–92) inhibited any success that the structural adjustment programme might have had while fuelling subsequent warfare. As is typical in similar situations, development aid was halted or converted into humanitarian assistance, while military aid seemed to have continued regardless of the UN embargo. Military aid by France and Zaire has remained an object of controversy, with allegations by the media and NGOs disputed by France.[55]

Table 9.5 illustrates aid flows to Rwanda in 1987–92, at the time when the groundwork for genocide had been laid down. France and Belgium were the largest bilateral donors and their association with Rwanda was also reflected in EUrope's

---

[53] UN in $1.4bn Rwanda plea, *Financial Times*, 18 January 1995; Crossette, B. – Rwanda calls for development aid, *International Herald Tribune*, 9 June 1995.

[54] *The International Response to Conflict and Genocide: Lessons from the Rwanda Experience, Historical Perspectives: Some Explanatory Factors*, Joint Evaluation of Emergency Assistance to Rwanda, Copenhagen, March 1996, Study 1, pp. 36–39.

[55] Human Rights Watch/Arms Project – *Arming Rwanda. The Arms Trade and Human Rights Abuses in the Rwandan War*, and *Rwanda/Zaire. Arming with Impunity. International Support for the Perpetrators of Genocide*, Human Rights Watch, Washington, D.C. 1994 and 1995; Rwanda: Guilty governments, *The Economist*, 3 June 1995; Paris denies supplying Hutus, *The European*, 24–30 August 1995.

Table 9.5: Aid to Rwanda, in 1987–92
(in million US$)

	1987	1988	1989	1990	1991	1992
European Union	20.6	39.1	32.5	36.0	21.4	82.6
Belgium	33.5	29.1	26.7	43.4	55.8	45.7
Germany	22.0	25.0	27.2	31.8	40.1	43.6
World Bank/IDA	39.0	25.0	27.0	22.0	49.0	31.8
France	33.2	23.7	19.6	37.2	43.1	30.2
ADB	20.7	21.0	16.7	19.4	12.0	23.5
Japan	8.0	10.4	17.1	14.4	9.2	16.8
Switzerland	9.4	12.9	9.1	10.2	17.1	13.8
Canada	6.0	7.6	12.7	13.8	21.2	13.6
UNDP	7.6	10.2	9.0	12.3	12.8	10.2
TOTAL AID	251.1	259.5	241.7	305.2	374.8	363.6

Note: The figures refer to $ million and donors are ranked by the volume of their aid in 1992. Because only the main donors are included, their aid does not add up to the total.
Source: *The International Response to Conflict and Genocide: Lessons from the Rwanda Experience, Historical Perspectives: Some Explanatory Factors*, Joint Evaluation of Emergency Assistance to Rwanda, Copenhagen, March 1996, Study 1, p. 73.

aid. Increased aid flows in 1991–92 were the consequence of the just-negotiated structural adjustment programme and are likely to have facilitated the preparation of genocide.

As a former colonial power and donor of many decades, Belgium could not dissociate itself from the fate of Rwanda, and indeed an explicit policy on aid to Africa followed the retroactive anguish related to Rwandan genocide. Belgium had discontinued military aid to Rwanda in 1990, at the same time protesting human rights violations.[56] Human rights came to the fore of domestic foreign-policy debates and a vocal domestic constituency demanded in 1993 the government to threaten Rwanda 'with the suspension of official aid and make it conditional on democratization and improvements in the human rights situation.'[57] Following a report on widespread killings in March 1993, Belgium announced that it would reconsider aid to Rwanda, but 'Habyarimana [the president of Rwanda at the time] made conciliatory statements and Belgian aid continued.'[58] The killing of Belgian

---

[56] Misser, F. – Belgium and France beg to differ, *New African*, June 1994, p. 15.

[57] *The Reality of Aid 95. An Independent Review of International Aid*, Earthscan Publications, London, 1995, p. 36.

[58] Steering Committee for the Joint Evaluation of Emergency Assistance to Rwanda – *The International Response to Conflict and Genocide: Lessons from Rwanda Experience*, Synthesis Report, p. 15, and Part 2: *Early Warning and Conflict Management*, Copenhagen, 1996, pp. 31–32.

blue helmets in 1994, on the eve of the genocide, hastened the withdrawal of all Belgian personnel and most UN personnel, accomplishing what had been intended. That sequence of events led to subsequent changes of public opinion in Belgium. A parliamentary inquiry that looked into Belgium's role in the build-up towards genocide in Rwanda had harsh words to say about the wisdom of many acts by Belgium's foreign-policy and military establishments.[59]

The sequence of events in 1993–94 shows how little effect mere availability of information on a forthcoming genocide had had, not only in Belgium but also within the United Nations. Complaints of human rights violations from Rwanda had been many[60] and they were dealt with under the confidential 1503 procedure. The Sub-Commission forwarded them to its parent body, the Commission on Human Rights, which decided to continue the confidential procedure (the official term is to 'keep Rwanda under review'), thus postponing any decision to its subsequent annual session in 1994. Bacre Waly Ndiaye, the UN Special Rapporteur on Summary Executions, documented in his 1993 report how and why massacres had been carried out. Being in charge of one of the special procedures and thus empowered to receive information from NGOs and to contact the respective government in order to clarify NGO allegations, Ndiaye had requested a visit to Rwanda from the Habyarimana government, obtained permission, and traveled to Rwanda in April 1993. His report concluded that massacres were taking place and were likely to continue and thus described the background:

There is a striking contrast between, on the one hand, the close control exercised over the population and the detailed partitioning of the territory (to such an extent that a residence permit is required simply to change prefectures), and, on the other, the absence of any structure for the protection of vulnerable populations, more particularly the Tutsi minority.
As in the past, the fact that persons responsible for [massacres] can be certain of impunity is the chief reason for the current renewed phenomenon of summary executions. Evidence of this state of affairs has been noted on numerous occasions: political-party militias who set up roadblocks in the vicinity of army posts make identity checks in defiance of the law and commit acts of violence against passers-by; soldiers who strangled a civilian in broad daylight in front of Kigali Central Post Office on 9 March 1993 calmly walked away once the crime has been committed. ... The country has already experienced many massacres of an

---

[59] Commission d'enquête parlementaire concernant les événements du Rwanda, rapport fait au nom de la commission par MM Philipe Mahoux et Guy Verhofstad, Sénat de Belgique, session 1997–1998, Doc. 1–611/13, 6 December 1997.

[60] An International Commission of Inquiry was fielded to Rwanda by NGOs in January 1993, and issued its report on human rights violations in 1990–1993. That report was publicised in March 1993 and the Habyarimana government acknowledged that massacres of civilians were taking place.

ethnic character. Such acts of violence recur periodically, and the persons responsible, who in most cases are known to everyone, go unpunished.

Despite the terrible lessons to be learned from the country's recent history, no effective system for the prevention of ethnically motivated massacres has been set up. [In the over-populated rural areas] everything is left to the diligence of local government officials, who, as has been seen on repeated occasions, are often accomplices in the massacres or even instigate them. The political and administrative commission which investigated the disturbances in the pre-fectures of Ginsenyi, Ruhengeri and Kibuye even noted that the region's tele-phone system had suddenly 'broken down' at the time of the events of January 1993, and had 'curiously' become operational again without any need for repairs.[61]

Despite this report and Ndiaye's plea for some international action to halt the impeding genocide, the Commission on Human Rights decided to do nothing in March 1994. Following the killing of the presidents of Burundi and Rwanda on 6 April 1994, just after the Commission's session had ended, bloodshed ensued. The silence of United Nations human rights bodies was exacerbated by the reduction of UNAMIR [United Nations Assistance Mission for Rwanda] from 2,500 to 400 soldiers,[62] thus leaving the United Nations with a legacy of having failed even to try to halt genocide. The Secretary-General, Kofi Annan, acknow-ledged this UN's failure in December 1999, following the Report of the Independent Inquiry into the conduct of the United Nations in 1994.[63]

Perhaps a sense of guilt or fears about the future reputation of the United Nations emerged already at the time of the genocide, and the Commission on Human Rights convened a special session on Rwanda in May 1994. Special sessions of the Commission are rare and only two had previously been held, both concerning the Former Yugoslavia, and one thereafter on East Timor in 1999. This session on Rwanda had first been suggested by the first UN High Commissioner for Human Rights and initiated by Canada. Noting that 'the principal responsibility for UN action in Rwanda remains with the Security Council,' Canada suggested that action to prevent further human rights violations be incorporated into subsequent United Nations response to developments in Rwanda.[64]

---

[61] Commission on Human Rights – Extrajudicial, summary or arbitrary executions. Report by Mr. B.W. Ndiaye, Special Rapporteur, on his mission to Rwanda from 8 to 17 April 1993, U.N. Doc. E/CN.4/1994/7/Add.1 of 11 August 1993, paras. 44–46 and 55.

[62] Minta, I. – The Rwanda conflict: With the failure of peacekeeping, is peacemaking still possible?, *African Yearbook of International Law*, 1997, p. 27–28.

[63] United Nations – Report of the Independent Inquiry into the Actions of the United Nations During the 1994 Genocide in Rwanda, New York, 15 December 1999. A the time of writing, this report was not available as a U.N. document; its text and the accompanying Secretary-General's statement were posted on the website (www.un.org/News/ossg/rwanda_report.htm) on 19 December 1999.

[64] Zoller, A.-C. – The Commission's emergency session on Rwanda, Human Rights Monitor, No. 25–26, September 1994, p. 4.

At that special session, the Commission concluded that 'genocidal acts may have occurred in Rwanda' and appointed a Special Rapporteur, 'assisted by a team of human rights field officers'. The initial suggestion of a 'strong human rights component' for any UN programme in Rwanda was thus reduced to what became known as 'human rights field presence'. A future international court was already contemplated and the Commission on Human Rights affirmed that

> all persons who commit or authorize violations of human rights or international humanitarian law are individually responsible and accountable for those violations and that the international community will exert every effort to bring those responsible to justice, while affirming that the primary responsibility for bringing perpetrators to justice rests with national judicial system.[65]

Human rights field officers were deployed in Rwanda, with a vast mandate[66] and without resources or powers to implement it. The Special Rapporteur on Rwanda, René Degni-Segui, was immediately appointed and submitted his first report in June 1994. He noted that massacres were continuing but probed beyond visible manifestations of violence into discerning the root causes and identifying the facilitating factors:

> The Rwandese have indeed been the victims of a number of massacres in the past, notably in 1959, 1963, 1966, 1973, 1990, 1991, 1992 and 1993. However, those perpetrated at present are unprecedented in the history of the country and even in that of the entire African continent. They have taken on an extent unequaled in space and in time.
>
> The massacres do seem to have been planned. There are various pieces of evidence pointing to this conclusion. The first is the campaign of incitement to ethnic hatred and violence orchestrated by the media belonging to the Government, or close to it, such as radio Rwanda, and above all *Radio Television Libre des Mille Collines* (RTLM). The second is the distribution of arms to the civilian population, and more particularly to members of the militias. ... Furthermore, the members of the militias are reported to have undergone intensive training at military installations from November 1993 to March 1994. To this must be added the reign or terror carried out by the militias and the assassinations of

---

[65] Commission on Human Rights – The situation of human rights in Rwanda, Report of the Commission on Human Rights on its Third Special Session (Geneva, 24 and 25 May 1994), U.N. Doc. E/CN.4/S-3/4 of 30 May 1994, pp. 4–8.

[66] The Security Council's description of their mandate was ambitious: 'to monitor the ongoing human rights situation, to help redress existing problems and prevent possible human rights violations from occurring, to help foster a climate of confidence and the establishment of a more secure environment and thus facilitate the return of refugees and displaced persons, and to implement programmes of technical cooperation in the field of human rights, particularly in the area of administration of justice.' Security Council resolution 965 (1994) of 30 November 1994, preamble.

political figures. The third sign is the exceptional speed of events after the death of the President of Rwanda: the 'provisional government' was formed within only a few hours after the accident. ... In addition, barricades were set up between 30 and 45 minutes after the crash of the aircraft, and even before the news of it had been announced on the national radio. ... Finally, the fourth indication is the existence of lists giving names of persons to be executed. It seems to have been on the basis of these lists that various opposition leaders were murdered.[67]

Degni-Segui's reports facilitated collecting evidence that a genocide had taken place, such as copies of radio broadcasts which called for massacring Tutsis: 'the enemies are among you, get rid of them.'[68] The process of getting rid of thus defined enemies was amply described in the veritable flood of literature that has been written about the genocide in Rwanda. The post-genocide international response was patterned after that for the Former Yugoslavia, and an international tribunal established to try the guilty Rwandese, against the wishes of the new government of Rwanda which proceeded with domestic trials. A mismatch between international and Rwandese norms for conduct soured post-genocide relations between the two. The Tribunal has been plagued with all the ills that bring the United Nations into disrepute – mismanagement, snail's speed, excessively high expenditure.[69] Rwanda has been routinely accused of breaching international human rights standards through its resort to the death penalty, the lack of respect for fair trial guarantees, and overcrowded prisons. The two worlds remained far apart – one reading about genocide in air-conditioned offices, perusing official documents in all six United Nations official languages, and another trying to cope with the impact of genocide and prevent its perpetuation.

A bit of sympathy for Rwanda ensued with increased armed intrusions into Rwanda by the *génocidaires* who had initially fled to Zaire. The UN Special Representative, has referred to 'thousands of *génocidaires* who were using refugees as human shield to cover their escape and as a conduit to receive humanitarian assistance,' and has urged the condemnation of the 'insurgent forces which have shown themselves bent on resuming the programme of genocide they launched in

---

[67] Commission on Human Rights – Report on the situation of human rights in Rwanda, submitted by Mr. R. Degni-Segui, Special Rapporteur, U.N. Doc. E/CN.4/1995/7 of 28 June 1994, paras. 20 and 26.

[68] Commission on Human Rights – Report on the situation of human rights in Rwanda, submitted by Mr. Rene Degni-Segui, Special Rapporteur, U.N. Doc. E/CN.4/1995/70 of 11 November 1994, para. 10.

[69] The Tribunal started the first trials two years after it had been established, and passed its first judgment two years thereafter, having in the meantime gone through a widely-publicised process of dismissing key officials for 'chaotic management and under-qualified legal staff' (Report damns Rwanda Tribunal, *Guardian Weekly*, 23 February 1997). *The Economist* estimated the cost of the Tribunal at $120 million for its then caseload of 23 defendants (Rwanda bleeds on, *The Economist*, 23 May 1998).

1994.'[70] These insurgent forces have had much to do with the multiple armed conflicts in Zaire/Congo.

Zaire/Congo

The fate of Zaire had been molded by the UN intervention in Congo (as Zaire had been called at independence) in 1960–64.[71] The secession of Katanga (later Shaba) was prevented as had been intended, but the door was opened for Mobutu's ascent to power in 1967 and his subsequent 32-year rule. The then UN Secretary-General, Dag Hammarskjold, had taken the initiative to assist a new African government to defend itself against external obstacles to its independence (led by Congo's former colonial power, Belgium) as well as a great deal of internal opposition (which peaked with Katanga's secession). The United Nations became embroiled in a multi-layered war, left Congo without having managed to accomplished what it had planned to do, and without its Secretary-General who had been killed under murky circumstances. The impact of this intervention was UN's subsequent reluctance to undertake any military intervention in Africa for three decades.

Belgium had played a prominent – and negative – role in Congo's early independent history. Relations between Belgium and Zaire (as it was re-named by Mobutu) did not always conform to assumed asymmetry between a powerful donor and a dependent recipient. In retaliation for the frequent and widespread media criticism of corruption in Zaire, especially the much-described late president Mobutu's wealth, Zaire cut off relations with Belgium in 1988. Zairean companies were ordered out of Belgium, Belgians in Zaire had their residence permits revoked, bilateral treaties were suspended, Zaire demanded compensation for its uranium which had been used to make the first US atomic bomb, and threatened to bring Belgium before the International Court of Justice.[72] That confrontation ended

---

[70] Commission on Human Rights – Report on the situation of human rights in Rwanda submitted by the Special Representative, Mr. Michel Moussalli, U.N. Doc. E/CN.4/1998/60 of 19 February 1998, paras. 15 and 40 (i).

[71] The United Nations Operation in the Congo (ONUC, or *Opération des Nations Unies au Congo*) lasted from July 1960 until June 1964. It had originally been mandated to provide the government of Congo with military and technical assistance against the military intervention by Belgian troops, in conditions of the collapse of all essential services in the country. Joseph Mobutu was the chief of staff in the Congolese army as of July 1960, at the time when Belgium's army invaded Congo while Moïse Tshombé proclaimed the independence of Katanga. The Security Council called upon Bellgium to withdraw its army (from all Congo, including Katanga) and authorized the UN Secretary-General to provide the government of Congo with military assistance. 20,000 UN troops tried to cope with a chaotic situation spread over a country approximately the size of Western Europe. Belgium withdrew its army, the secession of Katanga was prevented and ONUC was terminated. Multiple layers of appearances and realities behind this apparently simple factual description have been revealed by Conor Cruise O'Brien in his autobiographical book *To Katanga and Back: A UN Case History* (Simon and Schuster, New York, 1962).

[72] Misser, F. and Rake, A. – Mobutu's boomerang bounces back, *New African*, March 1989, pp. 17–19; Andriamirado, S. and Kerdellant, C. – Belgique-Zaïre: la grande colère de Mobutu, *Jeune Afrique*, No. 1458, 14 December 1988.

with Belgium writing off part of Zaire's public and commercial debt. Media reports at the time pointed out that Belgium was offering an olive branch and financial inducements,[73] adding that 'Zaire is being courted by Germany, France and America. It can afford to be beastly to the Belgians.'[74]

Similarly to corruption, human rights in Zaire remained beyond Belgium's cooperation with Zaire until the early 1990s. Zaire was on the United Nations human rights agenda in 1985–89, and again in 1991–92. In 1993, the 1503 confidential procedure was determined to have been ineffective and was transformed into a public procedure, and a Special Rapporteur was appointed in 1994. The government of Zaire deemed that the UN Commission on Human Rights breached procedural rules by acting publicly against Zaire, and suggested that 'the Commission should simply have noted the failure of the complainants to apply to the domestic courts.'[75] Alongside Belgium, Zaire enjoyed the support of the United States and France besides the customary solidarity of other African delegations, and the UN response to human rights violations in Zaire was much too delayed and then muted.

The first sanctions against Zaire by the United States, even if they had been only a token gesture, predated the mobilization of the United Nations, as did calls for sanctions by the European Parliament.[76] Sanctions could have been applied on human rights grounds at any point during president Mobutu's long rule (1965–96). His rule did not change with time, as donors' efforts to influence him showed when they proliferated in the early 1990s.

US sanctions against Zaire were few and far between. Seven consecutive US administrations supported Mobutu's Zaire. President Mobutu's military involvement in Burundi in 1972, or in Angola in 1975, or in Rwanda in 1990, were likely to have been deemed aid-worthy.[77] US sanctions were imposed in 1991[78] but they concentrated on denials of visas to individual officials rather than economic measures. Wendy Sherman, then assistant secretary of state, found them to have been 'one of our most effective measures to influence Mobutu and his entourage.'[79] No evidence of such influence was ever provided, but the US model was replicated by other donors. France suspended aid to Zaire in October 1991, having evacuated its

[73] Béjot, J.-P. – Zaïre-Belgique: Dette morale contre dette financière, *Jeune Afrique Économie*, No. 117, March 1989, pp. 42–43.

[74] Zaire and Belgium: A question of upbringing, *The Economist*, 11 February 1989, p. 80.

[75] Information provided by the government of Zaire in response to resolution 1993/61, in: Situation of human rights in Zaire. Report by the Secretary-General, U.N. Doc. E/CN.4/1994/49 of 23 December 1994, p. 4.

[76] Misser, F. – Mobutu gets a dressing down, *New African*, September 1988, p. 22.

[77] The day of the dictator: Zaire's Mobutu and the United States foreign policy, *Harvard Human Rights Journal*, vol. 4, 1991, pp. 139–151.

[78] Zaire: Shadow boxing, *West Africa*, 22 February 1988, p. 311; Africa Watch – Zaire: Two years without transition, vol. 4, No. 9, 7 July 1992, p. 40.

[79] Lippman, T.W. – Seeking U.S. visa, Mobutu enlists friends, *International Herald Tribune*, 7 August 1995.

citizens from a turmoil created by a soldiers' mutiny; it resumed aid to Zaire and rehabilitated diplomatically president Mobutu in 1994 because of logistic and political needs for its intervention in Rwanda.[80]

At the time of donors' vocal insistence on multi-party elections, president Mobutu announced in 1990 that donors' demands would be met. Constitutional amendments and legalization of political parties followed, as did announcements of forthcoming elections. These fell into an established patters of transition in Zaire being merely rhetorical – no less than five such transitions occurred in Zaire during 1965–95. What ensued in the 1990s was, however, a complete break-down of government. In 1990–94 four different transitions were announced and none materialized. This situation was ultimately diagnosed as *le mal zairois*, where 'the State is absent when it comes to providing services, [but] very much present when it comes to political repression.'[81] The rate of economic growth turned to retro-gression (–10%) in 1992, while inflation exceeded 4,000% in 1992 and 8,000% in 1993. The response of the international community continued as if the formal governmental structures and monetized economy still functioned.

Western policies were ambivalent. The United States reportedly insisted on president Mobutu's continued control over the armed forces[82] while EUrope focused on democratization.[83] In May 1990, Belgium suspended aid to Zaire in response to the killing of protesting students at the University of Lubumbashi.[84] That suspension of aid was too late to have an effect on the government because it had started disintegrating. Two governments vied for international legitimacy, one formed through a national conference, another by president Mobutu. Neither was running the country which slid into lawlessness and violence. Zaire was represented internationally by two different delegations, including at the World Conference on Human Rights, in June 1993.[85] Neither the human rights record nor the failure to carry out multi-party elections impeded French aid to Zaire. Marie-Pierre Subtil explained that France's commitment to democracy as a criterion for eligibility for French aid had been a misunderstanding: 'today, the president's advisers say Mitterand was only taking note of the inevitability of the democratization trend in

---

[80] Mobe, A. – Le jeu de Paris en faveur de Mobutu, *Le nouvel Afrique Asie,* No. 62, November 1994, pp. 20–21.

[81] Commission on Human Rights – Report on the situation of human rights in Zaire, prepared by the Special Rapporteur, Mr. Roberto Garretón, U.N. Doc. E/CN.4/1995/67 of 23 December 1994, para. 127.

[82] Huband, M. – Zaire: Pressure from abroad, *Africa Report,* vol. 37, No. 2, March/April 1992, p. 43; Braeckman, C. – L'impossible mutation du président Mobutu, *Le monde diplomatique,* March 1993, p. 20.

[83] EUrope's aid to Zaire was first halted in response to Mobutu's suspension of the Zairean National Conference at the beginning of 1992. (*The Courier,* No. 132, March-April 1992, News round-up, p. xvi.)

[84] Zaire: EC demands action, *West Africa,* 11–17 June 1990, p. 998.

[85] da Costa, P. – EC objects to Zairian group at WCHR, *Terra Viva,* 25 June 1993.

the world.'[86] The offer of UN experts to monitor human rights and provide advice to the government (agreed upon in 1995 by the UN Commission on Human Rights) was premised on the assumption that 'the government' existed and functioned. That approach had been proposed by France, whose delegation emphasized 'that the Government of Zaire has positively responded to several suggestions and that some improvements have been noted.'[87] Even if any such improvement had been made, they fell into oblivion when Zaire imploded.

The representative of the new Democratic Republic of the Congo had only harsh words for the 32 years of the Mobutu regime and even harsher about the lack of concern of 'Mobutu's masters' for human rights throughout those three decades. He singled out France as the 'executor' of the exodus of Rwandese refugees into Zaire and an actor who had facilitated the transfer of Rwandan genocide to Congo, as Zaire has named itself.[88]

These words were addressed to what is usually termed 'the international community' and prodded some soul-searching. It has been none too difficult to recall that the UN Commission on Human Rights adopted its first resolution on human rights violations in Zaire as late as 1994. It also appointed Roberto Garretón as the Special Rapporteur and has kept Zaire on the violators-agenda thereafter. The initial Commission's consensus was ruptured through a tug-of-war between Congo/Zaire and Garretón, and then between Congo (no longer Zaire) and the United Nations. The underlying issue was Zaire/Congo's refusal to allow an investigation into mass killings.

The problem came light through verbal duels between the UN Special Rapporteur and the government. Garretón, an experienced Chilean human rights activist rather than a diplomat, questioned both the behaviour and the human rights commitment of the AFDL (*Alliance des forces démocratiques pour la libération du Congo-Zaïre*) to become *a persona non grata*. His insistence that the fate of a large number of refugees who disappeared in Congo in 1996–97 be investigated was met by intransigent refusals by the AFDL and later the AFDL government. The Commission on Human Rights expressed in 1998 its concern about the government's refusal to allow Garretón access to the country and renewed his mandate.[89] That resolution was adopted by a majority vote, with African members of the

---

[86] Subtil, M-P. – Farewell to a questionable African record, *Le Monde*, 6–7 November 1994, reprinted in *Guardian Weekly*, 13 November 1994.

[87] Parker, P. – A summary of the major developments at the 1995 session of the UN Commission on Human Rights, *Netherlands Quarterly of Human Rights*, vol. 13, 1995, No. 3, p. 327.

[88] United Nations – Statement by the Minister of Justice of the Democratic Republic of Congo before the Commission on Human Rights of 14 April 1998, Summary record of the 42nd meeting, U.N. Doc. E/CN.4/1998/SR.42 of 16 April 1998, paras. 97–98 and 101.

[89] Commission on Human Rights – Situation of human rights in the Democratic Republic of the Congo, resolution 1998/61 of 21 April 1998, paras. 2 (c) and 5 (a). The Commission also expressed its concern at the forced withdrawal of the Investigative Team that had tried to clarify the fate of missing refugees under the authority of the Secretary-General of the United Nations.

Commission (except Cape Verde and South Africa) voting against or abstaining.[90] The Security Council noted that UN investigators had not been 'allowed to carry out [their] mission fully and without hindrance,'[91] accompanying this with a vague threat. The fate of these disappeared refugees became embroiled in a medley of simultaneous and overlapping wars and is unlikely ever to be clarified.

Explosive divisions by ethnic origin that have plagued Rwanda and Burundi have been carried over to Zaire through numerous population movements, some ancient, some new, some voluntary, some forced. Discerning the fate of a single ethnic group in a country composed of 450 different ethnic groups with more than 200 languages[92] would have been difficult even without the government's intransigence. The fate of *rwandophones*[93] went through ups and downs: they had been granted and denied citizenship, nobody quite knew who they were and how many since colonial archives had been destroyed, while Zaire never created a population register or carried out a census recently. Many different population movements in the ancient and recent history have muddled attempts at stocktaking, while many local conflicts – many of them armed – further complicated the picture. Killings of *rwandophones* had been reported from Kivu (the northeastern province of Congo/Zaire bordering with Rwanda) by Caritas and Médecins sans Frontières already in 1993 and the initial toll was estimated at 1,500 or 3,000. The planned UN inquiry, proposed by Garretón, was refused entry by the government.[94]

The influx of more then one million refugees from Rwanda followed on the heels of the military victory by the Rwandan Patriotic Front in 1994, and was likely to have fuelled anti-*rwandophonie* in Zaire. As the Special Rapporteur's attempts in 1996 to visit the area proved fruitless, the UN instituted a parallel track, fielding another mission to Kivu for humanitarian aspects of ethnic violence, and yet another for the preparation of hoped-for elections.[95] By that time, Zaire's government was accusing Garretón of 'displaying a lack of objectivity.'[96] At the same time, events started unfolding with a great deal of speed: an armed attack

---

[90] Resolution 1998/61 was adopted by 28 votes in favour (Western and Latin American members), 7 votes against (China, Congo, Congo/Zaire, Cuba, Indonesia, Rwanda and Uganda), and 18 abstentions (Asian members and Botswana, Guinea, Madagascar, Mali, Morocco, Mozambique, Senegal, Sudan, and Tunisia). Commission on Human Rights – Report on the Fifty-fourth session (16 March–24 April 1998), U.N. Doc. E/CN.4/1998/177, para. 318.

[91] Security Council – Statement by the President of the Security Council, Doc. S/PRST/1998/20 of 13 July 1998.

[92] Commission on Human Rights – Report on the situation of human rights in Zaire, prepared by the Special Rapporteur, Mr. Roberto Garretón, U.N. Doc. E/CN.4/1996/66 of 29 January 1996, para. 16.

[93] Garreton, R. – l'impossible enquête, *Le monde diplomatique*, December 1997.

[94] Misser, F. – Zaire: Massacres in Kivu, *New African*, September 1993; Ndovi, V. -Zaire: No protection without taxation, *Africa Events*, September 1993.

[95] Commission on Human Rights – Report on the situation of human rights in Zaire, prepared by the Special Rapporteur, Mr. Roberto Garretón, U.N. Doc. E/CN.4/1997/6/Add.1 of 16 September 1996, paras. 8–9 and 137–138.

[96] Commission on Human Rights – Report on the situation of human rights in Zaire, prepared by the Special Rapporteur, Mr. Roberto Garretón, U.N. Doc. E/CN.4/1997/6 of 28 January 1997, para. 18.

in October 1996 sent some 700,000 Rwandese and Burundian refugees fleeing from the camps in Zaire. The initial armed attacks had been attributed to *Banyamulengue*, the *rwandophones* who had been denied Zairean citizenship in 1981 to be threatened with collective expulsion in 1996. Remnants of the pre-1994 Rwandan armed forces (FAR, *Forces Armées Rwandaises*) as well as *interahamwé* (commonly referred to as *génocidaires* in post-1994 Rwanda) apparently joined the warfare, as did the armed forces of both Zaire and Rwanda. Efforts at retrospective discerning who-did-what-to-whom were (and remain) unsuccessful.[97] Garretón was concerned about some 140,000 disappeared refugees and formed a joint mission with the UN experts on summary executions and disappearances to try to investigate their fate.[98] That mission was refused entry into Zaire, whereupon the UN Secretary-General established another entity, the Investigative Team, making the Garretón mission redundant, while estimates of the number of possible victims of massacres increased.[99]

Disagreements about what happened will probably never diminish, but a factual summary could look something like this: refugees started fleeing from their camps after warfare had erupted between Kivu's *rwandophones*[100] and Congo/Zaire's

---

[97] Suffice it here to illustrate conflicting versions of what happened through one example:'between 1,000 (APR, *Armée Patriotique Rwandaise*, figure) and 300 (survivors' figure) fighters attacked the Congolese Tutsi camp at Mudende, Rwanda, on 12 December [1997], massacring between 270 (Rwandan figure) and 1,800 (Congolese figure) refugees.' Central Africa: The contras return, *Africa Confidential*, vol. 39, No. 4, 20 February 1998, p. 3–4.

[98] Commission on Human Rights – Report on the situation of human rights in Zaire, prepared by the Special Rapporteur, Mr. Roberto Garretón, U.N. Doc. E/CN.4/1998/65 of 30 January 1998, para. 90; Report on allegations of massacres and other human rights violations occurring in eastern Zaire (now the Democratic Republic of the Congo) since September 1996, prepared by Mr. Roberto Garretón, Special Rapporteur on the situation of human rights in the Democratic Republic of the Congo, Mr. Bacre Waly Ndiaye, Special Rapporteur on extrajudicial, summary or arbitrary executions, and Mr. Jonas Foli, member of the Working Group on Enforced or Involuntary Disappearances, U.N. Doc. E/CN.4/1998/64 of 23 January 1998, paras. 12–13.

[99] Estimates of the number of refugees who might have been killed, varied between 50,000 and 250,000. The lower figure was based on testimonies by relief agencies and the local population, while the higher figures reflected the number of refugees who had been recorded in Zaire in 1994 but could not be accounted for in 1997–98. It is possible that precise numbers will never be known: the registration of refugees fleeing from Rwanda in 1994, besides well-known tendency to inflate the numbers when seeking humanitarian aid, did not differentiate between armed and unarmed people, making it impossible to subsequently estimate the number of combatants amongst registered refugees. The flight from refugee camps following armed attacks at the end of 1996 led back to Rwanda. Those fleeing in the opposite direction were assumed to fear returning to Rwanda because of their involvement in the 1994 genocide. Whatever took place happened in the jungle. One crucial piece of evidence against the future government of Zaire/Congo was its systematic denial of access to international and foreign agencies and so nobody was able to gather evidence.

[100] Chris McGreal reported from Uvira that Banyamulenge were forced to flee after the deputy-governor, Lwasi Ngabo Lwabanji, ordered them out of the country within seven days, threatening them that they would be treated as rebels if they stayed on, 'exterminated and expelled,' and their property given to soldiers. McGreal. C. – Trapped in a bloody triangle of terror, *Guardian Weekly*, 27 October 1996.

army, probably with Rwandan and Burundian involvement, in October 1996. The following month Sergio Vieira de Mello (then with UNHCR) said:'We don't know where the [refugees] are. We can't say for certain if they are dying in large numbers but we know that their food probably ran out.'[101] The international response at the time was to plan an international military force that would, with UN's authorization, secure delivery of humanitarian aid. Although France seemed to have been the principal proponent of such a military force, its neutrality was in doubt[102] and Canada was to lead; these factors proved hypothetical since such a military force never materialized.

The process of clarifying the fate of disappeared refugees was plagued with verbal battles between Garretón and Zaire/Congo[103] while aid to Congo/Zaire was conditioned by the government's co-operation with the investigation.[104] The government did not co-operate, on the contrary: one team had to be withdrawn (mainly because it included Garretón as a member) to be replaced by another,[105] which was admitted to Zaire but precluded from carrying out an investigation. After the

---

[101] Orr, D. – Zaire aid fails to reach lost and hungry, *The Independent*, 13 November 1996.

[102] Rwanda's government held that the French *Operation Turquoise* made possible mass escape of *génocidaires,* whose rearmament was then facilitated in the refugee camps in Zaire. Aid in our time (editorial), *Financial Times*, 15 November 1996; McKinley, J.C. – Airdrop risks longer conflict: Zaire aid might help militias, *International Herald Tribune*, 3 December 1996.

[103] In brief, an initial UN mission by Roberto Garretón to eastern Zaire/Congo established *prima faciae* evidence that mass killings had taken place, having discovered, *inter alia*, mass graves where people had been buried naked, blindfolded, with their hands tied behind their backs (Commission on Human Rights – Report on the mission carried out at the request of the High Commissioner for Human Rights between 25 and 29 March 1997 to the area occupied by rebels in eastern Zaire, U.N. Doc. E/CN.4/1997/6/Add.2 of 2 April 1997). That mission had been intended to determine whether an in depth investigation was necessary and, having determined so, the Commission on Human Rights decided to field a three-person team composed of Special Rapporteurs (Garretón, Ndiaye and Foli), who arrived in Zaire in May for a preliminary investigation. The not-yet-government of Zaire/Congo objected to Garretón's participation and the team's investigation was cut short. They tried again in June and were denied permission to proceed, whereupon the UN Secretary-General composed another team, which arrived in Zaire/Congo in August but was also prevented from carrying out an investigation. This was followed by protracted diplomatic negotiations. (McGreal, C. – Truth that lies buried in Congo's killing fields, *Guardian Weekly*, 27 July 1997; Williams, P. – Kabila blocks UN investigation into massacres, *Human Rights Tribune/Tribune des droits humains*, vol. 4, No. 4, September 1997, pp. 22–23; Goshko, J.M. – Washington considers mission to Congo, *The Washington Post*, reprinted in *Guardian Weekly*, 12 October 1997; Congo: Who killed whom?, *The Economist*, 15 November 1997).

[104] Zaire's foreign debt of $14 was the first item to be negotiated with the donor community to make Zaire/Congo eligible for aid. Conditions for eligibility reported from the donors' meeting in September 1997 included the government's permission of a UN investigation into alleged mass killing of Rwandan/Hutu refugees. (Kabila sends a message to the world: 'Buzz off', and Congo: What's the world done to us, *The Economist*, 27 September and 29 November 1997).

[105] This change, decided by the UN Secretary-General, was attributed to the urging 'by the Clinton administration, which was trying to develop good relations with Mr. Kabila.' Crossette, B. – UN suspends inquiry into Hutu deaths, *International Herald Tribune*, 11–12 April 1998.

detention of one member whose files were examined, the team was withdrawn.[106] Congo/Zaire's allegation was that the team had been incompetent and inept at developing a working relationship with the government.[107] The effect was that the fate of the disappeared refugees was not clarified, with the likely consequence of fuelling subsequent *zaïrois v. rwandophone* retaliations.

Another consequence of this frustrated investigation has been continued suspension of aid to Zaire, leaving the country devastated by 32 years of misrule to slide into further warfare. In the first year of Zaire's reincarnation as Congo, the country received less than $100 million, out of which $30 million for a World Banks' trust fund that was expected to raise $4.5 billion for a three-year development programme.[108] The donors' logic seemed to have been that the mistake of funding Mobutu's Zaire (actually, Mobutu himself) should not be repeated and stringent conditions should be imposed upon the new government before aid is committed. From the Zairean side, the fact that Mobutu's Zaire (in effect, Mobutu himself) <u>was</u> funded while no aid has been given the new government undoubtedly did not look like a principled stance that the donors had in mind.

This type of argument immediately became purely rhetorical because within months of coming into power, the government of Congo/Zaire was embroiled in domestic and regional warfare. Having come into power through a military victory with a great deal of neighbours' involvement (Angola, Burundi, Eritrea, Ethiopia, Rwanda, Uganda, Zambia and Zimbabwe had been mentioned[109]), the government has remained involved in a regional war. A deadly game of chess ensued, with a multi-layered agenda. The explicit agenda was discussed during various efforts at pace-making; the foremost item on the implicit agenda was the exploitation of Zaire/Congo's wealth, much as it had been in the 1960s.

Throughout the Cold War and Mobutu's rule,[110] Zaire's involvement in armed conflicts in neighbouring countries was not seen as a problem since its role was, *inter alia*, to serve as a base for covert and overt military operations. Zaire reportedly hosted armed contingents fighting against the governments of Angola,

---

[106] Goshko, H.M. – U.N. accuses Congo over Hutu massacres, *Guardian Weekly*, 12 July 1998.

[107] Shearer, D. – Isolating Kabila just hastens Congo's slide, *International Herald Tribune*, 23–24 May 1998.

[108] New Congo, same old ways, *The Economist*, 2 May 1998.

[109] Zaire: Time for revenge, *The Economist*, 26 April 1997; Bucklet, S. – Zaire's neighbours cheer rebel gains, *The Washington Post*, reprinted in *Guardian Weekly*, 4 May 1997; Smith, P. – Kinshasa holds key to peace in Africa, *Guardian Weekly*, 25 May 1997; Misser, F. – Who helped Kabila?, *New African*, July/August 1997, pp. 9–10.

[110] One version of history linked the very beginning of Mobutu's rule to a CIA plot to kill Patrice Lumumba, the first prime minister of Congo, before helping Mobutu to seize control, to then keep him in control 'as a bastion against communism, supplying his with weapons and mercenaries when necessary.' Wrong, M. – Zaire lost in a world of its own, *Financial Times*, 26–27 April 1997.

Rwanda, Burundi or Uganda.[111] The involvement of these countries in the over-throw of Mobutu's government marked the end of the Cold War in Africa. Foreign and international involvement did not seize, however, but switched from ideo-logical to commercial alliances. Congo/Zaire's diamonds, gold, copper, cobalt, uranium, or oil provided ample grounds for them. A 'state' or 'government' has proved to be an empty shell. Since no public institution survived Mobutu (not even the army), his prediction what Zaire would be chaotic without him proved accurate. The scramble of foreign mining companies to sign contracts for the exploitation of mineral wealth during the inter-regnum[112] demonstrated the lack of confidence that a future 'state' or 'government' would be different from the previous one.

Such a government had hardly been formed when warfare erupted again. It was again attributed to the *rwandophones*[113] and immediately led to the involvement of the neighbouring states. Rwanda and Uganda were accused by the government of 'foreign invasion',[114] Zimbabwe and Angola (followed by Namibia, Chad and Sudan) sent troops to help the government.[115] The UN Special Rapporteur, Roberto Garretón, has pleaded for halting military assistance to combatants and the sale of weapons, as well as for a multinational military force to separate Zaire/Congo from its neighbours.[116] South Africa and then Zambia tried its hand at peace-making, which was none too easy with six involved African states and three major rebel groups (with changing leadership). A peace agreement was signed in July and August 1999, first by African presidents and then by rebel leaders,[117] but warfare continued.

Many African problems are attributed to the territorial division of Africa into separate countries along the colonial lines. The lack of correspondence between territorial and ethnic divisions was revealed in all phases of Zaire's demise –

---

[111] North-eastern Zaire provided shelter for armed opposition to governments in Burundi and Rwanda, as well as the Lord's Resistance Army fighting against Uganda; UNITA was operating against Angola's government from south-east Zaire. Braid, M. – Zaire's rebels prove a powerful force for change in Africa, *The Independent*, 5 April 1997.

[112] Ashurst, M. – Zaire mines privatization in doubt, *Financial Times*, 19 April 1997; Ashurst, M. & Wrong, M. – Anglo, De Beers in bid to secure Zairean interests, *Financial Times*, 21 April 1997; Gooding, K. – Confusion and concern over mining in Congo, *Financial Times*, 6 January 1998.

[113] According to Victoria Brittain, in August 1998 'Mr Kabila requested that a crack unit of the Rwandan army be stationed in Kinshasa. When this was refused, he angrily demanded that all Rwandans leave Congo, and launched his propaganda war against Tutsis.' Brittain, V. – Ethnic cataclysm looms in Congo, *Guardian Weekly*, 6 September 1998.

[114] Smith, P. – Rebels close in on Africa's trigger, *Guardian Weekly*, 16 August 1998.

[115] Congo: War turns commercial, *The Economist*, 24 October 1998.

[116] Commission on Human Rights – Report on the situation of human rights in the Democratic Republic of the Congo, submitted by the Special Rapporteur, Mr. Roberto Garretón, U.N. Doc. E/CN.4/1999/31 of 8 February 1999, paras. 144 and 146.

[117] Congo: The war is dead. Long live the war, and Split Congo, with peace treaties but no peace, *The Economist*, 17 July and 23 October 1999; Turner, M. – UN takes low-key role this time in Congo, *Financial Times*, 17 September 1999.

neither the problems nor possible solutions could be defined as 'domestic'. Moreover, the scramble for Zaire's wealth was as much evident in the warfare of the 1960s as in the 1990s. The donors' response was two-fold: Jacques Santer, then the President of EUrope's Commission, was quoted saying that EUrope's aid to countries militarily involved in Congo/Zaire should be reassessed to prevent aid from being diverted to financing warfare,[118] while the United Nations has been pleading for a mere $26 million in humanitarian aid for Zaire/Congo and could not obtain more than 60%.[119] The cost-consciousness that has become a prominent feature of Western foreign policies in the 1990s has not affected only Central Africa, but also the Horn of Africa, as the next section shows.

THE HORN OF AFRICA

Ethiopia, Somalia and Sudan have provided the background for a series of controversies in Western human rights policies. A chronological sequence whereby human rights violations in individual countries appeared on the UN agenda, shown in Table 9.1, is followed in this section. Ethiopia generated the first major controversy by pitting humanitarian and human rights policies against each other. Although Ethiopia has never been condemned for human rights violations by the United Nations, it was repeatedly denounced and penalized by individual donors. Somalia was first tackled for human rights violations in 1989, leading to a condemnation in 1992. Sudan followed with a faster sequence – it was placed on the agenda in 1991 to be condemned in 1992, and a great deal of investigative and condemnatory activity followed.

Somalia and Sudan provide the background against which the definition of 'human rights' has expanded in the 1990s. The United Nations has been trying to provide human rights assistance to Somalia after the failed international military intervention of 1992–95. No government has been formed to become responsible for human rights protection, however and it remained uncertain how human rights protection could be designed in the absence of a government.[120] A different but also challenging conceptual problem presented itself in Sudan: the Commission on Human Rights has found that the government was not the only violator and 'called upon all parties to the conflict to cooperate in order to ensure respect [of human rights].'[121] How parties at war against each other could be expected to cooperate so as to protect human rights was left un-explained.

---

[118] Misser, F. – Kabila refuses to compromise, *New African*, November 1998.

[119] Bayandor, D. – Look away from Kosovo to see the crisis in Central Africa, *International Herald Tribune*, 22 June 1999.

[120] Commission on Human Rights – Assistance to Somalia in the field of human rights, resolution 1998/59 of 17 April 1998.

[121] Commission on Human Rights – Situation of human rights in the Sudan, resolution 1998/67 of 21 April 1998, para. 4.

Ethiopia

Abuses by previous regimes ruling Ethiopia were well documented in an endless stream of publications and documents. As is customary in international human rights law, such abuses have been attributed to 'the state' while the process of retroactive individualization of responsibility remained burdened with legal and political problems. In 1992, the government of Ethiopia initiated trials against leaders of the Menghistu regime (1974–91) for crimes against humanity. The Office of the Special Prosecutor was established 'to create a historical record of the abuses of the Menghistu regime and bring those criminally responsible for human rights violations and/or corruption to justice.'[122] More than 3,000 people had been arrested in 1991–92 and the Office managed to decrease that number to 1,800 by 1994, when the first defendants were collectively charged with genocide and crimes against humanity. By 1997, more than 5,000 persons were charged; half of them were in detention and half were living abroad and charged *in absentia.*[123] The initial international and foreign enthusiasm for the trials soon turned into critiques of prolonged detention without trial, delays and unmet deadlines.[124] Critics have seldom failed to point out that the large number of indictments against former government officials has not been matched by a similar practice against officials of the government-in-power.

Regardless of how these trials will ultimately end, they have all targeted individual Ethiopian officials and are unlikely to shed much light on the external involvement in abuses that occurred in 1974–91 or international efforts to counter those abuses. Such efforts were few. The United Nations never condemned human rights violations in Ethiopia. Economic sanctions were used by Western countries, but it is difficult to extricate human rights from the multitude of grounds on which aid to Ethiopia was stopped, suspended or decreased.

Ethiopia was entangled in a proxy war between the main cold-war adversaries. Although the Menghistu regime declared its ideological programme as soon as it obtained power in 1974, Ethiopia's relations with the United States deteriorated three years later, in 1977, when the incipient US human rights policy coincided with a war between Ethiopia and Somalia. The United States supported Somalia while the Soviet Union supported Ethiopia. Even with the benefit of hindsight, it is impossible to discern whether Ethiopia was targeted by US sanctions for human rights violations or for changing sides from the US to the Soviet sphere of influence. Moreover, Ethiopia had not compensated previously expropriated US

---

[122] The Transitional Government of Ethiopia – Update No. 4 of the Office of the Special Prosecutor, December 1993, mimeographed, p. 1.

[123] Aadland, Ø. – Report of an assessment study of the status and context of the Dergue-trials in Ethiopia, Norwegian Institute of Human Rights, Oslo, May 1997, mimeographed, p. 4.

[124] Woubishet, D. – An end to governmental impunity in Ethiopia: The prosecution of former officials of the Dergue, *Human Rights Tribune/Tribune des droits humains*, August-September 1996, p. 16.

property, presenting additional grounds for sanctions. Yet additional grounds for economic sanctions stemmed from Ethiopia's agricultural policy and its failure to service the foreign debt. Out of these different grounds for sanctions, human rights violations provided a focus in 1977 because documents about the 'red terror' (1974–76) became available at the time and Ethiopia was targeted by US sanctions. They consisted of occasional aid cut-offs, but Ethiopia remained nevertheless a major aid recipient throughout the 1970s and 1980s.

As Table 9.6 shows, the United States was the leading donor in the 1970s and has retrospectively been held responsible for supporting Ethiopia's ideology of militarization.[125] Diminished flows of US aid in the 1980s did not affect total aid because humanitarian aid was, as is customary, exempt from sanctions. Aid to Ethiopia increased in 1980–89, as is shown in more detail in Table 9.7.

Table 9.6: Aid to Ethiopia, 1960–95
(in million US$)

	1960	1965	1970	1975	1980	1985	1990	1995
Canada	–	–	–	2.6	2.5	34.7	26.9	2.7
Denmark	–	–	–	0.1	0.1	2.2	0.9	4.3
France	–	–	–	0.8	3.5	6.5	15.4	12.6
Germany	–	1.4	5.0	15.1	14.9	25.4	46.7	87.7
Italy	6.1	1.4	9.0	2.0	7.5	81.6	169.1	62.3
Japan	–	–	–	4.6	1.0	6.6	10.3	61.9
Netherlands	–	–	–	2.7	3.8	8.0	24.9	37.5
Norway	–	–	0.2	0.3	1.0	12.0	25.5	24.6
Sweden	0.3	1.4	6.7	11.9	31.4	24.6	48.9	38.8
United Kingdom	–	–	–	6.3	4.4	36.1	35.2	42.2
USA	8.0	11.3	10.0	5.0	19.0	143.0	50.0	70.0
EUrope	–	–	–	–	66.1	271.5	351.5	381.4
Total bilateral	14.7	16.2	32.6	73.1	91.4	416.3	503.1	474.8
Total multilateral	5.1	10.5	7.3	60.3	120.4	285.5	385.1	379.4

Source: *Geographical Distribution of Financial Flows to Developing Countries*, various issues.

The most important reason for increased aid flows was publicity for the 1984–85 famine. Another famine in 1987–88 attracted less attention; yet another in 1994 was hardly noticed abroad; yet another in 1998 merited only a brief mention.[126] Another one might happen in 1999–2000, while all attention is focused on the

---

[125] Agyeman-Duah, B. – *The United States and Ethiopia: Military Assistance and the Quest for Security, 1953–1993*, University Press of America, Lanham, 1994, p. 160.
[126] Akol, J. – Ethiopia starving again, *New African*, September 1994; Steele, J. – Ethiopia faces new famine threat, *Guardian Weekly*, 1 March 1998.

Ethiopia-Eritrea war. The 1973–74 famine had facilitated the overthrow of the Selassie's regime, the famine in 1984–85 transformed Ethiopia into the foremost recipient of food aid at the time, with everybody – from professional photographers to pop stars – taking a turn at publicising the famine and organizing relief.

Foreign and international responses to that famine were entangled in conflicting aims – feeding the hungry and punishing the Menghistu regime; saving lives by providing food aid and imposing sanctions so as to hasten an end to repression.[127] The descriptors of Ethiopia at the time were 'drought-stricken' and 'conflict-torn'. Years of warfare and two droughts in the 1980s made Ethiopia a prime recipient of emergency relief. It was among the largest recipients of aid from EUrope, Italy, Finland, Sweden and the United Kingdom. As illustrated in Table 9.7, aid to Ethiopia rapidly grew in the 1980s to peak after the 1984–85 famine.

Inquiries into Ethiopia's human rights record led to divergence among donors. The effects of a linkage between aid flows and human rights at that time were statistically visible with regard to individual donors but did not affect total aid flows. Decreased aid from the United States in 1988 is visible from Table 9.7, as is increased aid from Italy; the United Kingdom decreased while Sweden increased aid. Jeremy Swift commented that 'the push by right-wingers in the US to isolate Ethiopia and let starvation and misery undermine the regime.'[128] The 1987 US *State Department Report* had found that 'Ethiopia's human rights record remained deplorable,'[129] and the United States banned coffee imports, commercial loans and investment, mandated a revocation of the MFN (Most Favoured Nation) status for Ethiopia, and US representatives were instructed to vote against World Bank's loans.[130] *Amnesty International* claimed in 1986–87 that there were 1,000 political prisoners in Ethiopia[131] while the European Parliament singled out Ethiopia among 'the most serious negative developments' in human rights in 1985–86. Funds earmarked for Ethiopia under the Lomé Convention were suspended but not on human rights grounds. The reason was an unmet condition for increased producer prices in agriculture.[132]

Different from donors' varying reactions to human rights violations in Ethiopia, the United Nations human rights bodies were silent. A series of resolutions on emergency assistance was adopted instead. As Table 9.7 illustrates, Ethiopia was receiving huge amounts of humanitarian aid, and the UN policy at the time was not to mix humanitarian and human rights agendas. And so in 1987, when EUrope and

---

[127] Tomaševski, K. – Starvation in Ethiopia: The missing link of human rights, *SIM Newsletter*, No. 9, January 1985, pp. 3–7.

[128] Swift, J. – Ethiopia: Trials and errors, *IWGIA (International Working Group on Indigenous Affairs) Newsletter*, No. 48, December 1986, p. 19.

[129] *Country Reports on Human Rights Practices for 1987*, Washington, D.C., February 1988, p. 96.

[130] The US applies the squeeze, *South*, December 1987, p. 21.

[131] Amnesty International – *Political Imprisonment and Torture in Ethiopia*, London, June 1987.

[132] Human rights in the world for the year 1985/86 and Community policy on human rights, European Parliament, resolution of 12 March 1987, para. 7 (d).

Table 9.7: Aid to Ethiopia, 1982–94
(in million US$)

	1982	1984	1985	1988	1990	1992	1994
Australia	6.5	11.9	16.5	−3.2	13.5	13.3	3.8
Canada	6.9	18.6	46.5	24.0	26.9	18.6	15.0
France	4.6	9.0	21.1	8.4	4.6	10.9	16.4
Germany	11.5	28.5	27.0	43.2	56.9	123.5	110.9
Italy	26.4	71.2	112.2	246.6	144.9	43.6	38.7
Sweden	19.5	18.3	24.6	53.2	41.0	39.3	27.2
United Kingdom	11.1	36.8	41.3	34.2	28.1	37.7	43.4
USA	–	18.0	142.0	62.0	49.0	65.0	122.0
EUrope	89.8	213.2	325.0	542.7	396.9	549.9	426.0
Total bilateral aid	100.2	242.8	488.4	587.0	482.3	438.5	496.3
Multilateral aid	221.1	417.4	778.8	987.8	992.4	1173.7	1007.7

Source:DAC/OECD- *Geographical Distribution of Financial Flows to Developing Countries*, various issues.

the USA imposed sanctions, the UN General Assembly appealed to donors 'to provide Ethiopia with adequate material, financial and technical assistance in order to carry out relief and rehabilitation programmes for displaced persons, voluntary returnees and refugees.'[133]

Much, if not most, emergency relief was delivered by non-governmental organizations. The Menghistu government was often accused of withholding food aid from rebel-controlled areas[134] and the rebels were also accused of impeding the work of relief agencies. Their attacks on the UN food aid convoys prompted a switch to airlifting food. The United Nations was praised for feeding the hungry but criticised for not trying to stop warfare.[135] Feeding the hungry can – in theory – be treated as a-political. In practice, humanitarian agencies had to take sides among domestic relief agencies (established by the government, Eritrean and Tigrean rebels), implicitly preferring some over others.[136] This dilemma became a veritable battleground in the policy and practice of delivering humanitarian relief a decade later. Food aid was, as elsewhere, criticised because it was curing symptoms while ignoring causes. The government was blamed for much of the causation of the

---

[133] General Assembly resolution 42/139 of 7 December 1987, para. 2.

[134] Don't feed Mengistu. If Ethiopia's boss won't let aid to rebel areas, he should get none too, editorial, *The Economist*, 16 April 1988, p. 18.

[135] Dede-Esi Amanor – Eritrea: No end to the conflict, *West Africa*, 28 March 1988, p. 548.

[136] Keller, E.J. – Drought, war, and the politics of famine in Ethiopia and Eritrea, *The Journal of Modern African Studies*, vol. 30, 1992, No. 4, p. 621.

consecutive famines and protests targeted especially Ethiopia's forced resettlement programme.[137]

In May 1991 Mengistu Haile-Mariam's government was overthrown. The military victory was attributed primarily to the *Ethiopian People's Revolutionary Democratic Front* (EPRDF) and its representative, Meles Zenawi, was elected president of the transitional government at the national conference held in July 1991. Twenty-seven political and ethnic organizations participated, and the subsequent Transitional Period Charter enumerated basic civil and political rights and committed the country to elections. The Charter also affirmed the right of each ethnic group – there are more than seventy – to the preservation of its identity. Ethiopia's structure was designed on the basis of ethnically based self-governing regions. (Eritrea held a referendum on independence in 1993 and its result was honoured, but the subsequent war between Ethiopia and Eritrea in 1998–2000 demonstrated that secession might have been accepted but was not forgiven.[138])

The international donor community assisted with demobilizing half of the army inherited from the Mengistu regime, canceled $300 million of Ethiopia's debt arrears and pledged $1.2 billion for an economic reform programme.[139] As with other countries, domestic budgetary constraints were expected to prevent these pledges from being translated into disbursements. Human rights concerns have re-emerged as one justification for rescinding promises of aid. The 1992 elections were criticised by a Norwegian electoral observer mission for their failure 'to bring the main political forces into a peaceful political process.'[140]

Neither electoral observers nor the donor community spoke with one voice. *Africa Confidential* commented that observers of the 1995 elections in the Donors' Election Unit 'were embarrassed because there was no real contest to observe' while OAU observers reported 'isolated irregularities' but concluded that the right to vote was freely exercised.[141] The electoral boycott by the opposition parties made the elections a foregone conclusion: 'the USA has failed to bring the opposition into the elections but will still back the winners.'[142] Danish electoral observers did not take part in the monitoring; Denmark claimed that they had been rejected, Ethiopia countered that the Danish request came too late. This contributed to Ethiopia's deletion from the list of Denmark's main aid recipients one year later, justified by Ethiopia's refusal to enter into a political dialogue on human rights.[143]

---

[137] Report of 20 Ethiopia Killings Raises Doubt on Resettlement, *International Herald Tribune*, 13–14 February, 1988.

[138] Lycett, A. – Ethiopia/Eritrea: The crazy war, *New African*, May 1999.

[139] Ethiopia: Meles Zenawi takes control, *New African*, February 1993.

[140] Norwegian Institute of Human Rights – Local and Regional Elections in Ethiopia, 21 June 1992. Report of the Norwegian Observer Group, Oslo, August 1992, [mimeographed], p. 3.

[141] Ethiopia: No contest, *Africa Confidential*, vol. 36, No. 11, 26 May 1995, p. 4; Ethiopia: Opposition boycotts polls, *Africa Research Bulletin*, vol. 32, No. 5, 27 June 1995, p. B11840.

[142] Ethiopia: The centre holds, *Africa Confidential,* vol. 36, No. 8, 14 April 1995, p. 2.

[143] Denmark keeps Ethiopia on ice, *Development Today*, 12/13–1995; Vague Danish arguments for a move out of Ethiopia, *Development Today*, 2/96.

Denmark was an exception as the donor community was increasing aid, praising Ethiopia's economic growth (an annual 5% in 1991–97), the privatization of state-owned enterprises and incentives for foreign investment. By 1998, Ethiopia became the major African recipient of loans from the World Bank ($700 million) and US aid ($83 million).[144] For the United States, Ethiopia was strategic ally, especially as a front-line state for containing Sudan. *Human Rights Watch* had this to say:

> For too long [US officials] had limited their interventions to requests to the Ethiopian government to come up with public responses to human rights concerns on high profile cases. The daily repressive practices in outlaying areas in the country, and the clampdowns on the freedoms of expression, association and assembly gradually slipped into a domain of accepted normality. Had the donor community put the same commitment it showed in backing the economic liberalization programs of the government in promoting the respect of basic human rights in the country, the current government might have reacted differently.[145]

Somalia

Human rights violations in Somalia were 'discovered' internationally in 1987–88, towards the end of the rule of Siad Barre (1969–91) and aid cutoffs aimed to hasten his demise. A series of international interventions followed in 1992–95 and thereafter Somalia was again forgotten.

The 1992–95 international military intervention in Somalia created a double negative precedent: international troops became a warring party, committed atrocities and also became their target. What had originally been intended as enforced delivery of humanitarian relief (*Operation Restore Hope*) became a war and was dubbed *Shoot To Feed Operation*. That intervention had been inspired by widespread publicity for a famine in Somalia and for the inability of international humanitarian agencies to relieve starvation. The human toll at the blue-helmets side was estimated at 150, Somali civilian casualties at 500.[146] A later assessment by an independent expert found twofold human rights violations: 'Somali violations of

---

[144] Buckley, S. – Foreign aid 'props up system of abuse,' *The Washington Post*, reprinted in *Guardian Weekly*, 26 April 1998.

[145] Human Rights Watch – Ethiopia: The Curtailment of rights, vol. 9, No. 8 (A), December 1997, p. 49–50.

[146] Media reports of Somali civilian casualties attributed to the blue helmets included between 20 and 150 killed in June 1993, then 54 died during US bombardment in July 1993, some 100 in September 1993, and an estimated 200 in October 1993. Somali mission turns to blood and tears (editorial), *Guardian Weekly*, 18 July 1993; Huband, M. – UN defends decision to open fire on civilians, *The Guardian*, 11 September 1993; Crawford, L. – Unrepentant UN ready to accept civilian casualties in Somalia, *Financial Times*, 11–12 September 1993.

the rights of other Somalis and violations of Somali human rights by the UNOSOM II forces.'[147]

Budgetary allocations illustrated the priorities in that intervention – $1.6 billion was spent to enforce the delivery of humanitarian relief whose value was estimated at $160,000 million.[148] Interest for that US/UN intervention was revived when blue helmets were brought before military courts and civilian commissions of inquiry in the United States, Canada, Belgium and Italy in response to the media exposure of killings, torture and ill-treatment of Somalis.[149]

Somalia could be an object of such an extreme type of international military intervention because it has not had a government since 1991 and confirmed the basic postulate that human rights protection ought to be domestic, and it is the responsibility of the government to ensure that human rights are protected. When Siad Barre's government dissolved in January 1991, the UN personnel left with all other expatriates. UNOSOM-1 followed, consisting of 'fewer than 100 lightly armed Pakistani troops [who] had to be guarded by the local militia' to be withdrawn in September 1991.[150] In December 1992, Operation Restore Hope had started, as a US operation approved by the Security Council, intended to create a secure environment for the delivery of humanitarian relief.[151] Some 28,000 soldiers from 28 countries created – or not – a secure environment for delivering humanitarian aid, depending on whose assessment one relies upon. Five months later UNOSOM-2 replaced the US-led military intervention, with halved troops and a vastly expanded mandate, which included disarming local political armies structured upon clan-based militias and creating a unified political structure for the whole country. A US armed contingent continued operating independently, outside UNOSOM, and attained notoriety for its consecutive attempts to capture General Aideed, who was for some reason identified as the culprit. The US military contingent was withdrawn in September 1994, after televised pictures of the corpses of

---

[147] Commission on Human Rights – Report by the independent expert, Mr. Fanuel Jariretundu Kozonguizi, on the conditions in Somalia, U.N. Doc. E/CN.4/1994/77/Add.1 of 9 February 1994, para. 23.

[148] Afwerki, I. – Can Somalia survive U.N.? *The Washington Post*, reprinted in *Guardian Weekly*, 24 October 1993.

[149] Hoagland, J. – Missteps in Somalia, but overall the operation is encouraging, *International Herald Tribune*, 15 April 1993; Farnsworth, C.H. – Alleged racism in military jolts Canada, *International Herald Tribune*, 18 May 1993; Clarke, H. and Rollnick, R. – Belgian 'racist' troops row, *The European*, 15–18 July 1993; Graham, R. – Italy to probe torture claims, *Financial Times*, 14–15 June 1997; Endean, C. – Did Somalia's saviours become torturers? *The European*, 19–25 June 1997; Bates, S. – Peacekeeping 'torturers' go on trial, *Guardian Weekly*, 29 June 1997.

[150] Dowden, R. The African tragedy: Apathetic, ill-informed, too late, *The Independent*, 16 July 1993.

[151] Security Council resolution 794 of 3 December 1992 authorized the use of all necessary means (the armed force in the UN jargon) to establish as soon as possible a secure environment for humanitarian relief operations. The Security Council anticipated that co-ordination between 'unified command and control' of the military forces and the United Nations would be arranged through dialogues between the Secretary-General and Member States, and the Secretary-General was asked to immediately prepare plans for UNOSOM-2 to follow upon the withdrawal of the Member States' (that is, US-led) military forces.

US soldiers, dragged by hostile and cheering Somalis, had been beamed world-wide; the withdrawal of the last *blue helmets* followed in March 1995.

Somalia furnished the first field-test for a new type of international intervention which combined humanitarian aid with fighting a war. It was justified by a newly created notion of a 'complex emergency,' denoting humanitarian disasters that particularly vicious and cruel wars create. International action was deemed necessary to save Somalis from starvation, but food was to be delivered by the military, which could secure access *to* victims, but could easily disregard the human rights *of* victims.

In this first field-testing in Somalia, the difference between the rights of expatriates (both military and civilian) and of domestic victims came painfully to light: a Commission of Inquiry was established to investigate armed attacks against UNOSOM II and a reward of $25,000 had been offered for the capture of general Aidid who was deemed guilty,[152] while the atrocities by the blue helmets against Somalis were defined as lying beyond the UN mandate and a mere clarification of facts had to wait until 1997–98.

The implosion of what had been assumed constitute 'the state' in Somalia opened the way for such an extreme international intervention. That state underwent a typical cold-war switch: an alignment with the Soviet Union in 1970–78 was followed by an alliance with the United States in 1978–90, with the corollary dependence on military and economic aid, as shown in Table 9.8. The Ogaden war prompted that change. Somalia's military aggression against Ethiopia brought the Soviet Union (and Cuba) to Ethiopia's side whereupon Somalia sought US aid.[153] Somalia first sought US aid during the Carter administration; human rights conditionality did not apply and aid to Somalia, first economic and later military, was granted and rapidly increased. It was guided by strategic criteria, for which Somalia's proximity to the oil exporting Middle Eastern countries and US military bases provided a sufficient justification.

A tug of war emerged between US Congress and the executive a decade later, towards the end of Siad Barre's regime. It was prompted by the widespread publicity for the warfare waged in the north of Somalia, by the government against the Isaak clan.[154] Abuses had been, however, reported ever since Siad Barre came to

---

[152] Commission on Human Rights – Report by the independent expert, Mr. Fanuel Jariretundu Kozonguizi, on the conditions in Somalia, U.N. Doc. E/CN.4/1994/77 of 15 December 1993, paras. 11 and 7.

[153] Hamrick, S.J. – Somalia: From cold war games to deadly chaos, *International Herald Tribune*, 11 February 1993.

[154] A mass grave was uncovered in May 1997, containing bodies of some 250 people, who had been bound by the wrist in groups of 10 and 15, and were assumed to have been killed by Somalia's army in 1988 for being members of presumed sympathizers of the Somali National Movement (Isaac clan). This retroactively confirmed many reports in 1988 that Somalia's army was summarily killing captured civilians and combatants in the north-west. Commission on Human Rights – Situation of human rights in Somalia. Report of the Independent Expert, Ms. Mona Rishmawi, U.N. Doc. E/CN.4/1998/96 of 16 January 1998, para. 60.

Table 9.8: Aid to Somalia in 1960–95 at five-year intervals
(in million US$)

	1960	1965	1970	1975	1980	1985	1990	1995
Canada	–	–	–	1.4	2.4	0.9	0.9	1.3
France	–	–	–	–	1.6	1.7	3.1	4.7
Germany	–	4.1	6.4	3.6	27.9	20.7	20.8	7.0
Italy	10.7	13.0	4.9	5.5	27.4	55.9	111.3	11.8
Netherlands	–	–	–	1.0	3.2	2.6	0.2	10.4
Sweden	–	–	–	4.7	6.8	1.0	2.5	13.5
United Kingdom	7.7	0.0	0.5	0.6	6.7	2.3	3.0	4.2
USA	3.0	7.9	6.0	5.0	60.0	54.0	72.0	54.0
EUrope	–	–	–	–	104.0	98.4	183.7	69.7
Total bilateral	21.4	25.0	17.8	23.1	139.4	163.5	259.8	119.2
Total multilateral	0.0	3.7	9.9	50.0	166.3	153.8	137.3	72.1

Source: *Geographical Distribution of Financial Flows to Developing Countries*, various issues.

power through a military coup in 1969. They were legalized and institutionalized, but Somalia was protected from any international opprobrium. US Congress conditioned aid to Somalia by 'meaningful dialogue between the government and the opposition' in 1987 and 1988,[155] but that did not have much effect on aid flows as can be seen from Table 9.8. US aid was to be cut down in 1991 because of Somalia's inability to service its foreign debt; by that time Somalia had already disintegrated.

Threats of cutting off aid were used against Somalia also by EUrope, also at the very end of Siad Barre's regime. In January 1988 a trial of twelve opposition leaders, detained since 1982, had started. It was held in camera and resulted in seven death sentences and five opposition leaders were sentenced to long-term imprisonment. Numerous protests were addressed to the Somali government, including those by donors who threatened to withhold aid. Thus on 21 January 1988 the European Parliament announced a 'reconsideration of aid'; the death sentences were commuted and imprisonment replaced by house arrests.[156] That gesture probably saved some lives but had little effect on the government.

This ping-pong in the late 1980s, with donors conditioning aid by improvements in the human rights situation and Barre's government releasing political prisoners or establishing commissions of inquiry to investigate massacres, could not improve the protection of human rights in Somalia because their protection had never been

---

[155] Fields, A. and Smith, L. – Somalia: United States response to human rights abuses, *Harvard Human Rights Journal*, vol. 3, 1990, p. 210.

[156] Tomaševski, K. – *Development Aid and Human Rights*, Pinter Publishers, London, 1989, p. 68–69.

established. Making Barre's government accountable to donors probably made things worse because extracted concessions were token and discretionary. One of the worst features of extracting token concessions is that both sides know that every and any of them is discretionary and reversible.

The UN human rights bodies were silent until the early 1990s. The Commission on Human Rights had Somalia 'under review' within the confidential 1503 procedure, as has been illustrated in Table 9.1. A great deal of information on the denial of human rights was kept under the cloak of confidentiality. One example:

> The National Security Service (NSS), [has been] empowered to search homes and arrest individuals without a warrant, to detain and imprison suspects for an unspecified period, and to confiscate the property of anyone accused of security-related offences. ... Entrusted to a son-in-law of the President, Ahmed Suleiman, the NSS acquired a reputation for terror. The NSS was reinforced by the creation of the 'victory pioneers' (*gullwadayal*), paramilitary youth groups who act as the government's security watch-dogs at the neighbourhood level. The pioneers report directly to the President. To instill a 'revolutionary spirit' they enforce 'voluntary labour' and they may arrest people for 'counter-revolutionary' attitudes, which may simply be the failure to attend, on a regular basis, political indoctrination lessons at the neighbourhood centres. The 'victory pioneers' have their own prisons in Mogadishu and in all provincial capitals. No court can modify or revoke their detention oders (nor those of the NSS); neither is there right of appeal.[157]

The Commission decided to appoint an expert to look into human rights in Somalia as late as 1992. The government against which complaints of human rights violations had been directed existed no longer. The Sub-Commission reacted in 1991 noting that twenty years of gross violations of human rights were followed by a civil war and called upon the international community to prevent starvation and collapse of Somalia,[158] providing a human-rights endorsement for the subsequent shoot-to-feed intervention which has been described above.

After the withdrawal of the *blue helmets*, Somalia has reverted to the conditions that had preceded Siad Barre's military coup in 1969, when elections for 123 parliamentary seats had been contested by more than 60 political parties.[159] After 1995, such political parties have been replicated in clan-based armies. International conferences and the signing of various agreements did not effect change and thinking about peace-making has shifted focus:'the process should be decentralized and build peace from below, from a sub-clan level out in the districts, using traditional

---

[157] Anonymous – Somalia: Eighteen years of tyranny, *Index on Censorship*, 8/87, p. 30.

[158] Sub-Commission on Prevention of Discrimination and Protection of Minorities – Resolution 1991/29 of 16 August 1991.

[159] Greenfield, R. – Siad's sad legacy, *Africa Report*, March-April 1991, p. 14.

Somali structures already in existence.'[160] Perhaps this will turn out to be possible and Somalia will continue as a country without a government.

Sudan

Sudan's history since independence in 1956 has been marked by military rule and warfare. It was ruled by the military in 1958–64, and warfare had already started in the south against the Arab domination of the government. Francis Deng and Khalid Medani have attributed the four decades of warfare to the racial/ethnic/religious fault-line which divides the north from the south:

> The northern Sudanese see themselves as Arabs and deny the strongly African element in their skin colour, physical features and cultural elements, even in the practice of Islam. The south, where the African identity had predominated, remained isolated, protected by natural barriers and the resistance of the Nilotic warrior tribes.[161]

An attempt had been made in 1972–73 to halt warfare through the introduction of a regional self-government, but warfare intensified after that promise had been abrogated and the first attempt to introduce *Sharia* law made in 1983. The SPLA (Sudanese People's Liberation Army) was formed in 1984 and one year later a military coup ousted President Nimeiri, leading to a relatively peaceful four-year period. A change of government in 1989 led to increased international interest for human rights violations in Sudan, those related to warfare as well as those related to the second introduction of *Sharia law* in 1991. The process of political change in mid-1990s encompassed elections in 1995–96, followed by a new Constitution.[162] Attempts at peace-making included in 1997 the Khartoum Agreement with some of the southern armed groups,[163] leaving out the biggest ones, including the SPLA, as well as new northern armed movements, based in Eritrea.[164]

Warfare has continued during the past four decades, and at least one million were killed in confusing shifts of alliances between the many actors loosely structured into two main warring parties, with considerable (albeit consistently denied) military involvement of the neighbouring countries, Eritrea, Ethiopia and Uganda,

---

[160] Normark, S. – Somalia: The rebuilding continues, *New Routes, A Journal of Peace Research and Action,* vol. 1, 1996, No. 1, p. 20.

[161] Keller, E.J. & Rothschild, D. (Eds.) – *Africa in the New International Order: Rethinking State Sovereignty and Regional Security,* Lynne Rienner, Boulder, 1996, p. 101.

[162] The Constitution was adopted through an unusual procedure, with two different drafts discussed until its adoption by the National Assembly and its approval, three days later, through a referendum with 91.9% turnout and 96.7% votes in favour. Suleiman, G. & Doebbler, C.F. – Human rights in Sudan in the wake of the new Constitution, *Human Rights Brief,* vol. 6, No. 1, Fall 1998, p. 10.

[163] Hubard, M. – Peace pact signed for south Sudan, *Financial Times,* 22 April 1997.

[164] Hirst, D. – Sudan: regime under threat from all sides, *Guardian Weekly,* 22 June 1997.

with US backing.[165] A whole menu of atrocities has taken place, from bombardment of civilian targets to denials of access to humanitarian relief, from mass
abductions of children and their conversion into slaves to forced conscription. The
most internationally publicised facet of warfare in southern Sudan have been
consecutive famines. In what John Ryle has called 'the culpable incoherence of
Western policy,'[166] *Operation Lifeline Sudan* was set up in 1989. The government
agreed that humanitarian relief could be delivered to rebel-held areas, but both
warring parties obtained powers to veto any delivery as well as to feed their troops
first and foremost out of every delivery. During its ten years of existence, Operation
Lifeline Sudan has become the largest relief programme in history, supplying food
at tenfold market cost (an annual $200 million) because of complicated and expens-
ive transportation and delivery.[167] Operation Lifeline Sudan required the agreement
of the government and its human rights record was thus not on the agenda. Human
rights was treated as a self-contained area, un-connected to humanitarian relief as if
the victims discussed under 'humanitarian relief' were not routinely the same as
those discussed under 'human rights.'

The UN General Assembly placed Sudan on the violators-list in 1992 and the
Commission on Human Rights appointed a Special Rapporteur in 1993 to keep
Sudan on the violators-agenda thereafter. Sudan challenged its placement on the
violators-agenda, claiming that it was an abuse aimed at attacking Islam. It accused
the Special Rapporteur of pursuing an agenda whose main objective was the abolition of Sharia law and suggested that he be brought to justice for his irresponsible
remarks.[168] Sudan's argument went like this:

> The situation of human rights in Sudan was discussed for the first time by the
> Commission on Human Rights at its forty-seventh session in 1991, and the most
> pertinent question that comes readily to mind is why had the discussion begun at
> that specific date, two years after the present Government of Sudan had assumed
> power on 30 June 1989, despite the fact that the early months of assumption of
> power by any revolutionary government are usually tainted with violations of
> human rights. ... one would comfortably reach the conclusion that the dis-
> cussion has begun at the forty-seventh session in 1991 because that session was
> the first session to be convened after the application of Shariah in the Sudan
> in early 1991. So one should not loose sight of the relationship between the

---

[165] Ottaway, D.B. – U.S. to aid opposition to Sudan, *The Washington Post*, reprinted in *Guardian Weekly*, 17 November 1996; Peninou, J.-L. – Grandes manœuvres autour du Soudan, *Le monde diplomatique*, September 1997; Sudan's rebels change their spots, *The Economist*, 28 March 1998.

[166] Ryle, J. – How famine sharpens the hunger for power, *Guardian Weekly*, 10 May 1998.

[167] Toolis, K. – Africa's famine is big business, *Guardian Weekly*, 6 September 1998.

[168] Commission on Human Rights – Comments by the Government of the Sudan on the Report of the Special Rapporteur, Mr. Gaspar Biro, Annex to U.N. Doc. E/CN.4/1994/122 of 1 March 1994, paras. 2–4.

application of Shariah and the beginning of the attack on the human rights record of the Sudan.[169]

The Special Rapporteur's appointment in 1993 followed two years after Sudan had been placed under the confidential 1503 procedure. The shift from confidential to public procedure is a sanction of public exposure imposed to punish a government for its failure to cooperate. A public scandal broke out in 1994 when Sudan called the UN Special Rapporteur a blasphemer, leading to a condemnatory resolution adopted by a large majority (35-9-9).[170] Annual resolutions on human rights violations in Sudan have continued, and an attempt was reportedly made in 1996 towards diminishing this confrontational atmosphere. The government of Sudan referred to 'an understanding' whereby the threatened placement of human rights observers into Sudan would be 'reconsidered' in exchange for Sudan's invitation to UN human rights bodies to carry out fact-finding missions in the country; that understanding apparently collapsed in 1997.[171] The Commission insisted on the placement of human rights monitors in Sudan upon the initiative of the United States by a large majority (31-6-16).[172]

The donor community had moved against Sudan before the United Nations. The European Parliament called for suspension of aid to Sudan in 1990; the ACP-EC Joint Assembly discussed Sudan in 1991 when a proposed resolution condemning human rights violations was rejected in favour of a resolution which appealed to the authorities to ensure delivery of humanitarian aid. The Parliament proposed that Sudan be excluded from the Lomé Convention in December 1993, but that proposal was would have necessitated a decision by all ACP and EC parties and thus calls for aid to be cut off have continued.[173]

As Table 9.9 shows, aid to Sudan noticeably decreased in the 1990s. Some of this was, donors' rhetoric aside, the consequence of the IMF's formal declaration of non-cooperation with Sudan in 1990, which routinely entails a halt in international

---

[169] Commission on Human Rights – Letter dated 29 March 1996 from the Permanent representative of the Sudan to the United nations Office at Geneva, addressed to the Assistant secretary-general for Human Rights, U.N. Doc. E/CN.4/1996/145 of 2 April 1996, paras. 28–29.

[170] Commission on Human Rights – Situation of human rights in the Sudan, resolution 1994/79 of 9 March 1994.

[171] Commission on Human Rights – The response of the Government of the Sudan to the Report by the Special rapporteur, Mr. Gaspar Biro, Annex to U.N. Doc. E/CN.4/1997/126 of 4 April 1997, paras. 2–4.

[172] Commission on Human Rights – Report on the fifty-fourth session (16 March–24 April 1998), U.N. Doc. E/CN.4/1998/177, paras. 358–362.

[173] European Parliament – Human rights violations in Sudan, resolution of 22 November 1990, para. 4; ACP-EEC: Low-key Joint Assembly in Amsterdam, *The Courier*, November-December 1991, p. 7; van der Klaauw, J. – European Community: Parliamentary position on European trade/aid relations, *Netherlands Quarterly of Human Rights*, No. 1, 1994, p. 73; European parliament asks that necessary preparations be made for excluding Sudan from the Lomé Convention, if this country does not stop violating human rights, *Europa/Development Monthly*, No. 51, February 1994; ACP/EC Joint Assembly, *Eurostep News*, No. 17, August-October 1994, p. 16.

Table 9.9: Aid to Sudan in 1970–1995
(in million US$)

	1970	1975	1980	1985	1990	1995
Denmark	–	0.5	22.4	0.5	13.4	0.5
France	–	–	7.7	5.5	6.4	3.9
Germany	–0.8	34.2	62.4	70.8	47.7	17.1
Italy	–0.8	0.8	–1.7	65.3	21.9	3.8
Japan	–	0.2	10.9	25.8	38.9	21.2
United Kingdom	0.9	5.9	49.8	54.2	37.2	10.9
USA	–2.0	8.0	60.0	346.0	143.0	8.0
EUrope	–	–	244.6	291.1	259.4	99.4
Arab donors	–	2.4	231.9	215.2	1.8	0.6
Bilateral (OECD)	–0.2	60.1	271.6	647.2	418.7	130.1
Multilateral	6.6	66.5	192.2	267.3	371.6	105.1

Source: OECD – *Geographical Distribution of Financial Flows to Developing Countries/Aid Recipients*, Paris, various issues.

and foreign financial flows. The Netherlands had cut down aid to Sudan already in 1989,[174] and in 1993 Denmark decided to discontinue aid to nine African countries; only for one, Sudan, human rights violations were cited as justification.[175] The donors' dilemma of sanctioning the government while feeding the people has been thus articulated:

> The donors said:'We need to save people from starving.' The Sudanese people replied:'For what? So that they will be shot? Or so that they will be able to starve again next year?'.[176]

In the early 1980s, Sudan had among the largest recipients of US aid. The United States first suspended aid in 1988 because Sudan failed to repay owed debt; in 1989 aid was suspended because Sudan failed to ensure that food aid reached intended beneficiaries; in June 1989 General Bashir took power through a military coup, and the United States suspended aid because of a statutory requirement not to provide aid to countries in which a democratically elected government was ousted through a military coup.[177] Concerns about war-related abuses led to linking aid to peace-

---

[174] Sudan: peace has been postponed, *The Economist*, 28 January 1989.
[175] Denmark withdraws from nine countries, *Development Today*, 10/93.
[176] Lacville, R. – Breeze of politics is refreshing Africa, *Guardian Weekly*, 28 July 1991.
[177] Morton, J. – *The Poverty of Nations: The Aid Dilemma in the Heart of Africa*, I.B. Tauris Publishers, London, 1996, pp. 200–232; Middleton, N. and O'Keefe, P. – *Disaster and Development. The politics of Humanitarian Aid*, Pluto Press, 1998, pp. 69–81; Prendergast, J. – *Crisis Response: Humanitarian Band-Aids in Sudan and Somalia*, Pluto Press, London, 1997, pp. 19–29.

negotiations, then Sudan's human rights record became the principal focus, then Sudan's support for Iraq during the Gulf war, and then terrorism. As Table 9.9 illustrates, the decrease of US aid to Sudan for a combination of these various reasons is evident.

In 1993, just after Sudan had been placed on the UN violators-list, the USA blacklisted Sudan for sponsoring international terrorism. This led further to a statutory prohibition of any financial transactions with governments listed as 'sponsors of terrorism,' from which Sudan was exempt in August 1996 so as to enable Occidental Petroleum to negotiate an investment in exploitation of oil.[178]

In 1995–96 international condemnation of Sudan for its alleged involvement in an assassination attempts against Egypt's president Mubarak led to sanctions. In January 1996 the Security Council called on Sudan to extradite three non-Sudanese, 'sheltered in Sudan', who had been suspected of having organized the attempted assassination of Egypt's President Mubarak in June 1995. Three months later the Council decided that sanctions should be imposed against Sudan unless it complied with the requested extradition as well as refraining from 'assisting, supporting and facilitating terrorist activities and from giving shelter and sanctuary to terrorist elements.'[179] One colourful aspect of Sudan's involvement in international terrorism had been the spectacular delivery of the legendary Carlos, 'a terrorist dinosaur in decline,'[180] to France. Another, deeply disturbing, was the US bombing of the Shifa pharmaceutical factory in 1998, presumed to have been producing chemical weapons and also linked to Osama bin Laden, but as likely could have been producing anti-malaria pills.[181] The publicity for a presumed association between Sudan and terrorism has been considerable, overshadowing all other developments in and around Sudan.

AFRICA'S COLONIAL AND COMMERCIAL DIVIDERS

In 1998–99, almost half of Africa was encompassed by warfare, not only the Horn of Africa and the Great Lakes. Both intra-state wars and military interventions by one African state in another proliferated, military coups for which Africa attained notoriety two decades ago have resumed, and the heritage of previous decades became painfully evidenced in collapsed states and rule-or-ruin warfare. 'The state'

---

[178] Tangle of commerce and terrorism (Editorial), *The Washington Post*, reprinted in *Guardian Weekly*, 2 February 1997.

[179] OAU: Conflict resolution meeting condemns Sudan, *Africa Research Bulletin*, vol. 32, No. 9, 26 October 1995, p. 11973A; Security Council resolutions 1044 (1996) of 31 January 1996, and 1054 (1996) of 29 April 1996.

[180] Sudan: rest camp for terrorists, *The Economist*, 17 September 1994.

[181] Risen, J. – A year later, U.S. officials' doubts over Sudan bombing surface, *International Herald Tribune*, 28 October 1999.

often exploded or imploded. Demanding human rights protection from a non-existent or disempowered state has become, however, part of the political vocabulary. Because so many African states have suffered from a similar malaise, the choice of those that should be publicly labeled as violators was ample. The exercise of this choice has demonstrated the complexity of contemporary Western foreign policies in which, as the title of this section indicates, colonial links and commercial interests have played a prominent role.

Warfare has generated the grossest abuses and elicited most attention. The previous distinction between human rights and humanitarian law was obliterated in the new political vocabulary. Condemnations for human rights violations and sanctions increased in number, in parallel with peace-making and emergency relief. Peace-making routinely guaranteed actors that had formerly been labeled as 'violators' complete impunity for their ill-deeds, clashing against amply used human rights rhetoric.

The series of case studies in this section illustrates different international responses originating in divergent foreign policies of the reacting Western countries. Foreign-policy concerns, such as the division of Africa into anglophone, francophone and lusophone, have had considerable influence on international responses to particular man-made disasters. The Anglo-Saxon enthusiasm for democracy (i.e. multi-party elections) of the early 1990s was not shared by France. Its support for militocracy at the expense of democracy is illustrated through a series of mini-cases, which are followed by a focus on the oil factor. Oil wealth has not brought prosperity to African countries where oil has been discovered. Nigeria is an obvious example, although Chad and Congo/Brazaville also highlight how much oil wealth impeded rather than facilitating domestic or international human rights protection.

SIERRA LEONE

Sierra Leone has never attained prominence in international human rights politics. It became known for particularly vicious and cruel warfare, which could not be easily legitimized by one human rights rationale or another. Nor could it be condemned: as shown in Table 9.1, attempts were made in 1996–97 but did not lead to a condemnation.

Political violence marked almost the entire history of independent Sierra Leone, as did political and economic emergencies. The most notable signposts were a transition from military to civilian regime in 1968, and the overthrowing of that civilian regime by the military in 1985. Each change was made in the name of combating corruption, for which every overthrown regime had been notorious. In 1987, the country was blacklisted because of its inability to service foreign debt; sixteen ministers were sentenced to death because of corruption.

Warfare started in 1991 with the emergence of RUF (Revolutionary United Front) in Sierra Leone from Liberia, after many had been trained in Libya. The RUF had been assisted by the Liberian troops of Charles Taylor's National Patriotic

Front,[182] while the involvement of Guinean and Nigerian armed forces was reported on the side of the government. Protracted warfare was followed by a new constitution, which was followed by a military coup, and by further negotiations which opened the way for elections in 1996, followed by a peace agreement and another military coup in 1997. Sierra Leone was torn apart by vicious warfare – agreements, elections or constitutions turned out to be more than parchment promises.

Outside commentators could not find in Sierra Leone an ethnic or religious dividing line to which the conflict could be attributed, as in Burundi or Rwanda or Sudan, and therefore labels of mindless violence were abundantly used to describe what is an easily understandable struggle for power and/or profit. A label of mindless violence diverts attention from the rationale for war, underpinning the routine international strategy of negotiating peace agreements and holding elections, based on the hope that those who lost elections would accept the loss of power that the rule by force gives them. To understand the rationale for warfare, it was necessary to relinquish the routine attribution of a noble cause to the main warring parties. In the case of RUF, Ibrahim Abdullah posited that a 'lumpen social movement bred a lumpen revolution,' arguing that *lumpens*, namely the unemployed and unemployable, semi-literate young males, who live by their wits and are prone to criminal behaviour, petty theft, drugs, drunkenness and gross indiscipline[183] produced warfare to fit their own image. International policy-makers or academics could not easily explain why such a warring party resorted to mutilating people or abrogated any formal commitment they ever made, looking for a noble cause behind their atrocities and searching for a commitment to the greater good behind their participation in peace-negotiations.

The conduct of key foreign and international actors has not appeared to have been particularly beneficial for the country against a frequent assessment that 'systemic corruption became the norm'[184] during the first decades of Sierra Leone's independence, and no indication of a change could be discerned thereafter. Aid could not have had much impact on what it was intended to accomplish if corruption was systemic, while economic sanctions could not fare better when they were based on an assumption that revenue was derived legally from legitimate sources. The United Kingdom suspended aid to Sierra Leone in response to a series of summary executions in December 1992, the European Union followed, which 'left the populace dependent in large measure on non-governmental aid agencies.'[185]

Cutting off aid when warfare had already broken out pressurized the government to replace official aid by other revenue necessary to continue the war. With

---

[182] Rake, A. and Saccoh, S. – Sierra Leone – hijacked, *New African*, April 1995, p. 9.

[183] Abdullah, I. – Bush path to destruction: The origin and character of the Revolutionary United Front/Sierra Leone, *The Journal of Modern African Studies*, vol. 36, 1998, No. 2, pp. 207–208 and 223.

[184] Kpundeh, S.J. – *Politics and Corruption in Africa: A Case Study of Sierra Leone*, University Press of America, New York, 1995, p. 98.

[185] Liasi, T. – Threat to aid may complete Sierra Leone's misery, *Financial Times*, 23 June 1993.

publicity for contracting out the security of diamond mining to Executive Outcomes by the government[186] parallels were drawn with Angola, which is discussed below. A clear-cut dividing line between official/legal and unofficial/illegal sources of income and expenditures was blurred when the government reportedly 'diverted part of $19 million from International Monetary Fund to the mercenaries, when they threatened to leave as unpaid government bills mounted.'[187] During peace negotiations, the government-Executive Outcomes contract was an object of challenge by the RUF; monthly payments to the Executive Outcomes were reportedly $1.2 million, much above the government's official annual revenue of $800,000.[188]

An attempt by the military government (then led by Valentine Strasser) to extract funds from seventeen former ministers who had allegedly plundered government coffers was abandoned 'because the international community, particularly the European Union, had agreed to withhold bilateral funds while the human rights violations persisted.'[189] Withheld aid was easily compensated by export of diamonds. The warring sides became indistinguishable and referred to as *sobels* (soldiers during daytime who turn into rebels at night) who made their living through diamond or gold racketeering, looting and plunder. Distinguishing between the supposedly two sides to the armed conflict became impossible; uniforms and weapons were easily sold and purchased; knowledge that all uniformed and armed men were unlikely to have any salaries rapidly spread terror because they were known to exact 'salaries' at gunpoint. The fiercest battles were fought for diamond mining areas and unrecorded exports of diamonds were estimated at $5 million per week.[190]

Aid (an estimated $30 million[191]) was provided for elections, which met the donors' conditions of having been free and fair.[192] William Shawcross has pointed out that elections were supported by 'the British High Commission and the US Embassy, but not of many more embassies.'[193] A cynical comment by *The Economist* followed:

Blame the British, who still carry much wight in Freetown, and had demanded [election] as a condition for aid. They believed that an election, for which they

[186] Picard, F. – When mercenaries are a junta's best friend, *Guardian Weekly*, 22 October 1995.
[187] Huband, M. – Africa's poorest trapped in war of mindless mutilation, *Guardian Weekly*, 11 February 1996.
[188] Saccoh, R.S. – Sierra Leone: Enter the Kamajohs, *New African*, December 1966, p. 24.
[189] Sierra Leone: Why war?, *New African*, December 1994, p. 32.
[190] Huband, M – Africa's poorest trapped in war of mindless mutilation, *Guardian Weekly*, 11 February 1996.
[191] Girard, D. – Freetown fights an unknown enemy, *Guardian Weekly*, 1 January 1995.
[192] King, D. – Sierra Leone: Ballot defies bullet – but wounds remain, *The Courier*, No. 157, May-June 1966, p. 18.
[193] Shawcross, W. – Sierra Leone defies fear and heads for polls, *International Herald Tribune*, 15 March 1996.

have pledged £3m, would marginalize the RUF and end the war. Few agree with them.[194]

Half of the population of an estimated 4.1 million was unable to register because they had been killed or displaced. A million voters registered, and 700,000 cast their votes. No candidate obtained majority; in the runoff 60% of votes were cast for Ahmed Tejan Kabbah.[195] The newly elected civilian government was supposed to stop warfare, having no more than international legitimacy as a tool although it was composed of no less than 23 ministers and 24 junior ministers. After the government had been inaugurated in March 1996, the RUF leader Foday Sankoh referred to having met 'a group of Sierra Leoneans'[196] with obvious disdain for a negotiating party without an army. The peace agreement was signed in December 1996 in Côte d'Ivoire but another military coup followed six months later, in May 1996, triggering a military intervention by the Nigerian military government to restore democracy in Sierra Leone. Predictably, foreign nationals were evacuated, the new military government of Sierra Leone suspended from the Commonwealth,[197] and the Security Council imposed sanctions. These consisted of an arms and oil embargo as well as travel restrictions for members of the military junta.[198]

The elected civilian government was returned to Sierra Leone by Nigeria's military intervention, which was hailed for its legitimate end rather than means.[199] The end was legitimate because all inter-governmental bodies called for the return of the elected government. The means were not discussed because none of these inter-governmental bodies specified how that end should be attained. That the means were not deemed particularly important was evidenced in a sideshow: a scandal erupted when Sandline, a British firm of security consultants (who some people refer to as mercenaries) had furnished weapons to Sierra Leone in breach of the Security Council's arms embargo but with alleged acquiescence of the United Kingdom. The initial United Kingdom's reaction was that the means justified the end. In the words of the prime minister, Tony Blair:'[We] were trying to help the democratically elected regime to restore its position from an illegal military coup.'[200] Things were retroactively clarified, with the Security Council specifying

[194] Sierra Leone: Little brother, *The Economist*, 20 January 1996, p. 45.

[195] Sierra Leone: Vote to nowhere, *The Economist*, 2 March 1996; Ganda, A. – Sierra Leone: What next? *New African*, April 1996, p. 21; Stevens, K.-R. – Sierra Leone: Dawn of a new republic, *African Topics*, No. 12, April- May 1966, p. 16.

[196] Orr, D. – Deal raises hopes of end to Sierra Leone carnage, *The Independent*, 27 April 1996.

[197] Commonwealth puts Sierra Leone on hold, *The Independent*, 12 July 1997.

[198] Security Council resolution 1132 (1997) of 8 October 1997, paras. 5–6.

[199] 'The United Nations secretary-general, Kofi Annan, and leaders at the Organization of African Unity summit in Zimbabwe on Monday implicitly endorsed Nigeria's assault on Freetown by saying all steps must be taken to restore the democratic government to Sierra Leone.' McElroy, C. – Freetown battle shatters peace hopes, *Guardian Weekly*, 8 June 1997.

[200] Abrams, F. & Buncombe, A. – Blair:'We did nothing wrong,' *The Independent*, 12 May 1998.

that the arms embargo referred to non-governmental forces, exempting 'the Government of Sierra Leone.'[201] Another layer of questionable means concerned the reversal of the military coup in Sierra Leone through Nigeria's military intervention. This was also a possible breach of sanctions because all military co-operation with the government of Nigeria had been suspended after the execution of Ken Saro-Wiva, as is discussed below. Arms deliveries to Nigeria's military[202] to be used in Liberia were apparently exempt while the bombing of Liberia's capital, apparently without distinguishing between military and civilian targets, also did not trigger challenges of questionable means.[203]

Twenty four junior military officers who had organized the 1997 military coup were executed, RUF's leader, Foday Sankoh, sentenced to death for treason, while Nigeria's army stayed on battling.[204] That sequence of events made silence about the means needed to accomplish the postulated ends very loud. Little publicity accompanied the process of peace-making, which bestowed legitimacy upon all key combatants by inviting them all to join the government[205] thus accepting the heritage of lawlessness that they were likely bring into the government with them.

The previous experiment with electoralism in Sierra Leone resulted in a government that had international legitimacy but no power to govern; a military intervention aimed at redressing that government's lack of power to govern was deemed legitimate on the basis of its postulated end. If one turns things around to ask whether an actor possessing the effective power to govern in a country obtains international legitimacy through an experiment in electoralism, seeking an answer to this question makes Liberia a good case study, which can be introduced with this sarcastic summary by *The Economist*:

It took Liberia's Charles Taylor seven bloody years to graduate from embezzler to warlord to elected president' and he was welcomed into ECOWAS with three bursts of applause by his peers; out of sixteen presidents of the ECOWAS members, twelve had also come to power through military force.[206]

---

[201] Security Council resolution 1171 (1998) of 5 June 1998, para. 2.

[202] The Economic Community of West African States (ECOWAS) was originally established in 1975 and restructured in 1991–93 to give the organization powers for the resolution of regional conflicts. The ECOWAS headquarters is based in Nigeria, and Nigeria contributed most to the budget and holds the chairmanship. ECOMOG is the abbreviation originally used for the ECOWAS Monitoring Group deployed in Liberia in 1990, described in the next section, and has also been used for Nigeria's military intervention in Sierra Leone in 1997 regardless of the absence of an ECOWAS decision to that effect.

[203] Britain/Sierra Leone: The Freetown fall-out, *Africa Confidential*, vol. 39, No. 10, 15 May 1998, p. 1–2; Ankomah, B. – Nigeria trounced in Sierra Leone, and How the West won in Sierra Leone, *New African*, July/August 1997 and April 1998.

[204] Sierra Leone: War without end, and The darkest corner of Africa, *The Economist*, 21 November 1998 and 9 January 1999.

[205] Ourdan, R. – Uneasy peace follows a brutal past, *Guardian Weekly*, 16–22 December 1999.

[206] West Africa: Ironies, *The Economist*, 6 September 1997.

Liberia

The elections in Liberia have added some international legitimacy to Charles Taylor's military victory in the seven-year-long war, against an obvious decision by the international donor community to express disapproval through continued denial of aid. The government's annual budget for 1998 was reported at $41 million, and Charles Taylor said that 'empty global promises' and 'donor delays' resulted from their wish to have somebody else as Liberia's president.[207] This was not to be. As Max Ahmadu Sesay predicted, 'those who have been engaged in much of the asset-stripping of rural Liberia, namely the wardlords, will be best placed to offer patronage on a scale that is likely to attract a considerable following.'[208]

The elections were held in July 1997, following many failed peace agreements. The 10-month lead-time from the cease-fire to the elections made them hasty and imperfect (the lack of a population register and identity papers made electoral registration fictitious) but the elections were declared to have been free and fair. They were facilitated and scrutinized by the ECOMOG (Economic Community of West African States' Monitoring Group), a Nigeria-led sub-regional peace-keeping operation, while the ECOMOG was itself monitored by the United Nations. The reason for this two-layered structure was that the ECOMOG had been criticised for its role of a warring party rather than a peace-maker, and the United Nations – having endorsed this first experiment in sub-regional peace-enforcement – sent observers.

The beginning of warfare in Liberia was attributed to the invasion of Charles Taylor's National Patriotic Front of Liberia (NPFL) from Côte d'Ivoire[209] in December 1989. Seven years of vicious warfare followed, with warring parties shifting sides and allegiances, distinctions between combatants and civilians blurred, much mutilation and looting.

The Security Council imposed an arms embargo in 1992. The ECOWAS (Economic Community of West African States) had reacted already in 1990, sending peace-keeping forces, the ECOMOG, to Liberia. There was no peace to keep, however, and the ECOMOG became embroiled in making peace. A great deal of controversy ensued because this was the first sub-regional military intervention with unclear mandate and powers, plagued by divisions amongst the ECOWAS members about what should be accomplished and how, as well as dotted with reported misbehaviour of the ECOMOG troops, who joined in fighting and looting. After a two-year silence, the United Nations retroactively legitimized

---

[207] Ankomah, B. – Knives out for Taylor, *New African*, September 1998.

[208] Sesay, M.A. – Politics and society in post-war Liberia, *The Journal of Modern African Studies*, vol. 34, 1996, No. 3, p. 410.

[209] Besides Côte d'Ivoire, Charles Taylor's supporters were reportedly also Libya and Burkina Faso. Ellis, S. – Liberia 1989–1994: A study of ethnic and spiritual violence, *African Affairs*, vol. 94, 1996, p. 181.

the ECOMOG and added the UNOMIL to monitor both domestic combatants and the ECOMOG.[210]

The first peace agreement was concluded in 1993, and followed by many others, none of which had stopped warfare.[211] The ECOMOG was much criticised for having become a party in warfare, and critiques encompassed its supporters, including the United Nations. *Médecins sans frontières* was literally bombed out of Liberia in April 1993:

> ECOMOG has shelled a number of towns under the control of Charles Taylor's NPFL rebel forces, causing considerable damage to hospitals and compounds of relief agencies. And the direct threats to humanitarian aid escalated further in April, when a clearly marked MSF aid convoy from the Ivory Coast was bombed by ECOMOG jets. … After a series of ECOMOG air raids that destroyed relief facilities, killed and wounded local people, the message has finally become clear: humanitarian aid was superfluous in a war aimed at bringing rebels to their knees.[212]

The ECOWAS imposed sanctions against Liberia in November 1992 and a blockade was imposed on the *Taylorland* (the area held by Taylor's NPFL), preventing delivery of disaster relief.[213] The UNOMIL (United Nations Observers Mission in Liberia) was supposed to monitor the arms embargo, conceding peace-enforcement to the ECOMOG and peace-making to the ECOWAS. The Security Council commended the positive role of the ECOWAS 'in its continuing efforts to restore peace, security and stability in Liberia' and condemned violations of international humanitarian law 'by the factions in Liberia.'[214] The General Assembly optimistically anticipated in December 1992 that a framework for peaceful resolution of the Liberian conflict had been found and conditions for free and fair elections created, under the threat of ECOWAS's comprehensive sanctions against any recalcitrant party.[215]

---

[210] Adibe, C.E. – The Liberian conflict and ECOWAS-UN partnership, *Third World Quarterly*, vol. 18, 1997, No. 3, pp. 471–488; Ramcharan, B.G. – Cooperation between the U.N. and regional/sub-regional organizations in internal conflicts: The case of Liberia, *African Yearbook of International Law*, 1997, pp. 3–17.

[211] Details about the many peace agreements including their texts have been published in *The Liberian Peace Process, 1990–1996, Accord. An International Review of Peace Initiatives*, Conciliation Resources, London, undated.

[212] Field report: Peacekeepers attack aid convoys in Liberia, *Médecins sans frontières International Newsletter*, No. 6, June 1993, p. 4.

[213] Ankomah, B. – Liberia: War or peace?, *New African*, February 1993, p. 15; Liberia: Peace, perhaps, *The Economist*, 31 July 1993;

[214] Security Council resolution 950 (1994) of 21 October 1994, preamble and para. 7.

[215] United Nations – Assistance for the rehabilitation and reconstruction of Liberia, General Assembly resolution 47/154 of 18 December 1992, preamble.

There had been fourteen cease-fire and peace agreements, two for each year of warfare. The thirteenth was concluded in Abuja in August 1995, and accompanied by high hopes. It gave 'every factional leader a voice in the new government, regardless of the soundness of his claim to power.'[216] Presidential elections were planned with all warlords having announced their intentions to win by a landslide. The Commission on Human Rights added its voice only in 1996 through a chairman's statement, which deplored indiscriminate destruction and urged aid to Liberia 'to cope with the humanitarian situation.'[218]

The ECOWAS decided in July 1996 that elections should be held within the next six months without disarmament, 'but with threats against any warring faction leaders who block the process.'[219] Elections were held exactly one year later, with partial disarmament, and without a great deal of enthusiasm for their outcome, as noted above. The most often mentioned actor displaying this lack of enthusiasm was the United States.

The one-and-a-half century of the US involvement in Liberia has necessarily raised questions about its past policy. Liberia had been originally settled by freed American slaves before the end of the civil war in the USA. In 1980–89, the United States aided Liberia with an estimated half-billion dollars, supporting a regime which has retroactively been assessed as particularly unworthy of aid. In 1985, Samuel Doe's government was transformed, with US support and endorsement, from a military regime to a democratically elected government. Liberia had a special claim on US aid because it hosted US military bases, including the largest communications installations in Africa. US aid was decreased at the very end of the Doe regime. Human rights violations were cited as one reason, but Liberia's inability to continue repayment of previous US loans had made Liberia ineligible for US aid and prompted the USA to provide in 1988 financial experts to the government so as to enable it to come to grips with the donors' requirements.[220] Aid was cut down by more than two-thirds in 1990,[221] just as Samuel Doe's regime was challenged militarily by Charles Taylor's NPFL. By April 1996, the USA reportedly funded the ECOMOG with $400 million and the US military remained 'the outside world's sole functioning representative in Liberia.'[222] All foreign, including UN, personnel had been evacuated.

---

[216] Purvis, A. – Liberia: Giving peace a chance, *Time*, 18 September 1995, p. 39.

[218] Chairman's statement on the situation of human rights in Liberia of 24 April 1996, Commission on Human Rights – Report on the Fifty-second Session (18 March–26 April 1996), U.N. Doc. E/CN.4/1996/177, p. 299.

[219] ECOWAS proposals, *Africa Research Bulletin*, vol. 33, No. 7, 1–31 July 1996, p. A12345.

[220] Harsch, E. – Liberia: Allegations of US 'shadow cabinet', *African Concord*, 4 March 1988, p. 21; Butty, J. – Liberia: A progress report, *West Africa*, 22 August 1988, p. 1525.

[221] Butty, J. – Liberia: Less money from Uncle Sam?, *West Africa*, 5–11 March 1990, p. 366; Stearns, S. – Liberia: Amidst the ruins, money is being made, *African Business*, August 1991, p. 21–23.

[222] Hammer, J. – Liberia: Running for the exits, *Newsweek*, 22 April 1996, p. 16.

US aid to the ECOMOG was $29 million in 1991, and $31 million was approved towards the end of 1993 to an 'expanded' ECOMOG.[223] The ECOMOG was controlled and manned mostly by Nigeria when it had been set up in August 1990. Francophone members of the ECOWAS neither approved nor participated. The United States pursued a carrot-and-stick strategy to 'expand' the ECOMOG, recalling its ambassador from Burkina Faso to protest alleged arming of the NPFL, financially and politically supporting Côte d'Ivoire's attempt at peace-making, and offering funding for Senegal's participation in the ECOMOG.[224]

As mentioned above, only the fourteenth attempt at peacemaking proved successful, leading to demobilization and elections. The process of demobilization revealed that one-third of combatants had been below 18 years of age,[225] which explained a great deal of the messy, vicious and cruel warfare that had just ended. That children can be trained to commit atrocities is well-known from the resistence of governments and armed movements to increasing the minimum age for participation in warfare to adulthood. That young boys are particularly prone to crime and violence is well-known from criminological research.

NIGERIA

A great deal of international attention and demands for sanctions against Nigeria were triggered by the execution of Ken Saro-Wiwa and eight other Ogoni activists in November 1995. Those were not the first calls for sanctions against Nigeria, but will almost certainly remain known as the most publicised case. Ken Saro-Wiwa had been a well-known author and campaigner, a charismatic figure fighting the battle of the Ogoni people against environmental degradation caused by the oil industry as well as the denial of individual rights and freedoms in Nigeria. He and eight other MOSOP (Movement for the Survival of the Ogoni People) activists were tried and convicted by a special tribunal,[226] and all international appeals for clemency did not prevent their execution, which coincided with a Commonwealth bi-annual conference. Immense publicity preceded and followed their execution:

---

[223] Human Rights Watch/Africa – Human rights in Africa and U.S. policy. A special report by Human Rights Watch/Africa for the White House Conference on Africa, Washington, D.C., June 26–29, 1994, mimeographed, p. 19.

[224] The danger in Liberia (editorial), *The Washington Post*, reprinted in *International Herald Tribune*, 10 November 1992; da Costa, P. – Liberia: Good neighbours, *Africa Report*, November-December 1991, p. 23; Liberia: The Abidjan round, *West Africa*, 13–19 May 1991, p. 751.

[225] French, H.W. – Liberian militias hand in guns, *International Herald Tribune*, 28 January 1997; Momoh, J. – Liberia: The road to peace, *New African*, April 1997, p. 25.

[226] The trial was held under the Civil Disturbances (Special Tribunals) Decree, with a military officer sitting as a member and defendants having no right to legal assistance or appeal. Their charge was having had instigated the killing of fellow Ogonis. All international human rights bodies that analysed that trial reached the same conclusion. For example, the Human Rights Committee found that the executions had been arbitrary deprivations of life. Human Rights Committee – Preliminary concluding observations: Nigeria, U.N. Doc. CCPR/C/79/Add. 64 of 3 April 1996, para. 9.

theirs was a specific, well-publicised grievance, Ken Saro-Wiwa was a hero and martyr whose side people could easily take, and there was a link between his fate and their governments' foreign policy since oil exports to the West were Nigeria's main source of revenue, while a British/Dutch oil company was the main actor in oil exploitation.

The sanctions that were imposed against Nigeria were minuscule since none of the Western importers of Nigeria's oil would even discuss an oil embargo; political sanctions embodied Nigeria's suspension from the Commonwealth; the arms embargo predating the execution of Ken Saro-Wiwa was strengthened; the amount of aid that was suspended was tiny and could not have affected Nigeria's budget. Investment in the oil and gas exploitation continued, despite assertions by the advocates of economic sanctions that Nigeria's rulers were misappropriating the oil wealth and could be affected by an oil embargo, while the population would not be harmed since it was not benefitting from Nigeria's oil wealth anyway. The counter-rationale went like this: 'British officials admit to preferring strong government in Nigeria to democracy. And all for the sake of British investment in Nigeria's oil industry.'[227] Indeed not even a full month after the executions had taken place, 'the British government [was] sponsoring businessmen to go to Nigeria to drum up trade.'[228] Britain is the largest exporter to Nigeria, as well as the largest investor together with the United States and the Netherlands.[229] Nigeria attracted 32% of investment in Africa in 1996, despite sanctions for human rights violations or military rule as well as the lack of compliance with the structural adjustment targets.[230]

Debates about sanctions against Nigeria predated the many calls for sanctions which followed the execution of Ken Saro-Wiva in 1995. Military rule has marked a large part of Nigeria's history as an independent country. Nigeria started its independence in1960 with an elected civilian government, but two years later the country was in turmoil; elections followed in 1964 and turmoil re-emerged in 1966, followed by an attempted military coup, whereupon the civilian government handed the government over to the military and another military coup followed. The Biafra war started in 1967 and ended in 1970 with Biafra's surrender. In 1975 yet another (internal that time) military coup took place. One year later one more internal military coup brought to power a military regime which led the country to an elected civilian government in 1979. In 1983 elections were accompanied by religious riots, violent conflicts and allegations of electoral fraud to lead to another military coup. Another (internal) military coup took place in 1985. In 1987–89 there was another beginning of transition to civilian rule, with a new constitution and the subsequent formation of two political parties by the military government.

---

[227] Africa's colonial favourites, *The Economist*, 28 October 1995.

[228] Crawshaw, S. – Trade trip to Nigeria backed by Whitehall, *The Independent*, 7 December 1995.

[229] Adams, P. – Oil: The regime's Achilles' heel?, *Financial Times*, 11–12 November 1995.

[230] African Development Bank: The bank that likes to say no, *The Economist*, 6 June 1998.

Elections for local authorities followed in 1990, as did an attempted military coup. Parliamentary elections were held in 1992 and presidential elections in 1993. The 1993 elections were canceled retroactively and the military regime established a transitional civilian government, whose reign was stopped shortly thereafter through another military coup. The military regime in 1993–98, headed by General Sani Abacha, became a prominent target of calls for sanctions. His rule ended in 1998 with his death and his successor, General Abubakar, promised return to an elected government and freed prominent political prisoners. Nigeria's diplomatic isolation was ended and sanctions lifted.[231]

The focus for condemnations and sanctions was the period between 1993 and 1998. The probable winner of the presidential elections in June 1993, Chief Abiola, was placed in detention to die in detention in 1998. Wole Soyinka had protested against Nigerians having been robbed of their dignity when electoral results were dismissed, the victor detained, and Soyinka forced into exile.[232] Those who could not leave were detained, harassed, silenced, sometimes killed. Summary trials were organized against former heads of state and/or government and held by special military or security courts; detention without trial was amply used. The government of the time protected itself against domestic political challenge through a variety of repressive practices, exempting all its decrees and decisions from judicial review. Human rights guarantees thus became legally non-existent:

> At present, no constitutional guarantee for the protection of the rights of the people of Nigeria exists due to the adoption of Decree No. 107 of 1993, namely the Constitution (Suspension and Modification) decree, which restores the 1979 Constitution while suspending the application of its human rights provisions.[233]

In response to the open challenge to the donors' insistence on democracy, embodied in the annulment of the 1993 elections, EUrope suspended aid, followed by the United States, while the United Kingdom imposed 'limited military sanctions.'[234] The European Union suspended military co-operation with Nigeria in July 1993 and introduced visa restrictions for military and security officials. Restrictions for arms export licenses as well as aid projects were added in December 1993. (The jargon term for such a scheme is case-by-case review with presumption of denial, meaning that export licenses or aid projects are to be rejected unless special circumstances justify an exception.) Those restrictions were thus in place at the time

---

[231] Black, I. – West warms to Nigeria's new regime, *Guardian Weekly*, 5 July 1998.

[232] Nigeria 'on the road to disaster', *Guardian Weekly*, 18 July 1993.

[233] Commission on Human Rights – Situation of human rights in Nigeria. Report submitted by the Special Rapporteur of the Commission on Human Rights, Mr. Soli Jehangir Sorabjee, U.N. Doc. E/CN.4/1998/62 of 16 February 1998, para. 23.

[234] *The Courier*, No. 141, September-October 1993; U.K. puts military sanctions on Nigeria, *International Herald Tribune*, 25 June 1993; Maier, K. – World fury as Nigeria sends writer to gallows, *The Independent*, 11 November 1995.

of calls for sanctions against Nigeria in response to the execution of Ken Saro-Wiwa. Total aid to Nigeria was minuscule and donors' suspensions had little effect although they were frequent 'because the government fails to comply with the conditions of even the most tolerant of donors.'[235] The European Parliament called for an oil embargo against Nigeria, but its initiative did not go far:'Britain and the Netherlands vetoed moves to agree to [an oil embargo], with an eye to the impact it would have on Shell, the Anglo-Dutch oil concern.'[236] The only oil-related economic sanction was the announcement by the IFC (International Financial Corporation) that it would not proceed with funding a multi-billion gas project, but the justification was the failure of Nigeria's government to undertake macro-economic reforms.[237] Sanctions also included sports boycotts but Nigeria's football team won the Olympic gold medal in Atlanta in 1996,[238] showing the boycott to have been selective.

In 1995, the condemnation of 40 people for an attempt to overthrow the government triggered further calls for sanctions. The trials had been conducted by the military in secret. Former President Olusegun Obasanjo (the only one to lead Nigeria to an elected government and then step down, to re-emerge as the elected president in 1999) was among the condemned. The execution of Ken Saro-Wiwa led to further calls for sanctions. The suspension of Nigeria from the Commonwealth in November 1995 marked a symbolic victory for Britain's former colonies. It was the first meeting at which South Africa participated after its re-admission, led by Nelson Mandela, who was sharply critical of Nigeria. The United Kingdom – while acquiescing to Nigeria's suspension – was quoted saying that it actually preferred a 'constructive dialogue'.[239] The decision on Nigeria's suspension had just one dissenter, the Gambia,[240] also ruled by the military.

While human rights violations in Nigeria were the object of all this international attention in 1993–95, the United Nations was much slower in forging its own response. The Working Group on Arbitrary Detention was faced with numerous cases of detention of human rights activists. One example was Femi Falana, an attorney and member of the Committee for the Defense of Human Rights who had repeatedly been detained and harassed, had his passport confiscated, his residence

---

[235] Nigeria: The general in his not-so-solitude, *The Economist*, 6 April 1996.

[236] McGreal, C. & Bates, S. – British and Dutch veto Nigeria oil ban, *Guardian Weekly*, 26 November 1995.

[237] Lascelles, D. Et al. – Shell 'regrets' execution but continues Nigeria strategy, *Financial Times*, 11–12 November 1995.

[238] Barber, J. – Reaching for values: The Commonwealth and Nigeria, *The World Today*, vol. 53, No. 1, January 1997, p. 19–20.

[239] Adams, P. – Nigeria seeks to avert sanctions, *Financial Times*, 24 June 1996.

[240] Crawshaw, S. – After the outrage, the action, *The Independent*, 13 November 1995.

and office searched.[241] The Special Rapporteur on Arbitrary Executions reported the use of excessive force against the Ogoni community and noted that special tribunals tended to impose capital punishment against Ogonis without fair-trial guarantees.[242] Moving such issues up to the UN Commission on Human Rights took a long time. An attempt at a condemnatory resolution against Nigeria in 1995, tabled by EUrope, was defeated (17-21-15) with all non-Western members voting against or abstaining. The following year a similar draft was narrowly adopted (28-19-6), with an attempt by the African group within the Commission to dilute the follow-up by eliminating establishment of a Special Rapporteur on Nigeria.[243] The previous tradition of solidarity amongst African governments facing condemnations for human rights violations was breached. Uganda hosted a special session of the African Commission on Human and Peoples' Rights – devoted to Nigeria – in December 1995.[244]

Gani Fawehinmi, a prominent Nigerian human rights lawyer expressed his disappointment with Western responses to the repression in Nigeria and suggested that all foreign property and investment of the military officers holding power in Nigeria should be frozen, and funds from oil exports placed in an escrow account until 'problems are resolved', as he put it.[245] His call, and many others along this line, remained unheeded. Negotiations between the IMF and the military government revolved around the government's expenditure and the lowering of inflation. The key problem was Nigeria's failure to service its foreign debt of $28 (or perhaps $33) billion.[246] The key shareholder in the IMF and the World Bank, the US government, was reported to condition its vote in favour of further loans to Nigeria on progress in curbing drugs trafficking.[247]

Demands for sanctions targeted Nigeria's oil exports, valued at an annual $12 billion, but impossible to determine with precision because oil revenue had been misappropriated.[248] Exports were destined mainly for the USA (close to one-

---

[241] Commission on Human Rights – Report of the Working group on Arbitrary Detention, U.N. Doc. E/CN.4/1994/27 of 17 December 1993, Decision No. 22/1993 (NIGERIA) of 30 April 1993, pp. 81–83.

[242] Commission on Human Rights – Extrajudicial, summary or arbitrary executions. Report by the Special Rapporteur, Mr. Bacre Waly Ndiaye, U.N. Doc. E/CN.4/1994/7 of 7 December 1993, paras. 463–464.

[243] Reekie, K. – Nigeria: UN Commission on Human Rights votes to appoint Special Rapporteur, *Human Rights Tribune/Tribune des droits humains*, vol. 4, No. 2–3, June 1997, p. 27–28.

[244] Nigeria: African human rights body reacts to the murder of Ogoni leaders, *ICJ Newsletter*, No. 64/1996, p. 7.

[245] No freedom without a fight. Interview with Gani Fawehinmi, *Newsweek*, 10 October 1994.

[246] Adams, P. – Few prospects in sight for an IMF agreement with Nigeria, *Financial Times*, 4 February 1994.

[247] Adams, P. – Reform test for Nigeria, *Financial Times*, 5 January 1994; Nigerian $4.3bn gas project hit by US ban, *Financial Times*, 21 April 1994; Lippman, T.W. – U.S. diplomacy fails to nudge Nigeria, *The Washington Post*, reprinted in *Guardian Weekly*, 30 July 1995.

[248] Nigeria's missing billions, *The Economist*, 22 October 1994; Adams, P. – Economic reforms on parole, *Financial Times*, 20 January 1995.

half) and Western Europe (mostly Spain, France and Germany). Alongside the largest importers of Nigerian oil, six individual oil companies (Shell, Chevron, Mobil, Elf, Texaco and Agip) found themselves in a crossfire. Demands that they pull out of Nigeria were countered by warnings against 'ongoing hostile activities' by their governments.[249] Shell's involvement in Nigeria was scrutinised to reveal its involvement in arms purchases 'on behalf of the Nigerian police force who guard Shell's facilities'; Shell's asset base in Nigeria was estimated at $14 billion, without a planned $3.6 billion natural gas project.[250] Other Western oil companies continued their involvement in Nigeria, not only British/Dutch Shell, but also French Elf and Total.[251]

The transition to an elected government in 1999 brought the involvement of oil companies back into focus. In times of the falling oil prices, an elected Nigeria's government was expected to try to maximize its oil revenue. The combined pressures of debt repayment and neglect by previous military governments were coming at the time when Nigeria's foreign exchange earnings were diminishing. The future will show whether foreign and international financial support to a new government of Nigeria, elected in 1999, will contribute to investment in human rights protection. All experiences thus far caution against such expectations.

THE END OF FRENCH *CHASSES GARDÉES*?

Different from publicity for human rights in Anglophone countries, French-speaking African countries have been immune to international scrutiny. A country such as Comoros has attracted little international attention although it had 17 attempted military coups in 20 years.[252] There was a French connection – several coups were attributed to Bob Denard, a well-known French mercenary; France sometimes reacted by cutting off aid and deploying the army[253] and in-between Comoros sank into oblivion.

Verbal and policy-duels between English- and French speaking donors have illustrated differences in Western foreign policies. Niger was an illustrative

---

[249] Maier, K. – Nigeria warns oil firms after British criticism, *The Independent*, 18 July 1995; Black, I. – Nigeria gives warning to oil companies, *Guardian Weekly*, 23 July 1995.

[250] Shell confirms Nigeria project, *Financial Times*, 15 November 1995; Bates, S. & Bowcott, O. – Shell undeterred by Nigeria hangings, *Guardian Weekly*, 19 November 1995; Duodu, C. – Shell admits arms imports into Nigeria, *Guardian Weekly*, 4 February 1996; Corzine, R. – Shell plays for high stakes in Nigeria, *Financial Times*, 8 July 1996.

[251] Maringues, M. – Paris starts to parley with Abacha regime, *Le Monde*, 15–16 February, reproduced in *Guardian Weekly*, 1 March 1998.

[252] Commission on Human Rights – Report on the question of the use of mercenaries as a means of violating human rights and impeding the exercise of the right of peoples to self-determination, submitted by Mr. Enrique Bernales Ballestros, Special Rapporteur, U.N. Doc. E/CN.4/1996/27 of 17 January 1996, para. 56.

[253] Mercenary surrenders to French forces in Comoros, *International Herald Tribune*, 6 October 1995.

example of two donors at cross purposes. The United States suspended aid to Niger in response to elections in July 1996, calling them fraudulent, while France wished the elected president success in leading Niger along the path of stability and development.[254] A military coup in January 1997 dismantled electoral results. Colonel Ibrahim Baré Maïnassara, who had led the coup, explained that the government had been paralysed due to a 'conflictuous cohabitation' between the president and the prime minister.[255] Conflicts revolved around directorships of state-owned companies and demands for budgetary allocations according to the relative political strength of different ethnic groups.[256] France had announced in 1995 that it would intervene in countries with which it had military co-operation agreements when an elected government is overthrown by the military, but did not do so.[257] Alongside EUrope, Canada, Germany and the USA,[258] France imposed sanctions against Niger on 27 January 1996 to lift them on 7 March 1996.[259] Those 38-day sanctions are probably the shortest in history.

The immunity of Francophone African countries to international scrutiny of their human rights performance has been somewhat ruptured in the 1990s. The UN Commission on human rights placed Togo on the agenda for human rights violations in 1993, 'deploring the repeated acts of violence' to take it off the agenda in 1995 to receive human rights assistance.[260] As is customary, the 1993 condemnatory resolution was forwarded to the government of Togo, which replied that violations were 'simply the result of profound lack of comprehension and understanding among different protagonists of the nation's political life.'[261] The opposition was accused of having organized militias which attacked the army. A different picture was presented by the UN Rapporteur on Summary Executions, who found that the army had killed probably 2,500 people in 1990–93 with impunity.[262] In 1994, when the Commission on Human Rights was in session, Togo submitted a general report under international human rights treaties, stressing 'ever-increasing importance attached to human rights', which are 'given pride of place in

---

[254] Niger: Election or 'coup'?, *Africa Research Bulletin*, vol. 33, No. 7, 1–31 July 1996, p. 12337–12338.

[255] Soudan, F. – Ça recommence!, *Jeune Afrique*, No. 1830, 31 January–6 February 1996, p.p. 9–10.

[256] Niger: Unhappy cohabitation. A democratic constitution is working very badly, tempting the army to intervene again, *Africa Confidential*, vol. 36, No. 17, 25 August 1995, p. 7.

[257] French, H.W. – On Gabon's ramparts, France. Its troops still show flag across Africa, *International Herald Tribune*, 23 May 1996.

[258] Niger coup leaders talk, *The European*, 1–7 February 1996.

[259] Cessou, S. et al. – Et si les sanctions économiques ne servaient á rien ..., *Jeune Afrique Économie*, No. 214, 18 March 1996, p. 54.

[260] Commission on Human Rights – Situation of human rights in Togo, resolution 1993/75; Situation of human rights in Togo. Report of the Secretary-General, U.N. Doc. E/CN.4/1996/89 of 5 January 1996.

[261] Commission on Human Rights – Situation of human rights in Togo. Report by the Secretary-General, U.N. Doc. E/CN.4/1994/59 of 20 January 1994, p. 5.

[262] U.N. Doc. E/CN.4/1994/7, para. 593.

fundamental legislation'. Democratic transition was blamed for 'substantial social and political tension, which has been reflected in inter-ethnic disturbances' and so 'the police and security forces have been hard put to perform their duties effectively.'[263]

Prerequisites for the rule of law, as different from the rule of force, were debated by the ACP-EC Joint Assembly when it was elaborating a blueprint for democratization, and it diagnosed 'non-subordination of the armed forces to the political authorities' as a major obstacle.[264] The national conference in Togo, convened after a great deal of public outcry, was dispersed by the 'over-large army'.[265] The military regime of General Eyadema (who came to power through a military coup in 1967) started transforming itself into a democracy in 1991–92. A multi-party system was legalized, a national conference followed, as did a new Constitution. France cut off aid to Togo in February 1993, following the killing of unarmed demonstrators by the military to resume aid as soon as elections were held.[266] General Eyadema was re-elected with 96% of the votes; the opposition boycotted the elections while the turnout was estimated at 36%.[267] President Eyadema's electoral victory was confirmed in the subsequent elections in 1998[268] while Togo had in the meantime been dropped from the UN human rights agenda.

The scarce publicity for human rights in Francophone African countries has continued with few exceptions. Stanley Cohen has summarized the pattern of international human rights politics as 'the Chad rule,'[269] capturing the determinants of case-creation. Few people can find Chad on the map, even fewer have ever been there, yet fewer would be able to say why anybody would go to Chad, and this is all componded by the human rights language being English rather than French.

Chad has been depicted as a 'hostage of politicians and rebels of all sorts'[270] and a large number of reports had been submitted to the United Nations, mainly by the *Fédération internationale des ligues de droits de l'homme*. An illustration conveys their typical message:

---

[263] United Nations – Core document forming the initial pert of State party reports under international human rights instruments: Togo, U.N. Doc. HRI/CORE/1/Add.38 of 15 February 1994, paras. 57–59.

[264] Resolution on democracy, human rights and development in the ACP countries, adopted by the ACP-EC Joint Assembly in Gabarone on 31 March 1993, Doc. ACP/EC 687/A/93/fin., para. A.

[265] Democracy tops the agenda at Joint Assembly, *The Courier*, No. 132, March-April 1992; Togo: A test for France, *The Economist*, 4 July 1998.

[266] Democracy in Africa: A lull in the wind, *The Economist*, 4 September 1993, p. 49; France and Africa: Dangerous liaisons, *The Economist*, 23 July 1994, p. 19.

[267] United Nations – Situation of human rights in Togo. Report by the Secretary-General, U.N. Doc. E/CN.4/1994/59 of 20 January 1994, para. 24.

[268] Togo: Mini-Mobutu okay?, *Africa Confidential*, vol. 38, No. 23, 21 November 1997, p. 6–7; Sotinel, T. – Togo leader re-elected in disputed poll, *Le Monde*, reproduced in *Guardian Weekly*, 5 July 1998.

[269] Cohen, S. – *Denial and Acknowledgment: The Impact of Information about Human Rights Violations*, Center for Human Rights, The Hebrew University of Jerusalem, 1995, p. 102.

[270] Placce, J.-B. – Tchad: Le plus dur reste à faire, *Jeune Afrique Economie*, No. 223, 5 August 1996, p. 60.

In a telegram dated 14 November 1996, the Specialized Units Command issued orders for no proceedings whatsoever to be taken against thieves. 'On catching a thief in the act, proceed immediately to physically eliminate him.' When explanations were demanded by human rights associations, the head of state and his Prime Minister openly acknowledged giving firm instructions for thieves to be summarily executed, on the ground that 'the justice system is powerless and corrupt.'[271]

Chad thereupon entered the confidential 1503 procedure and was kept there by decisions of the Commission on Human Rights, reached behind closed doors. The Sub-Commission broke silence in 1994 through a resolution that denounced flagrant and systematic human rights violations.[272] The Commission did not follow suit and France was repeatedly criticised for saving Chad from public exposure, 'using all her influence, notably with other members of the European Union.'[273] Prospects for inter-governmental action on Chad's human rights record are likely to diminish further because of discovery of oil: 'Exxon, Shell and Elf plan to spend $3.2 billion on developing three Chadian oilfields, and the World Bank will partly finance a 1,600km pipeline to the coast.'[274] Oil wealth valued in billions, for a government whose annual budget was reported at $80 million,[275] is going to make all the difference, although not necessarily towards respect of human rights.

Oil wealth and a population held hostage by the warring parties has characterized also Congo/Brazzaville. The Sub-Commission on Prevention of Discrimination and Protection of Minorities adopted a resolution in 1997, diagnosing the continuing loss of life to 'intercommunal strife,' pleading for the respect of the ceasefire and peace agreements, but also hinting at the causation of warfare by calling for 'transparency so that everyone will know how governmental revenues are being distributed and spent.'[276]

Oil wealth has been a curse rather than a blessing for Congo/Brazaville, Africa's fourth largest oil exporter. Before the 1992 elections, under the Sassou-Nguesso's regime (1979–92), Elf had been the largest oil company in Congo/Brazzaville. The

---

[271] Commission on Human Rights – Written statement submitted by the International Federation of Human Rights Leagues, U.N. Doc. E/CN.4/1997/NGO/21 of 5 March 1997, para. 11.

[272] Sub-Commission on Prevention of Discrimination and protection of Minorities – Situation of human rights in Chad, resolution 1994/19 of 25 August 1994.

[273] Vichniac, I. – Limited success for UN human rights body, *Le Monde*, 23 April, reproduced in *Guardian Weekly*, 4 May 1997; Numéro spécial: Tchad, *Codapement Vôtre*. Journal du CODAP, Centre de conseils et d'appuis pour les jeunes en matière de droits de l'homme, 1997, No. 1, p. 3.

[274] Brown, P. – Chad poised for oil boom, *Guardian Weekly*, 4 may 1997.

[275] Tuquoi, J.-P. – Chad under the shadow of the gun, *Le Monde*, 29 March, reproduced in *Guardian Weekly*, 14 April 1996.

[276] Sub-Commission on Prevention of Discrimination and protection of Minorities – Situation of human rights in the Congo, resolution 1997/1 of 20 August 1997. The resolution was adoped by a tight vote – 13 in favour, 10 against, and 2 abstentions.

newly elected president, Pascal Lissouba, rescinded Elf's oil extraction monopoly in favour of US-based Occidental Petroleum.'[277] Warfare ensued. As in similar cases, the cited reasons for the war were many, while the sources of funding of warfare remained cloaked in silence. Denis Sassou-Nguesso's military victory ended the war in 1997, after at least 6,000 people had been killed.[278] His military victory was facilitated by Angola's military intervention on his side,[279] and the inability of his opponent, Pascal Lissouba, to muster a foreign or international military intervention on his side. Following Sassou-Nguesso's military victory, Elf issued a communique saying that its chairman had gone to Congo to meet the victor.[280]

ANGOLA

The role of the oil factor in Angola has been as prominent as in Congo/Brazaville, but less publicised because Angola has been a cold-war orphan, while attention to the funding for warfare that has plagued its entire history tended to switch to diamonds (the source of the opposition's funds) rather than oil, which is the main source of revenue for the government.

Angola was a battlefield between a Soviet-Cuban supported government and US-South African supported rebels. Reduced external involvement in Angola after the Cold War ended created pressure towards peace-making and led to the 1991 peace agreement and the ill-fated elections in 1992. The underlying assumption was summarized by Norrie MacQueen as

> a perception of the Angolan conflict as one created and sustained essentially by external forces. Angola was seen as a 'Cold War conflict' which with the passing of the Cold War would be largely self-resolving – or resolvable with minimal external input.[281]

The 1991 Peace Accords for Angola, *Acordos de Paz para Angola*, (called alternatively Bicesse and Estorial Accords) envisaged unification of the warring political armies and elections of the winner-takes-all type. The United Nations

---

[277] The Congos: A local war turns regional, *The Economist*, 11 October 1997; Faligot, R. – Jospin finds Africa tricky, *The European*, 12–18 June 1997.

[278] Rake, A. – Sassou-Nguesso seizes power, *New African*, December 1997, p. 24.

[279] Rupert, J. – Africa nations more ready to intervene, *The Washington Post*, reprinted in *Guardian Weekly*, 2 November 1997.

[280] Gallois, D. – French oil firm plays down role in Africa, *Le Monde*, 30 October, reproduced in *Guardian Weekly*, 9 November 1997.

[281] MacQueen, N. – Peacekeeping by attrition: The United Nations in Angola, *The Journal of Modern African Studies*, vol. 36, 1998, No. 3, p. 401.

anticipated a modest budget and short involvement: the Security Council approved the 18-month mission with a budget of $132.3 million[282] and a total of $250 million was to be provided to Angola for the implementation of Peace Accords.[283] As described elsewhere,[284] this UN strategy did not work. The United Nations found on the eve of elections that disarming and demobilization of the two political armies had not materialized and there was no unified army. The elections proceeded as planned and the United Nations declared them to have been free and fair; whether anybody believed that the losers would accept their adversaries' victory is difficult to know. The announcement of electoral results was postponed because of complaints by the losers, with sporadic armed clashes expanding into warfare. The blame for resumption of warfare was placed on UNITA. Having lost the battle of ballots, it reverted to battling by bullets.

International responsibility for this unsuccessful electoral exercise was cloaked behind silence – international, foreign and domestic. Peace-making placed the two parties – MPLA and UNITA – on an equal footing and impunity for past abuses was bestowed upon both. No safeguards were anticipated to prevent abuses from continuing.

Attempts at peace-making continued after the failed 1992 elections, leading to the Lusaka Agreement in 1994 and a transition from war to peace started again after two years of post-war warfare. This second time, the United Nations prioritized disarming and demobilizing the political armies. Some 100,000 combatants were expected to disarm and a $65 million in aid, $650 per person, was allocated for their *civilianization*.[285] The UN registered an incoming 63,000 but not their subsequent departure from this 'all-expenses paid rest programme'; *The Economist* claimed that only the disabled and child soldiers had demobilized.[286] The UN's failure became evident in 1998–99, when warfare resumed.

Contrary to the previous UN policy of treating UNITA's leader Jonas Savimbi as the villain, the UN opted in 1994 for even-handedness and advocated power-sharing. The Lusaka Agreement granted UNITA four ministerial posts, six deputy-ministerial, and a dozen regional and communal governorships,[287] which was supposed to induce them to join a government of national unity and reconciliation, inaugurated in 1996. The Security Council accepted 'the special status of the leader

---

[282] UNAVEM II created to verify peaceful transition, *UN Chronicle*, September 1991, p. 28.

[283] *Africa Research Bulletin*, 1–31 October 1992, p. 10741.

[284] Tomaševski, K. – Angola, in Baehr, P. Et al. (Eds.) – *Human Rights in Developing Countries. Yearbook 1994*, Kluwer Law and Taxation Publishers/Nordic Human Rights Publications, 1994, pp. 113–149.

[285] Delay in merger of troops snags peace in Angola, *International Herald Tribune*, 17–18 August 1996.

[286] Chambon, F. – Savimbi stalls over Angola peace accords, *Le Monde*, 16 October, reproduced in *Guardian Weekly*, 27 October 1996; Angola: Still waiting for peace, and Angola on the way to war, *The Economist*, 29 March 1997 and 25 July 1998.

[287] Angola: Jaw-jaw and war-war, *Africa Confidential*, vol. 35, No. 7, 1 April 1994, p. 4.

of UNITA' and commended the government for the promulgation of an amnesty law.[288] The previous opponents went jointly fundraising, obtaining pledges for $1 billion out of which only $220 million was disbursed, mostly as food aid.[289]

Thereupon peace-making was officially ended and UNAVEM III was replaced by MONUA (*Missão de Observação das Nações Unidas em Angola*),[290] which had been deployed just before warfare resumed. The policy of even-handedness was changed to sanctions against UNITA. A travel, transit and transportation embargo was imposed and broadened to the closure of UNITA's offices abroad and the freezing of its assets.[291] The Security Council continued calling upon UNITA and Jonas Savimbi to join the government, envisaging a transformation of UNITA into a political party.[292] This strategy was based upon an unfounded assumption that a mere membership in parliament or executive constituted an attractive inducement. As UNITA possessed a large part of Angola, with diamond mines generating a monthly income of $30 million,[293] such inducements were simply not attractive. UN sanctions did not hamper UNITA's diamonds-for-arms trade. The government then launched a war against UNITA's allies in Congo/Brazzaville and Congo/Kinshasa[294] to cut off UNITA's export-import routes, while the United Nations regretted the resumed warfare.

Much criticism had been directed at the United Nations for its 1991–92 work in Angola, such as 'low-cost dabbling' or 'the bungled mission;'[295] the then Secretary-General acknowledged the UN's failure in Angola.[296] The second attempt at peace-making did not advocate elections but designed a power-sharing scheme, coupled with demilitarization of two political armies. The underlying causes of resumed warfare were not tackled, however. Both political armies had easy access to funds

---

[288] Security Council resolutions 1064 (1996) and 1075 (1996) of 11 July and 11 October 1996.

[289] Bates, S. – Angolan enemies ask Europe for funds, *Guardian Weekly*, 1 October 1995; Conchiglia, A. – Mensonges et diamants en Angola, *Le monde diplomatique*, April 1997.

[290] The Security Council thanked the international actors for 'assisting the parties in Angola to implement the peace process' in its resolution 1118 (1997) of 30 June 1997, established MONUA as an observer mission, urging the government and UNITA to complete the remaining 'political and milit aspects of the peace process.'

[291] Security Council resolutions 1127 (1997) of 28 August 1997 and 1173 (1998) of 12 June 199

[292] For example, the Security Council called upon UNITA to 'transform itself into a genuine poli party through the dismantling of its military structure' in its resolution 1195 (1998) of 15 Septen 1998, para. 4.

[293] Liebenberg, J. – Angola's diamond chaos, *New African*, December 1996.

[294] Angola's military joined the armed rebellion led by Laurent Kabila in Congo/Kinshasa, reported motivated by the previous support of the Mobutu regime for UNITA which had provided UNITA wi freedom to operate. The war waged by Denis Sassou-Nguesso against the then-president Pasc Lissouba of Congo/Brazzaville was also reportedly joined by Angola's army so as to deprive UNITA its previous territorial refuge in Congo/Brazzaville and gain military control of Cabinda.

[295] World fiddles, Africa burns, *New African*, May 1993, p. 23; Angola: relief and rivalry, *Afr Confidential*, vol. 34, No. 24, 3 December 1993, p. 7.

[296] Lewis, F. – The Secretary-General is right to give brinkmanship a try, *International Her Tribune*, 2 November 1993.

necessary to continue warfare and a great deal of commitment to obtaining and retaining power.

Table 9.10 shows aid flows to Angola since the time of independence at five-year intervals. Angola was the target of US sanctions in the 1970s because of its classification as a communist country. The war effort was funded by the government through the export of oil, and assisted by Soviet aid and Cuban armed forces. This is not reflected in aid statistics.

Table 9.10: Aid to Angola in 1975–95
(in million US$)

	1975	1980	1985	1990	1995
Belgium	0.1	0.5	0.1	4.1	0.6
Canada	–	–	1.8	11.2	3.8
Denmark	0.1	2.3	0.9	0.1	0.0
Germany	1.2	0.2	2.5	10.0	17.0
Italy	−1.2	43.2	16.3	37.7	9.5
Netherlands	0.6	8.0	8.1	12.6	23.3
Norway	–	16.9	0.3	7.3	28.8
Portugal	–	–	–	–	30.4
Sweden	1.1	0.2	18.7	38.3	26.5
Switzerland	0.9	0.0	0.8	4.2	3.6
United Kingdom	–	0.0	0.2	2.2	21.5
USA	–	7.0	7.0	1.0	31.0
EUrope	–	12.4	36.6	97.3	249.6
Total bilateral	4.0	35.8	59.6	142.6	247.7
Total multilateral	0.8	52.6	31.9	69.1	176.7

Source: *Geographical Distribution of Financial Flows to Developing Countries*, OECD, Paris, various issues.

The subsequent sanctions against UNITA are also not recorded in aid or any other official statistics because its revenue originated in illegal export of diamonds, ivory and timber, while the purchases of arms have been illegal as well. After the Security Council imposed sanctions against UNITA, EUrope followed suit targeting the illicit trade in diamonds. This could have reflected EUrope's commitment to peace-making in Angola, had it not been for an alternative explanation, the fears that UNITA's trade in diamonds would cause a crash in their price. EUrope's sanctions were announced in August 1998 as a response to a massacre by UNITA but interpreted as an attempt to keep the illicit stones off the market so as to stabilize diamond prices.'[297]

---

[297] Atkinson, D. – Angola rebels provoke crisis in diamond trade, *Guardian Weekly*, 9 August 1998.

UNITA had initially been supported by the US government. Victoria Brittain has chronologized US funding for their opposition to Angola's government in 1975–76, noting that it was interrupted in 1976–85 while in 1989 the United States provided $50 million for UNITA and cast a vote against Angola's IMF membership.[298]

The armed struggle for liberation had started in 1961; three liberation movements fought against the Portuguese and against each other. All skilled personnel had been Portuguese and used the local population as manual labour, no investment had been made into Angola's future development; aspirations for political independence had been brutally suppressed. Independence was granted hastily, following the a successful rebellion in Lisbon in April 1974. Angola's independence was proclaimed on 11 November 1975 in the midst of warfare between three liberation movements. The MPLA (*Movimento Popular de Libertação de Angola*) had been the oldest and was originally led by Agostinho Neto. The second liberation movement, FNLA (*Frente Nacional de Libertação de Angola*) subsequently disappeared, while UNITA (*União Nacional para la Independência Total de Angola*) continued war against MPLA. In Cabinda, an Angolan enclave encircled by Congo/Kinshasa with a population of 177,000 but much of Angola's oil, a multi-factional national liberation movement FLEC (*Frente da Libertação do Enclave de Cabinda*) has continued armed struggle.

The United Nations dealt with pre-independence Angola under the agenda item of decolonization.[299] National liberation movements were encouraged and supported; it was not anticipated that they would start fighting each other. The Sub-Commission on Prevention of Discrimination and Protection of Minorities discussed Angola in 1975, calling for non-interference by outside powers (this meant South Africa) but remaining silent about the struggle amongst Angolan liberation movements.[300] Besides internal actors, external involvement in warfare in Angola included (in alphabetical order) China, Cuba, France, Soviet Union, South Africa, SWAPO, USA, and Congo/Kinshasa. The United Nations Special Rapporteur on Mercenaries has diagnosed 'a typical case of an internal conflict being waged at the same time as an international conflict.'[301] Warfare continued

---

[298] Brittain, V. – *Death of Dignity: Angola's Civil War*, Pluto Press, London, 1998, p. 5, 23, and 41–42.

[299] A special United Nations body was formed for Angola in 1961 because of terrorist attacks on European settlements. It operated only one year (after 1962 Angola was dealt with by the all-encompassing Decolonization Committee), and during that time it heard representatives of no less than ten Angolan liberation movements. Zuijdwijk, T.J.M. – *Petitioning the United Nations. A Study in Human Rights*, Gower, Adlershot and St. Martin's Press, New York, 1982, p. 208.

[300] Sub-Commission on Prevention of Discrimination and Protection of Minorities – Report on the Twenty-eighth Session (1975), U.N. Doc. E/CN.4/1180, pp. 57–59.

[301] United Nations – Report on the question of the use of mercenaries as a means of violating human rights and impeding the exercise of the right of peoples to self-determination, submitted by Mr. Enrique Bernales Ballestros (Peru), Special rapporteur, U.N. Doc. E/CN.4/1992/12 of 13 December 1991, para. 64.

throughout Angola's history as an independent country, between 'a government that bombs its own cities and by an opposition movement willing to sacrifice thousands of civilians to pursue their leader's thirst for power.'[302]

The relative ease with which the international aspects of the Angolan conflict were solved overshadowed the need to look into the havoc which years of warfare created in Angola. Cold-war categorizations deemed the government as pro-Soviet and UNITA as pro-Western. The Soviet Union's support to Angolan government, including the much publicised Cuban troops, depicted Angola as part of the Soviet sphere of influence in Africa. US support for UNITA depicted Angola as a proverbial cold-war battlefield, while South Africa's direct and indirect war against Angola strangthened UNITA.[303] Jonas Savimbi had been cast in the role of freedom fighter until the late 1980s[304] to become the main culprit for failed peace-making in the 1990s, then an honoured statesman, and then again a target of sanctions and opprobrium. By the end of 1998 warfare resumed, showing that the United Nations had neither disarmed nor demilitarized the country.[305]

Oil brings Angola's government 90% of its export earnings. Military expenditure has constituted the largest single item in the government's budget throughout Angola's history; in the 1980s it was estimated at an annual $1 billion.[306] Angola's external debt was estimated at $8.8 billion by the World Bank and $9.5 billion by the Economist Intelligence Unit,[307] the difference originating in the calculation of Angola's military debt to the former Soviet Union. Angola reportedly acknowledged a $6 billion debt, to be repaid by awarding oil-and-diamond concessions to Russian companies.[308] Angola's deficit was placed at 42.7% of GDP by the IMF and 21.6% of GDP by Angola's Ministry of Planning.[309] These figures had been reported before the most recent outbreak of warfare in 1998–2000 and Angola's military intervention in Zaire/Congo, which is financed through loans mortgaging Angola's future oil and diamonds revenue.[310]

[302] Maier, K. – Angolans sink back towards year zero, *The Independent,* 8 February 1994.

[303] People's Republic of Angola – *White Paper on Acts of Aggression by the Racist South African Regime against the People's Republic of Angola, 1975–1982,* Luanda, 1982.

[304] Bridgland, F. – Jonas Savimbi: A Key to Africa, Paragon House, New York, 1986; Loiseau, Y. and de Roux, P.-G. – Portrait d'un révolutionnaire et général: Jonas Savimbi, Le Table Ronde, Paris, 1987; Bridgland, F. – Savimbi: Fallen idol of Angola, *Sunday Telegraph,* 12 March 1989.

[305] Conchiglia, A. – United Nations fails in Angola, *Le monde diplomatique,* (English edition), July 1999.

[306] Hodges, T. – *Angola to 2000. Prospects for Recovery,* EIU Research Report, London, February 1993, p. 32.

[307] The Economist Intelligence Unit – *Angola 1993/94. Country Profile,* London, 1993, p. 54–55.

[308] Iordansky, V. – Russia: No bear hugs for Africa, *Africa Recovery,* April 1992, p. 17; Angola's diamonds: De Beers's worst friend, *The Economist,* 22 August 1998.

[309] Ministry of Planning – Plan of Economic Rehabilitation (*Plano de recuperacao economica*) 1993–97, Luanda, mimeographed, 1992.

[310] 'In 1993 the government pledged on short-term loans the next five years of potential oil production – some $2 billion. In the first quarter of 1994, a further estimated $1 billion was spent.' Human Rights Watch/Africa – Human rights in Africa and U.S. policy, A special report by Human Rights Watch/Africa for the White House Conference on Africa, Washington, D.C., 26–27 June 1994, p. 5.

The accounts, as illustrated by the figures quoted above, consist of a great deal of guesswork because neither revenue nor expenditure is open to public scrutiny.

It might seem callous to end a section on human rights policies by discussing governmental revenue and the importance of the oil factor in it. And yet, human rights promises remain empty words – as this section has shown – unless governmental revenue (whether the government in question is a recipient or donor) prioritises promoting human rights over funding man-made disasters. The oil factor leads on to the next Chapter, devoted to Iraq, while the fate of human rights in Western foreign policies, whether towards Africa or towards Iraq, requires asking the question whether we are not entering a post-human-rights era.

Part IV

Towards a Post-human-rights Era?

Chapter 10

Sanctions against Iraq

The United Nations did not label Iraq as a human rights violator until after it had invaded Kuwait to then make it one of the foremost violators. Condemnations have been accompanied by sanctions, sanctions followed by bombing raids, and the Western public socialized into accepting this escalation by equalizing Iraq with its President. The United States then went yet one step further in organizing and supporting the Iraqi opposition,[1] at least those parts that proved amenable to US support. A blueprint has thus emerged whereby any harm inflicted upon the Iraqi population is justified by the objective of 'toppling Saddam,' which anticipates that – by some, as yet unknown, magic – all problems in and around Iraq would be solved once 'toppling Saddam' was accomplished. This type of scenario has become a feature of the 1990s, transposed from Iraq to Serbia, which is addressed in the next Chapter. Such individualization and personalization of problems and solutions fits extremely well with half-minute soundbites through which foreign policy is presented to the Western public. It bodes ill for the rule of law through allowing justification of the abuse of power by a noble cause rather than challenging it as the human rights rationale requires.

Before 1990, Iraq had been exempt from condemnations because of its oil wealth, despite its war against Iran or vast documentation about domestic abuses. Iraq's military invasion of Kuwait represented a threat to Kuwait's, and also to Saudi Arabia's oil wealth, and thus to the West. Iraq was punished by a military intervention which liberated Kuwait, and a comprehensive disarmament strategy has intended to prevent Iraq from militarily threatening its oil-rich neighbours or Israel. The sanctions prevent Iraq from exporting oil and importing anything except strictly and narrowly defined life-sustaining goods, wreaking havoc upon the population without harming or changing its government. The population has thus become a hostage in the geopolitical warfare fought between the governments of Iraq and the United States.

Condemnations of Iraq's human rights performance have been within the province of the Commission on Human Rights and thus subject to some democratic scrutiny, if of the imperfect inter-governmental type, while sanctions are exempt

---

[1] Myers, S.L. – U.S. will give military training to opponents of Saddam, *International Herald Tribune*, 29 October 1999; Don't trick or treat Saddam, *The Economist*, 6 November 1999; Hirst, D. – Is the US finally becoming serious about toppling Saddam?, *Guardian Weekly*, 11–17 November 1999.

from any legal scrutiny or democratic oversight. A great deal of disagreement amongst the five veto-wielding members of the Security Council has come to light, showing S-1 (the United States) to be intransigently punitive, S-3 (the United States, France and the United Kingdom) to be wavering, and the two non-Western members (Russia and China) the least punitive, although not for reasons associated with human rights. The operative United Nations rules have prevented any other UN body from dealing with Iraq as long as the Security Council is 'seized of the matter,' in the official jargon. Previous attempts to activate the Security Council to respond to human rights violations, including in Iraq, had failed. Similar attempts to constrain Security Council's sanctions against Iraq invoking human rights of the victimized population also failed.

The Security Council had used its enforcement powers sparingly during the first forty years of existence. In both cases (Rhodesia and South Africa, discussed in Chapter 2) enforcement stopped with sanctions. Security Council's enforcement powers include countering armed force with armed force, while sanctions have also replicated the means employed in warfare. Both people and their human rights have thus become collateral damage.

CREATING A SELF-GRANTED RIGHT TO PUNISH

Human rights violations (i.e. peacetime abuses) and wartime atrocities (breaches of humanitarian law) became intertwined in the early 1990s. The political vocabulary of the 1990s has merged wartime and peacetime abuses and abolished the difference between private and public ill-deeds. This effort to extend human rights protections into armed conflicts imposed upon human rights an impossible task: human rights law assumes the existence of a state which is both willing and able to guarantee human rights, and can then be made responsible for their protection. In contrast, humanitarian law acknowledges that this assumption does not apply in warfare and constrains its pursuit by prohibiting particular atrocities and holding individuals who have committed and ordered them personally responsible. In Iraq, the two have been blurred and the humanitarian logic has been misconstrued as a human rights rationale. The state has been personalized and its impersonation demonized, and then any means could be employed with the aim of destroying this one-person state.

Accordingly, Iraq has been the target of long and harsh sanctions, whose humanitarian consequences have been examined by endless humanitarian actors and UN agencies, which have sought funding to alleviate their worst manifestations. Supplies of humanitarian relief became equated with 'rights' to food or health, and charity mistaken for the recognition of such rights. The state could not be expected to recognize human rights because its unwillingness to do so has been confirmed in an endless stream of its condemnations, while its capacity to guarantee human rights has been diminished, if not eliminated, through sanctions. Iraq has been subjected to an intense pressure by the UN Commission on Human Rights to allow the stationing of monitors[2] so that additional documentation could be gathered in order to justify additional condemnations and sanctions.

Persistent condemnations of human rights violations in Iraq have all emphasized Iraq as the culprit, extending the same approach to sanctions. Because sanctions have originated from international rather than Iraqi decisions, the emphasis has been placed on Iraq's intransigence in refusing to meet the conditions for lifting sanctions. This line of argument has not obviated the fact that the population of Iraq has been caught in a crossfire, and the unavoidable question has been what to do. The proponents of *droit d'ingérence* (right to intervene) have posited their right to assist people,[3] demanding that foreign and international actors be granted access to victims so as to be able to help them. A corresponding duty, even an obligation to intervene, was derived from solidarity with people in dire need of assistance.[4] A merger between this right (or duty) to assist victimized people and the use of armed force characterized *Operation Provide Comfort* and set the precedent for the future. Its purpose was to deliver humanitarian aid but its objective was to halt abuses by the government in the Kurdish-populated north through detachment of that territory from Iraq's control.

OPERATION PROVIDE COMFORT

The US-led armed intervention in northern Iraq of April 1991 combined a multitude of unusual features. The Security Council authorized its humanitarian dimensions, without mentioning the military component. No consensus could be reached and 'a murky compromise was cobbled together.'[5] Humanitarian assistance was to be delivered to internally displaced Kurds, while the allied armed forces would ensure delivery of humanitarian relief to its recipients as well as their safety.

The idea of creating safe havens for displaced Kurds was publicly announced by Britain's prime minister of the time, John Major, on 8 April 1991.[6] His idea was that these safe havens should be sponsored by the United Nations, replacing the allied forces by a small UN armed contingent, and thus complying with Security

---

[2] In 1996, the Commission on Human Rights requested the UN Secretary-General to 'send a team of human rights monitors' to Iraq 'to facilitate improved information flows' (Resolution 1996/72 of 23 April 1996, adopted by a roll-call vote of 30-0-21) to subsequently call upon Iraq to 'allow the stationing of human rights monitors throughout Iraq.' (Resolution 1999/14 of 23 April 1999 adopted by a roll-call vote of 35-0-18).

[3] Bettati, M. and Kouchner, B. – *Le devoir d' ingérence*, Denoël, Paris, 1987.

[4] Federation Internationale des Ligues des Droits de l'Homme – Droits et devoir d'ingérence: vers une réforme de la Charte de l'ONU? *La Lettre Hebdomadaire de la FIDH*, Nos. 501/502, Septembre 1993, pp. 3–8.

[5] Friedman, T. – Nations at war with themselves: Today's threat to peace is the guy down the street, *The New York Times*, June 2, 1991.

[6] Cavalry to the rescue, *The Economist*, 20 April 1991, p. 41.

Council resolution 687 which demanded the termination of military presence of 'the Member States cooperating with Kuwait'.[7] Two days later, the airlift of relief supplies started and was secured by imposing an exclusion zone upon Iraq. *Operation Northern Watch* complemented this exclusion zone by policing an accompanying no-fly zone, which has continued thereafter.

A precedent was created in the agreement between Iraq and the United Nations by postulating an individual entitlement to humanitarian relief: 'all civilians in need, wherever they are located, are entitled to receive it.'[8] Such a right to receive assistance borrowed human rights language to apply it to humanitarian relief, implying that a right could exist without a remedy, that is, that an individual could have a right which can neither be realized nor enforced. This construct aimed to facilitate the return of displaced Kurds (mainly from Turkey) by ensuring their safety against Iraq's but not also Turkey's army.[9] Security Council resolution 688 of 5 April 1991 condemned the repression of the Iraqi civilian population, and demanded 'that Iraq allow immediate access by international humanitarian organizations to all those in need of assistance in all parts of Iraq,' adding a demand upon Iraq 'to ensure that the human and political rights of all Iraqi citizens are respected.'[10] It is possible to speculate that the Council intended by this formulation to exempt from protection non-citizens, such as the Kurdish population originating from Turkey, for example.

The Security Council's insistence on domestic repression to justify international military intervention ruptured the Council's previous inaction, as well as the inability of the Commission on Human Rights to act upon hundreds of documented violations of human rights in Iraq[11] Although the Security Council need not heed international law, there is no right of military intervention on the grounds of human rights violations. The International Court of Justice affirmed in 1986 that the use of armed force could not be the appropriate method to ensure respect of human rights.[12] Scholarly debates have proliferated but a legal challenge could not be mounted – decisions of the Security Council enforcing international peace and security are exempt from legal scrutiny.

Katherine Wilkens, a former staff director of the Sub-Committee on Middle East of the House Foreign Affairs Committee, has claimed that *Operation Provide*

[7] Security Council resolution 687 (1991) of 3 April 1991, Part B, para. 6.

[8] Memorandum of Understanding signed on 18 April 1991, *International Legal Materials,* vol. 30, 1991, at 861.

[9] Security Council resolution 678 (1990) of 29 November 1990.

[10] Security Council resolution 688 (1991) of 5 April 1991, reprinted in *International Legal Materials,* vol. 30, 1991, pp. 858–859.

[11] Tomaševski, K. – *Human Rights Violations and Development Aid: From Politics Towards Policy,* Human Rights in Development Series, Commonwealth Secretariat, London, May 1990, p. 4.

[12] International Court of Justice – *Military and Paramilitary Activities in and against Nicaragua, Nicaragua v. United States of America,* Merits, *1986 ICJ Report,* para. 268.

Comfort was 'less a way to ease the suffering of the Kurds than a US effort to assist Turkey', which benefitted additionally because all international aid was channeled through Turkey and air cover, that is, the policing of the exclusion zone, carried out from Turkish air bases.[13] Another view of *Operation Provide Comfort* came from Jim Hoagland:

> Few years ago, the United States was deeply involved in defending the liberated Kurdish enclave in northern Iraq as a springboard for overthrowing Saddam. But two incompetent CIA covert operations in Iraq canceled each other out and left a strategic vacuum. ... The debacle in Kurdistan rivals Somalia as the Clinton administration's greatest foreign policy defeat, and needs to be under wraps by the year 2000.[14]

Intra-Kurdish fighting resulted in an invitation to Baghdad to intervene militarily, which it did. To retaliate for Baghdad's military operation in the north of the country, the United States launched missile attacks against southern Iraq, extending the no-fly zone southwards. Nicholas Burns of the US State Department said in explanation that US strategic interests were in the south because Saudi Arabia and Kuwait lie to the south rather than north of Iraq.[15] Missile attacks and bombing then became a prelude, and subsequently a sideshow to NATO's bombing of the Former Yugoslavia in 1999.

S-1 AND SANCTIONS AGAINST IRAQ

In the early 1990s US unilateral sanctions plummeted (from a hundred in 1946–89 to one in 1990–93) while those imposed by the Security Council increased.[16] Oscar Schachter has commented that Council's determinations of who should be sanctioned and why were discretionary and final,[17] while Mohammed Bedjaouni has concluded that Security Council's sanctions were beyond legal challenge: 'everybody knows that whether or not this discretionary power is ever judicially challenged is entirely up to the Council itself.'[18] It was not up to the whole Council, however, with the United States wielding a veto over all proposals aimed at lifting sanctions against Iraq.

---

[13] Wilkens, K.A. – How we lost the Kurdish game, *Guardian Weekly*, 29 September 1996.

[14] Hoagland, J. – Clinton's troubles in northern Iraq aren't about to go away, *International Herald Tribune*, 22 May 1997.

[15] Mather, I. – Saddam gloats as missile raids backfire, *The European*, 12–18 September 1996.

[16] Elliott, K.A. – Sanctions: A look at the record, *The Bulletin of the Atomic Scientists*, vol. 49, No. 9, November 1993, p. 33.

[17] Schachter, O. – United Nations law, *American Journal of International Law*, vol. 88, 1994, No. 1, p. 12.

[18] Bedjaouni, M. – *The New World Order and the Security Council. Testing the Legality of Its Acts*, Martinus Nijhoff, 1994, p. 128.

Sanctions have been a response to the abuse of force by the government of Iraq (both outside and within its borders) and aimed to incapacitate it from doing so in the future. The inevitable price of harming Iraqi population while trying to incapacitate its ruler has been explained by a convoluted line of reasoning: the Iraqi ruler had been harming his own people and additional harm inflicted upon the people was justifiable because the ultimate aim of sanctions was to prevent future Iraq's rulers from harming the people. This logic has been faulted by many, accepted by a few, but the few have had the power to continue sanctions while the many had none to lift them. The victims of sanctions have been treated as an object of Western foreign policies rather than a subject of rights. The US secretary of state, Madeleine Albright, has elucidated what the decision-making process entails:

> In Iraq, 4,000 infants die every month as a direct result of Anglo-American-led sanctions. The US secretary of state, Madeleine Albright, was asked about this.'This is a very hard choice,' she replied,'but we think the price is worth it.'[19]

The decision-making process with regard to sanctions has undergone a decade of twists and turns. In 1992, the cited obstacle for lifting sanctions was the lack of Iraq's co-operation with the UN weapons inspectors, in 1994 it was Iraq's refusal to recognize Kuwait's sovereignty and its UN-determined borders, in 1996 sanctions were justified by intra-Kurdish warfare, in 1997–99 the cited obstacle has been again Iraq's refusal to co-operate with weapons inspectors. The initial set of conditions for lifting sanctions[20] was broadened to become open-ended. Obstacle have been extended to Iraq's 'sponsorship of assassinations'[21] and a great deal of human rights rhetoric has been added.[22]

The lack of public insight into decision-making within the Security Council was partially remedied by numerous newspaper reports about closed-door sessions. Public sessions are not particularly informative, coming on the heels of rounds of closed-door negotiations. Publicly reported disagreements within the Security Council have pitted China, France and Russia (reportedly in favour of lifting

---

[19] Pilger, J. – Moral sightseeing by the West, *Guardian Weekly*, 20 June 1999.

[20] The Security Council specified the conditions for lifting sanctions demanding that Iraq (1) rescind its actions purporting to annex Kuwait, (2) accept its liability for losses arising out of its invasion of Kuwait, (3) release all prisoners of war, and also all detained Kuwaiti and third country nationals, (4) return all Kuwaiti property, (5) cease 'hostile and provocative actions by its forces' against other countries, and (6) 'provide all information and assistance in identifying Iraqi mines, booby traps and other explosives as well as any chemical and biological weapons and material.' Security Council resolution 686 of 2 March 1991.

[21] Richards, C. – Clinton leads call to keep Iraq sanctions, *The Independent*, 4 August 1994.

[22] Guess who is still running Iraq, *The Economist*, 6 April 1991, p. 40; Iraq: The UN moves goalposts, *The Economist*, 25 December 1993–7 January 1994, p. 57–58; Iraq sanctions to stay in place, *Financial Times*, 19–20 March 1994.

sanctions) against the United Kingdom and the United States who were not. Periodic reviews by the Security Council created a great deal of interest for three different reasons:

- One reason has been the mounting evidence on the negative impact of sanctions on the population of Iraq and the related protests by professional and other non-governmental organizations, as well as concerns expressed by some United Nations human rights bodies; these seemed to have had little resonance in the Security Council debates.
- The second reason were media reports on diplomatic attempts to lift sanctions and speculation about the underlying reasons. A delegation of French business-men visited Iraq in 1994 to negotiate pre-contracts effective as soon as sanctions were lifted. France parted ways with US foreign policy by pulling out of Operation Provide Comfort to become in 1998 Iraq's main trading partner. Russia has needed repayment of large Iraq's debt for previous weapons pur-chases. China has concluded a production-sharing oil exploration agreement with Iraq and entered into a $500 million contract.[23]
- The third reason has been speculation that the real motive for sanctions – secur-ing the demise of Saddam Hussein – would not be accomplished by sanctions alone and the associated fears about the paths which Western foreign might adopt to secure this objective.

The ebb and flow of interest for developments in and around Iraq has relied on reports in the mass media. A decade is an immensely long period at the time when the attention span for crises in far-away countries is short and the crises are many. Endless disputes and scandals concerning UNSCOM's (United Nations Special Commission) efforts to cleanse Iraq off nuclear, chemical and biological weapons have raised much interest, less so the constant threat and occasional use of US/UK military force in Iraq. The creation of international law through states' practice has found a disturbing illustration: each subsequent bombing spree of missile attack provoked less public debate than the previous one, and their ever diminishing challenges have been reinforced by decreasing public exposure. The interest for decision-making within the Security Council has also diminished because actions

[23] Des Français á Bagdad, *Jeune Afrique*, No. 1747, 30 June–6 July 1994; Trueheart, C. – France ends Kurdish mission, *Guardian Weekly*, 5 January 1997; Naïm, M. – France draws a line in the sand over Iraq, *Le monde*, 5 September 1996, reprinted in *Guardian Weekly*, 15 September 1996; Walker, M and Tran, M. – US fears Saddam may get off hook, *Guardian Weekly*, 23 October 1994; Poole, T. – China in oil talks with Baghdad, *The Independent*, 12 November 1996; Burns, J. and Littlejohns, M. – London backs trade delegation visit to Iraq, *Financial Times*, 13 January 1995; Black, I. – Britons lose out in export battle for Iraq, *Guardian Weekly*, 12 February 1995; China: Oil deal set, *Far Eastern Economic Review*, 12 June 1997; Paris, G. – Traders beat a path to the door of UN-sanctioned Iraq, *Le Monde*, 18 November, reproduced in *Guardian Weekly*, 29 November 1998; Crossette, B. – France proposes end to oil ban on Iraq, *International Herald Tribune*, 14 January 1999; Iraq: Sanctions mess, *The Economist*, 4 December 1999.

against Iraq became identified with US foreign policy.[24] The US acknowledgment that it sought a change of regime in Iraq, evidenced in aid to Iraqi opposition[25] has exposed a self-granted US right to speak in the name of 'the international community' and hamper the work of the United Nations.[26] It has also diminished any incentives for the government Iraq to comply with conditions for lifting sanctions and thus facilitate its own overthrow.

This sequence of events has exposed the failure of condemnations, sanctions, and military interventions to produce a change of regime and left many question unanswered: Is it possible to change a government through international and foreign pressure alone? And if so, will a new government be better or worse than the previous one? Whether there is a new government or not, what will sanctions and bombing have done to the new generations of Iraqis and their vision of human rights?

PEOPLE AS COLLATERAL DAMAGE

Countering mountains of documents on Iraq's human rights violations generated to support continued sanctions, Iraq's strategy has been to publicise harmful effects of sanctions and assert that sanctions have been the main cause of violations.[27] Publicity for the harm inflicted through sanctions has been enhanced by opponents of sanctions in the West.

The contemporary demonization of Iraq could not wipe away the fact that Iraq had pursued a policy of providing education, health care and housing for all, and that food rationing has continued during the war and during sanctions. A veritable statistical war ensued with regard to the effects of sanctions, with a reported 380% increase in child mortality, for example.[28] UNICEF has estimated that an average

---

[24] A good illustration was the US decision to bomb Iraq of 16 December 1998, announced exactly at the time when the Security Council was in session, studying findings of weapons inspectors (UNSCOM and IAEA). That the US bombing had been announced when the reports were just being presented to the Security Council highlighted how irrelevant any assessment of the full Council was deemed to be.

[25] Gellman, B. – Clinton voices 2 policies on Iraq with big consequences (if he means it), *International Herald Tribune*, 17 November 1998; Iraq: Slippery Saddam, *The Economist*, 10 October 1998; Alkadiri, R. – Saddam's survival strategy, *The World Today*, January 1999, p. 7.

[26] Crossette, B. – UN chief rejects U.S. stance on Iraq, *International Herald Tribune*, 16 December 1998.

[27] Numerous notes verbales from the Permanent Mission of the Republic of Iraq to the United Nations Office described and quantified detrimental effects of sanctions. They included precise statistics, alluding to a complete immunity of Iraq's statistical services to all sanctions-related hardships or disruptions. A 1998 note verbale included, for example, statistics on the percentage of birthweights under 2.5 kg (it was 23.7% in January and 24.7% in December 1997) and the number of deaths in children under five attributed to the economic embargo (58,845 in 1997, out of which 5,405 in January and 4,793 in December).

[28] Human Rights Committee – Statement of the representative of Iraq before the Human Rights Committee during the consideration of Iraq's third periodic report under the International Covenant on Civil and Political Rights on 18 July 1991, U.N. Doc. CCPR/C/42/CRP.1/Add.17 of 25 July 1991, para. 14.

monthly salary in Baghdad had the purchasing power of $2 while the biggest health hazard has not actually been impoverishment but contaminated water.[29] The vicious circle of cause-and-effect has run into a series of obstacles: while humanitarian exceptions have accompanied sanctions, the repairs necessary to ensure the supply of safe water reached far beyond the usual food-and-medicine exceptions; sanctions had not been designed to last for a full decade and thus excluded the question whether new generations of Iraqis would grow up illiterate because schooling is not encompassed by humanitarian exemptions.

Although food and medicine have been exempted from sanctions, their import has been considerably slowed due to the needed approval of the Sanctions Committee. The prohibitions of many dual-use items (such as shoes or computer diskettes) could be understood, if not necessarily justified, but others raised eyebrows: medication containing nitrates (which are used for anesthetics) could not be imported so as to prevent its possible abuse for military purposes, while making any surgery extremely painful; the import of pencils for schoolchildren was banned because they contained lead, which could be extracted from pencils and used for some murky military purpose.[30]

Findings of the initial United Nations missions that went to Iraq to assess the state of humanitarian needs[31] led to an offer to Iraq to sell oil under UN supervision. Before sanctions, Iraq's imports of food and medicine were estimated at $2.5 billion and in 1991 they fell to $200 million.[32] The UN Secretary-General's proposal that Iraq be allowed to sell oil worth $2.5 billion had not been accepted by the Security Council and the figure was lowered to $1.6 billion. The oil-for-food arrangement was negotiated, after numerous disagreements and agreements, at the end of 1996.[33] Its apparent purpose was to ease the suffering of the Iraqi people, but Geoff Simons saw it differently:

> Drafted by American or US-proxy officials, 986 [the Security Council resolution authorizing oil-for-food arrangement] was aimed in part at feeding Iraqi oil money to Kuwait through the Compensation Fund to facilitate the payment of American contractors (not least the arms suppliers). Humanitarian pressure for the relief of Iraqi suffering was nicely exploited for the benefit of US companies.[34]

---

[29] UNICEF – Emergency Activities in Irak 1991–1995, Baghdad, January 1995.

[30] Rouleau, E. – Le peuple irakien, première victime de l'ordre américain, *Le monde diplomatique*, November 1994, p. 10–11; Waiting for the next Iraqi crisis, *The Economist*, 25 April 1998.

[31] Aga Khan, S. – The priority is getting food and medicine to Iraq, *International Herald Tribune*, 16 September 1991.

[32] Aid agencies say Iraq is on brink of famine, *Guardian Weekly*, 29 September 1991; Tuquoi, J.-P. – Iraqis still pay the price of Gulf war, *Guardian Weekly*, 11 September 1994.

[33] Baghdad, defying UN, exports oil, *International Herald Tribune*, 25 November 1991; Sanctions on Iraq, *The Economist*, 27 March 1993, p. 15.

[34] Simons, G. – *The Scourging of Iraq. Sanctions, Law and Natural Justice*, MacMillan Press, London, second edition, 1998, p. 233.

Iraq resumed exporting oil in December 1996 and increased food rations followed in April 1997.[35] Iraq has defined the impact of this arrangement as the imposition of an international trusteeship,[36] in a way anticipating the subsequent application of that term to Bosnia and Herzegovina and Kosovo. One-third of the proceeds from the sale of oil was earmarked for the compensation of Kuwaiti and other victims of the Gulf War, 10% for the expenses of the UN programme aimed at eliminating Iraq's weapons of mass destruction, and $150 million for the UN Inter-Agency Humanitarian Programme in the Northern Region.[37]

As often happens with such arrangements, the expected annual $600 million worth of food to be delivered to northern Iraq motived the local farmers not to grow food, expecting that it would be distributed free of charge.[38] International assistance for northern Iraq could not easily offset the triple embargo against the Kurdish population – as part of Iraq they were encompassed by sanctions against Iraq; as a rebellious part of Iraq, they were subjected to internal embargo by Baghdad; because aid was channeled through Turkey, deliveries were interrupted in retaliation for the assumed support of PKK.

Denis Halliday resigned in 1998 as the chief of the UN humanitarian mission in Iraq, having failed to do his job in impossible conditions – he could supervise the delivery of food aid but people were dying of contaminated water about which he could do nothing because repairing water and sewage plants was beyond the permitted humanitarian exemptions.[39]

Verbal duels about the suffering of the Iraqi population, and its consequences for the UN human rights policy, have taken suffering for granted. Madeleine Albright, then the US Ambassador to the United Nations, has pointed out that 'the tightest and most comprehensive sanctions ever imposed' would remain in place so as to 'prevent Saddam Hussein from using innocent civilians as bargaining chips'. To avoid any misunderstanding, she added: 'As a final protection, if the United States and the Security Council are not satisfied with Iraq's performance, the [oil-for-food arrangement] will not be renewed after its six-month trial period.'[40] The emphasis on Iraq's need to satisfy firstly the United States, and secondly the Security Council, has reflected the increasing lack of agreement in the Security Council and the ability of the United States to veto any decision.

---

[35] Hargreaves, D. – Oil prices tumble as Iraqi supplies return to market, *Financial Times*, 12 December 1996; Iraq and the UN: Oil but no food, *The Economist*, 15 February 1997; Iraqis queue for extra food rations, *Financial Times*, 3 April 1997.

[36] Commission on Human Rights – Note verbale dated 29 January 1996 from the Permanent Mission of Iraq to the United Nations Office at Geneva addressed to the Centre for Human Rights, U.N. Doc. E/CN.4/1996/119 of 19 March 1996, para. 20.

[37] Security Council resolution 986 (1995) of 14 April 1995.

[38] Cockburn, P. – Kurds fear starvation as aid is delayed, *The Independent*, 21 September 1996.

[39] Cockburn, P. – Gunning for the Iraqi people, *The Independent*, 7 August 1998.

[40] Albright, M.K. – A good deal for Iraqis and for the rest of us, *International Herald Tribune*, 24 May 1966.

DENIED RESPONSIBILITIES

The facts relating to detrimental effects of sanctions against Iraq have been much disputed while a tricky question – who is responsible for these effects? – has been avoided as much as possible. Advocates of sanctions have argued their case as a legitimate international response to repression. Opponents have argued that sanctions resulted in double victimization of the Iraqi population. Jason Burke has thus summed up the debate:

> President Saddam's enemies say he cynically spends less than he could on medicine because dying children are good propaganda material. His allies maintain that the money released by the UN is criminally insufficient. Either way, the effect is the same.[41]

The UN General Assembly has placed full responsibility for the sanctions and their effects on the government of Iraq by deploring Iraq's 'failure to provide the Iraqi population with access to adequate food and health care' through its refusal to implement pertinent Security Council resolutions.[42] In 1991, the Sub-Commission on Prevention of Discrimination and Protection of Minorities acknowledged the suffering of Iraq's population and appealed to all governments and international organizations to 'take urgent measures to prevent the death of thousands of innocent persons, in particular of children, and to ensure that their needs for food and health care were met.' One year earlier the Sub-Commission called upon 'all those participating in sanctions against Iraq not to prevent the delivery of necessary food and medicine.'[43] The Sub-Commission avoided intra-UN conflicts by referring to a 'humanitarian situation' in Iraq rather than human rights.

The former UN Special Rapporteur on Iraq has elaborated a two-pronged notion of human rights with his finding that 'the absence of respect for the rights pertaining to democratic governance is at the root of all the major violations of human rights in Iraq,' but the absence of democratic governance has not impeded, in theory at least, 'the Government's responsibility to take all necessary action to ensure the full realization of the rights to food and health care for all.'[44] The acceptance of an assertion that human rights to food or health could be dissociated from political rights, or reduced to receipts of Iraq's or UN's charity, has marked a

---

[41] Burke, J. – Iraq sanctions fuel the politics of hate, *Guardian Weekly*, 23–29 December 1999.

[42] United Nations – Situation of human rights in Iraq, General Assembly resolution 48/144 of 20 December 1993, preamble and para. 3.

[43] Sub-Commission on Prevention of Discrimination and Protection of Minorities – Appeal concerning the civilian population in Iraq, decision 1991/108 of 29 August 1991, and decision 1990/109 of 24 August 1990.

[44] Commission on Human Rights – Report on the situation of human rights in Iraq, submitted by the Special Rapporteur, Mr. Max van der Stoel, U.N. Doc. E/CN.4/1998/67 of 10 March 1998, para. 7.

departure from the UN policy whereby human rights are indivisible and necessitate individual freedom to be recognized as part of any and every human right. It has also marked a return to cold-war politics, when such a two-pronged approach prevailed, and 'rights' to food or health had been equalized with governmental handouts in denial of individual freedoms and political rights.

Such changes in the contents subsumed under the term 'human rights' are explored in the next Chapter which discusses Eastern Europe. There is a great deal of evidence of the previous Eastern European human rights concepts throughout international human rights law because most treaties were negotiated during the Cold War and the input of the Soviet Union and its allies was considerable. These treaties have not been altered thus creating an abyss between law and policy.

Chapter 11

Fortress Europe and Eastern Europe

Geographical proximity has greatly influenced EUrope's relations with its neighbourhood. If human rights criteria have been none too easy to apply with regard to faraway countries, those close by have created huge, often insurmountable problems. EUrope could easily impose sanctions against Burma or Haiti while a neighbouring country such as Algeria or the Former Yugoslavia has raised fears about a flood of refugees above human rights considerations. When distance is immense, commercial relations minute, and migration non-existent, abstract human rights principles are protected from multiple, often conflicting, foreign policy concerns. Domestic security routinely overrides commitment to the human rights of others. In the Balkans, the strategy of containment has escalated from condemnations and sanctions to bombing and establishment of international protectorates, and has been reflected in what Alain Gresh has called 'the brutalization of public opinion in Western countries.'[1] Protective walls keeping barbarians outside *Fortress Europe*[2] protected those inside from looking out through conceptual blinkers which, much as during the Cold War, lowered the constraints in Western foreign policies with regard to methods that can be employed to protect domestic security. This has allowed asking 'When do we have a legal right to bomb?'[3] and public acceptance of a positive answer.

Western foreign policies have expanded upon a self-granted right to judge and punish, which has been routinely justified by one definition of human rights or another. For an entity such as EUrope, which has laid down a host of human rights policies for its relations with *the other Europe*, forging a foreign policy in the absence of statehood has been a Herculean task. EUrope's rhetorical commitment to human rights in its relations with third countries preceded its normative commitment to a common foreign policy. Such a foreign policy was optimistically announced in the 1992 Maastricht Treaty, which declared: 'foreign policy is hereby established'. It has not yet been created, however. EUrope's pattern of condemnations and sanctions for human rights violations then cannot be assumed to have been guided by a foreign policy and it has thus been even more erratic than is the case for individual Western countries.

EUrope's responses to human rights violations can be examined through a comparison between two tracks: what EUrope said or did with regard to violators as

---

[1] Gresh, A. – The rules of war, *Le monde diplomatique*, English Edition, September 1999.

[2] Tomaševski, K. – New Europe, old divisions, in Gomien, D. (ed.) – *Broadening the Frontiers of Human Rights. Essays in Honour of Asbjørn Eide*, Scandinavian University Press, Oslo, 1993, p. 285.

[3] Wedgwood, D. – When do we have a legal right to bomb?, *Financial Times*, 10–11 April 1999.

determined by the United Nations, and which governments EUrope has identified as violators by its own criteria. These are not the extreme examples of the Kosovo or Chechnya type, but they were stepping stones on the way towards divergent international processes for identifying violations and violators. Because international law is formed through states' practice, particular conduct gains acceptance gradually, through repetition and justification, assertion of a right to pursue a particular path and progression along this path. The public education dimensions of this process create what Alain Gresh has termed 'brutalization of public opinion' through the gradual public acceptance of foreign policy decisions as facts. EUrope's practice of designing and enforcing political conditionality[4] has developed in the first post-cold-war decade, 1989–1999, through a series of *ad hoc* responses to emerging and evolving crises in its neighbourhood and the world at large. It is thus worthwhile to illustrate its evolution by chronologizing some of these *ad hoc* responses, which tend to be forgotten as soon as the media attention shifts to another country or controversy.

This Chapter limits the analysis to those countries that were placed on the UN agenda as violators or targeted by EUrope's sanctions for which human rights violations were cited amongst reasons. The two parallel tracks have only sometimes overlapped, showing that EUrope neither followed nor led the United Nations.

An important reason for this double track is the complexity of Europe's ever-changing definition of 'human rights'. Its rapid evolution followed the end of the Cold War, prioritizing democracy and subsuming human rights under democracy. Armed conflicts prompted a merger between human rights and humanitarian law and attempts to extend human rights requirements from peace-time into warfare. Since ethnicity was determined to be a cause (often *the* cause) of armed conflicts, minority rights emerged as a key demand. Definitions of minority rights mushroomed, leading the definition towards collective at the expense of individual rights. On the one hand, EUrope's recognition of new states bestowed legitimacy upon statehood based on ethnic homogeneity. On the other hand, ethnic cleansing was defined as a crime and minority rights inserted into the human rights conditions which Eastern European states were required to comply with. Legitimizing ethnic homogeneity as the end while condemning the means towards this end created endless controversies. These controversies translated into the behaviour of EUrope as an international actor, as cases discussed below illustrate.

EUrope's human rights policy developed through the grafting of human rights upon a long list of other items, to some of its future components (notably aid) but not others (migration or crime prevention). Denial of refuge to people fleeing from repression could then be dissociated from human rights: repression in their country of origin could be condemned as a human rights violation, even reinforced by eco-

---

[4] Political conditionality is defined as a complex and ever changing set of criteria relating to democracy, quality of governance, or human and minority rights, which has been included in foreign policy in the form of requirements which 'the third countries' have to comply with, while such compliance is subjected to EUrope's political judgments.

nomic sanctions, but access to EUrope for victims of these violations could be impeded by defining them as illegal immigrants. This line of reasoning was possible because human rights applied to EUrope's relations with third countries, legitimizing condemnations and sanctions, but did not bestow rights upon the citizens of 'the third countries' because legally recognized rights have been confined to EUrope's citizens.

Eastern Europe had consisted of eight countries during the Cold War, whereupon their number increased to thirty; it is possible that their number will grow further. Uncertain status of newly created but un-recognized states (such as Chechnya, Abkhazia, or Kosovo) added to uncertainties resulting from the breakup of the former eight countries. Within what had been Yugoslavia two successor states, Yugoslavia/Serbia and Montenegro and FYROM/Macedonia, have disputed names, while the emergence and *de facto* recognition of 'entities' within Bosnia and Herzegovina further complicated the identification of the main actors to be held responsible for human rights violations. The assumption of international law that a state necessitates a defined territory and effective control over that territory was turned on its head with the recognition of Bosnia and Herzegovina. Assuming that such control would somehow derive from its recognition as a state blurred the boundary between normative and empirical realms. The non-recognition of Chechnya between its military victory in 1996 and the second Russia's military intervention in 1999 explicitly assumed Russia's control over the respective territory and population and resulted in muted condemnations and minute sanctions against Russia for its second war against Checnya. The normative and empirical worlds became separated by an abyss in the really existing world and merged in the virtual world of foreign policy. It was then possible for EUrope to hail Bosnia and Herzegovina's commitment to the highest internationally recognized level of human rights protection, and impossible to say anything about human rights in Kosovo at the turn of the millennium, not knowing who the addressee should be. With such a gap between appearance and reality, no human rights policy could thrive.

EUrope has not been a passive observer of such apparent and real changes, on the contrary. Its articulated a policy for the recognition of new states and in practice recognized some but not others. It also developed a practice of condemning human rights violations, but, again, it was applied to some violations but not others. Furthermore, it threatened and applied economic sanctions against some violators, shielding others. A web of trade-and-aid agreements gave EUrope the opportunity to complement its political support for some countries or causes with financial benefits, while penalizing others through denials of such benefits.

THE SECOND AND THE THIRD COUNTRIES

EUrope's relations with 'the third countries' became part of the official vocabulary, never mentioning any 'second' countries. This has replicated the global geopolitical hierarchy where the widespread usage of the Third World omits a second while accepting the self-identification of the first world. As this un-named second world denoted Eastern Europe when the three worlds were being defined, it seems fitting to use the adjective 'second' for those Eastern European countries that are queuing for membership in the European Union, and denote as 'the third' those that have been defined as ineligible.

Intra-European relations can thus be structured in three concentric circles.[5] The European Union is the smallest and the most desirable, commonly identified as Europe in the narrowest sense of the word. Its planned enlargement eastwards had been confined a narrow circle of Central European countries.[6] The 41 members of the Council of Europe have stretched European borders eastwards to Russia and Georgia and form the second circle. The membership of the OSCE (Organization for Security and Cooperation in Europe) had included from the very outset the United States and Canada to extend well into Asia after the end of the Cold War.

This all-encompassing membership of the OSCE was designed for the broadest possible geographical and geopolitical definition of Europe. Except specifically excluded undesirable countries, membership is widely open. Admission to the second circle, the Council of Europe, was interpreted in the media as 'the first step to membership of the European Community,'[7] a step towards the innermost circle. The first Eastern European members created little controversy. This changed with the admission of the Baltic states because of contentious citizenship laws and minority rights, as discussed below. Hungary and Poland had been admitted to membership in 1990, as well as Czechoslovakia (as it was at the time). Bulgaria, Estonia, Latvia and Lithuania applied in 1991; Bulgaria was admitted in 1992, while inadequate human rights safeguards precluded immediate membership of the three Baltic states.[8] The Council of Europe decided to exclude from membership five Asian countries (Kazakhstan, Kyrgyzstan, Tadzhikistan, Turkmenistan and Uzbekistan), leaving open possible membership for Caucasian countries (Armenia, Azerbaidjan, and Georgia, out of which only Georgia was admitted in 1999).

These three different European organizations developed three different approaches to human rights. EUrope's leverage for the enforcement of its definition of human rights was based on two pillars: the first was eagerness of Eastern European countries to be considered for membership, and the second was their status as aid recipients. The Council of Europe had developed a host of programmes and activities to facilitate the adjustment of its new Eastern European

---

[5] This has been discussed in Tomaševski, K. – *Between Sanctions and Elections. Aid Donors and their Human Rights Performance*, Pinter/Cassell, London, 1997, pp. 41–61.

[6] The accession process was formally launched by the first European Conference in March 1998. Negotiations started with Hungary, Poland, Estonia, the Czech Republic, and Slovenia (and also with Cyprus), while five other Eastern European applicants (Bulgaria, Latvia, Lithuania, Romania and Slovakia) were called 'the second group.'

[7] Marshall, A. – Romania gets foot in door of the EC, *The Independent,* 29 September 1993.

[8] Pekkanen, R. and Danelius, H. – Human rights in the Republic of Estonia, Doc. AS/Ad Hoc-Bur-EE (43) 2 of 17 December 1991; De Meyer, J. and Rozakis, C. – Human rights in the Republic of Latvia, Doc. AS/Ad Hoc-Bur-EE (43) 4 of 20 January 1992.

membership to the international enforcement of civil and political rights. The OSCE's definition of human rights has been extra-legal from the very outset and its work spans a broad range of electoral and conflict-resolution issues.

In 1989–92 the first five Eastern European countries (Poland, Hungary, Czecho-slovakia, Romania, and Bulgaria) signed association agreements with Europe (the European Community at the time). The aim was noble: 'consolidation of reforms should take precedence over short-term commercial advantage for the existing member states.'[9] Eastern European countries had been promised access to Europe's market(s) as well as technical and financial assistance. Human rights became part of these 'Europe agreements' with second and third countries through a variety of human rights clauses. The first agreements with Poland and Hungary had been signed in 1991, just before human rights clauses entered EUrope's practice. This practice varied until a standard clause was developed in 1995 with the purpose of giving EUrope a unilateral right of suspension as a response to human rights vio-lations. An immensely complicated variety of formulations resulted from this nominally standard clause, and it can be summarized in three basic types:

–   The most far-reaching model defines human rights and respect for democratic principles as an essential provision of the treaty and gives EUrope the right to suspend it with immediate effect if this essential provision is breached. That clause was included in the agreement with Albania.
–   A somewhat milder version of the suspension clause anticipates seeking other solutions beforehand and was included in agreements with the Baltic countries, Bulgaria, Romania, the Czech Republic, Slovakia and Slovenia.
–   A yet milder version of the human rights clause envisages consultations before suspension and forms part of EUrope's agreement with Russia, accompanied with interpretative declarations concerning the meaning of the human rights clause and the anticipated procedure in the case of a dispute.[10]

It is unlikely that technicalities of legal draftsmanship will determine EUrope's resort to economic sanctions in the form of suspending cooperation, nor is it likely that a targeted country will take EUrope to court for a breach of its legal obligations if the suspension seems to be at odds with the treaty provisions. This Chapter describes EUrope's practice thus far. This practice makes law appear as the least relevant amongst those factors that shaped EUrope's responses to human rights crises in Eastern European countries.

---

[9]   Pinder, J. – *The European Community and Eastern Europe*, The Royal Institute of International Affairs, Pinter Publishers, London, 1992, p. 60.

[10]   This is described in Tomaševski, K. – Human rights conditionality, Steytler, N. (Ed.) – *Democracy, Human Rights and Economic Development in Southern Africa*, Lex Patria Publishers, Johannesburg, 1997, in pp. 327–346.

The nucleus of Europe's future policy towards second and third countries was formed in 1989–91[11] in conditions of the rapid transformation of the political landscape in Eastern Europe through elections and fragmentation. EUrope was an engine for change, having designed the model for the new (or 'transitioning') countries to follow in order to move geopolitically westwards.

EUrope's leverage was based, *inter alia*, on initial Western promises of aid amounting to tens of billions. In 1991, *The Economist* reported that $31 billion had been promised to Bulgaria, Czechoslovakia, Hungary, Poland and Romania; the *Financial Times* cited a promised $45 billion in aid and investment to Eastern Europe.[12] Aid to Eastern Europe was co-ordinated by the European Community (as it was then) under the name of 'assistance for economic restructuring' or for 'political and economic reform'.[13] The addition of 'political reform' created a whole new area of aid, alternatively termed democracy, human rights, good governance, rule of law or civil society. The EC's PHARE programme (the abbreviation stands for *Pologne/Hongrie, Assistance à la reconstruction économique*) started in January 1990, and was broadened to other countries as they complied with the political and economic conditionality. The former encompassed the rule of law, human rights, multi-party system, free elections, with the addition of suppression of organized crime or emigration westwards, or environmental protection, especially safeguards against possible nuclear contamination, or else suppression of corruption. The latter has been commonly defined as transition to the market economy. The first recipient of EUrope's aid was Poland in 1989, joined in 1990 by Romania, and in 1991 by Albania and Bulgaria. By 1992 PHARE grew to $1 billion and the largest items were humanitarian relief and technical assistance.[14] According to subsequent critics, the former represented a convenient means for disposing of EUrope's agricultural surplus through food aid, the latter has been an excellent market for the army of Western consultants.

The volume and composition of EUrope's aid is presented in Table 11.1. Eastern European countries were divided into three categories. The CEES (Central and Eastern European States) encompassed the closest, the least poor and those aspiring to membership in the European Union. The second category was NIS (New Independent States of the former Soviet Union), while the two poorest countries – Albania and Yugoslavia – qualified for official development assistance and formed a category of their own. The figures in Table 11.1 reflect EUrope's preference for

---

[11] This early period (1989–93) is described in Tomaševski, K. – Human rights in Eastern Europe, in Baehr, P. et al. (eds.) – *Human Rights in Developing Countries Yearbook 1994*, Kluwer Law and Taxation Publishers/Nordic Human Rights Publications, 1994, pp. 67–112.

[12] The IMF and the World Bank survey, *The Economist*, 12 October 1991; Robinson, A. and Wolf, M. – Europe's reluctant empire-builders, *Financial Times*, 2 December 1991.

[13] Commission of the European Communities – XXVth General report on the Activities of the European Communities 1991, Luxembourg, 1992, pp. 249 et seq.

[14] Commission of the European Communities – *XXVIth General Report on the Activities of the European Communities 1992*, Office for Official Publications of the European Communities, Luxembourg, 1993, p. 257.

Table 11.1: EUrope's aid to Eastern Europe in 1989–95
(in million US$)

	1989	1990	1991	1992	1993	1994	1995
DEVELOPING COUNTRIES							
Albania	10.4	11.1	324.2	389.7	265.6	164.7	181.0
[Yugoslavia]	43.0	46.7	158.8	1475.1	2579.1	1717.9	1637.9
NIS	–	–	877.9	438.6	624.2	1024.6	727.6
Belarus	–	–	187.0	273.1	185.9	119.0	222.6
Moldova	–	–	–	9.7	28.5	54.1	66.5
Russia	–	254.0	563.5	1935.0	2419.8	1843.9	1569.7
Ukraine	–	289.0	368.3	557.6	327.9	289.8	318.4
CEESs	–	79.7	438.1	299.7	479.7	753.4	458.8
Bulgaria	–	15.3	316.1	147.7	114.8	158.3	110.9
Czech Republic	–	3.3	230.6	130.4	100.2	143.1	146.8
Estonia	–	–	15.4	104.4	42.4	43.4	55.4
Hungary	–	67.3	626.0	222.9	165.9	200.5	–251.1
Latvia	–	–	3.4	84.0	33.4	51.5	61.1
Lithuania	–	–	4.0	93.8	62.2	71.2	176.7
Poland	–	1322.1	2508.3	1438.5	1031.2	1801.4	3789.0
Romania	–	243.1	321.1	258.0	167.6	144.6	271.5
Slovak Republic	–	1.7	114.5	63.8	50.6	78.5	96.3

Source: OECD – *Geographical Distribution of Financial Flows to Aid Recipients 1991–1995*, Paris, 1996.

Poland reflected in the high volume of aid. A comparison with Russia is illustrative: aid flows to Russia have been less than half of those to Poland, while a comparison between the size of the two countries points to aid to Poland being manifold larger than aid to Russia. The increase of aid, mostly humanitarian, to the Former Yugoslavia is also evident from the figures. The Slovak Republic, which is discussed below, was evidently the least favoured.

EUrope's Human Rights Criteria

Negotiations for the admission of new applicants has provided EUrope with an opportunity to articulate and apply human rights criteria. The initial circle of applicants bordering EUrope developed by the turn of the millennium into a declared ambition to almost double EUrope from 15 states in 1999 to 28[15] at some undefined point in the future.

---

[15] The initial circle of candidates for admission had been limited to three (Poland, the Czech Republic and Hungary), replicating the sequence at the end of the Cold War. Before the official listing had been made, Slovenia and Estonia were added, bringing the list to five. The final EU summit before the turn of the millennium broadened the list to include Latvia and Lithuania, Slovakia, Romania and Bulgaria. (Cyprus was part of every list, Malta had been part of some to disappear and re-emerge, and Turkey was added at the very end of 1999.)

The human rights criteria developed for applicants and potential applicants have varied a great deal, as is discussed below. The relatively small volume of aid would not have furnished a significant leverage (after initial hopes for another Marshall Plan turned into frustration) had it not been for the objective of many Eastern European countries to geopolitically move westwards, into EUrope. Those who actually wanted to move in the opposite direction, eastwards, were penalized. One can speculate as to whether EUrope's condemnatory and punitive policy towards Slovakia (during the Meciar government) or Belarus (throughout the Lukashenka government), ostensibly because of human rights violations, was motivated by anger at their leaning eastwards rather than westwards.

Human rights in Slovakia and Belarus created a great deal of attention within EUrope compared to paucity of attention within the United Nations. Moreover, EUrope's objections concerning both countries related primarily to democracy rather than human rights. The human rights performance of these two countries did not reach a level that would trigger a UN condemnation but EUrope developed and applied its own criteria.

Belarus

In 1997, the Human Rights Committee identified many faults in the human rights performance of Belarus, singling out in particular 'the persistence of political attitudes that are intolerant of dissent and criticism.'[16] The Committee's excursion into such political judgments was illustrative of the politicization and personalization of human rights assessments that penetrated even such nominally legal bodies. The president of Belarus, Alexandr Lukashenka, was singled out as the culprit, un-named but recognizable from the Committee's critique.

He had been elected to the presidency in 1994 on a political platform of reverting to an association with Russia, rather than the West, which was combined with his opposition to the expected transition of Belarus to the free market. The majority who voted for him had obviously endorsed this platform. A shift away from a parliamentary to a presidential system was legalized through a referendum in 1996, and a treaty with Russia signed in 1997. The 1996 referendum was criticised in the West and aid to Belarus diminished. EUrope conditioned resumption of aid by return to democracy, the Parliamentary Assembly of the Council of Europe suspended the guest status that had previously been given to Belarus.[17] Different from all its neighbours, Belarus was not admitted to membership.

The 1996 referendum was a means to legitimize vast presidential powers. The referendum was faulted by observers from the European Parliament, and Belarus

[16] Human Rights Committee – Concluding observations: Belarus, U.N. Doc. CCPR/C/79/Add. 86 of 19 November 1997, para. 7.
[17] Krushelnycky, A. – Belarus flirts with iron fist, *The European*, 21–27 November 1996; Lohman, D. – Can international pressure restore democracy in Belarus?, *Helsinki Monitor 1997*, No. 3, p. 74.

found below 'internationally accepted democratic and constitutional principles.'[18] The formulation used – internationally accepted democratic and constitutional principles – alluded to a non-existent body of criteria. The International Helsinki Federation for Human Rights took this one step further: 'a referendum, which failed to obtain international approval and can neither be considered legal nor legitimate.'[19] EUrope's aid, which had formed part of the Tacis programme and amounted to an estimated at 12 million ecu, was suspended. The EUrope-Belarus agreement had been signed in March 1995 but was not ratified. Loans to Belarus had already been suspended because of its lack of compliance with macro-economic conditions (or conditionalities, as they are usually called). Besides EUrope, the IMF, the World Bank, and EBRD also suspended their loans, citing non-performance in macro-economic benchmarks and indicators.[20] The United States followed suit and suspended a $40 million aid programme. The reasons were many, and one of them could have been the expulsion of a US diplomat (but a citizen of Belarus) who had been arrested at an anti-government demonstration.[21]

The UN Sub-Commission adopted a resolution on Belarus in 1998, benefitting from the procedural rule whereby it had been pre-empted from adopting resolutions on countries that its parent body was dealing with, and suggesting to the Commission to address human rights violations in Belarus. The Commission silently declined that suggestion. The Sub-Commission did not resort to the language of condemnations or violations, but denounced the harassment of political leaders, journalists and human rights activists as well as 'the concentration of the legislative power in the executive and a weak judiciary.'[22] There has been no follow-up to this resolution.

Slovakia

EUrope's relations with Slovakia were highly personalized and the country was seen through the personality of its leader, Vladimir Meciar. He had led the country throughout its almost entire existence as an independent country[23] and exited from

---

[18] Reeves, P. – All power to Europe's dictator, *The Independent*, 26 November 1996; Turner, M. – EU funding under threat as relations with Belarus worsen, *European Voice*, 9–15 January 1997.

[19] Belarus: Absence of the rule of law, *Human Rights and Civil Society Newsletter*, vol. 3, No. 2, 1997, p. 3.

[20] Regional focus: Belarus, *Business Central Europe*, October 1996.

[21] Reeves, P. – Belarus risks US revenge by expelling 'spy', *The Independent*, 25 March 1997; Belarus: Games without frontiers, *The Economist*, 29 March 1997.

[22] Sub-Commission on Prevention of Discrimination and Protection of Minorities – Situation of human rights in Belarus, resolution 1998/1 of 19 August 1998, para. 1; the voting record was 17-4-3.

[23] The government, led by Vladimir Meciar, came to power in 1992 on a nationalist platform, which it retained after the 'velvet divorce' from the Czech Republic in 1993. No less than six changes of government took place in 1989–95, but Vladimir Meciar always came back to power until his party lost the elections in 1998.

the government following his defeat in the 1998 elections.[24] After his demise, the image of the Slovak Republic immediately changed and hastened its acceptance as an applicant for membership of the European Union in December 1999.

Helmut Kohl, then Germany's Chancellor, reportedly informed the Meciar government that it would not be admitted to EUrope because of 'anti-democratic tendencies.'[25] Slovakia was warned in October 1995 by the European Parliament that Western aid would be suspended because of disrespect for democracy and human rights.[26] In April 1996, additional concerns were voiced after a legislative change threatened five years in prison for an offence of damaging 'the reputation and the interests of Slovakia abroad through wilful dissemination of wrong information.'[27] In October 1996, the litany of EUrope's complaints against Slovakia broadened to a law on universities and to the status of minority languages, but also to the postponement of privatization of the four largest banks. The prevalent critique of Slovakia was typically summed up in one sentence: 'the country doesn't have a hope of being accepted as long as Mr. Meciar remains in power.'[28] Karel Bartak has described the conflict as *le meciarisme* against *dogmes bruxellois*. It went much beyond human rights into the very model for the second and/or third countries. Bartak has listed EUrope's objections, such as to Slovakia's free-trade agreement with Russia or its threat of counter-protectionist measures against (heavily subsidized) imports from the European Union.[29]

One could easily write a whole book discussing reasons for Europe's punitiveness against Belarus or Slovakia (while not Bulgaria or Moldova, for example), and another bemoaning the application of undefined criteria as to who or what is un-democratic. Indeed, the ever-changing Europe's definition of human rights in its emerging foreign policy (perhaps policies is a better word) highlights this whole Chapter. The effects of such varied and varying definitions were compounded through challenges to EUrope as rapidly evolving events in the Balkans or Causacus forced instant decisions. This test has more often than not failed to exhibit anything resembling a foreign or human rights policy, as the mini case studies below illustrate.

THE UNITED NATIONS AND EUROPE COMPARED

István Bibó, a well-known Hungarian historian, has many times lamented the misery of Eastern European small states created at the beginning of the 20th

---

[24] Anderson, R. & Done, K.. – Slovaks must still persuade world to welcome them back, *Financial Times*, 29 September 1998.

[25] Zifcak, S. – Democracy and rule of law in Slovakia, *ICJ Review*, No. 53, 1994, p. 91.

[26] Bridge, A. – West voices fears for Slovak democracy, *The Independent*, 26 October 1995; Slovakia: Madness, *The Economist*, 2 December 1995, p. 30–31.

[27] Klau, T. – Slovakian defamation law rings EU alarm bells, *European Voice*, 3–10 April 1996.

[28] Lyons, R. – Something rotten, *Business Central Europe*, October 1996.

[29] Bartak, K. – La Slovaquie, 'mauvais élève' de l'Occident, *Le Monde diplomatique*, May 1997.

century. Something similar could well apply to the beginning of the 21st century. Misery is not on the human rights agenda, however. The post-cold-war re-definition of human rights excluded social and economic rights which had been championed by the losers of the Cold War. The Western definition rapidly shifted to democracy, then to minority rights, then to good governance, and became amenable to changing political judgments. As mentioned above, some countries were singled out as human rights violators by EUrope but not the United Nations, others were dealt with by the Security Council because of armed conflicts (such as Armania/ Azerbaijan or Tajikistan) but were not placed on the UN violations-agenda and EUrope remained silent, while conflicts in the Former Yugoslavia attained an unprecedented level of EUrope's attention.

Table 11.2 gives an overview of the Eastern European countries the UN violations-agenda. Few – only five – were determined as violators by the UN Commission on Human Rights. Eleven more were discussed under the confidential 1503 procedure, but the substance of complaints is not known. EUrope's criteria in determining violators were different. Sometimes they were higher than those applied by the UN because neither Belarus nor Slovakia figured on the UN agenda while singled out by EUrope as violators. In the case of Georgia, EUrope's criteria were lower since Georgia was determined by the United Nations but not by Europe to have been a violator. What were then EUrope's criteria for identifying human rights violations and responding to them? Answers are sought in this Chapter,

Table 11.2: Eastern Europe on the UN violations-agenda, 1989–98

Country	Commission	Sub-Commission	1503 procedure
Albania	1988–91, 1993–94	1985–88, 1994	1984–88, 1995
Armenia	–	–	1994–95
Azerbaijan	–	–	1994–95
Belarus	–	1998	–
Czech Republic	–	–	1997
Estonia	–	–	1994, 1997
Georgia	1994	–	–
Kyrgyzstan	–	–	1997–98
Latvia	–	–	1995, 1997
Lithuania	–	–	1997
Moldova	–	–	1995
Romania	1989–91, 1993	(1989)	–
Russia/Chechnya	(1995–96)	(1996)	–
Slovenia	–	–	1995, 1996
Uzbekistan	–	–	1996–97
[Former Yugoslavia]	1992–99	1992–96	–

Note: Resolutions relating to Bosnia and Herzegovina, Croatia, Serbia and Montenegro, and Kosovo are not listed separately but encompassed under 'Former Yugoslavia'.

which discusses pertinent cases following the parallel human rights agendas of the United Nations and the European Union.

The sequence followed in this Chapter is chronological. As Table 11.2 shows, Albania and Romania were the first targets of UN condemnations as the Cold War was ending. They were followed by a multitude of problems associated with pre-disintegration Soviet Union, in which the fate of the Baltic countries had figured prominently. The initial issue was denial of their right to re-gain statehood, sub-sumed on the UN agenda under the effort to facilitate the withdrawal of Soviet army. A reversal placed the Baltic countries on the human rights agenda with regard to the protection of 'Russian-speakers' as non-citizens and/or a minority. In 1992, Yugoslavia was placed on the human rights agenda to remain there there-after; condemnations were numerous and accompanied by sanctions and EUrope led in imposing and enforcing them.

Numerous armed conflicts took place geographically further from EUrope, in Caucasian countries and further east, around the Caspian Sea. Georgia was the only country that was identified by the UN Commission on Human Rights as a violator, as Table 11.2 shows. Armenia and Azerbaijan were placed on UN's agenda, the reason was warfare in Nagorno-Karabakh, but no formal condemnation ensued and the issue moved to the Security Council.

Russia followed China in having become a veto-wielding member of the Security Council that was almost condemned for human rights violations during its first war in Chechnya. The face-saving procedural device of a chairman's state-ment avoided a formal condemnation; the threatened economic sanctions were also a face-saving rather than enforcement measure, as is discussed below. The pre-cedent established by the first Chechnya war allowed its resumption in 1999 in an extreme rule-or-ruin form, with an even more muted Western response than in 1994–96.

Albania

The initial enthusiasm for human rights at the end of the Cold War and for Albania's emergence from decades of self-isolation were immediately replaced by concerns about the exodus triggered by a chaotic transition. The chosen destination was Italy, easily accessible across the Adriatic and known within Albania due to historical links and Italian media broadcasting into Albania. The exodus from Albania to Italy took place twice. The first one, in 1991, could be blamed on the previous decades of totalitarian rule, for which Albania was duly condemned by the United Nations. The second one, in 1997, was caused by ill-deeds of a post-communist, EU-supported regime. These two bouts of international attention for Albania were followed by silence until Albania became a key Western ally because of its proximity to Kosovo. This did not break the silence about human rights in Albania, however.

Pictures of rusty freighters packed to overflowing with hundreds of Albanians, sailing towards Italy symbolized Albania in 1991 and again in 1997. The first exodus was caused by anarchy following the collapse of the previous communist regime, the second by an armed anarchy following the collapse of get-rich-quick pyramid investment schemes, which typified Albania's transition to capitalism. International and foreign support concentrated on multi-party elections and human rights protection, without producing a visible domestic impact, or indeed heeding the common sense interpretation of capitalism as requiring the possession of capital.

At the time of the first Albanian exodus in 1991, the linkage of EUrope's aid to prevention of immigration had barely started.[30] Italy had reportedly offered $40 to each Albanian to go back, which was obviously not attractive enough as an inducement and 27,000 were returned by force.[31] Subsequent humanitarian aid was reportedly provided with an understanding that Albanian authorities would prevent further exodus. Albania's government seemed to have prevented emigration in 1992–96, although reports about trafficking in migrants highlighted loopholes.

With the benefit of hindsight, one could speculate that Western support to Albania's government(s) in 1992–96 might have been based on an erroneous equation between anti-communism and commitment to democracy. Another and more important reason was Albania's strategic position, its geographical and ethnic links with the Albanian population in Kosovo and Macedonia, and its endorsement of the Western policy towards Former Yugoslavia. Albania was assisted in carrying out elections, drafting a constitution, setting up bodies with 'human rights' in their titles and a thin veneer of formal human rights protection was put in place.

In parallel with Europe's aid, Albania was shifted to and fro between UN agenda items – assistance and violations – within the same year (1993–94).[32] Neither assistance nor mildly worded concerns about violations appeared to have had an impact. The Council of Europe admitted Albania in 1995. Fraudulent elections one year later and lawlessness following the collapse of pyramid investment schemes in 1996 did not testify to Albania's willingness and ability to guarantee human rights, however.

Different from political liberties and civil rights which were the focus of all international human rights assistance programmes, an economic system which would have enabled Albania's population to legally earn its livelihood was not even nominally in place. Sources of Albania's revenue consisted in roughly equal

---

[30] The shift from Western Europe's commitment to the right to leave one's country during the Cold War to Europe's support for prevention of migration from Eastern Europe is described in Tomaševski, K. – Frontiers to equal rights: New Europe, old divisions, in Gomien, D. (ed.) – *Broadening the Frontiers of Human Rights. Essays in Honour of Asbjørn Eide*, Scandinavian University Press, Oslo, 1993, pp. 271–286.

[31] Italy offers Albanians $40 to go home, *International Herald Tribune*, 13 August 1991; Parliamentary Assembly of the Council of Europe – Exodus of Albanian nationals (Rapporteur: Mr Böhm, Germany), Doc. AS/PR (43) 21, Strasbourg, 6 December 1991.

[32] Commission on human rights – Situation of human rights in Albania, Report of the Secretary-General, U.N. Doc. E/CN.4/1993/43 of 16 February 1993 and E/CN.4/1994/75 of 7 December 1994.

parts of the remittances by migrant workers (estimated at an annual $300–400 million) and foreign aid (some $500 million in 1991–95).[33] Albania was a favoured recipient of EUrope's aid in 1991–94 and subsequent to the 1995–96 turmoil, pledges of aid reached $600 million.[34] With the eruption of warfare in the neighbouring Kosovo, aid to Albania increased to $1.5 billion.[35] Much aid was committed but not disbursed, as is customary, while the aid that was disbursed often did not have development of the country as its primary purpose.

The pyramid investment schemes[36] which led to the turmoil of 1996 and the subsequent exodux had been based on a promise of a 50% monthly return on investment and probably seemed to may exactly what capitalism was all about. There was no regulation or licensing in place, no public information about the risk of such 'investments,' no warnings that those schemes were probably also used for money laundering. With the absence of a governmental policy defining what is legal and illegal, and of alternative means of generating income, pyramid schemes were estimated to have spread to 80% of the population.[37] The majority lost all their savings. For many, the money to invest had originated from the sale of their entire property. Questions about the government's complicity in those schemes remained unanswered.[38] Attention shifted to coping with the complete breakdown of public order which ensued from public protests that followed the collapse of pyramid schemes.

Conflicts in Eastern Europe were routinely attributed to ethnicity and their causation was not sought in rapid impoverishment. No ethnic fault-line could be found within Albania.[39] Western aid to Albania had been divided between electoral support and humanitarian relief, neither of which addressed the causes of popular unrest nor tackled widespread poverty and further impoverishment. After Albania's GNP decreased by half in 1991–94 and exports fell by two-thirds, Gramoz Pashko,

---

[33]   Barber, L. – Albania crisis poses new test for EU, *Financial Times*, 11 March 1997.

[34]   Albania: Not yet calm, *The Economist*, 7 February 1998.

[35]   The Balkans: Europe's roughest neighbourhood, *The Economist*, 24 January 1998.

[36]   Such investment schemes redistribute money from late-joiners to those who had joined early hence the name 'pyramid.' Everybody who joins must pay an entry fee, worth several annual salaries in Albania, and recruit six more people to join so as to create as many levels of the pyramid as possible.

[37]   Lennon, P. – Going to market only to be fleeced, *Guardian Weekly*, 3 March 1997.

[38]   Bevins, A. – The gangster regime we fund, and Gangsters' Whitehall link, *The Independent*, 14 and 15 February 1997.

[39]   Two exceptions to this assertion should be highlighted. Firstly, a Greek minority in Albania was an object of a dispute, leading Greece to block EUrope's aid to Albania to culminate in 1994 in the trial of four of leaders of the Greek community and a massive deportation of Albanian migrants workers from Greece in retaliation. (Mather, I. – Passport to deportation and despair, *The European*, 2–8 September 1994; Greece v Albania, *The Economist*, 17 September 1994) Secondly, a great deal of speculation about a north-south division within Albania has been based on the previous communist regime having drawn support from the south of the country, while the post-communist regime led by Sali Berisha has drawn support from the north of the country. (Schmidt, F. – Albania: An old system blends into the present, *Transition*, vol. 2, No. 18, 6 September 1996, pp. 50–52)

an opposition leader at the time, acknowledged that Albania's income derived from migrant workers' remittances, foreign aid, sanctions-busting, and crime.[40] A glimpse of everyday life in 1995 went like this:

> While Tirana's water supply is intermittent and its telephone system does not work properly, pavement stalls are full of American cigarettes, Italian biscuits and soft porn magazines.[41]

Electoral support formed a large part of international and foreign involvement in the field of human rights. The observers' verdicts of elections in Albania were not favourable and thus additional electoral support was probably seen as a way towards improving elections. The US Commission on Security and Cooperation in Europe found that the 1992 elections breached the CSCE norms because ethnic political parties had been banned.[42] The 1995 ban on political activities by former members of the communist leadership (which had ruled Albania in 1946–91) and a law on genocide were preparations for the 1996 elections.[43] The President at the time, Sali Berisha, questioned about an unusual definition of genocide in Albanian law explained that a cultural genocide had taken place; Albania's cultural heritage, such as churches and mosques, had been destroyed.[44] The law on genocide was applied against military officers who shot people trying to flee the country or officials who had ordered internal exile as punishment for dissidents.[45] That law was also useful in decreasing competition in the forthcoming elections by disqualifying opposition leaders. Not all, however. The then president of the Constitutional Court, Rustem Giata, who declared the genocide law constitutional, had previously been a judge and in 1973 allegedly condemned to death a priest for trying to flee Albania.[46] Some pre- and post-1989 government officials were tried for misappropriation of public funds. Such trials were suspected to have been abuse of law in political struggles because targeting was, again, selective.[47]

---

[40] Hansen, J. – Land of hope and no money, *International Herald Tribune*, 1–2 April 1995.

[41] Tuquoi, J.-P. – Albania struggles to embrace capitalism, *Le monde*, 26 May 1995, reproduced in *Guardian Weekly*, 25 June 1995.

[42] *Human Rights and Democratization in Albania*, Commission on Security and Cooperation in Europe, Washington, D.C., January 1994, p. 10 and 12.

[43] Law on genocide and crimes against humanity committed during the communist regime in Albania for political, ideological or religious reasons.

[44] Mather, I. – Albania proves a fast learner in slinging the political mud, *The European*, 22–28 February 1996.

[45] Life jail sentences urged for Albanian officials, *Financial Times*, 22 May 1996.

[46] Standish, A. – Anti-communist law backfires on Berisha, *The European*, 28 December 1995–3 January 1996.

[47] Albania dictator's widow given 9 years for corruption, *International Herald Tribune*, 28 January 1993; Former premier jailed for wasting *bc1.6m of state cash, *The European*, 2–5 September 1993; Bad gets worse in Albania, *The Economist*, 13 November 1993.

International and foreign electoral support did not result in better elections and those held in 1996 were not declared by anybody except their victors to have been free-and-fair.[48] Their results were short lived – the collapse of pyramid investment schemes led to exodus, the exodus to an international military intervention. The previous emphasis on elections as the path towards democratizing Albania was quietly dropped.

A military intervention was triggered by the 1997 exodus, which had forced Italy to receive 16,000 Albanians and promise them a three-month refuge. Thereupon Italy launched an international military intervention to restore some order in Albania so as to be able to repatriate the Albanians. Security Council's authorization endowed that military intervention with legality. The mandate had first been described as securing ports and airports[49] and suspicions were immediately voiced that the aim was to prevent further exodus from Albania to Italy rather that securing the delivery of humanitarian aid as was officially stated. The Security Council approved a multinational protection force offered 'by certain Member States' with the additional stipulation that the entire international should be financed by these 'certain Member States' alone. The declared aim had been 'to facilitate the safe and prompt delivery of humanitarian assistance' and was thereafter broadened (with China's abstention) to protect the OSCE mission during the forthcoming elections.[50] 7,000 soldiers and 450 electoral observers then provided security for another round of elections,[51] won again by Sali Berisha, who had been the head of state and government before and during the pyramid-scheme crisis. He was forced to resign shortly after the elections and subsequent attempts to bring him to court were reportedly impeded by EUrope and the United States with the justification that his trial might destabilize Albania.[52]

The 1997 Italian-led military intervention in Albania resembled the one in Somalia. There was no civil war but anarchy. The government had lost control over two-thirds of the country, most male population was heavily armed, the army depleted of soldiers and weapons. A variety of armed gangs did not fall under some unified command nor form discernable warring parties.

Italy's leadership of the Multilateral Protection Force was rife with problems. The heritage of invading Albania (twice in the 20th century) did not provide a good background for a humanitarian mission. Italy's policy of 'active dissuasion of

[48] Done, K. – New friends recoil as Albania's mask slips, *Financial Times*, 31 May 1996; Sullivan, M. – Doubt cast on Berisha 'win', *The European*, 30 May–6 June 1996.

[49] Krushelnycky, A. and Puccioni, M. – Italy's task force told to steer clear of Vlora, *The European*, 3–9 April 1997.

[50] Security Council resolutions 1101 (1997) of 28 March and 1114 (1997) of 19 June 1997.

[51] Raffone, P. – L'Europe peut-elle oublier l'Albanie?, *Le Monde diplomatique*, September 1997.

[52] Wood, P. – Masked troops patrol Tirana as parliament moves against 'coup' leader, *The Independent*, 19 September 1998; Bowcott, O. – Berisha faces coup charges in Albania, *Guardian Weekly*, 27 September 1998.

Albanian vessels carrying people illicitly into Italy'[53] resulted in the sinking of one Albanian ship and 80 people drowning, which did not make Italy welcome to Albania. The humanitarian purpose of this military intervention was hotly disputed.[54]

The declared purpose of the intervention was to 'escort humanitarian aid to the hungry', but there was not much need for food aid. Moreover, food aid was distributed without military escorts.[55] The multinational protection force then had its remit broadened to securing the elections to withdraw after they were held. *The Economist* asked 'what, apart from giving foreign troops an excuse to leave, even an internationally approved election might accomplish.'[56] Those were the fourth elections since 1990 and therefore skepticism about their effects. These elections were financed by the United States and EUrope. The OSCE chief of election monitoring, Brian Pridham, resigned saying that elections had been a whitewash to justify the withdrawal of foreign troops while the observers' verdict was that the elections were 'adequate and acceptable.'[57]

International responses to developments in Albania have been guided by varying foreign policy objectives, with much difference between and within Western foreign policies. Furthermore, many international actors were involved: EUrope, the Council of Europe, and OSCE were all providing human rights and electoral assistance, while the WEU and NATO overlapped on military and security issues. The United Nations and various agencies complicated matters further. For US military, Albania provided a staging post for the Former Yugoslavia and Andrew Gumbel claimed in 1997 that Albania's 'naval and air bases are under partial control of Nato.'[58] Reginald Hibbert summed up Albania's attraction for different components of Western foreign policies:

[Albania provided] the United States with bases for air operations over Bosnia, the Germans with a Balkan friend who could help to counterbalance Serbia, and the Italians with a law-and-order ally who would stop Albanians from trying to emigrate *en masse* across the Adriatic.[59]

---

[53] Graham, R. – Italy paves the way to lead Albania mission, *Financial Times*, 3 April 1997.

[54] Puccioni, M. – Rome re-examines 'Dr Good', *The European*, 20–26 February 1997; Graham, R. – Albania forces Italy to make hard decisions, *Financial Times*, 5 March 1997; Bohlen, C. – Prodi loses support for Albania force, *International Herald Tribune*, 9 April 1997.

[55] O'Connon, M. – Aid workers in Albania wonder why they need UN troops, *International Herald Tribune*, 22 April 1997; Tihon, F. – What are we doing here, ask saviours of Albania, *The European*, 19–25 June 1997.

[56] Albania: Ready, aim, vote, *The Economist*, 17 May 1997.

[57] Standish, A. – Opposition defy Berisha with election boycott call, *The European*, 15–21 May 1997; Albania: A long shot, *The Economist*, 28 June 1997; Steele, J. – Berisha bows to election defeat, *Guardian Weekly*, 6 July 1997.

[58] Albania: Berisha beacons, *The Economist*, 18 May 1996; Perlez, J. – Albania's autocrat: No postelection blush, *International Herald Tribune*, 3 June 1996; Gumbel, A. – Albania enters twilight zone, *The Independent*, 4 March 1997.

[59] Hibbert, R. – Dealing with the dispossessed, *The World Today*, May 1997, p. 120.

The ebb and flow of these varied foreign policy interests have resulted in bouts of activity in and around Albania, followed by silence, then another spasm of interventionism would ensue, and again silence. In 1999, attention shifted briefly to Albania while it was hosting close to half million refugees from Kosovo.[60] A post-Kosovo-crisis donors' meeting, a grouping known by the name Friends of Albania, found that 'progress on law and order, anti-corruption measures and the building of public institutions remained less than satisfactory.'[61] No self-criticism accompanied this finding and thus no soul searching ensued about the contribution made towards progress on law and order, suppression of corruption, or the building of public institutions by the Friends of Albania themselves.

Depending on the developments in (and around) Kosovo, Albania may or may not again sink into oblivion, but it is unlikely that a focus on developments in Albania itself will guide international and foreign involvement. A similar silence has followed international involvement in Romania after the end of the Ceausescu regime. Condemnations for human rights violations were followed by assistance and then by silence.

Romania

Romania followed Albania on the UN violations-agenda, with a similar sequence of events. Condemnations of human rights violations in 1989–91 were followed by human rights assistance, coupled with the admission to the Council of Europe and a Europe-agreement. EUrope's human rights concerns ranged from police abuses to criminalization of homosexuality, but were overwhelmed by efforts to decrease emigration from Romania as well as to tackle organized crime, to then shift to an exclusive focus to support for economic restructuring, to finally elevate Romania to the status of applicant for membership in the European Union in December 1999.

During the Cold War, Romania was a frequent target of Western human rights policies because the human rights record of the Ceausescu regime had been notorious while there was some leverage for applying economic sanctions. A ping-pong took place in the 1980s between the United States and Romania with regard to the annual renewal of Romania's most favoured nation status (MFN). Romania found itself an object of intense human rights scrutiny each summer, at the time when its MFN status was due for renewal. When Romania concluded a bilateral trade treaty with the United States, the 1974 Jackson-Vanik amendment applied and Romania ran the risk of losing MFN status for precluding its citizens from emigrating. Romania's emigration statistics became an object of scrutiny in 1982–84 with the

---

[60] Shearer, D. – Are there heroes?, *The World Today*, July 1999, p. 4–5.

[61] Wringht. R. – Optimism fades as Albania's pre-Kosovo problems come again to the fore, *Financial Times*, 14–15 August 1999.

number of emigrants increasing at the time when US Congress was discussing the renewal of Romania's MFN status to subsequently again decrease.[62]

The US deputy Secretary of State had reportedly informed Nicolae Ceausescu in February 1988 that 'the United States was dissatisfied with Romanian human rights policies' whereupon Romania informed the United States that it was renouncing its MFN status, whose benefits were estimated at an annual $250 million.[63] Romania's MFN status was written into the 1975 trade agreement with the United States, which followed Romania's admission to the IMF in 1972. An often cited reason was Ceausescu's maverick foreign policy, evidenced, *inter alia*, in Romania's condemnation of the Soviet military occupation of Czechoslovakia in 1968. Another reason was Romania's occasional grant of the right to leave to some of its citizens, with expensive exit visas paid by Israel or Germany. The grounds could not have been human rights because the US Commission on Security and Cooperation in Europe retrospectively assessed Ceausescu's regime as 'the most repressive and demoralizing of the Warsaw Pact countries.'[64]

After Romania had abrogated its MFN status in 1988, the UN Commission on Human Rights became concerned about serious human rights violations in Romania and appointed a Special Rapporteur on the eve of the killing of Nicolae Ceauscescu in December 1989.[65] The Special Rapporteur continued reporting in 1990–92 whereupon he became the executive director of the Romanian Human Rights Institute, established with financial assistance of the United Nations and the Council of Europe.[66] As was UN's practice, changes of regime were immediately rewarded by human rights assistance. In this particular case, a subsequent evaluation faulted the programme for the absence of objectives which were to be accomplished.[67]

At the time when human rights assistance was initiated, Romania was ruled by the Social Democratic Party of Romania (PDSR), whose leadership consisted of the previous *nomenklatura*. The PDSR was headed by Ion Iliescu, formerly a close aide to Nicolae Ceausescu, and ruled the country in 1990–96. It co-operated with

---

[62] Davidson, L.A. – Romania, CSCE and the most-favored-nation process, 1982–84, in Newson, D.D. (ed.) – *The Diplomacy of Human Rights*, Institute for the Study of Diplomacy, Georgetown University and University Press of America, 1986, pp. 187–200.

[63] Romania drops U.S. trade link, *International Herald Tribune*, 29 February 1988.

[64] Commission on Security and Cooperation in Europe – *Human Rights and Democratization in Romania*, Washington D.C., June 1994, p. 1.

[65] Commission on Human Rights – Report on the situation of human rights in Romania submitted by Mr. Joseph Voyame, Special Rapporteur, U.N. Doc. E/CN.4/1991/30 of 8 January 1991, paras. 1–3.

[66] Commission on Human Rights – Situation of Human Rights in Romania. Note by the Secretary-General transmitting the report of Mr. Joseph Voyame, former Special Rapporteur of the Commission and Executive Director of the Romanian Human Rights Institute, U.N. Doc. E/CN.4/1994/76/Add.1 of 21 January 1994.

[67] Commission on Human Rights – Report on the evaluation of the Romania Country Programme of Advisory Services and technical Assistance in the Field of Human Rights, U.N. Doc. E/CN.4/1995/90/Add.1 of 7 March 1995, para. 49.

the United Nations, allowed the setting up of hundreds of NGOs, adopted a stream of new laws. In 1991 alone, more than a hundred were adopted and another hundred prepared.[68]

While the trappings of human rights protection were being put in place, the government's performance remained unchanged. In June 1990, EUrope withdrew support for Romania citing repression against anti-government demonstrations as the reason. A year later, the United States refused to grant Romania MFN status.[69] Aid to Romania was at the time confined to humanitarian assistance, there was almost no foreign investment, while the IMF/World Bank made a $1 billion commitment as late as in 1996–97.[70]

German aid to Romania was from the very beginning of transition in January 1990 conditioned by 'moves towards democracy' and its aims included preventing the 200,000 ethnic Germans from exercising their right to emigrate to Germany. The then minister of foreign affairs, Hans-Dietrich Genscher said 'that Bonn hoped that guarantees of democracy would encourage ethnic Germans to remain.'[71] The subsequent repatriation of the Roma (often referred to as Gypsies) from Germany further slanted German aid towards its linkage with migration. The Roma had apparently decided *en masse* not to remain in Romania but rather to try their luck in Germany, and this luck proved absent or short-lived. Their repatriation was institutionalized through an agreement of 1992 and Romania subsequently signed similar agreements with France and Switzerland.[72] The 1992 Germany-Romania agreement replicated the previous exchange of ethnic Germans for hard currency during the Ceausescu regime.[73]

Romania was declared a democracy despite 'irregularities' noted by international observers who monitored the 1990 elections. Its admission to the Council of Europe in October 1993 was described in the media as 'conditional.'[74] Numerous shortcomings were identified, ranging from unaccountable secret services to legalized discrimination against minorities.[75] Lucian Mihai has noted that shortcomings

---

[68] Commission on Human Rights – Report on the situation of human rights in Romania submitted by Mr. Joseph Voyame, Special Rapporteur, U.N. Doc. E/CN.4/1992/28 of 3 January 1992, para. 66.

[69] Mistrust shadows Romanian regime, *International Herald Tribune*, 18 December 1992.

[70] Done, K. – Shock therapy is prescribed, Survey of Romania, *Financial Times*, 25 June 1997.

[71] Genscher, in Romania, links aid to the rights of German minority, *International Herald Tribune*, 16 January 1990.

[72] Chatelot, C. – Romania: False promise of the West lures easterners, *Le monde*, 30 August 1995, reproduced in *Guardian Weekly*, 17 September 1995.

[73] 'Ceausescu's regime allowed the mass emigration of Transylvanian Saxons and Banat Swabians to West Germany in exchange for much-needed hard currency and other economic and diplomatic advantages.' Ionescu, D. – Romanian leaders (and criminals) eye Germany's plenty, *Transition*, 9 February 1996, p. 30.

[74] Ionescu, D. – Romania admitted to the Council of Europe, *RFE/RL Research Report*, vol. 2, No. 44, 5 November 1993, p. 43.

[75] Koenig, F. – Report on the application by Romania for membership of the Council of Europe, Parliamentary Assembly, Doc. 6901, Strasbourg, 19 July 1993.

went further than poor implementation of law. Rather, Romania's legislation had not prohibited violations of rights and freedoms guaranteed by international treaties to which Romania was a party[76] and the legal basis for human rights protection was thus lacking. The ILO has found that 'discrimination based on national extraction and race continued to exist to a serious extent against the Roma and, to a lesser extent, against the Magyars, and no policy to promote equality of opportunity and treatment' was formulated.[77] The United Nations Rapporteur on Torture included Romania in his 1994 report because 'police officers resorted to torture and ill-treatment of detainees frequently in order to force them to make confessions which were later used as evidence in courts.'[78] The European Parliament added its own critique of Romania's penalization of homosexuality by five years in prison.[79]

This mixture of human rights problems did not uphold international attention for human rights in Romania; both condemnations and assistance stopped and Romania was silently deleted from the international human rights agenda. With the benefit of hindsight, this appears much too early because the first seven years of post-Ceauschescu Romania were retroactively assessed as a non-transition. Such negative assessments were reflected in the rejection of Romania's bid to join NATO in 1997[80] as well as its classification in the second tier of Eastern European countries to be admitted to the European Union. Non-governmental organizations have continued outlining shortcomings in Romania's human rights system, prioritizing demilitarization of the police and prison service[81] to little avail. Romania was taken off the international human rights agenda. Perhaps a revival of interest will ensue from Europe's decision to include Romania amongst the applicants for membership in the European Union in December 1999.

The Baltic Countries: Estonia, Latvia and Lithuania

The three Baltic states, defined by Russia as 'near abroad,' became a prominent issue in international human rights politics because of the large population of Russian origin that found itself in a foreign country after the Soviet Union had disintegrated. Mutually opposed grievances have not been easy to reconcile: the Baltic

---

[76] Michai, L. – On the provisions regarding human rights of the Romanian Constitution, in: Rzepliński, A. (ed.) – *International Conference on Human Rights and Freedoms in New Constitutions in Central and Eastern Europe,* Warsaw, 24–29 April 1992, Helsinki Foundations for Human Rights, Warsaw, 1992, p. 104.

[77] United Nations – Situation of human rights in Romania. Report by the Secretary-General submitted pursuant to resolution 1992/64 of the Commission on Human Rights, U.N. Doc. E/CN.4/1993/40 of 5 February 1993, para. 19, p. 29.

[78] United Nations – Report of the Special Rapporteur, Mr. Nigel S. Rodley, U.N. Doc. E/CN.4/1994/31 of 6 January 1994, para. 469.

[79] Turner, M. – Accusations fly over 'election rigging' in Romania, *European Voice*, 31 October–6 November 1996.

[80] Lieven, A. – Quest to join Nato in paramount, Survey of Romania, *Financial Times*, 25 June 1997.

[81] International Helsinki Federation for Human Rights – *1998 Annual Report*, Vienna, 1998, p. 176 and 179.

states had been occupied and russified by the Soviet Union, the 'Russian speakers' who found themselves in the Baltic states post-1991 have epitomized the previous *occupation cum russification* and have accumulated grievances against the Baltic states. Endless Western human rights missions traveled to the Baltics to investigate the treatment of the Russian minority. Russia's has threatened and reportedly imposed economic sanctions against Latvia for its denial of minority rights, creating a rare example of non-Western sanctions on the human rights grounds.

Estonia and Latvia were a particular target of international scrutiny relating to the rights of non-citizens and minority rights. Their regaining of independence in 1991, after fifty-one years of the Soviet occupation, was followed by the denial of citizenship to people referred to as 'Russian-speakers'. They moved – or were moved – to the Baltics while Estonia and Latvia were a part of the Soviet Union, while many Estonians and Latvians were forced to flee Soviet repression. Due to that pattern of migration, the balance between the indigenous and Russian-speaking population was altered. Had the Russian-speakers been given political rights after independence, the electoral arithmetic would have jeopardized victories of the indigenous – Estonian or Latvian – parties.

With independence came an urge to return to pre-Soviet times and blank out the in-between period, except for recording Soviet-imposed victimization. The living remnants of the five decades of Soviet rule, 'the Russian speakers,' became unwelcome foreigners. The policy of both governments was to define citizenship by reviving the legal and factual situation as it had been before the Soviet occupation, thus expunging the demographic changes that occurred from 1940 until 1991. The problem was compounded by the slow withdrawal of the Soviet/Russian military from the Baltics, for which the fate of Russian-speakers – persistent accusations of violations of human rights – was a useful excuse for the Soviet Union and then Russia.

In 1992–93, the UN General Assembly kept on its agenda two items, one on the withdrawal of foreign military forces, and another on human rights in Estonia and Latvia.[82] In December 1991 the European Council approved aid to the former Soviet Union, which was promptly suspended because of Soviet armed repression that tried to stifle the forthcoming independence of the Baltic states. The withdrawal of Russia's military was announced in October 1992, but translating this into practice was extremely slow. The justification were many, amongst them the lack of housing for the military personnel, whereupon Denmark and the United States offered housing aid.[83]

---

[82] General Assembly – Complete withdrawal of foreign military forces from the territories of the Baltic States, resolutions 47/21 of 25 November 1992 and 48/18 of 15 November 1993; Situation of human rights in Estonia and Latvia, resolutions 47/115 of 16 December 1992 and 48/155 of 20 December 1993.

[83] Kennan, G.F. – Building stability in Russia and the Baltics, *International Herald Tribune*, 10 November 1992.

The UN General Assembly noted 'the complaint of alleged violations of human rights with respect to the Russian-speaking population in Estonia and Latvia' and called for the application of 'generally accepted norms of international law in the field of human rights.'[84] There were – still are – few generally accepted norms in international law concerning citizenship, however, and states' practice varies a great deal. The goal of international law to accord rights to individuals by virtue of their being human clashes against the primordial legal link between the state and its own citizens. Assessments of Estonia's or Latvia's laws against international norms were many and they were accompanied with even more numerous recommendations with regard to facilitating access to citizenship for 'Russian-speakers.' Comparisons with other countries, to determine what the states' practice was, showed that criteria for citizenship were comparable to those applied in the many countries which applied stringent criteria for the granting of citizenship. Human rights missions and conferences proliferated nevertheless, as did critiques of Estonia's and Latvia's laws and practices. The European Union 'expressed grave concern at certain aspects of the law on foreigners adopted in Estonia and the law on citizenship adopted by Latvia.'[85] Russia routinely accused Estonia and Latvia of human rights violations, arguing, for example, in 1995 that 'hundreds of thousands of permanent residents have been declared aliens in their own country', adding an assertion that forced deportations from Estonia were taking place, and pointing out that in Latvia the League of Stateless Persons of Latvia had been formed but was refused registration.[86]

Admission of the Baltic states to the Council of Europe was postponed because of such controversies relating to citizenship laws and the protection of minorities. Estonia, Latvia and Lithuania had first applied in 1991[87] and then legal reform ensued, with much international and foreign involvement, towards their admission. Lithuania was deleted from the problem-list shortly thereafter, while the pressure upon the two remaining states, and their frequently changing governments, continued. The aim was to prevent the 'understandable anti-Soviet sentiments from degenerating into inter-ethnic violence.'[88]

---

[84] United Nations – Situation of human rights in Estonia and Latvia, General Assembly resolution 47/115 of 16 December 1992, preamble and para 4.

[85] European Commission – *General Report on the Activities of the European Union 1994*, Brussels/Luxembourg, 1995, para. 759.

[86] Sub-Commission on Prevention of Discrimination and Protection of Minorities – Note verbale dated 10 August 1995 from the Permanent Mission of the Russian Federation to the United Nations Office at Geneva addressed to the Chairman of the forty-seventh session of the Sub-Commission on Prevention of Discrimination and Protection of Minorities, U.N. Doc. E/CN.4/Sub.2/1995/44 of 10 August 1995.

[87] Pekkanen, R. and Danelius, H. – Human rights in the Republic of Estonia, Doc. AS/Ad Hoc-Bur-EE (43) 2 of 17 December 1991; De Meyer, J. and Rozakis, C. – Human rights in the Republic of Latvia, Doc. AS/Ad Hoc-Bur-EE (43) 4 of 20 January 1992.

[88] Schlager, E.B. – The right to have rights: Citizenship in newly independent OSCE countries, *Helsinki Monitor*, vol. 8, 1997, No. 1, p. 26.

In 1998, Estonia was placed on the first list of countries to start negotiations for admission to the European Union while Latvia became a target of Russia's economic sanctions.[89] Preparations of Estonia's membership have included the appointment of a (Russian) counselor for ethnocultural relations, a commission to review citizenship and language laws, as well as negotiations of an agreement on the borders between Estonia and Russia.[90] The European Union was faced with a dilemma relating to Russia's repetitive threats of economic sanctions against Latvia. The dilemma was whether to pressurize Russia to lift 'restrictive trade measures' against Latvia,[91] or to pressurize Latvia to make concessions. The latter prevailed and a first step towards liberalization of the law on citizenship was approved by a referendum in October 1998.[92] One can anticipate further steps to be taken in the year 2000 after Latvia had been added to the list of applicants for membership in the European Union.

Former Yugoslavia

By the end of the first post-cold-war decade, armed conflicts have become part of the geopolitical landscape close to the very borders of EUrope. Warfare further away, in Armenia-Azarbeijan or Chechnya, could be confined to occasional reports, which have resulted in lessened public revulsion as warfare dragged on, especially because most people in the West hardly know where these countries are. The number and persistence of armed conflicts have made such warfare part and parcel of the post-cold-war geopolitical landscape. Closer to Europe, warfare created waves of refugees and measures against their influx have been broadened and strengthened. Moreover, the identification with the victims has been easier when they looked almost as if they were Western. The warfare closest to Europe, in the Former Yugoslavia, has triggered the most vehement reactions.

These reactions had started with condemnations and sanctions, but then escalated through a merger of peace-making, peace-building and peace-keeping, to end with military interventions ostensibly justified by defending of human rights. The 78-day NATO bombing spree in 1999, whose daily cost was estimated at between $70 and $100 million[93] was justified by the prime minister of the United Kingdom as follows:

---

[89] Russia's parliament called for economic sanctions against Estonia in 1993 (Vallens, D. – The law on aliens controversy in the Baltic states, *The ICJ Review*, No. 54, 1995, p. 17) and sanctions against Latvia were reportedly imposed in 1998 (Baltic Assembly condemns Russian actions, *The Baltic Times*, vol. 3, No. 109, 14–20 May 1998).

[90] Saffrais, G. – Lente intégration des Russes dans les pays baltes, *Le Monde diplomatique*, February 1998.

[91] Turner, M. – Union considers increasing pressure on Moscow over Latvia, *European Voice*, 30 April–6 May 1998.

[92] Latvia votes for Europe, *The Economist*, 10 October 1998.

[93] If you know of a better 'ole, go to it, *The Economist*, 17 April 1999.

If we had not, we would have been complicit in the evil that was being wreaked on Kosovo. If we had not, we would have sent a message to every would-be violator of human rights in the world that they could go about their business unchallenged.[94]

The events of 1999 were not the beginning of Western interventionism in the Former Yugoslavia but rather an intermediate stage, leading to an uncharted future. The necessity for interventionism (as defined by EUrope) had first emerged in 1991, when Yugoslavia had started disintegrating.

The first responses were condemnations of human rights violations and economic sanctions. EUrope suspended Yugoslavia's trade concessions (granted in 1983) and then all co-operation in November 1991.[95] The atrocities that preceded and followed are known well enough to be omitted here. Security Council's arms embargo and economic sanctions against the Former Yugoslavia[96] followed intermittently. In 1991–99 sanctions were strengthened and lifted to exact specific acts or omissions, reimposed when such concessions proved apparent rather than real, to be lifted again to reward compliance and re-imposed when compliance was faulted. Objectives which were pursued through sanctions were changing following the dynamics of warfare and changing foreign policies of the principal actors. The grounds for sanctions were repetitive and voluminous condemnations of human rights violations. In 1996, the UN Commission on Human Rights adopted its longest resolution theretofore, twelve pages of single-spaced text, providing an exhaustive list of human rights violations and breaches of humanitarian law, and accompanying them with an even longer list of measures that should be put in place to right the on-going wrongs.[97] By 1999, this output further increased with the

---

[94] *Human Rights. Annual Report for 1999*, Foreign & Commonwealth Office and Department for International Development, London, July 1999, p. 10.

[95] The European Community (as it then was) first suspended and then abrogated its co-operation agreement with Yugoslavia (Council decision No. 91/602/EEC of 25 November 1991, *Official Journal of the European Communities*, 1991, L 325, p. 23). The subsequent legal challenge (Case C-162/96 *Racke v. Hauptzollamt Mainz*) probed into the legal basis for EUrope's abrogation of an international treaty as there had been no human rights clause at the time it was concluded, in 1983, but did not get very far because the *rebus sic stantibus* clause was accepted as a valid basis for abrogation. This clause allows parties to re-consider their treaty commitments when conditions for their implementation profoundly change. The issue was not pursued further because the affected party, Yugoslavia, was no longer and could not challenge that interpretation.

[96] Out of the new states originating from the disintegration of the Former Yugoslavia, the main target of economic sanctions has been Serbia and Montenegro, Croatia has been to a large extent exempt, while Slovenia and FYROM/Macedonia were not targeted at all. This pattern was similar to EUrope's policy of abrogating the co-operation agreement with Yugoslavia in November 1991 to re-institute tariff preferences for Bosnia and Herzegovina, Croatia, FYROM and Slovenia in December 1991.

[97] Commission on Human Rights – Situation of human rights in the Republic of Bosnia and Herzegovina, the State of Bosnia and Herzegovina, the Republic of Croatia and the Federal Republic of Yugoslavia (Serbia and Montenegro), resolution 1996/71of 23 April 1996 adopted without a vote.

12-page resolutions on the human rights in the Former Yugoslavia having become accepted practice, with the addition of a separate resolution on Kosovo.[98]

These and similar findings of human rights violations provided ample justifications for sanctions. Moreover, the World Bank had terminated Yugoslavia's membership in 1993. Successor states were admitted, except for Serbia/Yugoslavia, whose membership in the Bank has to wait until it can rejoin the IMF. One obstacle was cleared with an agreement on debt repayment[99] but others have not followed suit. The IMF/World Bank membership and thereby access to international and/or foreign capital has remained denied and justifications have been many. *The New York Times* has explained, for example, that 'Mr. Milosevic continued to abuse the rights of Albanians in Kosovo and harbor indicted war criminals.'[100]

Sanctions against the Former Yugoslavia have been enforced (if imperfectly) through a co-ordinated action led by EUrope. Their economic effects have not been disputed. Serbia's public spending climbed to 55% of GDP as the economy kept shrinking, the current account deficit reached $2 billion, the industry diminished to one-third of its pre-war capacity with unemployment reaching an estimated 50%.[101] The impact of sanctions was, however, not the expected change of leadership through elections or popular revolt. Similarly to Iraq, economic sanctions led to bombing and the 1999 NATO's 'air campaign' ruined Serbia's infrastructure, further damaging its economy.[102] Thereafter, Western support for opposition to Serbia's government has been merged with demands for surrendering Slobodan Milosevic, who was in the meantime charged with war crimes,[103] thus reinforcing the previously expected and now required change of leadership in Yugoslavia/Serbia.

Bosnia and Herzegovina

Alongside Serbia itself, international condemnations and sanctions have been orientated towards Serbia's conduct in its 'near abroad.' The disintegration of Yugoslavia had initially been opposed and then facilitated, to rapidly revert to

---

[98] Commission on Human Rights – The situation of human rights in the Federal Republic of Yugoslavia (Serbia and Montenegro), the Republic of Croatia and Bosnia and Herzegovina, resolution 1999/18 of 23 April 1999 adopted by a roll-call vote of 46-1-6, and Situation of human rights in Kosovo, resolution 1999/2 of 13 April 1999, adopted by a roll-call vote of 44-1-6.

[99] Robinson, A. – Yugoslavia seeks end to financial isolation, *Financial Times*, 20 June 1997; Graham, G. – Belgrade agrees outline of $1.7bn debt restructuring, *Financial Times*, 17 July 1998.

[100] Milosevic's grip (editorial), *The New York Times*, reprinted in *International Herald Tribune*, 26–27 July 1997.

[101] The Kosovo cauldron, *The Economist,* 14 March 1998; Dinmore, G. – Panic-buying empties shelves as Serbs guard against further western sanctions, *Financial Times*, 16 April 1998.

[102] Fitchett, J. – Is Serb economy the true target?, *International Herald Tribune*, 26 May 1999.

[103] EU plans 'carrot and stick' strategy to promote democracy in Balkan region, and Fresh EU bid to bolster Serb opposition, *European Voice*, 2–8 September and 4–9 November 1999.

opposition because the process of disintegration slid into warfare. Attempts to halt it quickly progressed from verbal condemnations to sanctions. Sanctions against Yugoslavia/Serbia and Montenegro were imposed by EUrope in 1991 and by the United Nations in 1992,[104] to be suspended in 1995 as an inducement for compliance with the Dayton Agreement, and then re-imposed on various occasions for different reasons. Sanctions had first been imposed on the grounds of Serbia's many ill-deeds in Bosnia and Herzegovina, to later increase the scope of its objectionable conduct to Kosovo, then also to Montenegro, while additional grounds have constantly been found in Serbia itself.

The Dayton Agreement was an outcome of NATO's bombing in the summer of 1995 and thus constituted an effort at enforced peace-making. It is an unusual document. It stopped warfare, as it was meant to, by bombing the warring parties to the negotiating table and secured their acceptance of foreign military presence so as to prevent resumption of warfare. The scheme created in Dayton was ambiguous in every possible procedural and substantive respect. The three ethnically-defined warring parties were re-named into the three constituent peoples of Bosnia and Herzegovina whereby each obtained a claim to collective rights. Bosnia obtained a constitution which committed it, as well as the two entities within it, to 'ensure the highest level of internationally recognized human rights and fundamental freedoms'[105] That commitment would have been difficult to translate into practice even if it was not – as it was – a result of closed-door negotiations in Dayton and thus it did not even originate in Bosnia. Such open-ended commitment to human rights has created open-ended vulnerability for accusations of human rights violations. These have originated from the parties 'witnessing' the Agreement, who had, according to Paul Szasz, 'an understandable aversion to accepting any direct legal ties to the details of the settlement.'[106] Many more accusations of human rights violations have originated from the multitude of international and foreign,

---

[104] Reasons for sanctions are well known from a veritable flood of literature which has been generated about the Former Yugoslavia and are thus not discussed here. Their legal background merits a clarification: Bosnia's formal accusation of genocide had been accepted – but not acted upon – by the International Court of Justice (Application of the Convention on the Prevention and Punishment of the Crime of Genocide, Bosnia and Herzegovina versus Yugoslavia (Serbia and Montenegro), Order of 8 April 1993, *1993 ICJ Report*, p. 3). The International Tribunal for Violations of International Humanitarian Law in the Former Yugoslavia subsequently came into being and shifted attention from the responsibility of the state, which the ICJ would have clarified had it dealt with the case, to individual responsibility under international humanitarian law and the Genocide Convention. This changed orientation from the previous state-centered approach towards the individualization of responsibility has not been reflected in an accompanying remolding of sanctions, which remained state-centered and affecting the whole population rather than only the individuals who have been identified as culprits.

[105] Article II of the Constitution of Bosnia and Herzegovina, which constituted Annex 4 to the Dayton Agreement. The whole text of the Dayton-Paris Agreement, officially termed the General Framework Agreement for Peace in Bosnia and Herzegovina, is reproduced in *International Legal Materials*, vol. 35, 1996, pp. 75–169.

[106] Szasz, P.C. – The protection of human rights through the Dayton/Paris Peace Agreement on Bosnia, *The American Journal of International Law*, vol. 90, 1996, p. 315.

governmental, inter-governmental and non-governmental actors that involved themselves in what became known as an international protectorate. The details of the settlement reached in the Dayton Agreement have proved important in view of the abyss between the promise of the highest level of internationally recognized human rights and the reality of Bosnia and Herzegovina, which, four years after Dayton, in the words of its president Alija Izetbegovic, did not have 'established borders, where joint institutions are not functioning, and which has at least two armies and two police forces.'[107]

The suspension of sanctions as an inducement for compliance with the Dayton Agreement meant that sanctions could be re-imposed with ease and threats of sanctions have been amply used. They have targeted Serbia (not only concerning its involvement in Bosnia but also relating to Kosovo, as is described below), Croatia (for its reluctance to re-admit the Serbian population forced out of the country) as well as Bosnia. The routinely unnamed entity (Republika Srpska) was initially deprived of aid so as to enforce a change in its leadership and compel its participation in multi-ethnic institutions which were anticipated as the key governing bodies for the whole state.[108] The ebb and flow of aid to Bosnia has been linked to a variety of conditions. The reasons for denying aid ranged from the surrender of persons indicted by the International Tribunal for trial to cutting off Bosnia's ties with Iran.[109]

Conflicts about the meaning and implications of the Dayton Agreement have been many, both between and within individual governments as well as between and within other intervening actors: Was Bosnia actually partitioned or was it supposed to be a single state? Was the military component of the Agreement supposed to carry out peace-keeping, peace enforcement, or policing, or all of these? Who was in charge of making the civilian part of implementation sustainable so that it could survive the departure of international and foreign agencies? In the meantime, calls for human rights conditionality have diversified:

> The fighting [over turf and budgets] has been replaced by differing perspectives on the use of conditionality – withholding funds until parties have complied with particular obligations as opposed to using economic assistance as a positive incentive to entice cooperation, withdrawing it later if the parties do not comply – and whether instituting harsher conditions for the Republika Srpska is a counterproductive tactic in the long run.[110]

---

[107] Hedges, C. – Bosnia get little relief, *International Herald Tribune*, 18 August 1999.

[108] Mervin, H. – Aid for Bosnian Serbs tied to ousting leaders, *Financial Times*, 15 April 1996; Political antagonism keeps Bosnia on 'critical list', *European Voice*, 15–22 May 1996.

[109] Black, I. And Fairhall, D. – Terms for Bosnia aid spelled out, *Guardian Weekly*, 15 December 1996; Dobbs, M. – Bosnia to get cash if it cuts ties to Iran, *International Herald Tribune*, 15 March 1996.

[110] Woorward, S.L. – The United States leads, Europe pays, *Transition*, 12 July 1996, p. 15.

The former UN Special Rapporteur on human rights opted for a punitive approach, expressing her conviction 'that local authorities must be kept aware that [economic] assistance (to be distinguished from emergency humanitarian aid) depends expressly on their demonstrated respect for the principles of international human rights.'[111] Elisabeth Rehn's rationale has been that rebuilding and reconstruction had to await until respect of human rights has been secured. She has substantiated this line of reasoning by recalling that roads and factories had existed in Bosnia before the war but did not prevent it, hence respect for human rights should precede reconstruction.[112] This rationale has created a Catch-22 situation: reconstruction has been delayed because of the lack of compliance with human rights guarantees, while these have been hampered by delayed reconstruction.

Post-1995 Bosnia has often been referred to as an international protectorate due to the vast self-granted powers of the various bodies acting in the name of 'the international community'. These were split: the military powers have been exercised by NATO, funding decided by each individual donor, while the non-military and non-economic issues have been left to a EU/US international administration. Cost-sharing has created frequent disagreements because the United Nations involvement stopped with Dayton and the associated costs formed no longer part of the UN budget. Foreign-funded and foreign-staffed military and civilian personnel was estimated at a cost of $5 billion in 1995–99 alone,[113] out of which military costs constituted the overwhelming part.

Non-military aid was made conditional on the compliance with Western demands, which ranged from the reform of property laws aimed at facilitating return of refugees to the design of a flag and inscriptions to be used in passports, and each has been accompanied with a deadline.[114] That type of governance could not be described using the donors' contemporary vocabulary and terms such as 'local ownership', 'the government in the driving seat' or 'sustainability.' Rather, it was defined as necessary for peace-building. Which direction peace-building was taking remained unclear, however. The Dayton Agreement was designed to form a state (Bosnia and Herzegovina), split into two entities (Moslem-Croat Federation and Republika Srpska), and built upon the collective rights of Muslims, Croats and Serbs. 'The state' had vague and weak sovereign powers. Jane Sharp has commented that two years after the Dayton Agreement, 'it was still not clear whether

---

[111] Commission on Human Rights – Situation of human rights in the territory of the former Yugoslavia. Periodic report submitted by Ms. Elisabeth Rehn, Special Rapporteur, U.N. Doc. E/CN.4/1997/56 of 29 January 1997, para. 174.

[112] Rehn, E. – Prologue, in Hedegaard, L. (ed.) – *Bosnia and the West. A Hearing 15–16 January 1996,* The Danish Foreign Policy Society, Copenhagen, October 1996, p. 10.

[113] Fairhall, D. – Bosnia bill is $5 billion and rising, *Guardian Weekly*, 20 October 1996.

[114] Aid warning for Bosnia, *Financial Times*, 6 December 1996; Barber, L. – Ex-rivals head for Bosnia aid meeting, *Financial Times*, 9 January 1997; Mather, I. – Only sanctions will bring Bosnians to their senses, *The European*, 5–11 June 1997.

the major donor countries favour integration or partition for Bosnia.'[115]
Commentators have praised the multitude of institutions with human rights in their
name that have been set up.[116] Counter-praise has emphasized that these institutions
were foreign-staffed, foreign-funded and protected by the foreign military.[117]
Jacques Klein, deputy High Representative, tilted the balance towards counter-
praise, lamenting the lack of the rule of law or independent judiciary in Bosnia and
Herzegovina.[118]

Alongside the rule of law and the judiciary, democracy has also been faulted
many times. The Security Council lifted sanctions in 1996, following elections in
Bosnia and Herzegovina. These had generated a flood of complaints, which
included the electoral turnout exceeding the number of people who had been registered to vote. The UN Special Rapporteur has held that 'the elections were surely
not 'free and fair'[119] while the OSCE certified them as free-and-fair, to then retroactively increase the number of people eligible to vote from 2.9 to 3.2 million in
response to evidence of some 600,000 'surplus voters.'[120] The reason for this
unusual procedure was immediately linked to the then forthcoming presidential
elections in the United States, which necessitated presenting Bosnia as a foreign
policy success, which then led to personnel changed within the OSCE:

> The head of the OSCE mission in Sarajevo is Robert Frowick, a US diplomat.
> Over the past month, the press department in the Bosnian capital has been grad-
> ually packed with US officials, while their European counterparts have been sent
> home or demoted, in effect making the OSCE press office an extension of the
> American Embassy.[121]

Differences in the assessment of elections illustrated the underlying differences in
defining the ends and means of international involvement in Bosnia. The first
generation of testimonies about the process of peace-making has appeared,[122]

---

[115] Sharp, J.M.O. – Doing better on Bosnia: Enforce the law, protect rights, *The World Today*, vol.
53, No. 2, February 1997, p. 37.

[116] Gemalmaz, M.S. – Constitution, ombudsperson and human rights chamber in 'Bosnia and
Herzegovina,' *Netherlands Quarterly of Human Rights*, vol. 17, 1888, No. 3, pp. 277–329.

[117] Chandler, D. – *Faking Democracy after Dayton*, Pluto Press, London, 1999; Zivkovic, A. – The
protectorate, a way to dominate, *Le monde diplomatique*, English Edition, July 1999.

[118] Bosnia: Better luck next time, *The Economist*, 1 May 1999.

[119] Commission on Human Rights – Situation of human rights in the territory of the Former
Yugoslavia. Periodic report submitted by Ms. Elisabeth Rehn, Special Rapporteur, U.N. Doc.
E/CN.4/1997/9 of 22 October 1996, paras. 6 and 9.

[120] Barber, T. – Bosnia election fraud hidden by OSCE figures, *The Independent*, 25 September 1996;
Strauss, J. – OSCE wounded in Bosnia, *The European*, 26 September–2 October 1996.

[121] Borger, J. – Massive vote-rigging taints Bosnia election, *Guardian Weekly*, 29 September 1996.

[122] The memoirs of two participants, Carl Bilt and Richard Holbrooke, have been published (Bildt, C.
– *Peace Journey*, Weidenfeld, 1998; Holbrooke, R. – *To End a War*, Random House, New York, 1998)
to present personalized accounts of what had taken place.

revealing how much disagreement there had been between the proponents of American and European foreign policy during and after negotiations. Whatever was negotiated then provided scope for further disagreements between international and foreign actors themselves. The outcome of the carrot-and-stick strategy whereby Bosnia and Herzegovina was to be pacified and democratized departed from the original purpose of international involvement – to un-do the ethnic engineering and cleansing. Jonathan Ayal noted that prospects were gloomy, 'an ethnic partition which theoretically is accepted by nobody, but ultimately supported by everyone.'[123]

Croatia

Although the main target of condemnations and sanctions was Serbia, Croatia was also affected by the denial of international loans for its ill-deeds in Bosnia and Herzegovina as well as domestic abuses, in particular the forced removal of its Serbian population out of the country. An unnamed World Bank official was thus quoted in 1993 :

> We simply can't lend money to Croatia when Croats are massacring Muslim civilians in central Bosnia. There is no way of ensuring that assets provided won't be misappropriated, since military expenditures gobble up everything else.[124]

Croatia's successful military offensive in Krajina in August 1995 was used as the main pillar for the subsequent elections in October 1995. During its war in Krajina 'the Croatian army has been observed wearing US uniforms, carrying US radios and eating German rations.'[125] The Sanctions Committee remained uninformed about these apparent breaches of sanctions because no government officially reported them, while foreign complicity in warfare did not, at least not yet, become a topic of official investigations. Almost one-third of Croatia's territory was re-conquered and cleansed of the Serbian population. The linkage between battles by bullets and then ballots was illustrated in the inability of the 150,000 or 200,000 Serbs who had been forced out of the country and could not vote, while 380,000 expatriate Croats were given the right to vote.[126] EUrope suspended negotiations of

---

[123] Ayal, J. – Bitter reality exposes Bosnia's poll charade, *Guardian Weekly*, 29 September 1996.

[124] Reforms under siege, *Business Central Europe*, September 1993.

[125] Bellamy, C. – Upgraded armament and tactics brought victory, *The Independent*, 8 August 1995.

[126] The EU foreign ministers in their joint statement of 30 October 1995 stated: 'The granting of reconstruction assistance to Croatia should be linked to the creation of real return option by the Croat government for the Serbs and to strict respect for human and minority rights.' Croatia accord set back, *European Voice*, 2–8 November 1995.

a co-operation agreement with Croatia in August 1995 in response to warfare[127] to resume them in October 1995, at the time of elections, while the EBRD also resumed its lending to Croatia at the same time.[128]

The free-but-not-fair verdict of international and foreign electoral observers with regard to the 1995 elections hid differences among them. The OSCE noted pre-election flows, including 'ongoing looting, house burning and killing of elderly Serbs' as well as gaps between the electoral practices and 'desired standards', but concluded that elections had been 'orderly and free.'[129] The US Commission on Security and Cooperation is Europe was not so generous. It noted that 'elections were scheduled a year in advance to capitalize politically on the Croatian Army's victories in retaking occupied territory', concluding that the elections 'seemed almost an expression of defiance of any democratic trend that may exist in Croatia.'[130]

Croatia's admission to the Council of Europe was approved by the Parliamentary Assembly in the spring of 1996 but blocked by the Council of Ministers. Reasons were many: denial of the right of return to the Serbian population and the associated denials of minority rights, the lack of co-operation with the International War Crimes Tribunal, as well as the harassment of human rights activists and journalists. President Franjo Tudjman argued that such a decision was surprising after countries such as Turkey, Albania, Moldova and Russia had been admitted.[131] His line of argument prevailed and Croatia was admitted in October 1996. *Le monde* commented that this gesture stripped the Council of Europe 'of a part of its significance and its mission.'[132]

In June 1997 Croatia was threatened with suspension of aid for impeding the return of the expelled Serbian population, who had fled from the onslaught of Croatia's army two years earlier.[133] The World Bank 'postponed the consideration' of a loan to Croatia the following month, citing concerns of its major shareholders over compliance with the Dayton Agreement. The media was explicit:

---

[127] An anonymous Phare official had this to say:The ink on the agreement allowing Croatia into the Phare programme was not even dry when they launched the Krajina offensive and when the agreement was revoked, they did not seem to care. Priorities differ prior to start of donors' conference, *European Voice*, 11–17 April 1996.

[128] Croatia accord set back, *European Voice*, 2–8 November 1995; EBRD to invest in Croatia, *Financial Times*, 1 November 1995.

[129] OSCE Parliamentary Assembly – Report on the elections to the House of Representatives in the Republic of Croatia, 29 October 1995, dated 5 November 1995, no place of issue, mimeographed.

[130] Commission on Security and Cooperation in Europe – *1995 Parliamentary Elections in Croatia*, Washington, D.C., February 1996, p. 1.

[131] Silber, L. and Robinson, A. – Tudjman furious over European bar, *Financial Times*, 16 May 1996.

[132] Recognition for Croatia undeserved, *Le monde*, 8 November 1996, reproduced in *Guardian Weekly*, 17 November 1996.

[133] Dobbs, M. – Albright sharply rebukes Balkan leaders, *The Washington Post*, reprinted in *Guardian Weekly*, 8 June 1997.

The World Bank has delayed indefinitely, at the request of the US government, a meeting which had been due to approve a $30 million loan for Croatia. Having handed over to the Hague Tribunal ten indictees, Croatia was promised not to be threatened by economic sanctions.'[134]

Croatia continued being a target of diplomatic and economic sanctions, however, until the death of its first president, Franjo Tudjman,[135] which was followed by hopes for a changed government to result from elections planned for January 2000.

Kosovo

Foreign-policy determinants that profiled strategies of different foreign and international actors involved in Bosnia also molded international responses to developments in and around Kosovo. Sanctions against Serbia followed warfare which erupted in 1998, after at least seven years of Kosovars' popular resistance against Serbia's governance. These seven years were inaugurated by a 1991 referendum, which reflected the overwhelming support for independence but has not been recognized by Serbia. Resistence to Serbian/Yugoslav authorities has been accompanied by the mobilization of international support. That support was not forthcoming for independence but rather for decreased repression and increased autonomy, which were reportedly amongst US conditions for lifting financial sanctions against Serbia/Yugoslavia.[136]

The Security Council imposed an arms embargo (with China's abstention), having determined 'the use of excessive force by Serbian police forces against civilians and peaceful demonstrators in Kosovo, as well as all acts of terrorism by the Kosovo Liberation Army.'[137] Neither side has been short of weapons at any point and thus the arms embargo seems to have been ineffective. Threats of the use of armed force[138] to suppress Serbia's repression in Kosovo had at first been deemed to constitute just threats; economic sanctions were initially used as the second best. As in 1991, EUrope led the way in sanctions against Yugoslavia/

[134] Robinson, A. – US action blocks loan for Croatia, *Financial Times*, 25 June 1997; Dinmore, G. – Croatians rejoining the club, *Financial Times*, 9 February 1998.

[135] Diplomats hope for thaw in EU's relations with Croatia, *European Voice*, 16 December 1999–5 January 2000.

[136] Williams, I. – US friends groomed to aid Kosovo, *The European*, 2–8 January 1997.

[137] Security Council resolution 1160 (1998) of 31 March 1998, preamble.

[138] The strategy of containment was put into practice through NATO's military co-operation with Albania and Macedonia, and Albania reportedly requested a NATO force alongside the border with Kosovo. (Buchan, D. – Nato prepares for Kosovo explosion, *Financial Times*, 29 May 1998) It was reportedly decided on 6 June 1998 that air strikes (patterned after NATO's bombing three years earlier) would be explored as an option, but planning was not set into motion and thus a discrepancy between political and military decision-making came into the open. (The descent into another Balkan war, *The Economist*, 13 June 1998.)

Serbia, with the Commission proposing a ban on new investment with a broad
formulation that would have outlawed 'ownership of any assets in the Republic
of Serbia' (indicatively not mentioning its official, albeit disputed name
'Yugoslavia'). That would have stopped companies with assets and/or investment
from routine operations such as replacing old machinery. A clarification followed,
whereby only new investment was banned, exempting also day-to-day commercial
transactions. Concerning enforcement, it transpired that only Finland's domestic
law included a possibility for applying sanctions against companies or individuals
for breaches of EUrope's sanctions against Serbia.[139]

Paradoxically, US sanctions against Yugoslavia/Serbia had been slightly eased
in February 1998[140] because the situation in Bosnia was perceived as improving, and then things took a turn for worse in Kosovo and sanctions followed
immediately.

An arms embargo was imposed in March 1998 and accompanied with a threat
that Yugoslavia's assets abroad would be frozen if repression in Kosovo continued.
Sanctions immediately fell into a *gringo's light switch* model: between March and
June sanctions were threatened, imposed, withdrawn and threatened again;[141] thereafter sanctions were eased again when Yugoslavia agreed to a 'meaningful dialogue' with Kosovars.[142] A ban on air traffic was imposed in June (with Russia
abstaining from the vote).[143] Demands for lifting sanctions ranged between the
withdrawal of Yugoslav/Serbian army and the police from Kosovo, 'a genuine dialogue' between the Yugoslav/Serbian government and Kosovar representatives
(whose definition and scope kept changing), and to differently defined autonomy
for Kosovo. The process of closed- and semi-open door negotiations precluded
public insight into the substance of various proposals and counter-proposals, the
identification of actors who were negotiating, as well as into the fate of human
rights in this process. What could be inferred was that preservation of territorial
integrity was initially given precedence over demands for self-determination, with
minority-rights guarantees for the Kosovar majority. Subsequent to the 1999
NATO military intervention, demands broadened to changing Serbia's leader,[144]
following the pattern established for Saddam Hussein.

[139] Turner, M. – Discord erodes force of Serbia sanctions, *European Voice*, 16–22 July 1998.
[140] Sanctions eased on Yugoslavia, *Financial Times*, 24 February 1998.
[141] Dinmore, G. – Talks edge closer over Kosovo, *Financial Times*, 12 March 1998; Black, I. – West
gets tough with Milosevic, *Guardian Weekly*, 15 March 1998; Clinton's empty threats (editorial),
The Washington Post, reprinted in *Guardian Weekly*, 14 June 1998; Walker, M. and Norton-Taylor, R. –
Europe warns Milosevic to pull out army, *Guardian Weekly*, 14 June 1998.
[142] Yugoslav sanctions on hold, *The Independent*, 19 May 1998.
[143] Buchan, D. – West and east demand action over Kosovo, *Financial Times*, 13–14 June 1998.
[144] Black, I. – Serbia must get rid of Milosevic, say summit leaders, *Guardian Weekly*, 5–11 August
1999.

When the threats of military intervention were transformed into action, a precedent was created for NATO military intervention without an authorization by the Security Council.[145] This widened the gulf between the United Nations and NATO. Post-Dayton NATO (without a role for the United Nations) further marginalized the United Nations as well as dispensing with the requirement that armed force should be authorized lest it be determined as illegal.

The practice of extra-legality, epitomized in denying the application of the legal prohibition of the use of armed force,[147] has also been reflected in resort to decision-making by actors without any status under international law. The main international actors involved in the Kosovo crisis have consisted of several overlapping groupings, with the Contact Group formally constituting the key negotiating and decision-making body. All members of the Contact Group (USA, Russia, France, Germany, Italy and the United Kingdom) have also been members of NATO except Russia, four out of six members have been veto-wielding members of the Security Council, and four out of six members of the European Union. Any of these separate groupings to which members of the Contact Group belonged (NATO, Security Council, EUrope) made statements and demands in the name of 'the international community' and, accordingly, this 'international community' became a weasel-word. Differing statements and demands have revealed the absence of hierarchical decision-making as well as the lack of a singularity of purpose that could have translated into a coherent strategy.

---

[145] The two grounds for resort to armed force under the United Nations Charter are self-defense and Security Council's enforcement action. Neither could be used for the 1999 NATO bombing spree. Moreover, the North Atlantic Treaty (*United Nations Treaty Series*, vol. 34, p. 243) explicitly committed NATO to the observance of the UN Charter (in Articles 1 and 7). The clarity of this legal case probably inspired Serbia's government to file a case against ten members of NATO (avoiding those, such as the United States, that do not recognize ICJ's jurisdiction) before the International Court of Justice on 10 May 1999. It is possible that this case will not go any further than the 1993 genocide case filed by Bosnia and Herzegovina against Yugoslavia/Serbia, thus leaving major crises of 1999 outside the remit of international law. The North Atlantic Treaty, however, has also included a commitment whereby its provisions would be carried out by its members 'in accordance with their respective constitutional processes' (Article 11), which has opened the possibility of domestic legal challenge because not a single participant in the NATO bombing seems to have followed domestic constitutional requirements for waging a war.

[147] It would be difficult to imagine any Western leader openly acknowledging a knowing breach of international law and so it was brushed aside as being inapplicable or non-existent. The British Foreign Secretary, Robin Cook, presented NATO's action as 'purely humanitarian' (Why Kosovo matters, *Guardian Weekly*, 4 April 1999), French President Jacques Chirac charged Serbia's president, Slobodan Milosevic, with responsibility for 200,000 deaths in the Balkans (Buchan, D. – Confusion's master-piece, *Financial Times*, 31 March 1999). Madeleine Albright and Robin Cook, the US and British foreign ministers, posited as the aim of NATO bombing as the creation of 'the conditions under which the ethnic cleansing of Kosovo can be reversed.' (Albright, M.K. and Cook, R. – The air campaign remains the right thing to do, *International Herald Tribune*, 17 May 1999.) The US Special Envoy to the Balkans at the time, Richard Holbrooke, was quoted saying that the reason for bombing had been 'to ensure the credibility of NATO.' (Pilger, J. – War in Europe, *New Statesman*, 2 April 1999, p. 13.)

The absence of a strategy that would have included some minimum human rights guarantees was revealed as soon as an international protectorate, patterned after Bosnia and Herzegovina, was established in Kosovo. Previous repression against Albanian population was merely re-targeted against Serbian and Roma population, whose estimated size was halved within the first few months.[148] Elizabeth Sellwood noted the absence of prospects for their human rights: 'advocating tolerance of Serb and other minority groups would be an electoral liability for Kosovar politicians.'[149] Elections are likely to follow nevertheless, while in the meantime multiple international actors involved in designing a blueprint for the future of Kosovo have seemed at odds with each other. Differences were particularly visible relating to the status of the KLA (Kosovo Liberation Army).[150] The Security Council demanded demilitarization of the KLA,[151] but it was instead 'transformed but not demilitarized' according to an agreement between NATO and KLA,[152] not furnishing grounds for optimism regarding a coherent and human-rights-based international strategy for Kosovo.

Georgia

Georgia's independence in 1992 was followed, with much delay, by its application for membership in the Council of Europe in 1996 (to which it was admitted in 1999) and an association agreement with the European Union in 1997. The years in-between were dotted with warfare: one war was fought in South Ossetia in 1992 because Ossetians wished to join North Ossetia, which was part of Russia. Another war was fought in Abkhazia in 1993–94 (with occasional eruptions thereafter) because Abkhazia wanted independence. In the capital, nightly gun battles were fought to conquer institutions of the newly established state.

Georgia's retrospective description of its first years of statehood states that the first democratically elected president, Zviad Gamsakhurida, won elections 'appeal-

---

[148] According to UNHCR data, the Serb population decreased by 63% and other minorities (including Roma) by 75%. Kosovo resurgent, *The Economist*, 25 September 1999.

[149] Sellwood, E. – Frustration grows, *The World Today*, December 1999, p. 9.

[150] The KLA seems to have been set up in 1992 out of previously existing Kosovar armed movements amongst the diaspora in Western Europe; there has been a great deal of concern about its sources of funding. Viktor Chernomyrdin, formed Russia's prime minister and special Russia's envoy for Kosovo, posited drug trafficking as the main source of funding (Chernomyrdin, V. – 'Impossible to talk as bombs fall,' *The Washington Post*, reprinted in Guarding Weekly, 6 June 1999) while Christophe Chiclet pointed to the imposition of compulsory financial contributions upon Kosovar diaspora. (Chiclet, C. – Rise of the Kosovar freedom fighters, *Le monde diplomatique*, English edition, May 1999.)

[151] Security Council resolution 1244 (1999) of 10 June 1999, paras. 9 (b) and 15.

[152] Wright, R. and Morris, H. – KLA determined to become a political force, *Financial Times*, 22 June 1999; Smith, J. – Confusion reigns in Kosovo, *The Washington Post*, reprinted in *Guardian Weekly*, 22–28 July 1999; LeBor, A. – KLA to become official Kosovo Corps, *The Independent*, 8 September 1999.

ing to the nationalistic and anti-communist sentiments of the masses'[153] and was subsequently ousted through a military coup. The subsequent president, Eduard Shevardnadze, was brought back from his duties in Moscow to lead his native land. Western support for democracy was faulted after 'Zviad Gamsakhurdia, an unattractive character but nevertheless the elected president of the republic, was forcibly removed from his post by Eduard Shevardnadze, to whom the West gave its full support,'[154]

Georgia's human rights performance could not have been impressive due to all these political and armed conflicts, aggravated by economic retrogression. Its assessment by the Human Rights Committee in 1997 was a depressive reading. The Committee deplored the absence of remedies for human rights violations, was concerned about torture, deplored widespread abuse of pre-trial detention and police custody, and found prisons to be disastrous.[155]

The first Georgia's president, Zviad Gamsakhurdia, made the abolition of autonomy for South Ossetia and Adjaria priorities in his political platform. A vicious circle of warfare was unleashed after the respective claimants sought Russia's assistance,[156] which then reinforced Georgia's political leadership in their determination to seek a militarily victory.

Four wars – two defined as such, two deemed minor – erupted within Georgia in quick succession; two were struggles to conquer the state and two to leave it. Warfare in South Ossetia (defined alternatively to have begun in 1989 or 1992) ended with an armed truce and deployment of an OSCE mission. It was immediately followed by warfare in Abkhazia in 1992–93. The first cease-fire, mediated by Russia, collapsed within a month and one year later Abkhazia won militarily, driving both Georgia's armed forces and Georgian population from its territory. A two-layered peace-keeping force (consisting of 3,000 CIS, mainly Russian, peace-keepers and 150 UN observers) was deployed to secure the border between the two warring parties.[157] Abkhazia deemed itself independent and held elections in 1996.[158] Those revealed intricacies that foreign and international involvement in

---

[153] United Nations – Core document forming part of the reports of States parties: Georgia, U.N. Doc. HRI/CORE/1/Add. 90 of 2 February 1998, para. 38.

[154] Vitaliev, V. – For Yeltsin, read Bolshevik, *The European*, 30 September–3 October 1993.

[155] Human Rights Committee – Concluding observations: Georgia, U.N. Doc. CCPR/C/79/Add.75 of 5 May 1997.

[156] Russia had initially supported the Abkhaz side and in 1993 shifted to Georgia's side; in 1996 it reportedly had 'a large military base in Georgia' (Williams, S. – Why Georgia has Europe on its mind, *The European*, 8–14 August 1996), but in 1997 Georgia joined GUAM (Georgia, Ukraine, Azerbaijan and Moldova), a grouping of four states that found a common interest in the fact that each claim that Russia was involved with a secessionist movement on its territory. (Radvanyi, J. – Transports et géostratégie au sud de la Russie, *Le monde diplomatique*, June 1998, p. 19.)

[157] MacFarlane, S.N. – On the front lines in the near abroad: The CIS and the OSCE in Georgia's civil wars, *Third World Quarterly*, vol. 18, 1997, No. 3, p. 517–518.

[158] Williams, S. – Abkhazia pays high price for self-rule, and Anger over Abkhazia poll 'farce', *The European*, 21–27 November and 28 November–4 December 1996.

conflict-resolution had to tackle: elections were denounced by Georgia because the Georgian population could not vote. It had been cleansed out of Abkhazia and was lingering in internal displacement. Had Abkhazia allowed their return, elections would have been influenced by Georgian votes as they had been 45% of Abkhazia's population before warfare started. The Security Council declared actions by 'Abkhaz authorities' jeopardizing territorial integrity of Georgia to be unacceptable and condemned their preventing refugees from returning.[159] Fears were that these precepts would be enforced through another war. A historic meeting between Abkhaz and Georgian presidents committed themselves not 'to allow a resumption of bloodshed.'[160] A truce continued without a solution to the underlying conflict.

Much as ethnicity was identified as the principal cause of warfare,[161] an important factor was pipeline politics, namely expected revenue from oil and gas extracted in Kazakhstan and Turkmenistan and shipped westwards. A pipeline for Caspian oil towards the Black Sea was expected to generate $130 million in investment and $8 million in annual revenues.[162] It was allegedly pipeline politics that threatened a resumption of warfare in 1998 and almost cost Georgia's president his life.[163] The location of the pipeline was hoped to solve chronic impoverishment.

The state of Georgia has found itself throughout its existence as an independent state having nothing to offer its population – neither peace and security, nor an economic basis for survival. A pipeline and the ensuing oil-and-gas wealth have then appeared as a cure for all ills and came to dominate both regional politics and foreign policies towards the region.

Nagorno Karabakh, Armenia and Azerbaijan

Overlapping territorial claims in the ethnic and religious patchwork of the Caucasus have led to a series of armed conflicts after the disintegration of the Soviet Union. Every and any of them led to allegations of human rights violations, routinely by all warring parties; every and any of them was justified by the right to self-determination by the warring parties. Conflicting territorial claims originated in desires to restore the previous borders. These claims overlapped because some actors aimed at pre-1944 or pre-1917 borders, while other insisted on the restoration of their pre-1917 territorial status, yet others went further back into history. The Soviet army tried to suppress aspirations towards secession in Georgia in 1989 and in Azerbaijan in 1990 leading to the spiraling ethnic and religious radicalization. The subsequent dissolution of the Soviet Union, and the corresponding division of the army in 1992, led to warfare.

---

[159] Security Council resolution 1065 (1996) of 12 July 1996, paras. 3 and 6.
[160] Meek, J. – Hopes high for peace in Georgia, *Guardian Weekly*, 24 August 1997.
[161] Cheterian, V. – Le Géorgie face à ses minorités, *Le monde diplomatique*, December 1998.
[162] Georgia: Great game, *The Economist*, 20 July 1996.
[163] Williams, S. – Pipeline row sparked unrest, says Georgia, *Financial Times*, 29 May 1998.

In October 1992 war erupted in North Ossetia, triggered by a proclamation of an Ingush Republic. Demands of statehood for Abkhazia, South Ossetia and Chechnya all resulted in warfare. Armenia and Azerbaijan have fought a war about the fate of Nagorno Karabakh. Consecutive military victories factually made Nagorno Karabakh part of Armenia, thus changing the borders on the ground, but these changed have not been not politically or legally recognized. International and foreign actors were faced with a flood of claims and counter-claims, allegations of abuses and counter-abuses, conflicting assertions of rights and wrongs.

The 1991–94 war for Nagorno Karabakh, a small Armenian enclave in Azerbaijan with a population of 100,000–200,000 (depending on the source and the time), brought a litany of abuses to the international human rights agenda. From forced removal of populations to the bombardment of civilian targets, from arbitrary detentions and torture to blockades aimed at starving civilians into exodus or submission, the war for Nagorno Karabakh exhibited the whole range of atrocities typifying warfare that is uninhibited by humanitarian considerations. The underlying rationale was to right layers of historical wrongs – to reunite Nagorno Karabakh with Armenia on the basis of ethnicity of the majority living there, and to preserve the territorial integrity of Azerbaijan by preventing this.

A demand of statehood was not conceded by the main inter-governmental mediator, the OSCE. The 1996 Lisbon Summit could not attain consensus due to Armenia's opposition to the denial of a right to statehood for Nagorno Karabakh. A chairman's statement was adopted instead, anticipating that Nagorno Karabakh would remain within Azerbaijan with 'the highest degree of self-rule.'[164] A ceasefire negotiated in 1994, and interrupted by sporadic warfare, was founded upon the acquiescence of the two main combatants to a final compromise. That had reportedly been the result of combined pressure of Russia and the United States,[165] with the latter being the major Armenia's donor with an annual $1 billion.[166] US aid has been to a large extent due to political activism of the Armenian diaspora, which constitutes one of the most influential 'ethnic lobbies,' not only in the United States. Compared with Armenia's population of a 3.7 million, the Armenian diaspora of 4 million[167] exercises a great deal of influence in keeping Nagorno Karabakh and Armenia in the limelight of international human rights politics, mobilizing financial aid and political support. The 1988 earthquake, the Nagorno Karabakh conflict, and the associated Azerbaijan's blockade and Turkey's

---

[164] Bloed, A. – OSCE: Lisbon Summit was no spectacular event, *Netherlands Quarterly of Human Rights*, 1997, No. 1, p. 90.
[165] Tordai, J. – An intractable conflict, *The Middle East*, February 1997, p. 14.
[166] Williams, S. – Hopes slim for progress on Karabakh, *Financial Times*, 16 April 1998.
[167] Armenia: Core document forming part of reports of States parties, U.N. Doc. HRI/CORE/1/Add. 57 of 30 June 1995, para. 2.

embargo, prompted humanitarian aid which made Armenia's ministry of social welfare 'a key player in the economy through control of humanitarian aid.'[168]

Historical wrongs affecting the Armenians of Karabakh originated in their unfortunate position on the very border between the Byzantine Empire and Zoroastrian Persia. The Armenians were victimized by the 1914–16 genocide, which cleansed away non-Muslim minorities in Turkey. Nagorno Karabakh was initially spared having been ruled by Russia until Turkey's offensive at the end of the First World War. Turkey's subsequent surrender led to Azerbaijan's sovereignty over Karabakh, which was confirmed by the 1921 decision of the Soviet Transcaucasian Bureau, albeit with a promise of 'a large measure of regional autonomy.'[169] Such regional autonomy never materialized. Attempts at declaring independence of Nagorno Karabakh during the demise of the Soviet Union led to the imposition of blockade by Azerbaijan so as to starve Nagorno Karabakh into submission and to the retaliation by Armenia in the form of mass expulsion of Azeris.[170]

Warfare started in 1992, after a referendum on independence and the setting up of parliament in Nagorno Karabakh. The background was the withdrawal of the Soviet army after the Soviet Union had been dissolved. The armed conflict was accompanied with the isolation of Armenia by its neighbours, which resulted in its passing one winter without electricity or heating and its industrial production coming to halt. Foreign and international support for Armenia aimed to counter these effects.

Militarily, the war for Nagorno Karabakh ended with the cleansing off of the Azeri population and effective (if unrecognized) Armenia's control, constantly challenged by Azerbaijan. There is virtually nothing that the two parties can agree upon, as evidenced in their interpretations of the beginning of the armed conflicts. Armenia's version goes like this:

> Ten years ago, in 1988, as a response to a peaceful and constitutional demand of the Nagorny-Karabakh people to exercise its right to self-determination, the Azeri authorities organized an armed mob which launched programs against Armenians living in the Azeri city of Sumgait. These massacres were the first acts of mass killings on the territory of the former Soviet Union, as documented by the criminal proceedings launched by the Soviet authorities. Immediately after declaring its independence, Azerbaijan freed the accused murderers and openly saluted them as national heroes in the mass media. ... Massacres in Ganja, Baku and other cities between 1988 and 1991 were far more barbaric and massive, leading to the deportation and ethnic cleansing of about half a million Armenians. These atrocities were followed by unprecedented Azeri military offensives and operations designed to implement a military solution by

---

[168] Bremmer, I. and Welt, C. – A break with the past? State and economy in post-communist Armenia, *Helsinki Monitor*, 1997, No. 1. p. 40.

[169] Cox, C. and Eibner, J. – *Ethnic Cleansing in Progress: War in Nagorno Karabakh*, Institute for Religious Minorities in the Islamic World, Zürich/London/Washington, 1993, p. 31.

[170] Human Rights Watch/Helsinki – Escalation of the armed conflicts in Nagorno-Karabakh, New York, September 1992.

annihilating the Nagorny-Karabakh population. It has to be finally and forever clarified that it was Azerbaijan which started an armed aggression against Nagorny-Karabakh.[171]

Azerbaijan's version:

The armed hostilities against Azerbaijan were preceded by anti-constitutional actions in the Nagorno-Karabakh region of Azerbaijan perpetrated by separatist groups receiving outside support; forming the backdrop to these actions were certain decisions taken by the Armenian authorities in contravention of international law. Of these decisions, the most notorious is the resolution 'Reunification of the Armenian Soviet Socialist Republic and Nagorno-Karabakh' adopted by the Armenian Parliament on 1 December 1989. Moreover, in Armenia's Declaration of Sovereignty of 23 August 1990, part of the territory of another State – the Nagorno-Karabakh region of Azerbaijan – is recognized as an integral part of the Republic of Armenia. These decisions by the Armenian Parliament were enacted by its armed forces with the widespread use of mercenary bands and a sudden upsurge in terrorist activity by the Armenian special services and terrorist organizations against sovereign Azerbaijan State with a view of wresting away part of its age-old lands. All-out hostilities began at the end of 1991 and the beginning of 1992 when Armenian armed formations initiated combat operations in the Nagorno-Karabakh region of Azerbaijan using most sophisticated weapons systems.[172]

The negotiated end of the 1991–94 war, an 'armed truce' rather than peace, was followed by a change of political leadership in Armenia. The previous president, Levon Ter-Petrosian, was forced out of office and the most often cited reason was his willingness to compromise on the final determination of Nagorno Karabakh's status.[173] Ter-Petrosian had started his political career through the Karabakh Committee (later re-named Armenian National Movement) and perhaps it was poetic justice that his career ended because of Karabakh. He was replaced by Robert Khotcharian, previously president of Nagorno Karabakh and later the prime minister in Ter-Petrosian's government.[174] Ter-Petrosian entered history having the

[171] Commission on Human Rights – Letter dated 14 April 1998 from the Permanent representative of Armenia to the United Nations Office at Geneva addressed to the Chairman of the Commission on Human Rights, U.N. Doc. E/CN.4/1998/166 of 15 April 1998, p. 2.

[172] Commission on Human Rights – Letter dated 9 March 1998 from the Permanent Representative of the Republic of Azerbaijan to the United Nations Office at Geneva addressed to the Chairman of the Committee on the Elimination of Racial Discrimination, U.N. Doc. E/CN.4/1998/131 of 12 march 1998, p. 2.

[173] Armenia: And presidents go, *The Economist*, 7 February 1998; Sheets, L. – Armenia poll under scrutiny, *Guardian Weekly*, 29 March 1998; Williams, D. – Armenians disappointed by freedom, *The Washington Post*, reprinted in *Guardian Weekly*, 15 March 1998.

[174] Can Armenia's new man deal?, *The Economist*, 4 April 1998.

1996 presidential elections (which he won) faulted by the OSCE, which was only the second time for the OSCE not to have passed its usual favourable verdict.[175] It had found a surplus of 22,013 ballots over the number of voters, while Ter-Petrosian won by a margin of 21,941 votes.[176] In the words of Edmund Herzig, these elections were

> the cover under which a small corrupt clique can concentrate wealth and power in its own hands, and at the same time present to international observers a picture of transition to democracy and market economy.[177]

On the Azeri side, the failure to keep military control over Nagorno Karabakh led to the ousting of two consecutive presidents, in 1992 and 1993. The latter followed Armenia's victory in the war in Nagorno Karabakh, which secured *de facto* independence for Nagorno Karabakh from Azerbaijan, Armenia's occupation of a swathe of territory around Karabakh and internal displacement of between 500,000 and 1 million Azeris. The territory from which Azeris had been cleansed was then populated by Armenians.[178]

Azerbaijan's economic prospects have considerably improved in the meantime. In 1994, an $8 billion contract with a consortium of oil companies was signed by the government of Azerbaijan and oil started flowing three years later.[179] Estimates of the total investment by oil companies were between $18 and $23 billion and Azerbaijan's revenue over the next thirty years was estimated at $60 billion.[180] International attention shifted from much reported abuses by the government of Azerbaijan to its forthcoming oil wealth. Aid politics did not become easier, however:

> While American companies pour billions of dollars into Baku, the American government is barred by Congress, thanks to its vigorous Armenian lobby, from giving almost any aid state aid to Azerbaijan.[181]

---

[175] The list of ODIHR election monitoring missions is annexed to Prins, D. And Würzner – Transition or tradition? The United Nations, the OSCE and electoral assistance, *Helsinki Monitor*, 1996, No. 4, pp. 30–31.

[176] ODIHR (the Office for Democratic Institutions and Human Rights of the OSCE) report on the presidential elections in Armenia, 22 September 1996, reproduced in *Helsinki Monitor*, 1996, No. 4, p. 109.

[177] Herzig, E. – Shame and gloom as everyone loses in Armenia, *The World Today*, November 1996, p. 293.

[178] Meek, J. – Armenians carve up Azeri regions, *Guardian Weekly*, 22 June 1997.

[179] Williams, S. – Azeri consortium rolls out the barrels, *Financial Times*, 12 November 1997.

[180] Collet, N. – Azerbaijan: Land of black gold, *The Middle East*, March 1997; Williams, S. – Oil boom that can't get started, *The European*, 12–18 June 1997.

[181] The Caucasus: That mountain conundrum, *The Economist*, 1 November 1997.

The 1992 Freedom Support Act precluded aid to Azerbaijan because of its blockade against Armenia,[182] but the two influential lobbies – the Armenian diaspora and oil companies – have continued pursuing incompatible agendas, the former lobbying for sanctions against Azerbaijan and aid to Armenia, the latter for aid to Azerbaijan to facilitate the exploration and exploitation of oil.

Settling armed conflicts was seen as the essential prerequisite for the anticipated profits from oil, and attaining stability became a keyword in foreign policy. Although international and foreign electoral observers had not endorsed elections in Azerbaijan,[183] the elected leaders were retroactively endorsed as guarantors of stability. In May 1998, foreign oil companies were reportedly looking for ways of advancing oil revenues to Azerbaijan so as to strengthen the country's stability.[184] Whether the prospects of oil wealth will strengthen or undermine stability is un-knowable.

Russia/Chechnya

The disintegration of the Soviet Union created a host of problems for Western foreign policies. Uniqueness of Russia was – and remains – grounded in the fear of explosion or implosion. Food aid was supplied at the time of the disintegration of the Soviet Union in 1991 and food aid became one of the principal issues in EUrope's relations with Russia in 1998–99. EUrope's practice of disposing of agricultural surplus through food aid has had a great deal of influence on the emphasis on food aid. The foremost priority concern was – and is – nuclear safety exemplified by fears of the lack of a centralized control over nuclear weapons and shaky security of nuclear power plants. It has been coupled with EUrope's fears of a flood of refugees and/or immigrants that could accompany any major crisis in Russia.

There were plenty of incidents which triggered calls for punitive conditionality against Russia, but these were overshadowed by principal foreign policy concerns. Russia's consecutive financial crises inevitably triggered Western loans, the many elections were determined to have been free and fair, the first war against Checnya (1994–96) received much publicity but neither inter-governmental condemnations nor unilateral sanctions followed, reactions to the second one have been equally muted.

The Russian (previously Soviet) military interventions were frequent. The early ones took place in Tbilsi in April 1989, in Baku in January 1990 and Erevan in

[182] Gall, C. – Nagorny Karabakh: Peace deal eludes ethnic conflict, Azerbaijan survey, *Financial Times*, 3 March 1998.

[183] LeVine, S. – Officials in Azerbaijan rigged elections openly, observers say, *International Herald Tribune*, 16 November 1995; Pope, H. – Poll shows weakness of Kazakh democracy, *The Independent*, 10 March 1994.

[184] Corzine, R. and Gall, C. – Move to speed oil cash to Baku, *Financial Times*, 15 May 1998.

May 1990, and in Lithuania and Latvia in January 1991. Each one prompted calls for a Western punitive response. After the Soviet Union demanded Western assistance for the first time, in May 1990, possibilities of applying economic inducements and sanctions by altering aid flows broadened Western choices. In June 1990, the MFN status was denied to the Soviet Union because of its economic blockade against Lithuania. In December 1990 the European Council first decided on aid to the former Soviet Union, which was suspended shortly thereafter as a response to the Soviet armed repression in the Baltics; aid was un-suspended again in September 1991.[185] One of the first joint actions of the European Union within common foreign and security policy was a EU observer mission to Russian parliamentary elections in December 1993 and EUrope's contribution to these elections also included trade concessions[186] to facilitate the victory of the favoured candidate. Europe was then in a self-congratulatory mood:

> The operation's success lent credibility to Russia's electoral process while demonstrating the European Union's capacity to provide effective electoral support for the democratic process.[187]

The many Russian elections, although hailed in the West, were accompanied by much anxiety. There was initially no shortage of elections – in March 1989, December 1993, and December 1995 parliamentary elections, in June 1991 presidential elections, in March 1990 referendum on constitutional amendments, in March 1991 referendum on preservation of the Soviet Union.[188] In April 1993 there was a referendum on the presidential powers. In-between various elections and referenda, a military coup took place in August 1991. It was condemned by Western countries, with a corollary suspension of aid.[189] The self-coup by President Yeltsin

---

[185] EC approves aid for Soviet states, *International Herald Tribune*, 5 September 1991.

[186] Barber, L. and Lloyd, J. – Russia wins European trade concessions, *Financial Times*, 10 November 1993.

[187] European Commission – *General Report on the Activities of the European Union 1994*, Brussels/Luxembourg, 1995, para. 739.

[188] The question posed to the electorate read as follows (in standard translation to English): 'Do you consider it necessary to preserve the Union of Soviet Socialist Republics as a renewed federation of equal sovereign republics, in which human rights and the freedoms of all nationalities will be fully guaranteed?' If the electorate did not know what the question meant, nor did the experts. The promise of guaranteed human rights sounded appealing, but guarantees of freedoms of all nationalities must have created many different interpretations of what was actually being promised. This, however, remains of historical interest only because the Soviet Union dissolved within six months of this referendum.

[189] Within a week of the coup, Europe, the United States and West European bilateral donors suspended aid to the Soviet Union, as it then was, to resume aid one week later. (Bush, back in capital, suspends Kremlin aid; EC cites 'violation', halts Kremlin aid; The coup finished, West resumes aid, *International Herald Tribune*, 20, 21 and 23 August 1991).

took place in September-October 1993. It was not condemned by the West. On the contrary, their increased aid commitments rewarded it. A meeting of EU's foreign ministers called for accelerated and increased aid to Russia and promised that negotiations of a free trade agreement would be accelerated.[190] A pre-electoral European Parliament's mission to Russia heard a 'litany of complaints' relating to the forthcoming parliamentary elections but Western support did not diminish.[191] Parliamentary elections were held in December 1995 and presidential in June 1996, while the first war in Chechnya continued.

The twenty-one-month war in Chechnya, between December 1994 and May 1996, ended with the withdrawal of the Russian army and *de facto* independence for Chechnya. A decision on Chechnya's status was postponed for five years, according to the wording of the Khasavyurt peace agreement signed in May 1997. Elections had been held and declared free-and-fair, the capital was renamed from Grozny to Jokhar-Gala, the country from Chechnya to Ichkeria, and ambassadors appointed to represent the country abroad,[192] although Chechnya was not recognized by any country and it was thus unknown where those ambassadors were to go. Shamil Basaev became the first acting prime minister. He was best known for the hostage-taking operation in Budyonnovsk in June 1995, whereby Chechnya's war was taken to Russia, some 1,200 people taken hostage, and at least 100 killed in the rescue operation by the Russian armed forces.[193] Basaev's intervention in the neighbouring Dagestan provoked the second Russian war in October 1999.

Some 40,000 Russian troops fought in Chechnya in 1994–96, almost 4,000 were killed. Casualties on the Chechen side were estimated at between 30,000 and 80,000. The capital, Grozny, was reduced from a population of 400,000 to 40,000 between November 1994 and February 1995 as Russia bombed the capital.[194] The Western governments had initially declared the war to be an internal affair.[195]

Chechnya had declared independence following a military coup in 1991 but not a single state recognized it. Justifying the use of armed force, Russia posited that

the initial cause of the tragedy in Chechnya was the seizure of power over a part of the Russian Federation by the illegal regime of Djokhar Dudaev, as a result of

---

[190] Savil, A. and Marshall, A. – The West unites in its support for President, *The Independent*, 5 October 1993.

[191] Yeltsin accused of impeding fair Russian election, *Financial Times*, 5 November 1993; Our Boris, right or wrong, *The Independent*, 7 October 1993; The West's reaction, *The Economist*, 25 September 1995.

[192] Chechnya: Taiwan on the Caucasus, *The Economist*, 22 February 1997; Chechnya: President names ambassadors, *Financial Times*, 21 April 1998.

[193] Russia and Chechnya: Still growling, *The Economist*, 24 January 1998.

[194] Facts and figures, *Challenges. ICRC Magazine*, June 1995, p. 6.

[195] In Europe, 'concern' on Chechen fighting, *International Herald Tribune*, 30 December 1994.

which an abnormal situation developed between 1991 and 1994 in the Chechen Republic.[196]

Russia's self-granted right to prevent secession prevailed, even if its inaction during the 'abnormal situation' in 1991–94 remained a mystery. The United States continued supporting Russia's right to prevent secession, while EUrope moved to condemnations of Russia's excessive and indiscriminatory use of the armed force. The US position was criticised by Human Rights Watch/Helsinki because an IMF loan of $6.8 billion was approved at the time, thus almost directly financing Russia's war effort.[197] The first statement by France, which held the EU Presidency at the time, announced that economic pressure would be used to compel Russia to respect human rights in Chechnya.[198] A month into the war, EUrope postponed signing an interim trade agreement with Russia as 'an unmistakable note of concern.'[199] Russia objected to such 'inadequate and hasty reactions' and refused access to Checnya for OSCE observers and/or mediators.[200] A compromise was forged, with the EUrope-Russia trade agreement further postponed while threats of sanctions were withdrawn, with Russia agreeing to an OSCE mission in Chechnya.[201] The trade agreement was signed in June 1995, after the OSCE mission was accepted by Russia and deployed in Chechnya but the war continued another year.[202]

A draft resolution was tabled before the Sub-Commission on Prevention of Discrimination and Protection of Minorities on Checnya but the draft was withdrawn.[203] The UN Commission on Human Rights opted for a chairman's statement, an optimal solution for situations where no condemnation could ensue while the underlying issue had to be addressed. A chairman's statement was thus adopted in 1995 and 1996, deploring grave violations of human rights before and after the shift from the political to armed conflict, as well as the disproportionate use of the armed force by Russia.[204]

---

[196] Commission on Human Rights – The situation of human rights in the Republic of Chechnya of the Russian Federation. Report of the Secretary-General, U.N. Doc. E/CN.4/1996/13 of 26 March 1996, para. 49.

[197] Russia: Partisan war in Chechnya on the eve of the World War II commemoration, HUman Rights Watch/Helsinki, vol. 7, No. 8, May 1995, p. 6.

[198] Bovay, N.M.L. – The Russian armed intervention in Chechnya and its human rights implications, *The Review of the International Commission of Jurists*, No. 54/1995, p. 34 and 53.

[199] Marshall, A. – EU holds back on treaty in war row, *The Independent*, 6 January 1995.

[200] Hiatt, F. – Russia assails West's stance and warns of risk to ties, *International Herald Tribune*, 13 January 1995.

[201] Marshall, A. and Crawshaw, S. – EU lets Kremlin off the hook, *The Independent*, 24 January 1995.

[202] Marshall, A. – Trade pact signed as Western Europe warms to Russia, *The Independent*, 18 July 1995.

[203] Report of the Sub-Commission on Prevention of Discrimination and Protection of Minorities, U.N. Doc. E/CN.4/1996/2-E/CN.4/Sub.2/1995/51, paras. 247–249.

[204] Commission on Human Rights – Chairman's statement in connection with the situation of human rights in the Republic of Chechnya of the Russian Federation, U.N. Docs. E/CN.4/1995/176, para. 594 and E/CN.4/1996/77, para. 371.

Effects of the war on Russia's budget were estimated at one-third of the planned Russia's budget deficit, equivalent to the $13 billion in loans that were at the time approved by the IMF and the World Bank.[205] If *The Economist* is to be believed, Chechnya demanded $260 billion from Russia as compensation but obtained a promise of $2million[206] which was subsequently not paid as Russia has lurched from one financial crisis to another.

As mentioned above, three years after the first Chechnya war had ended another began, initially in Dagestan, to which Shamil Basayev had taken his combatants along with plans to establish an Islamic state, apparently without support of Dagestani population.[207] Russia's bombing campaign ensued[208] trying to root out the combatants. They were labeled as terrorists because of a series of bombs that exploded in major Russian cities, killing hundreds, that were blamed on 'the Chechens.' Russia's army started its ground war in Chechnya in October 1999, enjoying a great deal of political and public support, and warfare has continued into the year 2000.

Western responses was even more muted that in 1994–96. Concerns over the cost of the war[209] prevailed over concerns about the methods used in waging it. An OSCE meeting in November 1999 resulted in Russia's acquiescence to the provision of humanitarian relief to Chechnya and to entry for a military observer, while a great deal of Western rhetoric about solving the conflict was called 'a pipe dream' by Zbigniew Brzezinski.[210] EUrope suspended some of its technical assistance to Russia at its Helsinki summit in December 1999,[211] which provided an excellent opportunity to make the necessary savings in programmes for Russia in order to fund the newly-decided aid for Kosovo.[212] Because Russia's bombing against Chechnya was a replica of NATO's 'air campaign' earlier in 1999, the circumstances for Western self-righteousness were none to propitious. Another factor in both Russia's and Western strategy is likely to have been pipeline politics.

The main sources of revenue for Chechnya were anticipated exports of oil and transit fees from the oil pipeline, originally anticipated to be the only one to carry the Caspian oil to the Black Sea.[213] According to cynics, wars in Chechnya may

---

[205] Chote, R. – Chechnya 'threat to Moscow budget', *Financial Times*, 6 February 1995; Lloyd, J. – Economy hostage to war, oil and Yeltsin, *Financial Times*, 30 December 1994.

[206] Chechnya: Year zero, and Chechnya: Habeas corpus, *The Economist*, 18 January and 23 August 1997.

[207] Matveeva, A. – Caucasus in flames, *The World Today*, October 1999, pp. 9–11.

[208] Jack, A. – Russia's running sore, *Financial Times*, 29 September 1999.

[209] World Bank warning to Russia over Chechnya, and IMF hints Chechnya puts Russia loans at risk, *Financial Times*, 15 October and 29 November 1999.

[210] Brzezinski, Z. – Self-determination for Chechnya is in Russia's interest, *International Herald Tribune*, 20–21 November 1999.

[211] European Council 10–11 December, *European Voice*, 16 December 1999–5 January 2000.

[212] Taylor, S. – Tacis and Meda face cuts to fund aid for Kosovo, *European Voice*, 24–30 June 1999.

[213] In April 1999 another, Western-supported, pipeline opened between Baku (Azerbaijan's capital on the Caspian Sea) and the Black Sea port of Supsa in Georgia, reportedly constituting the first step by a group of Western-supported countries (Georgia, Ukraine, Azerbaijan and Moldova) towards rupturing Russia's monopoly over pipelines between the Caspian and the Black Sea. Radvanyi, Y. – Moscow's designs on Chechnya, *Le monde diplomatique*, English Edition, November 1999.

have been not been fought primarily to preempt secession but rather the loss of control over the oil pipeline(s), particularly important in the oil-rich Caucasus. The pipeline linking the Caspian and Black Sea passes through Chechnya and its security was guaranteed against an estimated annual income of $10 million in transit fees.[214] Pipeline politics is thus likely to influence further developments in Chechnya as well as in the entire Caucasus. Whenever and wherever oil is at issue, human rights fare ill.

---

[214] Hardings, A. – Moscow retreats to a Chechen stalemate, *The World Today*, vol. 53, No. 1, January 1997, p. 5–6; Thornhill, J. – Breakthrough on Caspian pipeline plan, *Financial Times*, 4 July 1997; Gall, C. – Chechnya: Risks and returns, *Financial Times*, 16 April 1998.

Part V

A Look Back and a Look Forward

Chapter 12

The Pattern of Condemnations and Sanctions

Western, especially American, responses to human rights violations have been dubbed *Gringo's light switch*. *Gringo* is a common South American expression for the Northerners also used for white people in general, while pressing the *light switch* on and off depicts responses to violations. An incentive to press the switch on can be any well-publicised abuse. Cosmetic concessions can halt condemnatory or punitive responses as the light switch is easily pressed off. Any halt in abuses that might have taken place is easily reversed, also by pressing the light switch. The repressive apparatus responsible for abuses routinely remain untouched, with its operation suspended, to be re-activated by merely pressing the light switch.

Cynical generalizations follow along this line. A common generalization is that only remote, small, friendless and poor countries are condemned and sanctioned for human rights violations, or else the existing pattern is attributed to the vagaries of international and domestic politics. This book has mapped out this pattern and it is summarized in this Chapter.

The chronological and regional overview in the preceding Chapters have high-lighted the two parallel tracks, multilateral and unilateral, that have been a prominent feature of the pattern of responses to violations in the past decades. The list of countries against which sanctions have been imposed does not correspond to the governments that have been determined by the United Nations to be violators. Non-Western countries constitute the majority in the United Nations and proposals to condemn individual governments are funnelled through a democratic decision-making process. The Western group (WEOS) wields an influence disproportionate to its small number of votes, but the number of UN-determined violators is nevertheless much smaller than the number decreed to be violators by the West alone. Furthermore, there are differences within the Western group and additional differences between foreign-policy and economic-exchange decisions within individual countries, and thus differences between political judgments and the imposition of economic sanctions. This accounts for an apparently arbitrary pattern of condemnations and sanctions.

CONDEMNATIONS

There are two ways of assessing the record of the United Nations in identifying and condemning individual governments as violators: one can hail UN's powers to hold governments accountable through peer pressure, or bemoan the fact that this peer pressure has accomplished so little. Condemnation for violations is a political sanctions against a particular government by its peers and is thus fiercely resisted. Table 12.1 shows how many governments have been placed on UN's agenda and how few were publicly identified as violators. The choice of 'were,' past finished, in describing UN's record in identifying and condemning violators originates in the growing tendency of the Commission on Human Rights towards consensus. This is a consequence of the imbalance between the large numbers of Western condemnatory proposals and the much larger number of non-Western votes in the Commission. The outcome is a constantly diminishing number of governments that are named-and-shamed by their peers. Against the immunity of regional or subregional potentates to such opprobrium, condemnations seem destined to demise.

Table 12.1 lists alphabetically all countries placed on the violations-agenda thus far, presenting the complete record of public and confidential procedures. The data is derived from resolutions and decisions of the Commission on Human Rights and its Sub-Commission. The 1503 procedure has generated the largest number of potential condemnations and is presented in the right-hand column. This procedure seemed doomed to disappearance when in 1999 the Commission on Human Rights did not leave a single case pending.[1] The numbers diminish as one moves leftwards through the Sub-Commission (nominally independent) to the Commission (officially inter-governmental).

The outcome of inter-governmental policing as of 1967, when it started, is impressive: almost two-thirds of UN's members – 104 altogether – have been placed on the violations-agenda. Not all were targeted for gross abuses of governmental powers embodied arbitrary killings or mass arrests. In some cases, denial of property rights was at issue, in others it was restrictive access to citizenship. The obstacles in the passage of the initiatives through the inter-governmental decision-making structures are immense. Although the 1503 procedure is confidential and only leaked information becomes publicly available, its outcomes indicate diminishing rates of return on attempts to have governments condemned as violators.

In the public domain, the necessity of mobilizing a sufficient number of votes requires WEOS, the Western group, which routinely initiates condemnations, to build cross-regional alliances. The reasons for casting a vote against a particular government do not necessarily originate in a wish to publicly expose its dismal human rights record. They range between intra-regional solidarity, to yielding to extra-regional (usually Western) blackmail, or to trading favours. Inter-governmental politics operates by rules that have little to do with the formally established procedures or the substance in hand. And yet, collective condemnations of governments by their peers were inconceivable thirty years ago. The nature of inter-governmental politics has not changed and thus the addition of human rights

---

[1] In a closed session, as is customary, the Commission discontinued consideration of alleged human rights violations in the Gambia, Saudi Arabia, Nepal and Yemen; it moved Chad from violations- to assistance-agenda, and Sierra Leone from confidential to public procedure. Commission on Human Rights – Report on the Fifty-fifth Session (22 March–30 April 1999), U.N. Doc. E/CN.4/1999/167, paras. 246–251.

Table 12.1: UN violations-agenda, 1967–1999

Country	Commission	Sub-Commission	1503 procedure
Afghanistan	1980–91, 1993–99	1981–88, 1998–99	1981–84
Albania	1988–91, 1993–94	1985–88, 1994	1984–88, 1995
Algeria	–	(1997–98)	–
Angola	1994	–	–
Antigua and Barbuda	–	–	1997
Argentina	–	(1976), (1978)	1980–84
Armenia/Azerbaijan	–	–	1994–95
Bangladesh	–	–	(1988)
Bahrain	–	1997	1991–93
Belarus	–	1998	–
Benin	–	–	1984–85, 1988
Bhutan	–	–1998	–
Bolivia	1981–83	1980	1977–81
Botswana	–	–	1997
Brazil	–	–	1974–76
Brunei Darussalam	–	–	1988–90
[Burma] Myanmar	(1989–90), 1992–99	1991, 1993	1979–80, 1990–92
Burundi	1994–99	1988, 1994–96	1974–75
Cambodia [Kampuchea]	1979–80, 1984–89, 1994–95	1978–88, 1991	1979
Central African Republic	–	–	1980–81
Chad	–	1993–94	1991–99
Chile	1975–90	1974–88	1975–76, 1978–79, 1981
China/Tibet	(1993–97), (1999)	1989–91, (1993)	–
Colombia	(1995–99)	1995, (1996)	1990
Congo/Brazzaville	–	1997, 1999	–
Cuba	(1988), 1990–97, 1999	–	–
Cyprus	1975–88, 1990, 1996, 1999	1974–88, (1996)	–
Czech Republic	–	–	1997
El Salvador	1981–91	1981–92	1981
Equatorial Guinea	1979–85, 1989–90, 1992–99	1979–80	1976–79
Estonia	–	–	1994, 1997
Ethiopia	(1986)	–	1978–81
Gabon	–	–	1986
Gambia	–	–	1997–99
Germany	–	–	1994
[East Germany]	–	–	1981–83
Greece	–	–	(1972)
Grenada	1984	–	1988
Guatemala	1980–86, 1992, 1994	1982–86, 1989–95	1981

Table 12.1: *continued*

Country	Commission	Sub-Commission	1503 procedure
Georgia	1994	–	–
Guyana	–	–	1974–75
Haiti	1984,1987–90, 1992–94	1988, 1992–94	1981–87, 1989–90
Honduras	–	–	1988–89
India/Pakistan (Kashmir)	–	1997	–
Indonesia/East Timor	1983, (1993–96), 1997, (1998–99)	1982–84, 1987, 1989–90, 1992–93	(1973–75), 1978–81, 1983–85
Iran	1982–99	1980–96	1974–75, 1983
Iraq	(1989), 1991–99	(1989), 1990–91, 1993–96	1988–89
Israel/Occupied Territories	1968–99	1968–96	1975–77
Japan	–	–	1981, 1998
Kenya	–	–	1993
Korea, North	–	1997–98	–
Korea, South	–	–	1977–82
Kuwait/Iraq	1991	1990	1994
Kyrgyzstan	–	–	1997–98
Laos	–	–	1995
Latvia	–	–	1995, 1997
Lebanon	1985–97	1982–90	1997
Liberia	(1996–97)	–	–
Lithuania	–	–	1997
Malawi	1980	–	1977–80
Malaysia	–	–	1984
Mali	–	–	1996
Mauritania	1982, 1985	1982, 1984–85	(1990)
Mexico	–	1998	–
Moldova	–	–	1995
Mozambique	–	–	1981
Nepal	–	–	1996, 1998–99
Nicaragua	1979	1979	–
Nigeria	(1995), 1996–98	–	–
Pakistan	1985	1985	1984, 1985, 1988
Panama	1990	1990	–
Papua N.G./Bougainville	1993–95	1992, 1994	–
Paraguay	1985	1983–85, 1989	1978–90, 1998
Peru	–	1992–93	(1990), 1998
Philippines	–	–	1984–86

Table 12.1: *continued*

Country	Commission	Sub-Commission	1503 procedure
Poland	1982–83	–	–
Portugal/African colonies	–	–	(1972), 1974–75
Romania	1989–91, 1993	(1989)	–
Russia/Chechnya	(1995–96)	(1996)	–
Rwanda	1994–99	1994–96	1993–95
Saudi Arabia	–	–	1995–99
Sierra Leone	1999	–	1996–98
Slovenia	–	–	1995, 1996
Somalia	1992, 1994	1991–92	1989–94
South Africa	1967–94	1967–93	–
Sri Lanka	1984, 1987, (1994)	1983–84	–
Sudan	1992–99	–	1991–93
Syria	–	–	1989,1992, 1997
Tajikistan	–	–	1998
Tanzania/Zanzibar	–	–	1974–75, 1997
Thailand	–	–	1995, 1996
Togo	1993–95	1994	(1993)
Turkey	–	(1995–97)	1983–86, (1990)
Uganda	–	(1972), (1979)	1975–81, 1995
United Kingdom/ N. Ireland	–	–	1974–75
Uruguay	1985	1983–84	1978–85
USA	(1995–96)	–	1997
Uzbekistan	–	–	1996–97
Venezuela	–	–	1982
Viet Nam	–	–	(1974–75), 1994
Western Sahara	1981–87, 1989–90, 1993, 1995–96, 1998–99	1987	–
Zaire/Congo	1992–93, 1995–99	–	1985–89, 1991–93
Yemen	–	–	1998–99
[Yugoslavia]	1992–99	1992–96, (1998)	–

Note: The first column lists outcomes of the consideration of specific countries on the violations-agenda item by the Commission on Human Rights, the second one to its Sub-Commission, and the third one to the 1503 procedure for investigating a consistent pattern of gross and reliably attested violations of human rights.

Square brackets denote countries which changed name or exist no longer, while round brackets indicate that a tabled resolution or decision was voted upon but not adopted, or replaced by a chairman's statements as a milder substitute for a condemnatory resolution. The countries that have been moved from the violations- to assistance-agenda (such as Cambodia, Guatemala or Haiti) are not listed subsequent to such a decision, although the contents of resolutions adopted under the agenda item of 'assistance' has often confirmed that violations continued.

can be deemed to be a genuine success because it forced upon a reluctant collective of governments an issue which goes far beyond politics of whatever kind. The first steps had been triggered by non-Western majorities that mobilized the United Nations against South Africa and Israel, and broadened when Western foreign policies included human rights in the 1970s, to peak at the end of the Cold War and start dwindling in the late 1990s. One reason has been *the West versus the Rest* pattern.

A widespread generalization whereby small, poor and friendless countries such as Haiti or North Korea get condemned for human rights violations is, like all generalizations, descriptive of the general pattern and allows for exceptions. Small and poor countries are not targeted by condemnations if they are not friendless (such as Bangladesh or Nepal, Niger or Uganda, Honduras or Peru). A powerful actor in its region, such as Nigeria, was condemned for human rights violations, not so Argentina during the *dirty war* or Mexico, while India and Pakistan have illustrated different facets of their acquired immunity to UN's opprobrium.

In Africa, Anglophone countries have been targets of international human rights politics much more than Francophone. The emergence of Francophone countries amongst human rights violators on the UN agenda and targets of economic sanctions resulted from changing French policy towards its *domaine-préservé*. Different, often conflicting, Western foreign policies made human rights records of individual countries into only one among many different factors that led to – or did not – condemnations and/or sanctions. The Chad rule (formulated by Stanley Cohen before Chad found itself on the UN violations-agenda, if for a short time) captures the main determinants for case-creation. The language obstacle is compounded by too few people being able to find Chad on the map, even fewer have ever been there, yet fewer know anybody from Chad. Without familiarity with a country, creation of a human rights case depends on publicity accompanying a major man-made disaster. Military coups and warfare are not sufficient. Two countries that have been on the UN violations-agenda, Western Sahara and Mauritania, have not prompted much publicity nor economic sanctions. The former was accepted as a OAU member but not recognized as a state, and is being assisted by the United Nations towards statehood. Mauritania attracted the attention of UN human rights bodies for a variety of human rights violations, ranging from slavery to harassment of opposition, but has never attracted international publicity.

It is not only African countries that are cloaked by the lack of publicity. The military coup in Fiji in 1987 and the consequent institutionalized discrimination against Asian Fijians never made it to the UN agenda.[2] The Philippines was an early and an abundantly used example of inability of the UN human rights bodies to respond to violations at the time, and for the role of the USA in keeping the Philippines immune during the Marcos regime. James Hamilton-Paterson gave his

---

[2] Sadiq Ali, S. – Fiji: Institutionalized racial discrimination, *Peoples for Human Rights: IMADR (International Movement against Discrimination and Racism) Yearbook 1991*, vol. 4, 1992, pp. 56–67.

book about Ferdinand Marcos (and his wife Imelda) the title *America's Boy*[3] so as to highlight the US link. Vietnam's human rights record could not be discussed during the Vietnam war or in its aftermath. US economic sanctions (first imposed in 1964) continued long after the war had ended. Consular relations were established in 1994, accompanied by two US conditions for normalization. The first related to American prisoners of war and the missing-in-action, the second was formulated as a 'bilateral dialogue on human rights issues.'[4] Diplomatic relations followed in 1995, preceded by an agreement on the settlement of mutual property claims, which led to the unblocking of Vietnam's assets.[5] A waiver from the Jackson-Vanik amendment (targeting communist countries that do not allow free emigration) was discussed in 1997. Predictably, suggestions that the waiver be conditioned by the release of political and religious prisoners were promptly launched.[6] Congressional debates about granting the most favoured nation (MFN) status to Vietnam followed in 1998 and were immediately entangled into congressional initiatives to impose trade sanctions on the grounds of religious persecution.

Bangladesh is a good exception to the popular generalization whereby poor countries are easily condemned for human rights violations and targeted by sanctions. Neither the military rule nor the protracted armed conflict in Chittagong Hills led to aid withdrawals, although the country has been for decades one of the major aid recipients, dubbed as *the basket case* by Henry Kissinger. The rule of General Ershad (1982–90) provided ample incidents which donors could have interpreted as grounds for withholding aid, especially the Chittagong Hill Tracts, where armed suppression of struggles for self-protection of the tribal populations prompted much international concern in 1986–87.[7] Aid continued nevertheless, with the donor community displaying 'a sympathetic indulgence'[8] towards Bangladesh.

The transition of military to electoral regime was achieved by widespread public mobilization, which culminating in a popular uprising against General Ershad, leading to his resignation,[9] similarly to the ousting of the Marcos regime in the

---

[3] Hamilton-Paterson, J. – *America's Boy: The Marcoses and the Philippines*, Granta, London, 1997.

[4] United States-Vietnam liaison offices, *American Journal of International Law*, vol. 88, 1994, p. 729.

[5] Claims settlement agreements – United States-Vietnam, *American Journal of International Law*, vol. 89, 1995, pp. 366–370.

[6] Mann,J. – U.S. prepares to exempt Vietnam from trading curb, *International Herald Tribune*, 19 December 1997.

[7] Tomaševski, K. – *Foreign Aid and Human Rights. Case Studies of Bangladesh and Kenya*, The Danish Center of Human Rights, Copenhagen, 1988, pp. 1–69.

[8] Kamaluddin, S. – Bangladesh: Misplaced hope, *Far Eastern Economic Review*, 25 June 1998.

[9] General Ershad had subsequently been tried and convicted for 'illegally amassing wealth' (Bangladesh court convicts Ershad, *International Herald Tribune*, 4 February 1992) and released from prison in June 1996 so as to go to parliament and be sworn in as a newly elected member, and then return to prison. (Kamaluddin, S. – Bangladesh: Down to work, *Far Eastern Economic Review*, 4 July 1996.)

Philippines. Similarly to the Philippines, the transition itself was hailed, its aftermath less so. Bangladesh became virtually paralysed by what became known as a 'power struggle between two ladies.' The victor of the first post-Ershad election, Begum Khaleda Zia, is the widow of General Zia ul Rahman (killed in 1981), and leads the Bangladesh Nationalist Party. The victor of the 1996 election, Sheikh Hasina Wazed is the daughter of Sheik Mujibur Rahman (killed in 1975), leads the Awami League. This background has led *The Economist* to sum up the 1991 elections as 'two dead men locked in electoral battle.'[10] Political polarization and violence, mass demonstrations and strikes, started in 1991 and increased in 1995–96 to lead to a change of government, and then increased again in 1998–2000. This illustrated how personalized and urbanized power politics was – and is – and also how much more could have been accomplished outside power politics. Rural Bangladesh is home to some of the world-famous development schemes, such as the Grameen Bank, which showed ingenuity by providing loans rather than perpetuating charity, combining financial with vocational support, and satisfying the basic criterion of sustainability.

It is unlikely that there will be any condemnations of any South American government, with the exception of Cuba, thus illustrating two changes which distinguish today's international human rights politics from the era when South American governments were the target of UN's condemnations. The political transitions in the 1980s have altered the political landscape of the region, while the parallel process of regionalization within the UN Commission on Human Rights has endowed the governments of the region with the power to veto any proposal for a condemnation of any of its own (again, the exception is Cuba as well as Haiti). The second change highlights the slant which international human rights politics has adopted in the 1990s, which confines the violations-agenda to civil liberties and political rights. Were economic or indigenous rights placed on the agenda, the listing of issues and countries would look much different.

The biggest change has affected Eastern Europe, which used to be a regional block with considerable powers in halting most Western initiatives during the Cold War, while in the 1990s it has lost any recognizable identity. The spokesperson for the European Union routinely refers to the endorsement of EUrope's positions by its members-to-be, the voting records show Russia to be a one-state-region having lost all its previous followers, while the draft resolution tabled by the Czech Republic against Cuba in 1999 illustrated how much the post-cold-war geopolitics has changed.

These changes can be depicted as a shift from geopolitics to *geoeconomics*, and have been reflected in the changing pattern of economic sanctions for human rights violations.

---

[10] Bangladesh: Voting for memory, *The Economist,* 2 March 1991.

ECONOMIC SANCTIONS

Economic sanctions have been defined by the Dutch Advisory Committee on Human Rights as 'any restrictions on economic exchanges with a particular country which are intended to serve as instruments of human rights policy.'[11] International law was traditionally inter-state law and its enforcement was based on self-help: the state which was a target of wrongdoing had to react against harm inflicted by another. Such reactions are called *sanctions* instead of *countermeasures* as law would require. Thereby one state responds to a wrongful act by another. The Security Council is authorized by the UN Charter to impose sanctions while an individual government has no authority to sanction another. Much as the Security Council has the authority to impose sanctions, it does not have power to enforce them. Enforcement is left to individual states and to peer pressure. Where such pressure is strong sanctions are enforced, where it is lacking sanctions are ignored.

When wrongdoing harms a state's own population rather than another state, international law shifts from providing answers to asking questions. Endless scholarly disputes testify to the diversity of opinion as to what the law is. This book does not add to them. Rather, it examines states' practice in order to clearly pose and openly argue the many questions that emerge when condemnations and sanctions are treated as a an extra-legal foreign-policy phenomenon.

One can track sanctions through a series of successive phases: from the initial political decision that sanctions should be imposed, to a later political decision imposing sanctions, to legislative and/or administrative instructions translating the previous political decision into specific sanctions, and finally to decisions mandating their enforcement and monitoring compliance. This decision-making process can stop at any of these stages; information about such stoppages may never become publicly available. Evidence that sanctions have or have not been imposed often does not exist beyond the initial political decision.

Sanctions should be, but are often not, observable phenomena. This book has described and discussed all cases of economic sanctions justified by human rights violations so as to present comprehensive empirical evidence. The first layer of analysis, fitting the arbitrary pattern of sanctions into any form of their systematic presentation, was a difficult task: political decisions imposing sanctions have often lacked translation into corresponding economic measures; sanctions were imposed, lifted and reimposed with great speed; justifications for sanctions changed or one country was targeted by sanctions on different grounds. The process of decision-making is difficult to research because primary sources are virtually non-existent. Investigative journalism or NGO newsletters, or else memoirs of retired government officials, shed some light on the sequence of events that led to a particular foreign-policy decision and the corollary economic sanctions of their absence. This

---

[11] Advisory Committee on Human Rights and Foreign Policy – *Human Rights and International Economic Relations*, Report No. 12, The Hague, 29 May 1991, mimeographed, p. 47.

wealth of empirical material was structured chronologically for the first decades, and then regionally after sanctions proliferated.

The second layer of analysis are consequences of such governmental conduct in the country imposing sanctions. The area of foreign policy falls between the cracks of established research disciplines and methods. Human rights were meant to be based upon the rule of law and constitute domestic governmental responsibility. Each government is responsible for human rights within its own territory and international law never anticipated that one government would purport to police and sanctions another. Foreign policy decisions and economic sanctions have remained beyond law. One cannot start a legal case against a minister of foreign affairs for the damage to human rights attributed to his or her decision to impose economic sanctions against another country. Foreign policy remains in the realm of political accountability which is domestic. The biggest obstacle for coming to grips with economic sanctions is that the population victimized by sanctions does not have a political voice in the country imposing sanctions. Calls for political account-ability are increasingly heard when commercial interests of a domestic political constituency are harmed by economic sanctions against another country. Few voices are raised against the punishment of people for the sins of their rulers.

The third layer of analysis has been made necessary by the unanticipated ele-vation of human rights to one of the prominent items in Western foreign and aid policies towards the end of the Cold War and changes in international human rights activism followed suit. Discerning the meaning and impact of this whole process is thus necessary because the concept of human rights informing it has become blurred.

Table 12.2 lists those countries against which economic sanctions were imposed as a response to human rights violations, in which a change of regime took place and was positively assessed whereupon sanctions were lifted. These cases are termed *conclusive*. The proverbial problem with sanctions – they are easy to impose but difficult to lift – is confirmed by the small number of conclusive cases, those in which sanctions have not been subsequently threatened, showing that the initial judgment about a regime change from violative to protective was made on some dubious grounds. Cases such as Malawi or South Korea, where the change used as the background for lifting sanctions was apparent rather than real, are frequent.

The most frequent type of sanctions for human rights violations has been cutting off government-to-government aid. Economic sanctions against non-recipients of aid have been rare, a handful of cases thus far; South Africa was the first and is best known. At the beginning of the linkage between condemnations and sanctions, Rhodesia and South Africa were targeted but not Portugal. Portugese colonialism in Africa was declared by the Security Council to constitute a threat to peace and security in 1960. The General Assembly that same year defined Portugese 'overseas provinces' as non-self-governing territories and condemned Portugal for conduct incompatible with the UN Charter. Portugal's conduct in Angola was condemned in 1962, and the General Assembly asked states 'to refrain from offering the Portugese Government any assistance which would enable it to continue its

Table 12.2: Economic sanctions for human rights violations: Conclusive cases

Period	Target country	Sanctioning governments and organizations
1946–93	South Africa	India, OAU, UN, OAPEC, Parties to the Convention against Apartheid, Nordic countries, Australia, Austria, Canada, New Zealand, EUrope, USA, South Korea, Singapore, Japan
1965–79	[Rhodesia]	United Kingdom, UN, OAPEC
1972–79	Uganda	United Kingdom, Canada, Norway, Denmark, EUrope, USA
1973–88	Chile	Netherlands, Norway, Sweden, Denmark, Italy, United Kingdom, USA, EUrope
1973–79	South Korea	USA, Japan, Germany
1947/1975–89	[Soviet Union & allies]	USA
1977–79; 1980–89	Nicaragua	OAS, USA; USA
1977–94	Guatemala	USA, Canada, Japan, EUrope
1977–92	El Salvador	USA, Canada
1978–90	Mozambique	USA, EUrope
1978–93	Vietnam	USA, Australia, Canada, Denmark, Norway
1981–83	Grenada	USA
1982–87	Poland	USA, Canada
1987–97	Fiji	Australia, New Zealand, United Kingdom
1987–89	Panama	USA
1988–93	Romania	USA, EUrope
1991–93	Malawi	Denmark, Norway, EUrope, USA, Japan, Germany

Note: Those sanctions that were never implemented, such as UN-recommended sanctions against Portugal in 1964–74 for denial of self-determination to its African colonies, are not included, nor is a series of token US sanctions for human rights violations against Uruguay (1976–81), Argentina (1977–81), Brazil (1977–84), Bolivia (1977–82), the Philippines (1985–86), and Paraguay (1987–89).

repression.'[12] In 1963–65 the Security Council first recommended withholding assistance that would facilitate Portugal's repression and then a weapons embargo. The General Assembly went further and recommended the withholding of all assistance to Portugal and breaking off trade, transport and diplomatic relations.[13] These recommendations never materialized because Portugal was a European

---

[12] United Nations – *Everyman's United Nations. A Basic History of the Organization 1945 to 1963*, New York, 1964, p. 368.

[13] United Nations – *Everyman's United Nations. A Complete Handbook of the Activities and Evolution of the United Nations During Its First Twenty Years*, New York, 1968, p. 410–411.

country and a member of NATO. Julius Nyerere had this to say about the US conduct:

> Despite America's verbal criticism of Portugese colonialism, American arms and equipment were used by Portugal in its military operations in Angola, Guinea-Bissau and Mozambique.[14]

Economic sanctions multiplied after the entry of human rights into Western foreign policies, which institutionalized suspensions or decreases of aid as a response to violations. Further proliferation was caused by the end of the Cold War because the alternative to Western aid existed no longer and the criteria for eligibility could be constantly changed. This has generated a large number of cases, most of them inconclusive. Table 12.3 lists inconclusive cases, the majority of countries thus far targeted by sanctions.

Sanctions have been announced or imposed ostensibly because of human rights violations, in some cases several times, and thus typify a pattern of conduct marked by contradictory impulses. A clearly delineated beginning and end is an exception rather than the rule. The US sanctions against Cuba or Iran have been changed with respect to the grounds and justification. African countries such as Equatorial Guinea or Burundi have had sanctions imposed and lifted many times. Sanctions were sometimes lifted without any change in the target government's human rights performance, an implicit acknowledgment that they were ineffective. Moreover, nominally imposed sanctions were sometimes minuscule and aid to the sanctioned countries actually increased (China in 1990–99 and Indonesia in 1992–95 are prominent examples).

African countries have been the most frequent target of economic sanctions for human rights violations – no less than twenty-five – and thus every second African country has been targeted. In a quick succession, aid suspensions targeted Kenya, Malawi, Cameroon, Togo, Congo/Brazzaville, Gambia, Comores, Zambia and Niger. Reasons ranged from demands for multi-party elections, to dissatisfaction with elections, disapproval of military coups (with or without an involvement of mercenaries), outrage at publicised atrocities (within or without war), opposition to corruption, or suspicions of governmental involvement in drug or arms trafficking. Human rights violations were often tagged on to whatever other reasons were cited.

The easiest explanation for this haphazard pattern of sanctions is that cutting off aid is cost-saving for the country imposing sanctions and decision is within the discretion of the donor government. This explains minuscule sanctions against Nigeria highlighting the immunity of oil exporters (with the notable exception of Iraq) to economic sanctions, in Africa much as elsewhere. Alongside Iraq, a range of cold-war orphans illustrates the changed fate of human rights in international politics. Ethiopia and Cambodia became a political battlefield between advocates and

---

[14] Nyerere, J.K. – America and southern Africa, *Foreign Affairs*, vol. 55, No. 4, July 1997, p. 671.

Table 12.3: Economic sanctions for human rights violations: Inconclusive cases

Period	Target country	Sanctioning governments and organizations
1948–	Israel	League of Arab States, OAPEC, OAU, EU
1960–	Cuba	USA, OAS
1971–	Equatorial Guinea	Canada, EUrope
1972–	Burundi	Belgium, USA, EUrope, OAU
1975–	Cambodia	USA, UN, Denmark, Canada
1976–91; 1994–	Angola & Unita	USA, EUrope; UN
1978–	Ethiopia	USA, United Kingdom, EUrope, Denmark
1979–	Central African Republic	Canada, UN
1979–	Iran	USA, EUrope
1980–	Afghanistan & Taliban	UN, Canada, USA
1980–	Liberia	Canada, EUrope, USA
1980–	Zaire/Congo	USA, EUrope, France, Belgium, Japan, Germany
1982–	Turkey	Germany, EUrope
1982–88	Suriname	Netherlands, Canada, USA
1985–94	Sri Lanka	Canada, Norway, Denmark, EUrope, United Kingdom
1987–	Haiti	USA, OAS, UN, EUrope, Japan, Canada, France, Germany
1988–	Burma/Myanmar	Germany, USA, Denmark, United Kingdom, EUrope, Canada, Japan
1988–	Somalia	United Kingdom, USA, EUrope, Denmark, UN
1989–	Sudan	USA, Denmark, EUrope, United Kingdom, Japan
1989–92	China	EUrope, World Bank, USA, Canada, Japan, Denmark
1990–	Kenya	Norway, Denmark, World Bank, EUrope, United Kingdom, USA, Japan, Germany
1990–	Iraq	USA, EUrope, UN
1991–95	Russia	EUrope, USA
1992–	[Former Yugoslavia]	EUrope, UN, USA
1992–	Cameroon	EUrope
1992–	Congo/Brazaville	EUrope
1992–	Togo	France, EUrope, Germany
1993–	Nigeria	USA, United Kingdom, EUrope, Belgium, Netherlands, Canada, Germany
1993–	Sierra Leone	United Kingdom, EUrope, Japan
1995–	Rwanda	Belgium, Netherlands, EUrope
1992–	Indonesia	Netherlands, Canada, USA
1992	Peru	USA, Japan, Germany, Spain
1992–	Azerbaijan	USA
1994–96	Gambia	United Kingdom, EUrope, USA, Japan
1995	Comores	France
1995–	Zambia	USA, United Kingdom, Norway, EUrope
1996	Niger	France, EUrope, USA, Denmark, Germany, Canada
1997–	Belarus	EUrope, USA

opponents of sanctions. The conflict between the desire to punish violators and to assist victims was reflected in different foreign and international responses, often dissociated from developments within the targeted countries. Warfare in Afghanistan and Angola, which had previously been the justification for condemnations and sanctions, outlived both. In was fairly easy during the Cold War to identify the target for condemnations and sanctions and the beneficiary of political support and aid. Warfare has often not ended as anticipated, and the previous objects of political support and aid shifted to become targets for condemnations and sanctions. The meaning of 'human rights' thus necessarily changed.

There has been hardly any opposition in the donor countries to cutting down or cutting off aid and using human rights violations as justification, on the contrary. Such sanctions, perceived as costless in donor countries, were first imposed against Equatorial Guinea and Burundi in the early 1970s while an international response to institutionalized denials of human rights in both countries emerged in the 1990s. The donor-recipient relations made sanctions against African countries (with the exception of South Africa) numerous but often ineffective. Occasional aid cutoffs were applied by some individual donors while not by others (France, Japan and United Kingdom lagged behind) and were intertwined with cold-war politics. The patron-client relationship was reflected in the pattern of sanctions: favoured client countries have been immune. Countries such as Pakistan or Algeria have been conspicuously absent from targets of sanctions for human rights violations, while Turkey has been a huge political problem for EUrope during the past two decades.

Since aid represents taxpayers' money, domestic political processes determine its size and allocation. Domestic support for human rights in foreign policy is high, much as for cutting off aid to human rights violators. Cutting off aid is the most popular sanction because people are easily mobilized against their money being used to fund foreign dictatorships. The current revival of the previous anti-apartheid attempts to impose a human rights rationale upon trade and investment (notably with regard to trade with Burma or oil companies in Congo/Brazzaville) will show in the future whether the abyss between political and economic governance can be bridged. While cutting off aid saves taxpayers' money, cutting off trade or investment constitutes self-imposed sanctions. By no coincidence, opposition to economic sanctions in countries imposing them, especially the United States, started after sanctions were moved from public to private, from aid cutoffs to restrictions upon trade and investment.

If sanctions are seen as cost-saving for those imposing them, they tend to be imposed frequently and arbitrarily. Because 'human rights' was tacked on to foreign policy rather than integrated into it, nobody is ever sure about what a government should or should not be doing about 'human rights.' Current efforts to alter the donor-client relationship include insistence on the client's ownership of whatever the donor has chosen to provide. The earlier reversal of roles, the donor's 'ownership' of the fate of the client, has made abuses in aid-receiving countries a prominent issue for human rights lobbies. It was donors' complicity in the abuses by the government receiving its aid that triggered calls for sanctions. In countries without colonial or neo-colonial heritage the donor-client relationship prompted domestic constituencies in the donor countries to demand their government's to stop support for an abusive recipient. Thus the Netherlands cut off aid to its former colony Suriname apparently contradicting its own policy that people should not be punished for the sins of their rulers, while Denmark and Norway underwent agonizing debates about suspending aid to Kenya. Suspending aid dissociates the donor from abuses by a misbehaving recipient but also questions donors' previous support (including financial) to the institutional arrangement which institutionalized abuse of power.

In the 1970s, the focus of human rights activism was on public flows and the incipient NGO lobbying targeted donor governments. In the 1990s, public flows diminished while private flows increased. The focus of human rights lobbying shifted accordingly. Since private capital follows commercial rather than developmental or human rights criteria, the developing world was divided in two – one able to attract private funding and another dependent on the diminishing public funds. For aid dependent countries, the linkage with human rights has continued, for countries attractive to private investors that linkage became, at best, tenuous but more often than not irrelevant. For countries where aid constituted a minuscule fraction of financial flows, a linkage with human rights was sought in targeting Western commercial actors.

Granting or withholding aid are political decisions in which donor governments exercise discretion. Numerous efforts were made throughout the past decades to translate the aid relationship into a language of mutual rights and obligations; many recommendations were adopted by the majority of potential recipients with the dissenting minority of donors. Different from private capital flows and trade, intergovernmental aid is inherently subjected to governmental interference. Different ministerial agendas, competing values and modes of operation by different ministries do not add up to a foreign policy. The correlation between diminished aid flows and increased donors' punitiveness has exacerbated the notorious ineffectiveness of economic sanctions that consist solely of aid cutoffs.[15] The accumulation of different conditions for aid and grounds for cutoffs facilitates an easy summing up: when it is not human rights, it is something else. The nobility of human rights is obviously tainted with a suspicion that human rights violations have been merely one of many reasons used to justify diminished aid flows. Two conflicting rationales have emerged: aid has been defined as a necessary complement to domestic efforts of the recipient to improve its human rights performance[16] with the counterargument that the recipient's human rights performance will improve if aid is

---

[15] Research on the effectiveness of economic sanctions by Gary Hufbauer, Jeffrey Schott and Kimberly Ann Elliott at the Institute for International Economics has amply demonstrated the ineffectiveness of the manipulation of aid flows, as they termed it, regardless of the grounds upon which sanctions have been imposed. This point is summarized in Elliott, K.A. – Sanctions: A look at the record, *The Bulletin of the Atomic Scientists*, vol. 49, No. 9, November 1993, p. 33–34.

denied. These conflicting demands within Western foreign policies have influences the pattern of Western condemnations and sanctions, which has been slanted against aid recipients.

As has been noted above, punitive decisions by inter-governmental human rights fora triggered by human rights violations have been few, showing the absence of peer pressure that would pull in this direction. Unilateral decisions have been prevalent as Table 12.4 illustrates through a comparison of the outcomes of UN's condemnatory processes with the Western sanctions.

The left-hand column lists those countries whose governments were condemned for human rights violations by the United Nations and also were targeted by economic sanctions. A generous interpretation has been applied in both cases. Cuba has been included although a condemnation for human rights violations followed sanctions (not initially imposed on human rights grounds) by almost twenty years, while condemnations and sanctions against El Salvador and Guatemala in the 1980s were neither matched in time nor were they commensurate to the ill-deeds subsequently revealed by the truth commissions.

The right-hand column lists countries that were targeted by economic sanctions for which human rights violations were cited among other reasons, but there was no UN condemnation. Only aid receiving countries are found on that list, with the sole exception of the former Soviet Union, which does not necessitate any further comment.

REACHING GOVERNMENTS IMMUNE TO CONDEMNATIONS AND SANCTIONS

Discrepancies between condemnations and sanctions signify the parallel existence of two tracks and highlight different notions of human rights and their violations that inform the two. Looking into the Western unilateral track, one can look for those governments that were condemned for human rights violations but economic

---

[16] In earlier decades it was possible for a donor to announce that aid would be increased to recipients with good human rights performance so as to reward it, while in the times of constantly decreasing aid budgets this is no longer possible. Human rights have been added as a separate item in donors' budgets with the aim of providing some incentive. This type of aid consists of technical assistance, which is notoriously the least useful type of aid. Krishna Kumar's two main objections to this kind of aid were 'the limited relevance and high costs of training and technical assistance,' and luring away of professional staff from the recipient governments by high salaries offered by aid agencies. Kumar, K. – The nature and focus of international assistance for rebuilding war-torn societies, in Kumar, K. (ed.) – *Rebuilding Societies after Civil War. Critical Roles for International Assistance*, Lynne Rienner Publishers, Boulder, 1997, p. 6–7

Table 12.4: Discrepancies between multilateral condemnations and unilateral sanctions

Correspondence between condemnations and sanctions	Sanctions without UN condemnation
Afghanistan	Angola
Burma/Myanmar	Azerbaijan
Burundi	Cameroon
Cambodia	Central African Republic
Chile	China
Cuba	Comores
El Salvador	Ethiopia
Equatorial Guinea	Fiji
Guatemala	Gambia
Haiti	Grenada
Indonesia	Liberia
Iran	Kenya
Iraq	Nicaragua
Nigeria	Malawi
Peru	Mozambique
Poland	Niger
[Rhodesia]	Panama
Romania	Russia
Rwanda	Sierra Leone
Somalia	South Korea
South Africa	[Soviet Union]
Sudan	Suriname
Sri Lanka	Turkey
Togo	Uganda
Vietnam (Cambodia)	Zambia
Zaire/Congo	
Former Yugoslavia	

sanctions did not follow. The four tables in this Chapter provide a ready-made listing. Israel appears as the most visible case, accompanied with Albania, Cyprus (that is, Turkey), Georgia, Mauritania, Pakistan, Papua New Guinea, and Western Sahara (namely, Morocco). Some of these have been discussed in this book, others have not because neither the United Nations nor the West could forge a policy that would have led out of a deadlock (notably Cyprus and Western Sahara).

The proverbial deadlock which has impeded a condemnation for human rights violations of governments capable of mobilizing a defensive shield amongst their peers has been overcome through the development of thematic procedures as has been noted in Chapter 1. Such governments cannot be found under country-specific resolutions and procedures, but they can be identified, as Table 12.5 demonstrates. Gross and systematic violations, the situations where severity and continuity of violations could not be explained in terms of isolated incidents or individual excesses but apparently constituted the policy of the respective government, have been to a large extent captured by the shift from country-specific to thematic procedures as Table 12.5 reveals.

As mentioned in Chapter 6, attempts to add Argentina to the list of violators during the dirty war (1976–83) led to the first thematic procedure, for disappearances, in 1980. The background was frustration generated by the inability of UN human rights bodies to explicitly condemn the military government of Argentina

Table 12.5: Torture, disappearances and summary executions – Country list 1993–99

1993–94	1994–95	1995–96	1996–97	1998–99
...	...	...	Afghanistan	...
...	Algeria	Algeria	Algeria	Algeria
Angola	Angola	Angola	...	...
...	Argentina	Argentina	Argentina	...
...	Bolivia	Bolivia	Bolivia	...
Brazil	Brazil	Brazil	Brazil	Brazil
Burundi	Burundi	Burundi	Burundi	Burundi
Cameroon	Cameroon	Cameroon	Cameroon	...
Chad	...	...	Chad	...
Chile	Chile	Chile	Chile	...
China	China	China	China	China
Colombia	Colombia	Colombia	Colombia	Colombia
...	...	...	Cyprus	...
Ecuador	Ecuador	Ecuador	Ecuador	...
Egypt	Egypt	Egypt	Egypt	Egypt
...	El Salvador	...	...	...
Equatorial Guinea	...	Equatorial Guinea	...	...
Ethiopia	Ethiopia	Ethiopia	Ethiopia	Ethiopia
Guatemala	Guatemala	Guatemala	Guatemala	Guatemala
Haiti	Haiti	...	...	...
...	...	...	Honduras	Honduras
India	India	India	India	India
Indonesia	Indonesia	Indonesia	Indonesia	Indonesia
Iran	Iran	Iran	Iran	Iran
Iraq	Iraq	Iraq	Iraq	...
Israel	Israel	Israel	Israel	Israel
...	Lebanon	...	...	...
...	...	Libya	...	...
...	...	...	...	Malaysia
Mauritania	...	Mauritania	...	
Mexico	Mexico	Mexico	Mexico	Mexico
Morocco	...	Morocco	...	Morocco
Nepal	Nepal	Nepal	Nepal	Nepal
Nigeria	...	...	...	Nigeria
Pakistan	Pakistan	Pakistan	Pakistan	Pakistan
...	...	...	[Palestinian Authority]	[Palestinian Authority]
...	...	...	...	Paraguay
Peru	Peru	Peru	Peru	Peru
...	Philippines	Philippines	...	Philippines
...	...	...	Russia	Russia
Rwanda	...	...	Rwanda	Rwanda
Saudi Arabia	Saudi Arabia	Saudi Arabia	Saudi Arabia	Saudi Arabia
South Africa	South Africa	South Africa	...	...
Sri Lanka	Sri Lanka	Sri Lanka	Sri Lanka	Sri Lanka
Sudan	Sudan	Sudan	...	Sudan
Syria	Syria	Syria	...	...
Tajikistan	...	...	...	...
...	Togo	Togo	...	...
Turkey	Turkey	Turkey	Turkey	
...	Uzbekistan	Uzbekistan	...	...
...	Venezuela	Venezuela	Venezuela	Venezuela
...	Yemen	Yemen	Yemen	...

Table 12.5: *continued*

1993–94	1994–95	1995–96	1996–97	1998–99
Yugoslavia	Yugoslavia	Yugoslavia	Yugoslavia	...
Zaire	Zaire	Zaire	Zaire/Congo	Zaire/Congo

Source: Documentation of the United Nations Commission on Human Rights – Reports of the Special Rapporteur on torture (U.N. Doc. E/CN:4/1994/31 of 6 January 1994, E/CN.4/1995/34 of 12 January 1995, E/CN.4/1996/35 of 9 January 1996, E/CN.4/1998/38 of 24 December 1997, and E/CN.4/1999/61 of 12 January 1999), Reports of the Working Group on Enforced or Involuntary Disappearances (U.N. Doc. E/CN.4/1994/26 of 22 December 1993, E/CN.4/1995/36 of 30 December 1994, E/CN.4/1996/38 of 15 January 1996, E/CN.4/1998/43 of 12 January 1998, and E/CN.4/1999/62 of 28 December 1998), and reports of the Special Rapporteur on summary executions (U.N. Doc. E/CN.4/1994/7 of 7 December 1993, E/CN.4/1995/61 of 14 December 1994, E/CN.4/1996/4 of 25 January 1996, E/CN.4/1998/68/Add.1 of 19 December 1997, and E/CN.4/1999/39/Add. 1 of 6 January 1999).

for gross and systematic violations, exemplified by disappearances. The underlying rationale was that particular phenomena would be easier to tackle because the targeted government was not identified, that is named-and shamed, and would thus not mobilize all political allies to block such a procedure. Disappearances were followed by summary executions (in 1982) and torture (in 1985), typical forms of governmental abuse of power, outlawed by the very spirit of international human rights law. In 1986 another thematic mechanism was created for religious intolerance, largely orientated to investigating the situation in Eastern Europe (as it was at the time) and Iran, and many more followed. These thematic mechanisms included in the 1990s sale of children, child prostitution and pornography (1990), arbitrary detention (1991), internally displaced persons (1992), freedom of opinion and expression and racism in 1993, violence against women and independence of judges and lawyers in 1994, illicit dumping of toxic waste in 1995, the right to education in 1998, and the rights of migrants in 1999.

These procedures have enabled the United Nations to tackle a range of countries where a country-orientated approach would have been impossible. The focus on the type of violations, condemned by all governments on their own merits, opened the door for an examination of human rights violations in a much larger number of countries than would have been possible through the country-orientated approach. The very collection and subsequent public availability of such data extended the scope of UN's violations agenda worldwide. The powers of the United Nations to expose and oppose disappearances, torture and summary executions have been implicitly accepted by the entire membership. This tacit agreement has enabled the corresponding institutions to monitor compliance with the underlying prohibition of governmental abuse of power. Because results of that work are lost in the existing labyrinth, a summary chart is presented in Table 12.5 to single out those countries for which all three phenomena were documented in 1993–96. For those countries one can assume that safeguards against abuse of physical power are not effective, and therefore an inquiry into UN's response presents an illustrative test of the effectiveness of the global institutional human rights framework.

One reason for the global acceptance of thematic procedures that UN's investigatory powers are not followed by condemnatory action. The listing of countries with documented torture, disappearances and arbitrary executions indeed does not correspond to those that are condemned for human rights violations by the Commission on Human Rights, as a comparison between Tables 12.5 and 12.1 demonstrates. Another reason is the implicit acceptance of the underlying prohibition of gross abuses of physical power by all governments in the world. Quite a few countries included in Table 12.5 remain immune to UN's condemnations (Algeria, Brazil, Egypt, India, Mexico, Pakistan, Saudi Arabia, Turkey, and Venezuela) because there is generally not much correspondence between results of investigative work by special rapporteurs and working groups and condemnations agreed upon by the Commission on Human Rights, as has been described elsewhere.[17]

THE PAST AS PROLOGUE

Many innovations have been introduced into UN's human rights work, often for worse rather than for better. The 1990 session of the Commission on Human Rights revealed a newly created, layer of conceptual difficulties in defining human rights violations. The previous attempt of the US government to label abuses committed by armed opposition or terrorists as human rights violations appeared on the Commission's agenda with the draft resolution submitted by Colombia, Peru and the Philippines on terrorists and drug traffickers. Subsequent annual resolutions of the Commission have broadened the definition of human rights violations to acts 'perpetrated by terrorist groups.'[18] That broadened the notion of violations to abuses by governments, warlords, insurgents, terrorists, or drug-traffickers. The original meaning of human rights as safeguards against abuse of power by governments has disappeared. Violations became a label covering every and any manifestation of violence – war-related killings were declared to constitute human rights violations, violence against women was declared to be a human rights violation, terrorism was declared to violate human rights. That endless stream of violations has conflicted with the original purpose of human rights to constitute safeguards against abuse of power by the government.

The previous differentiation between governments, which have human rights obligations, and armed groups or terrorists which do not, also disappeared in the 1990s. Jan Bauer's description of the 1996 compromise on Colombia, for which neither an investigative nor a condemnatory UN action could be agreed upon despite extensive documentation on the need for it, has highlighted this change. The compromise was to set up an office of the High Commissioner on Human Rights in Colombia, with the task to monitor 'violations committed by agents of the

---

[17] Tomaševski, K. – Human rights, in Childers, E. (ed.) – *Challenges to the United Nations. Building a Safer World*, CIIR (Catholic Institute of International Relations), London, 1994, pp. 82–112; *Between Sanctions and Elections. Aid Donors and their Human Rights Performance*, Pinter Publishers/Cassell, London, 1997, pp. 77–83.

[18] Commission on Human Rights – Human rights and terrorism, resolution 1996/47 of 19 April 1996, preamble.

state as well as paramilitary groups, guerrilla groups and, possibly, persons involved in drug trafficking and the cartels.'[19] The chairman's statement, which conveyed that agreement, noted that arbitrary killings, disappearances and torture were taking place in Colombia with impunity for the involved agents of the state. The future office of the High Commissioner was mandated to 'assist the Colombian authorities in developing policies and programmes for the promotion and protection of human rights and to observe violations of human rights in the country, making analytical reports to the High Commissioner.'[20] Because human rights assistance had been provided to Colombia since 1988, little enthusiasm accompanied the 1996 compromise.

Abuses of physical power are notoriously widespread in armed conflicts and human rights rhetoric has become abundantly used in international responses to armed conflicts. Three emergency sessions of the UN Commission on Human Rights (the first two on the Former Yugoslavia in 1992, then on Rwanda in 1994, and on East Timor in 1999) marked this change. External monitoring followed from these sessions as did two international tribunals. The principal function of human rights to provide safeguards against abuses of power in peacetime was forgotten in efforts to extend human rights protections into warfare. The fragile legal framework of human rights was burdened by a task which it could not possibly accomplish. Insistence on human rights protection in circumstances where a government does not have control over its territory (and would not qualify for international recognition by pre-cold-war rules) imposes an impossible condition. In March 1996 the Italian Minister of Foreign Affairs, speaking on behalf of the European Union, referred to the Dayton/Paris agreements and hailed 'the commitment entered into by all parties to the peace agreements to guarantee to all persons within their jurisdiction the highest level of internationally recognized human rights and fundamental freedoms.'[21] Provided that 'all parties' (Bosnia and Herzegovina, recognized as a state by the United Nations, and two unrecognized and unmentionable entities, namely Herceg-Bosna and Republika Srpska) had the willingness to guarantee all rights and freedoms, none of them had the ability to do so. Virtual states have proliferated, from Bosnia and Herzegovina to Afghanistan, from Angola to Zaire/Congo. Calls upon such states to respect and protect human rights have fallen on deaf ears – there was no state, in the sense of public administration operating throughout the country and able to guarantee human rights. When such states lost the key defining attribute – the monopoly over armed force – the definition of violations was broadened to include abuses by any armed group.

---

[19] Bauer, J. – Highlights of the 1996 Commission on Human Rights, *Human Rights Tribune*, August-September 1996, p. 40.

[20] Chairman's statement on the situation of human rights in Colombia of 23 April 1996, Commission on Human Rights – Report on the Fifty-Second Session, U.N. Doc. E/CN.4/1996/177, p. 299.

[21] United Nations – Summary record of the 2nd meeting of fifty-second session of the Commission on Human Rights, 19 March 1996, U.N. Doc. E/CN.4/1996/SR.2 of 22 March 1996, para. 27.

Future historians might define human rights as a phenomenon of the second half of the twentieth century and may well conclude that the discrepancy between human rights as a normative statement and an empirical reality made the demise of human rights predictable and inevitable. Another possible conclusion could be that economic sanctions ostensibly imposed for human rights violations have contributed to the demise of human rights. As shown in this book, such sanctions were most frequently used in 1975–1991, with the United States starting beforehand and carrying on thereafter. Justifications for sanctions have changed, definitions of human rights and violations have changed as well. A necessary question follows: was 'human rights' just one of the many justifications for the abuse of economic power?

And yet, mobilization around human rights cannot be reduced to uses and abuses of the human rights rhetoric in foreign policy. The ideals of human rights activism cannot and should not be sullied by abuses of human rights language. There is a whole world of pragmatic idealism that has advanced the cause of human rights during the past decades. Nevertheless, developments in inter-governmental human rights politics necessitate reviewing what has been accomplished and assessing what the cost of these accomplishments has been.

Chapter 13

After this Past, What Future?

Research tends to be backward rather than forward looking and risks drawing retrospective conclusions. If the past is prologue, prediction requires a historical base. Any history of events which are still unfolding lacks the perspective that time brings. Most, if not all, developments discussed in previous Chapters are unfinished history. Perhaps the key lesson for human rights advocacy is that investment in exposing and opposing abuses yields return, although in a long-term perspective. The recognition of political accountability and legal responsibility for facilitating the Holocaust takes place in Western and Eastern European countries that were until recently deemed to have been neutral or victims. A distance of more than fifty years after the Second World War had ended was necessary to identify victimizers and accomplices and compensate victims and a great deal of activism throughout that time.

One should anticipate that history will be sitting in judgment of today's human rights policies fifty years from now, half-way through the twenty-first century. Parts of this history have already been rewritten by truth commissions, revising the official governmental and inter-governmental records at the time of dictatorships in Argentina, Chile or El Salvador. These truth commission were generous towards outside involvement and did not mention it, with the exception of Guatemala, depicting developments as if they had been purely domestic. It was much too early to tackle foreign and international support for dictatorships and this issue has been postponed into the next century. The attention devoted to opposition to human rights violations has created an erroneous image that this had been the states' practice.

Perhaps foreign and international involvement in the transition from Rhodesia to Zimbabwe, or from Idi Amin's to Museveni's Uganda, will be revisited again in a generation or so. One can speculate about an Indonesian verdict of foreign and international support for the regime that governed the country from 1965 until 1999. Hints of external, especially US support, for previous governments of South Korea have been many. Political accountability for facilitating abuses abroad is rare, legal responsibility beyond the pale.

The explanation of events in the past provides the background for predicting their future unfolding. While a clear perspective is impossible while events are unfolding, as soon as they finish unfolding, these events and the countries that triggered them fall into oblivion. This book has been written to impede this oblivion.

CHANGED WESTERN HUMAN RIGHTS NGOs

International human rights activism started with the maxim that people whose rights were protected should act for those who were less fortunate. In the 1960s, its motto was formulated simply: exposing human rights violations was the first step towards opposing them. Globalization of human rights activism was derived from universality of human rights – the adjective *human* implied everybody's duty to defend the rights of all fellow humans; allowing their violations to continue un-exposed and un-opposed undermined this very <u>human</u> in human rights. A right to speak on behalf of victims of human rights violations was followed by a right to act on their behalf. 'Amnesty International does not consult the prisoners about whether they want to be adopted,' argued Cosmas Desmond in a critique that created quite a stir at the time, 'it assumes that if a person is in prison the most is to get him or her out, regardless of any wider political implications.'[1] The underlying dilemma has reached far beyond the political implications of activism to probe into its rationale, which can transform the beneficiaries from subjects of rights into objects of protection.

A right to speak and act on behalf of victims was followed by a right to monitor their victimization, accompanied by lobbying for condemnations and sanctions, and later also military interventions. Applying a criminal-justice model, such activism sought to condemn and punish victimizers but neglected victims. As in criminal justice, the victim had no role. Condemnations of their governments sought to acknowledge their victimhood by rejecting a self-granted right of a state to abuse its population. Advocacy of sanctions implied a right to cause harm, to compound victimization by their government through economic hardship inflicted by another government.

The growth of human rights organizations started in earnest in the 1970s, when human rights entered foreign policies of Western governments, creating demand for information on human rights violations in other countries. Responses to human rights violations broadened from international political and/or legal judgments to economic sanctions, first bilateral and then also multilateral. The institutional-ization of human rights conditionality followed suit. Activism addressing human rights in other countries became part of domestic politics. Research was no longer purely academic because its findings could – and did – influence foreign policy. Advocacy could no longer be classified as international, or foreign, or domestic; human rights in other countries entered domestic politics with a view to influencing foreign policy to apply it in order to mold other countries.

The appeal of human rights to left-leaning parties, many of which define them-selves as liberal, has led human rights into 'the fatal liberal combination of a lofty goal and inadequate resources.'[2] The moral crusade of putting the world to rights has obtained an a-historical allure of instant universalism. Regardless of their past and present, it was an article of faith that any and every country could be re-molded into a human-rights-respecting state. A host of assumptions has been necessary to

---

[1] Desmond, C. – *Persecution East and West: Human Rights, Political Prisoners and Amnesty International*, Penguin, Harmondsworth, 1983, p. 26.
[2] Ferguson, N. – Bleeding hearts and bloody messes, *Financial Times*, 3–4 April 1999.

buttress this universalistic crusade. One had to assume that individual rights and freedoms are already recognized and one just needed to constrain their violations, and therefrom followed another assumption whereby human rights in other countries could be safeguarded at little or no cost, and a third one which individualized and personalized victimizers and victims.

Exposure of abuses abroad aimed to mobilize people into action against the government which was deemed responsible. This mobilization initially targeted one's own government to nudge it into action against another, embarrassing and publicly shaming it when it failed to act. A mere protest was rarely deemed to constitute a satisfactory response, condemnations and sanctions were urged, later to be followed by military interventions under some palatable name that included the adjective 'humanitarian' or rhetorically transformed bombing into an 'air campaign.'[3]

Human rights organizations, spreading their activities from the nucleus in Western countries, globalized their reach. The entry of human rights into Western foreign policies multiplied condemnations and sanctions. In contrast to the United Nations, individual Western governments needed no agreement or acquiescence of their non-Western peers. Aid-receiving countries were the most frequent target because the interest for them was the biggest and wielding the Western aid lever expected to change their behaviour. NGO reports (and the associated media coverage) became scheduled to coincide not only with annual sessions of the United Nations Commission on Human Rights or General Assembly, but also with decision-making on development finance for countries that were the object of such reports. After non-Western sources of development finance had dwindled, conditionalities proliferated. Asymmetry was reinforced by marginalizing inter-governmental fora. Multilateralism was quietly but effectively redefined. The United Nations no longer constituted a functional equivalent of the international community, this terms could be applied to G-7 or NATO.

The audiences for NGO reports on human rights violations multiplied. Foreign ministries, development aid agencies, parliamentary foreign affairs committees, political parties, the mass media, needed and demanded information about human rights in countries which were placed, or were likely to be placed, on the foreign policy agenda. Siegfried Pausewang has pointed out that allegations of human rights violations are not necessarily a tool for improving human rights protection but can be utilized to de-legitimize a particular government.[4] The boundary between human rights work and political partisanship became blurred.

Inter-governmental bodies that were set up to assess human rights performance of governments by their peers sank low on the foreign policy agenda. The United Nations attracts little publicity, the Inter-American or African human rights systems

---

[3] Fisk, R. – How to manipulate hearts and minds: Lies and more damned lies, *Le monde diplomatique*, English Edition, August 1999.

[4] Pausewang, S. – Ethiopia, in Baehr, P. Et al. (Eds) – *Human Rights in Developing Countries. 1996 Yearbook*, Kluwer Law International & Nordic Human Rights Publications, 1995, p. 206.

have remained absent from the Western mass media. Controversies about how best to respond to human rights violations in other countries have been routinely confined to globalized bilateralism, sometimes dubbed *the West versus the Rest.*

The punitive linkage between violations and aid flows split human rights organizations. Some lobby for their imposition, others against their use. Amnesty International does not support the imposition of sanctions. In 1997, the Human Rights Watch thus presented its strategy for sanctions against Bosnia and Herzegovina:

> First, a mechanism should be established whereby human rights organizations, … can report to and work with international financial institutions (IFIs) on the question of whether local authorities are truly complying with the Dayton Peace Accords – including the surrender of indictees – and are otherwise not violating basic international human rights standards. This would allow the IFIs to receive accurate, timely and specific information on which entities should receive assistance and which should not, and would enable IFIs to outline specific steps that jurisdictions must undertake to receive assistance, as well as to specify the conduct that would trigger the reduction or termination of assistance.[5]

Elevating human rights organizations into an officially recognized source of information on violations that would trigger sanctions illustrates the path traveled thus far: from a right to do good in the 1960s to a right to inflict harm in the 1990s. The proposal that NGO-created information should trigger suspension of funding by multilateral agencies that have neither mandate nor competence in human rights, vividly portrays how much the idea of championing human rights has changed in the past three decades.

DOMESTICATED FOREIGN POLICY

The distinction between public and private in foreign policy was blurred in the 1990s and foreign policy was *domesticated.* The big ideological struggle of the previous decades was replaced by a vacuum, reflected in the inability of scholars to find a term other than post-cold-war or post-foreign-policy or perhaps even post-human rights. The language of human rights and violations was also changed. At its worst, this confusing new vocabulary posits that people are violating each other's rights and abolishes the crucial difference between governments (that have human rights obligations) and, for example, terrorists (who do not). The inflation of human

---

[5] Human Rights Watch – Human rights groups call upon the European Union and World Bank to promote compliance with the Dayton Peace Accords through effective conditionality, Press release, Brussels, 10 January 1997.

rights rhetoric inevitably led to its devaluation. The arbitrariness of human rights rhetoric then justifies the arbitrary pattern of sanctions.

Foreign policy is a prerogative of the executive, exempt from human rights safe-guards embodied in the rule of law and only partially constrained by democratic safeguards. The absence of constraints upon domestic self-interest through demo-cratic procedures results from the foreign population being an object of decision-making but excluded from the process of making decisions; foreigners do not have political rights in another country. There is no access to decision-making for the Iraqi population to articulate their freedom from being bombed.[6] Division of labour, mandated by the separation of powers, also exempts foreign-policy decisions from judicial oversight.[7]

The state (represented by its government) is defined as the key actor in inter-national relations. Its foreign policy is supposed to guide these international relations. The inter-state level of analysis focuses on external determinants of state behaviour, treating 'the state' as a single actor. States have included human rights in their foreign policies late and have not become dominant actors, perhaps never will be.

If the state speaks with a forked tongue, with one part of the government advo-cating and another opposing condemnations-cum-sanctions, this state is pursuing several foreign policies at the same time. A separate domestic constituency exists for each separate foreign policy: a militant human-rights lobby may advocate aid cutoffs, joining forces with anti-aid constituencies, against the aid establishment and associated lobbies. Links between aid and export promotion may not be explicit in a formally adopted foreign policy, but this policy would not exist without support of those constituencies which export their goods and services through aid. These contradictions come into the open when there is a need for a single foreign policy while there are several, thus dismantling the myth whereby foreign policy is an integrated whole rather than patchwork.

Commitment to human rights in foreign policy (used here to denote the formally adopted document) is a self-contained addition to other commitments with which it often clashes. It is routinely written in beautiful rhetoric of moral imperatives, articulated at such a high level of abstraction to resemble Delphic utterances, while eschewing domestic self-interest as petty or tawdry. Such foreign policy may promise to make human rights its cornerstone. A selfless commitment to benefitting others can never be an outcome of domestic politics, however. Human rights guar-antees were intended to regulate relations between the state and its own citizens, not the state's relations with citizens of other countries. These guarantees are an outcome of political processes from which citizens of other countries are excluded.

---

[6] A leader in *Guardian Weekly* has found that 'parliamentary democracy has not served Britain especially well over the bombing of Iraq,' (At war over the bombing, *Guardian Weekly*, 27 December 1998).

[7] This is discussed in Tomaševski, K. – Foreign policy and torture, Dunér, B. (ed.) – *An End to Torture. Strategies for Its Eradication*, Zed Books, London, 1998, pp. 183–202.

As a consequence, a state cannot be brought to court for violating human rights of citizens of another state.[8]

Subordination of domestic self-interest to human rights of others, through an embargo impeding the import of oil from a repressive regime which happens to be the sole source of oil, has never happened. Lisa Martin has argued that governments imposing sanctions routinely fail to demonstrate their willingness to suffer economic losses themselves.[9] David Leyton-Brown took this line of reasoning one step further to conclude that sanctions are used as a weapon of first resort, an easy way for governments to be seen to act.[10] The increased cost-consciousness in the 1990s has made human-rights-on-the-cheap immensely popular. Cost-consciousness has become a defining feature of foreign policy in the 1990s, and the low status of human rights within foreign policy required the attainment of human rights in other countries to be presented as costless.

In a TV interview after the NATO's bombing of Serbia and Kosovo, in June 1999, President Clinton defined US strategy for intervening by emphasizing 'an acceptable cost'[11] while Steven Burg and Paul Shoup, writing about international intervention in Bosnia and Herzegovina, emphasized the importance for the West 'to look virtuous while doing the absolute minimum.'[12]

As long as Western sanctions consist of cutting off aid, there is little domestic protest, but when they are broadened to trade and investment a chorus of protestors challenges them. The thrust of these protests is domestic cost: cutting off aid is cost-saving, restrictions upon trade and investment constitute self-denial of profits-to-be-made. The National Association of Manufacturers calculated that US sanctions targeted thirty-five countries in 1993–97 with foregone exports of $790 billion.[13] Similar bombastic assessments of domestic costs of sanctions have followed as did rebuttals.

When sanctions result from advocacy by a domestic target audience, the following worst case scenario can be depicted as a caricature: a domestic lobby calling for sanctions draws benefits (in terms of publicity for its championing of human rights) while displacing the burdens to the population affected by sanctions. The public

---

[8]   This assertion lays down the principle which, as all legal principles, allows exceptions. Before human rights entered the scene, foreigners had legal protection against abuses by whatever state might have abused them if their own state was strong enough to assert and protect their rights. Human rights attempted to derive the protection of individuals from their shared humanity and eliminate the power of the state of citizenship as the determining factor. This has remained an objective but has not become a binding rule.

[9]   Martin, L. – *Coercive Cooperation: Explaining Multilateral Economic Sanctions*, Princeton University Press, Princeton, 1992.

[10]   Leyton-Brown, D. – Problems and prospects for economic sanctions, *Third World Affairs 1987*, Third World Institute, London, 1987, p. 97.

[11]   Ching, F. – Sovereignty vs. human rights, *Far Eastern Economic Review*, 22 July 1999.

[12]   Burg, S.L. and Shoup, P.S. – *The War in Bosnia and Herzegovina: Ethnic Conflict and International Intervention*, M.E. Sharpe, 1999, p. 133.

[13]   Dunne, N. – Trade sanctions are hurting US business, Congress is told, *Financial Times*, 5 March 1997.

education effect of this political process, routinely played out in the glare of media exposure, is the creation (or reinforcement) of a belief that human rights in other countries can be promoted through purposeful impoverishment.

BLURRED DOMESTIC-FOREIGN-INTERNATIONAL BOUNDARY

Former Chinese political prisoners[14] have become major actors in the NGO community in the United States, blurring the borders between domestic and foreign. The release of many was extracted by Western delegations who travelled to China with their lists, and quite a few adopted the United States as their base. In earlier decades, a widely accepted definition of human rights organizations contained working for the rights of others as an essential element.[15] The era of idealism demanded activists to refrain from addressing any issue where they might be suspected of abusing human rights to promote self-interest. By the 1990s, this fell into oblivion. Women organized themselves to champion the rights of women, indigenous organizations preceded them, minority groups followed. The human as *genus proximum* yielded to *diferentia specifica*, a vast number of human rights organizations embodied an endless range of different agendas, the creation of new rights followed.

The blurring of the boundary between foreign and domestic was not a creation of human rights organizations. Rather, it resulted from migration[16] (mostly forced) of persecuted movements, groups, and individuals. Exiles and refugees from Latin American dictatorships were an important NGO actor in the 1970s. Chile, Argentina and Uruguay generated a large number because exile was used as a form of punishment, or else individuals were given a choice of leaving the country instead of remaining in detention. Refuge in the West, through which attention is

---

[14] Registers of political prisoners were published by Human Rights Watch/Asia (*Detained in China and Tibet: A Directory of Political and religious Prisoners*, New York, 1994) and, with addition of other victims, by Amnesty International (*China: Repression in the 1990s. A Directory of Victims*, London, 1966).

[15] In the words of José Zalaquett, 'the central purpose of the [human rights] organization is not to work for the advancement or respect of its own rights or the rights of its members, but rather for the rights of others.' Zalaquett, J. – *The Human Rights Issue and the Human Rights Movement. Characterization, Evolution, Propositions*, World Council of Churches, Geneva, 1981, p. 30–31.

[16] Exiles, asylum-seekers, refugees, immigrants, migrant workers, or foreign students diminish geographical distance through their physical presence in the country contemplating economic sanctions making the issue visible. Although not constituting a political constituency in the narrow sense of that term, their influence on European human rights policies towards their countries of origin has often been considerable. Where human rights organizations have been established by exiles or refugees in host countries to deal solely with human rights issues in their countries of origin, this influence was formalized by giving exile organizations a recognized standing concerning the host country's human rights policy towards their country of origin. Regretfully, this phenomenon does not seem to have been analysed as yet.

being focussed on abuses at home, has also been the fate of Tamils from Sri Lanka or Kurds from Turkey. The effects on the forging of a foreign policy in countries providing refuge can be gleaned from twists and turns in the responses to human rights violations by their 'new' states of affiliation towards their 'old' homeland. It is these effects, *inter alia*, that have resulted in the reluctance of the favoured destinations in seeking refuge to import the underlying conflicts through admission of people seeking refuge. Containment of conflicts at their origin has thus emerged as an important foreign policy goal.

PERSONALIZATION AND INDIVIDUALIZATION

The British government has joined the foreign-policy and development-aid ministries in producing a joint brochure on human rights (an unusual event since the two ministries, wherever they exist as separate actors, tend to define human rights differently). Coloured photographs on thick glossy paper, which characterizes governmental human rights policies and reports, were interspersed with the need for a dialogue with China and this statement:'We regularly raise the cases of individuals and have received information about all those on the EU's list.'[17] Equalizing human rights with the fate of few internationally known individuals facilitates reporting accomplishments – a detainee liberated, human rights problem solved, the country can be taken off the agenda. Summarizing the record of the Carter administration, which was often credited for institutionalizing human rights in foreign policy, David Heaps listed 'the release of political prisoners in Indonesia; the imposition of less harsh punishment on foes of the regime in South Korea; the more conciliatory treatment of political opponents in the Philippines; the liberation of prominent dissenters such as Jacobo Timmerman in Argentina.'[18]

Personalization of crusades for sanctions around the fate of Daw Aung San Suu Kyi in Burma or the late Ken Saro-Wiwa in Ogoniland/Nigeria has highlighted the pressure upon Western governments to be seen to act. A human rights story told through statistics of victims and procedural hurdles to prosecute victimizers lacks the human factor, human faces and voices, individual tragedies that people can identify with.

This individualization conforms to the individualism which is in-built in international human rights law, where an individual victim of an individualized violation is given access to a retroactive remedy. It does not facilitate systemic and structural approaches that are necessary for building human rights protection for all. These would necessitate a long-term commitment and an investment far beyond

---

[17] Foreign & Commonwealth Office/Department for International Development – *Annual Report on Human Rights 1998*, London, April 1998, p. 40.

[18] Heaps. D. – *Human Rights and U.S. Foreign Policy: The First Decade 1973–1983*, American Association for the International Commission of Jurists, New York, 1984, p. 26.

minuscule sums allocated for human rights. Preference for an easy and costless alternative – confining human rights to individual cases – satisfies many difference audiences.

On the victimizers side, this individualization works against the very purpose of human rights, namely protection against abuses by the state. El Salvador's Truth Commission embarked upon the identification of responsible individuals[19] within 1980–91 military and civilian institutions, recommending that they be cleansed out of these institutions. This precedent triggered both applause and criticism. It came at a time when individualization of responsibility for atrocities gained ground at the expense of institutional responsibility of states and therefore applause. It publicly condemned individuals who had stood no trial and thus breached an ancient legal principle, and therefore criticism. Outsiders' (in this case foreigners') identification of responsible individuals weakens institutions, deprives them of the responsibility – and necessary power – by removing the task of enacting and enforcing internal rules of conduct to outsiders.

Just before international human rights started developing, a much quoted statement from the Nüremberg trials put it differently:

> Crimes against international law are committed by men, not by abstract entities, and only by punishing individuals who commit such crimes can the provisions of international law be enforced.[20]

Numerous proposals have been made to freeze financial assets of political elites[21] rather than imposing sanctions against virtually existing states. They were joined by Kofi Annan, who has argued for 'sanctions aimed at decision-makers and their families, including the freezing of personal and organizational assets as well as restrictions on travel.'[22]

---

[19] The Commission paraphrased the well-known dictum originating from the Nuremberg Trials (quoted above) to say that 'it is individuals that commit crimes, not the institutions they have created. As a result, it is to individuals and not their institutions that the corresponding penalties established by law must be applied,' arguing that 'this approach protects institutions and punishes criminals.' The Commission did not take a further step to ask whether institutions that have lost credibility through the process of self-criminalization are worthy of protection, and whether new ones will gain credibility in the absence of institutional responsibility. Report of the Commission on the Truth for El Salvador: From Madness to Hope. The 12-year war in El Salvador, U.N. Doc. S/25500 of 1 April 1993, p. 13

[20] Official documents of the Trial of the Major War Criminals before the International Military Tribunal, Nuremberg, 14 November 1945–1 October 1946, 1947, p. 223.

[21] Economic sanctions and international relations: An April 1993 Conference summary, *Scandinavian Journal of Development Alternatives*, vol. 12, No. 4, December 1993, p. 162.

[22] United Nations – The causes of conflict and the promotion of durable peace and sustainable development in Africa. Report of the Secretary-General, U.N. Doc. S/1998/318 of 13 April 1998, para. 25.

The year 1999 was marked by court proceedings against General Pinochet, for command responsibility, to use the humanitarian law jargon, as the head of state of Chile in 1973–89, and the first indictment of an acting head of state, Slobodan Milosevic by the International War Crimes Tribunal. Rumours were widespread about a forthcoming indictment of Saddam Hussein. Karin von Hippel and Michael Clarke have attributed this fixation on a particular ruler to a US stereotype which assumed 'that if such rulers were only removed, democracy and/or stability would neatly fall in place.'[23] The systemic, institutional and/or structural factors that institutionalize denials and violations of human rights have thus been wished away because they are too expensive and time-consuming to tackle.

ACTING AND REACTING FOR DIFFERENT TARGET AUDIENCES

Condemnations and sanctions are triggered by highly visible events which prompt instant reactions. Foreign-policy decisions can be made rapidly, particularly if they consist of symbolic statements (such as a verbal condemnation of an atrocity) and gestures (such as suspension of a minute aid package) and typically accommodate the government's need to be seen to act. Outcomes of such decisions reflect the relative weight of different constituencies, balancing divergent, often conflicting interests and values advocated by the relevant constituencies.

The object of condemnations and sanctions is another state but their target audience is much broader – it is domestic, foreign and international; it is governmental and non-governmental; its consists of militant zealots and profit-seeking businessmen; it includes TV crews seeking 30-seconds diagnosis of the problem and recipe for solution. Accommodating their different expectations would be impossible was it not for the ample leeway between saying and doing, acting and being seen to act, which the conduct of foreign policy had developed. George Kennan thus depicted the world of foreign policy through its bias towards virtual reality:

> Form means a great deal in international life. What is important, in other words, is not so much what is done as how it is done. And, in this sense, good form in outward demeanor becomes more than a means to an end, more than a subsidiary attribute: it becomes a value in itself, with its own validity and its own effectiveness, and – human nature being what it is – the greatest value of all.[24]

There is a range of target audiences and messages addressed to them can vary a great deal, creating layers of appearances and realities below the surface:

---

[23] von Hippel, K. and Clarke, M. – Something must be done, *The World Today*, March 1999, p. 6.

[24] Kennan, G.F. – *Memoirs: 1925–1950*, Little Brown, Boston, 1967, pp. 408.

- domestic constituencies lobbying for condemnations and sanctions have to see them materialize; if domestic constituencies lobbying against condemnations and sanctions have to be re-assured that condemnations are devoid of effects and sanctions virtual rather than real, then the government will be apparently speaking with a forked tongue while really doing its utmost to accommodate all relevant domestic constituencies;
- friendly governments who joined in condemnations and imposed sanctions have to be convincing that rules of conduct developed within the peer group are observed; group solidarity spreads of the burden of anticipated retaliation by the object of condemnations and sanctions (and its peer group, if it has any to mobilize);
- unfriendly governments ought to be alerted to the possibility of being targeted;
- the object of condemnations and sanctions has to be publicly shown that peer-group rules are applied and enforced; this message can be altered if the nominal target of sanctions has to be assured that condemnations are purely verbal and sanctions merely symbolic;
- the population of the condemned and sanctioned country is given a self-contradictory message: on the one hand, its human rights have been elevated to a major foreign-policy concern; on the other hand, condemnations seem to promise that wrongs will be righted while sanctions reinforce victimization.

Such a variety of possible messages to diverse audiences shows that different ends necessitate corresponding means.

MEANS *VERSUS* ENDS

Aid is often defined as the way to improve human rights in recipient countries, but undermined by demands for cutting off aid in response to violations. Both providing aid and its denial can be defined as human-rights-friendly. Although common sense rebels against this contradiction, foreign policy has to accommodate such mutually conflicting demands.

Thus far, aid has not been particularly successful, probably because the bulk of human rights aid consists of technical assistance which is notoriously the least helpful type of aid. Although exceptions have not been unknown, aid has not been harmful, in contrast to sanctions or military interventions. The failure of condemnations and sanctions to achieve their ambitious aim of engineering a political transformation in the target country results from the incapacity of foreign policy to accomplish what it apparently promises to do. Freeing political prisoners or adopting a new constitution can be accomplished. However, political bargaining between governments which such gestures require enhances discretionary use of power and undermines the very basis for human rights protection. The ease with which a government can free political prisoners or adopt a new constitution cautions against the equal ease with which such actions can be – and often are – reversed.

The aim of sanctions can be translated into preventing evil deeds, but this makes them a lesser evil rather than something good. However justified, economic sanctions include purposeful impoverishment which leads also to disempowerment. The population of the targeted country finds itself in the crossfire between its own government and those applying sanctions. Both sides are likely to point to the evil deeds of the other side and argue that their own represent a lesser evil.

When the spotlight is directed towards means rather than ends, the framework elaborated for assessing warfare provides ready-made guidance. Restrictions upon warfare are intended to protect the civilian population against being targeted and to constrain the situations is which it becomes collateral damage. Prohibitions embodied in the law of armed conflicts protect civilians against purposeful destruction, intentional harm, and becoming collateral damage through gross negligence. By analogy civilians should be at least equally protected in peacetime. Hans-Peter Gasser, the then legal adviser of the ICRC (International Committee of the Red Cross) defined economic sanctions as instruments of warfare arguing that humanitarian exceptions should apply as they do in warfare.[25] UNICEF has proposed that all sanctions should have an *ex ante* child impact assessment which would detail the expected impact of proposed sanctions on children and include 'the offsetting measures proposed to be taken.[26] Graça Machel noted that sanctions were seen 'as a safer recourse that can be applied at lower cost.'[27]

Economic sanctions follow the logic of warfare, aiming to 'deprive the enemy of the material means of resistance',[28] while deterring potential providers of such material means of resistance. Effects of sanctions that were enforced, such as against Iraq, Haiti or the Former Yugoslavia, were opposite of those intended – detrimental for the population, negligible (at best) for the government. Sanctions against Haiti were faulted from their very design because neither the OAS nor the UN differentiated between legitimate and prohibited purposes of sanctions[29] as these are inferred from the legal restrictions upon warfare.

The hardship imposed upon the population in the target country is hidden behind the rhetoric of law whereby sanctions are imposed against the state rather than its population. The responsibility for protecting the population against the hardship created by sanctions falls into a legal gap: by legal rules, this responsibility pertains

---

[25] In Post, H.H.G. (ed.) – *International Economic Law and Armed Conflict*, Martinus Nijhoff Publishers, Dordrecht, 1994, p. 179.

[26] Commission on human rights – Human rights and unilateral coercive measures. Report of the Secretary-General, U.N. Doc. E/CN.4/1995/43 of 13 January 1995, para. 83.

[27] United Nations – Impact of armed conflicts on children, U.N. Doc. A/51/306 of 26 August 1996, para. 127.

[28] Medlicott, W.N. – *The Economic Blockade*, HM Stationary Office, London, 1952, reprinted in 1978, p. 16.

[29] Simunovic, M. – Sanctions studies pose dilemmas, *PHR Record*, vol. 7, No. 1, Winter/Spring 1994, pp. 14–15.

to the government of the sanctioned state. Sanctions, however, aim to disempower that government, to make it unable to perform ordinary governmental functions even if it wished to do so. Those who have imposed sanctions do not have a legal responsibility towards the population of another country, hence this legal gap.

The costs of sanctions is a weak link among the articles of faith upon which sanctions are based. While people are easily mobilized in favour of sanctions against a foreign dictator, purposefully starving the children of that country raises eyebrows, then questions, then protests. The means used by the dictator and by those working for his demise become uncomfortably similar. A prototype Saddam Hussain is accused on violating human rights of the population of Iraq and then come international sanctions imposing upon the population impoverishment and starvation so as to force Saddam Hussain to respect their human rights. Since this rationale does not quite add up, there is a great deal of effort in *sanctionology* to shift attention from means to ends. The means employed might be unpleasant but are necessary to attain the worthwhile ends.

The means are, however, the essential criterion used in conceptualizing abuses of power as human rights violations. Every government's rhetoric promises worthwhile ends, domestically and internationally. The essential test is to determine whether the means employed are leading to the professed ends and whether they are compatible with the declared ends. Alarm bells ring when the employed means apparently defy the professed end.

TRICKLE DOWN *VERSUS* TRICKLE UP APPROACH

It is assumed that the original cause for condemnations and sanctions (human rights violations) necessitates a change in the government (or of the government) and this can be accomplished through external and international pressure. An additional assumption is that such change will be positive – external and international pressure is seen as capable not only of inducing change but guiding it in a desired direction. The belief that a change will be for the better is necessary to justify the cost of sanctions for their victims. Economic deprivation is seen as a means to convert a government from a violator to protector of human rights. It is expected to force the guilty government to comply with conditions for resumed economic exchanges or to nudge the people to renounce their government. The implicit assumption is that economic deprivation is human-rights-friendly and leads to a beneficial political change.

The process of political change routinely defies outsiders' assumptions. Thomas Carothers, an American with extensive experience in Latin America has thus defined a typical US bias:

when Americans involve themselves in other societies, they usually work from an ahistorical point of view, reflecting their lack of knowledge about the other society and with a culturally ingrained attitude about the unimportance of history to bind the present.[30]

Sanctions rely on economic means to achieve political change through psychological pressure. The assumption that psychological and/or political pressure is generated through economic hardship necessitates analysing whether sanctions have the intended economic effects, and whether their economic effects lead towards desired political changes. Data on economic hardship resulting from economic sanctions suffer 'from a large extent of indeterminacy'[31] and cause-and-effect studies easily reach opposite conclusions about the same case. An assessment of the political impact of economic sanction comes from Vojin Dimitrijević, a human rights scholar and activist as well as a participant-observer of the impact of sanctions in Serbia. Having examined detrimental material effects of sanctions in Yugoslavia, Dimitrijević has confirmed that the faith in sanctions as a means to changing governance (or at least the government) was wrong. As intended, sanctions resulted in economic deprivation, which did not lead to rebellion against the government but resignation. Since no difference was made between the government and the population, sanctions were seen as collective punishment and intensified an anti-Westernism. The combination of purposeful impoverishment caused by sanctions and the international ostracism ultimately confined the domestic political agenda to survival.[32] Dimitrijevic added that sanctions did not increase respect for the West (NATO and USA) as promoters of democracy and human rights; rather 'they are respected as stronger and more technologically advanced.'[33]

Sanctions undermine the ability of the target government to implement human rights obligations. The underlying reason for sanctions is illegitimacy of that government and sanctions are expected to deprive that government of revenue. The implicit logic is that diminishing the ability to implement human rights guarantees will enhance the willingness of that government to guarantee human rights. Because that logic is not persuasive, a change of government is routinely sought, but it may not point in the desired direction. The application of *electoralism*[34] to Africa has shown that many changes in government and of governments have not

---

[30] Carothers, T. – The resurgence of United States political development assistance to Latin America in the 1980s, in Whitehead, L. (ed.) – *The International Dimensions of Democratization: Europe and the Americas*, Oxford University Press, 1996, p. 143.

[31] van Bergeijk, P.A.G. – The effectivity of economic sanctions: Illusion or reality?, *Peace Economics, Peace Science and Public Policy*, vol. 2, 1994, No. 1, p. 32.

[32] Dimitrijević, V. and Pejić, J. – UN sanctions against Yugoslavia: Two years later, in: Bourantonis, D. and Wiener, J. (eds.) – *The United Nations in the New World Order: The World Organization at Fifty*, Macmillan, London, 1995, pp. 138, 143, 145 and 147.

[33] Dimitrijević, V. – Post scriptum to UN sanctions against Yugoslavia (Serbia and Montenegro), in Tanner, F. (ed.) – *Effects of International Sanctions*, Mediterranean Academy of Diplomatic Studies, Malta, January 1996, p. 52.

[34] Tomaševski, K. – *Between Sanctions and Elections*, Pinter/Cassell, London, 1997, pp. 181–206.

yielded beneficial effects. If a change takes place, which results from domestic processes to which outside pressure can only provide support, the willingness of a new government will then be hampered by its diminished capacity to translate human rights into practice as the outcome of impoverishment caused by sanctions.

Human rights necessitate substantial and continuous investment. Conventional wisdom, according to which any government can safeguard human rights and freedoms if is willing to do so, runs against reality: a government may wish to secure the independence of the judiciary but will fail to do so if it cannot adequately pay the judges. Political will is indispensable but insufficient. All human rights, civil and political liberties included, necessitate developed infrastructure and continuous investment. No country has ever managed to secure freedom from torture unless it paid well its police. If their salaries are lower than their living expenses, their dedication to professional policing will yield to securing survival of their families.

Extra-Legality

Condemnations and sanctions requires a quadrilateral analytical scheme to capture multiple relations: horizontal relations between the two governments, vertical relations between each government and its own population as well as diagonal relations between one government and the population in another country. No ready-made human rights framework exists for these cross-cutting relations because they were not anticipated and no law exists to regulate them.

Globalized bilateralism has depleted human rights of the grounding in law. Any substantive issue could be labelled as a human rights violation and the government deemed responsible called a violator. While a lively dispute about universality of human rights goes on amongst academics, three decades of Western human rights activism have accustomed the general public to accept violations, violators and victims as defined in political debates.

Condemnations and sanctions borrow from international law the postulate that the state is responsible for human rights violations and should be penalized, but omit the corollary, namely that international law requires other states to resort to law. The authority of international law is not based on an international capacity to govern but on the willingness of states to adjust their conduct to the requirements of the rule of law. Forcible action to mold the conduct of states has been envisaged only when international peace and security is threatened and the authority to impose sanctions is vested in the Security Council. The United Nations does not have an enforcement mandate for human rights, only for peace and security.

There is no inducement for states to comply with their human rights obligations, nor is there an incentive for them to induce others to comply. There also is no authority bestowed upon one state to hold another in breach of human rights violations. The European Commission on Human Rights has held that international human rights law does not 'create subjective and reciprocal rights' for states. The standing of a state under the European Convention on Human Rights against another accused of having breached the Convention 'is not to be regarded as exercising a right of action for the purpose of enforcing its own rights, but rather as bringing before the Commission an alleged violation of the public order in Europe.'[35] This rationale shows why international law is studiously avoided: human rights problems would become depoliticised as they would be submitted for adjudication to an international court-like institution, few of the phenomena labeled as violations would be determined as such.

Although the term 'sanctions' is a misnomer and law requires the use of countermeasures, the continued usage of 'sanctions' is not only a reflection of the unlikely acceptance of an ugly legal term like 'countermeasures' as a household word, but rather the mobilizing power of 'sanctions' as a law-based response to an illegal act. The accompanying assumption is that everything labeled as a human rights violation for the purpose of justifying sanctions is a breach of international human rights law.

The International Law Commission (ILC) has tried to restrain freedom of action in conditions of deep inequalities between states, which favours the strong at the expense of the weak. The ILC found that 'countermeasures were an exercise in power'[36] and should be subsumed under the rule of law so as to prevent abuses. Its attempt to impose this 'should' upon the unruly 'is' has thus far not been successful.

Economic sanctions pertain to the menu of coercion applied to mould another state's conduct. Because unequal power is an essential prerequisite for the effectiveness of sanctions, resort to sanctions is based on a perceived power over the target state. Recommended prohibitions of abuse of economic power by one state against another aim at altering unequal power through the assertion of equal rights. States are equal under international law, much as all humans have equal rights. The use and abuse of economic power remains beyond the rule of law.

A government imposing sanctions implicitly creates for itself a right to punish, *ius puniendi*. This *ius puniendi* divided the international community along the line of sanctioning *versus* sanctioned, the North versus the South. The Commission on Human Rights has denounced coercive unilateral economic measures and proclaimed them to be in clear contradiction with international law.[37] The formulation 'clear contradiction with international law' was repeated several times. The Commission condemned 'certain countries [which] using their predominant position in the world economy, continue to intensify the adoption of unilateral coercive

---

[35] European Commission on Human Rights – Austria v. Italy, *Yearbook of the European Convention on Human Rights*, vol. 4, 1961, p. 140.

[36] United Nations – Report of the International Law Commission on the work of its forty-fifth session, U.N. Doc. A/48/10, para. 228.

[37] Resolution 1995/45 of 5 March 1995 cited as authorities the UN Charter, the Declaration on the Principles of International Law concerning Friendly Relations and Cooperation among States in accordance with the Charter, the Charter of Economic Rights and Duties of States, and the Vienna Declaration and Programme of Action.

measures.'[38] These resolutions reflect predictable anger of the South at the abuse of economic power by the North. The voting pattern reveals, predictably, the minority of governments using economic coercion on one side and the majority of those likely to become objects of sanctions on the other side.

A right to punish is the counterpart of a right to reward. A decision to grant aid for a specific purpose or to a particular country is based on a decision that this issue or that country is aid-worthy. Donors publicise the criteria for their aid as well as listing the recipients. These, however, are formulated as such a high level of abstraction that a great deal of discretion is implied in their interpretation and application.

Henry Kissinger, while he was the US Secretary of State, argued that non-discrimination was an obstacle to using economic sanctions in response to human rights violations. Reports were compiled by US embassies following the 1974 statutory requirement for the assessment of human rights performance for recipients of US aid. Kissinger's response was that all governments violated human rights and action against some should not be undertaken because it would be discriminatory.[39] Menno Kamminga has concluded that interventions and intercessions 'on behalf of the human rights of foreign nationals often consists of one-way traffic from stronger toward weaker states.'[40] Detlev Dicke predicted in 1987 that the pattern of sanctions would change when some developing countries felt powerful enough to take a public stand against sanctions and take the consequences.[41] East Asian countries did in the early 1990s, but their need for Western assistance halted that attempt.

EXTERNALIZATION OF RESPONSIBILITY

Condemnations and sanctions result in externalization of responsibility. Contrary to the insistence of international human rights law on <u>domestic</u> human rights protection, sanctions rely on foreign and/or international substantive and procedural standards weakening the accountability of governments to their own citizens.

Anthony Hazlitt Heard has raised a crucial, but unanswered question about long-term effect of sanctions: 'What sort of people will emerge when sanctions and

---

[38] United Nations – Human rights and unilateral coercive measures, resolutions 1995/45 and 1994/47 of the Commission on Human Rights of 3 March 1995 and 4 March 1994. The 1995/45 resolution was adopted by 24 votes in favour, 17 against and 12 abstentions; resolution 1994/47 was adopted by 23 delegations voting in favour, with 18 against and 12 abstaining.

[39] Martin, L.L. – *Coercive Cooperation. Explaining Multilateral Economic Sanctions*, Princeton University Press, Princeton, 1992, p. 104.

[40] Kamminga, M.T. – *Inter-state Accountability for Violations of Human Rights*, Pennsylvania Studies in Human Rights, University of Pennsylvania Press, Philadelphia, 1992, p. 2.

[41] Dicke, D.C. – The concept of economic coercion: A wrong in itself, in: de Waart, P. et al. (eds.) – *International Law and Development*, Martinus Nijhoff Publishers, Dordrecht, 1988, p. 190.

repression end?'[42] Ninety years ago, the Western sanctions against the Soviet Union following the October Revolution elicited this description:

> The continuance of the blockade of Russia renders helpless the quite innocent population, engenders in the people of Russia a feeling of hostility to the allies, and only serves to intensify the disordered state of the country.[43]

Similar descriptions have been many in the past nine decades, arguing that sanctions punish people for the sins of their rulers. Such descriptions do not vary for those sanctions that have been ostensibly imposed in the name of human rights.

This book has argued that resort to human rights language to legitimize external policing and sanctioning undermines the very basis for human rights protection, which ought to be domestic. The implicit rationale for condemnations and sanctions is remote-controlled political development. A momentum for change that could not be generated within the country's domestic political processes is expected, as is the orientation of such change against the guilty government but in favour of human rights protection. That rationale remains implicit because it conflicts with what is known about political effects of sanctions in the sanctioned countries, which routinely strengthen the (guilty) government and often channel political changes in the direction of increased repression. Repression is then justified by the combination of impoverishment attributed to sanctions and the external enemy that caused that impoverishment.

Sanctions make the targeted government accountable to other governments, who are accountable to their own electorates. People in the sanctioned countries – in the name of whose rights sanctions are imposed – are not factored into that equation. Human rights are thus removed from their grounding in the rule of law into the realm of politics. Human rights developed as correctives for domestic political processes but exclude foreign policy. The design that evolved during the past decades obliges each government to protect human rights of its own population, but abuses of power by other governments are beyond the reach of the existing safeguards. Developing such safeguards is a challenge for the future.

---

[42] Hazlitt Heard, A. – Sanctions can work, but apply them with care, *International Herald Tribune*, 28 May 1993.

[43] Berkenheim, A. – The economic blockade of Russia, *International Review*, London, vol. 1, January-June 1919, p. 250.

Index of acronyms and abbreviations

Index of geographical and personal names

Analytical index

International Studies in Human Rights

1. B. G. Ramcharan (ed.): *International Law and Fact-finding in the Field of Human Rights.* 1982
   ISBN 90-247-3042-2

2. B. G. Ramcharan: *Humanitarian Good Offices in International Law.* The Good Offices of the United Nations Secretary-General in the Field of Human Rights. 1983
   ISBN 90-247-2805-3

3. B. G. Ramcharan (ed.): *The Right to Life in International Law.* 1985
   ISBN 90-247-3074-0

4. P. Alston and K. Tomaševski (eds.): *The Right to Food.* 1984   ISBN 90-247-3087-2

5. A. Bloed and P. van Dijk (eds.): *Essays on Human Rights in the Helsinki Process.* 1985
   ISBN 90-247-3211-5

6. K. Törnudd: *Finland and the International Norms of Human Rights.* 1986
   ISBN 90-247-3257-3

7. H. Thoolen and B. Verstappen: *Human Rights Missions.* A Study of the Fact-finding Practice of Non-governmental Organizations. 1986   ISBN 90-247-3364-2

8. H. Hannum: *The Right to Leave and Return in International Law and Practice.* 1987
   ISBN 90-247-3445-2

9. J. H. Burgers and H. Danelius: *The United Nations Convention against Torture.* A Handbook on the Convention against Torture and Other Cruel, Inhuman or Degrading Treatment or Punishment. 1988   ISBN 90-247-3609-9

10. D. A. Martin (ed.): *The New Asylum Seekers: Refugee Law in the 1980s.* The Ninth Sokol Colloquium on International Law. 1988   ISBN 90-247-3730-3

11. C. M. Quiroga: *The Battle of Human Rights.* Gross, Systematic Violations and the Inter-American System. 1988   ISBN 90-247-3687-0

12. L. A. Rehof and C. Gulmann (eds.): *Human Rights in Domestic Law and Development Assistance Policies of the Nordic Countries.* 1989   ISBN 90-247-3743-5

13. B. G. Ramcharan: *The Concept and Present Status of International Protection of Human Rights.* Forty Years After the Universal Declaration. 1989   ISBN 90-247-3759-1

14. A. D. Byre and B. Y. Byfield (eds.): *International Human Rights Law in the Commonwealth Caribbean.* 1991   ISBN 90-247-3785-0

15. N. Lerner: *Groups Rights and Discrimination in International Law.* 1991
   ISBN 0-7923-0853-0

16. S. Shetreet (ed.): *Free Speech and National Security.* 1991   ISBN 0-7923-1030-6

17. G. Gilbert: *Aspects of Extradition Law.* 1991   ISBN 0-7923-1162-0

18. P.E. Veerman: *The Rights of the Child and the Changing Image of Childhood.* 1991
   ISBN 0-7923-1250-3

19. M. Delmas-Marty (ed.): *The European Convention for the Protection of Human Rights.* International Protection versus National Restrictions. 1991   ISBN 0-7923-1283-X

International Studies in Human Rights

20. A. Bloed and P. van Dijk (eds.): *The Human Dimension of the Helsinki Process.* The Vienna Follow-up Meeting and its Aftermath. 1991   ISBN 0-7923-1337-2

21. L.S. Sunga: *Individual Responsibility in International Law for Serious Human Rights Violations.* 1992   ISBN 0-7923-1453-0

22. S. Frankowski and D. Shelton (eds.): *Preventive Detention.* A Comparative and International Law Perspective. 1992   ISBN 0-7923-1465-4

23. M. Freeman and P. Veerman (eds.): *The Ideologies of Children's Rights.* 1992
ISBN 0-7923-1800-5

24. S. Stavros: *The Guarantees for Accused Persons Under Article 6 of the European Convention on Human Rights.* An Analysis of the Application of the Convention and a Comparison with Other Instruments. 1993   ISBN 0-7923-1897-8

25. A. Rosas and J. Helgesen (eds.): *The Strength of Diversity.* Human Rights and Pluralist Democracy. 1992   ISBN 0-7923-1987-7

26. K. Waaldijk and A. Clapham (eds.): *Homosexuality: A European Community Issue.* Essays on Lesbian and Gay Rights in European Law and Policy. 1993
ISBN 0-7923-2038-7; Pb: 0-7923-2240-1

27. Y.K. Tyagi: *The Law and Practice of the UN Human Rights Committee.* 1993
ISBN 0-7923-2040-9

28. H.Ch. Yourow: *The Margin of Appreciation Doctrine in the Dynamics of European Human Rights Jurisprudence.* 1996   ISBN 0-7923-3338-1

29. L.A. Rehof: *Guide to the* Travaux Préparatoires *of the United Nations Convention on the Elimination of All Forms of Discrimination against Women.* 1993 ISBN 0-7923-2222-3

30. A. Bloed, L. Leicht, M. Novak and A. Rosas (eds.): *Monitoring Human Rights in Europe.* Comparing International Procedures and Mechanisms. 1993   ISBN 0-7923-2383-1

31. A. Harding and J. Hatchard (eds.): *Preventive Detention and Security Law.* A Comparative Survey. 1993   ISBN 0-7923-2432-3

32. Y. Beigbeder: *International Monitoring of Plebiscites, Referenda and National Elections.* Self-determination and Transition to Democracy. 1994   ISBN 0-7923-2563-X

33. T.D. Jones: *Human Rights: Group Defamation, Freedom of Expression and the Law of Nations.* 1997   ISBN 90-411-0265-5

34. D.M. Beatty (ed.): *Human Rights and Judicial Review.* A Comparative Perspective. 1994   ISBN 0-7923-2968-6

35. G. Van Bueren, *The International Law on the Rights of the Child.* 1995
ISBN 0-7923-2687-3

36. T. Zwart: *The Admissibility of Human Rights Petitions.* The Case Law of the European Commission of Human Rights and the Human Rights Committee. 1994
ISBN 0-7923-3146-X; Pb: 0-7923-3147-8

37. H. Lambert: *Seeking Asylum.* Comparative Law and Practice in Selected European Countries. 1995   ISBN 0-7923-3152-4

International Studies in Human Rights

International Studies in Human Rights

56. M. Jones and L.A. Basser Marks (eds.): *Disability, Divers-ability and Legal Change.* 1998
ISBN 90-411-1086-0

57. T. Barkhuysen, M.L. van Emmerik and P.H.P.H.M.C. van Kempen (eds.): *The Execution of Strasbourg and Geneva Human Rights Decisions in the National Legal Order.* 1999
ISBN 90-411-1152-2

58. S. Coliver, P. Hoffman, J. Fitzpatrick and S. Bowen (eds.): *Secrecy and Liberty: National Security, Freedom of Expression and Access to Information.* 1999
ISBN 90-411-1191-3

59. W.S. Heinz and H. Frühling: *Determinants of Gross Human Rights Violations by State and State-Sponsored Actors in Brazil, Uruguay, Chile, and Argentina.* 1960-1990. 1999
ISBN 90-411-1202-2

60. M. Kirilova Eriksson: *Reproductive Freedom.* In the Context of International Human Rights and Humanitarian Law. 1999
ISBN 90-411-1249-9

61. M.B. Eryilmaz: *Arrest and Detention Powers in English and Turkish Law and Practice in the Light of the European Convention on Human Rights.* 1999
ISBN 90-411-1269-3

62. K. Henrard: *Devising an Adequate System of Minority Protection.* Individual Human Rights, Minority Rights and the Right to Self-Determination. 2000
ISBN 90-411-1359-2

63. K. Tomaševski: *Responding to Human Rights Violations.* 1946–1999. 2000.
ISBN 90-411-1368-1

This series is designed to shed light on current legal and political aspects of process and organization in the field of human rights.

MARTINUS NIJHOFF PUBLISHERS – THE HAGUE / BOSTON / LONDON